A Bibliography Of Canada's Peoples
1980–1989

A Bibliography Of Canada's Peoples 1980–1989

Part 1: Thematic Entries

Compiled by
Renée Rogers and Gabriele Scardellato

Multicultural History Society of Ontario
1996

Published with the assistance of the Ontario Ministry of Citizenship and the Ministry of Culture, Tourism and Recreation.

Canadian Cataloguing in Publication Data

Rogers, Renée, 1956—
 A bibliography of Canada's peoples, 1980–1989

 Bibliographies series)
 Contents: pt.1. Thematic entries.
 Includes index
 ISBN 0-919045-69-3 (pt. 1)

 1. Minorities – Canada – Bibliography. 2. Canada – Population – Ethnic groups – Bibliography. I. Scardellato, Gabriele Pietro, 1951–
 II. Multicultural History Society of Ontario.
 III. Title. IV. Series.

 Z1395.E4R6 1996   016.3058'00971   C96–930207–X

Cover design by Tapanainen Graphics, Toronto
Printed and bound by the University of Toronto Press

A Bibliography of Canada's Peoples **is available from:**
 University of Toronto Press
 5201 Dufferin Street
 North York, Ontario, Canada M3H 5T8
 Order Fulfilment 1-800-565-9523

Preface

The appearance of the *Bibliography of Canada's Peoples, 1980—1989* reiterates the commitment of the Multicultural History Society of Ontario (MHSO) to continue publishing original research tools to assist in the further study of all the peoples who inhabit Canada. This second instalment in our decanal bibliography differs from the first (covering the years 1972—1979) in several ways.

In contrast to the 1970s bibliography, which was based largely on the volume of Andrew Gregorovich, work on the 1980s bibliography has been carried out entirely by staff-members at the MHSO, Gabriele Scardellato and Renée Rogers. Whereas the division between works dealing with specific themes and with various ethnocultural groups has been maintained, the number of themes and groups has changed and increased. The classification framework for the ethnocultural groups in volume 2 reflects the schema used in another MHSO publication, the forthcoming *Encyclopedia of Canada's Peoples*.

Finally, the actual number of entries in the 1980s bibliography is nearly double the number that appeared in the 1970s bibliography. This reflects both an expansion in the field of ethnic studies in Canada, as well as an improvement in the process of gathering bibliographical material. Because there are so many more entries, it was decided to divide the 1980s bibliography into two volumes, the first dealing with themes, the second with ethnocultural groups.

The compilers have made an important contribution to Canadian studies with the publication of this bibliography. The nearly 8,000 entries provide a wide array of information about individual ethnocultural groups and about how they function and become integrated into Canadian society. The anticipation that all those interested in Canada are likely to benefit from these volumes will surely encourage the compilers as they continue their current work on the volumes concerning the 1990s.

Paul Robert Magocsi
Toronto, Ontario
January 1996

Contents

Introduction

The present bibliography is a continuation of the Multicultural History Society of Ontario's bibliographic project which began with an update of Andrew Gregorovich's 1972 *Canadian Ethnic Groups Bibliography*. The volume that resulted from that undertaking was published in 1993 as *A Bibliography of Canada's Peoples: Supplement 1, 1972-1979*. In the course of preparing it the editors decided to move to a decennial bibliographic format and some of the early 1980s citations, totalling no more than three hundred titles, that had been gathered by Mr Gregorovich and others, were set aside and have been retrieved for the current volume. Additionally, good use was made of the annual bibliographies published in *Canadian Ethnic Studies/Études ethniques au Canada* and similar journals, as well as those published in a steadily increasing number of monographs in the field of Canadian ethnic studies and other sources. The compilers were also extremely fortunate to obtain access to an electronic bibliographic database compiled and maintained by Ms Iza Laponce of the library of the University of British Columbia. Access to these types of resources has become increasingly important in particular because of the growth of the number of publications of all types in this field.

Mr Gregorovich's 1972 bibliography totalled 2,120 entries of which almost 500 were listed under various subject headings and the remainder were organized by individual ethnic groups. This format was followed in the 1970s update which was published with a total of 3,775 entries—with 439 subject entries—for only an eight-year period. The current volume is devoted exclusively to broad subject areas in the study of Canada's peoples and at 4,131 entries it is larger than both of the earlier volumes. Moreover, it is only the first of what will be a two-volume set with the second volume devoted exclusively to individual ethnic groups. Together, these volumes are ample testimony to the continued growth in the field of Canadian ethnic studies that occurred through the 1980s.

Some quantitative analysis of this volume's contents might prove useful to illustrate this growth. First, the types of citations can be subdivided into three relatively distinct categories. The first of these categories consists of monographs which, in turn, can be subdivided into two distinct groupings. One subcategory is composed of monographs written either by one or by a number of authors and in the current volume a total of 671 titles of this type have been cited. The other subcategory is composed of monographs that consist of writings by a number of authors brought together or "edited by" an editor or a number of editors and a total of 168 titles of this type are cited here and these were the sources for 698 citations in this portion of the bibliography. The overwhelming majority of these titles, approximately 700 in all, regardless of type, were published in Canada and roughly 60 others were produced in the United States of America. Another 20 were published in the United Kingdom and the remainder in a scattering of European states, with one citation from India and another from Japan.

The second category of entries is composed of articles derived from serials publications; namely, academic or scholarly and other journals and, occasionally, articles published in newspapers. Because of space considerations, the latter type of entry has been kept to a minimum in both this volume and its companion. Even so, in the current work alone, about 55 per cent of the entries or more than 2,200, are derived from serials publications. These were obtained from some 530 publications for an average of four entries per serial title.

The third category of citations in the bibliography is formed by academic theses written either at the masters or the doctoral level. This grouping totals some 315 entries, most of which (more than 260) were produced through the graduate schools of Canadian universities and more than a third of these (approximately 115 titles) were doctoral theses. This is a only brief quantitative analysis of the types of publications that have been cited in volume one of this decennial bibliography and at some point a comparative analysis of this and preceding volumes might provide an interesting overview of the general growth of the study of Canada's peoples. In the meantime, a number of acknowledgements are necessary.

A project that requires a long period of time to bear fruit almost inevitably produces a long list of individuals who have participated in it and have made significant contributions. Almost equally inevitable is the risk one runs in acknowledging some contributions while possibly omitting others. Bohdan Tkachenko was available for various phases of this volume at the MHSO, just as he was on hand for the revision work for its predecessor and he proved himself extremely effective as always.

Renée Rogers, Library Technician in the MHSO's Resource Centre, was my co-compiler and editor and also accomplished the bulk of the keyboarding and related work. It is unlikely that our work would have proceeded as smoothly had it not been for her dedication, in particular, as well as that of many other individuals. Without all of them the present volume could not have been completed.

Gabriele Scardellato
Toronto, Ontario
1995

Bibliographies

0001 **American and Canadian Immigrant and Ethnic Folklore**
American and Canadian Immigrant and Ethnic Folklore: An Annotated Bibliography. New York: Garland Publishing, 1982. 484 p.

0002 **Anderson, W.W., ed.**
Caribbean Orientations: A Bibliography of Resource Material on the Caribbean Experience in Canada. Toronto: The Organization for Caribbean Canadian Initiatives (OCCI) and Williams-Wallace Publishers, Inc., 1985.

0003 **Barrier, N. Gerald**
India and America: American Publishing on India, 1930-1985. New Delhi, India: American Institute of Indian Studies, 1986. 333 p.

0004 **Benjamin, Steven M.**
The German-Canadians: A Working Bibliography. Toronto: German-Canadian Historical Association, 1982. 23 p.

0005 **Biskupski, Mieczyslaw B.**
"Bibliography/Bibliographie: A Selected, Annotated Bibliography of Articles and Books in the Humanities and Social Sciences Published in Poland, 1981." *East-Central Europe/L'Europe du centre-est*, vol. 13 no. 2 (1986) p. 149-228.

0006 **Blake, Raymond B.**
"Recent Publications Relating to Canada." *Canadian Historical Review*, vol. 70 no. 3 (1989) p. 366-381.

0007 **Bloomfield, Elizabeth**
"International Urban Bibliography: Recent Publications In Urban History/Bibliographie du monde urbain: publications récentes en histoire urbaine." *Urban History Review/Revue d'histoire urbaine*, vol. 16 no. 1 (1987) p. 78-118; vol. 16 no. 2 (1987) p. 196-221.

0008   **Bogusis, Ruth, Liba Blazek, and Sabine Sonnemann, comps.**
        *Checklist of Canadian Ethnic Serials/Liste des publications en série
        ethniques du Canada.* Ottawa: National Library of Canada,
        Newspaper Division, Public Services Branch, 1981, viii, 381 p.

0009   **Bombas, Leonidas C.**
        Canada's Hellenism: A Bibliographic Guide. Athens: Greek-Canadian
        Documentation Series, 1989. 76 p.

0010   **Boshyk, Yury and Boris Balan**
        *Political Refugees and Displaced Persons, 1945-54: A Selected
        Bibliography and Guide to Research with Special Reference to
        Ukrainians.* Edmonton: Canadian Institute of Ukrainian Studies,
        University of Alberta, 1982.

0011   **Brown, Mary and Patricia Sharon**
        *Catalogue of the Rodolphe Joubert Collection on French Canada in
        Department of Rare Books and Special Collections.* Montreal: McGill
        University Libraries, 1984.

0012   **Brown, Mary and Patricia Sharon**
        Eastern Arctic Study: Annotated Bibliography. Kingston, Ontario:
        Centre for Resource Studies, Queen's University, 1984.

0013   **Brumble, H. David**
        *An Annotated Bibliography of American Indian and Eskimo Autobio-
        graphies.* Lincoln: University of Nebraska Press, 1981.

0014   **Brye, David L., ed.**
        *European Immigration and Ethnicity in the United States and
        Canada: A Historical Bibliography.* Clio Bibliography Series no. 7.
        Santa Barbara, California: ABC-Clio, 1983.

0015   **Buchanan, Jim**
        Canadian Indian Policy: A Bibliography Supplement, 1979-1986.
        Monticello, Ill.: Vance Bibliographies, 1986. 23 p.

0016   **Buchholtzer, Guy P.**
        *La côte du Pacifique nord-ouest 1753-1984: contribution française à
        la connaissance des langues et sociétés amérindiennes de l'Amérique
        du Nord.* Paris: A. E. A., 1985. 131 p.

0017 **Buchignani, Norman**
"Social Science Research on Asians in Canada." In: *Asian Canadians: Aspects of Social Change*, edited by K. Victor Ujimoto and Josephine Naidoo. [Ottawa: Canadian Asian Studies Association] 1984, p. 1-29. Proceedings of Asian Canadian Symposium VI, University of Guelph, Guelph, Ontario, June 6 to 8, 1984.

0018 **Budrys, Milda**
"Lithuanian Physicians Affiliated with U.S. and Canadian Universities (Part III)." *Lituanus*, vol. 35 no. 4 (1989) p. 27-43.

0019 **Caldwell, Gary**
Les études ethniques au Québec. Québec: Institut québécois de recherche sur la culture, 1983.

0020 **Canada. Department of the Secretary of State**
Canadian Ethnic Groups Bibliography. 2nd ed. Ottawa: Department of the Secretary of State, Departmental Library, 1985. 96 p.

0021 **Canadian Institute of Ukrainian Studies**
"Audio-visual Materials in the Ukrainian Language Resource Centre." *Multicultural Education*, vol. 7 no. 1 (1984) p. 35-42.

0022 **Canadian Plains Research Center**
"Index [To Ten Years of *Prairie Forum*]." *Prairie Forum*, vol. 11 no. 1 (1986) p. 147-164.

0023 **CANPLAINS Data Base**
"Prairie Theses, 1984-85." *Prairie Forum*, vol. 11 no. 1 (1986) p. 101-111.

0024 **Carrier, Anne, Barbara Walther, and Harold Lass**
"The Holocaust in Literature." *History and Social Science Teacher*, vol. 21 no. 4 (1986) p. 214-216.

0025 **Centre de bibliographie historique de l'Amérique française**
"Bibliographie d'histoire de l'Amérique française (publications récentes)." *Revue d'histoire de l'Amérique française*, vol. 43 no. 1 (1989) p. 130-162.

0026 **Chojnacki, Wojciech**
"Bibligrafia Publikacji Prasowych O Najnowszej Emigracji Z Lat 1980-1987/A Bibliography of Press Publications on the Most Recent Emigration of 1980-1987." *Przeglad Polonijny*, vol. 15 no. 4 (1989) p. 129-143.

0027   **Cline, Scott**
"Jewish-ethnic Interactions: A Bibliographical Essay." *American Jewish History*, vol. 77 no. 1 (1987) p. 135-154.

0028   **Cohen, Yolande**
Les thèses québécoises sur les femmes. Québec: Institut de recherche sur la culture, 1983.

0029   **Commission des droits de la personne du Québec. Service de la recherche**
Bibliographie analytique de recherche, 1976-1989. Québec: La Commission, 1989. 68 p.

0030   **Cooke, Dorothy**
An Index to Acadiensis 1901-1908. Halifax, N.S.: Dalhousie University Libraries and Dalhousie University School of Library Science, 1983.

0031   **Cordasco, Francesco**
The New American Immigration: Evolving Patterns of Legal and Illegal Emigration - A Bibliography of Selected References. New York: Garland Publishing, 1987. 418 p.

0032   **Corley, Nora T.**
Resources for Native Peoples Studies. Ottawa: National Library of Canada, Resources Survey Division, 1984.

0033   **Dempsey, Hugh A. and Lindsay Moir**
Bibliography of the Blackfoot. Native American Bibliography Series no. 13. Metuchen, N.J.: The Scarecrow Press, 1989. 24 p.

0034   **Dennis, Mike and Martin Watson**
"Bibliography/Bibliographie: A Selected Bibliography of Articles and Books in the Social Sciences and Humanities Published in the German Democratic Republic in 1985." *East-Central Europe/ L'Europe du centre-est*, vol. 13 no. 1 (1986) p. 45-77.

0035   **Dorais, Louis-Jacques**
"La recherche sur les inuit du nord québécois: bilan et perspectives." *Études Inuit Studies*, vol. 8 no. 2 (1985) p. 99-115.

0036 **Drolet, Gaëtan**
"ASTIS Bibliography, un instrument de repérage de l'information scientifique sur le monde nordique." *Études Inuit Studies*, vol. 8 no. 1 (1984) p. 181-89.

0037 **Durst, Russel K. and James D. Marshall**
"Annotated Bibliography of Research in the Teaching of English." *Research in the Teaching of English*, vol. 22 no. 2 (1988) p. 213-227; vol. 22 no. 4 (1988) p. 434-452.

0038 **Dworaczek, Marian**
Human Rights Legislation in Canada: A Bibliography. Monticello, Ill.: Vance Bibliographies, 1983. 35 p.

0039 **Dwyer, Aldrich J.**
"An Ore Body of Note: Theses and Dissertations on Indians, Metis and Inuit at the University of Alberta." *Canadian Journal of Native Education*, vol. 13 no. 2 (1986) p. 40-51.

0040 **Dwyer, Melva J.**
"Bibliography of British Columbia." *B.C. Studies*, no. 77 (1988) p. 80-97; no. 78 (1988) p. 96-104.

0041 **Elliott, Lorris**
Literary Writing by Blacks in Canada: A Preliminary Survey. Edited by Michael S. Batts. Ottawa: Department of the Secretary of Canada, Multiculturalism/Multiculturalisme, 1988. 40 p.

0042 **Elliott, Lorris**
The Bibliography of Literary Writings by Blacks in Canada. Toronto: Williams-Wallace, 1986. 48 p.

0043 **Ethnic and Immigration Groups: The United States, Canada, and England**
Ethnic and Immigration Groups: The United States, Canada, and England. New York: The Institute for Research in History and the Haworth Press, 1983. 126 p.

0044 **Finley, E. Gault**
*Education in Canada: A Bibliography/L'éducation au Canada: Une bibliographie.*Toronto: Dundurn Press, 1988. 600 p.

0045   **Foley, Kathryn Shred**
Research in Core French: Annotated Bibliography. [Canada:]
Canadian Association of Second Language Teachers, 1987.
167 p. French language title: *Recherches sur le français de base:
bibliographie analytique.*

0046   **Fowke, Edith**
A Bibliography of Canadian Folklore in English. Toronto: University
of Toronto Press, 1981. 272 p.

0047   **Frittz, Linda**
Native Law Bibliography. Saskatoon, Sask: Native Law Centre,
University of Saskatchewan, 1984.

0048   **Getty, Ian A.L. and Antoine S. Lussier, eds.**
As Long as the Sun Shines and Water Flows. Vancouver: University
of British Columbia Press, 1983.

0049   **Govia, Francine**
Blacks in Canada: In Search of the Promise: A Bibliographic Guide.
Edmonton, Alberta: Harambee Centres Canada, 1988.

0050   **Green, Howard**
Ivan Halasz de Beky: A Bibliography. Toronto: L. Bush, 1983.

0051   **Green, Howard**
The NESA Bibliography Annotated for Native Studies. Vancouver:
Tilla-cum Library, 1983.

0052   **Gregorovich, Andrew**
"Ukrainians in Ontario: A Selected Bibliography." *Polyphony: The
Bulletin of the Multicultural History Society of Ontario*, vol. 10 no.
1/2 (1988) p. 271-285.

0053   **Griffith, Curt Taylor**
*Native North Americans: Crime, Conflict and Criminal Justice, A
Research Bibliography.* 2nd ed. Burnaby, B.C.: Criminology
Research Centre, Simon Fraser University and the Northern
Conference, 1984. 209 p.

0054   **Hackett, Christopher, ed.**
*A Bibliography of Manitoba Local History: A Guide to Local and
Regional Histories Written About Communities in Manitoba.*
Winnipeg: Manitoba Historical Society, 1989. 152 p.

0055 **Hayden, Jean and Isla Dafoe**
"Using Resources By and About Natives: Resources for Native Education." *The Medium,* vol. 28 no. 3 (1987) p. 46-55.

0056 **Hiebert, Stephanie**
"Radical Reformation and Mennonite Bibliography, 1985." *Mennonite Life,* vol. 41 no. 2 (1986) p. 15-31.

0057 **Hogan, Brian F.**
"A Current Bibliography of Canadian Church History/Bibliographie récente de l'histoire de l'église canadienne." *Canadian Catholic Historical Association: Historical Studies/La société canadienne d'histoire de l'Église catholique: Sessions d'étude,* no. 55 (1989) p. 149-193.

0058 **Howard, Lynda M., comp.**
Issues of Public Interest Regarding Northern Development: An Annotated Bibliography. Edited by Lynda M. Howard and Paul Davies. Calgary: Pallister Resource Management, 1984. 431 p.

0059 **Indra, Doreen M.**
"A Bibliography of Research on Southeast Asian Refugee Resettlement in Canada." In: *Uprooting, Loss and Adaptation: The Resettlement of Indochinese Refugees in Canada,* edited by Kwok B. Chan and Doreen Marie Indra. Ottawa: Canadian Public Health Association, 1987, p. 176-190.

0060 **Indra, Doreen M.**
Southeast Asian Refugee Settlement in Canada: A Research Bibliography. Ottawa: Canadian Asian Studies Association, Carleton University, 1984. 29 leaves.

0061 **International Sociological Association/Association internationale de sociologie**
"Bibliography: Involuntary Migration." *Current Sociology/La sociologie contemporaine,* vol. 36 no. 2 (1988) p. 115-153.

0062 **Jackson, Bruce, Michael Taft, and Harvey S. Axelrod**
"The Centennial Index: One Hundred Years of the Journal of American Folklore." *Journal of American Folklore,* vol. 101 no. 402 (1988) p. 1-506.

0063　**Janssen, Viveka K.**
"Bibliography on Swedish Settlement in Alberta, 1890-1930,"
Swedish-American Historical Quarterly. vol. 33 no. 2 (1982) p. 111-
123.

0064　**Jarvis, Eric and Melvin Baker**
"Clio in Hogtown: A Brief Bibliography [of Toronto]." *Ontario
History: Journal of the Ontario Historical Society,* vol. 74 no. 3
(1984) p. 287-294.

0065　**Johnson, Gregory A.**
"Recent Publications Relating to Canada." *Canadian Historical
Review,* vol. 69 no. 4 (1988) p. 513-530.

0066　**Jonasson, Eric**
"An Index to the Poetry Published in the *Icelandic Canadian* Volumes 1-40 (1942-1982)." *The Icelandic Canadian,* vol. 44 no. 4
(1986) p. 27-32.

0067　**Jonasson, Eric**
"Icelandic Service Personnel of the Second World War: An Index of
the Biographies Published in the 'Icelandic-Canadian Magazine'."
The Icelandic Canadian, vol. 44 no. 4 (1986) p. 41-47.

0068　**Kaganoff, Nathan M.**
"Judaica Americana: An Annotated Bibliography of Monographic and
Periodical Literature Published Since 1960 and Received in the
Library of the American Jewish Historical Society." *American Jewish
History,* vol. 77 no. 2 (1987) p. 285-315.

0069　**Kerst, Catherine Hiebert**
*Ethnic Folklife Dissertations from the United States and Canada,
1960-1980: A Selected Bibliography.* Washington, D.C.: American
Folklife Center, Library of Congress, 1986. 69 p.

0070　**Klippenstein, Lawrence**
"Canadian Mennonite Writings: A Bibliographic Survey, 1970-1980."
German-Canadian Yearbook/Deutschkanadisches jahrbuch, vol. 6
(1981) p. 284-293.

0071　**Krech, Shepard**
Native Canadian Anthropology and History: A Selected Bibliography.
Winnipeg: Rupert's Land Research Centre, University of Winnipeg,
1986. 214 p.

0072   **Larose, André**
"Bibliographie: bibliographie courante sur l'histoire de la population canadienne et la démographie historique au Canada, 1985/Bibliography: A Current Bibliography on the History of Canadian Population and Historical Demography in Canada, 1985." *Histoire sociale/ Social History*, vol. 19 no. 38 (1986) p. 461-465.

0073   **Larose, André**
"Bibliographie courante sur l'histoire de la population canadienne et la démographie historique au Canada, 1982/Bibliography: A Current Bibliography on the History of Canadian Population and Historical Demography in Canada, 1982." *Histoire sociale/Social History*, vol. 15 no. 30 (1982) p. 489-494.

0074   **Leduc, Marcel and Douglas Vaisey**
"The Canadian Labour Bibliography/La bibliographie du mouvement ouvrier canadien, 1983 and 1984." *Labour/Le Travail*, 16 (1985) p. 245-270.

0075   **Legros, Dominique**
"Bibliographie des amérindiens de la côte nord-ouest (1973-1982)." *Recherches amérindiennes au Québec*, vol. 14 no. 2 (1984) p. 56-70.

0076   **Levine, Marc V.**
"The Language Question in Quebec: A Selected, Annotated Bibliography." *Quebec Studies*, no. 8 (1989) p. 37-41.

0077   **Liddel, Peter C.**
A Bibliography of Germans in British Columbia. Vancouver: CAUTG, 1982.

0078   **Loganbill, Marilyn**
"Radical Reformation and Mennonite Bibliography 1987." *Mennonite Life*, vol. 43 no. 2 (1988) p. 24-31.

0079   **Lonardo, Michael**
"The Canadian Labour Bibliography/La bibliographie du mouvement ouvrier canadien 1988." *Labour/Le Travail*, no. 24 (1989) p. 195-218.

0080   **Lovejoy, James**
Bibliography of the Salish People of British Columbia and Northwestern Washington. [Vancouver: s.n., 1983.] 31 leaves.

0081   **Mackey, William R., ed.**
Bibliographie internationale sur le bilinguisme/International Bibliography on Bilingualism. 2e éd. Québec, P.Q.: Presses de l'université Laval, 1982. 575 p.

0082   **Madill, Dennis**
Select Annotated Bibliography on Metis History and Claims. Ottawa: Indian and Northern Affairs, 1983. 45 p.

0083   **Madill, Dennis**
Select Annotated Bibliography of British Columbia Indian Policy and Land Claims. Ottawa: Treaties and Historical Research Centre, Research Branch, Corporate Policy, Dept. of Indian and Northern Affairs, 1982. 27 p.

0084   **Magocsi, Paul Robert**
"Ucrainica Collections and Bibliography in North America: Their Current Status." *Journal of Ukrainian Studies/Zhurnal Ukrajinoznavchykh Studij,* vol. 12 no. 2 (1987) p. 77-91.

0085   **Magocsi, Paul Robert**
Galicia: A Historical Survey and Bibliographic Guide. Toronto: Canadian Institute of Ukrainian Studies, University of Toronto, 1983. 299 p.

0086   **Malycky, Alexander**
Ukrainian Book Imprints of Edmonton, Alberta: First Supplement. Publication no. 2. Edmonton: Ukrainian Bibliographical Society of Alberta, 1985.

0087   **Malycky, Alexander**
"German-Albertans: A Bibliography Part 2." *German-Canadian Yearbook/Deutschkanadisches jahrbuch,* vol. 7 (1982).

0088   **Malycky, Alexander**
"German-Albertans: A Bibliography Part 1." *German-Canadian Yearbook/Deutschkanadisches jahrbuch,* vol. 6 (1981).

0089   **Malycky, Alexander and Mykola Woron**
Ukrainian Publishing Activity of Alberta: 1. Publication no. 1. Calgary: Ukrainian Bibliographical Society of Alberta, 1984.

0090   **Metress, Seamus P.**
"The Irish in the Great Lakes: Selected Bibliography of
Sociohistorical Sources." *Ethnic Forum*, vol. 7 no. 1
(1987) p. 97-109.

0091   **Metropolitan Toronto Central Library. Languages Centre**
*A Bibliography of Inuit (Eskimo) Linguistics in Collections of the
Metropolitan Toronto Library.* Toronto: Metropolitan Toronto Library
Board, Languages Centre, 1982.

0092   **Millar, Michael M.**
*Researching the Germans from Russia: Annotated Bibliography of the
Germans from Russia Heritage Collection.* Fargo: North Dakota
Institute for Regional Studies, North Dakota State University, 1987.
224 p.

0093   **Miller, Carman**
"Research Resources on Canada and the South African War."
Archivaria no. 26 (1988) p. 116-121.

0094   **Miller, Joseph C. and David F. Appleby**
"Slavery: Current Bibliographical Supplement (1986)." *Slavery and
Abolition*, vol. 8 no. 3 (1987) p. 353-386.

0095   **Miska, John P., comp.**
*Canadian Studies on Hungarians, 1886-1986: An Annotated
Bibliography of Primary and Secondary Sources.* Regina: Canadian
Plains Research Center, University of Regina, 1987. 245 p.

0096   **Moir, Michael B.**
"Scottish Manuscripts in Canadian Repositories." *Archivaria*, 17
(1983-84) p. 145-161.

0097   **Monzon, Susana**
"Bibliographie américaniste." *Journal de la société des américanistes*,
vol. 75 (1989) p. 251-271.

0098   **Morrison, James H.**
*Common Heritage: An Annotated Bibliography of Ethnic Groups in
Nova Scotia.* Halifax, N.S.: Saint Mary's University, 1984. 130 p.

0099   **Moskal, Susan**
        *Contemporary Canadian Indian Statistics Published by the Federal
        Government, 1960-1985: A Selective Bibliography and Subject Index
        to Sources Available in the University of Waterloo Library.* Waterloo,
        Ont.: University of Waterloo Library, 1987. 25 p.

0100   **Myroniuk, Halyna**
        Ukrainians in North America: A Selected Bibliography. Toronto:
        Multicultural History Society of Ontario, 1981.

0101   **Nadkarni, Meena**
        Citizenship in Canada: A Retrospective Bibliography. Monticello, Ill.:
        Vance Bibliographies, 1985. 29 p.

0102   **Narby, Jeremy**
        *Resource Development and Indigenous Peoples: A Comparative
        Bibliography.* Boston: Anthropology Resource Center, 1983. 32 p.

0103   **National Ethnic Archives**
        A Guide to Sources for the Study of Ukrainian Canadians. Ottawa:
        National Ethnic Archives, 1984.

0104   **Native Indian Pre-school Curriculum Research Project**
        Native Indian Pre-school Curriculum Resources Bibliography.
        Vancouver: Urban Native Indian Education Society, 1983.

0105   **Orfalea, Gregory**
        "On Arab-Americans: A Bibliographical Essay." *American Studies
        International*, vol. 27 no. 2 (1989) p. 26-41.

0106   **Palmer, Gregory, ed.**
        *A Bibliography of Loyalist Source Material in the United States,
        Canada and Great Britain.* Westport. Conn.: Meckler Publ., 1982.

0107   **Passerieux, Catherine et Louis Le Borgne**
        Guide bibliographique sur les relations ethniques et l'immigration.
        Montréal: Université du Québec à Montréal, Service des
        bibliothèques, 1985. 11 p.

0108   **Peeters, Yvo J.D.**
        "Bibliography on Ethnic and Linguistic Conflict." *Plural Societies*,
        vol. 16 no. 1 (1986) p. 87-90

0109   **Pentland, H. and H. Christoph Wolfort**
        Bibliography of Algonquin Linguistics. Winnipeg: University of
        Manitoba Press, 1983.

0110   **Perin, Roberto**
        "Clio as an Ethnic: The Third Force in Canadian Historiography."
        Canadian Historical Review, vol. 53 (1983) p. 441-467.

0111   **Pernal, Andrew B.**
        "Recent Polish Publications on Canada and the Emigration from
        Poland to Canada." *Manitoba History,* vol. 17 (1989) p. 37-43.

0112   **Perron, J.**
        *Bibliographie des thèses et mémoires sur les communautés culturelles
        et l'immigration.* Montréal: Ministère des communautés culturelles et
        de l'immigration, 1983. 43 p.

0113   **Peters, Evelyn J.**
        Aboriginal Self-government in Canada: A Bibliography 1986. King-
        ston: Institute of Intergovernmental Relations, Queen's University,
        1986. 112 p.

0114   **Petryshyn, Roman and Natalia Chomiak**
        *Political Writing of Post-World War Two Ukrainian Emigres:
        Annotated Bibliography and Guide to Research.* Edmonton: Canadian
        Institute of Ukrainian Studies, University of Alberta, 1984.

0115   **Poirier, Marie**
        Les femmes immigrées au Québec: bibliographie annotée. Montréal:
        Direction des communications et direction de la recherche, Ministère
        des communautés culturelles et de l'immigration, 1985. 51 p.

0116   **Potvin, Claude**
        Acadiana, 1980-1982: une bibliographie annotée. Moncton, New
        Brunswick: Éditions CRP, 1983. 110 p.

0117   **Ramrattan, Annette and Nick Kach**
        "Native Education in Alberta: A Bibliography." *Canadian Journal of
        Native Education,* vol. 12. no. 3 (1985) p. 55-68.

0118   **Ray, Douglas and Beatriz Franco**
        "Bibliography—Human Rights in Education: Recently Published
        Canadian Sources and an Index." *Canadian Journal of Education/
        Revue canadienne de l'éducation,* vol. 11 no. 3 (1986) p. 364-382.

0119   **Reimer, Margaret Loewen**
One Quilt. Many Pieces. A Concise Reference Guide to Mennonite Groups in Canada. Waterloo, Ont.: Mennonite Publishing Services, 1983.

0120   **Rome, David, Judith Nefsky et Paule Obermeir**
Les juifs du Québec, bibliographie rétrospective annotée. Québec: Institut québécois de recherche sur la culture, 1981. 317 p.

0121   **Rutkowski, Alan and Nadia Cyncar**
Ukrainica on Microform: A Checklist of Non-serial Publications in The University of Alberta Library. Edmonton: Canadian Institute of Ukrainian Studies, University of Alberta, 1984. 91 p.

0122   **Rutkowski, Alan and Nadia Cyncar**
Ukrainian Serials. A Checklist of Ukrainian Journals, Periodicals and Newspapers at the University of Alberta Library. Edmonton: Canadian Institute of Ukrainian Studies, University of Alberta, 1983. 62 p.

0123   **Scantland, Anna Cecile**
Bibliography: Study of Historical Injustice to Japanese Canadians. Vancouver: Parallel Publishers, 1986. Typescript (loose-leaf).

0124   **Senecal, Andre Joseph**
Quebec Studies: A Selected Annotated Bibliography. Burlington, Vt.: Information Center on Canada, 1982.

0125   **Sherman, William C.**
Prairie Mosaic: An Ethnic Atlas of Rural North Dakota. Fargo, North Dakota: Institute for Regional Studies, 1983.

0126   **Shermis, Michael**
"Recent Publications in the Jewish-Christian Dialogue: An Annotated Bibliography." *American Journal of Theology and Philosophy*, vol. 9 no. 1 and 2 (1986) p. 137-142

0127   **Slavutych, Yar**
An Annotated Bibliography of Ukrainian Literature in Canada: Canadian Book Publications, 1908-1986. Edmonton: Slavuta Publishers, 1987. 166 p.

0128   **Social Science Federation of Canada/La fédération canadienne des sciences sociales**
Directory of Social Science Research Centers and Institutes at Canadian Universities/Répertoire des centres et instituts de recherche en sciences sociales dans les universités canadiennes. Ottawa: University of Ottawa Press/Les presses de l'université d'Ottawa, 1987. 196 p.

0129   **Strathern, Gloria**
Alberta Newspapers, 1880-1982: An Historical Directory. Edmonton: University of Alberta Press, 1988. 568 p.

0130   **Stymeist, David H., Lilia Salazar, and Graham Spafford**
A Selected Annotated Bibliography on the Filipino Immigrant Community in Canada and the United States. University of Manitoba Anthropology Papers, no. 31. Winnipeg: University of Manitoba, Department of Anthropology, 1989. 131 p.

0131   **Sugunasiri, Suwanda H.J.**
The Literature of Canadians of South Asian Origins: An Overview and Preliminary Bibliography. Toronto: Multicultural History Society of Ontario, 1987. 62 p.

0132   **Surtees, Robert J.**
Canadian Indian Policy: A Critical Bibliography. Bloomington: University of Indiana Press, 1982. 107 p.

0133   **Swanick, Eric L.**
The Lake Meech Accord (Canadian Constitution): A Bibliography. Monticello, Ill.: Vance Bibliographies, 1988. 22 p.

0134   **Swanick, Eric L., ed.**
"Recent Publications Relating to the History of the Atlantic Region." *Acadiensis: Journal of the History of the Atlantic Region/Revue de l'histoire de la région atlantique,* vol. 19 no. 1 (1989) p. 209-231.

0135   **Swyripa, Frances A.**
Guide to Ukrainian Canadian Newspapers, Periodicals and Calendar-Almanacs on Microfilm, 1903-1970. Edmonton: Canadian Institute of Ukrainian Studies, University of Alberta, 1985.

0136   **Swyripa, Frances A. and Andrij Makuch**
Ukrainian Canadian Content in the Newspaper 'Svoboda,' 1893-1904. Edmonton: Canadian Institute of Ukrainian Studies, University of Alberta, 1985.

0137   **Tupling, Donald M.**
Canada: A Dissertation Bibliography, 1983 Supplement/Une bibliographie de dissertations, 1983 supplément. Ann Arbor, Mich.: University Microfilms International, 1983. 31 p.

0138   **Tupling, Donald M.**
Canada, a Dissertation Bibliography. Une bibliographie de dissertations. Ann Arbor, Mich.: University Microfilms International, 1980. 131 p.

0139   **Turcotte, Paul-André**
"Bibliographie générale sélective sur le nationalisme canadien-français ou québécois." *Social Compass,* vol. 31 no. 4 (1984) p. 427-438.

0140   **Ukrainian Bibliographical Society of Alberta**
Ukrainian Publishing Activity of Alberta. Publication no. 1. Calgary, Alta: Library of St. Vladimir's Ukrainian Orthodox Congregation, 1984.

0141   **Wai, Lokky**
The Native Peoples of Canada in Contemporary Society: A Demographic and Socio-economic Bibliography. London, Ont.: Population Studies Centre, University of Western Ontario, 1989. 82 p.

0142   **Wiebe, Victor G.**
Alberta/Saskatchewan Mennonite and Hutterite Bibliography, 1962-1981. Saskatoon: Mennonite Historical Society of Alberta and Saskatchewan, 1981.

0143   **Williams, Wiley J.**
"United States Government Information Resources and Ethnic Research: An Introduction." *Ethnic Forum,* vol. 6 no. 1/2 (1986) p. 150-166.

0144   **Young, Judy**
"Some Thoughts about the Present State of Bibliography in the Area of Canadian Ethnic Studies." In: *Bibliography for Canadian Studies: Present Trends and Future Needs* (Association for Canadian Studies), vol. 6 (1982) p. 38.

0145   **Young, Rod**
"Labour Archives: An Annotated Bibliography." *Archivaria*, no. 27 (1988-89) p. 97-110.

0146   **Zaporzan, Shirley and Robert B. Klymasz**
Film and the Ukrainians in Canada, 1921-1980: A Filmography Index of Film Titles with Bibliography. Edmonton: Canadian Institute of Ukrainian Studies, University of Alberta, 1982.

0147   **Zimmerman, Diana**
Ojibwa Cree Resource Centre Catalogue. Timmins, Ontario: Ojibwa Cree Resource Centre, 1982.

General and Encyclopedic Works

0148   **Alberta Culture**
"Profiles of Ethno-cultural Groups in Alberta: Black, Chinese, Sikh, Dutch." *Heritage Link*, vol. 1 no. 3 (1986) p. 35-43.

0149   **Anctil, Pierre**
"Double majorité et multiplicité ethnoculturelle à Montréal." *Recherches sociographiques*, vol. 25 no. 3 (1984) p. 441-456.

0150   **Bathalon, Réal**
Répertoire des organismes ethno-culturels du Québec. Montréal: Ministère des communautés culturelles et de l'immigration, 1983. 124 p.

0151   **Bathalon, Réal et Nicole Jetté**
Répertoire ethnoculturel du Québec 1986/Ethnocultural Directory of Quebec 1986. Montréal: Centre intercultural Monchanin Montréal, 1986. 49/51 p.

0152   **Beaulieu, Agnès**
"Répertoire des recherches en cours dans les universités québécoises sur les communautés culturelles et l'immigration au Canada." *Sociologie et Sociétés*, vol. 15 no. 2 (1983) p. 167-174.

0153   **Bibby, Reginald W.**
The Emerging Generation: An Inside Look at Canada's Teenagers. Toronto: Irwin Publishing, 1985. 220 p.

0154   **Boulet, Jac-Andre**
"Socio-economic Achievements of Montreal Language Groups in 1971." *Canadian Review of Sociology and Anthropology/Revue canadienne de sociologie et d'anthropologie*, vol. 18 no. 2 (1981) p. 239-248.

0155   **Breton, Raymond**
"West Indian, Chinese and European Ethnic Groups in Toronto." In:
Two Nations, Many Cultures: Ethnic Groups in Canada, edited by
Jean Leonard Elliott. 2nd ed. Scarborough, Ont.: Prentice-Hall of
Canada, 1983, p. 425-443.

0156   **Broadfoot, Barry**
The Immigrant Years, 1945-1967. Vancouver: Douglas and McIntyre,
1986. 240 p.

0157   **Buchignani, Norman**
"Canadian Ethnic Research and Multiculturalism." *Journal of
Canadian Studies/Revue d'études canadiennes*, vol. 17 no. 1
(1982) p. 16-34.

0158   **Burnet, Jean R. and Howard Palmer**
*Coming Canadians: An Introduction to a History of Canada's
Peoples*. Toronto: McClelland and Stewart, 1988. 253 p.

0159   **Canada. Department of the Secretary of State. Multiculturalism
Directorate**
*Visible Minorities in Government Communications: A Matter of
Balance*. Ottawa: Department of Supply and Services, 1988. 15 p.

0160   **Canada. Parliament. House of Commons. Special Committee on
Participation of Visible Minorities in Canadian Society**
Equality Now: Report. Bob Daudlin, chairman. Ottawa: Supply and
Services Canada, 1984. 166 p.

0161   **Canada. Statistics Canada**
Profile of Ethnic Groups. Dimensions. Census Canada, 1986. Ottawa:
Statistics Canada, 1989. 383 p. French language title: *Profil des
groupes ethniques*. Catalogue no.: 93-154.

0162   **Canada. Statistics Canada**
Profile of the Immigrant Population. Dimensions. Census Canada,
1986. Ottawa: Statistics Canada, 1989. French language title: *Profil
de la population immigrante*. Catalogue no.: 93-155.

0163   **Charon, Milly**
Worlds Apart: New Immigrant Voices. Dunvegan, Ontario: Cormorant
Books, 1989. 430 p.

0164   **Coates, Ken and Fred McGuinness**
Manitoba: The Province and the People. Edmonton: Hurtig
Publishers, 1987. 203 p.

0165   **Disman, Miloslav**
"Immigrants and Other Grieving People: Anthropological Insights for
Counselling Practices and Policy Issues." *Canadian Ethnic Studies/
Études ethniques au Canada,* vol. 15 no. 3 (1983) p. 106-118.

0166   **Elliott, Jean Leonard, ed.**
Two Nations, Many Cultures: Ethnic Groups in Canada. 2nd ed.
Scarborough, Ont.: Prentice-Hall of Canada, 1983. 493 p.

0167   **Forward, Charles N., ed.**
British Columbia: Its Resources and People. Western Geographical
Series, vol. 22. Victoria: University of Victoria, Department of
Geography, 1987. 433 p.

0168   **Froeschle, Hartmut**
Ethnic Groups and Canadian Identity. Toronto: German-Canadian
Historical Association, 1983. 10 p.

0169   **Fry, A. and Charles Forceville, eds.**
Canadian Mosaic: Essays on Multiculturalism. Amsterdam: Free
University Press, 1988. 64 p.

0170   **Harney, Robert F., ed.**
*Gathering Place: Peoples and Neighbourhoods of Toronto, 1834-
1945.* Toronto: Multicultural History Society of Ontario, 1985. 304 p.

0171   **Harvey, Fernand**
"The Other Ethnic Groups in Quebec." *Language, Culture, and
Curriculum,* vol. 1 no. 3 (1988) p. 197-202.

0172   **Herberg, Edward Norman**
Ethnic Groups in Canada: Adaptations and Transitions, Scarborough,
Ontario: Nelson Canada, 1989. 329 p.

0173   **Lamothe, Aleida**
Les autres québécoises. Montréal: Ministère des communautés
culturelles et de l'immigration, Direction de la recherche, 1985.
110 p.

0174   **Langlois, André**
L'analyse factorielle à Trois Entrées: une application à l'espace ethnique montréalais. Unpublished PhD thesis, Université Laval, 1983. 4 microfiches. Canadian theses on microfiche, 67115.

0175   **Lautard, E. Hugh**
"Regional Variation in Canada's Cultural Mosaic." *Canadian Issues,* vol. 5 (1983) p. 59-67.

0176   **Linteau, Paul-André**
"La montée du cosmopolitisme montréalais." *Questions de culture,* no. 2 (1982) p. 28-53.

0177   **Miodunka, Wladyslaw**
"Immigrants and Ethnic Groups in Canadian Cities: Conference Organized by Canadian Ethnic Studies Association." *Przeglad Polonijnuy,* vol. 13 no. 2 (1987) p. 77-80, 129.

0178   **Morton, William Lewis**
"The Historical Phenomenon of Minorities: The Canadian Experience." *Canadian Ethnic Studies/Études ethniques au Canada,* vol. 13 no. 3 (1981) p. 1-39.

0179   **Nett, Emily M.**
Canadian Families: Past and Present. Toronto: Butterworths, 1988. 342 p.

0180   **Pucci, A. and J. Potestio, eds.**
"Thunder Bay's People." Monographic issue of *Polyphony: The Bulletin of the Multicultural History Society of Ontario,* vol. 9 no. 2 (1987) 114 p. Monographic issue of *Polyphony.*

0181   **Rao, G. Lakshmana, Anthony H. Richmond, and Jerzy Zubrzycki**
Immigrants in Canada and Australia. 3 volumes, edited by Anthony H. Richmond and Freda Richmond. Downsview, Ont.: York University, Institute for Behavioural Research, 1984. vol. 1, *Demographic Aspects and Education*; vol. 2, *Economic Adaptation*; vol. 3, *Urban and Ecological Aspects.*

0182   **Samuel, T. John**
"Visible Minorities in Canada." In: *Contributions to Demography: Methodological and Substantive: Essays in Honour of Dr. Karol J. Krotki.* Edmonton: University of Alberta, Department of Sociology, 1987, p. 641-658.

0183   **Sharpe, Robert**
        Regional Variations Among Ethnic Groups in Ontario: A Core-periphery Model. Unpublished MA thesis, Wilfred Laurier University, 1983. Canadian theses on microfiche, 61735.

0184   **Stefura, Mary, ed.**
        "Sudbury's People." *Polyphony: The Bulletin of the Multicultural History Society of Ontario*, vol. 5 no. 1 (1987) 114 p. Monographic issue of *Polyphony.*

0185   **Wood, Colin J.B.**
        "Population and Ethnic Groups." In: *British Columbia: Its Resources and People*, edited by Charles N. Forward. Victoria: Department of Geography, University of Victoria, 1987, p. 309-332.

Migration and Immigration

0186   **Abella, Irving**
"The German-Jewish Intellectual and Canadian Immigration, 1933-1945." *Annalen: Deutschkanadische Studien*, vol. 4 (1983) p. 167-184.

0187   **Adelman, Howard, ed.**
The Three S's: Selection, Status Determination, Settlement. Downsview, Ontario: Refugee Documentation Project, 1984.

0188   **Akbari, Ather H.**
"The Benefits of Immigrants to Canada: Evidence on Tax and Public Services." *Canadian Public Policy/Analyse de politiques*, vol. 15 no. 4 (1989) p. 424-435.

0189   **Aldridge, J.R.**
"The Refugee Process in Canada." *Canadian Council on International Law. Proceedings of Annual Conference*, vol. 10 (1981) p. 117-135.

0190   **Allen, Rebecca**
"The Social Organization of Migration: An Analysis of Uprooting and Flight of Vietnamese Refugees." *International Migration/Migrations Internationales/Migraciones Internacionales*, vol. 23 no. 4 (1985) p. 439-452.

0191   **Allen, Rebecca**
The Social Organization of Migration: An Analysis of the Uprooting and Flight of Vietnamese Refugees. Unpublished MA thesis, University of Calgary, 1983. 3 microfiches. Canadian theses on microfiche, CT 87-20788-1.

0192   **Angus, William H.**
"Canadian Immigration and Refugee Policies: A Blurred Boundary."
In: *Doing it Right*, edited by John C. Munro. Toronto: James Lorimer
and Co. Publishers, 1987, p. 106-115.

0193   **Atchison, John**
"Immigration in Two Federations." In: *Federalism in Canada and
Australia*, edited by Bruce W. Hodgins et al. Peterborough, Ont.: The
Frost Centre for Canadian Heritage and Development Studies, Trent
University, 1989, p. 200-227.

0194   **Atchison, John**
"Immigration in Two Federations: Canada and Australia."
*International Migration/Migrations Internationales/Migraciones Inter-
nacionales*, vol. 26 no. 1 (1988) p. 5-32.

0195   **Audet, Benoit**
Immigration temporaire au Québec en 1984. Montréal: Ministère des
communautés culturelles du Québec, Direction de la recherche, 1985.
16 p.

0196   **Audet, Benoit**
*Importance et caractéristiques des personnes immigrées recevant des
prestations d'aide sociale au Québec: de janvier 1981 à janvier
1984*. Montréal: Ministère des communautés culturelles du Québec,
Direction de la recherche, 1984. 24 p. annexes statistiques.

0197   **Audet, Benoit**
L'immigration temporaire au Québec en 1982. Montréal: Ministère
des communautés culturelles et de l'immigration, Direction de la
recherche, 1983. 42 p.

0198   **Avery, Donald**
"Canada's Response to European Refugees, 1939-1945: The Security
Dimension." In: *On Guard for Thee: War, Ethnicity and the
Canadian State, 1939-1945*, edited by Norman Hillmer, Bohdan
Kordan, and Lubomyr Luciuk. Ottawa: Canadian Committee for the
History of the Second World War, 1988, p. 179-216.

0199   **Avery, Donald**
"Canadian Immigration Policy Towards Europe 1945-1952: Altruism
and Economic Self-interest." *Zeitschrift für Gesellschaft für Kanada-
Studien*, vol. 6 no. 1 (1986) p. 37-56.

0200   **Avery, R.**
"The Impact of International Migration on Canada's Population Growth: An Application of the Stationary Population Equivalent Model." In: *Contributions to Demography: Methodological and Substantive, Essays in Honour of Dr. Karol J. Krotki.* Edmonton: University of Alberta, Department of Sociology, 1987, p. 245-290.

0201   **Badets, Jane**
"Canada's Immigrant Population." *Canadian Social Trends*, no. 14 (1989) p. 2-6.

0202   **Bailey, Thomas**
"The Influence of Legal Status on the Labor Market Impact of Immigration." *International Migration Review*, vol. 19 no. 2 (1985) p. 220-238.

0203   **Balakrishnan, T.R.**
Immigration and the Changing Ethnic Mosaic of Canadian Cities. Ottawa: Health and Welfare Canada, 1988. 69 leaves.

0204   **Bandera, Marika**
"The Canadian Ukrainian Immigrant Aid Society: A Decade of Service." *Polyphony: The Bulletin of the Multicultural History Society of Ontario*, vol. 10 no. 1/2 (1988) p. 245-246.

0205   **Barbara, Augustin**
Marriage Across Frontiers. Clevedon, U.K.: Multilingual Matters, 1989. 214 p.

0206   **Bassler, Gerhard P.**
"Newfoundland and Refugees from the Third Reich, 1933-41." *Newfoundland Studies*, vol. 3 no. 1 (1987) p. 37-70.

0207   **Bassler, Gerhard P.**
"Central Europeans in Post-Confederation St. John's, Newfoundland: Immigration and Adjustment." *Canadian Ethnic Studies/Études ethniques au Canada*, vol. 18 no. 3 (1986) p. 37-46.

0208   **Beach, Charles M. and Alan G. Green, eds.**
Policy Forum on the Role of Immigration in Canada's Future. Kingston, Ont.: John Deutsch Institute for the Study of Economic Policy, Queen's University, 1989. 102 p.

0209   **Beattie, Betsy**
"Opportunity Across the Border: The Burlington Area Economy and the French Canadian Worker in 1850." *Vermont History*, vol. 55 no. 3 (1987) p. 133-152.

0210   **Beaujot, Roderic P.**
"The Link Between Immigration and Emigration in Canada, 1945-1986." *Canadian Studies In Population*, vol. 16 no. 2 (1989) p. 201-216.

0211   **Beaujot, Roderic P.**
Income of Immigrants in Canada: A Census Data Analysis. Ottawa: Statistics Canada, 1988. 98 p. French language title: *Le revenu des immigrants au Canada*.

0212   **Beaujot, Roderic P.**
The Role of Immigration in Changing Socio-demographic Structures. Ottawa: Health and Welfare Canada, 1988. 255 p.

0213   **Beck, Brenda E.F.**
"Perceptions des relations parentales entre parent et enfant chez des immigrants au Canada: variations selon qu'ils proviennent d'Inde, du Japon ou de Hongrie." In: *Asian Canadians: Regional Perspectives*, edited by K. Victor Ujimoto and Gordon Hirabayashi. Guelph: University of Guelph, 1982, p. 207-221. Paper presented at the 5th Asian Canadian Symposium held at Mount Saint Vincent University, Halifax, Nova Scotia, May 23 to May 26, 1981.

0214   **Bennett, Doug**
"No Strangers in Paradise: Canada's Refugee Policy." *Canadian Forum*, vol. 47 no. 771 (1987) p. 6-13.

0215   **Bercuson, David and Howard Palmer**
Settling the Canadian West. Focus on Canadian History Series. Toronto: Grolier Ltd., 1984. 96 p.

0216   **Bergman, E.**
"Social Effects of Migration in Receiving Countries: A Theoretical Approach." *International Migration/Migrations Internationales/ Migraciones Internacionales*, vol. 27 no. 2 (1989) p. 217-224.

0217   **Bernéche, Francine**
"Immigration et espace urbain: les regroupements de population
haïtienne dans la région métropolitaine de Montréal." *Cahiers
québécois de démographie*, vol. 12 no. 2 (1983) p. 295-324.

0218   **Berton, Pierre**
The Promised Land: Settling the West, 1896-1914. Toronto:
McClelland and Stewart, 1984.

0219   **Blanc, Bernadette**
"Problématique de la localisation des nouveaux immigrants à
Montréal." *Canadian Ethnic Studies/Études ethniques au Canada*,
vol. 18 no. 1 (1986) p. 89-108.

0220   **Bolaria, B. Singh**
"The Brain Drain to Canada: The Externalization of the Cost of
Education." In: *The Political Economy of Canadian Schooling*, edited
by Terry Wotherspoon. Toronto: Methuen, 1987, p. 301-322.

0221   **Bolduc, Denis**
*L'opinion des québécois en matière d'immigration: une analyse poly-
tomique ordinale.* Québec, P.Q.: Département d'économique, Université
Laval, 1988. 75 p. Communication presentée aux Congrès de la Société
canadienne de science économique, Lac Delage, P.Q., 18-20 mai 1988, et
de la Canadian Economic Association, Windsor, Ont.: 3-5 juin 1988.

0222   **Boshyk, Yury and Boris Balan**
*Political Refugees and Displaced Persons, 1945-54: A Selected
Bibliography and Guide to Research with Special Reference to
Ukrainians.* Edmonton: Canadian Institute of Ukrainian Studies,
University of Alberta, 1982.

0223   **Bothwell, Robert**
"Weird Science: Scientific Refugees and the Montreal Laboratory."
In: *On Guard for Thee: War, Ethnicity and the Canadian State,
1939-1945*, edited by Norman Hillmer, Bohdan Kordan, and
Lubomyr Luciuk. Ottawa: Canadian Committee for the History of the
Second World War, 1988, p. 217-240.

0224   **Bourbeau, Robert**
"Mobilité linguistique et migration: analyse de leur relation dans quelques pro-
vinces canadiennes en 1971 et 1981." In: *Contributions to Demography:
Methodological and Substantive, Essays in Honour of Dr. Karol J. Krotki.*
Edmonton: University of Alberta, Department of Sociology, 1987, p. 349-376.

0225   **Bourque, Jean-Louis**
"Pour une véritable politique québécoise en matière d'immigration."
Action nationale, vol. 76 no. 7 (1987) p. 583-594.

0226   **Bouthillier, G.**
"L'immigration internationale: un fait politique." *Cahiers québécois de démographie*, vol. 12 no. 2 (Octobre 1983) p. 181-199.

0227   **Boyd, Monica**
"The American Emigrant in Canada: Trends and Consequences."
International Migration Review, vol. 15 no. 4 (1981) p. 650-670.

0228   **Brown, Michael**
"The Push and Pull Factors of Aliyah and the Anomalous Case of Canada: 1967-1982." *Jewish Social Studies*, vol. 48 no. 2 (1986) p. 141-162.

0229   **Brown, Ron**
"Roads of Broken Dreams: It Was a Noble Experiment That Failed."
History of the Canadian West, no. 3 (1984) p. 65-76.

0230   **Bruce, Jean**
After the War. Toronto: Fitzhenry and Whiteside, 1982. 192 p.

0231   **Brun, Henri**
"Les statuts respectifs de citoyen, résident et étranger, à la lumière des Chartes des droits." *Cahiers de droit*, vol. 29 no. 3 (1988) p. 689-731.

0232   **Brunet, Michel**
"Les immigrants en Amérique du Nord: Des partenaires d'une même aventure." In: *Questions de culture,* série 2. Québec: Institut québécois de recherche sur la culture, 1983.

0233   **Buchignani, Norman**
Continuous Journey: Social History of South Asians in Canada.
Toronto: McClelland and Stewart in association with the Multiculturalism Directorate, Department of the Secretary of State and the Canadian Government Publishing Centre, Supply and Services, Canada, 1985. 250 p.

0234   **Buchignani, Norman**
"Accommodation, Adaptation and Policy: Dimensions of the South
Asian Experience in Canada." In: *Visible Minorities and Multicul-
turalism: Asians in Canada*, edited by K. Victor Ujimoto and Gordon
Hirabayashi. Toronto: Butterworths, 1980, p. 121-150.

0235   **Buchignani, Norman**
"The Economic Adaptation of Southeast Asian Refugees in Canada."
In: *Southeast Asian Exodus: From Traditions to Resettlement;
Understanding Refugees from Laos, Kampuchea and Vietnam in
Canada*, edited by Elliot L Tepper. Ottawa: Canadian Asian Studies
Association, 1980, p. 191-204.

0236   **Bumsted, J.M.**
*Land, Settlement, and Politics on Eighteenth-Century Prince Edward
Island.* Montreal: McGill-Queen's University Press, 1987. 256 p.

0237   **Burke, Mary Anne**
"Immigration." *Canadian Social Trends*, no. 2 (1986) p. 23-27.

0238   **Burnet, Jean R. and Howard Palmer**
Coming Canadians: An Introduction to a History of Canada's Peoples.
Toronto: McClelland and Stewart, 1988. 253 p.

0239   **Busch, R.L.**
"Edmonton's Elderly Soviet Immigrants." In: *Central and East
European Ethnicity in Canada: Adaptation and Preservation*, edited
by T. Yedlin. Edmonton: Central and East European Studies Society
of Alberta, 1985, p. 43-62.

0240   **Campbell, Charles M.**
A Time Bomb Ticking: Canadian Immigration in Crisis. Toronto:
Mackenzie Institute for the Study of Terrorism, Revolution and
Propaganda, 1989. 39 p.

0241   **Canada. Employment and Immigration Canada (Department) Policy
and Program Development Branch**
Corporate Priorities in Immigration Planning, 1985. Ottawa:
Employment and Immigration Canada, 1984. 8, 9 p.

0242   **Canada. Employment and Immigration Canada**
Immigration Statistics: 1980. Ottawa: Employment and Immigration
Canada, 1980. 85 p.

0243 **Canadian Museum of Civilization**
Ukrainians in Canada, 1891-1991. Ottawa: Canadian Museum of
Civilization, National Museum of Science and Technology, 1989.
127 p. French language title: *Les ukrainiens au Canada, 1891-1991.*

0244 **Canadian Task Force on Mental Health Issues Affecting**
Immigrants and Refugees
After the Door Has Been Opened: Mental Health Issues Affecting
Immigrants and Refugees in Canada: Report ... Ottawa: Department
of the Secretary of State of Canada, Multiculturalism Sector, 1988.
113 p. French language title: *Puis: la porte s'est ouverte: problèmes*
mentaux affligeant immigrants et réfugiés au Canada; une étude. . .

0245 **Cannon, Margaret**
China Tide: The Revealing Story of the Hong Kong Exodus to
Canada. Toronto: Harper and Collins, 1989. 263 p.

0246 **Carrigan, D. Owen**
"The Immigrant Experience in Halifax, 1881-1931." *Canadian Ethnic*
Studies/Études ethniques au Canada, vol. 20 no. 3 (1988) p. 28-41.

0247 **Center for Migration Studies**
"Migration and Health." *International Migration Review,* vol. 21 no.
3 (1987) p. 491-907.

0248 **Chan, Anthony B.**
Gold Mountain: The Chinese in the New World. Vancouver: New
Star Books, 1983. 223 p.

0249 **Chan, Kwok B. and Doreen Marie Indra, eds.**
Uprooting, Loss and Adaptation: The Resettlement of Indochinese
Refugees in Canada. Ottawa: Canadian Public Health Association,
1987. 195 p.

0250 **Chandrasekhar, S.**
"A History of Canadian Legislation with Respect to Immigration
from India." *Plural Societies,* vol. 16 no. 3 (1986) p. 254-280.

0251 **Chandrasekhar, S.**
"A History of Canadian Legislation with Respect to Immigration
from India." *Population Review,* vol. 29 no. 1/2 (1985) p. 11-34.

0252   **Chimbos, Peter D.**
The Canadian Odyssey: The Greek Experience in Canada. Toronto:
McClelland and Stewart, 1980. 176 p.

0253   **Chow, Donna**
"Opportunities and Challenges Created by Hong Kong Immigration to
Vancouver." *Business Review (U.B.C. Commerce Undergraduate
Society)*, vol. 23 (1988) p. 73-82.

0254   **Coelho, A. Bento**
"Effects of Migration on Social Change in the Country of Origin."
*International Migration/Migrations Internationales/Migraciones Inter-
nacionales*, vol. 27 no. 2. (1989) p. 183-190.

0255   **Con, Harry, Ronald J. Con, Graham Johnson, et al.**
*From China to Canada: A History of the Chinese Communities in
Canada.* Toronto: McClelland and Stewart, 1982. 369 p.

0256   **Copeland, Nancy**
Adaptation to Resettlement by Southeast Asian Adolescents. Unpub-
lished MSc thesis, University of Manitoba, 1984. 2 microfiches.
Canadian theses on microfiche, 62422.

0257   **Creese, Gillian Laura**
"Immigration Policies and the Creation of an Ethnically Segmented
Working Class in British Columbia, 1880-1923." *Alternate Routes*,
vol. 7 (1984) p. 1-34.

0258   **D'Costa, Ronald**
"Canadian Immigration Policy: A Chronological Review with
Particular Reference to Discrimination." *Canada 2000: Race
Relations and Public Policy*, edited by O.P. Dwivedi et al. Guelph,
Ont.: Department of Political Studies, University of Guelph,
1989, p. 44-52.

0259   **D'Costa, Ronald**
"Canadian Immigration Policy: A Chronological Review with
Particular Reference to Discrimination." *CPSA Papers/ACSP
Contributions 1987*, Section Ba, paper 2, fiche 1. Paper presented at
the 59th annual meeting of the Canadian Political Science
Association, June 6-8, 1987, McMaster University, Hamilton,
Ontario.

0260   **Dahlie, Hallvard, ed.**
Varieties of Exile: The Canadian Experience. Vancouver: University of British Columbia Press, 1986. 216 p.

0261   **Danys, Milda**
DP: Lithuanian Immigration to Canada After the Second World War. Toronto: Multicultural History Society of Ontario, 1986. 365 p.

0262   **Davis, Morris**
"U.S. Citizens as Canadian Aliens." *Dalhousie Review,* vol. 60 no. 2 (1980) p. 251-263.

0263   **Delfino, Angelo**
"Italian Immigrant Aid Society: an Historical Outline." *Polyphony: The Bulletin of the Multicultural History Society of Ontario,* vol. 7 no. 2 (1985) p. 114-117.

0264   **De Voretz, Don**
"The Immigration of Third World Professionals to Canada: 1968-1973." *World Development,* vol. 11 no. 1 (1983) p. 55-64.

0265   **Del Negro, Luciano**
Immigration et unité ouvrière. Montréal: Confédération des syndicats nationaux, Comité d'immigration, 1982. 59 p.

0266   **Deonandan, Kalowatie**
"The Evolution of Canada's New Refugee Policy and its Impact on Central American Refugees." *CPSA Papers/ACSP Contributions 1989,* Section B paper 5, fiche 2. Paper presented at the 61st annual meeting of the Canadian Political Science Association, June 1-3, 1989, Laval University, Quebec, P.Q.

0267   **Deschamps, Gilles**
"Economic Adaptation of Indochinese Refugees in Quebec." In: *Uprooting, Loss and Adaptation: The Resettlement of Indochinese Refugees in Canada,* edited by Kwok B. Chan and Doreen Marie Indra. Ottawa: Canadian Public Health Association, 1987, p. 97-115.

0268   **Devereaux, Mary Sue**
Canada's Immigrants. Ottawa: Minister of Supply and Services Canada, 1984. 40, 40 p. French language title: *Les immigrants au Canada.*

0269 **Devoretz, Don**
"The Immigration of Third World Professionals to Canada, 1968-1973." *World Development*, vol. 11 no. 1 (1983) p. 55-64.

0270 **Dirks, Gerald E.**
"Immigration Policy." In: *The Canadian Encyclopedia*, Volume 2. Edmonton: Hurtig Publishers, 1988.

0271 **Dirks, Gerald E.**
"World Refugees: The Canadian Response." *Behind the Headlines*, vol. 45 no. 5 (1988) p. 1-18.

0272 **Dirks, Gerald E.**
"A Policy Within Policy: The Identification and Admission of Refugees to Canada." *Canadian Journal of Political Science*, vol. 17 no. 2 (1984) p. 279-308.

0273 **Dirks, Gerald E.**
"The Canadian Rescue Effort: The Few Who Cared." In: *Canadian Jewish Mosaic*, edited by M. Weinfeld, W. Shaffir and I. Cotler. Toronto: John Wiley and Sons, 1981, p. 77-92.

0274 **Draper, Paula Jean**
"Fragmented Loyalties: Canadian Jewry, The King Government and the Refugee Dilemma." In: *On Guard for Thee: War, Ethnicity and the Canadian State, 1939-1945*, edited by Norman Hillmer, Bohdan Kordan, and Lubomyr Luciuk. Ottawa: Canadian Committee for the History of the Second World War, 1988, p. 151-178.

0275 **Dreisziger, Nandor A.F.**
"Immigration and Re-migration: The Changing Urban-Rural Distribution of Hungarian Canadians, 1886-1986." *Hungarian Studies Review*, vol. 13 no. 2 (1986) p. 20-41.

0276 **Drystek, Henry F.**
"The Simplest and Cheapest Mode of Dealing with Them: Deportation from Canada Before World War II." *Histoire social/Social History*, vol. 15 no. 30 (1982) p. 407-43.

0277 **Dubeau, Sharon**
New Brunswick Loyalists: A Bicentennial Tribute. Agincourt, Ont.: Generation Press, 1983.

0278   **Dumon, W.A.**
"Family and Migration." @*International Migration/Migrations Internationales/Migraciones Internacionales*, vol. 27 no. 2 (1989) p. 251-270.

0279   **Dunae, Patrick A.**
"Waifs: the Faibridge Society in British Columbia, 1931-1951." *Histoire sociale/Social History*, vol. 21 no. 42 (1988) p. 224-250.

0280   **Dunae, Patrick A.**
"Promoting the Dominion: Records and the Canadian Immigration Campaign, 1872 to 1915." *Archivaria*, no. 19 (1984/85) p. 73-93.

0281   **Dunsiger, Jane Catherine**
A Comparative Study of Narrative Accounts of Visits Home Drawn from the Immigrant Ethnic Community in St. John's, Newfoundland. Unpublished MA thesis, Memorial University of Newfoundland, 1983. Canadian theses on microfiche, 63563.

0282   **Eisenbruch, Maurice**
"The Mental Health of Refugee Children and Their Cultural Development." *International Migration Review*, vol. 22 no. 2 (1988) p. 282-300.

0283   **Elliott, Jean Leonard**
"Canadian Immigration: A Historical Assessment." In: *Two Nations, Many Cultures: Ethnic Groups in Canada*, edited by Jean Leonard Elliott. 2nd ed. Scarborough, Ont.: Prentice-Hall of Canada, 1983, p. 289-301.

0284   **Epp, George K.**
"Mennonite Immigration to Canada After World War II." *Journal of Mennonite Studies*, vol. 5 (1987) p. 108-119.

0285   **Finkel, Alvin**
"Canadian Immigration Policy and the Cold War, 1945-1980 [sic]" *Journal of Canadian Studies/Revue d'études canadiennes*, vol. 21 no. 1 (1986) p. 53-70. Dates should read: 1945-1960.

0286   **Finkelstein, Mont S.**
"The Johnson Act, Mussolini and Fascist Emigration Policy: 1921-1930." *Journal of American Ethnic History*, vol. 8 no. 1 (Fall 1988) p. 38-55.

0287   **Foot, David K.**
Population Aging and Immigration Policy in Canada: Implications and Prescriptions. Ottawa: Policy and Program Development, Immigration Canada Employment and Immigration Commission, 1986. 23, 26 p. French language title: *Vieillissement de la population et politique canadienne d'immigration: Répercussions et recommandations.*

0288   **Francis, R. Douglas**
Images of the West: Responses to the Canadian Prairies. Saskatoon: Western Producer Prairie Books, 1989. 268 p.

0289   **Francis, R. Douglas**
"Outopia to Eutopia: How Dreams Filled the 'Desolate' West." *NeWest Review*, vol. 15 no. 1 (1989) p. 10-18.

0290   **Francis, R. Douglas**
"The Ideal and the Real: The Image of the Canadian West in the Settlement." In: *Rupert's Land: A Cultural Tapestry*, edited by Richard C. Davis. Waterloo, Ont.: Wilfrid Laurier University Press, 1988, p. 253-274.

0291   **Fulford, Robert**
"Displaced Persons: The Grassy Narrows Reserve." *Saturday Night*, vol. 100 no. 5/3662 (1985) p. 9-15.

0292   **Gagné, Madeleine**
"L'insertion de la population immigrée sur la marche du travail au Québec." *Revue internationale d'action communautaire*, vol. 21 no. 1 (1989) p. 153-163.

0293   **Gagné, Madeleine, M. Baillargeon, C. Benjamin, et B. Audet**
"Déterminer un niveau d'immigration pour le Québec: pourquoi, comment?" *Cahiers québecois de démographie*, vol. 12 no. 2 (1983) p. 207-215.

0294   **Gagnon, Jean**
"Les migrations du nord de la Saskatchewan: symbole et réalite de l'intégration des indigènes." *Cahiers de géographie du Québec*, vol. 32 no. 86 (1988) p. 151-172.

0295   **Ganzevoort, Herman**
A Bittersweet Land: The Dutch Experience in Canada, 1890-1980.
Toronto: McClelland and Stewart, 1988. 133 p.

0296   **Ganzevoort, Herman and Mark Boekelman**
"Introduction." In: *Dutch Immigration to North America*, edited by
Herman Ganzevoort and Mark Boekelman. Toronto: Multicultural
History Society of Ontario, 1983, p. xi-xvi.

0297   **Garcea, Joseph**
"Provincial Initiatives in Immigration 1966-1986: Asymmetry and
Special Status." *CPSA Papers/ACSP Contributions 1986*, Section C,
paper 1, fiche 10. Paper presented at the 58th annual meeting of the
Canadian Political Science Association, June 6-8, 1986, University of
Manitoba, Winnipeg, Manitoba.

0298   **Gartner, Lloyd P.**
"Jewish Migrants en Route from Europe to North America:
Traditions and Realities." *Jewish History*, vol. 1 no. 2 (1986) p. 49-
66.

0299   **Gerber, Jean Miriam**
*Immigration and Integration in Post-war Canada: A Case Study of
Holocaust Survivors in Vancouver, 1947-1970.* Unpublished MA
thesis, University of British Columbia, 1989. 112 leaves. Canadian
theses on microfiche, 551305.

0300   **Gerber, Linda M.**
"Community Characteristics and Out-migration from Canadian Indian
Reserves: Path Analyses." *Canadian Review of Sociology and
Anthropology/Revue canadienne de sociologie et d'anthropologie*,
vol. 21 no. 2 (1984) p. 145-165.

0301   **Girard, Philip**
"From Subversion to Liberation: Homosexuals and the Immigration
Act 1952-1977." *Canadian Journal of Law and Society/Revue
canadienne de droit et société*, vol. 2 (1987) p. 1-28.

0302   **Goh, Maggie and Craig Stephenson, eds.**
Between Worlds. Oakville, Ont.: Rubicon Publ., 1989. 139 p.

0303   **Goldring, Philip**
"Governor Simpson's Officers: Elite Recruitment in a British
Overseas Enterprise, 1834-1870." *Prairie Forum*, vol. 10 no. 2
(1985) p. 251-281.

0304   **Grant, E. Kenneth and John Vanderkamp**
"A Descriptive Analysis of the Incidence and Nature of Repeat
Migration Within Canada 1968-71." *Canadian Studies in Population*,
vol. 11 no. 1 (1984) p. 61-77.

0305   **Grant, E. Kenneth and Alun E. Joseph**
"The Spatial Aspects and Regularities of Multiple Interregional
Migration Within Canada." *Canadian Journal of Regional Science/
Revue canadienne des science régionales*, vol. 6 no. 1 (1983) p. 75-
96.

0306   **Gray, Charlotte**
"Refugee Run-Around: Slick Red Tape Seems to Have Triumphed
Over Human Need." *Saturday Night*, vol. 104 no. 1/3706
(1989) p. 11-13.

0307   **Grenier, Gilles**
"Earnings by Language Group in Quebec in 1980 and Emigration
From Quebec Between 1976 and 1981." *Canadian Journal of
Economics/Revue canadienne d'économique*, vol. 20 no. 4
(1987) p. 774-791.

0308   **Grey, Julius H.**
Immigration Law in Canada. Toronto: Butterworths, 1984. 237 p.

0309   **Groberman, Ruth**
"The Foreign Student Experience in Canada Today." In: *Visible
Minorities and Multiculturalism: Asians in Canada*, edited by K.
Victor Ujimoto and Gordon Hirabayashi. Toronto: Butterworths,
1980, p. 151-162.

0310   **Groniowski, Krzysztof**
"The Socio-economic Base of Polish Emigration to North America,
1854-1939." In: *Polish Presence in Canada and America*, edited by
Frank Renkiewicz. Toronto: Multicultural History Society of Ontario,
1982, p. 1-10.

0311   **Guendelman, Sylvia and Auristela Perej-Itriago**
"Migration Tradeoffs: Men's Experiences with Seasonal Lifestyles."
International Migration Review, vol. 21 no. 3 (1987) p. 709-727.

0312   **Guillaume, Pierre**
"L'immigration européenne au Canada depuis la deuxième guerre
mondiale." *Études canadiennes/Canadian Studies*, vol. 12 no. 1
(1986) p. 7-24.

0313   **Hall, David J.**
Clifford Sifton: Volume Two; A Lonely Eminence, 1901-1929.
Vancouver: University of British Columbia Press, 1985.

0314   **Harney, Robert**
"Preface." In: *Dutch Immigration to North America*, edited by
Herman Ganzevoort and Mark Boekelman. Toronto: Multicultural
History Society of Ontario, 1983, p. vii-x.

0315   **Hawkins, Freda**
"Canadian Immigration and Refugee Policies." In: *De Mackenzie
King à Pierre Trudeau: quarante ans de diplomatie canadienne*, sous
la direction de Paul Painchaud. Sainte-Foy, P.Q.: les Presses de
l'Université Laval, 1989, p. 631-667.

0316   **Hawkins, Freda**
Critical Years in Immigration: Canada and Australia Compared.
Montreal: McGill-Queen's University Press, 1989. 368 p.

0317   **Heisler, Barbara Schmitter**
"Sending Countries and the Politics of Emigration and Destination."
International Migration Review, vol. 19 no. 3 (1985) p. 469-483.

0318   **Helly, Denise**
"Immigrants aux États-Unis, au Canada et au Québec: un schéma."
Revue internationale d'action communautaire, vol. 21 no. 61
(1989) p. 35-42.

0319   **Hertzman, Lewis, et al.**
"L'immigration au Canada avant et après la Confédération." In:
*Commission internationale d'histoire des mouvements sociaux et des
structures sociales. Les migrations internationales de la fin du
XVIIIème siècle à nos jours*. Paris: Éditions du C.N.R.S., 1980, p. 79-
107.

0320   **Howard, Rhoda**
"The Canadian Government Response to Africa's Refugee Problem."
Canadian Journal of African Studies, vol. 15 no. 1 (1981) p. 95-116.

0321   **Howard, Rhoda**
"Contemporary Canadian Refugee Policy: A Critical Assessment."
Canadian Public Policy/Analyse de politiques, vol. 6 no. 2
(1980) p. 361-373.

0322   **Howith, H.G.**
Immigration Levels Planning: The First Decade. Ottawa:
Employment and Immigration Canada, 1988. 41 p. French language
title: *Planification des niveaux d'immigration: la première décennie.*

0323   **Immigration and Refugee Board**
"Refugee Determination: What It Is and How It Works?" *Heritage
Link*, vol. 4 no. 2 (1989) p. 34-36.

0324   **Indra, Doreen M.**
"Changes in Canadian Immigration Patterns Over the Past Decade
with Special Reference to Asia." In: *Visible Minorities and Multiculturalism: Asians in Canada*, edited by K. Victor Ujimoto and Gordon
Hirabayashi. Toronto: Butterworths, 1980, p. 163-179.

0325   **Innes, Frank C.**
"Some Possible Implications of Recent Canadian Immigration
Experience: An Example of Geographic Concern with Respect to
Public Policy." In: *German-Canadian Studies: Critical Approaches*,
edited by Peter Liddell. Vancouver: CAUTG, 1983, p. 28-38.

0326   **International Law Association**
"Conference Report: Legal Status of Refugees Resolution -
International Law Association 62nd Conference Held in Seoul, 24-29,
August, 1986." *International Migration Review*, vol. 20 no. 4
(1986) p. 1048-1053.

0327   **Islam, Nasir**
"Canada's Immigration Policy: Compassion, Economic Necessity or
Lifeboat Ethics?" In: *How Ottawa Spends 1989/90: The Buck Stops
Where*, edited by Katherine A. Graham. Ottawa: Carleton University
Press, 1989, p. 209-246.

0328   **Ivany, Kathryn**
        The History of the Barr Colonists as an Ethnic Experience, 1903-1928. Unpublished MA thesis, University of Alberta, 1985. 2 microfiches. Canadian theses on microfiche, CT86-29463-3.

0329   **Jacob, André et Francine Sercongs**
        Les politiques sociales et les travailleurs immigrants. Montréal: Confédération des syndicats nationaux, Comité d'immigration, 1982. 85 p.

0330   **Jensen, Leif**
        The New Immigration: Implications for Poverty and Public Assistance Utilization. Westport, Conn.: Greenwood Press, 1989. 205 p.

0331   **Johnston, Hugh**
        The Voyage of the Komagata Maru: The Sikh Challenge to Canada's Colour Bar. Vancouver, University of British Columbia Press, 1989. 162 p.

0332   **Jones, Lloyd**
        "Thunder Bay and the Post-1979 Refugees." *Polyphony: The Bulletin of the Multicultural History Society of Ontario,* vol. 9 no. 2 (1987) p. 113-114.

0333   **Kaprielian-Churchill, Isabel**
        "Migratory Caravans: Armenian Sojourners in Canada." *Journal of American Ethnic History,* vol. 6 no. 2 (1987) p. 20-38

0334   **Kastelik, Wieslawa**
        An Application of Family-Centered Ecosystemic Approach with Immigrant/Refugee Families. Unpublished MSW thesis, University of Manitoba, 1988. 2 microfiches. Canadian theses on microfiche, CT89-28515-2.

0335   **Khatun, Hafiza**
        Intra-urban Residential Migration of East-Indian People in Edmonton. Unpublished MA thesis, University of Alberta, 1984. 3 microfiches. Canadian theses on microfiche, CT87-23548-6.

0336   **Knight, Sheilagh**
        L'immigration latino-américaine au Québec, 1973-1986: élements politiques et économiques. Unpublished MA thesis, Université Laval, 1988. 4 microfiches. Canadian theses on microfiche, CT90-23141-6.

0337 **Kobayashi, Audrey**
"Focus: Asian Migration to Canada." *Canadian Geographer/Le géographe Canadien*, vol. 32 no. 4 (1988) p. 351-362.

0338 **Kobayashi, Audrey**
"Emigration to Canada and Development of the Residential Landscape in a Japanese Village: The Paradox of the Sojourner." *Canadian Ethnic Studies/Études ethniques au Canada*, vol. 16 no. 3 (1984) p. 111-131.

0339 **Kobayashi, Audrey**
Emigration from Kaideima, Japan, 1885-1950: An Analysis of Community and Landscape Change. Unpublished PhD thesis, University of California, 1983. 347 p.

0340 **Kolcon-Lach, Emilia**
"Immigration Doors to Canada: Too Narrow or Too Wide?" *Perception*, vol. 11 no. 1 (1987) p. 8-10.

0341 **Kosinski, Leszek A.**
"Immigration from East Central Europe to Canada, 1956-1980." In: *Central and East European Ethnicity in Canada: Adaptation and Preservation*, edited by T. Yedlin. Edmonton: Central and East European Studies Society of Alberta, 1985, p. 9-24.

0342 **Kovàcs, Martin L.**
"New Settlers on the Prairie: Problems of Adaptation." In: *Central and East European Ethnicity in Canada: Adaptation and Preservation*, edited by T. Yedlin. Edmonton: Central and East European Studies Society of Alberta, 1985, p. 63-86.

0343 **Kovàcs, Martin L., ed.**
Roots and Realities Among Eastern and Central Europeans. Edmonton: Central and East European Studies Association of Canada, 1983. 334 p.

0344 **Krimer, Ester**
The Psychological Impact of Immigration: An Experience of Change, Loss, and Gain. Unpublished PhD thesis, University of Toronto, 1986. 4 microfiches. Canadian theses on microfiche, CT88-21737-5.

0345   **Krishnan, P.**
"Towards a Prediction of Third World Immigrants Into Canada,
1973-1985." *International Migration Review*, vol. 18 no. 1/2
(1980) p. 34-39.

0346   **Labelle, Micheline**
"La question fédérale de l'immigration internationale au Canada."
L'ère des Liberaux: Le pouvoir fédéral de 1963 à 1984. Yves
Bélanger, Dorval Brunelle et collaborateurs. Sillery, P.Q.: Presses de
l'université du Québec, 1988, p. 313-342.

0347   **Labelle, Micheline**
"Immigration internationale et minorités ethniques." *Cahiers de
recherche sociologique*, vol. 2 no. 2 (1984) p. 5-7.

0348   **Labelle, Micheline**
"Émigration et immigration: les haïtiens au Québec." *Sociologie et
sociétés*, vol. 15 no. 2 (1983) p. 73-88.

0349   **Labelle, Micheline**
"Politique d'immigration et immigration en provenance de la Caraïbe
anglophone au Canada et au Québec, 1900-1979." *Canadian Ethnic
Studies/Études ethniques au Canada*, vol. 15 no. 2 (1983) p.1-24.

0350   **Labelle, Micheline, Serge Larose et Victor Piché**
*Politique d'immigration et immigration en provenance de la Caraïbe
anglophone au Canada et au Québec.* Collection de titrés à part.
Montréal: Département de démographie, Université de Montréal,
1983. 24 p.

0351   **Lachapelle, Rejean**
*Immigration and the Ethnolinguistic Character of Canada and
Quebec.* Ottawa: Statistics Canada, 1988. 31, 32 p. French language
title: *L'immigration et le caractère ethnolinguistique du Canada et du
Québec.*

0352   **Lachapelle, Rejean**
"Population Exchanges Between Quebec and the United States Over
the Last Two Decades." In: *Problems and Opportunities in U.S.-
Quebec Relations*, edited by Alfred O. Hero, Jr. and Marcel Daneau.
Boulder, Colorado: Westview Press, 1984 p. 64-79.

0353   **Lam, Lawrence**
Vietnamese-Chinese Refugees in Montreal: Long-term Resettlement.
Toronto: University of Toronto - York University Joint Centre on
Modern East Asia, 1985. 25 leaves.

0354   **Land, Stephen N.**
"Western Settlement, 1896-1914: The Role of the Liberal Govern-
ment in Ensuring the Colonization of Western Canada." *Fort Calgary
Quarterly*, vol. 8 no. 1 (1988) p. 2-7.

0355   **Landry, Yves**
"The Life Course of Seventeenth Century Immigrants to Canada."
Journal of Family History, vol. 12 no. 1-3 (1987) p. 201-212.

0356   **Lanphier, C. Michael**
"Dilemmas of Decentralization: Refugee Sponsorship and Service in
Canada and United States." In: *The Southeast Asian Environment*,
edited by Douglas H. Webster. Ottawa : University of Ottawa Press,
1983, p. 173-190. Proceedings of the annual conference of the
Canadian Council for Southeast Asian Studies held at the Faculty of
Environmental Design, University of Calgary, Calgary, Alberta,
November 13 to 15, 1981.

0357   **Lanphier, C. Michael**
"Indochinese Resettlement and the Development of Canadian Refugee
Policy." In: *Two Nations, Many Cultures: Ethnic Groups in Canada*,
edited by Jean Leonard Elliott. 2nd ed. Scarborough, Ontario:
Prentice-Hall of Canada, 1983, p. 412-424.

0358   **Lanphier, C. Michael**
"Canada's Response to Refugees." *International Migration Review*,
vol. 15 no. 1/2 (1981) p. 113-130.

0359   **Larose, Serge**
*Procès migratoire et trajectoire de classe des immigrantes et
immigrants haïtiens au Québec.* Montréal: Centre de recherche des
Caraïbes, Université de Montréal, 119 p.

0360   **Lehmann, Heinz**
*The German Canadians 1750-1937: Immigration, Settlement and
Culture*, edited and translated by Gerhard P. Bassler. St. John's,
Newfoundland: Jesperson Press, 1986. 541 p.

0361   **Lehr, John C.**
"Government Perceptions of Ukrainian Immigrants to Western
Canada, 1896-1902." *Canadian Ethnic Studies/Études ethniques au
Canada*, vol. 19 no. 2 (1987) p. 1-12.

0362   **Lehr, John C. and D. Wayne Moodie**
"The Polemics of Pioneer Settlement: Ukrainian Immigration and the
Winnipeg Press." *Canadian Ethnic Studies/Études ethniques au
Canada*, vol. 12 no. 2 (1980) 88-101.

0363   **Lemieux, Valerie Matthews**
"Immigration: A Provincial Concern." *Manitoba Law Journal*, vol. 13
no. 1 (1983) p. 111-140.

0364   **Lemoine, M.**
"Effects of Migration on Family Structure in the Receiving Country."
*International Migration/Migrations Internationales/Migraciones Inter-
nacionales*, vol. 27. no. 2 (1989) p. 271-279.

0365   **Lemon, Anthony, and Norman Pollock, eds.**
Studies in Overseas Settlement and Population. New York: Longman,
1980. 337 p.

0366   **Lewry, Marilyn Lesley**
*A Study of the Locational Changes Among Hebridean Immigrants in
Southeast Saskatchewan, 1883 to 1926.* Unpublished MA thesis,
University of Regina, 1985. 3 microfiches. Canadian theses on
microfiche, CT87-25966-0.

0367   **Liberati, Luigi Bruti**
"Le relazioni tra Canada e l'Italia e l'emigrazione Italiana nel primo
novecento." *Studi Emigrazione*, vol. 22 no. 77 (1985) p. 44-67.

0368   **Lightman, Jacob B.**
*Social Change and the Soviet Jewish Immigrant: A Canadian Profile:
Results of a Survey of the Settlement and Integration of Jews from
the Soviet Union Who Arrived as Landed Immigrants in Canada from
1973 to 1978.* Montreal: Jewish Immigrant Aid Services of Canada,
1984. 151 p.

0369   **Ljungmark, Lars**
"Canada: An Alternative for Swedish Emigration to the New World,
1873-1875." *Swedish-American Quarterly*, vol. 35 no. 3
(1984) p. 253-266.

0370   **Locher, Uli**
        Les anglophones de Montréal: Émigration et evolution des attitudes,
        1978-1983. Québec, P.Q.: Éditeur officiel du Québec, 1988. 219 p.

0371   **Lockwood, Glenn J.**
        Eastern Upper Canadian Perceptions of Irish Immigrants, 1824-1868.
        Unpublished PhD thesis, University of Ottawa, 1988. 8 microfiches.
        Canadian theses on microfiche, CT90-23676-0.

0372   **Luciuk, Lubomyr Y.**
        "'Trouble All Around': Ukrainian Canadians and Their Encounter
        with the Ukrainian Refugees of Europe, 1943-1951." *Canadian*
        Ethnic Studies/Études ethniques au Canada, vol. 21 no. 3
        (1989) p. 37-54.

0373   **Lyaschuk, Dmytro**
        "The First Emigration from Pre-Carpathian Ukraine." *Ukrainian*
        Canadian, vol. 41 no. 734/228 (1989) p. 35-38.

0374   **Malarek, Victor**
        Haven's Gate: Canada's Immigration Fiasco. Toronto: Macmillan of
        Canada, 1987. 262 p.

0375   **Malpas, Nicole**
        Étude d'un mouvement migratoire: l'immigration italienne au Québec
        (1931-1971). Unpublished MSc thesis, Université de Montréal, 1984.
        1 microfilm.

0376   **Mannion, John J.**
        "Old World Antecedents, New World Adaptations: Inistioge (Co.
        Kilkenny) Immigrants in Newfoundland." *Newfoundland Studies,* vol.
        5 no. 2 (1989) p. 103-175.

0377   **Marr, William L.**
        "Immigration Policy and Canadian Economic Growth." In: *Domestic*
        Policies in the International Economic Environment. John Whalley
        and Roderick Hill, research coordinators. Toronto: published and
        edited by the University of Toronto Press, 1985, p. 57-109.

0378   **Marr, William L.**
        "Sons of Immigrants' Earnings: Canada and the United States."
        Canadian Studies in Population, vol. 8 no. 1 (1981) p. 49-55.

0379   **Martinez, Ana Isabel Guada**
       *The Process of Adaptation of an Ethnic Group: The Case of
       Spaniards in Ottawa.* Unpublished MA thesis, Carleton University,
       1986. 3 microfiches. Canadian theses on microfiche, CT87-25854-0.

0380   **Mata, Fernando G.**
       "Latin American Immigration to Canada: Some Reflections on the
       Immigration Statistics." *Canadian Journal of Latin American and
       Caribbean Studies/Revue canadienne des études latino-américans et
       carraïbes,* vol. 10 no. 20 (1985) p. 27-42.

0381   **Matas, David**
       "Fairness in Refugee Determination." *Manitoba Law Journal,* vol. 18
       no. 1 (1989) p. 71-103.

0382   **Matas, David and Ilana Smith**
       Closing the Doors: The Failure of Refugee Protection. Toronto:
       Summerhill Press, 1989. 336 p.

0383   **Mathews, Georges**
       Le choc démographique: le déclin du Québec est-il inévitable?
       Montréal: Boréal Express, 1984. 204 p.

0384   **McDade, Kathryn**
       Barriers to Recognition of the Credentials in Immigrants in Canada.
       Ottawa: Institute for Research on Public Policy, 1988. 60 p.

0385   **McEvoy, F.J.**
       "A Symbol of Racial Discrimination: The Chinese Immigration Act
       and Canada's Relations with China, 1942-1947." *Canadian Ethnic
       Studies/Études ethniques au Canada,* vol. 14 no. 3 (1982) p. 24-42.

0386   **McKee, B. Brian**
       "An Analysis of Current Canadian Emigration to the United States."
       Canadian Studies in Population, vol. 15 no. 1 (1988) p. 67-86.

0387   **McLaughlin, N.**
       "The Labour Force Participation of Canada's Immigrants." *Labour
       Force/La population active,* vol. 41 no. 9 (1985) p. 87-113.

0388   **Meintel, Deirdre**
       "Les québécois vus par les jeunes d'origine immigrée." *Revue
       internationale d'action communautaire,*vol. 21 no. 61 (1989) p. 81-
       94.

0389   **Menchions, Pamela O.**
        Federal-provincial Consultation on Immigration Policy in Canada.
        Unpublished MA thesis, Queen's University, 1984. 2 microfiches.
        Canadian theses on microfiche, CT87-21600-7.

0390   **Michalowski, Margaret**
        "Adjustment of Immigrants in Canada: Methodological Possibilities
        and Its Implications." *International Migration/Migrations Internation-*
        ales/Migraciones Internacionales, vol. 25 no. 1 (1987) p. 21-39.

0391   **Moore, Christopher**
        The Loyalists: Revolution, Exile and Settlement. Toronto: Macmillan,
        1984.

0392   **Morrocco, Frank N. and Henry M. Goslett**
        The Annotated Immigration Act of Canada. Toronto: Carswell, 1988.
        446 p.

0393   **Munro, Kenneth**
        "The Chinese Immigration Act, 1885: Adolphe Chapleau and the
        French Canadian Attitude." *Canadian Ethnic Studies/Études ethniques*
        au Canada, vol. 19 no. 3 (1987) p. 89-101.

0394   **Murison, Barbara C.**
        "Poverty, Philanthropy and Emigration to British North America:
        Changing Attitudes in Scotland in the Early Nineteenth Century."
        Journal of Canadian Studies/Revue d'études canadiennes, vol. 2 no.
        2 (1987) p. 263-288.

0395   **Nash, Alan E.**
        International Refugee Pressures and the Canadian Public Policy
        Response. Ottawa: Institute for Research on Public Policy, Studies in
        Social Poicy, 1989. 128 p.

0396   **Neary, Peter**
        "Canadian Immigration Policy and the Newfoundlanders. 1912-1939."
        Acadiensis, vol. 11 no. 2 (1982) p. 69-83.

0397   **Neill, Ghyslaine**
        Les trajectoires socio-professionelles des immigrantes et des
        immigrants haïtiens au Québec. Unpublished MSc thesis, Université
        de Montréal, 1983. 1 microfilm.

0398   **Neuwirth, Gertrud**
"Refugee Resettlement." *Current Sociology/La sociologie contemporaine*, vol. 36 no. 2 (1988) p. 27-41.

0399   **Neuwirth, Gertrud**
"Indochinese Refugees in Canada: Sponsorship and Adjustment." *International Migration Review*,vol. 15 nos. 53-54 (1981) p. 131-141.

0400   **Nguyen, San Duy**
"Maslow's Need Hierarchy and Refugee Resettlement." In: *Uprooting, Loss and Adaptation: The Resettlement of Indochinese Refugees in Canada*,edited by Kwok B. Chan and Doreen Marie Indra. Ottawa: Canadian Public Health Association, 1987, p. 42-51.

0401   **Noivo, Edite Almeida**
Migration and Reactions to Displacement: The Portuguese in Canada. Unpublished MA thesis, Carleton University, 1985.

0402   **Nord, Douglas C.**
"MPs and Senators as Middlemen: The Special Joint Committee on Immigration Policy." In: *Parliament, Policy and Representation*, edited by Harold D. Clarke, Colin Campbell, F.Q. Quo and Arthur Goddard. Toronto: Methuen, 1980, p. 181-193.

0403   **Ohndorf, W.**
"Social Effects of Migration in Receiving Countries: Similarities and Differences." *International Migration/Migrations Internationales/ Migraciones Internacionales*, vol. 27 no. 2 (1989) p. 209-216.

0404   **Ornstein, Michael D.**
Adjustment and Economic Experience of Immigrants in Canada: An Analysis of 1976 Longitudinal Survey of Immigrants. rev. ed. Downsview Ont.: York University, Institute for Behavioural Research, 1983. 66 leaves. A Report to Employment and Immigration Canada, April 1, 1981.

0405   **Palmer, Howard**
"Patterns of Immigration and Ethnic Settlement in Alberta, 1920-1985." In: *Peoples of Alberta: Portraits of Cultural Diversity*, edited by Howard and Tamara Palmer. Saskatoon: Western Producer Prairie Books, 1985, p. 28-49.

0406   **Palmer, Howard**
"Canadian Immigration and Ethnic History in the 1970's and
1980's." *Journal of Canadian Studies/Revue d'études canadiennes*,
vol. 17 no. 1 (1982) p. 35-50.

0407   **Palmer, Howard**
"Canadian Immigration and Ethnic History in the 1970's and
1980's." *International Migration Review*, vol. 15 no. 3 (1981) p. 471-
501.

0408   **Paquet, Gilles and Wayne R. Smith**
"L'émigration des canadiens français vers les États-Unis 1790-1940:
problématique et corps de sonde." *L'actualité économique*, vol. 59
no. 3 (1983) p. 423-455.

0409   **Papp, Susan M.**
"Flight and Settlement: the '56ers." *Polyphony: The Bulletin of the
Multicultural History Society of Ontario*, vol. 2 no. 2/3 (1980) p. 63-
70.

0410   **Passaris, Constantine E.**
"Immigration to Canada in the Post Second World War Period:
Manpower Flows from the Caribbean." In: *White Collar Immigrants
in the Americas and the Caribbean*, edited by A.F. Marks and
H.M.C. Vessuri. Leiden: Royal Institute of Linguistics and
Anthropology, 1983, p. 73-118.

0411   **Patrias, Carmela**
"From Emigration Save Us Oh Lord." *Polyphony: The Bulletin of the
Multicultural History Society of Ontario*, vol. 9 no. 1 (1987) p. 17-
22.

0412   **Pekin, H.**
"Effects of Migration on Family Structure." *International Migration/
Migrations Internationales/Migraciones Internacionales*, vol. 27 no. 2
(1989) p. 281-293.

0413   **Penisson, B.**
"Un siècle d'immigration française au Canada, 1881-1990." *Revue
Européenne des migrations internationales*, vol. 2 no. 2
(1986) p. 111-125.

0414   **Percy, Michael B.**
"American Homesteaders and the Canadian Prairies." *Explorations in Economic History*, vol. 24 no. 1 (1987) p. 77-100.

0415   **Perin, Roberto**
"The Immigrant: Actor or Outcast." In: *Arrangiarsi: The Italian Immigration Experience in Canada*, edited by Roberto Perin and Franc Sturino. Montreal: Guernica, 1989, p. 9-35.

0416   **Perruchoud, R.**
"Family Reunification." *International Migration/Migrations Internationales/Migraciones Internacionales*, vol. 27 no. 4 (1989) p. 509-524.

0417   **Petryshyn, Jaroslav**
Peasants in the Promised Land: Canada and the Ukrainians, 1891-1914. Toronto: James Lorimer and Co., 1985. 265 p.

0418   **Philips, Trevor J.**
"Juvenile Emigration to Canada: A Glimpse at a Subculture's Health." *Journal of Canadian Culture*, vol. 1 no. 2 (1984) p. 97-89.

0419   **Plaut, W. Gunther**
Refugee Determination in Canada. Proposals for a New System. Ottawa: Minister of Supplies and Services Canada, 1985.

0420   **Beach, Charles M. and Alan G. Green, eds.**
Policy Forum on the Role of Immigration in Canada's Future. Kingston, Ont.: John Deutsch Institute for the Study of Economic Policy, 1989. 102 p.

0421   **Polyzoi, Eleoussa**
"Psychologists' Perceptions of the Canadian Immigrant Before World War II." *Canadian Ethnic Studies/Études ethniques au Canada*, vol. 18 no. 1 (1986) p. 52-65.

0422   **Proudfoot, Bruce**
"The Setting of Immigration Levels in Canada Since the Immigration Act, 1976." *Journal of Canadian Studies/Revue d'études canadiennes*, vol. 4 no. 2 (1989) p. 233-256.

0423 **Pryor, Edward T.**
"The Canada-United States Joint Immigration Study: Issues in Data Comparability." *International Migration Review*, vol. 21 no. 4 (1987) p. 1038-1066.

0424 **Ramcharan, Subhas**
"South Asian Immigration: Current Status and Adaptation Modes." In: *South Asians in the Canadian Mosaic*, edited by Rabindra N. Kanungo. Montreal: Kala Bharati Foundation, 1984, p. 33-47.

0425 **Ramirez, Bruno**
"Operai senza una 'causa'? I manovali Italiani a Montreal, 1900-1930." *Studi Emigrazione/Études migrations*, vol. 22 no. 77 (1985) p. 98-111.

0426 **Ramirez, Bruno**
The Italians of Montreal: From Sojourning to Settlement, 1880-1921. Montreal: Editions du Courant; B. Ramirez/M. Del Balso, 1980. 54 p.

0427 **Rasporich, Anthony W.**
For a Better Life: A History of the Croatians in Canada. Toronto: McClelland and Stewart in association with the Multiculturalism Directorate, Department of the Secretary of State and the Canadian Govenment Publishing Centre, Supply and Services Canada, 1982. 279 p.

0428 **Reczynska, Anna**
"Kanada a Problemy Polskich Uchodzcow W Okresie Drugiej Wojny Swiatowej." *Studia Historyczne*, vol. 32 no. 3 (1989) p. 437-452.

0429 **Reczynska, Anna**
Emigracja Z Polski Do Kanady W Okresie Miedzywojennym. Wroclaw: Zaklad Narodowy im Ossolinskich, 1986. 223 p.

0430 **Reitz, Jeffrey G.**
"Immigrants, Their Descendants, and the Cohesion of Canada." In: *Cultural Boundaries and the Cohesion of Canada*, edited by Raymond Breton. Montreal: Institute for Research on Public Policy, 1980, p. 331-417.

0431 **Richard, Madeline A.**
Immigration Policy, Ethnic History and Intermarriage, Canada 1871 and 1971. Unpublished PhD thesis, York University, 1989.

0432   **Richmond, Anthony H.**
"Some Consequences of Third World Migration to Canada." In: *The Impact of International Migration on Developing Countries*, edited by Reginald Appleyard. Paris: Development Centre of the Organisation for Economic Co-operation and Development, 1989, p. 335-359.

0433   **Richmond, Anthony H.**
"Caribbean Immigrants in Britain and Canada: Socio-economic Adjustment." *International Migration/Migrations Internationales/ Migraciones Internacionales*, vol. 26 no. 4 (1988) p. 365-386.

0434   **Richmond, Anthony H.**
"Caribbean Immigrants in Britain and Canada." *Revue Européenne des migrations internationales*, vol. 3 no. 3 (1987) p. 129-150.

0435   **Richmond, Anthony H.**
"Immigration and Unemployment in Canada and Australia." *International Journal of Comparative Sociology*, vol. 25 nos. 3-4 (1984) p. 243-254.

0436   **Richmond, Anthony H.**
Factors in the Adjustment of Immigrants and Their Descendants. Ottawa: Statistics Canada, 1980. 481 p.

0437   **Roberts, Barbara**
"Shovelling Out the 'Mutinous': Political Deportations from Canada Before 1936." *Labour/Le Travail*, no. 18, (1988) p. 77-110.

0438   **Roberts, Barbara**
Whence They Came: Deportation from Canada, 1900-1935. Ottawa: University of Ottawa Press, 1988. 260 p.

0439   **Roberts, Barbara**
"Doctors and Deports: The Role of the Medical Profession in Canadian Deportation, 1900-1920." *Canadian Ethnic Studies/Études ethniques au Canada*, vol. 18 no. 3 (1986) p. 17-36.

0440   **Robertson, M.**
"A Longitudinal Perspective on Unemployment Experience of Principal Applicant Immigrants to Canada: 1977-1981." *Canadian Studies in Population*, vol. 13 no. 1 (1986) p. 37-56.

0441   **Robinson, W.G.**
"Illegal Immigrants in Canada: Recent Developments." *International Migration Review*, vol. 18 no. 3 (1984) p. 474-485.

0442   **Robinson, W.G.**
A Report to the Honourable Lloyd Axworthy, Minister of Employment and Immigration on Illegal Migrants in Canada. Ottawa: Minister of Supply and Services Canada, 1983. xxxv, 121, 214 p.

0443   **Robinson, W.G.**
The Refugee Status Determination Process: A Report of the Task Force on Immigration Practices and Procedure. Ottawa: Government of Canada, 1981. xxiii, 132 p.

0444   **Rockett, I.R.H. and S.L. Putnam**
"Physician-Nurse Migration to the United Stated: Regional and Health Status Origins in Relation to Legislation and Policy." *International Migration/Migrations Internationales/Migraciones Internacionales*, vol. 27 no. 3 (1989) p. 389-410.

0445   **Rogge, J.R.**
"The Indochinese Diaspora: Where Have All the Refugees Gone." *Canadian Geographer/Le géographe Canadien*, vol. 29 no. 1 (1985) p. 65-71.

0446   **Sabet-Esfahani, Afsaneh**
The Experience of Immigration: The Case of Iranian Women. Unpublished MA thesis, University of British Columbia, 1988. 237 leaves. Canadian theses on microfiche, CT90-20361-7.

0447   **Sampat-Mehta, R.**
"First Fifty Years of South Asian Immigration: A Historical Perspective." In: *South Asians in the Canadian Mosaic*, edited by Rabindra N. Kanungo. Montreal: Kala Bharati Foundation, 1984, p. 13-31.

0448   **Samuel, T. John**
"Immigration and Visible Minorities in the Year 2001: A Projection." *Canadian Ethnic Studies/Études ethniques au Canada*, vol. 20 no. 2 (1988) p. 92-100.

0449   **Samuel, T. John**
"National Recording Systems and the Measurement of International
Migration in Canada: An Assessment." *International Migration
Review*, vol. 21 no. 4 (1987) p. 1170-1211.

0450   **Satzewich, Victor (Vic) N.**
"Racism and Canadian Immigration Policy: The Government's View
of Caribbean Migration, 1962-1966." *Canadian Ethnic Studies/Études
ethniques au Canada*, vol. 21 no. 1 (1989) p. 77-97.

0451   **Sauriol, Micheline**
*Une approche éducative pour les immigrants adultes ayant des
difficultés d'appentissage du français.* Unpublished MA thesis,
University of Montreal, 1986.

0452   **Scardellato, Gabriele P.**
"Beyond the Frozen Wastes: Italian Sojourners and Settlers in British
Columbia." In: *Arrangiarsi: The Italian Immigration Experience in
Canada*, edited by Roberto Perin and Franc Sturino. Montreal:
Guernica, 1989, p. 135-161.

0453   **Schoenfeld, Stuart**
"Wandering Jews and Local Jews: Migration and Jewish Community
Structure." In: *Canadian Jewry Today: Who's Who in Canadian
Jewry*, edited by Edmond Y. Lipsitz. Downsview, Ont.: J.E.S.L.
Educational Products, 1989, p. 86-91.

0454   **Schultz, John A.**
"White Man's Country: Canada and the West Indian Immigrant,
1900-1965." *American Review of Canadian Studies*, vol. 12 no. 1
(1982) p. 53-64.

0455   **Segal, Gary L.**
*Immigrating to Canada: Who is Allowed? What is Required? How to
Do It.* 5th ed. Vancouver: International Self-counsel Press, 1983.
179 p.

0456   **Serio, Nicoletta**
"Canada as a Target of Trade and Emigration in Post-Unification
Italian Writing." In: *Arrangiarsi: The Italian Immigration Experience
in Canada*, edited by Roberto Perin and Franc Sturino. Montreal:
Guernica, 1989, p. 91-117.

0457   **Shanks, Connie**
"The Orphans' Odyssey [in the latter 1800's and early 1900's
Thousands of British 'Orphans' Were Sent to Homes in Canada.
Many Ended Up in Atlantic Canada]." *Atlantic Advocate*, vol. 80 no.
3 (1989) p. 36-38.

0458   **Sherbaniuk, Richard**
"Settlement Services: A Practical Welcome." *First Reading: Edmonton Social Planning Council*, vol. 3 no. 6 (1984) p. 4-5.

0459   **Simone, Nick**
Italian Immigrants in Toronto: 1890-1930. Working Papers, no. 26.
Toronto: Department of Geography, York University, 1981. 51 p.

0460   **Smith, Charles D.**
"Refuge Or Asylum? Does Canada Have a Choice?" *International
Migration Review*, vol. 21 no. 1 (1987) p. 155-158. Report on the
conference held at Glendon College, York University, Toronto, May
27-30, 1986.

0461   **Southcott, Chris**
"Ethnicity and Community in Thunder Bay." *Polyphony: The Bulletin
of the Multicultural History Society of Ontario*, vol. 9 no. 2
(1987) p. 10-20.

0462   **Stolarik, M. Mark**
"From Field to Factory: The Historiography of Slovak Immigration to
U.S. and Canada, 1976-1987." *Ethnic Forum*, vol. 8 no. 1
(1988) p. 23-39.

0463   **Sturino, Franc**
"Italian Emigration: Reconsidering the Links in Chain Migration." In:
Arrangiarsi: The Italian Immigration Experience in Canada, edited by
Roberto Perin and Franc Sturino. Montreal: Guernica, 1989, p. 63-90.

0464   **Sullivan, Teresa A.**
*Different Paths to Diversity: Canadian Immigration Patterns, 1971-
1981*. Texas Population Research Center papers, ser. 11, no. 11. 09
Austin, Texas: University of Texas, Texas Population Research
Center, 1989. 16 p.

0465   **Surrey, David S.**
Choice of Conscience: Vietnam Era Military and Draft Resisters in Canada. New York: Praeger, 1982. 207 p.

0466   **Surrey, David S.**
The Assimilation of Vietnam Era Draft Dodgers and Deserters Into Canada: A Matter of Class. Unpublished PhD thesis, New School for Social Research, 1980. Canadian theses on microfiche, 1094.

0467   **Szacka, Alexandra E.**
Ethnicité et fragmentation du mouvement ouvrier: La situation des immigrants juifs au Québec, 1920-1940. Unpublished MA thesis, Université Laval, 1981. 2 microfiches. Canadian theses on microfiche, 56243.

0468   **Szalaszcnyj, Kadilyn**
"Memoirs: Estella and Her Husband Seward T. St. John Homesteaded Near Wilcox in 1902. Her Early Impressions Were Recorded in Her Diary." *Liaison: Magazine of Museum Association of Saskatchewan,* no. 1 (September 1989) p. 12-15.

0469   **Takata, Toyo**
Nikkei Legacy: Story of Japanese Canadians from Settlement to Today. Toronto: NC Press, 1983. 176 p.

0470   **Taschereau, Sylvie**
"L'histoire de l'immigration au Québec: une invitation à fuir les ghettos." *Revue d'histoire de l'Amérique française,* vol. 14 no. 4 (1988) p. 575-589.

0471   **Tepper, Elliot L.**
Asia's Refugeees and the Western Tradition: The Political and Constitutional Legacy of Indochina. Ottawa: Citizenship Registration Branch, Government of Canada, 1983. 48, 48 p. French language title: *Les réfugiés asiatiques et la tradition occidentale: L'héritage constitutionnel et politique de l'Indochine.*

0472   **Tepper, Elliot L., ed.**
Southeast Asian Exodus: From Tradition to Resettlement, Understanding Refugees from Laos, Kampuchea, and Vietnam in Canada. Ottawa: Canadian Asian Studies Association, 1980. 230 p. French language title: *D'un continent à l'autre: les réfugiés du sud-est asiatique: pour mieux comprender ceux qui arrivent du Laos, du Kampuchéa et du Viêt-nam au Canada.*

0473   **Ternowetsky, Gordon W.**
        *The Impact of Immigration on Unemployment, Poverty, Inequality
        and State Dependency: Counting the Costs.* Regina: Regina Social
        Administration Research Unit, Faculty of Social Work, University of
        Regina, 1986. 30 leaves.

0474   **Thornton, Patricia A.**
        "The Problem of Out-migration from Atlantic Canada, 1871-1921: A
        New Look." *Acadiensis*, vol. 15 no. 1 (1985) p. 3-34.

0475   **Thraves, Bernard D.**
        An Analysis of Ethnic Intra-urban Migration: The Case of Winnipeg.
        Unpublished PhD thesis, University of Manitoba, 1986.

0476   **Trovato, Frank**
        "The Inter-urban Mobility of the Foreign Born in Canada."
        International Migration Review, vol. 22 no. 3 (1988) p. 59-86.

0477   **Trovato, Frank**
        "Ethnicity and Migration in Canada." *International Migration Review*,
        vol. 17 no. 2 (1983) p. 245-267.

0478   **Tyhurst, L.**
        "Coping with Refugees: A Canadian Experience, 1948-1981."
        International Journal of Social Psychiatry, vol. 28 no. 2 (1982)
        p.105-110.

0479   **Van Esterik, Penny**
        "Cultural Factors Affecting the Adjustment of Southeast Asian
        Refugees." In: *Southeast Asian Exodus: From Tradition to Resettle-
        ment: Understanding Refugees from Laos, Kampuchea, and Vietnam
        in Canada*, edited by Elliot L. Tepper. Ottawa: Canadian Asian
        Studies Association, 1980, p. 151-172.

0480   **Vineberg, R.A.**
        "Federal-provincial Relations in Canadian Immigration." *Canadian
        Public Administration/Adminstration publique au Canada*, vol. 30 no.
        2 (1987) p. 299-317.

0481   **Virtanen, Keijo**
        "'Counter-Current': Finns in the Overseas Return Migration
        Movement." In: *Finnish Diaspora I: Canada, South America, Africa,
        Australia and Sweden*, edited by Michael G. Karni. Toronto:
        Multicultural History Society of Ontario, 1981, p. 183-202.

0482   **Wade, Mason**
"France's Belated Conquest of New England: The Great Migration
from Canada." *Journal of American Culture*, vol. 9 no. 1 (1986) p. 77-
82.

0483   **Weatherbe, Steve, Tim Gallagher, and Paul Bunner**
"B.C.'s Terrorist Mouthpiece [Francisco Nota Moises]: Three West
Coast Cases [Moises, Pastora and Torres] Underscore Canada's
Politically Inconsistent Immigration Process." *Alberta Report*, vol. 15
no. 29 (1988) p. 9-10.

0484   **Weaver, John C.**
"Hamilton and the Immigration Tide." *Families*, vol. 20 no. 4
(1981) p. 197-208.

0485   **Weiner, Gerry**
"Immigration to the Year 2000: A Canadian Perspective." *Atlantic
Community Quarterly*, vol. 25 no. 1 (1987) p. 83-90.

0486   **Wetmore, Donald and Lester B. Sellick**
Loyalists in Nova Scotia. Hantsport, N.S.: Lancelot Press, 1983.

0487   **Whitaker, Reginald**
Double Standard: The Secret History of Canadian Immigration.
Toronto: Lester and Orpen Dennys, 1987. 348 p.

0488   **Whyte, David**
A Dictionary of Scottish Emigrants to Canada Before Confederation.
Toronto: Ontario Genealogical Society, 1986. 443 p.

0489   **Wilkinson, Daphne Rose**
*Immigration, Aspirations and Adjustment: A Study of South Asian
Families.* Unpublished MA thesis, McGill University, 1985. 2
microfiches. Canadian theses on microfiche, CT86-28876-5.

0490   **Wisenthal, Christine Boas**
*Insiders and Outsiders: Two Waves of Jewish Settlement in British
Columbia, 1858-1914.* Unpublished MA thesis, Department of
Geography, U.B.C. 1987. 160 leaves. Canadian theses on microfiche,
400579.

0491 **Wood, John R.**
"Well Founded Fear: The Controversy Over Canada's Refugee Policy." *CPSA Papers/ACSP Contributions 1989*, Section B paper 24, fiche 8. Paper presented at the 61st annual meeting of the Canadian Political Science Association, June 1-3, 1989, Laval University, Quebec, P.Q.

0492 **Woon, Yuen-Fong**
"Indo-Chinese Refugee Sponsorship: The Case of Victoria, 1979-1980." *Canadian Ethnic Studies/Études ethniques au Canada*, vol. 16 no. 1 (1984) p. 57-77.

0493 **Wynn, Graeme**
"Ethnic Migrations and Atlantic Canada: Geographical Perspectives." *Canadian Ethnic Studies/Études ethniques au Canada*, vol. 18 no. 1 (1986) p. 1-16.

0494 **Young, Margaret**
Canada's Immigration Program. Backgrounder, BP-190E. Ottawa: Prepared and edited by Library of Parliament, Research Branch, Law and Government Division, 1989. 28, 9 p.

0495 **Young, Margaret**
Canada's New Refugee Status Determination System. Backgrounder, BP-185E. Ottawa: Prepared and edited by Library of Parliament, Research Branch, Law and Government Division, 1989. 19 p.

0496 **Young, Margaret**
The Convention Refugee Determination Process in Canada. Ottawa: Library of Parliament, Research Branch, Law and Government Division, 1987. 13 p.

0497 **Zimmerman, Diana**
Refugees: Holdings of the Center for Migration Studies Library/ Archives. Staten Island: Center for Migration Studies Publications, 1987. 423 p.

0498 **Zucchi, John E.**
Italians in Toronto: Development of a National Identity, 1875-1935. Kingston: McGill-Queen's University Press, 1988. 255 p.

Demography

0499 **Alberta. Policy and Planning Branch, Native Affairs Secretariat**
A Demographic Overview of the Native Populations in Alberta.
Alberta: Policy and Planning Branch, Native Affairs Secretariat,
1985. 35 p.

0500 **Bakvis, Herman**
"The Political Significance of Demographic Change: Comments on
'Aspects Linguistiques de l'évolution démographique au Canada'."
Canadian Issues, (1989) p. 105-120. Special monographic volume in
the *Canadian Issues* series titled *Demolinguistic Trends and the
Evolution of Canadian Institutions.* Montreal: Association for Canadian Studies, 1989. French language title: "L'incidence politique de
l'évolution démographique: commentaires sur les 'Aspects linguistiques de l'évolution démographique au Canada'." p. 107-124. Paper
presented at a Colloquium on Demolinguistic Trends and the Evolution of Canadian Institutions, held in Hull, 10 February 1989.

0501 **Balakrishnan, T.R.**
Class and Ethnicity in the Internal Structure of Canadian Cities.
Discussion paper, no. 89-5. London, Ont.: University of Western
Ontario, Population Studies Centre, 1989. 13 p.

0502 **Balakrishnan, T.R.**
"Changing Patterns of Residential Segregation in the Metropolitan
Areas of Canada." *Canadian Review of Sociology and Anthropology/
Revue canadienne de sociologie et d'anthropologie*, vol. 19 no. 1
(1982) p. 92-110.

0503 **Banks, Brian**
"History's Lessons: A New Atlas Provides a Fascinating Vision of
Canada and its Development." *Equinox*, no. 35 (1987) p. 72-79.

0504   **Basavarajappa, K.G.**
"Spouse Selection in Canada, 1921-78: An Examination of Age, Sex and Religion." *Journal of Biosocial Science*, vol. 20 no. 2 (1988) p. 211-223.

0505   **Basavarajappa, K.G.**
"Fertility of Asian Ethnic Groups in Canada, 1971-1981." In: *Contributions to Demography: Methodological and Substantive: Essays in Honour of Dr. Karol J. Krotki.* Edmonton: University of Alberta, Department of Sociology, 1987, p. 311-322.

0506   **Basavarajappa, K.G.**
"Asian Immigrants in Canada: Some Findings from 1981 Census." *International Migration/Migrations Internationales/Migraciones Internacionales*, vol. 23 no. 1 (1985) p. 97-121.

0507   **Basavarajappa, K.G.**
"Fertility Levels of Asian Indians in Canada, 1971-1981." *Population Review (Indian Institute for Population Studies)*, vol. 29 no. 1/2 (1985) p. 136-147.

0508   **Baskin, Bernard**
"[Jewish population in] Canada." *American Jewish Yearbook*, vol. 84 (1984) p. 175-186.

0509   **Beaujot, Roderic P.**
The Relative Economic Situation of Immigrants in Canada: Review of Past Studies and Multivariate Analysis on 1981 Data. Ottawa: Health and Welfare Canada, 1986. 60, 12 p. Report prepared for the Review of Demography and its Implications for Economic and Social Policy.

0510   **Beaujot, Roderic P.**
Growth and Dualism: The Demographic Development of Canadian Society. Toronto: Gage, 1982. 249 p.

0511   **Béland, Francois**
"A Comparison of the Mobility Structures of Francophones and Anglophones in Quebec: 1954, 1964, 1974." *Canadian Review of Sociology and Anthropology/Revue canadienne de sociologie et d'anthropologie*, vol. 24 no. 2 (1987) p. 232-251.

0512   **Bernéche, Francine et J.C. Martin**
"Immigration, emploi et logement: La situation de la population haïtienne dans certaines zones de la région métropolitaine de Montréal," *Anthropologie et sociétés*, vol. 8 no. 2 (1984) p. 5-29.

0513   **Bilash, Radomir Borislaw**
The Colonial Development of East Central Alberta and its Effect on Ukrainian Immigrant Settlement to 1930. Unpublished MA thesis, University of Manitoba, 1983. 3 microfiches. Canadian theses on microfiche, 54658.

0514   **Boxhill, Walton O.**
1981 Census Information on Place of Birth, Citizenship and Immigration: Some Facts and Figures. Ottawa: Statistics Canada, Housing, Family and Social Statistics Division, 1986. 69 p. French language title: *Statistiques du recensement de 1981 sur le lieu de naissance, la citoyenneté et l'immigration: quelques faits et chiffres.*

0515   **Boxhill, Walton O.**
A User's Guide to 1981 Census Data on Ethnic Origin. Ottawa: Statistics Canada, 1986. 77 p. French language title: *Guide de l'utilisateur des donnees de recensement de 1981 sur l'origine ethnique.*

0516   **Boxhill, Walton O.**
Limitations to the Use of Ethnic Origin Data to Quantify Visible Minorities in Canada. Ottawa: Statistics Canada, 1984. 48 p. French language title: *Restrictions relatives à l'utilisation des données sur l'origine ethnique pour dénombrer les minorites visiblés au Canada.*

0517   **Brym, Robert J.**
"The Rise and Decline of Canadian Jewry? A Socio-demographic Profile." In: *Canadian Jewry Today: Who's Who in Canadian Jewry*, edited by Edmond Y. Lipsitz. Downsview, Ont.: J.E.S.L. Educational Products, 1989, p. 37-51.

0518   **Caldwell, Gary**
"The Quebec Question: A Matter of Population." *Canadian Journal of Sociology/Cahiers canadiens de sociologie*, vol. 12 nos. 1-2 (1987) p. 16-41.

0519   **Caldwell, Gary**
"Anglo-Quebec: Demographic Realities and Options for the Future."
In: *Conflict and Language Planning in Quebec*, edited by Richard Y.
Bourhis. Clevedon, Avon: Multilingual Matters, 1984, p. 205-221.

0520   **Canada. Census 1986**
Federal Electoral Districts - 1987. Profiles - Profils. Ottawa:
Minister of Supply and Services, 1988. 2 vol. French language title:
*Circonscriptions électorales fédérales - Ordonnance de
representation de 1987.*

0521   **Canada. Indian and Inuit Affairs**
*Schedule of Indian Bands, Reserves and Settlements Including
Membership and Population, Location and Area in Hectares, June 1,
1987*. Ottawa: Indian and Inuit Affairs, 1987. 187 p. French language
title: *Répertoire des bandes, réserves et établissements indiens;
effectif et population, location et superficie en hectares, le 1er juin
1987*. Earlier published as: *Registered Indian population, 1965-1973*.

0522   **Canada. Multiculturalism Directorate**
*Socio-economic Profiles of Selected Ethnic Visible Minority Groups:
1981 Census*. Ottawa: Multiculturalism Canada, 1986. 103 p.

0523   **Canada. Review of Demography and Its Implications for
Economic and Social Policy**
Charting Canada's Future: A Report of the Demographic Review.
Ottawa: Health and Welfare Canada, 1989. 74, 74 p. French language
title: *Esquisse du Canada de demain.*

0524   **Canada. Royal Commission on Equality in Employment**
Report. Ottawa: Supply and Services Canada, 1984. 393 p. Rosalie
Silberman Abella, Commissioner. French language title: *Rapport de
la Commission sur l'égalite en matière d'emploi.*

0525   **Canada. Task Force on Program Review**
Major Surveys: A Study Team Report ... Ottawa: The Task Force,
1985. 224 p. Chairman: Erik Nielsen, team leader: James M.
Stanley. French language title: *Principales enquêtes.*

0526   **Careless, J.M.S.**
"Cabbagetown." *Polyphony: The Bulletin of the Multicultural History
Society of Ontario*, vol. 6 no. 1 (1984) p. 15-18.

0527   **Castonguay, Charles**
"Virage démographique et Québec francais." *Cahiers québécois de démographie*, vol. 17 no. 1 (1988) p. 49-60.

0528   **D'Costa, Ronald**
"Statistical Profile of Visible Minorities in Canada (1981)." In: *Canada 2000: Race Relations and Public Policy*, edited by O.P. Dwivedi. Guelph, Ont.: Department of Political Studies, University of Guelph, 1989, p. 143-169.

0529   **D'Costa, Ronald**
The Age Composition of Selected Ethnic Groups in Canada. Ottawa, 1988. 20 p.

0530   **D'Costa, Ronald**
"Asian Immigration to Canada, 1968-1982: Characteristics of Immigrants from South, Southeast, and East Asia." In: *Asian Canadians: Aspects of Social Change*, edited by K. Victor Ujimoto and Josephine Naidoo. [Ottawa: Canadian Asian Studies Association], 1984, p. 30-48.

0531   **Davids, Leo**
"The Canadian Jewish Population Picture: Today and Tomorrow." In: *Canadian Jewry Today: Who's Who in Canadian Jewry*, edited by Edmond Y. Lipsitz. Downsview, Ont.: J.E.S.L. Educational Products, 1989, p. 52-60.

0532   **Davids, Leo**
"Canadian Jewry: Some Recent Census Findings." *American Jewish Yearbook*, vol. 85 (1985) p. 191-201.

0533   **DeRoche Constance P.**
The Village, The Vertex: Adaptation to Regionalism and Development in a Complex Society. Occasional Papers in Anthropology, no. 12. Halifax: Department of Anthropology, St. Mary's University, 1985.

0534   **DeVries, John**
"Explorations in the Demography of Language and Ethnicity: The Case of Ukrainians in Canada." In: *Central and East European Ethnicity in Canada: Adaptation and Preservation*, edited by T. Yedlin. Edmonton: Central and East European Studies Society of Alberta, 1985, p. 111-132.

0535   **Driedger, Leo**
Aging and Ethnicity: Towards an Interface. Perspectives on Individual
and Population Aging Series. Toronto: Butterworths, 1987. 131 p.

0536   **Driedger, Leo**
"Urbanization of Ukrainians in Canada: Consequences for Ethnic
Identity." In: *Changing Realities: Social Friends Among Ukrainian
Canadians,* edited by W.R. Petryshyn. Edmonton: Canadian Institute
of Ukrainian Studies, 1980 p. 107-133.

0537   **Duhaine, Gérard**
"La catastrophe et l'État: Histoire démographique et changements sociaux
dans l'Arctique." *Études Inuit Studies,* vol. 13 no. 1 (1989) p. 75-114.

0538   **Duncan, James S.**
"Ethnic Segregation in North American Urban Environments, "
Ethnic Studies Report, vol. 1 no. 2 (1983) p. 19-21.

0539   **Gaffield, Chad**
"Boom or Bust: The Demography and Economy of the Lower Ottawa
Valley in the Nineteenth Century." *Historical Papers, Ottawa 1982,*
Canadian Historical Association, 1982.

0540   **Gauthier, Hervé**
"Des conditions démographiques nouvelles." *Journal of Canadian
Studies/Revue d'études canadiennes,* vol. 23 no. 4 (1988/89) p. 16-36.

0541   **George, Peter J.**
"Aspects et tendances de la population canadienne." *Annales de
géographie,* vol. 95 no. 527 (1986) p. 3-25.

0542   **Hagey, N. Janet**
*Highlights of Aboriginal Conditions 1981-2001: Part I, Demographic
Trends.* [Ottawa] Qualitative Analysis and Socio-demographic
Research, Indian and Northern Affairs Canada, 1989. 28 p. French
language title: *Faits saillants des conditions autochtones, 1981- 2001:
1 ère partie, tendances démographiques.*

0543   **Hagey, N. Janet**
*Highlights of Aboriginal Conditions 1981-2001: Part II, Social
Conditions.* [Ottawa:] Qualitative Analysis and Socio-demographic
Research, Indian and Northern Affairs Canada, 1989. 35 p. French
language title: *Faits saillants des autochtones, 1981-2001: 2 ème
partie, conditions sociales.*

0544   **Hagey, N. Janet**
Highlights of Aboriginal Conditions 1981-2001: Part III, Economic Conditions. [Ottawa] Qualitative Analysis and Socio-demographic Research, Indian and Northern Affairs Canada, 1989. 40 p. French language title: *Faits saillants des conditions autochtones, 1981-2001: 3 ème partie, conditions economiques.*

0545   **Hamm, Bemd, Raymond F. Currie, and David R. Forde**
"A Dynamic Typology of Urban Neighbourhoods: The Case of Winnipeg." *Canadian Review of Sociology and Anthropology/Revue canadienne de sociologie et d'anthropologie,* vol. 25 no. 3 (1988) p. 439-455.

0546   **Heaton, Tim B.**
"Sociodemographic Characteristics of Religious Groups in Canada." *Sociological Analysis,* vol. 47 no. 1 (1986) p. 54-65.

0547   **Henripin, Jacques**
"Le québecois dont la langue est flottante et la mobilité linguistique." *Cahiers québécois de démographie,* vol. 14 no. 1 (1985) p. 87-98.

0548   **Hiller, Harry H.**
Canadian Society: A Macro Analysis. Scarborough, Ontario: Prentice-Hall Canada, 1985. 245 p.

0549   **Hryniuk, Stella**
"Ukrainian Immigration to Ontario: An Overview." *Polyphony: The Bulletin of the Multicultural History Society of Ontario,* vol. 10 no. 1/2 (1988) p. 21-26.

0550   **Hudson, Douglas**
"The Plateau: A Regional Overview." In: *Native Peoples: The Canadian Experience,* edited by R. Bruce Morrison and C. Roderick Wilson. Toronto, McClelland and Stewart, 1986, p. 436-444.

0551   **Jansen, Clifford J.**
Fact Book on Italians in Canada. 1st ed. Toronto: Department of Sociology, York University, 1981. 85 p.

0552   **Johansson, S.R.**
"The Demographic History of the Native Peoples of North America: A Selective Bibliography." *Yearbook of Physical Anthropology,* vol. 25 (1982) p. 133-152.

0553   **Joy, Richard J.**
"Canada's Official Language Populations, as Shown by the 1981
Census." *American Review of Canadian Studies*, vol. 15 no. 1 (1985)
p.90-96.

0554   **Kalbach, Warren E.**
"Growth and Distribution of Canada's Ethnic Population, 1871-
1981." In: *Ethnic Canada: Identities and Inequalities*, edited by Leo
Driedger. Toronto: Copp Clark Pitman, 1987, p. 82-110.

0555   **Kalbach, Warren E.**
"A Demographic Overview of Racial and Ethnic Groups in Canada."
In: *Race and Ethnic Relations in Canada*, edited by Peter S. Li. Don
Mills, Ontario: Oxford University Press, 1980, p. 18-49.

0556   **Khondakar, Nizamuddin**
*Some Changes in Socioeconomic and Spatial Characteristics of
Ethnic Groups in London, Ontario, 1961-1971.* Unpublished PhD
thesis, University of Western Ontario, 1981. 4 microfiches. Canadian
theses on microfiche, 53828.

0557   **Kim, Uichol**
*Acculturation of Korean Immigrants to Canada: Psychological,
Demographic and Behavioural Profiles of Emigrating Koreans, Non-
emigrating Koreans and Korean-Canadians.* Unpublished PhD thesis,
Queen's University, 1988.

0558   **Kogler, Rudolf K.**
"The Canadian Polish Community in the Light of the 1976 Census
Results." In: *The Canadian Alternative: Cultural Pluralism and the
Canadian Unity*, edited by Hedi Bouraoui. Downsview, Ontario:
ECW Press, 1980, p. 55-63. Paper presented at the Conference on
Cultural Pluralism and Canadian Unity held at Stong College, York
University, 26-27 October 1979.

0559   **Kordan, Bohdan S.**
"Ukrainians in Ontario and the 1981 Canada Census: A Research
Note." *Polyphony: The Bulletin of the Multicultural History Society
of Ontario*, vol. 10 no. 1/2 (1988) p. 11-16.

0560   **Kovacsics, Joszef**
"Torteneti demografiai attekintes a Kanadaba vaandorolt Magya-
rokrol." (Historical Demographic Survey on the Hungarians Migrated
to Canada). *Demografia*, nos. 2-3 (1981) p. 243-269.

0561   **Kralt, John**
Atlas of Residential Concentration for the Census Metropolitan Area of Montreal. Ottawa: Multiculturalism Canada, 1986. 131 p. French language title: *Atlas des populations de la région métropolitaine de recensement de Montréal.*

0562   **Kralt, John**
Atlas of Residential Concentration for the Census Metropolitan Area of Toronto. Ottawa: Multiculturalism Canada, 1986. 127 p. French language title: *Atlas des populations de la région métropolitaine de recensement de Toronto.*

0563   **Kubat, Daniel**
"Le rôle de l'élément démographique dans la planification de l'immigration au Canada." *Cahiers québécois de démographie*, vol. 15 no. 2 (1986) p. 253-265.

0564   **Kutner, Nancy G. and Michael H. Kutner**
"Ethnic and Residence Differences Among Poor Families." *Journal of Comparative Family Studies*, vol. 18 no. 3 (1987) p. 463-470.

0565   **Lachapelle, Réjean**
Aspects linguistiques de l'évolution démographiques au Canada. Ottawa: Health and Welfare Canada, 1988. 205 p. Report prepared for the Review of Demography and its Implications for Economic and Social Policy.

0566   **Lachapelle, Réjean**
L'avenir démographique du Canada et les groupes linguistiques. Studies in social policy. Discussion paper on demographic review, 87. A. 8. Ottawa: Institute for Research on Public Policy, 1987. 21 leaves.

0567   **Lachapelle, Réjean**
"La démolinquistique et le destin des minorités françaises vivant a l'exterieur du Québec." *Royal Society of Canada. Proceedings and Transactions*, ser. 5 vol. 1 (1986) p. 123-142.

0568   **Lachapelle, Réjean**
"Definition et analyse des mobilités demographiques: l'example de la mobilité linguistique." In: *Association internationale des démographes de langue française.* Démographie et destin des sous-populations, Colloque de Liége. Paris: l'Association, 1983, p. 237-248.

0569 **Lachapelle, Réjean**
La situation démolinguistique au Québec: evolution passée et prospective. Montréal: Institut de recherches politiques, 1980. 391 p.

0570 **Lai, Chuen-Yan David**
"The Population Structure of North American Chinatowns in the Mid-twentieth Century: A Case Study." In: *Visible Minorities and Multiculturalism: Asians in Canada*, edited by K. Victor Ujimoto and Gordon Hirabayashi. Toronto: Butterworths, 1980, p. 13-22.

0571 **Langlois, André**
"La diversité de la population d'origine française dans l'espace ethnique d'Ottawa." *Canadian Ethnic Studies/Études ethniques au Canada*, vol. 19 no. 1 (1987) p. 42-51.

0572 **Langlois, André**
"Le comportement résidential de la population d'origine française à Ottawa, 1961, 1971, 1981." *Recherches sociographiques*, vol. 27 no. 3 (1986) p. 261-273.

0573 **La Rose, André**
"Bibliographie: bibliographie courante sur l'histoire de la population canadienne et la démographie historique au Canada, 1985/Bibliography: A Current Bibliography on the History of Canadian Population and Historical Demography in Canada, 1985." *Histoire sociale/Social History*, vol. 19 no. 38 (1986) p. 461-465.

0574 **Li, Peter S.**
"Immigration Laws and Family Patterns: Some Demographic Changes Among Chinese Families in Canada, 1885-1971." *Canadian Ethnic Studies/Études ethniques au Canada*, vol. 12 no. 1 (1980) p. 58-73.

0575 **Loaiza, Edilberto**
Socio-demographic Characteristics and Economic Attainment of Latin-American Immigrants in Canada: A Census Data Assessment, 1981, 1986. Unpublished PhD thesis, University of Western Ontario, 1989. 270 leaves.

0576 **Lux, André**
"Un Québec qui vieillit: Perspectives pour le XXIè me siècle." *Recherches sociographiques*, vol. 24 no. 3 (1983) p. 325-377.

0577   **Marr, William L.**
Consumption and Saving Patterns of the Foreign-born in Canada.
Ottawa: Health and Welfare Canada, 1988. 9 leaves. Report prepared
for the Review of Demography and its Implications for Economic
and Social Policy.

0578   **Masse, Sylvain**
"Le déclin de l'empire démographique québécois." *Quebec Studies*,
no. 8 (1989) p. 111-118.

0579   **Mathews, Georges**
Politiques natalistes européennes et politique familiale canadienne.
Montréal: INRS-Urbanisation, 1989. 65 p.

0580   **Mathews, Georges**
Le choc démographique: le déclin du Québec est-il inevitable?
Montréal: Boréal Express, 1984. 204 p.

0581   **Mercer, John**
"Asian Migrants and Residential Location in Canada." *New
Community*, vol. 15 no. 2 (1989) p. 185-202.

0582   **Mondale, Clarence**
"Concepts and Trends in Regional Studies." *American Studies
International*, vol. 27 no. 1 (1989) p. 13-37.

0583   **Morawska, Ewa**
"A Cultural Profile of Toronto Poles." *Polyphony: The Bulletin of the
Multicultural History Society of Ontario*, vol. 6 no. 2 (1984) p. 93-
100.

0584   **Normandeau, Louise et Victor Piché, eds.**
*Les populations amérindiennes et inuits du Canada: aperçu
démographique*, sous la direction de Louise Normandeau et Victor
Piché. Montréal: Presses de l'Université de Montréal, 1984. 282 p.

0585   **Passaris, Constantine E.**
"Canada's Demographic Outlook and Multicultural Immigration."
*International Migration/Migrations Internationales/Migraciones Inter-
nacionales*, vol. 25 no. 4 (1987) p. 361-384.

0586   **Pereira, Cecil**
        A Study of the Ethnic and Non-ethnic Factors on the Resettlement of the Ugandan Asian Refugees in Canada. Unpublished PhD Thesis, University of Wisconsin, Madison, 1981.

0587   **Piché, Victor**
        L'immigration Carabéene au Canada et au Québec: Aspects statistiques. Montréal: Centre de recherches caraïbes, Université de Montréal, 1983. 189 p.

0588   **Prattis, J. Ian**
        "Ethnic Succession in the Eastern Townships of Quebec." *Anthropologica,* vol. 22 no. 2 (1980) p. 215-234.

0589   **Ram, Bali**
        "Regional Distribution of India's Immigrant Community in Canada." *Population Review,* vol. 29 nos. 1-2 (1985) p. 80-94.

0590   **Reserves and Trust, Indian and Inuit Affairs Program**
        Registered Indian Population by Band, Responsibility Centre, Region, Language or Dialect and Linguistic Group. Ottawa: Reserves and Trust, Indian and Inuit Affairs Program, 1982. French language title: *Population indienne inscrite selon la bande, centre de responsibilité, région, langue ou dialecte, et groupe linguistique.*

0591   **Richmond, Anthony H.**
        Caribbean Immigrants: A Demo-economic Analysis. Ottawa: Statistics Canada, 1989. 85 p.

0592   **Robert-Lamblin, J.**
        "An Historical and Contemporary Demography of Akutan, an Aleutian Village." *Études Inuit Studies,* vol. 6 no. 1 (1982) p. 99-126.

0593   **Robitaille, Norbert**
        An Overview of Demographic and Socio-economic Conditions of the Inuit in Canada. Ottawa: Indian and Northern Affairs Canada, 1985. 112 p. French language title: "Aperçu de la situation démographique et socio-économique des inuits du Canada."

0594   **Schoenfeld, Stuart, ed.**
        The Changing Jewish Community: A Symposium on Current Research, Held at York University, January 2, 1982. Toronto: Institute for Behavioural Research, York University, 1983. 240 leaves.

0595   **Seward, Shirley B.**
"Demographic Change, the Canadian Economy and the Role of Immigration." In: *The Future of Social Welfare Systems in Canada and the United Kingdom*, edited by Shirley B. Seward. Halifax, N.S.: Institute for Research on Public Policy, 1987, p. 231-246.

0596   **Siggner, Andrew J.**
"The Socio-demographic Conditions of Registered Indians." *Canadian Social Trends*, (1986) p. 2-9.

0597   **Siggner, Andrew J.**
An Overview of Selected Demographic Patterns and Trends Among Registered Indians for Canada and the Regions, with Observations on Intra-regional Differences in Saskatchewan. Ottawa: Research Branch, Corporate Policy, Dept of Indian Affairs and Northern Development, 1980. 57 p. Prepared for Workshop on Indian Demographic Patterns and Trends and their Implications for Policy and Planning (1980: Ottawa).

0598   **Siggner, Andrew J.**
An Overview of Demographic, Social and Economic Conditions Among Saskatchewan's Registered Indian Population. Ottawa: Indian and Northern Affairs Canada, 1980. 39 p.

0599   **Statistics Canada**
Population Projections for Canada, Provinces and Territories, 1984-2006, prepared by M.V. George and J. Perreault. Ottawa: Statistics Canada, 1985. 346 p. Text in English and French.

0600   **Statistics Canada**
Report on the Demographic Situation in Canada. Current Demographic Analysis. Ottawa: Statistics Canada, 1983. Catalogue 91-209E.

0601   **Tepper, Elliot L.**
"Demographic Change and Pluralism." *Canadian Studies in Population*, vol. 14 no. 2 (1987) p. 223-235.

0602   **Termote, Marc**
La situation démolinguistique du Québec. Québec, P.Q.: Éditeur officiel, 1988. 292 p., 524 p.

0603   **Termote, Marc**
"La place de la migration dans la recherche démographique." *Cahiers québécois de démographie*, vol. 12 no. 2 (1983) p. 175-179.

0604   **Tolvanen, Ahti**
"The Finnish Experience: Population Development of Finns in Port Arthur." *Polyphony: The Bulletin of the Multicultural History Society of Ontario*, vol. 9 no. 2 (1987) p. 43-45.

0605   **Trovato, Frank**
"Mortality Differentials in Canada, 1951-1971: French, British and Indians." *Culture, Medicine and Psychiatry*, vol. 12 no. 4 (1988) p. 459-477.

0606   **Trovato, Frank**
"Mortality Differences Among Canada's Indigenous and Foreign-born Populations, 1951-1971." *Canadian Studies in Population*, vol. 12 no. 1 (1985) p. 49-80.

0607   **Trovato, Frank**
"Ethnicity, Education and Fertility in Canadian Society." *Sociological Focus*, vol. 14 no. 1 (1981) p. 57-74.

0608   **Trovato, Frank**
"Minority Group Status and Fertility in Canada." *Canadian Ethnic Studies/Études ethniques au Canada*, vol. 8 no. 3 (1980) p. 1-18.

0609   **Vernex, Jean-Claude**
"La francophonie canadienne hors du Québec: quelques jalons pour une géographie ethnolinguistique du Canada."In: *La géographie du Canada*, textes recueillis par Pierre George. Bordeaux: Presses universitaires de Bordeaux, 1986, p. 215-229.

0610   **White, Pamela M.**
"Ethnic Origins of the Canadian Population." *Canadian Social Trends*, no. 13 (1989) p. 13-16.

0611   **Wien, Frederic Carl**
Socioeconomic Characteristics of the Micmac in Nova Scotia.
Halifax: Institute of Public Affairs, Dalhousie University, 1983.
167 p.

0612   **Wong, Amy Chor Yee**
An Examination of the Geographic and Socioeconomic Spaces of Ethnic Groups in Toronto: A Core-periphery Perspective.
Unpublished MA Thesis Wilfrid Laurier University, 1982, 3 microfiches. Canadian theses on microfiche, 56188.

0613   **Wood, Colin J.B.**
"Population and Ethnic Groups." In: *British Columbia: Its Resources and People*, edited by Charles N. Forward. Victoria: Department of Geography, University of Victoria, 1987, p. 309-332.

Ethnicity and Inter-ethnic Relations

0614　**Abele, Frances and D. Stasiulis**
"Canada as a 'White Settler Colony': What About Natives and Immigrants?" In: *The New Canadian Political Economy*, edited by Wallace Clement and Glen Williams. Kingston, Ontario: McGill-Queen's University Press, 1989, p. 240-277.

0615　**Abernathy, Thomas J.**
"Status Integration and Ethnic Intramarriage in Canada." In: *Racial Minorities in Multicultural Canada*, edited by Peter S. Li and B. Singh Bolaria. Toronto: Garamond Press, 1982, p. 97-102.

0616　**Aboud, Frances E.**
"Self and Ethnic Concepts in Relation to Ethnic Constancy." *Canadian Journal of Behavioural Science/Revue canadienne des sciences de comportement*, vol. 15 no. 1 (1983) p. 14-26.

0617　**Aboud, Frances E.**
"Ethnic Self-identity." In: *Canadian Social Psychology of Ethnic Relations*, edited by Robert C. Gardner and Rudolf Kalin. Toronto: Methuen, 1981, p. 37-56.

0618　**Aboud, Frances E.**
"A Test of Ethnocentricity with Young Children." *Canadian Journal of Behavioural Science/Revue canadienne des sciences de comporte-ment*, vol. 12 no. 3 (1980) p. 195-209.

0619　**Abu-Laban, Baha**
"Cultural Pluralism and Varieties of Ethnic Politics." *Canadian Ethnic Studies/Études ethniques au Canada*, vol. 13 no. 3 (1981) p. 44-63.

0620   **Adam, Heribert**
"Combatting Racism." *Queen's Quarterly*, vol. 89 no. 4
(1982) p. 785-793.

0621   **Adelman, Mara B.**
"Cross-cultural Adjustment: A Theoretical Perspective on Social
Support." *International Journal of Intercultural Relations*, vol. 12 no.
3 (1988) p. 183-204.

0622   **Ages, Arnold**
"Anti-semitism: The Uneasy Calm." In: *Canadian Jewish Mosaic*,
edited by M. Weinfeld, W. Shaffir and I. Cotler. Toronto: John Wiley
and Sons, 1981, p. 383-395.

0623   **Akoodie, Mohammed Ally**
"Identity and Self-concept in Immigrant Children." In: *Multicul-
turalism in Canada: Social and Educational Perspectives*, edited by
Ronald J. Samuda, John W. Berry and Michel Laferriére. Toronto:
Allyn and Bacon Inc., 1984, p. 253-265.

0624   **Akoodie, Mohammed Ally**
*Immigrant Students: A Comparative Assessment of Ethnic Identity,
Self-concept and Locus of Control Amongst West Indian, East Indian
and Canadian Students.* Unpublished PhD thesis, University of
Toronto, 1980. Canadian theses on microfiche, no. 43608

0625   **Ames, Michael M.**
"Reaction to Stress: A Comparative Study of Nativism." *Northwest
Anthropological Research Notes*, vol. 21 no. 1/2 (1987) p. 401-414.

0626   **Anctil, Pierre**
"Via Crucis et Lupini: sur les pistes d'une nouvelle ethnohistoire de
Montreal." *Vice Versa*, vol. 1 no. 5-6 (1984) p. 26-27.

0627   **Anderson, Alan B.**
"Generation Differences in Ethnic Identity Retention in Rural
Saskatchewan." *Prairie Forum*, vol. 7 no. 2 (1982) p. 171-195.

0628   **Anderson, Alan B.**
Ethnicity in Canada: Theoretical Perspectives. Toronto: Butterworths,
1981. 334 p.

0629 **Andiappan, Palaniappan**
"Racial Discrimination in Employment in Canada." *Relations industrielles/Industrial Relations*, vol. 44 no. 4 (1989) p. 827-849.

0630 **Angus, Ian H., ed.**
Ethnicity in a Technological Age. Edmonton: Canadian Institute of Ukrainian Studies, University of Alberta, 1988. 210 p. A collection of essays based on a May 1986 symposium held at Peter Robinson College, Trent University, Peterborough, Ontario.

0631 **Annis, Robert C.**
"The Effects of a White or Indian Model Upon White Children's Awareness." In: *Ethnic Psychology: Research and Practice with Immigrants, Refugees, Native Peoples, Ethnic Groups and Sojourners*, edited by J.W. Berry and R.C. Annis. Lisse: Swets and Zeitlinger, 1988, p. 198-206. Paper presented to the North American Regional International Association of Cross-cultural Psychology on Ethnic Psychology held in Kingston, Canada, August 16-21, 1987.

0632 **Annis, Robert C.**
"Effect of Test Language and Experimenter Race on Canadian Indian Children's Racial Self-identity." *Journal of Social Psychology*, vol. 126 no. 6 (1986) p. 761-774.

0633 **Annis, Robert C.**
"Self-identification and Race Preferences Among Canadian Indian children." In: *Ethnic Minorities and Immigrants in a Cross-cultural Perspective: Selected Papers*, edited by Lars H. Ekstrand. Berwyn: Swets North America, 1986, p. 79-86.

0634 **Armitage, Peter**
"Redbaiting and Racism on Our Frontier: Military Expansion in Labrador and Quebec." *Canadian Review of Sociology and Anthropology/Revue canadienne de sociologie et d'anthropologie*, vol. 26 no. 5 (1989) p. 798-817.

0635 **Armour, Leslie**
"History, Community, Ethnicity and the Thrust of Technology in Canada." In: *Ethnicity in a Technological Age*, edited by Ian H. Angus. Edmonton: Canadian Institute of Ukrainian Studies, University of Alberta, 1988, p. 157-175.

0636   **Armour, Leslie**
The Idea of Canada and the Crisis of Community. Ottawa: Steel Rail
Publishers, 1981. 180 p.

0637   **Bacchi, Carol Lee**
"Race Regeneration and Social Purity: A Study of the Social
Attitudes of Canada's English-speaking Suffragists." In: *Interpreting
Canada's Past*, edited by J.M. Bumsted. 2 volumes. Toronto: Oxford
University Press, 1986, vol. 2, p. 192-206.

0638   **Baer, Douglas E.**
"Differences in Achievement Values of French Canadians and
English Canadians." In: *Social Inequality in Canada: Patterns,
Problems, Policies*, edited by James E. Curtis, Edward Grabb, Neil
Guppy and Sid Gilbert. Scarborough, Ontario: Prentice-Hall Canada,
1988, p. 476-484

0639   **Baer, Douglas E.**
"French Canadian - English Canadian Differences in Values: National
Survey Findings." *Canadian Journal of Sociology/Cahiers canadiens
de sociologie*, vol. 9 no. 4 (1984) p. 405-428.

0640   **Bagley, Christopher**
"The Adaptation of Asian Children of Migrant Parents: British
Models and Their Application to Canadian Policy." In: *The South
Asian Diaspora in Canada: Six Essays*, edited by Milton Israel.
Toronto: Multicultural History Society of Ontario, 1987, p. 15-35.

0641   **Baird, Richard**
"The State and Value of Central and Eastern European Groups and
Culture in Canada." In: *Central and East European Ethnicity in
Canada: Adaptation and Preservation*, edited by T. Yedlin. Edmon-
ton: Central and East European Studies Society of Alberta,
1985, p. 25-34.

0642   **Balakrishnan, T.R.**
"Segregation of Visible Minorities in Montreal, Toronto and
Vancouver." In: *Ethnic Canada: Identities and Inequalities*, edited by
Leo Driedger. Toronto: Copp Clark Pitman, 1987, p. 138-157.

0643   **Balan, Jars, ed.**
Identifications, Ethnicity and the Writer in Canada. Edmonton:
Canadian Institute of Ukrainian Studies, 1982. 154 p.

0644   **Banks, James A.**
        "The Social Studies, Ethnic Diversity, and Social Change."
        Elementary School Journal, vol. 87 no. 5 (1987) p. 531-543.

0645   **Banks, Sherrie Leigh**
        *The Influence of the Ethnicity of the Experimenter on Verbal
        Conditioning of Self-acceptance Responses.* Unpublished MA thesis,
        York University, 1988. 3 microfiches. Canadian theses on microfiche,
        CT90-23406-7.

0646   **Barger, W. Ken**
        "Eskimos on Trial: Adaptation, Inter-ethnic Relations, and Social
        Control in the Canadian North." *Human Organization*, vol. 39 no. 3
        (1980) p. 242-249.

0647   **Barrett, Stanley R.**
        Is God a Racist? The Right Wing in Canada. Toronto: University of
        Toronto Press, 1987. 377 p.

0648   **Barrett, Stanley R.**
        "Fascism in Canada." *Contemporary Crises*, vol. 8 no. 4
        (1984) p. 345-378.

0649   **Barrett, Stanley R.**
        "White Supremacists and Neo-fascists: Laboratories for the Analysis
        of Racism in Wider Society." *Canadian Ethnic Studies/Études
        ethniques au Canada*, vol. 16 no. 1 (1984) p. 1-15.

0650   **Barsh, Russel L.**
        "The Ethnocidal Character of the State and International Law." *The
        Journal of Ethnic Studies*, vol. 16 no. 4 (1989) p. 1-30.

0651   **Basavarajappa, K.G.**
        "Ethnic Fertility Differences in Canada, 1926-71: An Examination of
        Assimilation Hypothesis." *Journal of Biosocial Science*, vol. 16 no. 1
        (1984) p. 45-54.

0652   **Basran, Gurcharn S.**
        "Canadian Immigration Policy and Theories of Racism." In: *Racial
        Minorities in Multicultural Canada*, edited by Peter S. Li and B.
        Singh Bolaria. Toronto: Garamond Press, 1983, p. 3-14.

0653   **Bassler, Gerhard P.**
"Newfoundland's 'Dangerous' Internees Who Never Were: The
History of Victoria Camp, 1940-1943." *Newfoundland Studies*, vol. 5
no. 1 (1989) p. 39-51.

0654   **Bassler, Gerhard P.**
"The Enemy Alien Experience in Newfoundland 1914-1918."
Canadian Ethnic Studies/Études ethniques au Canada, vol. 20 no. 3
(1988) p. 42-62.

0655   **Baureiss, Gunter**
"Discrimination and Response: The Chinese in Canada." In: *Ethnicity
and Ethnic Relations in Canada: A Book of Readings*, edited by Rita
M. Bienvenue and Jay E. Goldstein. 2nd ed. Toronto: Butterworths,
1985, p. 241-261.

0656   **Baureiss, Gunter**
"Ethnic Organizational Theory: The Chinese Case." In: *Racial
Minorities in Multicultural Canada*, edited by Peter S. Li and B.
Singh Bolaria. Toronto: Garamond Press, 1982, p. 103-120.

0657   **Baureiss, Gunter**
"Ethnic Resilience and Discrimination: Two Chinese Communities in
Canada." *The Journal of Ethnic Studies*, vol. 10 no. 1 (1982) p. 69-87.

0658   **Beagle, Mickey**
"Segregation and Discrimination in the West Coast Fishing Industry."
Canadian Issues, vol.3 no. 1 (1980) p. 141-150.

0659   **Beaujot, Roderic P.**
"Analysis of Ethnic Fertility Differentials Through the Consideration
of Assimilation." *International Journal of Comparative Sociology*,
vol. 23 no. 1/2 (1982) p. 62-70.

0660   **Belair Lockhead, Joanne**
Le contact inter-ethnique: antecedents, processus et consequents.
Unpublished PhD thesis, Université d'Ottawa, 1988. 6 microfiches.
Canadian theses on microfiche, CT90-22718-4.

0661   **Bentley, Sid**
*Religions of Our Neighbours: A Comprehensive, Non-academic
Overview of Several Religious Traditions.* [Hinduism - Sikhism -
Judaism - Christianity - Islam - Zoroastrianism] Coquitlam, B.C.:
Bentley West Pub. Co., 1989. 259 p.

0662   **Bercuson, David Jay**
        A Trust Betrayed: The Keegstra Affair. Toronto: Doubleday, 1985.
        288 p.

0663   **Bercuson, David Jay**
        "Regionalism and 'Unlimited Identity' in Western Canada." *Journal
        of Canadian Studies/Revue d'études canadiennes,* vol. 15 no. 2
        (1980) p. 121-126.

0664   **Berlin, Mark L.**
        "Hate Unbridled." *Policy Options/Options politiques,* vol. 6 no. 6
        (1985) p. 31-32.

0665   **Bernard, A.**
        "Les attitudes des Canadiens français à l'égard des autres groupes
        ethniques." *Conjoncture politique au Québec,* no. 4 (1983) p. 81-86.

0666   **Bernéche, Francine**
        "Les mariages d'Indiennes et non-Indiens au Québec: caracteristiques
        et conséquences démographiques." *Recherches amérindiennes au
        Quebec,* vol. 9 no. 4 (1980) p. 313-321.

0667   **Bernier, Jacques**
        "Les minorités ethnoculturelles et l'État au Canada." *Études
        canadienne/Canadian Studies,* vol. 21 no. 2 (1986) p. 177-184.

0668   **Berry, John Widdup**
        "Acculturation Attitudes in Plural Societies." *Applied Psychology,*
        vol. 38 no. 2 (1989) p. 185-206.

0669   **Berry, John Widdup**
        "Psychological Acculturation of Immigrants." In: *Cross-cultural
        Adaptation: Current Approaches,* edited by Young Yun Kim and
        William B. Gudykunst. Beverly Hills, Calif.: Sage Publications,
        1988, p. 62-89.

0670   **Berry, John Widdup**
        "Finding Identity: Separation, Integration, Assimilation, or Margin-
        ality." In: *Ethnic Canada: Identities and Inequalities,* edited by Leo
        Driedger. Toronto: Copp Clark Pitman, 1987, p. 223-239.

0671   **Berry, John Widdup**
"Cultural Relations in Plural Societies: Alternatives to Segregation and Their Sociopsychological Implications." In: *Groups in Contact: The Psychology of Desegregation*, edited by Norman Miller and Marilynn B. Brewer. Orlando: Academic Press, 1984, 11-27.

0672   **Berry, John Widdup**
"Native Peoples and the Larger Society." In: *Canadian Social Psychology of Ethnic Relations*, edited by Robert C. Garner and Rudolf Kalin. Toronto: Methuen, 1981, p. 214-230.

0673   **Berry, John Widdup and R.C. Annis, eds.**
Ethnic Psychology: Research and Practice with Immigrants, Refugees, Native Peoples, Ethnic Groups and Sojourners. Lisse: Swets and Zeitlinger, 1988. 332 p.

0674   **Berry, John Widdup, et al.**
"Comparative Studies of Acculturative Stress." *International Migration Review*, vol. 21 no. 3 (1987) p. 491-511.

0675   **Bhargava, Gura**
"Seeking Immigration Through Matrimonial Alliance: A Study of Advertisements in an Ethnic Weekly." *Journal of Comparative Family Studies*, vol. 19 no. 2 (1988) p. 245-259.

0676   **Biakabutuka, Mulenga-Wa**
Difference ethnique et communication dans une situation d'intervention. Unpublished PhD thesis, Université de Montréal, 1984. 1 microfilm.

0677   **Bienvenue, Rita and Jay E. Goldstein, eds.**
Ethnicity and Ethnic Relations in Canada: A Book of Readings. 2nd ed. Toronto: Butterworths, 1985. 335 p.

0678   **Birch, Anthony H.**
Nationalism and National Integration. London: Unwin Hyman, 1989. 253 p. Contains a chapter: "National Integration in Canada", p. 138-182.

0679   **Blake, Larry**
"Students' View of Inter-group Tensions in Quebec: The Effect of Language Immersion Experience." *Canadian Journal of Behavioural Science/Revue canadienne des sciences de comportement*, vol. 13 no. 2 (1981) p. 144-160.

0680   **Blinn, Lynn**
"The Family Photo Assessment Process (FPAP): A Method of
Validating Cross-cultural Comparisons of Family Social Identities."
Journal of Comparative Family Studies, vol. 19 no. 1 (1988) p. 17-
35.

0681   **Block, W.E. and M.A. Walker, eds.**
*Discrimination, Affirmative Action, and Equal Opportunity: An
Economic and Social Perspective.* Vancouver: Fraser Institute, 1982.
271 p.

0682   **Blue, A.W.**
"Developmental Trends in Racial Preference and Identification in
Northern Native Canadian Children." In: *Growth and Progress in
Cross-cultural Psychology: Selected Papers*, edited by C. Kagitcibasi.
Berwyn: Swets North America, 1987, p. 311-320. Papers presented at
the 8th International Association for Cross-cultural Psychology.
International Conference, 1986, Istanbul, Turkey.

0683   **Boekelman, Mark**
"The Letters of Jane Aberson, Everday Life on the Prairies During
the Depression: How Immigration Turns Conservatives into Social
Democrats." In: *Dutch Immigration to North America*, edited by
Herman Ganzevoort and Mark Boekelman. Toronto: Multicultural
History Society of Ontario, 1983, p. 111-130.

0684   **Boekestijn, Cees**
"Intercultural Migration and the Development of Personal Identity:
The Dilemma Between Identity Maintenance and Cultural Adaptation." *International Journal of Intercultural Relations*, vol. 12 no. 2
(1988) p. 83-106.

0685   **Bolaria, B. Singh**
"Race and Racism." In: *Racial Oppression in Canada*, edited by B.
Singh Bolaria and Peter S. Li. Toronto: Garamond Press, 1985, p. 7-
18.

0686   **Bolaria, B. Singh**
"On the Study of Race Relations." In: *Contradictions in Canadian
Society*, edited by John A. Fry. Toronto: John Wiley, 1983, p. 219-
247.

0687   **Bolaria, B. Singh**
"Dominant Perspectives and Non-white Minorities." In: *Racial Minorities in Multicultural Canada*, edited by Peter S. Li and B. Singh Bolaria. Toronto: Garamond Press, 1982, p. 157-169.

0688   **Bolger, Rory M.**
"Ethnic Identity and Assimilation: A Seven Generation Risk - Canadian Lineage." *Central Issues in Anthropology*, vol. 6 no. 1 (1985) p. 11-18.

0689   **Bolin, Robert and Daniel J. Klenow**
"Older People in Disaster: A Comparison of Black and White Victims." *Aging and Human Development*, vol. 25 no. 1 (1988) p. 29-43.

0690   **Bonato, M.**
"Elle, moi et les autres." *Conjoncture politique au Québec*, no. 4 (1983) p. 113-117.

0691   **Bong, Nguyen Quy**
"The Vietnamese in Canada: Some Settlement Problems." In: *Visible Minorities and Multiculturalism: Asians in Canada*, edited by K. Victor Ujimoto and Gordon Hirabayashi. Toronto: Butterworths, 1980, p. 247-256.

0692   **Bouchard, Claude**
"Genetic Basis of Racial Differences [In Performance]." *Canadian Journal of Sport Sciences/Journal canadien des sciences du sport*, vol. 13 no. 2 (1988) p. 103-108.

0693   **Bouchard, Gerard**
"Les saguenayens et les immigrants au début du 20éme siécle: légitime défense ou xénophobie?" *Canadian Ethnic Studies/Études ethniques au Canada*, vol. 21 no. 3 (1989) p. 20-36.

0694   **Boulay, Marcel B., Pierre F.M. Ama, and Claude Bouchard**
"Racial Variation in Work Capacities and Powers." *Canadian Journal of Sport Sciences/Journal canadien des sciences du sport*, vol. 13 no. 2 (1988) p. 127-135.

0695   **Boulet, Jac-Andre**
L'evolution des disparités linguistiques de revenus du travail au Canada de 1970 à 1980. Ottawa: Conseil économique du Canada, 1983. 71 p.

0696 **Bouraoui, Hedi, ed.**
The Canadian Alternative: Cultural Pluralism and Canadian Unity.
Downsview, Ontario: ECW Press, 1980. 110 p. Papers presented at
the conference held at Stong College, York University, October 26-
27, 1979.

0697 **Bourhis, Richard Y.**
"Cross-cultural Communication in Montreal: Two Field Studies Since
Bill 101." *International Journal of the Sociology of Language*, no. 46
(1984) p. 33-47.

0698 **Bourne, L.S., et al. prep.**
*Canada's Ethnic Mosaic: Characteristics and Patterns of Ethnic
Origin Groups in Urban Areas.* Toronto: Centre for Urban and
Community Studies, University of Toronto, 1986. 174 p.

0699 **Boyd, Monica**
"Status Attainment of Immigrant and Immigrant Origin Categories In
the United States, Canada, and Israel." *Comparative Social Research*,
vol. 3 (1980) p. 199-228.

0700 **Brand, Dionne**
Rivers Have Sources, Trees Have Roots: Speaking of Racism.
Toronto: Cross Cultural Communication Centre, 1986.

0701 **Brandt, Godfrey L.**
The Realization of Anti-racist Teaching. London, U.K.: Faimer Press,
1986. 210 p.

0702 **Bray, R. Matthew**
"A Conflict of Nationalisms: The Win the War and National Unity
Convention, 1917." *Journal of Canadian Studies/Revue d'études
canadiennes*, vol. 15 no. 3 (1980-81) p. 18-30.

0703 **Brazeau, Jacques**
"Pertinence de l'enseignement des relations ethniques et caractér-
isation de ce champ d'études au Canada et au Quebec." *Sociologie et
sociètés*, vol. 15 no. 2 (1983) p. 133-146.

0704 **Breton, Raymond**
"French-English Relations." In: *Understanding Canadian Society*,
edited by James Curtis and Lorne Tepperman. Toronto: McGraw-Hill
Ryerson, 1988, p. 557-585.

0705   **Breton, Raymond**
"From Ethnic to Civic Nationalism: English Canada and Quebec."
Ethnic and Racial Studies, vol. 11 no. 1 (1988) p. 85-102.

0706   **Breton, Raymond**
"Stratification and Conflict Between Ethnolinguistic Communities
with Different Social Structures." In: *Ethnicity and Ethnic Relations
in Canada: A Book of Readings*, edited by Rita M. Bienvenue and
Jay E. Goldstein. 2nd ed. Toronto: Butterworths, 1985, p. 45-59.
Reprinted from *Canadian Review of Sociology and Anthropology/
Revue canadienne de sociologie et d'anthropologie*, vol. 15 no. 2
(1978) p. 148-157.

0707   **Breton, Raymond**
"The Production and Allocation of Symbolic Resources: An Analysis
of the Linguistic and Ethnocultural Fields in Canada." *Canadian
Review of Sociology and Anthropology/Revue canadienne de
sociologie et d'anthropologie*, vol. 21 no. 2 (1984) p. 123-144.

0708   **Breton, Raymond**
"La communauté ethnique, communauté politique." *Sociologie et
sociétés*, vol. 15 no. 2 (1983) p. 23-38.

0709   **Breton, Raymond**
"Linguistic Boundaries and the Cohesion of Canada." In: *Cultural
Boundaries and the Cohesion of Canada*, edited by Raymond Breton
et al. Montreal: The Institute for Research on Public Policy,
1980, p. 137-328.

0710   **Breton, Raymond, et al. eds.**
Cultural Boundaries and the Cohesion of Canada. Montreal: The
Institute for Research on Public Policy, 1980. 422 p.

0711   **Brym, Robert J.**
From Culture to Power: The Sociology of English Canada. Don
Mills, Ontario: Oxford University Press Canada, 1989. 222 p.

0712   **Brym, Robert J.**
"Anomie, Opportunity, and the Density of Ethnic Ties: Another View
of Jewish Outmarriage in Canada." *Canadian Review of Sociology
and Anthropology/Revue canadienne de sociologie et d'anthropologie*,
vol. 22 no. 1 (1985) p. 102-112.

0713   **Buchignani, Norman**
"Some Practical Points on Doing Contract Research on One's Own
Society." In: *Anthropology in Praxis*, edited by Philip Spaulding. Calgary:
Department of Anthropology, University of Calgary, 1986, p. 145-161.

0714   **Buchignani, Norman**
Cultures in Canada: Strength in Diversity. Regina: Weigel Educational Publishers, 1983. 96 p.

0715   **Buchignani, Norman**
"Inter-group Conflict and Community Solidarity: Sikhs and South
Asian Fijians in Vancouver." *Canadian Journal of Anthropology/
Revue canadienne d'anthropologie*, vol. 1 no. 2 (1980) p. 149-158.

0716   **Buckner, H. Taylor**
"A Study of Canadian Attitudes Towards Jews, Italians and Poles: A
Three Year Analysis." *Review of Anti-semitism in Canada*,
(1985) p. 11-36.

0717   **Burnet, Jean R.**
"Taking into Account the Other Ethnic Groups and the Royal
Commission on Bilingualism and Biculturalism." In: *Multiculturalism
and Intergroup Relations*, edited by James S. Frideres. New York:
Greenwood Press, 1989, p. 9-17.

0718   **Burnet, Jean R.**
"The Social and Historical Context of Ethnic Relations." In:
Canadian Social Psychology of Ethnic Relations, edited by Robert C.
Gardner and Rudolf Kalin. Toronto: Methuen, 1981, p. 17-35.

0719   **Butler, Pamela Jean**
Ottawa and Quebec: The Politics of Confrontation, 1967. Unpublished PhD thesis, McGill University, 1980. Canadian theses on
microfiche, no. 50405.

0720   **Byrnes, Deborah**
"Children and Prejudice." *Social Education*, vol. 52 no. 4
(1988) p. 267-271.

0721   **Caldwell, Gary**
"Discovering and Developing English-Canadian Nationalism in
Quebec." *Canadian Review of Studies in Nationalism/Revue
canadienne des études sur le nationalisme*, vol. 11 no. 2
(1984) p. 245-256.

0722   **Caldwell, Gary**
Les études ethniques au Québec: Bilan et perspective. Instruments de travail no. 8. Québec, P.Q.: Institut québécois de recherche sur la culture, 1983. 106 p.

0723   **Calloway, Colin G.**
Crown and Calumet: British-Indian Relations, 1783-1815. 1st ed. Norman, Ok.: University of Oklahoma Press, 1987. 345 p.

0724   **Calloway, Colin G.**
"Foundations of Sand: The Fur Trade and British-Indian Relations, 1783-1815." In: Le castor fait tout, edited by Bruce G. Trigger, Toby Morantz, and Louise Dechene. Montreal: Lake St. Louis Historical Society, 1987, p. 144-163.

0725   **Canada. Indian and Northern Affairs**
An Overview of Some Recent Research on Attitudes in Canada Towards Indian People. Ottawa: Research Branch, Policy Research and Evaluation, Indian and Inuit Affairs Program, Indian and Northern Affairs Canada, 1983. 22 p.

0726   **Canada. Minister of State, Multiculturalism**
Race Relations and the Law. Ottawa: Minister of State, Multiculturalism, 1983. 131 p. Report of a symposium held in Vancouver, British Columbia, April 22-24, 1982.

0727   **Canada. Statistics Canada**
Ethnicity, Immigration and Citizenship. 1 vol. Ottawa: Statistics Canada, 1989. French language title: Origine ethnique, immigration et citoyenneté.

0728   **Canadian Bar Association. Special Committee on Racial and Religious Hatred**
Report of the Special Committee on Racial and Religious Hatred. Ken Norman, Chairman. Ottawa: The Canadian Bar Association, 1984. 32 p.

0729   **Canadian Review of Sociology and Anthropology**
"Porter, John 1921-1979." Canadian Review of Sociology and Anthropology/Revue canadienne de sociologie et d'anthropologie vol. 18 no. 5 (1981) p. 583-657. Special issue in memory of John Porter, the author of The Vertical Mosaic.

0730 **Cannon, Gordon E.**
"Consociationalism [sic] vs. Control: Canada as a Case Study."
Western Political Quarterly, vol. 35 no. 1 (1982) p. 50-64.

0731 **Cartwright, Donald G.**
"Changes in the Patterns of Contact Between Anglophones and
Francophones in Quebec." *Geojournal*, vol. 8 no. 2 (1984) p. 109-
122.

0732 **Cassidy, Grant R.**
"Multiculturalism and Dutch Canadian Ethnicity in Metropolitan
Toronto." In: *Dutch Immigration to North America*, edited by
Herman Ganzevoort and Mark Boekelman. Toronto: Multicultural
History Society of Ontario, 1983, p. 197-220.

0733 **Cassin, Agnes Marguerite**
"Class and Ethnicity: Producing the Difference that Counts."
Canadian Ethnic Studies/Études ethniques au Canada, vol. 13 no. 1
(1981) p. 109-129.

0734 **Castonguay, Charles**
"Inter-marriage and Language Shift in Canada, 1971 and 1976."
Canadian Journal of Sociology/Cahiers canadiens de sociologie, vol.
7 no. 3 (1982) p. 263-278.

0735 **Castonguay, Charles**
*Exogamie et anglicisation dans les régions de Montréal, Hull, Ottawa
et Sudbury.* Québec: Centre international de recherche sur le bilinguisme, 1981. 112 p.

0736 **Castonguay, Charles**
"Sur quelques indices de propension a l'exogamie et au transfert
linguistique." *Cahiers québécois de démographie*, vol. 9 no. 3
(1980) p. 53-70.

0737 **Cerroni-Long, E.L.**
"Marrying Out: Socio-cultural and Psychological Implications of
Intermarriage." *Journal of Comparative Family Studies*, vol. 16 no. 1
(1985) p. 25-46.

0738 **Champagne, Mireille G.**
*Children's Racial Attitudes: A Cross Cultural and Historical
Analysis.* Unpublished PhD thesis, York University, 1984. 3
microfiches. Canadian theses on microfiche, 61510.

0739   **Chan, Kwok B.**
"Perceived Racial Discrimination and Response: An Analysis of Indochinese Experience in Montreal, Canada." *Canadian Ethnic Studies/Études ethniques au Canada*, vol. 19 no. 3 (1987) p. 125-147.

0740   **Chandrasekhar, S., ed.**
From India to Canada: A Brief History of Immigration: Problems of Discrimination, Admission and Assimilation. La Jolla, Calif.: Population Review Books, 1986. 217 p.

0741   **Charland, Maurice**
"Constitutive Rhetoric: The Case of the 'Peuple quebecois'." *Quarterly Journal of Speech*, vol. 73 no. 2 (1987) p. 133-150.

0742   **Chebat, Jean Charles**
"Proposition methodologique pour mesurer les perceptions internationales." *Recherches sociographiques*, vol. 28 no. 3 (1987) p. 209-229.

0743   **Cheung, Yuet-Wah**
"Explaining Ethnic and Racial Variations in Criminality Rates: A Review and Critique." *Canadian Criminology Forum/Forum canadien de criminologie*, vol. 3 (1980) p. 1-14.

0744   **Chiswick, Barry R.**
"Earnings in Canada: The Roles of Immigrant Generation, French Ethnicity and Language." *Research in Population Economics*, vol. 6 (1988) p. 183-228.

0745   **Chiswick, Barry R., Carmel U. Chiswick, and Paul W. Miller**
"Are Immigrants and Natives Perfect Substitutes in Production?" *International Migration Review*, vol. 19 no. 4 (1985) p. 674-685.

0746   **Choiniere, Robert**
"Aperçu des minorités ethniques du Québec." *Apprentissage et socialisation*, vol. 19 no. 2 (1987) p. 81-86.

0747   **Cholewinski, Ryszard Ignacy**
The Positive Cultural and Linguistic Right of Ethnic Minorities. Unpublished LLM thesis, University of Saskatchewan, 1988.

0748   **Christensen, Carole Pigler**
"Cross-cultural Social Work: Fallacies, Fears and Failings." *Intervention*, no. 74 (1986) p. 6-15.

0749   **Clark, Gerald**
Montreal: The New Cité. Toronto: McClelland and Stewart, 1982. 243 p.

0750   **Clark, Lovell**
"Nativism or Just Plain Prejudice?" *Acadiensis*, vol. 10 no. 1 (1980) p. 163-171.

0751   **Clement, Richard**
"Peur d'assimilation et confiance en soi: leur relation à l'alternance des codes et à la compétence communicative en langue seconde." *Canadian Journal of Behavioural Science/Revue canadienne des sciences de comportement*, vol. 18 no. 2 (1986) p. 187-196.

0752   **Clement, Richard**
"Aspects socio-psychologiques de la communication inter-ethnique et de l'identité sociale." *Recherches sociologiques*, vol. 15 no. 2/3 (1984) p. 293-312.

0753   **Clement, Richard**
"Ethnicity, Contact and Communicative Competence in a Second Language." In: *Language: Social Psychological Perspectives*, edited by Howard Giles, W. Peter Robinson, and Philip M. Smith. Oxford and New York: Pergamon Press, 1980, p. 147-154. Paper presented at the first International Conference on Social Psychology and Language, July 1979, University of Bristol, England.

0754   **Clift, Dominique**
The English Fact in Quebec. Montreal: McGill-Queen's University Press, 1980. 239 p.

0755   **Clifton, Rodney A.**
"Has Ethnic Prejudice Increased in Winnipeg Schools? A Comparison of Bogardus Social Distance Scales in 1971 and 1981." *Canadian Ethnic Studies/Études ethniques au Canada*, vol. 17 no. 1 (1985) p. 72-80.

0756   **Cloutier, Edouard**
"What's in a Name? Problems of Group Identity in Quebec." In:
English of Quebec: From Majority to Minority Status, edited by Gary
Caldwell and Eric Waddell. Quebec, P.Q.: Institut quebecois de
recherche sur la culture, 1982, p. 127-142.

0757   **Coates, Kenneth Stephen**
*Best Left as Indians: Native-white Relations in the Yukon Territory,
1840-1950*. Unpublished PhD thesis, University of British Columbia,
1984. 364 leaves.

0758   **Coates, Kenneth Stephen**
"Best Left as Indians: The Federal Government and the Indians of
the Yukon, 1894-1950." *Canadian Journal of Native Studies*, vol. 4
no. 2 (1984) p. 179-204.

0759   **Cohen, Maxwell**
"Hate Propaganda in Canada." In: *Communications in Canada*, edited
by Benjamin D. Singer. Don Mills, Ontario: Addison-Wesley Publishers, 1983, p. 248-267.

0760   **Cohen, Tannis**
Race Relations and the Law. Montreal: Canadian Jewish Congress,
1987. 124 p.

0761   **Cohn, Werner**
"The Persecution of Japanese Canadians and the Political Left in
British Columbia, December 1941–March 1942." *B.C. Studies*, no. 68
(1985/1986) p. 3-22.

0762   **Colby, Dorothy**
"Foreigners in Your Land: The Author Tells of a Christmas
Experience with Neighbors of Another Culture." *Canada Lutheran*,
vol. 4 no. 11 (1989) p. 6-7.

0763   **Collin, Dominique**
"L'ethno-ethnocentrisme: représentations d'identité chez de jeunes
autochtones du Québec." *Anthropologie et sociètés*, vol. 12 no. 1
(1988) p. 59-76.

0764   **Collin, Dominique**
*Crise d'identité ou identité de crise: conscience sociale et projet
existentiel chez quelques jeunes Inuit du Nouveau-Quebec.*
Unpublished MSc thesis, Université de Montréal, 1984. 1 microfilm.

0765   **Comeau, Paul-Andre**
"Les rélations federales provinciales: l'année des paradoxes feutrés."
Année politique Au Québec, vol. 1 (1987/88) p. 101-108.

0766   **Constantinides, Stephanos**
"The Relative Autonomy of Ethnicity as an Ideological Construct."
Canadian Ethnic Studies/Études ethniques au Canada, vol. 18 no. 2
(1987) p. 102-114.

0767   **Cooke, Katie**
*Images of Indians Held by Non-Indians: A Review of Current
Research.* Ottawa: Indian and Northern Affairs Canada, 1984. 90 p.

0768   **Coombo, Vivienne and Alan Little, eds.**
Race and Social Work. A Guide to Training. London, U.K.:
Tavistock Publications, 1986. 233 p.

0769   **Corenblum, B.**
"Racial Identity and Preference in Native and White Canadian
Children." *Canadian Journal of Behavioural Science/Revue
canadienne des sciences de comportement*, vol. 19 no. 3
(1987) p. 254-265.

0770   **Corenblum, B.**
"Ethnic Preference and Identification Among Canadian Indian and
White Children: Replication and Extension." *Canadian Journal of
Behavioural Science/Revue canadienne des sciences de
comportement*, vol. 14 no. 1 (1982) p. 50-59.

0771   **Cottrell, Michael**
"John O'Donohoe and the Politics of Ethnicity in Nineteenth Century
Ontario." *Canadian Catholic Historical Studies*, no. 56 (1989) p. 67-84.

0772   **Courtis, Kenneth S.**
*Fondements, forme et structure du sentiment d'appartenance
nationale chez les jeunes franco-québécois.* [Quebec]: Laboratoire
d'études politiques et administratives, Département de science
politique, 1983. 94 p.

0773   **Couturier, Hermel**
*Ethnicity as a Determinant of the Values, Preferences and Behaviour
of French and English Speaking Cross-country Skiers in the Province
of New Brunswick, Canada.* Unpublished PhD thesis, Texas A & M
University, 1988. 154 leaves.

0774   **Coyne, Andrew**
"Let This Please Be the Last Essay on the Canadian Identity."
Saturday Night, vol. 104 no. 7/3712 (1989) p. 25-30.

0775   **Craig, Richard G.**
Racial Discrimination: Asian Immigrants in B.C. Vancouver: Schools
Program, Legal Services Society of B.C., 1982. 73 p.

0776   **Craig, Terrence**
*Attitudes Toward Race in Canadian Prose Fiction in English, 1905-
1980.* Unpublished PhD thesis, University of Toronto, 1982. 4
microfiches. Canadian theses on microfiche, 55757.

0777   **Cranwell, Ford R.**
*A Cross-cultural Comparison of the Development of Self-concept in
Indian and White Children.* Unpublished MA thesis, Lakehead
University, 1985. 103 leaves. Canadian theses on microfiche, CT86-
28439-5.

0778   **Creese, Gillian Laura**
"Race, Gender and Socialism in British Columbia." [Vancouver: s.n.]
University of British Columbia Library, Humanities and Social
Sciences Division, 1988. 51 p.

0779   **Cruise, Eleanor Edith**
*The Effects of Acculturation and Attitudes Toward Inter-group
Relations on Well-being and Assertiveness in a Coast Salish Group.*
Unpublished MA thesis, Simon Fraser University, 1986.
178 p. Canadian theses on microfiche, CT88-21360-4.

0780   **Cryderman, Brian and Chris O'Toole, eds.**
Police, Race and Ethnicity: A Guide for Law Enforcement Officers.
Scarborough, Ontario: Butterworths, 1986. 241 p.

0781   **Cummins, Jim**
"Linguistic Minorities and Multicultural Policy in Canada." In:
Linguistic Minorities: Policies and Pluralism, edited by John
Edwards. London: Academic Press, 1984, p. 81-105.

0782   **Curat, Hervé**
*Ethnic and Immigration Groups: The United States, Canada, and
England.* New York: The Institute for Research in History and the
Haworth Press, 1983. 126 p.

0783   **Czernis, Loretta M.**
The Report of the Task Force on Canadian Unity: Reading a (re) Writing of Canada. Unpublished PhD thesis, York University, 1989. 2 microfiches.

0784   **D'Ardenne, Patricia and Aruna Mahtani**
Transcultural Counselling in Action. London: Sage Publications, 1989. 130 p.

0785   **D'Oyley, Vincent, ed.**
Perspectives on Race, Education and Social Development: Emphasis on Canada. Vancouver: Centre for the Study of Curriculum and Instruction, University of British Columbia, 1982. 134 p. Proceedings of a conference held by the Race Relations Institute, July 1982, at the University of British Columbia, Vancouver.

0786   **Dackiw, Boris Y.**
"Denaturalization of Suspected Nazi War Criminals: The Problem of Soviet Source Evidence." *Ukrainian Quarterly*, vol. 44 no. 1/2 (1988) p. 108-118.

0787   **Dahlie, Jorgen and Tissa Fernando, eds.**
Ethnicity, Power and Politics in Canada. Toronto: Methuen, 1981. 291 p.

0788   **Darroch, A. Gordon**
"Another Look at Ethnicity, Stratification and Social Mobility in Canada." In: *Ethnicity and Ethnic Relations in Canada: A Book of Readings*, edited by Rita M. Bienvenue and Jay E. Goldstein. Toronto: Butterworths, 1985, p. 153-179. Reprinted from the *Canadian Journal of Sociology/Cahiers canadiens de sociologie*, vol. 4 no. 1 (1979) p. 1-25.

0789   **Darroch, A. Gordon**
"Urban Ethnicity in Canada: Personal Assimilation and Political Communities." *Canadian Review of Sociology and Anthropology/ Revue canadienne de sociologie et d'anthropologie*, vol. 18 no. 1 (1981) p. 93-100.

0790   **Davis, Nanciellen**
Ethnicity and Ethnic Group Persistence in an Acadian Village in Maritime Canada. New York: AMS Press, 1985. 233 p.

0791   **Dawson, Don**
"Social and Cultural Reproduction and the School's Role in Social Mobility." In: *Racial Minorities in Multicultural Canada*, edited by Peter S. Li and B. Singh Bolaria. Toronto: Garamond Press, 1982, p. 31-38.

0792   **De la Luz, Reyes and John J. Halcon**
"Racism in Academia: The Old Wolf Revisited." *Harvard Educational Review*, vol. 58 no. 3 (1988) p. 299-314.

0793   **De Volder, Guido**
Cooperation and Conflict in Bi-ethnic or Dual Societies: The Development of French-Canadian and Afrikaner Nationalism. Unpublished MA thesis, McGill University, 1985. 2 microfiches. Canadian theses on microfiche, CT86-29704-7.

0794   **Decima Research**
A Study of Canadian Attitudes Toward Aboriginal Self-Government: Cross Tabulations. Toronto: Decima Research #2243, 1987. 470 p.

0795   **Deconde, Alexander**
"Clio, Clientage, Ethnocentrism, and War: Some Reflections." *Pacific Historical Review*, vol. 55 no. 1 (1986) p. 1-26.

0796   **Del Balso, Michele**
"L'assimilation et les études ethniques en Amérique du Nord." *Cahiers de recherche sociologique*, vol. 2 no. 2 (1984) p. 49-67.

0797   **Deshaies, Denise**
"Contacts interethniques: leur effets sur l'attitude et la motivation en langue seconde." *Canadian Modern Language Review*, vol. 37 no. 2 (1981) p. 141-150.

0798   **DeVries, John**
"Some Methodological Aspects of Self-reporting on Language and Ethnicity." *Journal of Multilingual and Multicultural Development*, vol. 6 no. 5 (1985) p. 347-368.

0799   **DiKaiou, M.**
"Peer Interaction in Migrant Children: Observation Data and Parent's Evaluations." *International Migration/Migrations Internationales/ Migraciones Internacionales*, vol. 27 no. 1 (1989) p. 49-68.

0800 **Dion, Kenneth**
"Ethnicity and Personality in Canadian Context." *Journal of Social Psychology: Political, Racial and Differential Psychology*, vol. 127 no. 2 (1987) p. 175-182.

0801 **Dofny, Jacques**
"Ethnic Cleavages, Labor Aristocracy, and Nationalism in Quebec." In: *New Nationalisms of the Developed West: Toward Explanation*, edited by Edward A. Tiryakian and Ronald Rogowski. Boston: Allen and Unwin, 1985, p. 353-373.

0802 **Dorais, Louis-Jacques**
"Les autochtones canadiens et leur identité." In: *Minorités et l'état*, sous la direction de Pierre Guillaume, Jean-Michel Lacroix, Rejean Pelletier, Jacques Zylberberg. Bordeaux: Presses universitaires de Bordeaux, 1986, p. 89-100.

0803 **Driedger, Leo**
"Alternate Models of Assimilation, Integration and Pluralism." In: *Canada 2000: Race Relations and Public Policy*, edited by O.P. Dwivedi et al. Guelph, Ontario: Department of Political Studies, University of Guelph, 1989, p. 349-370.

0804 **Driedger, Leo**
The Ethnic Factor: Identity in Diversity. Toronto: McGraw-Hill Ryerson, 1989. 450 p.

0805 **Driedger, Leo**
"Conformity vs. Pluralism: Minority Identities and Inequalities." In: *Minorities and the Canadian State*, edited by Neil Nevitte and Allan Kornberg. Oakville, Ontario: Mosaic Press, 1985, p. 157-174.

0806 **Driedger, Leo**
"Ethnic Stereotypes: Images of Ethno-centrism, Reciprocity or Dissimilarity?" *Canadian Review of Sociology and Anthropology/ Revue canadienne de sociologie et d'anthropologie*, vol. 21 no. 3 (1984) p. 287-301.

0807 **Driedger, Leo**
"Ethnic Intermarriage: Student Dating and Mating." In: *Marriage and Divorce in Canada*, edited by K. Ishwaran. Toronto: Methuen, 1983, p. 213-231.

0808   **Driedger, Leo**
"Attitudes of Winnipeg University Students Toward Immigrants of European Origin." *Prairie Forum*, vol. 7 no. 2 (1982) p. 213-226.

0809   **Driedger, Leo**
"Ethnic Identification: Variations in Regional and National Preferences." *Canadian Ethnic Studies/Études ethniques au Canada*, vol. 14 no. 3 (1982) p. 57-68.

0810   **Driedger, Leo**
"Ethnic Prejudice and Discrimination in Winnipeg Schools."
Canadian Journal of Sociology/Cahiers canadiens de sociologie, vol. 6 no. 1 (1981) p. 1-18.

0811   **Driedger, Leo, ed.**
Ethnic Canada: Identities and Inequalities. Toronto: Copp Clark Pitman, 1987. 442 p.

0812   **Driedger, Leo and Neena Chappell**
Aging and Ethnicity: Toward an Interface. Perspectives on Individual and Population Aging Series. Toronto: Butterworths, 1987. 131 p.

0813   **Drummond, L.**
"Analyse sémiotique de l'ethnicité au Québec." *Questions de culture* no. 2 (1982) p. 139-153.

0814   **DuCharme, Michele**
"The Segregation of Native People in Canada: Voluntary or Compulsory?" *Currents*, vol. 3 no. 4 (1986) p. 3-4.

0815   **Dusenberry, Lynne Marie**
Whites Learning the Indian Way. Unpublished MA thesis, University of Calgary, 1987. 1 microfiche. Canadian theses on microfiche, CT88-25341-X.

0816   **Dutcher, Stephen Wayne**
Power Theory and the Historical Record: Aboriginal-European Relations Revisited. Unpublished MA thesis, University of New Brunswick, 1988. 2 microfiches. Canadian theses on microfiche, CT89-28159-9.

0817 **Dutton, Alan**
Capitalism, the State and Minority Ethnic Relations in British Columbia. Unpublished MA thesis, University of Victoria, 1984. 115 p. Canadian theses on microfiche, 68024.

0818 **Dwivedi, O.P.**
"Moral Dimensions of Public Policy and Race Relations." In: *Canada 2000: Race Relations and Public Policy,* edited by O.P. Dwivedi et al. Guelph, Ontario: Department of Political Studies, University of Guelph, 1989, p. 286-295.

0819 **Dwivedi, O.P., et al. eds.**
Canada 2000: Race Relations and Public Policy. Guelph, Ontario: Department of Political Studies, University of Guelph, 1989.

0820 **Eastman, Julia Antonia**
Race, Ethnicity and Class: The Response to Discrimination of East Indians in Toronto. Unpublished MA thesis, Queen's University, 1980. 2 microfiches. Canadian theses on microfiche, 50126.

0821 **Edwards, John**
"Ethnic Salience, Identity and Symbolic Ethnicity." *Canadian Ethnic Studies/Études ethniques au Canada,* vol. 19 no. 1 (1987) p. 52-62.

0822 **Eliefja, Chaya**
Jewish-Christian Relations in Canada: The "United Church Observer" Controversy. Unpublished MA thesis, Carleton University, 1987. Canadian theses on microfiche, CT89-24145-7.

0823 **Elliott, Jean Leonard**
"Emerging Ethnic Nationalism in the Canadian Northwest Territories." *Canadian Review of Studies in Nationalism/Revue canadienne des études sur le nationalisme,* vol. 11 no. 2 (1984) 231-244.

0824 **Emihovich, Catherine, ed.**
"Toward Cultural Pluralism: Redefining Integration in American Society." *Urban Review,* vol. 20 no.1 (1988) p. 1-72.

0825 **Ennis, James G., et al.**
"Combating Campus Racism." *Radical Teacher,* no. 34 (1988) p. 2-15.

0826   **Esonwanne, Uzoma Martin**
        Difference, Interpretation and Referentiality. Unpublished PhD thesis,
        University of New Brunswick, 1988. 4 microfiches. Canadian theses
        on microfiche, CT89-27958-6.

0827   **Everett, Craig A., ed.**
        "Minority and Ethnic Issues in the Divorce Process." *Journal of
        Divorce*, vol. 11 no. 2 (1987) p. 1-127.

0828   **Exell, Robert**
        "British Columbia and the Native Community." In: *Governments in
        Conflict? Provinces and Indian Nations in Canada*, edited by J.
        Anthony Long and Menno Boldt; in association with Leroy Little
        Bear. Toronto: University of Toronto Press, 1988, p. 93-101.

0829   **Fainella, John G.**
        Ethnicity and Housing Adaptation: The Italians in Montreal.
        Unpublished MA thesis, McGill University, 1986. 2 microfiches.
        Canadian theses on microfiche, CT88-24673-1.

0830   **Fairburn, Kenneth J.**
        "Residential Segregation and the Intra-urban Migration of South
        Asians in Edmonton." *Canadian Ethnic Studies/Études ethniques au
        Canada*, vol. 21 no. 1 (1989) p. 45-64.

0831   **Fellin, Philip A. and Thomas J. Powell**
        "Mental Health Services and Older Adult Minorities: An
        Assessment." *The Gerontologist*, vol. 28 no. 4 (1988) p. 442-447.

0832   **Fenwick, Rudy**
        "Social Change and Ethnic Nationalism: A Historical Analysis of the
        Separatist Movement in Quebec." *Comparative Studies in Society and
        History*, vol. 23 no. 2 (1981) p. 196-216.

0833   **Ferazzi, Gabriele**
        "Forging Aboriginal/Non-Aboriginal Partnerships: The Joint Venture
        Model." *Canadian Journal of Native Studies*, vol. 9 no. 1
        (1989) p. 15-32.

0834   **Fernando, Sumon**
        Race and Culture in Psychiatry. London, U.K.: Croom Helm, 1988.
        216 p.

0835 **Filson, Glen**
"Class and Ethnic Differences in Canadians' Attitudes to Native People's Rights and Immigration." *Canadian Review of Sociology and Anthropology/Revue canadienne de sociologie et d'anthropologie*, vol. 20 no. 4 (1983) p. 454-482.

0836 **Fine, Mark A. and Andrew I. Schwebel**
"An Emergent Explanation of Differing Racial Reactions to Single Parenthood." *Journal of Divorce*, vol. 11 no. 2 (1987) p. 1- 16.

0837 **Fisher, A.D.**
"Alcoholism and Race: The Misapplication of Both Concepts in North American Indians." *Canadian Review of Sociology and Anthropology/Revue canadienne de sociologie et d'anthropologie*, vol. 24 no. 1 (1987) p. 81-98.

0838 **Fitzpatrick, Rory**
God's Frontiersmen: The Scots-Irish Epic. London: Weidenfeld and Nicolson in Association with Channel Four Television Co. and Ulster Televsion, 1989. 296 p.

0839 **Flanagan, Thomas**
"The Manufacture of Minorities." In: *Minorities and the Canadian State*, edited by Neil Nevitte and Allan Kornberg. Oakville, Ontario: Mosaic Press, 1985, p. 107-124.

0840 **Forbes, Hugh Donald**
Nationalism, Ethnocentrism, and Personality: Social Science and Critical Theory. Chicago: University of Chicago Press, 1985. 255 p.

0841 **Forcese, Dennis**
"Policing in a Settler Society: Canada and Visible Minorities." In: *Canada 2000: Race Relations and Public Policy*, edited by O.P. Dwivedi et al. Guelph, Ontario: Department of Political Studies, University of Guelph, 1989, p. 260-263.

0842 **Fraser, Peter**
A Cross-cultural Study of Personality Styles Among West Indian, Canadian, and Mixed Immigrant High School Students. Unpublished thesis, York University, 1987. 98 leaves. Canadian theses on microfiche, CT89-20963-4.

0843   **Frideres, James S., ed.**
        Multiculturalism and Intergroup Relations. New York: Greenwood
        Press, 1989. 182 p.

0844   **Fritz, Wayne**
        "Comparisons: Indian and Non-Indian Use of Psychiatric Services."
        In: *Racial Minorities in Multicultural Canada*, edited by Peter S. Li
        and B. Singh Bolaria. Toronto: Garamond Press, 1982, p. 68-85.

0845   **Gabelko, Nina Hersch**
        "Prejudice Reduction in Secondary Schools." *Social Education*, vol.
        52 no. 4 (1988) p. 276-279.

0846   **Gaffield, Chad**
        *Language, Schooling, and Cultural Conflict: The Origin of the
        French-language Controversy in Ontario.* Kingston, Ontario: McGill-
        Queen's University Press, 1987. 249 p.

0847   **Gall, Nicholas, Jerrold S. Greenberg, and Frances Tobin**
        "Health Education and Sensitivity to Cultural, Religious and Ethnic
        Beliefs." *Journal of School Health*, vol. 57 no. 5 (1987) p. 177-180.

0848   **Gardner, Robert C.**
        "Ethnic Stereotypes: Implications of Measurement Strategy." *Social
        Cognition*, vol. 6 no. 1 (1988) p. 40-60.

0849   **Gardner, Robert C. and Rudolf Kalin, eds.**
        A Canadian Social Psychology of Ethnic Relations. Toronto:
        Methuen, 1981. 244 p.

0850   **Garland, Robert, ed.**
        Ethnicity in Atlantic Canada. St. John, N.B.: Division of Social
        Science, University of New Brunswick, 1985. 117 p.

0851   **Gauhar, Altaf**
        "Ethnicity in World Politics." *Third World Quarterly*, vol. 11 no. 4
        (1989) p. 1-357.

0852   **Gauthier, Charles A.J.**
        *The Role of Zoning in the Socio-cultural Evolution of an Ethnic
        Neighbourhood.* Unpublished PhD thesis, University of Manitoba,
        1986. 3 microfiches. Canadian theses on microfiche, CT88-22767-2.

0853   **Gelfand, Donald E. and Charles M. Barresi, eds.**
        Ethnic Dimensions of Aging. Springer Series on Adulthood and
        Aging. New York: Springer Publishing, 1987. 299 p.

0854   **Gendron, Gaetan**
        *L'affirmation ethnique chez les Métis et Indiens sans statut du
        Québec: ambiguites et tensions.* Unpublished MA thesis, Université
        Laval, 1984. 2 microfiches. Canadian theses on microfiche, CT87-
        21724-0.

0855   **Genesee, Fred**
        "Change and Stability in Intergroup Perceptions." *Journal of
        Language and Social Psychology*, vol. 8 no. 1 (1989) p. 17-38.

0856   **George, Peter J.**
        "'Going in Between': The Impact of European Technology on the
        Work Patterns of the West Main Cree of Northern Ontario." *Journal
        of Economic History*, vol. 47 no. 2 (1987) p. 447-460.

0857   **Gerber, Linda M.**
        "Ethnicity Still Matters: Socio-demographic Profiles of the Ethnic
        Elderly in Ontario." *Canadian Ethnic Studies/Études ethniques au
        Canada*, vol. 15 no. 3 (1983) p. 60-80.

0858   **Gillmor, Don**
        "The Shooting of J.J. Harper: Add Thirty Seconds of Violence to a
        History of Racism and the Outcome is Death." *Saturday Night*, vol.
        103 no. 12/3705 (1988) p. 42-52.

0859   **Glazer, Nathan**
        "Toward a Sociology of Small Ethnic Groups: A Discourse and
        Discussion." *Canadian Ethnic Studies/Études ethniques au Canada*,
        vol. 12 no. 2 (1980) 1-16.

0860   **Glickman, Yaacov**
        "Anti-Semitism and Jewish Social Cohesion in Canada." In: *Ethnicity
        and Ethnic Relations in Canada: A Book of Readings*, edited by Rita
        M. Bienvenue and Jay E. Goldstein. 2nd ed. Toronto: Butterworths,
        1985, p. 263-284.

0861   **Goldstein, Jay E.**
        "Ethnic Intermarriage and Ethnic Identity." *Canadian Ethnic Studies/
        Études ethniques au Canada*, vol. 17 no. 3 (1985) p. 60-71.

0862   **Goldstein, Jay E.**
"The Prestige Dimensions of Ethnic Stratification." In: *Ethnicity and Ethnic Relations in Canada: A Book of Readings*, edited by Rita M. Bienvenue and Jay E. Goldstein. 2nd ed. Toronto: Butterworths, 1985, p. 181-198.

0863   **Goldstein, Jay E. and Rita M. Bienvenue, eds.**
Ethnicity and Ethnic Relations in Canada: A Book of Readings.
Toronto: Butterworths, 1980. 336 p.

0864   **Gordon, Richard Irving**
The Nationalist Prism: A Study of Ethnicity, Social Class, and Nationalism in Quebec Province: 1919-1936. Unpublished PhD thesis, University of California, Irvine, 1982. 165 p.

0865   **Gosselin, Luc**
Qui sommes-nous: étude de la composition ethnique des syndicats du conseil central de Montréal. Montréal: Confédération des syndicats nationaux, Conseil central de Montréal, 1985. 44 p.

0866   **Goyder, John C.**
"Ethnicity and Class Identity: The Case of French and English-speaking Canadians." *Ethnic and Racial Studies*, vol. 6 no. 1 (1983) p. 72-89.

0867   **Grabb, Edward G.**
"Sense of Control over Life Circumstances: Changing Patterns for French and English Canadians." *Canadian Review of Sociology and Anthropology/Revue canadienne de sociologie et d'anthropologie*, vol. 19 no. 3 (1982) p. 360-376.

0868   **Grabb, Edward G.**
"Sense of Personal Control Among French and English Canadians: A Reassessment and Reformulation." *Canadian Ethnic Studies/Études ethniques au Canada*, vol. 20 no. 1 (1988) p. 95-111.

0869   **Gradie, Margaret I. and Danielle Gauvreau**
"Migration and Hereditary Disease in the Saguenay Population of Eastern Quebec." *International Migraton Review*, vol. 21 no. 3 (1987) p. 592-608.

0870   **Grant, Carl A.**
"The Persistent Significance of Race in Schooling." *Elementary School Journal*, vol. 88 no. 5 (1988) p. 561-569.

0871   **Green, Joyce**
"Unassimilated." *Policy Options/Options politiques*, vol. 5 no. 6 (1984) p. 38-42.

0872   **Grenier, L.**
"Sous la rubrique des objets perdus: une réflexion méthodologique sur le racisme," *Sociologie et sociétés*, vol 15 no. 2 (1983) p. 148-153.

0873   **Gurdin, J. Barry**
"Naturalistic Categories of Ethnic Identity in Quebec." In: *Culture, Ethnicity, and Identity: Current Issues in Research*, edited by William C. McCready. New York: Academic Press, 1983, p. 149-180.

0874   **Haile-Michael, Yonas**
"Community and Race Relations Training for the Police." *Currents*, vol. 1 no. 3 (1983) p. 35.

0875   **Halli, Shiva S.**
Asian Ethnic Fertility in Canada: An Application of the Minority Group Status Hypothesis. Unpublished PhD thesis, University of Western Ontario, 1984. 4 microfiches. Canadian theses on microfiche, 61760.

0876   **Halloran, Mary**
"Ethnicity, the State and War: Canada and its Ethnic Minorities, 1939-45." *International Migration Review*, vol. 21 no. 1 (1987) p. 159-167.

0877   **Halloran, Mary**
"Ethnicity, the State and War: Canada and its Ethnic Minorities, 1939-45." *Journal of Ukrainian Studies/Zhurnal Ukrajinoznavchnyk Studij*, vol. 12 no. 1 (1987) p. 55-65.

0878   **Harney, Robert F.**
"'So Great a Heritage as Ours': Immigration and the Survival of the Canadian Polity." In: *In Search of Canada*, edited by Stephen R. Graubard. New Brunswick: Transaction Publishers, 1989, p. 51-97.

0879   **Harney, Robert F.**
"The Immigrant City [Toronto and Montreal]." *Vice Versa*, no. 24 (1988) p. 4-6.

0880   **Harney, Robert F.**
"'So Great a Heritage as Ours': Immigration and the Survival of the Canadian Polity." *Daedalus*, vol. 117 no. 4 (1988) p. 51-98.

0881   **Harney, Robert F.**
"'E Pluribus Unum': Louis Adamic and the Meaning of Ethnic History." *The The Journal of Ethnic Studies*, vol. 14 no. 1 (1986) p. 29-46.

0882   **Harney, Robert F.**
"Italophobia: An English-speaking Malady?" *Polyphony: The Bulletin of the Multicultural History Society of Ontario*, vol. 7 no. 2 (1985) p. 54-60.

0883   **Harney, Robert F.**
"Introduction." *Polyphony: The Bulletin of the Multicultural History Society of Ontario*, vol. 6 no. 1 (1984) p. 1-14. Introduction to a monographic issue of *Polyphony* "Toronto's People."

0884   **Harvey, Fernand**
"Les groupes ethniques: Enjeu de la lutte linguistique au Québec." *Journal of Canadian Studies/Revue d'études canadiennes*, vol. 23 no. 4 (1988/89) p. 37-43.

0885   **Hawkins, Freda**
"Race Relations in a Comparative Perspective." In: *Canada 2000: Race Relations and Public Policy*, edited by O.P. Dwivedi et al. Guelph, Ontario: Department of Political Studies, University of Guelph, 1989, p. 301-307.

0886   **Hazzan, Moise**
Différenciateur sémantique: attitudes d'un groupe d'étudiants en anthropologie sur la santé et les stéréotypes ethniques. Unpublished MSc thesis, Université de Montréal, 1984. 1 microfilm. Archives, microfilm section.

0887   **Head, Wilson A.**
"Historical, Social and Cultural Factors in the Adaptation of Nonwhite Students in Toronto Schools." In: *Multiculturalism in Canada: Social and Educational Perspectives*, edited by Ronald J. Samuda, John W. Berry and Michel Laferrière. Toronto: Allyn and Bacon Inc., 1984, p. 266-281.

0888   **Head, Wilson A.**
Adaptation of Immigrants: Perceptions of Ethnic and Racial Discrimination. Toronto: York University, 1980. 146 p.

0889   **Head, Wilson A. and Donald H. Clairmont**
Discrimination Against Blacks in Nova Scotia: The Criminal Justice System. Prepared for the Royal Commission on the Donald Marshall Jr., Prosecution. Halifax: The Commission, 1989.

0890   **Heber, R. Wesley**
Chipewyan Ethno-adaptations: Identity Expression for Chipweyan Indians of Northern Saskatchewan. Unpublished PhD thesis, University of Manitoba, 1989.

0891   **Heber, R. Wesley**
"Indians as Ethnics: Chipewyan Ethnic-adaptations." *The Western Canadian Anthropologist*, vol. 6 no. 1 (1989) p. 55-77.

0892   **Heller, Monica**
"Language and Ethnic Identity in a Toronto French-language School." *Canadian Ethnic Studies/Études ethniques au Canada*, vol. 16 no. 2 (1984) p. 1-14.

0893   **Henry, Frances**
"Racial Discrimination in Employment." In: *Social Inequality in Canada: Patterns, Problems, Policies*, edited by James E. Curtis et al. Scarborough, Ontario: Prentice-Hall Canada, 1988, p. 214-220.

0894   **Henry, Frances**
Who Gets the Work?: A Test of Racial Discrimination in Employment. Toronto: The Urban Alliance on Race Relations and the Social Planning Council of Metropolitan Toronto, 1985. 87 p.

0895   **Hiess, Arthur**
"Canada: A Survey of Anti-semitic Incidents in 1985." *Review of Anti-Semitism in Canada*, (1985) p. 2-10.

0896   **Hiller, Harry H.**
"Nationality, Relevance, and Ethnocentrism: An Essay in the Sociology of Canadian Book Publishing." *Social Forces*, vol. 59 no. 4 (1981) p. 1297-1307.

0897   **Hilton, Anthony**
"Ethnic Relations in Rental Housing: A Social Psychological
Approach." *Canadian Journal of Behavioural Science/Revue
canadienne des sciences de comportement*, vol. 21 no. 2
(1989) p. 121-131.

0898   **Hobart, Charles W.**
"Native White Relationships in a Northern Oil Town." *Canadian
Journal of Native Studies*, vol. 6 no. 2 (1986) p. 223-240.

0899   **Hofley, John R.**
"John Porter: His Analysis of Class and His Contribution to Canadian
Sociology." *Canadian Review of Sociology and Anthropology/Revue
canadienne de sociologie et d'anthropologie*, vol. 18 no. 5
(1981) p. 595-606.

0900   **House, John Douglas**
"Ethnicity and Social Change in Coastal Labrador." In: *Ethnicity in
Atlantic Canada*, edited by Robert Garland. Saint John, N.B.:
Division of Social Science, University of New Brunswick,
1985, p. 103-117.

0901   **Ieroncig, Anna**
*Le contact interculturel au travail chez un groupe d'immigrants
italiens: l'attitude envers l'acculturation et l'écart perçu entre leurs
valeurs personnelles de travail et celles des franco-québécois.*
Unpublished M.Ps. thesis, Université de Montréal, 1986. 1 microfilm.

0902   **Ijaz, M. Ahmed**
"Ethnic Attitude Change: A Multidimensional Approach." In:
Multiculturalism in Canada: Social and Educational Perspectives,
edited by Ronald J. Samuda, John W. Berry and Michel Laferriere.
Toronto: Allyn and Bacon Inc., 1984, p. 128-138.

0903   **Ijaz, M. Ahmed**
"Racism, Attitudes of Behaviour." *Currents*, vol. 1 no. 3
(1983) p. 12.

0904   **Indra, Doreen M.**
"Invisible Mosaic: Women, Ethnicity and the Vancouver Press, 1905-
1976." *Canadian Ethnic Studies/Études ethniques au Canada*, vol. 13
no. 1 (1981) p. 63-74.

0905   **Indra, Doreen M.**
"Community and Inter-ethnic Relations of Southeast Asian Refugees in Canada." In: *Southeast Asian Exodus: From Traditions to Resettlement: Understanding Refugees from Laos, Kampuchea and Vietnam in Canada*, edited by Elliot L. Tepper. Ottawa: Canadian Asian Studies Association, 1980, p. 173-190.

0906   **Isaacs, Marla B. and George H. Leon**
"Race, Marital Dissolution and Visitation: An Examination of Adaptive Family Strategies." *Journal of Divorce*, vol. 11 no. 2 (1987) p. 17-32.

0907   **Isajiw, Wsevolod W.**
"Definition of Ethnicity." In: *Ethnicity and Ethnic Relations in Canada: A Book of Readings*, edited by Rita M. Bienvenue and Jay E. Goldstein. 2nd ed. Toronto: Butterworths, 1985, p. 5-17. Reprinted from *Ethnicity*, vol. 1 no. 2 (1974) p. 111-124.

0908   **Isajiw, Wsevolod W.**
"How to Understand Today's Ethnic Group." *Canadian Ethnic Studies/Études ethniques au Canada*, vol. 12 no. 2 (1980) p. v-ix.

0909   **Jabbra, Nancy W.**
"Ethnicity in Atlantic Canada: A Survey." *Canadian Ethnic Studies/ Études ethniques au Canada*, vol. 20 no. 3 (1988) p. 6-27.

0910   **Jabbra, Nancy W.**
"Assimilation and Acculturation of Lebanese Extended Families in Nova Scotia." *Canadian Ethnic Studies/Études ethniques au Canada*, vol. 15 no. 1 (1983) p. 544-572.

0911   **Jackson, John D.**
Community and Conflict: A Study of French-English Relations in Ontario. Toronto: Canadian Scholars Press, 1988.

0912   **Jacob, André**
"L'accessibilité des services sociaux aux communautés ethniques." *Intervention*, no. 74 (1986) p. 16-24.

0913   **Jaenen, Cornelius J.**
"Assessing Early Native-European Contact." *Journal of Canadian Studies/Revue d'études canadiennes*, vol. 23 no. 1/2 (1988) p. 243-247.

0914   **Jaenen, Cornelius J.**
"French Attitudes Towards Native Society." In: *Old Trails and New Directions*, edited by Carol M. Judd and Arthur J. Ray. Toronto: University of Toronto Press, 1980, p. 59-72.

0915   **Jain, Harish C.**
"Affirmative Action: Employment Equity Programs and Canada's Visible Minorities." In: *Proceedings of the National Symposium on Progress Towards Equality, September 16-18, 1988 at Vancouver*, edited by Aziz Khaki. Vancouver: Committee for Racial Justice, [1989], p. 7-16.

0916   **Jain, Harish C.**
"Affirmative Action: Employment Equity Programs and Visible Minorities in Canada." In: *Canada 2000: Race Relations and Public Policy*, edited by O.P. Dwivedi et al. Guelph, Ontario: Department of Political Studies, University of Guelph, 1989, p. 170-177.

0917   **Jain, Harish C.**
"The Recruitment and Selection of Visible Minorities in Canadian Police Forces." In: *Canada 2000: Race Relations and Public Policy*, edited by O.P. Dwivedi et al. Guelph, Ontario: Department of Political Studies, University of Guelph, 1989, p. 264-278.

0918   **Jain, Harish C.**
"The Recruitment and Selection of Visible Minorities in Canadian Police Organizations: 1985 to 1987." *Canadian Public Administration /Administration publique au Canada*, vol. 31 no. 4 (1988) p. 463-482.

0919   **Jain, Harish C.**
"Racial Discrimination in Employment in Canada: Issues and Policies." In: *South Asians in the Canadian Mosaic*, edited by Rabindra N. Kanungo. Montreal: Kala Bharati Foundation, 1984, p. 69-84.

0920   **Jain, Harish C.**
"Employment and Pay Discrimination in Canada: Theories, Evidence, and Policies." In: *Union-management Relations in Canada*, edited by John Anderson and Morley Gunderson. Don Mills, Ontario: Addison-Wesley Publishers, 1982, p. 503-522.

0921   **Jain, Harish C.**
Equal Employment Issues: Race and Sex Discrimination in the United States, Canada and Britain. New York: Praeger, 1981. 256 p.

0922   **Jansen, Clifford J.**
"Inter-ethnic Marriages." *International Journal of Comparative Sociology*, vol. 23 no. 3/4 (1982) p. 225-235.

0923   **Jarvenpa, Robert**
"The Political Economy and Political Ethnicity of American Indian Adaptations and Identities." *Ethnic and Racial Studies*, vol. 8 no. 1 (1985) p. 29-48.

0924   **Jayasuriya, D.L.**
"Mental Health in a Multicultural Society: Some Key Issues of Policy and Practice." *Multicultural Australian Papers*, no. 55 (1986).

0925   **Johnson, Nan E.**
"The Pace of Births Over the Life Course: Implications for the Minority Group Status Hypothesis." *Social Science Quarterly*, vol. 69 no. 1 (1988) p. 95-107

0926   **Journal of Ukrainian Studies**
"The Tragedy of Canada's White Ethnics: A Constitutional Post-mortem." *Journal of Ukrainian Studies/Zhurnal Ukrajinoznavchnyk Studij*, vol. 7 no. 1 (1982) p. 3-15.

0927   **Juteau, Danielle**
"From French Canadian to Franco-Ontarians and Ontarois: New Boundaries, New Identities." In: *Two Nations, Many Cultures: Ethnic Groups in Canada*, edited by Jean Leonard Elliott. 2nd ed. Scarborough, Ontario: Prentice-Hall of Canada, 1983, p. 173-186.

0928   **Juteau, Danielle**
"La production de l'ethnicité ou la part réelle de l'idéal," *Sociologie et sociétés*, vol. 15 no. 2 (1983) p. 39-59.

0929   **Juteau, Danielle**
"Les autres 'ethniques'." *Sociologie et sociétés*, vol. 15 no. 2 (1983) p. 3-8.

0930   **Kahn, Joan R.**
"Immigrant Selectivity and Fertility Adaptation in the United States."
Social Forces, vol. 67 no.1 (1988) p. 108-128.

0931   **Kalbach, Warren E.**
*Ethnic-religious Identity, Acculturation, and Social and Economic
Achievement of Canada's Post-war Minority Populations: A Report.*
Ottawa: Health and Welfare Canada, 1988. 66 p. Report prepared for
the Review of Demography and its Implications for Economic and
Social Policy.

0932   **Kalbach, Warren E.**
"Ethnic-connectedness: How Binding is the Tie?" In: *Central and
East European Ethnicity in Canada: Adaptation and Preservation*,
edited by T. Yedlin. Edmonton: Central and East European Studies
Society of Alberta, 1985, p. 99-110.

0933   **Kalbach, Warren E.**
"Propensities of Intermarriage in Canada as Reflected in Ethnic
Origins of Husbands and Their Wives." In: *Marriage and Divorce in
Canada*, edited by K. Ishwaran. Toronto: Methuen, 1983, p. 196-212.

0934   **Kalin, Rudolf**
"The Development of Ethnic Attitudes." In: *Multiculturalism in
Canada: Social and Educational Perspectives*, edited by Ronald J.
Samuda, John W. Berry and Michel Laferrière. Toronto: Allyn and
Bacon Inc., 1984, p. 114-127.

0935   **Kalin, Rudolf**
"Canadian Ethnic Attitudes and Identity in the Context of National
Unity." *Journal of Canadian Studies/Revue d'études canadiennes*,
vol. 17 no. 1 (1982) p.103-110.

0936   **Kalin, Rudolf**
"The Social Ecology of Ethnic Attitudes in Canada." *Canadian
Journal of Behavioural Science/Revue canadienne des sciences de
comportement*, vol. 14 no. 2 (1982) p. 97-109.

0937   **Kalin, Rudolf**
"Ethnic Attitudes." In: *Canadian Social Psychology of Ethnic
Relations*, edited by Robert C. Gardner and Rudolf Kalin. Toronto:
Methuen, 1981, p. 132-150.

0938   **Kalin, Rudolf**
"Geographic Mobility and Ethnic Tolerance." *Journal of Psychology*,
vol. 112 no. 1 (1980) p. 129-134.

0939   **Kalin, Rudolf**
"The Perceptions and Evaluation of Job Candidates with Four
Different Ethnic Accents." In: *Language: Social Psychological
Perspectives*, edited by Howard Giles, W. Peter Robinson, and Philip
M. Smith. New York: Oxford: Pergamon Press, 1980, p. 197-203.
Paper presented at the First International Conference on Social
Psychology and Language, held at the University of Bristol, England,
July 1979.

0940   **Kallen, Evelyn**
"Academics, Politics and Ethics: University Opinion on Canadian
Ethnic Studies/Études ethniques au Canada." *Canadian Ethnic Studies
/Études ethniques au Canada*, vol. 13 no. 2 (1981) p. 112-123.

0941   **Kallen, Evelyn**
"Ethnicity and Human Rights in Canada; Constitutionalizing a
Hierarchy of Minority Rights." In: *Race and Ethnic Relations in
Canada*, edited by Peter S. Li. Don Mills, Ontario: Oxford University
Press, 1980, p. 77-98.

0942   **Kaplan, David H.**
"'Mai'tres Chez Nous': The Evolution of French Canadian Spatial
Identity." *American Review of Canadian Studies*, vol. 19 no. 4
(1989) p. 407-428.

0943   **Kehoe, John W.**
"Ethnocentrism, Self-esteem and Appreciation of Cultural Diversity."
Canadian Ethnic Studies/Études ethniques au Canada, vol. 14 no. 3
(1982) p. 69-78.

0944   **Kennedy, John C.**
"The Changing Significance of Labrador Settler Ethnicity." *Canadian
Ethnic Studies/Études ethniques au Canada*, vol. 20 no. 3
(1988) p. 94-111.

0945   **Kennedy, John C.**
*Holding the Line: Ethnic Boundaries in a Northern Labrador
Community*. St. John's, Newfoundland: Institute of Social and
Economic Research, Memorial University, 1982. 171 p.

0946 **Kienetz, Alvin**
"Ethnic Identity in Northern Canada." *The Journal of Ethnic Studies*, vol. 14 no. 1 (1986) p. 129-134.

0947 **Koch, Eric**
"Enemy Aliens in Canada: The Genesis of 'Deemed Suspect'." In: *German-Canadian Studies: Critical Approaches*, edited by Peter Liddell. Vancouver: CAUTG, 1983, p. 87-94.

0948 **Kostash, Myrna**
"Domination and Exclusion: Notes of a Resident Alien." In: *Ethnicity in a Technological Age*, edited by Ian H. Angus. Edmonton: Canadian Institute of Ukrainian Studies, University of Alberta, 1988, p. 57-66.

0949 **Kroeh-Sommer, Helma**
Ethnicity, Individual Modernity, and Academic Attributions. Unpublished MA thesis, University of Concordia, 1986. 2 microfiches. Canadian theses on microfiche, CT88-20756-6.

0950 **Lachapelle, Rejean**
"Evolution of Ethnic and Linguistic Composition." In: *Cultural Boundaries and Cohesion of Canada*, edited by Raymond Breton et al. Montreal: Institute for Research on Public Policy, 1980, p. 15-44.

0951 **Lacy, Ella P.**
"Enhancing Interpersonal Skills for Ethnic Diversity in Medical Practice." *International Migration Review*, vol. 22 no. 2 (1988) p. 301-311.

0952 **Laferrière, Michel**
"Les idéologies ethniques de la société canadienne: du conformisme colonial au multiculturalisme." In: *Le facteur ethnique aux États-Unis et au Canada*, études réunies par Monique Lecomte et Claudine Thomas. Lille, France: Université de Lille, 1983, p. 203-212.

0953 **Lai, Chuen-Yan David**
"The Issue of Discrimination in Education in Victoria 1901-1923." *Canadian Ethnic Studies/Études ethniques au Canada*, vol. 19 no. 3 (1987) p. 47-67.

0954   **Lalonde, Michèle**
"Speak White." In: *A Passion for Identity: Introduction to Canadian Studies*, edited by Eli Mandel and David Taras. Toronto: Methuen, 1987, p. 264-266.

0955   **Lalonde, Michèle**
Cause commune: manifeste pour une internationale des petites cultures. Montreal, L'Hexagone, 1981. 41 p.

0956   **Lalonde, Richard N.**
"An Intergroup Perspective on Stereotype Organization and Processing." *British Journal of Social Psychology*, vol. 28 no. 4 (1989) p. 289-303.

0957   **Lalonde, Richard N.**
Ethnic Stereotype Processing and Organization as a Function of Group Membership. Unpublished PhD thesis, University of Western Ontario, 1986. 3 microfiches. Canadian theses on microfiche, CT87-25618-1.

0958   **Lam, Lawrence**
"The Whites Accept Us Chinese Now": The Changing Dynamics of Being Chinese in Timmins. Toronto: Ethnic Research Programme, York University, 1983. 58 leaves.

0959   **Lambert, Ronald D.**
"Quebecois and English Canadian Opposition to Racial and Religious Intermarriage, 1968-1983." *Canadian Ethnic Studies/Études ethniques au Canada*, vol. 16 no. 2 (1984) p. 30-46.

0960   **Lambert, Wallace E.**
"Greek Canadians' Attitudes Toward Own Group and Other Canadian Ethnic Groups: A Test of Multiculturalism Hypothesis." *Canadian Journal of Behavioural Science/Revue canadienne des sciences de comportement*, vol. 18 no. 1 (1986) p. 35-51.

0961   **Lambert, Wallace E.**
"Social Influences on the Child's Development of Identity." In: *Canadian Social Psychology of Ethnic Relations*, edited by Robert C. Gardner and Rudolf Kalin. Toronto: Methuen, 1981, p. 57-75.

0962   **Lamothe, Aleida**
Conditions de travail des néo-québécois dans l'entretien ménager d'édifices publics. Montréal: Ministère des communautés culturelles et de l'immigration, Direction de la recherche, 1982. 32 p.

0963   **Lautard, E. Hugh**
"Ethnic Stratification in Canada, 1931-1971." *Canadian Journal of Sociology/Cahiers canadiens de sociologie,* vol. 9 no. 3 (1984) p. 333-343.

0964   **Lavoie, Marc**
"Discrimination Versus English Proficiency in the National Hockey League: A Reply." *Canadian Public Policy/Analyse de politiques,* vol. 15 no. 1 (1989) p. 98-101. A reply to Michael Krashinsky's critique, "Do Hockey Teams Discriminate Against French-Canadians ...?" *Canadian Public Policy/Analyse de politiques,* vol. 15 no. 1 (1989) p. 94-97.

0965   **Lavoie, Marc**
"Discrimination and Performance Differentials in the National Hockey League." *Canadian Public Policy/Analyse de politiques,* vol. 13 no. 4 (1987) p. 407-422.

0966   **Le Bourdais, Celine**
Spatialisation des composantes ethniques, socio-économiques et familiales à Montréal en 1981. Montréal: I.N.R.S., Urbanisation, 1987. 79 p.

0967   **League for Human Rights of B'nai Brith**
"Ontario and Quebec: A Survey of Anti-semitic Incidents in 1983." *Review of Anti-semitism in Canada,* (1983) p. 3-9.

0968   **League for Human Rights of B'nai Brith**
"Research Project on Anti-semitism: Study of Canadian Attitudes Towards Jews, Italians and Poles." *Review of Anti-semitism in Canada,* (1983) p. 31-55.

0969   **LeBorgne, Louis**
"Les questions dites 'ethniques'." *Recherches sociographiques,* vol. 25 no. 3 (1984) p. 421-439.

0970 **Lecomte, Monique et Claudine Thomas, comp.**
Le facteur ethnique aux États-Unis et au Canada. Études réunies par Monique Lecomte et Claudine Thomas. Lille: Université de Lille, 1983. 251 p.

0971 **Leslie, Peter M.**
Ethnonationalism in a Federal State: The Case of Canada. Kingston, Ontario: Institute of Intergovernmental Relations, Queen's University, 1988. 48 p. Published also as an essay in: *Ethnoterritorial Politics, Policy and the Western World,* edited by Joseph R. Rudolph Jr. and Robert J. Thompson. Boulder, Colo.: Lynne Rienner Publishers, 1989, p. 45-90.

0972 **Leung, Tina Wai-Ching**
Ethnic Variations in the Relationship Between Income and Fertility. Unpublished MA thesis, University of Alberta, 1987. 3 microfiches. Canadian theses on microfiche, CT-89-20677-5

0973 **Levitt, Cyril**
"The Swastika as Dramatic Symbol: A Case-study of Ethnic Violence in Canada." *Jewish Journal of Sociology,* vol. 31 no. 1 (1989) p. 5-24.

0974 **Levitt, Cyril**
The Riot at Christie Pits. Toronto: Lester and Orpen Dennys, 1987. 305 p.

0975 **Levitt, Cyril**
The Christie Pits Riot: A Case Study in the Dynamics of Ethnic Violence; Toronto, August 16, 1933. Downsview, Ontario: York University, 1985. 49 p.

0976 **Levitt, Joseph**
"Race and Nation in Canadian Anglophone Historiography." *Canadian Review of Studies in Nationalism/Revue canadienne des études sur le nationalisme,* vol. 8 no. 1 (1981) p. 1-16.

0977 **Lewycky, Laverne**
"Politics, Race Relations and Public Policy." In: *Canada 2000: Race Relations and Public Policy Policy,* edited by O.P. Dwivedi et al. Guelph, Ontario: Department of Political Studies, University of Guelph, 1989, p. 240-259.

0978   **Li, Peter S.**
Ethnic Inequality in a Class Society. Toronto: Wall and Thompson,
1988. 165 p.

0979   **Li, Peter S.**
"Race and Ethnicity." In: *Race and Ethnic Relations in Canada,*
edited by Peter S. Li. Don Mills, Ontario: Oxford University Press,
1980, p. 3-17.

0980   **Little, J.I.**
*Ethno-Cultural Transition and Regional Identity in the Eastern
Townships of Quebec.* Ottawa: Canadian Historical Association,
Booklet no. 13, 1989. 31 p.

0981   **Lortie-Lussier, Monique**
"Value Orientations of English, French, and Italian Canadian
Children: Continuity of the Ethnic Mosaic?" *Journal of Cross-
cultural Psychology,* vol. 17 no. 3 (1986) p. 283-299.

0982   **Macdonald, Norman**
"Putting on the Kilt: The Scottish Stereotype and Ethnic Community
Survival in Cape Breton." *Canadian Ethnic Studies/Études ethniques
au Canada,* vol. 20 no. 3 (1988) p. 132-146.

0983   **Maciejko, Bill**
"'Ethnicity': Myth and History in Western Canada: The Case of
David C. Jones and the 'Ruthenians'." *History of Education Review,*
vol. 18 no. 2 (1989) p. 57-63. A critique of David C. Jones "So
Petty, so Middle Europe, so Foreign: Ruthenians and Cana-
dianization." *History of Education Review,* vol. 16 no. 1
(1987) p. 13- 30.

0984   **Mackie, Marlene**
"Ethnic Identification: Both Sides of the Border." *Canadian Ethnic
Studies/Études ethniques au Canada* vol. 20 no. 2 (1988) p. 101-113.

0985   **Mackie, Marlene**
"Stereotypes, Prejudice, and Discrimination." In: *Ethnicity and Ethnic
Relations in Canada: A Book of Readings,* edited by Rita M.
Bienvenue and Jay E. Goldstein. Toronto: Butterworths,
1985, p. 219-239.

0986   **Mackie, Marlene**
"Measuring Ethnic Salience." *Canadian Ethnic Studies/Études ethniques au Canada*, vol. 16 no. 1 (1984) p. 114-131.

0987   **Mackie, Marlene**
"Ethnic Relations in the Prairies." In: *Canadian Social Psychology of Ethnic Relations*, edited by Robert C. Gardner and Rudolf Kalin. Toronto: Methuen, 1981, p. 194-213.

0988   **Mackie, Marlene**
"Ethnic Stereotypes and Prejudice: Alberta Indians, Hutterites and Ukrainians." In: *Ethnicity and Ethnic Relations in Canada*, edited by J.E. Goldstein and Rita M. Bienvenue. Toronto: Butterworths, 1980, p. 233-246. Reprinted from *Canadian Ethnic Studies/Études ethniques au Canada*, vol. 6 no. 1/2 (1974) 39-52.

0989   **MacLean, Michael J.**
"Ethnic Elderly People in Long-term Care Facilities of the Dominant Culture: Implications for Social Work Practice and Education." *International Social Work*, vol. 29 no. 3 (1986) p. 227-236.

0990   **Mair, Debra Louise**
National Conflict Agenda Settling: Explaining Ethnic Content on the Conflict Agenda of Quebec. PhD thesis, University of Michigan, 1988. 421 p. Canadian theses on microfiche, CT89-27308-1.

0991   **Mak, Magdalen Shunyee**
A Cross-cultural Study on Achievement, Causal Attribution, and Adolescent Perception of Parent Behaviour Among Euro-Canadian, Chinese-Canadian and Hong Kong Chinese Adolescents. Unpublished PhD thesis, Univesity of Manitoba, 1988.

0992   **Mallea, John R.**
"Canadian Dualism and Pluralism; Tensions, Contradictions and Emerging Resolutions." In: *Ethnic Psychology: Research and Practice with Immigrants, Refugees, Native Peoples, Ethnic Groups and Sojourners*, edited by John W. Berry and R.C. Annis. Lisse: Swets and Zeitlinger, 1988, p. 13-37. Paper presented to the North American Regional International Association of Cross-cultural Psychology on Ethnic Psychology held in Kingston, Canada, August 16-21, 1987.

0993   **Mandell, Nancy**
"Socialization, Subcultures, and Identity." In: *Understanding Canadian Society*, edited by James Curtis and Lorne Tepperman. Toronto: McGraw-Hill Ryerson, 1988, p. 395-422.

0994   **Mannette, Joy A.**
"'A Trial in Which No One Goes to Jail': The Donald Marshall Inquiry as Hegemonic Renegotiation." *Canadian Ethnic Studies/ Études ethniques au Canada*, vol. 20 no. 3 (1988) p. 166-180.

0995   **Manuel, George**
"The Fourth World in Canada." In: *Two Nations, Many Cultures: Ethnic Groups in Canada*, edited by Jean Leonard Elliott. 2nd ed. Scarborough, Ontario: Prentice-Hall of Canada, 1983, p. 15-18.

0996   **Marasinghe, Lakshman**
"Canada: Two Nations and Many Cultures." *Ethnic Studies Report*, vol. 2 no. 2 (1984) p. 21-49.

0997   **Marger, Martin N.**
"Emergent Ethnicity Among Internal Migrants: The Case of Maritimers in Toronto." *Ethnic Groups*, vol. 7 no. 1 (1987) p. 1-17.

0998   **Marr, William L.**
Consumption and Saving Patterns of the Foreign-born in Canada. Ottawa: Health and Welfare Canada, 1988. 9 leaves. Report prepared for the Review of Demography and its Implications for Economic and Social Policy.

0999   **Martin-Guillerm, Marguerite**
"Sudbury: structures ethniques et socio-économiques." *Laurentian University Review/Revue de l'université Laurentienne*, vol. 15 no. 1 (1982) p. 93-108.

1000   **Massey, Douglas S.**
"Ethnic Residential Segregation: A Theoretical Synthesis, and Empirical Review." *Sociology and Social Research*, vol. 69 no. 3 (1985) p. 315-350.

1001   **McAlpine, John D.**
Report Arising Out of the Activities of the Ku Klux Klan in British Columbia as Presented to the Honourable J.H. Heinrich, Minister of Labour for the Province of British Columbia. Vancouver: [s.n.] 1981. 79 [27] leaves.

1002   **McAndrew, Marie**
Rélations inter-ethniques et implication du Système scolaire public dans l'enseignement des langues d'origine: une analyse comparative du "Heritage Language Program" en Ontario et du programme d'enseignement des langues d'origine au Québec. Unpublished PhD thesis, Université de Montréal, 1988. 1 microfilm.

1003   **McAndrew, Marie**
"Le traitement du racisme de l'immigration et de la réalité multi-ethnique dans les manuels scolaires francophones au Québec." *Canadian Ethnic Studies/Études ethniques au Canada*, vol. 18 no. 2 (1986) p. 130-142.

1004   **McCarrey, Michael**
"Work and Personal Values of Canadian Anglophones and Francophones: Implications for Organizational Behaviour." *Canadian Psychology/Psychologie canadienne*, vol. 29 no. 1 (1988) p. 69-83.

1005   **McCormack, Ross**
"Cloth Caps and Jobs: The Ethnicity of English Immigrants in Canada, 1900-1914." In: *Interpreting Canada's Past*, edited by J.M. Bumsted. 2 volumes. Toronto: Oxford University Press, 1986, vol. 2, p. 175-191.

1006   **McCurley, Donna Anne**
The Effect of Ethnic Diversity Within Catholicism on Differential Catholic Fertility in Canada, 1971. Unpublished PhD thesis, Tulane University, 1983. 208 p. Canadian theses on microfiche, CT86-24161-0.

1007   **McGillivray, Ann**
"Transracial Adoption and the Status Indian Child." *Canadian Journal of Family Law/Revue canadienne de droit familial*, vol. 4 no. 4 (1985) p. 437-467.

1008   **McKee, B. Brian**
"Les franco-ontariens: A New Ethnic Identity in Canada." *Europa Ethnica*, vol. 45 nos. 2-3 (1988) p. 86-94.

1009   **McKee, B. Brian**
"Ethnic Maintenance in an Internal Colony: The Case of the Acadians of New Brunswick, Canada." *Plural Societes*, vol. 17 no. 2 (1987) p. 1-24.

1010   **McKee, B. Brian**
        Ethnic Maintenance in the Periphery: The Case of Acadia. Ottawa:
        Center for Research on Ethnic Minorities. 1984. 29 p.

1011   **McLaren, Peter**
        Cries from the Corridors: The New Suburban Ghettos. Markham,
        Ontario: Paperjacks, 1981.

1012   **McLeod, K. David**
        *A Study of Metis Ethnicity in the Red River Settlement: Quantification
        and Pattern.* Unpublished MA thesis, University of Manitoba, 1985.
        2 microfiches. Canadian theses on microfiche, CT87-25125-2.

1013   **McNeill, William H.**
        Polyethnicity and National Unity in World History. Toronto:
        University of Toronto Press, 1986. 85 p.

1014   **Micone, Marco**
        "La culture immigrée au Québec." *Conjoncture politique au Québec*
        no. 4 (1983) p. 107-112.

1015   **Midy, Franklin**
        *Condition immigrante et situation ethnique: Notes sur les conditions
        d'intégration de la communauté immigrée.* Montréal: Centre interna-
        tional de documentation et d'information haïtienne, caraïbe et afro-
        canadienne (C.I.D.I.H.C.A.) 1984.

1016   **Miller, James R.**
        *Skyscrapers Hide the Heavens: A History of Indian-white Relations
        in Canada.* Toronto: University of Toronto Press, 1989. 330 p.

1017   **Millett, David**
        "Defining the 'Dominant Group'." *Canadian Ethnic Studies/Études
        ethniques au Canada*, vol. 13 no. 3 (1981) p. 64-79.

1018   **Minton, Henry**
        "Emancipatory Social Psychology as a Paradigm for the Study of
        Minority Groups." In: *Racial Minorities in Multicultural Canada*,
        edited by Peter S. Li and B. Singh Bolaria. Toronto: Garamond
        Press, 1982, p. 148-156.

1019   **Moeno, Sylvia Ntlanta**
        The "Non-white" South Africans in Toronto: A Study of the Effects of
        "Institutionalized" Apartheid in a Multicultural Society. Unpublished
        PhD thesis, York University, 1981. Canadian theses on microfiche,
        no. 47851.

1020   **Moghaddam, Fathali M.**
        "Individualistic and Collective Integration Strategies Among
        Immigrants: Toward Mobility Model of Cultural Integration." In:
        Ethnic Psychology: Research and Practice with Immigrants,
        Refugees, Native Peoples, Ethnic Groups and Sojourners, edited by
        John W. Berry and R.C. Annis. Lisse: Swets and Zeitlinger,
        1988, p. 69-79.

1021   **Monet, Jacques**
        Le Canada: un cheminent vers la solidarité et la tolérance. Montréal:
        Parti libéral du Québec, 1980. 89 p.

1022   **Montcalm, Mary Beth**
        Class in Ethnic Nationalism: A Quebec Nationalism in Comparative
        Perspective. Unpublished PhD thesis, Carleton University, 1983. 5
        microfiche. Canadian theses on microfiche, no. 59906.

1023   **Morisset, Jean**
        L'identité usurpée. Montréal: Nouvelle optique, 1985.

1024   **Muszynski, Leon**
        Racial and Ethnic Discrimination in Employment. Toronto: Social
        Planning Council of Metropolitan Toronto: 1982. 76 p.

1025   **National Council for the Social Studies**
        "Countering Prejudiced Beliefs and Behaviours." *Social Education,*
        vol. 52 no. 4 (1988) p. 264-291.

1026   **Nevitte, Neil**
        "Minorities as an Attitudinal Phenomenon: A Comparative Analysis
        of Youth Elites." In: *Minorities and the Canadian State,* edited by
        Neil Nevitte and Allan Kornberg. Oakville, Ontario: Mosaic Press,
        1985, p. 257-274.

1027   **Nevitte, Neil and Allan Kornberg, eds.**
        Minorities and the Canadian State. Oakville, Ontario: Mosaic Press,
        1985. 324 p.

1028   **Ng, Roxana**
"Sex, Ethnicity Or Class? Some Methodological Considerations."
Studies in Sexual Politics, no. 1 (1984) p. 14-45.

1029   **O'Neil, John D.**
"The Cultural and Political Context of Patient Dissatisfaction in
Cross-cultural Clinical Encounters: A Canadian Inuit Study." *Medical
Anthropology Quarterly*, vol. 3 no. 4 (1989) p. 325-344.

1030   **Ogmundson, Richard**
"Toward Study of the Endangered Species Known as the Anglophone
Canadian." *Canadian Journal of Sociology/Cahiers canadiens de
sociologie*, vol. 5 no. 1 (1980) p. 1-12.

1031   **Olzak, Susan M.**
"Ethnic Mobilization in Quebec." *Ethnic and Racial Studies*, vol. 5
no. 3 (1982) p. 253-275.

1032   **Ontario. Race Relations and Policing Task Force**
The Report of the Race Relations and Policing Task Force. Toronto:
The Task Force, 1989. 294 p.

1033   **Onufrijchuk, Roman**
"Post-modern or Perednovok: Deconstructing Ethnicity." In: *Ethnicity
in a Technological Age*, edited by Ian H. Angus. Edmonton:
Canadian Institute of Ukrainian Studies, University of Alberta,
1988, p. 3-16.

1034   **Palmer, Bryan D.**
"What the Hell: Or Some Comments on Class Formation and Cultural Reproduction." In: *Popular Cultures and Political Practices*,
edited by Richard Gruneau. Toronto: Garamond Press, 1988, p. 33-
42.

1035   **Palmer, Howard**
"Etnicidad y pluralismo en America del Norte: comparación de las
perspectivas canadiense y estadounidense." *Estudios Migratorios
Latinoamericanos*, vol. 12 (1989) p. 257-286.

1036   **Palmer, Howard**
"Mosaic Versus Melting Pot? Immigration and Ethnicity in Canada
and the United States." In: *A Passion for Identity: Introduction to
Canadian Studies*, edited by Eli Mandel and David Taras. Toronto:
Methuen, 1987, p. 82-96.

1037   **Palmer, Howard**
"William Irving and the Emergence of Political Radicalism in
Calgary, 1906-1921." *Fort Calgary Quarterly*, vol. 7 no. 2
(1987) p. 1-19.

1038   **Palmer, Howard**
"Reluctant Hosts: Anglo-Canadian Views on Multiculturalism in the
Twentieth Century." In: *Cultural Diversity and Canadian Education:
Issues and Innovations*, edited by John R. Mallea and Jonathan C.
Young. Ottawa: Carleton University Press, 1984, p. 21-40.

1039   **Palmer, Howard**
Patterns of Prejudice: A History of Nativism in Alberta. Toronto:
McClelland and Stewart, 1982.

1040   **Palmer, Howard and Tamara**
Peoples of Alberta: Portraits of Cultural Diversity. Saskatoon, Sask.:
Western Producer Prairie Books, 1985.

1041   **Palmer, Tamara**
"Ethnic Response to the Canadian Prairies, 1900-1950: A Literary
Perspective on Perceptions of the Physical and Social Environment."
Prairie Forum, vol. 12 no. 1 (1987) p. 49-73.

1042   **Parker, Keith D.**
"Black-White Differences in Perceptions of Fear of Crime." *The
Journal of Social Psychology*, vol. 128 no. 4 (1988) p. 487-494.

1043   **Pate, Glenn S.**
"Research on Reducing Prejudice." *Social Education*, vol. 52 no. 4
(1988) p. 287-289.

1044   **Patterson, G. James**
"The Persistence of White Ethnicity in Canada: The Case of the
Romanians." *East European Quarterly*, vol. 19 no. 4 (January
1986) p. 493-500.

1045   **Payne, Barbara Jean**
*Aging, Ethnicity and Family Social Support: A Test of the
Modernizations and Aging Thesis.* Unpublished MSc thesis,
University of Toronto, 1989.

1046   **Pelletier, Gérard**
"Quebec: Different But in Step with North America." In: *In Search of Canada*, edited by Stephen R. Graubard. New Brunswick: Transaction Publishers, 1989, p. 265-282.

1047   **Pelletier, Gérard**
"Quebec: Different But in Step with North America." *Daedalus*, vol. 117 no. 4 (1988) p. 265-282.

1048   **Penning, M.J.**
"Multiple Jeopardy: Age, Sex, and Ethnic Variations." *Canadian Ethnic Studies/Études ethniques au Canada*, vol. 15 no. 3 (1983) p. 81-105.

1049   **Peppard, Nadine**
"Race Relations Training Today." *Currents*, vol. 1 no. 3 (1983) p. 6.

1050   **Philip, Tom and Byron Rempel**
"Oppression All the Same: Alberta Medical Authorities Ponder How to be Fair to Foreign-trained Doctors." *Alberta Report*, vol. 16 no. 42 (1989) p. 35-36.

1051   **Ponterotto, Joseph G.**
"Racial/Ethnic Minority Research in the 'Journal of Counseling Psychology': A Content Analysis and Methodological Critique." *Journal of Counseling Psychology*, vol. 35 no. 4 (1988) p. 410-418.

1052   **Ponting, J. Rick**
"Conflict and Change in Indian/Non-Indian Relations in Canada: Comparison of 1976 and 1979 National Attitude Surveys." *Canadian Journal of Sociology/Cahiers canadiens de sociologie*, vol. 9 no. 2 (1984) p. 137-158.

1053   **Ponting, J. Rick**
"The Reactions of English Canadians and French Quebecois to Native Indian Protest: A Note." *Canadian Review of Sociology and Anthropology/Revue canadienne de sociologie et d'anthropologie*, vol. 18 no. 2 (1981) p. 222-238.

1054   **Quebec Movement to Combat Racism (QMCR)**
Racism in Quebec. Montreal: Quebec Movement to Combat Racism, 1980. 58 p. Working papers delivered at the QMCR Conference, Montreal, May 25 and 26, 1979.

1055   **Quenneville, Ginette**
       Les nationalistes québécois et les juifs, 1939-1948. Unpublished MA
       thesis, Université de Montréal, 1986. 1 microfilm.

1056   **Race and Sex Equality in the Workplace: A Challenge and**
       Opportunity, Hamilton, Ontario, 1979.
       Race and Sex Equality in the Workplace: A Challenge and an Oppor-
       tunity. Ottawa: Women's Bureau, Labour Canada, 1980. 236 p.
       Proceedings of the Conference on Race and Sex Equality in the
       Workplace.

1057   **Ramcharan, Subhas**
       Social Problems and Issues: A Canadian Perspective. Scarborough,
       Ontario: Nelson Canada, 1989. 218 p.

1058   **Ramcharan, Subhas**
       Racism: Non-whites in Canada. Scarborough: Butterworths and Co.,
       1982. 138 p.

1059   **Ramirez, Bruno**
       "Les minorités: le multiculturalisme appliqué." In: *L'ère des liberaux:*
       le pouvoir fédéral de 1963 à 1984, edited by Yves Bélanger, Dorval
       Brunelle et collaborateurs. Sillery, P.Q.: Presses de l'Université du
       Québec, 1988, p. 383-404.

1060   **Reed, T. Edward**
       "Ethnic Differences in Alcohol Use, Abuse and Sensitivity: A
       Review with Genetic Interpretation." *Social Biology,* vol. 32 no. 3/4
       (1985) p. 195-209.

1061   **Reitz, Jeffrey G.**
       "The Institutional Structure of Immigration as a Determinant of Inter-
       racial Competition: A Comparison of Britain and Canada." *Interna-*
       tional Migration/Migrations Internationales/Migraciones Internacion-
       ales, vol. 22 no. 1 (1988) p. 117-145.

1062   **Reitz, Jeffrey G.**
       "Less Racial Discrimination in Canada, or Simply Less Racial
       Conflict? Implications of Comparisons with Britain." *Canadian*
       Public Policy/Analyse de politiques, vol. 14 no. 4 (1988) p. 424-441.

1063   **Remiggi, F.W.**
"Quelques origines spatiales du présent conflit francophone-anglophone au Québec: exemple de la Basse-Côte-Nord." *Cahiers de géographie du Québec*, vol. 24 no. 61 (1980) p. 157-166.

1064   **Rettig, Andrew**
"A Nativist Movement at Metlakatla Mission." *B.C. Studies*, vol. 46 (1980) p. 28-39.

1065   **Rex, John**
Race Relations in Sociological Theory. London and Boston: Routledge and Kegan Paul, 1983. 208 p.

1066   **Richmond, Anthony H.**
Immigration and Ethnic Conflict. Houndmills, Basingstoke, Hampshire: Macmillan Press, 1988. 218 p.

1067   **Richmond, Anthony H.**
"Ethnic Nationalism and Post-industrialism." In: *Two Nations, Many Cultures: Ethnic Groups in Canada*, edited by Jean Leonard Elliott. 2nd ed. Scarborough, Ontario: Prentice-Hall of Canada, 1983, p. 302-318.

1068   **Richmond, Anthony H., ed.**
After the Referenda: The Future of Ethnic Nationalism in Britain and Canada. Downsview: York University, 1982. 481 p.

1069   **Robinson, J. Lewis**
"Vancouver: Changing Geographical Aspects of a Multicultural City." *B.C. Studies*, no. 79 (1988) p. 59-81.

1070   **Robyak, James E., Mark Prange, and Melissa Sands**
"Drinking Practices Among Black and White Alcoholics and Alcoholics of Different Personality Types." *Journal of Personality Assessment*, vol. 52 no. 3 (1988) p. 487-498.

1071   **Rose, Courtice**
"The Concept of 'Reach' and the Anglophone Minority in Quebec." *Canadian Ethnic Studies/Études ethniques au Canada*, vol. 17 no. 3 (1985) p. 1-16.

1072   **Rosen, Evelyn**
*Attitudes Toward Women and Women's Roles As Related to
Education, Age, Ethnicity, and Religion.* Unpublished PhD thesis,
University of Wisconsin, 1984. Canadian theses on microfiche,
CT86-23134-8.

1073   **Rosen, Philip**
Hate Propaganda. Ottawa: Library of Parliament, Research Branch,
1985. 19 p.

1074   **Rosen, Rheta Ann**
*Filial Responsibility, Ethnicity and Social Exchange: A Study of
Helping Behaviour in the Older Family.* Unpublished PhD thesis,
York University, Toronto, 1987. Canadian theses on microfiche,
CT89-20461-6.

1075   **Routhier, Ghislaine**
*Étude exploratoire concernant l'influence des attitudes parentales sur
l'identité raciale des enfants noirs adoptés par des parents de race
blanche au Québec.* Unpublished MA thesis, Université du Québec à
Montréal, 1986. Canadian theses on microfiche, CT89-23948-7.

1076   **Roy, Patricia E.**
"British Columbia's Fear of Asians 1900-1950." In: *A History of
British Columbia: Selected Readings*, edited by Patricia Roy.
Toronto: Copp Clark Pitman Ltd., a Longman Co., 1989, p. 285-299.
Originally published in: *Histoire sociale/Social History*, vol. 13 no.
25 (1980) p. 161-172.

1077   **Royal Commission on the Donald Marshall, Jr., Prosecution
(N.S.)**
*Royal Commission on the Donald Marshall, Jr., Prosecution: Digest
of Findings and Recommendations.* Halifax, N.S.: The Royal
Commission, 1989. 41 p.

1078   **Rubin, Max**
"Alberta's Jews: The Long Journey." In: *Peoples of Alberta:
Portraits of Cultural Diversity*, edited by Howard and Tamara
Palmer. Saskatoon: Western Producer Prairie Books, 1985, p. 228-
247.

1079   **Rushton, J. Philippe and Anthony F. Bogaert**
"Race Versus Social Class Differences in Sexual Behavior: A
Follow-Up Test of the r/k Dimension." *Journal of Research in
Personality*, vol. 22 no. 3 (1988) p. 259-272.

1080   **Ryan, Claude**
"La dualité canadienne." *Policy Options/Options politiques*, vol. 3 no.
4 (1982) p. 17-23.

1081   **Saarinen, O.W.**
"Ethnicity and the Cultural Mosaic in the Sudbury Area." *Polyphony:
The Bulletin of the Multicultural History Society of Ontario*, vol. 5
no. 1 (1983) p. 86-92.

1082   **Sapon-Shevin, Mara**
"A Minicourse for Junior High Students [on Prejudice]." *Social
Education*, vol. 52, no. 4 (1988) p. 272-275.

1083   **Satzewich, Victor (Vic) N.**
"Racism: The Reactions to Chinese Migrants in Canada at the Turn
of the Century." *International Sociology*, vol. 4 no. 3 (1989) p. 311-
328.

1084   **Satzewich, Victor (Vic) N.**
Ethnic and Racial Stratification of Canadian Immigrants.
Unpublished MA thesis, University of Saskatchewan, 1984. 99
leaves.

1085   **Schissel, Bernard**
"Social and Economic Content and Attitudes Towards Immigrants in
Canadian Cities." *International Migration/Migrations Internationales/
Migraciones Internacionales*, vol. 23 no. 2 (1989) p. 289-308.

1086   **Schmidt, Joseph**
"Germanophilia: Still a French-Canadian Attitude?" *Annalen:
Deutschkanadische Studien*, vol. 4 (1983) p. 34-41.

1087   **Scott, Colin**
"Ideology of Reciprocity Between the James Bay Cree and the
Whiteman State." In: *Outwitting the State*, edited by P. Skalink. New
Brunswick, U.S.A. and London: Transaction Publishers, 1989, p. 81-
108.

1088   **Scott, Gilbert H.**
"Race Relations and Public Policy: Uncharted Course." In: *Canada 2000: Race Relations and Public Policy*, edited by O.P. Dwivedi et al. Guelph, Ontario: Department of Political Studies, University of Guelph, 1989, p. 227-232.

1089   **Scott, Gilbert H.**
"Race Relations and Public Policy: Unchartered Course." *CPSA Papers 1987/ACSP Contributions*, Section B (a), Public policy paper 6, fiche 2. Paper presented at the 59th annual meeting of the Canadian Political Science Association, June 6-8, 1987, McMaster University, Hamilton, Ontario.

1090   **Senior, Elinor Kyte**
"Suppressing Rebellion in Lower Canada: British Military Policy and Practice, 1837-1838." *Canadian Defence Quarterly/Revue canadienne de défense*, vol. 17 no. 4 (1988) p. 50-55.

1091   **Shadd, Adrienne L.**
The Regional Dynamics of Racial Inequality: A Comparative Study of Blacks in Ontario and Nova Scotia. Unpublished MA thesis, McGill University, 1983. Canadian theses on microfiche, CT87-23060-3.

1092   **Sheng, Jennifer**
Vancouver South: A Progressive Cultural Study. Vancouver: [s.n.], 1980. 118 leaves.

1093   **Shepard, R. Bruce**
"Plain Racism: The Reaction Against Oklahoma Black Immigration to the Canadian Plains." *Prairie Forum*, vol. 10 no. 2 (1985) p. 365-382.

1094   **Sher, Julian**
White Hoods: Canada's Ku Klux Klan. Vancouver: New Star Books, 1983. 229 p.

1095   **Short, Thomas**
"A 'New Racism' on Campus?" *Commentary*, vol. 86 no. 2 (1988) p. 46-50.

1096   **Simard, Lise M.**
"Cross-cultural Interaction: Potential Invisible Barriers." *Journal of Social Psychology*, vol. 113 no. 2 (1981) p. 171-192.

1097   **Simard, Lise M.**
"Intergroup Communication." In: *Canadian Social Psychology of Ethnic Relations*, edited by Robert C. Gardner and Rudolf Kalin. Toronto: Methuen, 1981, p. 172-194.

1098   **Simon, Michael P.**
Indigenous People in Developed Fragment Societies: A Comparative Analysis of Internal Colonialism in the United States, Canada and Northern Ireland. Unpublished PhD thesis, University of Arizona, 1986.

1099   **Simon-Barouh, I.**
"Rélations inter-ethniques et problèmes de minorité: quelques rémarques méthodologiques." *Sociologie et sociétés*, vol. 25 no. 2 (1983) p. 155-165.

1100   **Skop, Nadia Helen**
Ethnic Singlehood As a Sociological Phenomenon: Ukrainian-Canadians As a Case Study. Unpublished PhD thesis, University of Toronto, 1988. Canadian theses on microfiche, CT89-27778-8.

1101   **Smart, Patricia**
"Our Two Cultures." In: *A Passion for Identity: Introduction to Canadian Studies*, edited by Eli Mandel and David Taras. Toronto: Methuen, 1987, p. 196-205.

1102   **Smith, Allan**
"National Images and National Maintenance: The Ascendancy of the Ethnic Idea in North America." *Canadian Journal of Political Science/Revue canadienne de science politique*, vol. 14 no. 2 (1981) p. 227-257.

1103   **Smith, Carl F.**
French-English Relations in Canada. Scarborough, Ontario: Prentice-Hall of Canada, 1980. 141 p.

1104   **Smith, M.G.**
"Some Problems with Minority Concepts and a Solution." *Ethnic and Racial Studies*, vol. 10 no. 4 (1987) p. 341-362.

1105   **Smolak, Roman**
Factors Influencing the Retention of Ethnic Identity. Unpublished MA thesis York University, 1986. Canadian theses on microfiche, CT87-26100-2.

1106 **Sonnenschein, Frances M.**
"Countering Prejudiced Beliefs and Behaviours: The Role of the Social Studies Professional." *Social Education*, vol. 52 no. 4 (1988) p. 264-266.

1107 **Special Council Committee on Race Relations (Vancouver)**
At First a Dream: One Hundred Years of Race Relations in Vancouver. Vancouver: The Special Council Committee on Race Relations, 1986. 32 p.

1108 **Stelter, Gilbert A.**
"The People of Sudbury: Ethnicity and Community in an Ontario Mining Region." *Polyphony: The Bulletin of the Multicultural History Society of Ontario*, vol. 5 no. 1 (1983) p. 3-16.

1109 **Sterritt, Neil J.**
"Unflinching Resistance to an Implacable Invader." In: *Drumbeat: Anger and Renewal in Indian Country*, edited by Boyce Richardson. Toronto: Summerhill Press, 1989, p. 265-294.

1110 **Strain, Laurel A.**
"Social Networks of Urban Native Elders: A Comparison with Non-natives." *Canadian Ethnic Studies/Études ethniques au Canada*, vol. 21 no. 2 (1989) p. 104-117.

1111 **Strickland, Peter John**
Performance Attribution in the Job Selection Interview As a Function of Racial/Ethnic Origin, Performance Primacy, and Cognitive Set. Unpublished MA thesis, University of Saskatchewan, 1981. 101 leaves.

1112 **Symons, T.H.B.**
"Cultural Diversity, Canadian Identity and Canadian Federalism." In: *Public Policies in Two Federal Countries: Canada and Australia*, edited by R.L. Mathews. Canberra: Centre for Research on Federal Financial Relations, Australian National University, 1982, p. 225-236.

1113 **Tator, Carol**
"The Selling of Race Relations." *Currents*, vol. 1 no. 1 (1983) p. 14.

1114 **Taylor, Donald M.**
"Social Comparison in an Intergroup Context." *Journal of Social Psychology*, vol. 129 no. 4 (1989) p. 499-515.

1115   **Taylor, Donald M.**
Theories of Intergroup Relations: International Social Psychological Perspectives. New York: Praeger, 1987. 223 p.

1116   **Taylor, Donald M.**
"Stereotypes and Intergroup Relations." In: *Canadian Social Psychology of Ethnic Relations,* edited by Robert C. Gardner and Rudolf Kalin. Toronto: Methuen, 1981, p. 151-171.

1117   **Teitelbaum, Benjamin**
"Note on Ethnic and Race Relations in Quebec." In: *Canada 2000: Race Relations and Public Policy,* edited by O.P. Dwivedi et al. Guelph, Ontario: Department of Political Studies, University of Guelph, 1989, p. 344-348.

1118   **Tepper, Elliot L.**
"Demographic Change and Pluralism." In: *Canada 2000: Race Relations and Public Policy,* edited by O.P. Dwivedi et al. Guelph, Ontario: Department of Political Studies, University of Guelph, 1989, p. 20-43.

1119   **Tepper, Elliot L.**
Changing Canada: The Institutional Response to Polyethnicity. [Ottawa: s.n.] 1988. 257 p. Report prepared for the Review of Demography and its Implications for Economic and Social Policy.

1120   **Tepper, Elliot L.**
"Demographic Change and Pluralism." *Canadian Studies in Population,* vol. 14 no. 2 (1987) p. 223-235.

1121   **Thaler, Carol-Lyn Sakata**
Development of Ethnocentrism Scale for Junior High School Students in British Columbia. Unpublished MA thesis, Faculty of Education, University of British Columbia, 1985. 144 leaves.

1122   **Thomson, Dale Cairns**
"Canadian Ethnic Pluralism in Context." *Plural Societies,* vol. 11 no. 1 (1980) p. 55-75.

1123   **Thomson, Duncan Duane**
A History of the Okanagan: Indians and Whites in the Settlement Era, 1860-1920. Unpublished PhD thesis, University of British Columbia, 413 leaves. Canadian theses on microfiche, no. 241845.

1124   **Thorburn, H.G.**
"Ethnic Pluralism in Canada." In: *Three Faces of Pluralism: Political, Ethnic and Religious,* edited by Stanislaw Ehrlich and Graham Wooton. Farnborough, England: Gower, 1980, p. 151-168. A paper presented at the 10th World Congress of the International Political Science Association in Edinburgh.

1125   **Tobias, J.L.**
"Indian Reserves in Western Canada: Indian Homelands or Devices for Assimilation?" In: *Native People, Native Lands: Canadian Indians, Inuit and Metis,* edited by Bruce Alden Cox. Ottawa: Carleton Univeristy Press, 1988, p. 148-157.

1126   **Toner, Peter M.**
"Ethnicity and Regionalism in the Maritimes." In: *Ethnicity in Atlantic Canada,* edited by Robert Garland. Saint John, N.B.: Division of Social Science, University of New Brunswick, 1985, p. 1-18.

1127   **Tournon, Jean**
"Le Québec, plaque tournante des ethnies et nations du Canada français." *Études canadiennes/Canadian Studies,* no. 25 (1988) p. 55-65.

1128   **Tremblay, Marc-Adelard**
"L'identité des québécois francophones: perspectives théoretiques et tendances. The Identity of Francophone Quebecers: Theoretical Perspectives and Trends." *Royal Society of Canada. Proceedings and Transactions/Société royale du Canada. Mémoirs et comptes rendus,* Ser. 4 vol. 22 (1984) p. 3-18. Text mostly in English.

1129   **Triandis, Harry C., Richard Brislin, and C. Harry Hui**
"Cross-cultural Training Across the Individualism-collectivism Divide." *International Journal of Intercultural Relations,* vol. 12 no. 3 (1988) p. 269-290.

1130   **Trigger, Bruce Graham**
"Ethnohistory: Problems and Prospects." *Ethnohistory,* vol. 29 no. 1 (1982) p. 1-19.

1131   **Trovato, Frank**
"Immigrant Suicide in Canada: 1971 and 1981." *Social Forces,* vol. 65 no. 2 (1986) p. 433-457.

1132   **Trovato, Frank**
"Suicide and Ethnic Factors in Canada." *International Journal of Social Psychiatry*, vol. 32 no. 3 (1986) p. 55-64

1133   **Trovato, Frank**
"Ethnicity and Migration in Canada." *International Migration Review*, vol. 17 no. 2 (1983) p. 245-267.

1134   **Turner, David H.**
"Canadian Ethnology Today: Solitudes and Shifts." *Anthropology Today*, vol. 1. no. 4 (1985) p. 13-16.

1135   **Tuzlak, Aysan Sev'er**
"Joint Effects of Race and Confidence on Perceptions and Influence: Implications for Blacks in Decision-making Positions." *Canadian Ethnic Studies/Études ethniques au Canada*, vol. 21 no. 3 (1989) p. 103-119.

1136   **Tyhurst, L.**
"Coping with Refugees: A Canadian Experience, 1948-1981." *International Journal of Social Psychiatry*, vol. 28 no. 2 (1982) p. 105-110.

1137   **Ubale, Bhausaheb**
"Administrative Aspects of Race Relations Policies and Programs." In: *Racial Minorities in Multicultural Canada*, edited by Peter S. Li and B. Singh Bolaria. Toronto: Garamond Press, 1982, p. 15-25.

1138   **Ujimoto, Koji Victor**
"Aging Ethnic Minorities and Social Policy: The Role of Information Technology." In: *Canada 2000: Race Relations and Public Policy*, edited by O.P. Dwivedi et al. Guelph, Ontario: Department of Political Studies, University of Guelph, 1989, p. 279-285.

1139   **Ujimoto, Koji Victor**
"Theories of Race Relations: An Overview." In: *Canada 2000: Race Relations and Public Policy*, edited by O.P. Dwivedi et al. Guelph, Ontario: Department of Political Studies, University of Guelph, 1989, p. 76-91.

1140   **Ujimoto, Koji Victor**
"The Ethnic Dimension of Aging in Canada." In: *Aging in Canada: Social Perspectives*, edited by V.W. Marshall. 2nd ed. Toronto: Fitzhenry and Whiteside, 1987, p. 111-137.

1141   **Ujimoto, Koji Victor**
"Institutional Controls and Their Impact on Japanese Canadian Social Relations." In: *Racial Minorities in Multicultural Canada*, edited by Peter S. Li and B. Singh Bolaria. Toronto: Garamond Press, 1982, p. 121-147.

1142   **Ungerleider, Charles S.**
"Intercultural Awareness and Sensitivity of Canadian Police Officers." *Canadian Public Administration/Administration publique au Canada*, vol. 32 no. 4 (1989) p. 612-622.

1143   **Ungerlieder, Charles S.**
"Police Intercultural Education: Promoting Understanding and Empathy Between Police and Ethnic Communities." *Canadian Ethnic Studies/Études ethniques au Canada*, vol. 17 no. 1 (1985) p. 51-66.

1144   **Vachon, R. and J. Langlais, eds.**
Who is a Quebecois? Translated from the French by Frances E. Morgan. Ottawa: Tecumseh Press, 1983. 104 p.

1145   **Vaillancourt, Suzanne**
L'intégration sociale des immigrants par les classes d'accueil.
Unpublished MA thesis, Université de Montréal, 1983. 1 microfiche.

1146   **Vallee, Frank G.**
"Inequality and Identity in Multi-ethnic Societies." In: *Social Issues: Sociological Views of Canada*, edited by Dennis Forcese and Stephen Richer. Scarborough, Ontario: Prentice-Hall Canada, 1982, p. 124-166.

1147   **Vallee, Frank G.**
"The Sociology of John Porter: Ethnicity as Anachronism." *Canadian Review of Sociology and Anthropology/Revue canadienne de sociologie et d'anthropologie*, vol. 18 no. 4 (1981) p. 639-650.

1148   **Van Horne, Winston and Thomas V. Tonnesen, eds.**
Ethnicity and Health. Ethnicity and Public Policy Series, vol. 7. Milwaukee: University of Wisconsin System, Institute on Race and Ethnicity, 1988. 212 p.

1149   **Vaux, Alan**
"Variations in Social Support Associated with Gender, Ethnicity and Age." *Journal of Social Issues*, vol. 41 no. 1 (1985) p. 89-110.

1150   **Verdery, Katherine**
"Ethnicity as Culture: Some Soviet-American Contrasts." *Canadian Review of Studies in Nationalism/Revue canadienne des études sur le nationalisme*, vol. 15 no. 1/2 (1988) p. 107-110.

1151   **Vincent, Sylvie**
"Le racisme: idéologie et pratiques." *Recherches amérindiennes au Québec*, vol. 16 no. 4 (1986) p. 3-16.

1152   **Vipond, Mary**
"Nationalism and Nativism: The Native Sons of Canada in the 1920s." *Canadian Review of Studies in Nationalism/Revue canadienne des études sur le nationalisme*, vol. 9 no. 1 (1982) p. 81.

1153   **Wakil, S. Parvez**
"Between Two Cultures: A Study in Socialization of Children of Immigrants." *Journal of Marriage and the Family*, vol. 43 no. 4 (1981) p. 929-940.

1154   **Waldram, James B.**
"Ethnostatus Distinctions in Western Canadian Subarctic: Implications for Inter-ethnic and Interpersonal Relations." *Culture*, vol. 7 no. 1 (1987) p. 29-37.

1155   **Walker, James W. St. G.**
"Race and Recruitment in World War I: Enlistment of Visible Minorities in the Canadian Expeditionary Force." *Canadian Historical Review*, vol. 70 no. 1 (1989) p. 1-26.

1156   **Walker, James W. St. G.**
"'Race' Policy in Canada: A Retrospective." In: *Canada 2000: Race Relations and Public Policy*, edited by O.P. Dwivedi et al. Guelph, Ontario: Department of Political Studies, University of Guelph, 1989, p. 1-19.

1157   **Walker, James W. St. G.**
Racial Discrimination in Canada: The Black Experience. Ottawa: Canadian Historical Association, 1985. 28 p.

1158   **Wanner, Richard A.**
"The Vertical Mosaic in Later Life: Ethnicity and Retirement in Canada." *Journal of Gerontology*, vol. 41 no. 5 (1986) p. 662-671.

1159   **Ward, Peter W.**
"Class and Race in the Social Structure of British Columbia, 1870-
1939." *B.C. Studies*, vol. 45 (1980) p. 17-35.

1160   **Watson, G.**
"The Re-ification of Ethnicity and its Political Consequences in the
North." *Canadian Review of Sociology and Anthropology/Revue
canadienne de sociologie et d'anthropologie*, vol. 18 no. 4 (1981)
p.453-469.

1161   **Weaver, Sally M.**
"Struggles of the Nation-state to Define Aboriginal Ethnicity; Canada
and Australia." In: *Minorities and Mother Country Imagery*, edited
by Gerald L. Gold. St. John's, Nfld.: Institute of Social and
Economic Research, Memorial University of Newfoundland,
1984, p. 182-210.

1162   **Weimann, Gabriel**
*Hate on Trial: The Zundel Affair, the Media, Public Opinion in
Canada*. Oakville, Ontario: Mosaic Press, 1986. 201 p.

1163   **Weimann, Gabriel**
"'Hate on Trial': Origins and Strategic Implications of a Project."
Review of Anti-semitism in Canada, (1985) p. 37-48.

1164   **Wein, Fred**
"Racial Minorities and Recruitment/Hiring in Nova Scotia." In:
Ethnicity in Atlantic Canada, edited by Robert Garland. Saint John,
N.B.: Division of Social Science, University of New Brunswick,
1985, p. 36-61.

1165   **Weinfeld, Morton**
"Ethnic and Race Relations." In: *Understanding Canadian Society*,
edited by James Curtis and Lorne Tepperman. Toronto: McGraw-Hill
Ryerson, 1988, p. 587-616.

1166   **Weinfeld, Morton**
"Myth and Reality in the Canadian Mosaic: 'Affective Ethnicity'."
In: *Ethnicity and Ethnic Relations in Canada: A Book of Readings*,
edited by Rita M. Bienvenue and Jay E. Goldstein. 2nd ed. Toronto:
Butterworths, 1985, p. 65-86. Reprinted from *Canadian Ethnic
Studies/Études ethniques au Canada*, vol. 13 no. 3 (1981) p. 80-100.

1167   **Weinfeld, Morton**
"Affirmative Action in Quebec: Middle and Upper Management in the Private Sector." In: *Culture, Ethnicity, and Identity: Current Issues in Research*, edited by William C. McCready. New York: Academic Press, 1983, p. 361-380.

1168   **Weinfeld, Morton**
"Intermarriage: Agony and Adaptation." In: *The Canadian Jewish Mosaic*, edited by M. Weinfeld, W. Shaffir and I. Cotler. Toronto: John Wiley and Sons, 1981, p. 365-382.

1169   **Weinfeld, Morton, William Shaffir, and Irwin Cottler, eds.**
The Canadian Jewish Mosaic. Toronto: John Wiley and Sons, 1981. 511 p.

1170   **Whishaw, Iona**
"Cross-cultural Detective Work in Child Care." *Canadian Children*, vol. 10 nos. 1/2 (1985-86) p. 69-71.

1171   **Williams, Colin H.**
"Identity Through Autonomy: Ethnic Separatism in Quebec." In: *Political Studies from Spacial Perspectives: Anglo-American Essays on Political Geography*, edited by Alan D. Burnett and Peter J. Taylor. New York: John Wiley, 1981, p. 389-418.

1172   **Williams, Colin H.**
"The Desire of Nations: Quebecois Ethnic Separatism in Comparative Perspective." *Cahiers de géographie du Québec*, vol. 24 no. 61 (1980) p. 47-68.

1173   **Williams, Colin H.**
"Ethnic Separatism." *Cahiers de géographie du Québec*, vol. 24 no. 61 (1980) p. 47-68.

1174   **Williams, Margaret Jeanne Meyers**
Ethnicity and Class Conflict at Maillardville/Fraser Mills: The Strike of 1931. Unpublished MA thesis, Simon Fraser University, 1983. 2 microfiches. Canadian theses on microfiche, 62357.

1175   **Winn, Conrad**
"Affirmative Action and Visible Minorities; Eight Premises in Quest of Evidence." *Canadian Public Policy/Analyse de politiques*, vol. 11 no. 4 (1985) p. 684-700.

1176   **Wolfgang, Aaron and Michelle Cohen**
"Sensitivity of Canadians, Latin Americans, Ethiopians and Israelis to Interracial Facial Expression of Emotions." *International Journal of Intercultural Relations*, vol. 12 no. 2 (1988) p. 139-152.

1177   **Wong, Paul T.P., Valerian J. Derlega, and William Colson**
"The Effects of Race on Expectancies and Performance." *Canadian Journal of Behavioural Science/Revue canadienne des sciences de comportement*, vol. 20 no.1 (1988) p. 29-39.

1178   **Woo, Wendy Ellen**
Reactions to Racial Victimization: An Attribution Perspective. Unpublished MA thesis, University of Guelph, 1983. 2 microfiches. Canadian theses on microfiche, no. 63364.

1179   **Woon, Yuen-Fong**
"Ethnic Identity and Ethnic Boundaries: The Sino-Vietnamese in Victoria, British Columbia." *Canadian Review of Sociology and Anthropology/Revue canadienne de sociologie et d'anthropologie*, vol. 22 no. 4 (1985) p. 534-558.

1180   **Worrall, Persis H.**
Henri Tajfel's Approach to Intergroup Behaviour: Quebec Ethnicity in the 1960s. Unpublished MA thesis, McGill University, 1982. 2 microfiches. Canadian theses on microfiche, no. 61111.

1181   **Wright Jr., Roosevelt and Thomas D. Watts, eds.**
"Alcohol Problems and Minority Youth." *Journal of Drug Issues*, vol. 18 no. 1 (1988) p. 1-137.

1182   **Yasmin, Marziya**
Ethnicity and Socioeconomic Status in Canada, 1981. Unpublished PhD thesis, University of Alberta, 1989.

1183   **Yedlin, T., ed.**
Central and East European Ethnicity in Canada: Adaptation and Preservation. Edmonton: Central and East European Studies Society of Alberta, 1985. 177 p.

1184   **Yelaja, Shankar A., ed.**
Canadian Social Policy. Waterloo, Ontario: Wilfrid Laurier University Press, 1987. 428 p.

1185   **Yinger, J. Milton**
"Ethnicity and Social Change: The Interaction of Structural, Cultural, and Personality Factors." *Ethnic and Racial Studies*, vol. 6 no. 4 (1983) p. 395-409.

1186   **Young, Jon, ed.**
Breaking the Mosaic: Ethnic Identities in Canadian Schooling. Toronto: Garamond Press, 1984. 302 p. Papers presented at a working symposium titled: Race, Ethnicity, and Education: Critical Perspectives, held at the Ontario Institute for Studies in Education, in October 1984.

1187   **Zaffaroni, Irene Genevieve Marie**
The Great Chain of Being: Racism and Imperialism in Colonial Victoria, 1858-1871. Unpublished MA thesis, University of Victoria, 1987. 207 p. Canadian theses on microfiche, CT89-25627-6.

1188   **Ziegler, Suzanne**
"Measuring Inter-ethnic Attitudes in a Multi-ethnic Context." *Canadian Ethnic Studies/Études ethniques au Canada*, vol. 12 no. 3 (1980) p. 45-55.

1189   **Zielyk, I.V.**
"The Study of Ethnicity in American Sociology." *Ethnic Forum*, vol. 6 no. 1/2 (1986) p. 3-16.

Economic Conditions

1190 **Akbari, Syed Ather Hussain**
Some Economic Impacts of the Immigrant Population in Canada.
Unpublished PhD thesis, Simon Fraser University, 1988.

1191 **Armstrong, Robin**
"Factors of Indian Economic Development On-reserve: An Initial
Analysis." In: *Native Socio-economic Development in Canada:
Adaptation, Accessibility and Opportunity*, edited by Paul Kariya.
Winnipeg: Institute of Urban Studies, University of Winnipeg,
1989, p. 5-18.

1192 **Asch, Michael**
"Capital and Economic Development: A Critical Appraisal of the
Recommendations of the Mackenzie Valley Pipeline Commission."
In: *Native People, Native Lands: Canadian Indians, Inuit and Metis*,
edited by Bruce Alden Cox. Ottawa: Carleton Univeristy Press,
1988, p. 232-240.

1193 **Bartlett, Richard H.**
"Provincial Jurisdiction and Resource Development on Indian
Reserve Lands." In: *Managing Natural Resources in a Federal State*,
edited by J. Owen Saunders. Toronto: Carswell, 1986, p. 189-211.
Paper presented at the second Banff Conference on Natural
Resources Law, Banff, Alberta, April 17-20, 1985.

1194 **Bartlett, Richard H.**
Indians and Taxation in Canada. Saskatoon: Native Law Centre,
University of Saskatchewan, 1980. 65 p.

1195   **Bélanger, Yves**
L'entreprise québécoise: développement historique et dynamique contemporaine. Montréal: Hurtubise HMH, 1987. 187 p.

1196   **Bonacich, Edna**
"The Social Costs of Immigrant Entrepreneurship." *Amerasia Journal*, vol. 14 no. 1 (1988) p. 119-128.

1197   **Bouchard, Russel**
Le Saguenay des fourrures, 1534-1859: histoire d'un monopole. Chicoutimi-Nord, Québec: R. Bouchard, 1989. 269 p.

1198   **Brettel, Caroline B.**
"Ethnicity and Entrepreneurs: Portuguese Immigrants in a Canadian City." In: *People, Power, and Process: A Reader*, edited by Alexander Himelfarb and C. James Richardson. Toronto: McGraw-Hill Ryerson, 1980, p. 300-308.

1199   **Burrows, James K.**
"'A Much-needed Class of Labour': The Economy and Income of the Southern Interior Plateau Indians, 1897-1910." *B.C. Studies*, no. 71 (1986) p. 27-46.

1200   **Canadian Conference of the Arts**
"Free Trade and Culture: Who Cares?" *Arts Bulletin*, vol. 11 no. 1 (1986) p. 1-25. French language title: "Le libre-échange et la culture: qui s'en fiche?"

1201   **Chan, Kwok B.**
"Unemployment, Social Support and Coping: The Psychological Response of Indochinese Refugees to Economic Marginality." In: *Uprooting, Loss and Adaptation: The Resettlement of Indochinese Refugees in Canada*, edited by Kwok B. Chan and Doreen Marie Indra. Ottawa: Canadian Public Health Association, 1987, p. 116-131.

1202   **Clement Wallace**
"The Canadian Corporate Elite: Ethnicity and Inequality of Access." In: *Ethnicity and Ethnic Relations in Canada: A Book of Readings*, edited by Rita M. Bienvenue and Jay E. Goldstein. 2nd ed. Toronto: Butterworths, 1985, p. 143-151.

1203   **Clodman, Joel**
Immigration and Unemployment. Downsview, Ont.: York University, Institute for Behavioural Research, 1982. 146, 15 leaves.

1204   **Cosper, Ronald L.**
Ethnicity and Occupation in Atlantic Canada: The Social and Economic Implications of Cultural Diversity. Halifax, N.S.: International Education Centre, Saint Mary's University, 1984. 47 p.

1205   **Cox, Bruce Alden**
"Changing Perceptions of Industrial Development in the North." In: *Native People, Native Lands: Canadian Indians, Inuit and Metis,* edited by Bruce Alden Cox. Ottawa: Carleton University Press, 1988, p. 223-231.

1206   **Cox, Bruce Alden**
"Prospects for the Northern Native Economy." In: *Native People, Native Lands: Canadian Indians, Inuit and Metis,* edited by Bruce Alden Cox. Ottawa: Carleton University Press, 1988, p. 256-264.

1207   **Cunningham, Alain**
Socio-economic Impact Assessment, Development Theory, and Northern Native Communities. Vancouver: University of British Columbia, School of Community and Regional Planning, 1984. 18 p.

1208   **Davidson, Malcolm**
"Indian Economic Development in 'The Indian News', 1954-1982." *Canadian Journal of Native Studies,* vol. 3 no. 2 (1983) p. 321-340.

1209   **Duhaine, Gérard**
Ni chien, ni loup: l'économie, l'État et les inuits du Québec arctique. Unpublished PhD thesis, Université Laval, 1988. 7 microfiches. Canadian theses on microfiche, CT89-26081-8.

1210   **Fenwick, Rudy**
"Ethnic Culture and Economic Structure: Determinants of French-English Earnings Inequality in Quebec." *Social Forces,* vol. 61 no. 1 (1982) p. 1-23.

1211   **Gagnon, Alain G.**
"Towards Maitres Chez-nous: The Ascendancy of a Balzacian Bourgeoisie in Quebec." *Queen's Quarterly,* vol. 93 no. 4 (1986) p. 731-747.

1212   **Gauthier, Bernard**
Évaluation des impacts socio-économiques des politiques gouvernementales sur les inuits du Nouveau-Québec. Montréal, Unpublished MSc thesis, Université de Montréal, 1986. 1 microfilm.

1213   **Ghosh, Jayati**
An Analysis of the Spatial and Economic Variations of Ethnic
Groups, Ontario. Unpublished MA thesis, Wilfred Laurier University,
1986. 3 microfiches. Canadian theses on microfiche, CT88-22992-6.

1214   **Goldring, Philip**
"Inuit Economic Responses to Euro-American Contacts: South-east
Baffin Island, 1824-1940." In: Interpreting Canada's North: Selected
Readings, edited by Kenneth S. Coates and William R. Morrison.
Toronto: Copp Clark Pitman Ltd., 1989, p. 252-277.

1215   **Grenier, Gilles**
"Une analyse microéconomique des déterminants des transferts
linguistiques des minorités hors Québec en 1971." Actualité
économique, vol. 60 no. 2 (1984) p. 149-163.

1216   **Grove, D. John**
"Who Benefits from Ethnic Income Redistribution?" Social Science
Research, vol. 18 no. 1 (1989) p. 70-81.

1217   **Guimond, Serge**
"La représentation des causes de l'infériorité économique des
québécois francophones." Canadian Journal of Behavioural Science/
Revue canadienne des sciences de comportement, vol. 21 no. 1
(1989) p. 28-39.

1218   **Hall, John L.**
"Ethnic Tensions and Economics: Indian-white Interaction in a
British Columbia Community." Canadian Journal of Anthropology/
Revue canadienne d'anthropologie, vol. 1 no. 2 (1980) p. 179-190.

1219   **Hecht, Alfred**
"The Socio-economic Core-periphery Structures in Canada; A Present
Analysis." Zeitschrift der Gesellschaft für Kanada-Studien, vol. 8 no.
1 (1988) p. 23-52.

1220   **House, J.D.**
"Towards Sustainable Native Communities: Lessons from Newfound-
land Outports." In: Native Socio-economic Development in Canada:
Change, Promise and Innovation, edited by Paul Kariya. Winnipeg:
Institute of Urban Studies, 1989, p. 47-60.

1221   **Institute for Behavioural Research, York University**
Ethnogenerational Factors in Socio-economic Achievement in Toronto: The Second Generation During the 1970's. Downsview, Ont.: Institute for Behavioural Research, York University, 1984. 50 leaves.

1222   **Jain, Harish C.**
"The Impact of Recession on Equal Opportunities for Minorities and Women in the United States, Canada and Britain." *Columbia Journal of World Business*, vol. 18 no. 2 (1983) p. 16-27.

1223   **Januario, Ilda**
Les activités économiques des immigrants portugais au Portugal et à Montréal à travers les récits de vie. Unpublished MSc thesis, Université de Montréal, 1988. 1 microfilm.

1224   **Kanary, Joseph Michael**
A Formula for Native Economic Self-reliance: The Native Economic Development Program. Unpublished MA thesis, Dalhousie University, 1986. 2 microfiches. Canadian theses on microfiche, CT87-25498-7.

1225   **Kariya, Paul, ed.**
Native Socio-economic Development in Canada: Adaptation, Accessibility and Opportunity. Native issues, no. 1. Winnipeg: Institute of Urban Studies, University of Winnipeg, 1989. 55 p.

1226   **Krech, Shepard, ed.**
The Subarctic Fur Trade: Native Social and Economic Adaptations. Vancouver: University of British Columbia Press, 1984. 194 p.

1227   **Li, Peter S.**
"The Economic Cost of Racism to Chinese-Canadians." *Canadian Ethnic Studies/Études ethniques au Canada*, vol. 19 no. 3 (1987) p. 102-113.

1228   **Li Puma, Edward**
"Capitalism and the Crimes of Mythology: An Interpretation of the Mafia Mystique." *The Journal of Ethnic Studies*, vol. 17 no. 2 (1989) p. 1-22.

1229   **Mackie, Cam**
"Some Reflections on Indian Economic Development." In: *Arduous Journey: Canadian Indians and Decolonization*, edited by J. Rick Ponting. Toronto: McClelland and Stewart, 1986, p. 211-226.

1230   **Marr, William L.**
"Immigration Policy and Canadian Economic Growth." In: *Domestic Policies in the International Economic Environment*, John Whalley and Roderick Hill, research coordinators. Toronto: University of Toronto Press, 1985, p. 57-109.

1231   **Marr, William L.**
"Sons of Immigrants' Earnings: Canada and the United States." *Canadian Studies in Population*, vol. 8 no. 1 (1981) p. 49-55.

1232   **McArthur, Douglas**
"The New Aboriginal Economic Development Institutions." In: *Native Socio-economic Development in Canada: Change, Promise and Innovation*, edited by Paul Kariya. Winnipeg: Institute of Urban Studies, 1989, p. 33-46.

1233   **Meng, Ronald**
"The Earnings of Canadian Immigrant and Native-born Males." *Applied Economics*, vol. 19 no. 8 (1987) p. 1107-1120.

1234   **Morazain, Jeanne**
"Culture et marketing: un marriage possible?" *Le Devoir économique*, vol. 4 no. 1 (1988) p. 20, 23, 27.

1235   **Nash, Alan E.**
"Our Enterprising Immigrants." *Policy Options/Options politiques*, vol. 9 no. 10 (1988) p. 19-23.

1236   **Nash, Alan E.**
The Economic Impact of the Entrepreneur Immigrant Program. Ottawa: Institute for Research on Public Policy, 1987. 56, [37] p.

1237   **Osberg, Lars and Fazley Siddiq**
"The Inequality of Wealth in Britain's North American Colonies: The Importance of the Relatively Poor." *The Review of Income and Wealth*, vol. 34 no. 2 (1988) p. 143-163.

1238   **Overbeek, Johannes**
"The Economic Dilemma of Canadian Immigration: 1970-1980." *American Review of Canadian Studies*, vol. 13 no. 1 (1983) p. 108-118.

1239   **Passaris, Constantine E.**
"The Economic Determinants of Canada's Multicultural Immigration." *International Migration/Migrations Internationales/ Migraciones Internacionales*, vol. 22 no. 2 (1984) p. 90-100.

1240   **Ponting, J. Rick**
"Economic Development Provisions of the New Claims Settlements." In: *Arduous Journey: Canadian Indians and Decolonization*, edited by J. Rick Ponting. Toronto: McClelland and Stewart, 1986, p. 194-210.

1241   **Prasad, Kamal Kant**
Canada and the Changing Economy of the Pacific Basin: The Historical Development of East Indian Economic Activities in British Columbia, 1900-1940. Vancouver: Institute of Asian Research, University of British Columbia, 1983. 52 p.

1242   **Rhyme, Darla**
Visible Minority Business in Metropolitan Toronto: An Exploratory Analysis. Toronto: Ministry of Labour, Ontario Human Rights Commission, Race Relations Division, 1982. 134 p.

1243   **Richardson, Miles**
"The Fisheries Co-management Initiative in Haida Gwaii." In: *Co-operative Management of Local Fisheries*, edited by E. Pinkerton. Vancouver: University of British Columbia Press, 1989, p. 249-261.

1244   **Richmond, Anthony H.**
"Canadian Unemployment and the Threat to Multiculturalism." *Journal of Canadian Studies/Revue d'études canadiennes*, vol. 17 no. 1 (1982) p. 64-80.

1245   **Richmond, Anthony H.**
Comparative Studies in the Economic Adaptation of Immigrants in Canada: A Literature Review. Downsview, Ont.: York University, Institute for Behavioural Research, 1982. 226 p.

1246   **Richtik, James M.**
"Competition for Settlers: The Canadian Viewpoint." *Great Plains Quarterly*, vol. 3 no. 1 (1983) p. 39-49.

1247   **Ridler, Neil B.**
"An Economic Analysis of Canadian Language Policies: A Model and Its Implementation." *Language Problems and Language Planning*, vol. 10 no. 1 (1986) p. 42-58.

1248   **Rosenbluth, David**
        *Economic Inequality in Canada: The Effects of Region, Ethnicity and
        Gender on Earnings.* Unpublished PhD thesis, York University, 1985.
        Canadian theses on microfiche, 66194.

1249   **Rugman, Alan M.**
        "United States Protectionism and Canadian Trade Policy." *Journal of
        World Trade Law*, vol. 20 no. 4 (1986) p. 363-380.

1250   **Samuel, T. John**
        "Economic Adaptation of Indochinese Refugees in Canada." In:
        *Uprooting, Loss and Adaptation: The Resettlement of Indochinese
        Refugees in Canada*, edited by Kwok B. Chan and Doreen Marie
        Indra. Ottawa: Canadian Public Health Association, 1987, p. 65-76.

1251   **Samuel, T. John**
        "Economic Adaptation of Refugees in Canada: Experience of a
        Quarter Century." *International Migration/Migrations Internationales/
        Migraciones Internacionales*, vol. 22 no. 1 (1984) p. 45-55.

1252   **Sawchuk, Joseph Samuel**
        "Development or Domination: The Metis and Government Funding."
        In: *The Other Natives: The Metis*, edited by Antoine S. Lussier and
        D. Bruce Sealey. Winnipeg: Manitoba Metis Federation Press, 1980,
        vol. 3, p. 73-94.

1253   **Seward, Shirley B.**
        "Demographic Change, the Canadian Economy and the Role of
        Immigration." In: *The Future of Social Welfare Systems in Canada
        and the United Kingdom: Proceedings of a Canada/UK Colloqium,
        October 17-18, 1986, Ottawa/Meech Lake*, edited by Shirley B.
        Seward. Halifax, N.S.: Institute for Research on Public Policy,
        1987, p. 231-246.

1254   **Tepper, Elliot L.**
        *Self-employment in Canada Among Immigrants of Different
        Ethnocultural Backgrounds.* Ottawa: Research Division, Policy and
        Program Development Branch, Canadian Employment and
        Immigration Commission, 1988. 157 p.

1255   **Tough, Frank J.**
        *Native People and the Regional Economy of Northern Manitoba,
        1870-1930.* Unpublished PhD thesis, York University, 1987.

1256   **Verma, Ravi B.P.**
"Employment Income of Immigrants in Metropolitan Areas of Canada, 1980." *International Migration/Migrations Internationales/ Migraciones Internacionales*, vol. 27 no. 3 (1989) p. 441-453.

1257   **Verma, Ravi B.P.**
"Incomes of Asian Indians in Canada." *Population Review*, vol. 29 nos. 1/2 (1985) p. 125-135.

1258   **Weick, Edward R.**
"Northern Native People and the Larger Canadian Society: Emerging Economic Relations." *American Review of Canadian Studies*, vol. 18 no. 3 (1988) p. 317-329.

1259   **Wenzel, George W.**
"Sealing at Clyde River, NWT: A Discussion of Inuit Economy." *Études Inuit Studies*, vol. 13 no. 1 (1989) p. 3-22.

1260   **Wenzel, George W.**
"Marooned in a Blizzard of Contradictions: Inuit and the Antisealing Movement." *Études Inuit Studies*, vol. 9 no. 1 (1985) p. 77-91.

1261   **Wien, Frederic Carl**
Rebuilding the Economic Base of Indian Communities: The Micmac in Nova Scotia. Montreal: Institute for Research on Public Policy, 1986. 200 p.

1262   **Winn, Conrad**
"The Socio-economic Attainment of Visible Minorities: Facts and Policy Implications." In: *Social Inequality in Canada: Patterns, Problems, Policies*, edited by James E. Curtis, Edward Grabb, L. Neil Guppy, and Sid Gilbert. Scarborough, Ont.: Prentice-Hall Canada, 1988, p. 195-213. A revision of the author's "Affirmative Action and Visible Minorities: Eight Premises in Quest of Evidence." *Canadian Public Policy/Analyse de politiques*, vol. 11 no. 4 (1985) p. 684-700.

1263   **Wolfe, Jackie**
"Supporting Native Canadian Micro-enterprises: A Southern Ontario Case Study." In: *Native Socio-economic Development in Canada: Change, Promise and Innovation*, edited by Paul Kariya. Winnipeg: Institute of Urban Studies, 1989, p. 19-32.

Labour

1264   **Akenson, Donald H.**
        "An Agnostic View of the Historiography of the Irish-Americans."
        Labour/Le Travail, no. 14 (1984) p. 123-159.

1265   **Association haïtienne des travailleurs du taxi (A.H.T.T.)**
        La situation des travailleurs noirs dans l'industrie du taxi. Montréal:
        Association haïtienne des travailleurs du taxi, 1983. 35 p.

1266   **Association haïtienne des travailleurs du taxi (A.H.T.T.)**
        *Enquête sur les travailleurs haïtiens de l'industrie de taxi à
        Montréal.* Montréal: Association haïtienne des travailleurs du taxi,
        1982. 25 p.

1267   **Avery, Donald**
        "The Radical Alien and the Winnipeg General Strike of 1919." In:
        Interpreting Canada's Past, edited by J.M. Bumsted. 2 volumes.
        Toronto: Oxford University Press, 1986, vol. 2, p. 222-239.

1268   **Bauer, Jozef**
        "The Youngest Soldier." *Polyphony: The Bulletin of the Multicultural
        History Society of Ontario*, vol. 6 no. 2 (1984) p. 124-127.

1269   **Baureiss, Gunter**
        "Chinese Immigration, Chinese Stereotypes, and Chinese Labour."
        Canadian Ethnic Studies/Études ethniques au Canada, vol. 19 no. 3
        (1987) p. 15-34.

1270   **Beasley, Thomas F.**
        "The 1909 Freight Handlers Strike: Col. Sam Steele Searches Strikers
        for Guns." *Papers and Records: Thunder Bay Historical Museum
        Society*, vol. 17 (1989) p. 18-24.

1271   **Berson, Seemah Cathline**
The Immigrant Experience: Personal Recollections of Jewish Garment Workers in Canada, 1900-1930. Unpublished MA thesis, University of British Columbia, 1980. 254 leaves. Canadian theses on microfiche, 49898.

1272   **Bischoff, Peter**
"La formation des traditions de solidarité ouvrière chez les mouleurs montréalais: Le longue marche vers le syndicalisme (1859-1881)" *Labour/Le Travail*, no. 21 (1986) p. 9-43.

1273   **Blais, Andre**
"Can a Party Punish Its Faithful Supporters? The Parti Quebecois and Public Sector Employees." *Canadian Public Administration\Administration publique au Canada*, vol. 32 no. 4 (1989) p. 623-632.

1274   **Bolaria, B. Singh**
"Migrant Workers in the Canadian Labour Force." In: *Labour Force/ La population active*, edited by K. Victor Ujimoto and Gordon Hirabayashi. [Guelph, Ont.: University of Guelph, 1989] p. 98-115. Paper presented at the 5th Asian Canadian Symposium held at Mount Saint Vincent University, Halifax, Nova Scotia, May 23 to May 26, 1981.

1275   **Bolaria, B. Singh**
"The Health Effects of Powerlessness: The Case of Immigrant Farm Labour." In: *The Political Economy of Agriculture in Western Canada*, edited by G.S. Bahrain and D.A. Hay. Toronto: Garamond Press, 1988, p. 109-124.

1276   **Bolaria, B. Singh**
"Racial Problems and Foreign Labour." In: *Racial Oppression in Canada*, edited by B. Singh Bolaria and Peter S. Li. Toronto: Garamond Press, 1985, p. 183-198.

1277   **Bolaria, B. Singh**
"Migrants, Immigrants, and the Canadian Labour Force." In: *Labour Force/La population active*, edited by John A. Fry. Toronto: John Wiley, 1983, p. 130-139.

1278   **Bowen, Lynne**
Boss Whistle: The Coal Miners of Vancouver Island Remember. Lantzville, B.C.: Oolichan Books, 1982. 280 p.

1279   **Boyd, Monica, Chris Taylor, and Paul Delaney**
"Temporary Workers in Canada: A Multifaceted Program."
International Migration Review, vol. 20 no. 4 (1986) p. 929-950.

1280   **Burrows, James K.**
"'A Much-needed Class of Labour': The Economy and Income of the
Southern Interior Plateau Indians, 1897-1910." *B.C. Studies*, no. 71
(Fall 1986) p. 27-46.

1281   **Busch, Briton Cooper**
"The Newfoundland Sealers' Strike of 1902." *Labour/Le Travail*, no.
14 (Fall 1984) p. 73-102.

1282   **Calliste, Agnes M.**
"Blacks on Canadian Railways." *Canadian Ethnic Studies/Études
ethniques au Canada*, vol. 20 no. 2 (1988) p. 36-53.

1283   **Calliste, Agnes M.**
"Sleeping Car Porters in Canada: An Ethnically Submerged Labour
Market." *Canadian Ethnic Studies/Études ethniques au Canada*, vol.
19 no. 1 (1987) p. 1-20.

1284   **Calliste, Agnes M.**
*Educational and Occupational Expectations of High School Students:
The Effects of Socioeconomic Background, Ethnicity and Sex.*
Unpublished PhD thesis, University of Toronto, 1980. 4 microfiches.
Canadian theses on microfiche, 47020.

1285   **Cambie Consulting Group**
The Vancouver Urban Indian Needs Assessment Study. 1 volume.
Victoria, B.C.: Alcohol and Drug Program, Ministry of Labour and
Consumer Services, 1989.

1286   **Canada. Task Force on Program Review**
*Citizenship, Labour and Immigration: A Plethora of 'People'
Programs: A Study Team Report...* Ottawa: The Task Force, 1985.
261 p. French language title: *Citoyenneté, travail et immigration.*
Chairman: Erik Nielsen. Team leader: Duncan R. Campbell.

1287   **Capling, M. Ann**
"Drumheller Strike of 1925." *Alberta History*, vol. 31 no. 4
(1983) p. 11-19.

1288 **Carraro, Joseph**
"Unions and the Italian Community." *Polyphony: The Bulletin of the Multicultural History Society of Ontario*, vol. 7 no. 2 (1985) p. 105-106.

1289 **Cass, James**
Oyai. The Salmon Fisherman and the Woodworker: Indians of the North Pacific Coast. Toronto: D.C. Heath Canada Ltd. and The Royal Ontario Museum, 1983.

1290 **Centre for Resource Studies**
Native Participation in Mineral Development Activities. Kingston, Ont.: Centre for Resource Studies, Queen's University, 1984. 99 p.

1291 **Chan, Anthony B.**
"Chinese Bachelor Workers in Nineteenth Century Canada." *Ethnic and Racial Studies*, vol. 5 no. 4 (1982) p. 513-534.

1292 **Chimbos, Peter D.**
"Occupational Distribution and Social Mobility of Greek-Canadian Immigrants." *Journal of the Hellenic Diaspora*, vol. 14 no. 1/2 (1987) p. 131-143.

1293 **Chiu, Siu Miu Luda**
The English Language Needs of Chinese Immigrant Workers: A Case Study. Unpublished MA thesis, University of Toronto, 1980.

1294 **Conley, James R.**
"Frontier Labour, Crafts in Crisis and the Western Labour Revolt: The Case of Vancouver, 1900-1919." *Labour/Le Travail*, no. 23 (1989) p. 9-38.

1295 **Cosper, Ronald**
Ethnicity and Occupation in Atlantic Canada: The Social and Economic Implications of Cultural Diversity. Halifax, N.S.: International Education Centre, Saint Mary's University, 1984. 47 p.

1296 **Creese, Gillian Laura**
"Class, Ethnicity and Conflict: The Case of Chinese and Japanese Immigrants, 1880-1923." In: *Workers, Capital, and the State in British Columbia*, edited by Rennie Warburton and David Coburn. Vancouver: University of British Columbia Press, 1988, p. 55-85.

1297 **Creese, Gillian Laura**
"Organizing Against Racism in the Workplace: Chinese Workers in Vancouver Before the Second World War." *Canadian Ethnic Studies/ Études ethniques au Canada*, vol. 19 no. 3 (1987) p. 35-46.

1298 **Cruikshank, Douglas and Gregory S. Kealey**
"Strikes in Canada, 1891-1950: I. Analysis, II. Methods and Sources, III. The Data." *Labour/Le Travail* no. 20 (1987) p. 85-122, p. 123-132, p. 133-145.

1299 **Cruise, David and Alison Griffiths**
Lords of the Line: The Men Who Built the CPR [Canadian Pacific Railway]. Markham: Viking-Penguin Books, 1988. 486 p.

1300 **D'Costa, Ronald**
"The Occupational Composition of Asian Indians in Canada." *Population Review*, vol. 29 no. 1/2 (1985) p. 113-124.

1301 **Dacks, Gurston**
"Worker-controlled Native Enterprises: A Vehicle for Community Development in Northern Canada?" *Canadian Journal of Native Studies*, vol. 3 no. 2 (1983) p. 289-310.

1302 **De Lottinville, Peter**
"Life in an Age of Restraint: Recent Developments in Labour Union Archives in English Canada." *Archivaria*, no. 27 (1988-89) p. 8-24.

1303 **De Lottinville, Peter**
"Joe Beef of Montreal: Working Class Culture and the Tavern, 1869-1889." *Labour/Le Travailleur*, no. 8/9 (1981-82) p. 9-40.

1304 **Del Negro, Luciano**
Canada's Immigration Policy, Immigration Legislation, and Immigrant Labour in the 1970's. Unpublished MA thesis, Université du Québec, 1984. 324 leaves. 6 microfiches. Canadian theses on microfiche, 2809525.

1305 **Donegan, Rosemary**
"The Iconography of Labour: An Overview of Canadian Materials." *Archivaria*, no. 27 (1988-89) p. 35-56.

1306 **Dutton, Alan**
"Ethnicity and Class in the Farm Labour Process." In: *Workers, Capital, and the State in British Columbia*, edited by Rennie Warburton and David Coburn. Vancouver: University of British Columbia Press, 1988, p. 161-176.

1307   **Earle, Michael J.**
"The Coalminers and Their 'Red' Union: The Amalgmated Mine Workers of Nova Scotia." *Labour/Le Travail*, no. 22 (1988) p. 99-138.

1308   **Earle, Michael J., ed.**
Workers and the State in Twentieth Century Nova Scotia. Fredericton: Gorsebrook Research Institute of Atlantic Canada Studies by Acadiensis Press, 1989. 265 p.

1309   **Earle, Michael J. and H. Gamberg**
"The United Mine Workers and the Coming of the CCF [Cooperative Commonwealth Federation] to Cape Breton." *Acadiensis*, vol. 19 no. 1 (1989) p. 3-26.

1310   **Eversole, Linda**
"John Robert Giscombe: Jamaican Miner and Explorer." *British Columbia Historical News*, vol. 18 no. 3 (1985) p. 11-15.

1311   **Ferlzind, Jacques**
"Syndicalisme 'parcellaire' et syndicalisms 'collectif': Une interprétation socio-technique des conflits ouvriers dans deux industries québécoises, 1880-1914." *Labour/Le Travail*, no. 19 (1987) p. 49-88.

1312   **Finkel, Alvin**
"The Cold War, Alberta Labour, and the Social Credit Regime." *Labour/Le Travail*, no. 21 (1988) p. 123-152

1313   **Finkel, Alvin**
"Alberta Social Credit Reappraised: The Radical Character of the Early Social Credit Movement." *Prairie Forum*, vol. 2 no. 1 (1986) p. 69-86.

1314   **Finkel, Alvin**
"Social Credit and the Cities." *Alberta History*, vol. 34 no. 3 (Summer 1986) p. 20-26.

1315   **Finkel, Alvin**
"The Rise and Fall of the Labour Party in Alberta, 1917-42." *Labour/ Le Travail*, no. 16 (1985) p. 61-96.

1316   **Frager, Ruth A.**
"The Undermining of Unity within the Jewish Labour Movement of Toronto, 1928-35." *Polyphony: The Bulletin of the Multicultural History Society of Ontario*, vol. 9 no. 1 (1987) p. 47-50.

1317   **Ganzevoort, Herman**
"Sharks in Wooden Shoes." In: *Dutch Immigration to North America*, edited by Herman Ganzevoort and Mark Boekelman. Toronto: Multicultural History Society of Ontario, 1983, p. 147-166.

1318   **Gobel, Thomas**
"Becoming American: Ethnic Workers and the Rise of the CIO [Congress of Industrial Organizations]" *Labor History*, vol. 29 no. 2 (1988) p. 173-198.

1319   **Hak, Gordon**
"British Columbia Loggers and the Lumber Workers Industrial Union, 1919-1922." *Labour/Le Travail,* no. 23 (1989) p. 67-90.

1320   **Hak, Gordon**
"Red Wages: Communists and the 1934 Vancouver Island Loggers' Strike." *Pacific Northwest Quarterly*, vol. 80 no. 3 (1989) p. 82-90.

1321   **Hannant, Larry**
"The Calgary Working Class and the Social Credit Movement in Alberta, 1932-35." *Labour/Le Travail*, vol. 16 (1985) p. 97-116.

1322   **Harney, Robert F.**
"Chiaroscuro: Italians in Toronto, 1885-1915." *Polyphony: The Bulletin of the Multicultural History Society of Ontario*, vol. 6 no. 1 (1984) p. 44-49.

1323   **Harney, Robert F.**
"The Padrone System and Sojourners in the Canadian North, 1885-1920." In: *Pane e Lavoro: The Italian American Working Class*, edited by George E. Pozzetta. Toronto: Multicultural History Society of Ontario, 1980, p. 119-137.

1324   **Hartmann, Norbert and Wsevolod W. Isajiw**
"Ethnicity and Occupation: An Assessment of the Occupational Structure of Ukrainian-Canadians in the 1960s." *Canadian Ethnic Studies/Études ethniques au Canada*, vol. 12 no. 2 (1980) 55-73.

1325   **B.H. [Benedykt Heydenkorn]**
"Changes in Structure." *Polyphony: The Bulletin of the Multicultural History Society of Ontario*, vol. 6 no. 2 (1984) p. 80-81.

1326   **Hobart, Charles W.**
"Native Trainees and White Co-workers: A Study of Prejudice in an Individual Setting". *Canadian Journal of Native Studies*, vol. 4 no. 1 (1984) p. 67-83.

1327   **Hobart, Charles W.**
"Industrial Employment of Rural Indigenes: The Case of Canada." *Human Organization*, vol. 41 (1982) p. 54-63.

1328   **Hoffman, George**
"The New Party and the Old Issues: The Saskatchewan Farmer-Labour Party and the Ethnic Vote, 1934." *Canadian Ethnic Studies/ Études ethniques au Canada*, vol. 14 no. 2 (1982) p. 1-20.

1329   **Hopkin, Deian R. and Gregory S. Kealey, eds.**
Class, Community and Labour Movement: Wales and Canada, 1850-1930. St. John's, Nfld.: LLAFUR/CCLH, 1989. 275 p.

1330   **Hujanen, Taisto**
"The Role of Information in the Realization of the Human Rights of Migrant Workers." *International Migration Review*, vol. 23 no. 1 (1989) p. 105-119.

1331   **Hune, Shirley**
"Drafting an International Convention on the Protection of the Rights of All Migrant Workers and Their Families." *International Migration Review*, vol. 19 no. 3 (1985) p. 570-615.

1332   **Industrial Relations Research Association**
Race and Sex Equality in the Workplace: A Challenge and an Opportunity. Ottawa: Women's Bureau, Labour Canada, 1980. 236 p. Proceedings of a conference sponsored by Industrial Relations Research Association, Hamilton, and the District Chapter Faculty of Business, McMaster University, Hamilton, Ontario, September 28-29, 1979.

1333   **Isajiw, Wsevolod W.**
"Participation of Ukrainians in Business Occupations in Canada." In: *Changing Realities: Social Friends Among Ukrainian Canadians*, edited by W.R. Petryshyn. Edmonton: Canadian Institute of Ukrainian Studies, 1980, p. 97-103.

1334   **Jenkins, Richard**
"Acceptability, Suitability and the Search for the Habituated Worker:
How Ethnic Minorities and Women Lose Out." *Employers and
Recruitment: Explorations in Labor Demand*, vol. 11 no. 7
(1984) p. 64-76.

1335   **Jhappan, Carol Radha**
*Resistance to Exploitation: East Indians and the Rise of the Canadian
Farmworker's Union in B.C. Vancouver.* Unpublished MA thesis,
University of British Columbia, 1983. 129 leaves.

1336   **Judd, Carol M.**
"Native Labour and Social Stratification in the Hudson's Bay
Company's Northern Department 1770-1870." *Canadian Review of
Sociology and Anthropology/Revue canadienne de sociologie et
d'anthropologie*, vol. 17 no. 4 (1980) p. 305-314.

1337   **Kealey, Gregory S.**
"The Royal Canadian Mounted Police, the Canadian Security
Intelligence Service, the Public Archives of Canada, and Access to
Information: A Curious Tale." *Labour/Le Travail*, no. 21
(1988) p. 199-226.

1338   **Kealey, Gregory S., ed.**
"Women and Work/Les femmes et le travail." *Labour/Le Travail*, no.
24 (1989) 368 p.

1339   **Kerr, Kevin B.**
Immigration and the Canadian Labour Market. Backgrounder, BP-
153E. Ottawa: Library of Parliament, Research Branch, Economics
Division, 1986. 24 p.

1340   **Kogler, Rudolf K.**
"Occupational Trends in the Polish Canadian Community, 1941-71."
In: *Polish Presence in Canada and America*, edited by Frank
Renkiewicz. Toronto: Multicultural History Society of Ontario,
1982, p. 211-228.

1341   **Kostiainen, Auvo**
"Contacts Between the Finnish Labour Movements in the United
States and Canada." In: *Finnish Diaspora I: Canada, South America,
Africa, Australia and Sweden*, edited by Michael G. Karni. Toronto:
Multicultural History Society of Ontario, 1981, p. 33-48.

1342   **Kovàcs, Martin L.**
"From Industries to Farming." *Hungarian Studies Review*, vol. 8 no. 1 (1981) p. 45-60.

1343   **Krawchuk, Peter**
Mathew Popovich: His Place in the History of Ukrainian Canadians.
Toronto: Canadian Society for Ukrainian Labour Research, 1987.
119 p.

1344   **Lautard, E. Hugh**
"The Vertical Mosaic Revisited: Occupational Differentials Among Canadian Ethnic Groups." In: *Race and Ethnic Relations in Canada*, edited by Peter S. Li. Don Mills, Ontario: Oxford University Press, 1980, p. 189-208.

1345   **Le Blanc, André**
"Tracking the Worker's Past in Quebec." *Archivaria*, no. 27 (1988-89) p. 23-34.

1346   **Le Blanc, André**
"French Canada's Diaspora and Labour History." *Labour/Le Travail*, no. 20 (1987) p. 213-220.

1347   **Leir, Mark**
"Solidarity on Occasion: The Vancouver Free Speech Fights of 1909 and 1912." *Labour/Le Travail*, no. 23 (1989) p. 39-66.

1348   **Levine, Gilbert**
"Patrick Lenihan and the Alberta Miners." *Labour/Le Travail*, no. 16 (1985) p. 167-178.

1349   **Lindström-Best, Varpu**
"Tailor-maid: The Finnish Immigrant Community of Toronto Before the First World War." In: *Gathering Place: Peoples and Neighbourhoods of Toronto, 1834-1945*, edited by Robert F. Harney. Toronto: Multicultural History Society of Ontario, 1985. p. 205-238.

1350   **Makahonuk, Glen**
"Class Conflict in a Prairie City: The Saskatoon Working-class Response to Prairie Capitalism, 1909-19." *Labour/Le Travail*, no. 19 (1987) p. 89-124.

1351   **Makahonuk, Glen**
"Labour Relation and the Saskatchewan Coal Miners' Strike of 1948-1949." *Saskatchewan History*, vol. 39 no. 1 (1986) p. 1-20.

1352   **Makahonuk, Glen**
"The Saskatoon Relief Camp Workers' Riot of May 8, 1933: An Expression of Class Conflict." *Saskatchewan History*, vol. 37 no. 2 (1984) p. 55-72.

1353   **Manley, John**
"Communists and Auto Workers: The Struggle for Industrial Unionism in the Canadian Automobile Industry, 1925-36." *Labour/Le Travail*, no. 17 (1986) p. 105-133.

1354   **Marcuse, Gary**
"Labour's Cold War: The Story of a Union That Was Not Purged." *Labour/Le Travail*, no. 22 (1988) p. 199-210.

1355   **Marr, William L.**
"Are the Canadian Foreign Born Under-represented in Canada's Occupational Structure?" *International Migration/Migrations Internationales/Migraciones Internacionales*, vol. 24 no. 4 (1986) p. 769-775.

1356   **Martin, Michele**
"Feminization of the Labour Process in the Communications Industry: The Case of the Telephone Operators, 1876-1904." *Labour/Le Travail*, no. 22 (1988) p. 139-162.

1357   **Mary-Rousselière, Guy**
"Une remarquable industrie dorsétienne de l'os de caribou dans le nord de Baffin." *Études Inuit Studies*, vol. 8 no. 2 (1985) p. 41-59.

1358   **McLaughlin, N.**
"The Labour Force Participation of Canada's Immigrants." *Labour Force/La population active*, vol. 41 no. 9 (1985) p. 87-113.

1359   **Mellor, John**
Cape Breton Coal Miners, 1900-1925. New York: Doubleday, Inc., 1983.

1360   **Mellor, John**
The Company Store: James Bryson McLachan and the Cape Breton Coal Miners. Toronto: Doubleday, 1983.

1361   **Michell, Tom**
"Brandon 1919: Labour and Industrial Relations in the Wheat City in the Year of the General Strike." *Manitoba History*, no. 17 (1989) p. 2-11.

1362   **Miles, Robert**
Racism and Migrant Labour. Don Mills, Ont.: Oxford University Press, 1982.

1363   **Miner, Michael**
"Legal and Justice Imperatives: Police-Minority Relations in Canada and the Future." In: *National Symposium on Progress Towards Equality*, compiled and edited by Aziz Khaki. Vancouver: Committee for Racial Justice, 1988, p. 21-34. Proceedings of the National Symposium on Progress Towards Equality September 16-18, 1988, Vancouver.

1364   **Montgomery, David**
"Trends in Working-class History." *Labour/Le Travail*, no. 19 (1987) p. 13-22.

1365   **Mouat, Jeremy**
"The Politics of Coal: A Study of the Wellington Miners Strike of 1890-91." *B.C. Studies*, no. 77 (Spring 1988) p. 3-29.

1366   **Mullan, B.P.**
"The Inpact of Social Networks on the Occupational Status of Migrants." *International Migration/Migrations Internationales/Migraciones Internacionales*, vol. 27 no. 1 (1989) p. 69-86.

1367   **Ng, Ignace and Dennis Maki**
"Strike Activity of U.S. Institutions in Canada." *British Journal of Industrial Relations*, vol. 26 no. 1 (1988) p. 63-74.

1368   **Parr, Joy**
"Hired Men: Ontario Agricultural Wage Labour in Historical Perspective." *Labour/Le Travail*, no. 15 (1985) p. 91-104.

1369   **Peterson, Larry**
"Revolutionary Socialism and Industrial Unrest in the Era of the Winnipeg General Strike: The Origins of Communist Labour Unionism in Europe and North America." *Labour/Le Travail*, no. 13 (1984) p. 115-131.

1370   **Petroff, Lillian**
        "Sojourner and Settler: The Macedonian Presence in the City, 1903-1940." In: *Gathering Place: Peoples and Neighbourhoods of Toronto, 1834-1945*, edited by Robert F. Harney. Toronto: Multicultural History Society of Ontario, 1985, p. 177-204.

1371   **Petroff, Lillian**
        "Macedonians in Toronto: Industry and Enterprise, 1903-40." *Polyphony: The Bulletin of the Multicultural History Society of Ontario*, vol. 6 no. 1 (1984) p. 38-43.

1372   **Radforth, Ian**
        "Social History of Finns in Ontario: Finnish Lumber Workers in Ontario, 1919-46." *Polyphony: The Bulletin of the Multicultural History Society of Ontario*, vol. 3 no. 2 (1981) p. 23-34.

1373   **Ramirez, Bruno**
        "Workers Without a Cause: Italian Immigrant Labour in Montreal, 1880-1930." In: *Arrangiarsi: The Italian Immigration Experience in Canada*, edited by Roberto Perin and Franc Sturino. Montreal: Guernica, 1989, p. 119-134.

1374   **Ramirez, Bruno**
        "Brief Encounters: Italian Immigrant Workers and the CPR 1900-30." *Labour/Le Travail*, no. 17 (1986) p. 9-27.

1375   **Ramirez, Bruno**
        "French-Canadian Canadian Immigrants in the New England Cotton Industry: A Socioeconomic Profile." *Labour/Le Travailleur*, no. 11 (1983) p. 125-145.

1376   **Razzolini, Esperanza Maria**
        All Our Fathers: The North Italian Colony in Industrial Cape Breton. Ethnic Heritage Series no. 8. Halifax: International Education Centre, St. Marys University, 1983.

1377   **Reitz, Jeffrey G.**
        Ethnic Group Control of Jobs. Toronto: Centre for Urban and Community Studies, University of Toronto: 1982. 42 p.

1378   **Renaud, Louise**
        A Study in the Persistance of Poor Working Conditions and Low Status: Immigrant Domestic Workers in Canada. Unpublished MA thesis, Carleton University, 1984. Canadian theses on microfiche, CT86-29871-X.

1379 **Repo, Satu**
"Rosvall and Voutilainen: Two Union Men Who Never Died."
Labour/Le Travailleur, no. 8/9 (1981-82) p. 79-102.

1380 **Ridington, Robin**
"From Artifice to Artifact: Stages in the Industrialization of a
Northern Hunting People." In: *Sa Ts' e: Historical Perspectives on
Northern British Columbia*, edited by Thomas Thorner. Prince
George, B.C.: College of New Caledonia Press, 1989, p. 273-284.

1381 **Ridington, Robin**
"From Artifice to Artifact: Stages in the Industrialization of a
Northern People," *Journal of Canadian Studies/Revue d'études
canadiennes*, vol. 18 no. 3 (1983) p. 55-66.

1382 **Ritchie, Laurell**
"A Warning for Workers." *Policy Options/Options politiques*, vol. 7
no. 7 (1986) p. 27-29.

1383 **Robson, Robert S.**
"Strike in the Single Enterprise Community: Flin Flon-1934." *Labour
/Le Travailleur*, no. 12 (1983) p. 7-42.

1384 **Rosenstein, Carolyn Nancy**
*The Effects of Immigration on the Occupational Careers of Recent
Immigrants to Canada*. Unpublished PhD thesis, University of
California, Los Angeles, 1985. Canadian theses on microfiche, CT87-
23929-5.

1385 **Ross, Philip D.**
*Working on the Margins: A Labour History of the Native Peoples of
Northern Labrador*. Unpublished PhD thesis, McGill University,
1986. Canadian theses on microfiche, CT88-23309-5.

1386 **Rouillard, Jacques**
"Les travailleurs juifs de la confection à Montréal, 1910-1980."
Labour/Travailleur, no. 8/9 (1981-82) p. 253-259.

1387 **Sadowski, Chester**
"The Hard and Difficult Years." *Polyphony: The Bulletin of the
Multicultural History Society of Ontario*, vol. 6 no. 2 (1984) p. 130-
133.

1388   **Samuel, T. John**
"Canada's Visible Minorities and the Labour Market: Vision 2000."
In: *Canada 2000: Race Relations and Public Policy*, edited by O.P.
Dwivedi et al. Guelph, Ont.: Department of Political Studies,
University of Guelph, 1989, p. 178-186.

1389   **Samuel, T. John**
"Family Class Immigrants to Canada: Pt. 1, Labour Force Activity
Aspects." *International Migration/Migrations Internationales/Migra-
ciones Internacionales*, vol. 26 no. 2 (1988) p. 171-186.

1390   **Samuel, T. John**
"The Labour Market Experiences of Canadian Immigrants."
*International Migration/Migrations Internationales/Migraciones Inter-
nacionales*, vol. 23 no. 2 (1985) p. 225-250.

1391   **Satzewich, Victor (Vic) N.**
"Unfree Labour and Canadian Capitalism: The Incorporation of
Polish War Veterans." *Studies in Political Economy*, no. 28
(1989) p. 89-110.

1392   **Satzewich, Victor (Vic) N.**
"Immigrant Labour in Canada: The Cost and Benefit of Ethnic Origin
in the Job Market." *Canadian Journal of Sociology/Cahiers
canadiens de sociologie*, vol. 12 no. 3 (1987) p. 229-241.

1393   **Scardellato, Gabriele P.**
"Italian Immigrant Workers in Powell River, B.C.: A Case Study of
Settlement Before World War II." *Labour/Le Travail*, no. 16
(1985) p. 145-163.

1394   **Seager, Allen**
"Socialists and Workers: The Western Canadian Coal Miners, 1900-
1921." *Labour/Le Travail*, no. 16 (1985) p. 23-59.

1395   **Seager, Allen**
"Social History of Finns in Ontario: Finnish Canadians and the
Ontario Miners' Movement." *Polyphony: The Bulletin of the
Multicultural History Society of Ontario*, vol. 3 no. 2 (1981) p. 35-
45.

1396   **Seward, Shirley B.**
Immigrants in the Canadian Labour. Halifax, N.S.: Institute for
Research on Public Policy, 1989. 71 p.

1397   **Shadd, Adrienne L.**
"Dual Labour Markets in 'Core' and 'Periphery' Regions of Canada:
The Position of Black Males in Ontario and Nova Scotia." *Canadian
Ethnic Studies/Études ethniques au Canada*, vol. 19 no. 2
(1987) p. 91-109.

1398   **Sharma, Hari P.**
"Institutional Racism and the Labour Market: The Case of British
Columbia's Farmworkers." In: *Perspectives on Race, Education and
Social Development: Emphasis on Canada*, edited by Vincent
D'Oyley and Odette Jobidon. Vancouver: Centre for the Study of
Curriculum and Instruction, University of British Columbia,
1982, p. 29-32. Proceedings of a conference given by the Race
Relations Institute, July 1982, at the University of British Columbia,
Vancouver.

1399   **Singh, Hira**
"The Political Economy of Immigrant Farm Labour: A Study of East
Indian Farm Workers in British Columbia." In: *The South Asian
Diaspora in Canada: Six Essays*, edited by Milton Israel. Toronto:
Multicultural History Society of Ontario, 1987, p. 87-112.

1400   **Stein, James Frederick**
*The Religious Roots of the Canadian Labour Movement: The
Canadian Labour Press from 1873-1900*. Unpublished MA thesis,
University of Manitoba, 1986. 2 microfiches. Canadian theses on
microfiche, CT88-22851-2.

1401   **Swierenga, Robert**
"Dutch International Labour Migration to North America in the
Nineteenth Century." In: *Dutch Immigration to North America*, edited
by Herman Ganzevoort and Mark Boekelman. Toronto: Multicultural
History Society of Ontario, 1983, p. 1-34.

1402   **Taylor, Don and Bradley Dow**
*The Rise of Industrial Unionism in Canada - A History of the CIO
[Committee on Industrial Organization]*. Research and Current Issues
Series, no. 56. Kingston: Industrial Relations Centre, Queen's
University, 1988. 145 p.

1403   **Teal, Gregory L.**
"Organisation du travail et dimensions sexuelle et ethnique dans une
usine de vêtements (Montreal)" *Anthropoligie et societés: travail,
industries et classes ouvrières*, vol. 10 no. 1 (1986) p. 33-57.

1404   **Toner, Peter M.**
"Occupation and Ethnicity: The Irish in New Brunswick." *Canadian Ethnic Studies/Études ethniques au Canada*, vol. 20 no. 3 (1988) p. 155-165.

1405   **Wai-Man, Lee**
"Dance No More: Chinese Hand Laundries in Toronto." *Polyphony: The Bulletin of the Multicultural History Society of Ontario*, vol. 6 no. 1 (1984) p. 32-34.

1406   **Walaszek, Adam**
"Krnabrni przybysze: Przemysl amerykanski polscy imigranci, praca i zwiazki zawodowe na poczatku XXw/Stubborn Immigrants: Polish Immigants, Unions and Workers' Control in America at the Beginning of the XXth Century." *Przeglad Polonijny*, vol. 25 no. 3 (1989) p. 5-24, 161.

1407   **Walaszek, Adam**
"Emigranci Polscy wsrod 'robotnikow przemyslowych swiata', 1905-1917/Polish Emigrants Among 'The Industrial Workers of the World', 1905-1917." *Przeglad Polonijny*, vol. 14 no. 2 (1988) p. 43-55, 160-161.

1408   **Wenzel, George W.**
"The Integration of 'Remote' Site Labour into the Inuit Economy of Clyde River, N.W.T." *Arctic Anthropology*, vol. 20 no. 2 (1983) p. 79-92.

1409   **Wong, Lloyd Lee**
Migrant Seasonal Agricultural Labour: Race and Ethnic Relations in the Okanagan Valley. Unpublished PhD thesis, York University, 1988. 4 microfiches. Canadian theses on microfiche, CT90-2344.

1410   **Wong, Lloyd T.**
"Canada's Guestworkers: Some Comparisons of Temporary Workers in Europe and North America." *International Migration Review*, vol. 18 no. 1 (1984) p. 85-98.

1411   **Wotherspoon, T.**
"Immigration and the Production of a Teaching Force: Policy Implications for Education and Labour." *International Migration/ Migrations Internationales/Migraciones Internacionales*, vol. 27 no. 4 (1989) p. 543-562.

1412   **Yeo, David P.**
"Rural Manitoba Views the 1919 Winnipeg General Strike." *Prairie Forum*, vol. 14 no. 1 (1989) p. 9-22.

1413   **Young, Rod**
"Labour Archives: An Annotated Bibliography." *Archivaria*, no. 27 (1988-89) p. 97-110.

1414   **Zucchi, John E.**
"Mining, Railway Building and Street Construction: Italians in Ontario Before World War One." *Polyphony: The Bulletin of the Multicultural History Society of Ontario*, vol. 7 no. 2 (1985) p. 7-13.

1415   **Zucchi, John E.**
"Occupations, Enterprise, and the Migration Chain: The Fruit Traders from Termini Imerese in Toronto: 1900-1930." *Studi Emigrazione*, vol. 22 no. 77 (1985) p. 68-80.

1416   **Zureik, Elia**
The Experience of Visible Minorities in the Work World: The Case of M.B.A. Graduates: Report Submitted to the Race Relations Division of the Ontario Human Rights Commission. Toronto: Ontario Ministry of Labour, Ontario Human Rights Commission, Race Relations Division, 1983. 158, 17 p.

Multiculturalism and Multicultural Policy

1417   **Ayabe, Tsuneo, ed.**
Ethnicity and Multiculturalism in Canada: An Anthropological Study.
Ibaraki, Japan: Institute of History and Anthropology, University of
Tsukuba, 1986. 283 p.

1418   **Béranger, Jean, Jean Cazemajou, Jean-Michel Lacroix, et al. eds.**
*Multilinguisme et multiculturalisme en Amerique du Nord: diversité
régionale.* Recueil de travaux de Elytte Andouard-Labarthe [et al.].
Talence, France: Maison des sciences de l'homme d'Aquitaine, 1987.
246 p.

1419   **Berry, John Widdup**
"Multiculturalism and Psychology in Plural Societies." In: *Ethnic
Minorities and Immigrants in a Cross-cultural Perspective: Selected
Papers.* Lisse, Sweden: Swets and Zeitlinger, 1986, p. 35-51. Paper
presented at the Circum Mediterranean Regional Conference of the
International Association for Cross-cultural Psychology, held in
Malmo, Sweden, June 25-28, 1985.

1420   **Berry, John Widdup**
"Multicultural Attitudes and Education." In: *Multiculturalism in
Canada: Social and Educational Perspectives,* edited by Ronald J.
Samuda, John W. Berry, and Michel Laferrière. Toronto: Allyn and
Bacon Inc., 1984, p. 103-113.

1421   **Berry, John Widdup**
"Multicultural Policy in Canada: A Social Psychological Analysis."
*Canadian Journal of Behavioural Science/Revue canadienne des
sciences de comportement,* vol. 16 no. 4 (1984) p. 353-370.

1422   **Bhatnagar, J.**
"Multiculturalism and Education of Immigrants in Canada." In:
Educating Immigrants, edited by J. Bhatnagar. London: Croom
Helm, p. 69-95.

1423   **Bibby, Reginald W.**
"Bilingualism and Multiculturalism: A National Reading." In: *Ethnic
Canada: Identities and Inequalities*, edited by Leo Driedger. Toronto:
Copp Clark Pitman, 1987, p. 158-169.

1424   **Burnet, Jean R.**
Multiculturalism in Canada. Ottawa: Department of the Secretary of
State of Canada, 1988. 26, 29 p. French language title: *Le
multiculturalisme au Canada.*

1425   **Burnet, Jean R.**
"Myths and Multiculturalism." In: *Multiculturalism in Canada: Social
and Educational Perspectives*, edited by Ronald J. Samuda, John W.
Berry and Michel Laferrière. Toronto: Allyn and Bacon Inc.,
1984, p. 18-29.

1426   **Burnet, Jean R.**
"Multiculturalism Ten Years Later." In: *Two Nations, Many Cultures:
Ethnic Groups in Canada*, edited by Jean Leonard Elliott. 2nd ed.
Scarborough, Ont.: Prentice-Hall of Canada, 1983, p. 235-242.

1427   **Buyniak, Victor O.**
"Fifteen Years of Official Multiculturalism in Canada: Its Impact on
Heritage Languages and Cultures." *Hungarian Studies Review*, vol.
13 no. 2 (1986) p. 75-80.

1428   **Christopher, T.C.**
"Recent Developments in Multiculturalism." *CPSA Papers/ACSP
Contributions 1989*, Section A, paper 2, fiche 1. Paper presented at
the 61st annual meeting of the Canadian Political Science Association, June 1-3, 1989, Laval University, Quebec, P.Q.

1429   **Connell, Graeme**
"A Decade of Multiculturalism: An Overview and Assessment." In:
Asian Canadians: Regional Perspectives, edited by K. Victor Ujimoto
and Gordon Hirabayashi. [Guelph, Ont.: University of Guelph,
1989] p. 3-34. Paper presented at the 5th Asian Canadian Symposium
held at Mount Saint Vincent University, Halifax, Nova Scotia, May
23 to May 26, 1981.

1430   **Cornelius, J.**
"A Multicultural Canada: Origins and Implications." In: *German-Canadian Studies: Critical Approaches*, edited by Peter Liddell. Vancouver: CAUTG, 1983, p. 11-26.

1431   **Cutler, Rosaleen**
Preparation for Social Work in a Multicultural Society. Unpublished MSW thesis, York University, 1987. 2 microfiches. Canadian theses on microfiche, CT89-20196-X.

1432   **DeFaveri, Ivan**
"Multiculturalism and Education." In: *Essays on Canadian Education*, edited by Nick Kach et al. Calgary: Detselig Enterprises, 1986, p. 183-196.

1433   **Dorotich, Dan**
"Multicultural Education and Society in Canada and Yugoslavia." In: *Education in Multicultural Societies*, edited by Trevor Corner. London: Published on the behalf of the British Comparative and International Education Society, by Croom Helm, 1984, p. 96-116.

1434   **Dreisziger, Nandor A.F.**
"The Rise of a Bureaucracy for Multiculturalism: The Origins of the Nationalities Branch, 1939-1941." In: *On Guard for Thee: War, Ethnicity and the Canadian State, 1939-1945*, edited by Norman Hillmer, Bohdan Kordan, and Lubomyr Luciuk. Ottawa: Canadian Committee for the History of the Second World War, 1988, p. 1-30.

1435   **Driedger, Leo**
"Conformity vs. Pluralism: Minority Identities and Inequalities." In: *Minorities and the Canadian State*, edited by Neil Nevitte and Allan Kornberg. Oakville, Ont.: Mosaic Press, 1985, p. 157-174.

1436   **Elkins, David J.**
"The Canadian Kaleidoscope: Research on Identity, Values and Attitudes." In: *Proceedings of the Workshop on the Challenge of Research on Canadian Communities*, organized by Richard Simeon. Ottawa: Social Sciences and Humanities Research Council of Canada, 1980, p. 29-53.

1437   **Elliott, Jean Leonard**
"Immigration and the Canadian Ethnic Mosaic." In: *Race and Ethnic Relations in Canada*, edited by Peter S. Li. Don Mills, Ont.: Oxford University Press, 1980, p. 51-76.

1438   **Ethnic Forum**
"Librarianship and Multiculturalism in Canada." *Ethnic Forum*, vol. 2 no. 1 (1982) p. 36-49.

1439   **Fleras, Augie**
"Bridging the Gap: Towards a Multicultural Policing in Canada." *Canadian Police College Journal/Journal du Collège canadien de police*, vol. 13 no. 3 (1989) p. 153-164.

1440   **Fleras, Augie**
"Toward a Multicultural Reconstruction of Canadian Society." *American Review of Canadian Studies*, vol. 19 no. 1 (1989) p. 307-320.

1441   **Fleras, Augie**
"Multiculturalism: Policy and Ideology in the Canadian Context." In: *Police, Race and Ethnicity: A Guide for Law Enforcement Officers*, edited by Brian K. Cryderman. Toronto: Butterworths, 1986, p. 17-24.

1442   **Forbes, Hugh Donald**
"Cultural Pluralism and the Modern State: Canada as a Model for the World." In: *Proceedings of the 12th Annual Conference of the Atlantic Provinces Political Studies Association, October 23-25, 1986*. Halifax: Atlantic Provinces Political Studies Association, 1986, paper no. 2.

1443   **Foster, Lois**
"Themes in the Analysis of Multiculturalism: Canada and Australia." *Australian-Canadian Studies*, vol. 1 (1983) p. 78-95.

1444   **Foster, Lois**
"Themes in the Analysis of Multiculturalism: Canada and Australia." In: *Theory and Practice in Comparative Studies: Canada, Australia, and New Zealand*, edited by Peter Crabb. Sydney: ANZACS, 1983, p. 23-46. Papers from the first conference of the Australian and New Zealand Association for Canadian Studies held at Macquarie University, Sydney, August 1982.

1445   **Fraser, Susan Margaret Murray**
The Development of a Model for a Multicultural Pre-school Centre in British Columbia. Unpublished MA thesis, University of British Columbia, 1984. 117 leaves. Canadian theses on microfiche, 257296.

1446   **Friesen, John**
"Multicultural Policy and Practices: What About the Indian?"
Canadian Journal of Native Education, vol. 14 no. 1 (1987) p. 30-40.

1447   **Friesen, John**
When Cultures Clash: Case Studies in Multiculturalism. Calgary:
Detselig Enterprises Ltd., 1985. 171 p.

1448   **Furness, Anne Marie**
"Development of Local Sevices and Community Action on Behalf of
Multiculturalism." *Social Work Papers*, vol. 17 (1983) p. 15-25.

1449   **Gagnon, Alain G.**
"Le fédéralisme en pays multicommunautaires: un cadre d'analyse
theoretique et comparatif." *CPSA Papers/ACSP Contributions 1982*,
Section: G, paper 4, fiche 20. Paper presented at the Canadian
Political Science Associaton 54th annual meeting, June 7-9, 1982,
University of Ottawa, Ontario.

1450   **Gall, Gerald**
"Multiculturalism and the Fundamental Freedom: Section 27 and
Section 2." In: *Multiculturalism and the Charter: A Legal Perspective*, edited by the Canadian Human Rights Foundation. Toronto:
Carswell, 1987, p. 29-58.

1451   **Gatner, Joe A.**
The Development of a Federal Multicultural Policy. Background
paper for parliamentarians, BP-130E. Ottawa: Library of Parliament,
Research Branch, Political and Social Affairs Division, 1985. 20 p.

1452   **Godin, Gérald**
Conférence fédérale-provinciale sur le multiculturalisme. Montréal:
Ministère des communautés culturelles et de l'immigration, mai 1985.

1453   **Harney, Robert F.**
"A History of the Multicultural History Society." *Polyphony: The
Bulletin of the Multicultural History Society of Ontario*, vol. 9 no. 1
(1987) p. 1-16.

1454   **Harvey, Fernand**
"L'ouverture du Québec au multiculturalisme, 1900-1981." *Études
canadiennes/Canadian Studies*, vol. 2 no. 21 (1986) p. 219-228.

1455   **Hawkins, Freda**
"Multiculturalism in Two Countries: The Canadian and Australian Experience." *Journal of Canadian Studies/Revue d'études canadiennes*, vol. 17 no. 1 (1982) p. 64-80.

1456   **Head, Wilson A.**
"Citizenship, Limited and Unlimited: Implications for a Multiracial and Multicultural Society." In: *Challenging the Concept of Citizenship*, edited by Rene R. Gadacz. Edmonton: CSC Consulting Services, 1986, p. 76-85.

1457   **Herberg, Dorothy Chave**
"Issues in Multicultural Child Welfare: Working with Families Originating in Traditional Societies." *Social Work Papers*, vol. 17 (1983) p. 45-57.

1458   **Hiemstra, John L.**
Trudeau's Political Philosophy: Its Implications for Liberty and Progress. Toronto: Institute for Christian Studies, 1983. 107 p.

1459   **Hirabayashi, Gordon**
"Some Issues Regarding Ethnic Relations Research." In: *Visible Minorities and Multiculturalism: Asians in Canada*, edited by K. Victor Ujimoto and Gordon Hirabayashi. Toronto: Butterworths, 1980, p. 379-388.

1460   **Hudson, Michael R.**
"Multiculturalism, Government Policy and Constitutional Enshrinement: A Comparative Study." In: *Multiculturalism and the Charter: A Legal Perspective*, edited by the Canadian Human Rights Foundation. Toronto: Carswell, 1987, p. 59-122.

1461   **Isajiw, Wsevolod W.**
"Multiculturalism and the Integration of Canadian Community." *Canadian Ethnic Studies/Études ethniques au Canada*, vol. 15 no. 2 (1983) p. 107-117.

1462   **Jaworsky, John**
A Case Study of the Canadian Federal Government's Multiculturalism Policy. Unpublished MA thesis, Carleton University, 1980. 2 microfiches. Canadian theses on microfiche, 44409.

1463   **Jensen, Alan**
Multiculturalism and Community-Wide Agencies in the Lower Mainland: Overcoming Systemic Barriers to Access. Unpublished M.S.W. major paper, University of British Columbia, School of Social Work, 1988. 125 leaves.

1464   **Kallen, Evelyn**
"Multiculturalism as Ideology, Policy and Reality." In: *Social Inequality in Canada: Patterns, Problems, Policies,* edited by James E. Curtis. Scarborough, Ontario: Prentice-Hall Canada, 1988, p. 235-246.

1465   **Kallen, Evelyn**
"Multiculturalism, Minorities and Motherhood: A Social Scientific Critique of Section 27." In: *Multiculturalism and the Charter: A Legal Perspective,* edited by the Canadian Human Rights Foundation. Toronto: Carswell, 1987, p. 123-138.

1466   **Kirschbaum, Stanislav J.**
"Cultural Diversity and Canadian Unity: The Political Imperative." In: *The Canadian Alternative: Cultural Pluralism and Canadian Unity,* edited by Hedi Bouraoui. Downsview, Ontario: ECW Press, 1980, p. 32-42. Paper presented at the Conference on Cultural Pluralism and the Canadian Unity held at Stong College, York University, 1979.

1467   **Laferrière, Michel**
"Languages, Ideologies, and Multicultural Education in Canada: Some Historical and Sociological Perspectives." In: *Multiculturalism in Canada: Social and Educational Perspectives,* edited by Ronald J. Samuda, John W. Berry and Michel Laferrière. Toronto: Allyn and Bacon Inc., 1984, p. 171-183.

1468   **Lambert, Ronald D.**
"Opposition to Multiculturalism Among Quebecois and English-Canadians." *Canadian Review of Sociology and Anthropology/Revue canadienne de sociologie et d'anthropologie,* vol. 20 no. 2 (1983) p. 193-207.

1469   **Latouche, Daniel**
"Le pluralisme ethnique et l'agenda publique au Québec." *Revue internationale d'action communautaire,* no. 21 (1989) p. 11-26.

1470   **Leslie, Peter M.**
"Canada as a Bicommunal Polity." In: *Recurring Issues in Canadian Federalism*, Clare F. Beckton and A. Wayne MacKay, research coordinators. Toronto: University of Toronto Press, 1986, p. 113-144.

1471   **Ley, David F.**
"Pluralism and the Canadian State." In: *Geography and Ethnic Pluralism*, edited by Colin Clarke, David Ley, and Ceri Peach. London: George Allen and Unwin, 1984, p. 87-110.

1472   **Lin, Tsung-yi**
"Multiculturalism and Canadian Psychiatry: Opportunities and Challenges." *Canadian Journal of Psychiatry*, vol. 31 no. 7 (1986) p. 681-690.

1473   **Love, James H.**
"Nationalism and Multiculturalism in Canadian Education." *Journal of Canadian Culture*, vol. 2 no. 2 (1985) p. 55-70.

1474   **Lupul, Manoly R.**
"Networking, Discrimination and Multiculturalism as a Social Philosophy." *Canadian Ethnic Studies/Études ethniques au Canada*, vol. 21 no. 2 (1989) p. 1-12.

1475   **Lupul, Manoly R.**
"Multiculturalism and Canada's White Ethnics." *Canadian Ethnic Studies/Études ethniques au Canada*, vol. 15 no. 1 (1983) p. 99-107.

1476   **Magnet, Joseph Eliot**
"Interpreting Multiculturalism." In: *Multiculturalism and the Charter: A Legal Perspective*, edited by the Canadian Human Rights Foundation. Toronto: Carswell, 1987, p. 145-154.

1477   **Magocsi, Paul R.**
"On the Tenth Anniversary of the Multicultural History Society." *Polyphony: The Bulletin of the Multicultural History Society of Ontario*, vol. 9 no. 1 (1987) p. 95.

1478   **Makuto, Moffatt S.**
"International Students Organization." *Polyphony: The Bulletin of the Multicultural History Society of Ontario*, vol. 9 no. 2 (1987) p. 109-110.

1479   **Mazurek, Kas**
"Multiculturalism, Education and the Ideology of the Meritocracy."
In: *The Political Economy of Canadian Schooling*, edited by Terry
Wotherspoon. Toronto: Methuen, 1987, p. 141-179.

1480   **McLeod, Keith A.**
"Multiculturalism and Multicultural Education: Policy and Practice."
Canadian Society for the Study of Education, Eighth Yearbook,
(1981) p. 12-26.

1481   **McLeod, Keith A., ed.**
Multicultural Early Childhood Education. Toronto: Guidance Centre,
Faculty of Education, University of Toronto: 1984. 155 p.

1482   **Mitges, Gus**
Multiculturalism: Building the Canadian Mosaic. Ottawa: House of
Commons, Standing Committee on Multiculturalism, 1987. 164 p.

1483   **Moodley, Kogila A.**
"Canadian Multiculturalism as Ideology." *Ethnic and Racial Studies*,
vol. 6 no. 3 (1983) p. 320-331.

1484   **Moore, Dorothy E.**
Multiculturalism: Ideology or Social Reality. Unpublished PhD thesis,
Boston University Graduate School, 1980. 510 leaves.

1485   **Munro, John**
"Multiculturalism: A Policy and Program for All Canadians." In:
Munro, by Sherry Sleightholm. Ancaster, Ont.: Sleightholm
Publishing Limited, 1984, p. 95-100.

1486   **National Forum on Multiculturalism in Broadcasting**
*Reflections from the Electronic Mirror: Report of the National Forum
on Multiculturalism in Broadcasting in Toronto, Ontario, May 13 and
14, 1988*. [s.l.:] Canadian Multiculturalism Council, 1988. 155, 165 p.

1487   **Ollivier, Emile**
"Quatre thèses sur la transculturation." *Cahiers de recherche sociologique*, vol. 2 no. 2 (1984) p. 75-90.

1488   **Paquet, Gilles**
"Multiculturalism as National Policy." *Journal of Cultural Economics*, vol. 13 no. 1 (1989) p. 17-34.

1489   **Peter, Karl A.**
"The Myth of Multiculturalism and Other Political Fables." In:
Ethnicity, Power and Politics in Canada, edited by Jorgen Dahlie and
Tissa Fernando. Toronto: Methuen, 1981, p. 56-67.

1490   **Poisson, Rene Emile**
*Teacher Perception of Socio-cultural Factors Affecting Education in
Multicultural Classrooms.* Unpublished MEd thesis, University of
Saskatchewan, 1982. 113 leaves.

1491   **Porter, James N.**
"On Multiculturalism as a Limit of Canadian Life." In: *The Canadian
Alternative: Cultural Pluralism and Canadian Unity*, edited by Hedi
Bouraoui. Downsview, Ont.: ECW Press, 1980, p. 64-79. Paper
presented at the Conference on Cultural Pluralism and the Canadian
Unity held at Stong College, York University, 1979.

1492   **Pucci, Antonio and John Potestio, eds.**
"Thunder Bay's People." Introduction to a monographic issue of
*Polyphony: The Bulletin of the Multicultural History Society of
Ontario*, vol. 9 no. 2 (1987) p. 3-4.

1493   **Ramcharan, Subhas**
"Multiculturalism and Inequality: Non-white Migrants in Canadian
Mosaic." *California Sociologist*, vol. 7 no. 1 (1984) p. 1-12

1494   **Roberts, Lance W.**
"Exploring the Ideology of Canadian Multiculturalism." *Canadian
Public Policy/Analyse de politiques*, vol. 8 no. 1 (1982) p. 88-94.

1495   **Rubinoff, Lionel**
"Multiculturalism and the Metaphysics of Pluralism." *Journal of
Canadian Studies/Revue d'études canadiennes*, vol. 17 no. 1
(1982) p. 122-130.

1496   **Samuda, Ronald J.**
"The Canadian Brand of Multiculturalism: Social and Educational
Implications." In: *Multicultural Education: The Interminable Debate*,
edited by Sohan Modgil et al. London: Falmer Press, 1986, p. 101-111.

1497   **Samuda, Ronald J., John W. Berry, and Michel Laferrière, eds.**
Multiculturalism in Canada: Social and Educational Perspectives.
Toronto: Allyn and Bacon, Inc., 1984. 446 p. Papers presented at a
symposium on Multicultural Education, held at Queen's University,
November 7-11, 1981.

1498   **Scott, Gilbert H.**
"Multicultural Policy and Practice in Canada." In: *Ethnic Psychology: Research and Practice with Immigrants, Refugees, Native Peoples, Ethnic Groups and Sojourners*, edited by John W. Berry and R.C. Annis. Lisse: Swets and Zeitlinger, 1988, p. 7-12. Paper presented to the North American Regional International Association of Cross-Cultural Psychology on Ethnic Psychology held in Kingston, Canada, August 16-21, 1987.

1499   **Shapson, S.M. and Vincent D'Oyley, eds.**
Bilingual and Multicultural Education: Canadian Perspectives. Avon, England: Multicultural Matters, 1984. 170 p.

1500   **Stasiulis, Daiva K.**
"The Symbolic Mosaic Reaffirmed: Multiculturalism Policy." In: *How Ottawa Spends, 1988/89: The Conservatives Heading into the Stretch*, edited by Katherine A. Graham. Ottawa: Carleton University Press, 1988, p. 81-112.

1501   **Stefura, Mary**
"Organizing Sudbury's Multicultural Past." *Polyphony: The Bulletin of the Multicultural History Society of Ontario*, vol. 9 no. 1 (1987) p. 39.

1502   **Stefura, Mary, ed.**
"Sudbury's People." Monographic issue of *Polyphony: The Bulletin of the Multicultural History Society of Ontario*, vol. 9 no. 1 (1987).

1503   **Stockley, David**
"The Politics of Multiculturalism: Some Australian and Canadian Comparisons." *Australian-Canadian Studies*, vol. 2 (1984) p. 21-35.

1504   **Stockley, David**
"The Politics of Multiculturalism: Some Australian and Canadian Comparisons." In: *Theory and Practice in Comparative Studies: Canada, Australia, and New Zealand*, edited by Peter Crabb. Sydney: ANZACS, 1983, p. 47-63. Papers from the First Conference of the Australian and New Zealand Association for Canadian Studies held at Macquarie University, Sydney, August 1982.

1505   **Strong, Jean K.**
Ethnicity and the Development of Multiculturalism in Canada: An Essay on Political Process. Unpublished MA thesis, University of Alberta, 1984. 2 microfiches. Canadian theses on microfiche, CT87-22173-6.

1506   **Thomas, Barb**
Multiculturalism at Work: A Guide to Organizational Change.
Toronto: YWCA of Metropolitan Toronto: 1987. 157 p.

1507   **Tse, Linda**
Families in East Vancouver: Our Multicultural Neighbourhood.
Edited by Arline Oishi. Vancouver, B.C.: Mount Pleasant Family
Centre, 1988. 71 p.

1508   **Ujimoto, Koji Victor**
"Visible Minorities and Multiculturalism: Planned Social Change
Strategies for Next Decade." *Journal of Canadian Studies/Revue
d'études canadiennes*, vol. 17 no. 1 (1982) p. 111-121.

1509   **Ujimoto, Koji Victor and Gordon Hirabayashi, eds.**
Visible Minorities and Multiculturalism: Asians in Canada. Toronto:
Butterworths, 1980. 388 p. Papers originally presented at the annual
meetings of the Canadian Asian Studies Association, in 1977 and
1978.

1510   **Watson, Susan Karen**
*The Relationship Between Canadian Immigration and
Multiculturalism Policies: A Case Study.* Unpublished MSW thesis,
University of Calgary, 1985. 2 microfiches. Canadian theses on
microfiche, CT86-26656-7.

1511   **Waugh, Earle H., Baha Abu-Laban, and Regula B. Qureshi, eds.**
Muslim Community in North America. Edmonton: University of
Alberta Press, 1983. 316 p. The majority of the studies were
originally presented at the Symposium on Islam in North America
held at the University of Alberta, Edmonton, May 27-31, 1980.

Politics and Law

1512 **Ajzenstat, Janet**
"Liberalism and Assimilation: Lord Durham Reconsidered." In: *Political Thought in Canada*, compiled and edited by Stephen Brooks. Toronto: Irwin Publishing, 1984, p. 239-257.

1513 **Alia, Valerie**
"Changing Names: Clues in the Search for a Political Onomastics." *Onomastica Canadiana*, no. 67/1 (1985) p. 25-34.

1514 **Allaire, Yvan**
Canadian Business Response to the Legislation on Francization in the Workplace. Montreal: C.D. Howe Research Institute, 1980. 77 p.

1515 **Alliance Quebec**
"A Minority's Plea for the Supremacy of the Charter." In: *Meech Lake Primer: Conflicting Views of the 1987 Constitutional Accord*, edited by Michael D. Behiels. Ottawa: University of Ottawa Press, 1989, p. 225-231.

1516 **Angel, Sam Sumayya**
Language, Culture and the Political Process in Canada: A Critical Analysis. Unpublished MEd thesis, University of Saskatchewan, College of Education, 1985. 119 leaves.

1517 **Ares, Georges**
"The Accord Abandons Canada's Battered and Defenceless Minorities." In: *Meech Lake Primer: Conflicting Views of the 1987 Constitutional Accord*, edited by Michael D. Behiels. Ottawa: University of Ottawa Press, 1989, p. 219-224.

1518   **Arsenault, Pierre**
L'enchâssement des droits de la minorité canadienne-française dans la constitution du Canada. Moncton, N.B.: École de droit; Éditions de l'Université de Moncton, 1982. 54 p.

1519   **Association Canadienne-Française de l'Ontario**
Le droit de véto constitutionnel de Québec: un droit au service des franco-ontariens. Ottawa: L'Association canadienne-française de l'Ontario, 1982.

1520   **Barman, Jean**
"Neighbourhood and Community in Interwar Vancouver: Residential Differentiation and Civic Voting Behaviour." *B.C. Studies*, nos. 69/70 (1986) p. 97-141.

1521   **Barrett, Stanley R.**
"The Far Right in Canada." In: *Dissent and the State*, edited by C.E.S. Franks. Toronto: Oxford University Press, 1989, p. 224-246.

1522   **Bartlett, Richard H.**
The Indian Act of Canada. Saskatoon: University of Saskatchewan, Native Law Centre, 1980. 36 p. Originally published in the *Buffalo Law Review*, vol. 27 no. 4 (1978) p. 581-615.

1523   **Bastarache, Michel**
"L'accord constitutionnel de 1987 et la protection des minorités francophones hors Québec." *McGill Law Journal/Revue de droit de McGill*, vol. 34 no. 1 (1989) p. 119-129.

1524   **Beaudoin, Gérald A.**
"Les Accords Meech Langevin." *University of New Brunswick Law Journal/Revue de droit de l'Université du Nouveau-Brunswick*, vol. 38 (1989) p. 227-250.

1525   **Beaulieu, Marie**
Le criminologue québécois et l'intervention auprès des groupes ethniques. Unpublished MSc thesis, Université de Montréal, 1986. 1 microfilm.

1526   **Beaupre, Remi Michael**
"Vers l'interpretation d'une constitution bilingue." *Cahiers de droit*, vol. 25 no. 4 (1984) p. 939-958.

1527   **Beaupre, Remi Michael**
Construing Bilingual Legislation in Canada. Toronto: Butterworths, 1981. 161 p.

1528   **Behiels, Michael D.**
Prelude to Quebec's Quiet Revolution: Liberalism vs Neo-nationalism, 1945-1960. Montreal and Kingston: McGill-Queen's University Press, 1985.

1529   **Behiels, Michael D., ed.**
The Meech Lake Primer: Conflicting Views of the 1987 Constitutional Accord. Ottawa: University of Ottawa Press, 1989. 564 p.

1530   **Bell, David V.J.**
"Political Education and Political Culture." In: *Political Education in Canada*, edited by Jon H. Pammett and Jean-Luc Pepin. Halifax: Institute for Research on Public Policy, 1988. p. 3-14.

1531   **Bercuson, David Jay**
"The Zionist Lobby and Canada's Palestine Policy 1941-1948." In: *The Domestic Battleground: Canada and the Arab-Israeli Conflict*, edited by David Taras and David H. Goldberg. Montreal: McGill-Queen's University Press, 1989, p. 17-36.

1532   **Bergeron, Gerard**
"Il faut quelque chose, mais comment?" In: *Mécanismes pour une nouvelle constitution*, en collaboration Edmond Orban, Gérard Bergeron, Edward McWhinney, and Gérald A. Beaudoin. Ottawa: Éditions de l'Université d'Ottawa, 1981, p. 25-64.

1533   **Binavince, Emilio S.**
"The Judicial Aspects of Race Relations." In: *Canada 2000: Race Relations and Public Policy*, edited by O.P. Dwivedi et al. Guelph, Ont.: Department of Political Studies, University of Guelph, 1989, p. 312-319.

1534   **Bittar, Patricia**
"L'accès au statut de refugé: une analyse strategique en région Montréalaise." *Canadian Ethnic Studies/Études ethniques au Canada*, vol. 21 no. 1 (1989) p. 30-44.

1535   **Black, Jerome H.**
"Immigrants and Political Involvement in Canada: The Role of the
Ethnic Media." *Canadian Ethnic Studies/Études ethniques au
Canada*, vol. 20 no. 1 (1988) p. 1-20.

1536   **Black, Jerome H.**
"Age, Resistance, and Political Learning in a New Environment: The
Case of Canadian Immigrants." *Comparative Politics*, vol. 20 no. 1
(1987) p. 73-84.

1537   **Black, Jerome H.**
"The Practice of Politics in Two Settings: Political Transferability
Among Recent Immigrants to Canada." *Canadian Journal of Political
Science/Revue canadienne de science politique*, vol. 20 no. 4
(1987) p. 731-754.

1538   **Black, Jerome H.**
"Immigrant Political Adaptation in Canada: Some Tentative
Findings." *Canadian Journal of Political Science/Revue canadienne
de science politique*, vol. 15 no. 1 (1982) p. 3-28.

1539   **Boldt, Menno**
"Tribal Traditions and European-western Political Ideologies: The
Dilemma of Canada's Native Indians." In: *The Quest for Justice:
Aboriginal Peoples and Aboriginal Rights*, edited by Menno Boldt, J.
Anthony Long, and Leroy Little Bear. Toronto: University of Toronto
Press, 1985, p. 333-346.

1540   **Boldt, Menno**
"Tribal Traditions and European-western Political Ideologies: The
Dilemma of Canada's Native Indians." *Canadian Journal of Political
Science/Revue canadienne de science politique*, vol. 17 no. 3
(1984) p. 537-554.

1541   **Boldt, Menno**
"Philosophy, Politics and Extralegal Action: Native Indian Leaders in
Canada." *Ethnic and Racial Studies*, vol. 4 no. 2 (1981) p. 205-221.

1542   **Bourassa, Guy**
"Les rélations ethniques dans la vie politique montréalaise." *Le
système politique de Montréal: recueil de textes*. Sous la direction de
Guy Bourassa et Jacques Léveillée. Montréal: Association
canadienne-française pour l'avancement des sciences, 1986, p. 59-86.

1543   **Brassard, Jacques**
"L'immigration ententes politiques et droit constitutionnel." *Revue juridique thémis*, vol. 19 no. 3 (1985) p. 305-323.

1544   **Breton, Raymond**
"The Vesting of Ethnic Interests in State Institutions." In: *Multiculturalism and Intergroup Relations*, edited by James S. Frideres. New York: Greenwood Press, 1988, p. 35-56.

1545   **Buchignani, Norman**
"The Political Organization of South Asians in Canada." In: *Ethnicity, Power and Politics in Canada*, edited by Jorgen Dahlie and Tissa Fernando. Toronto: Methuen, 1981, p. 202-232.

1546   **Cairns, Alan C.**
Ritual, Taboo and Bias in Constitutional Controversies in Canada, or Constitutional Talk Canadian Style. Saskatoon: University of Saskatchewan, 1989. 32 p. (Timlin lecture).

1547   **Cairns, Alan C.**
"Citizens (Outsiders) and Governments (Insiders) in Constitution-making: The Case of Meech Lake." *Canadian Public Policy/Analyse de politiques*, vol. 14, Supplement (1988) p. 121-145.

1548   **Cairns, Alan C.**
"The Canadian Constitutional Experiment." *Dalhousie Law Journal*, vol. 9 no. 1 (1984) p. 87-114.

1549   **Canada. Commission of Inquiry on War Criminals**
Inquiry on War Criminals. Report. 2 volumes. Commissioner, Jules Deschenes. Ottawa: The Commission, 1986.

1550   **Cardozo, Andrew**
"Lobbying: How Communities Influence Public Opinion." In: *Canada 2000: Race Relations and Public Policy*, edited by O.P. Dwivedi et al. Guelph, Ont.: Department of Political Studies, University of Guelph, 1989, p. 92-102.

1551   **Carson, Bruce**
The Meech Lake Accord: A Constitutional Conundrum. Ottawa: Library of Parliament, Research Branch, 1989. 26 p.

1552   **Carty, R. Kenneth**
"The Making of a Canadian Political Citizenship." In: *National Politics and Community in Canada*, edited by R. Kenneth Carty and W. Peter Ward. Vancouver, B.C.: University of British Columbia Press, 1986, p. 65-79.

1553   **Clarke, Harold D., Allan Kornberg and Marianne Stewart**
"Politically Active Minorities: Political Participation in Canadian Democracy." In: *Minorities and the Canadian State*, edited by Neil Nevitte and Allan Kornberg. Oakville, Ont.: Mosaic Press, 1985, p. 275-300.

1554   **Coleman, William D.**
The Independence Movement in Quebec 1945-1980. Toronto: University of Toronto Press, 1984. 274 p.

1555   **Coleman, William D.**
"From Bill 22 to Bill 101: The Politics of Legitimation Under the Parti Quebecois." *CPSA Papers/ACSP Contributions 1980*, Section: Provincial Politics, paper 2, fiche 1. Paper presented at the 52nd annual meeting of the Canadian Political Science Association, June 2-4, 1980, Université du Québec à Montréal.

1556   **Conley, Marshall W.**
"The Protection of Refugees and Foreign Policy: Canada's Role." *CPSA Papers/ACSP Contributions 1983*, Section C, paper 1, fiche 5. Paper presented at the 55th annual meeting of the Canadian Political Science Association, June 6-8, 1983, University of British Columbia, Vancouver.

1557   **Cook, George Ramsay**
"Alice in Meechland or the Concept of Quebec as 'a Distinct Society'." In: *Navigating Meech Lake: The 1987 Constitutional Accord*, edited by Clive Thomson. Kingston, Ont.: Institute of Intergovernmental Relations, Queen's University, 1988, p. 53-64. Reprinted from: *Queen's Quarterly*, vol. 94 no. 4 (1987) p. 772-792.

1558   **Covell, Maureen**
"Ambiguous Majorities: Language Use and Political Institutions in Canada." *Canadian Issues*, vol. 11 (1989) p. 141-155. French language title: "Des majorités équivoques: les pratiques linguistiques dans les institutions politiques au Canada." p. 145-160.

1559   **Cowie, Ian B.**
"Issues of Jurisdiction Between Aboriginal and Non-Aboriginal
Governments." In: *Issues in Entrenching Aboriginal Self-government*,
edited by David C. Hawkes and Evelyn Peters. Kingston, Ont.:
Institute of Intergovernmental Relations, Queen's University,
1987, p. 119-132.

1560   **Culhane Speck, Dara**
*An Error in Judgement: The Politics of Medical Care in an Indian/
White Community.* Vancouver: Talonbooks, 1987. 281 p.

1561   **Dahlie, Jorgen and Tissa Fernando, eds.**
Ethnicity, Power and Politics in Canada. Toronto: Methuen, 1981.
291 p.

1562   **Daniels, Doug**
"The White Race is Shrinking: Perceptions of Race in Canada and
Some Speculations on the Political Economy of Race Classification."
Ethnic and Racial Studies, vol. 4 no. 3 (1983) p. 353-356.

1563   **Daugherty, Wayne**
A Guide to Native Political Associations in Canada. Ottawa: Treaties
and Historical Research Centre, Department of Indian and Northern
Affairs, 1982. 33 p.

1564   **Denis, Wilfrid B.**
"The Politics of Language." In: *Race and Ethnic Relations in
Canada*, edited by Peter S. Li. Don Mills, Ont.: Oxford University
Press, 1980, p. 148-188.

1565   **Dutil, P.A.**
"The Politics of Progressivism in Quebec: The Gouin 'Coup' Revisited."
Canadian Historical Review, vol. 69 no. 4 (1988) p. 441-465.

1566   **Ebona, Andrew**
"Federal Government Policies and Indian Goals of Self-government."
In: *Pathways to Self-determination: Canadian Indians and the
Canadian State*, edited by Leroy Little Bear, Menno Boldt and J.
Anthony Long. Toronto: University of Toronto Press, 1984, p. 90-96.

1567   **Elkins, David J.**
"The Horizontal Mosaic: Immigrants and Migrants in the Provincial
Political Cultures." In: *Small Worlds: Provinces and Parties in
Canadian Political Life*, by David J. Elkins, Richard Simeon, with
Donald E. Blake et al. Toronto: Methuen, 1980, p. 106-130.

1568 **Esman, Milton J.**
"The Politics of Official Bilingualism in Canada." In: *Language Policy and National Unity*, edited by W.R. Beer and J.E. Jacob. Totawa, N.J.: Rowman and Allanheld, 1985, p. 45-66.

1569 **Fanjoy, Emery M.**
"Language and Politics in New Brunswick." *Canadian Parliamentary Review*, vol. 7 no. 1 (1984) p. 2-7.

1570 **Flanagan, Thomas**
"The Agricultural Argument and Original Appropriation: Indian Lands and Political Philosophy." *Canadian Journal of Political Science/Revue canadienne de science politique*, vol. 22 no. 3 (1989) p. 589-602.

1571 **Fontaine, Yvon**
"La politique linguistique au Canada: l'impasse?" In: *Canada: The State of the Federation 1989*, edited by Ronald L. Watts and Douglas M. Brown. Kingston, Ont.: Institute of Intergovernmental Relations, Queen's University, 1989, p. 137-149.

1572 **Forsey, Eugene**
"No! [to Lake Meech Accord]" *University of New Brunswick Law Journal*, vol. 38 (1989) p. 251-277.

1573 **Fortin, Pierre**
"Would Quebec be Better In or Out?" In: *Politics: Canada*, edited by Paul Fox. 5th ed. Toronto: McGraw-Hill Ryerson, 1982, p. 209-218.

1574 **Fournier, Marcel**
"Culture et politique au Québec." *Canadian Journal of Sociology/Cahiers canadiens de sociologie*, vol. 12 no. 1/2 (1987) p. 64-83.

1575 **Frideres, James S.**
"Becoming Canadian: Citizen Acquisition and National Identity." *Canadian Review of Studies in Nationalism/Revue canadienne des études sur le nationalisme*, vol. 14 no. 1 (1987) p. 105-121.

1576 **Gaboury, Jean-Pierre**
"La culture politique des francophones de l'est ontarien et de l'Outaouais." *Bulletin du Centre de recherche en civilisation canadienne-française*, no. 27 (1983) p. 10-12.

1577   **Gagnon, Alain G.**
"The Evolution of Political Forces in Quebec: The Struggle for
Supremacy." In: *Quebec: State and Society*, edited by Alain G.
Gagnon. Toronto: Methuen, 1984, p. 262-283.

1578   **Gibbins, Roger**
"The Interplay of Political Institutions and Political Communities."
In: *Federalism and Political Community: Essays in Honour of
Donald Smiley*, edited by David P. Shugarman and Reg Whitaker.
Peterborough, Ont.: Broadview Press, 1989, p. 423-438.

1579   **Gibbins, Roger**
"An Assessment of the Probable Impact of Aboriginal Self-
government in Canada." In: *The Politics of Gender, Ethnicity and
Language in Canada*. Alan Cairns and Cynthia Williams, research
coordinators. Toronto: University of Toronto Press, 1986, p. 176-245.

1580   **Gibbins, Roger**
"Citizenship, Political, and Intergovernmental Problems with Indian
Self-government." In: *Arduous Journey: Canadian Indians and
Decolonization*, edited by J. Rick Ponting. Toronto: McClelland and
Stewart, 1986, p. 369-378.

1581   **Gibbins, Roger**
"Canadian Political Ideology: A Comparative Analysis." *Canadian
Journal of Political Science/Revue canadienne de science politique*,
vol. 18 no. 3 (1985) p. 577-598.

1582   **Gibbins, Roger**
"Canadian Indian Policy: The Constitutional Trap." *Canadian Journal
of Native Studies*, vol. 4 no. 1 (1984) p. 1-9.

1583   **Goldberg, David Howard**
"Keeping Score: From the Yom Kippur War to Palestine Uprising."
In: *The Domestic Battleground: Canada and the Arab-Israeli
Conflict*, edited by David Taras and David H. Goldberg. Montreal:
McGill-Queen's University Press, 1989, p. 102-122.

1584   **Goldberg, David Howard**
*Ethnic Interest Groups as Domestic Sources of Foreign Policy: A
Theoretical and Empirical Inquiry*. Unpublished PhD Thesis, McGill
University, 1986. 7 microfiches. Canadian theses on microfiche,
CT89-21172-8.

1585   **Graham, Katherine A.**
"Indian Policy and the Tories: Cleaning up After the Buffalo Jump."
In: *How Ottawa Spends: 1987/88: Restraining the State*, edited by
Michael J. Prince. Toronto: Methuen, 1987, p. 237-267.

1586   **Gregorovich, John B., ed.**
On the Record: The Debate Over Alleged War Criminals in Canada.
Letters to the Editors of 'The Whig-Standard'. Toronto: The Justinian
Press, 1987. 52 p.

1587   **Guillaume, Pierre, et al. eds.**
Minorités et l'État. Bordeaux: Presses universitaires de Bordeaux,
1986. 276 p.

1588   **Guillaume, Pierre, J.M. Lacroix, et P. Spriet, eds.**
Canada et canadiens. Bordeaux: Presses universitaires de Bordeaux,
1984. 382 p.

1589   **Hamel, J.M.**
"Native Participation in Free Elections: The Case of the Northwest
Territories." *Electoral Studies*, vol. 2 no. 2 (1983) p. 149-154.

1590   **Hammer, Tomas**
"Dual Citizenship and Political Integration." *International Migration
Review*, vol. 19 no. 3 (1985) p. 438-450.

1591   **Handler, Richard**
Nationalism and the Politics of Culture in Quebec. Madison, Wisconsin: The University of Wisconsin Press, 1988. 217 p.

1592   **Hawkins, Freda**
Canada and Immigration: Public Policy and Public Concern. 2nd ed.
Kingston, Ontario: McGill-Queen's University Press, 1988. 476 p.

1593   **B.H. [Benedykt Heydenkorn]**
"The Left in Canadian Polonia." *Polyphony: The Bulletin of the
Multicultural History Society of Ontario*, vol. 6 no. 2 (1984) p. 57-
59.

1594   **Hillmer, Norman, Bohdan Kordan, and Lubomyr Luciuk, eds.**
On Guard for Thee: War, Ethnicity and the Canadian State, 1939-1945.
Ottawa: Canadian Committee for the History of the Second World War,
1988. 282 p. Papers presented at the symposium Ethnicity, the State, and
War: Canada and Its Ethnic Minorities, 1939-1945, held at Queen's
University, Kingston, Ontario, 25-27 September 1986.

1595   **Howell, Susan E. and Deborah Fagan**
"Race and Trust in Government: Testing the Political Reality Model."
Public Opinion Quarterly, vol. 52 no. 3 (1988) p. 343-350.

1596   **Indra, Doreen M.**
"Bureaucratic Constraints, Middlemen and Community Organization:
Aspects of the Political Incorporation of Southeast Asians in
Canada." In: *Uprooting, Loss and Adaptation: The Resettlement of
Indochinese Refugees in Canada*, edited by Kwok B. Chan and
Doreen Marie Indra. Ottawa: Canadian Public Health Association,
1987. p. 147-170.

1597   **Indra, Doreen M.**
"Bureaucratic Constraints, Middlemen and Community Organization:
Aspects of the Political Incorporation of Southeast Asians in
Canada." In: *Aspects of Social Change*, edited by K. Victor Ujimoto
and Josephine Naidoo. Guelph, Ont.: University of Guelph,
1984, p. 164-202. Selections from the proceedings, Asian Canadian
Symposium VI, University of Guelph, June 6 to 8, 1984.

1598   **Jayasuriya, D.L. and Peter Sheldrake**
"Mainstreaming: Meeting the Needs of Ethnic Minorities in the
1980's." *Multicultural Australian Papers*, no. 52 (1986).

1599   **Jedwab, Jack**
"Uniting Uptowners and Downtowners: The Jewish Electorate and
Quebec Provincial Politics: 1927-39." *Canadian Ethnic Studies/
Études ethniques au Canada*, vol. 18 no. 2 (1986) p. 7-19.

1600   **Johnson, Richard and Andre Blais**
"Meech Lake and Mass Politics: The 'Distinct Society' Clause."
Canadian Public Policy/Analyse de politiques, vol. 14, Supplement
(1988) p. 25-42.

1601   **Jones, Ted**
Both Sides of the Wire: The Fredericton Internment Camp. 2 vols.
Fredericton, N.B.: New Ireland Press, 1988-1989.

1602   **Katz, Elliot H.**
*The Participation of a Cultural Minority in Politics: Jewish Voting
Preferences in Seven Oaks and River Heights, 1969 and 1973.*
Unpublished MA thesis, University of Manitoba, 1980. 3 microfiches.
Canadian theses on microfiche, CT89-28585-3.

1603   **Kealey, Gregory S. and Reg Whitaker, eds.**
R.C.M.P. Security Bulletins, 1939-1941, edited by Gregory S. Kealey
and Reg Whitaker. St. John's, Nfld.: Committee on Canadian Labour
History, 1989. 438 p.

1604   **Kelly, Michael J.**
"Post Referendum Quebec: The Potential for Conflict." *Conflict
Quarterly*, vol. 1 no. 1 (1980) p. 15-19.

1605   **Kolasky, John**
"The Decline of the Ukrainian Pro-communist Organization."
*Polyphony: The Bulletin of the Multicultural History Society of
Ontario*, vol. 10 no. 1/2 (1988) p. 119-120.

1606   **Kruhlak, Orest M.**
"Constitutional Reform and Immigration." In: *Meech Lake and
Canada: Perspectives from the West*, edited by Roger Gibbins et al.
Edmonton: Academic Printing and Publishing, 1988, p. 201-213.

1607   **L'Allier, Jean-Paul**
Les années qui viennent. Montreal: Boreal, 1987. 269 p.

1608   **Lacroix, Jean-Michel**
"Le vote minoritaire: les slovaques à Toronto pendant l'ère Trudeau."
In: *Minorités et l'État*, sous la direction de Pierre Guillaume et al.
Bordeaux: Presses universitaires de Bordeaux, 1986, p. 189-211.

1609   **Laforest, Guy**
"Penser l'État: Gérard Bergeron, un Aufklarer québécois." *Politique*,
no. 9 (1986) p. 147-166. A critique of G. Bergeron's "Pratique de
l'État au Québec."

1610   **Laponce, J.A.**
"Left or Centre? The Canadian Jewish Electorate 1953-1983."
*Canadian Journal of Political Science/Revue canadienne de science
politique*, vol. 21 no. 4 (1988) p. 691-714.

1611   **Laponce, J.A.**
"Left or Center: The Canadian Jewish Electorate." *CPSA Papers/
ACSP Contributions*, Section A, paper 6, fiche 3-5. Paper presented
at the 60th annual meeting of the Canadian Political Science
Association, June 9-11, 1988, Windsor University, Windsor, Ontario.

1612   **Laponce, J.A.**
"Assessing the Neighbour Effect on the Vote of Francophone
Minorities in Canada." *Political Geography Quarterly*, vol. 6 no. 1
(1987) p. 77-87.

1613   **Laponce, J.A.**
"L'ethnie comme consommatrice d'espace: exemples canadiens." In:
Minorités et l'État, sous la direction de Pierre Guillaume et al.
Bordeaux: Presses Universitaires de Bordeaux, 1986, p. 61-76.

1614   **Laponce, J.A.**
"Ruling Elites in a Multi-lingual Society: Quebec Within Canada."
In: *Political Elites and Social Change: Studies of Elite Roles and
Attitudes*, edited by Moshe M. Czudnowski. DeKalb, Ill.: Northern
Illinois University Press, 1983, p. 39-63.

1615   **Lecavalier, Guy and Patricia Fitzsimmons-Lecavalier**
"Political Constraints and Communal Movements: The Mobilization
Dilemmas of Quebec's Nonfrancophone Minority." *CPSA Papers/
ACSP Contributions 1984*, Section D, paper 8, fiche 12. Paper
presented at the 56th annual meeting of the Canadian Political
Science Association, June 10-12, 1984, University of Guelph,
Guelph, Ontario.

1616   **Lefèbre, Jean-Paul**
*Entre deux fêtes: la politique au Québec, de 1966 à 1976 - ce qui
s'est passé entre la révolution tranquille et l'avènement du Parti
Québécois, raconté par un participant à l'action.* Montréal: Stanké,
1987. 227 p.

1617   **Legendre, Camille**
"Altering Citizenship Status: Some Preliminary Thoughts." *Canadian
Review of Studies in Nationalism/Revue canadienne des études sur le
nationalisme*, vol. 11 no. 2 (1984) 257-270.

1618   **Lennox, John, ed.**
Se connai'tre: Politics and Culture in Canada. Toronto: Robarts
Centre for Canadian Studies, York University Department of
Communications, 1985. Papers presented at a conference held at
York University, May 15-16, 1985.

1619   **Leslie, Peter M.**
"Bicommunalism and the Canadian Constitutional Reform." *Publius*,
vol. 18 no. 2 (1988) p. 115-129.

1620   **Levine, Marc V.**
"Nationalism in Quebec: Past, Present and Future." *Quebec Studies*,
no. 8 (1989) p. 119-130.

1621   **Lewycky, Laverne**
"Politics, Race Relations and Public Policy." In: *Canada 2000: Race
Relations and Public Policy*, edited by O.P. Dwivedi et al. Guelph,
Ontario: Department of Political Studies, University of Guelph,
1989, p. 240-259.

1622   **Lijphart, Arend**
"Language, Religion, Class and Party Choice: Belgium, Canada,
Switzerland and South Africa Compared." In: *Electoral Participation:
A Comparative Analysis*, edited by Richard Rose. Beverly Hills,
Calif.: Sage Publications, 1980, p. 283-328.

1623   **Lindström-Best, Varpu**
"National Finnish Organizations in Canada: Central Organization of
the Loyal Finns in Canada." *Polyphony: The Bulletin of the
Multicultural History Society of Ontario*, vol. 3 no. 2 (1981) p. 97-
103.

1624   **Long, J. Anthony**
"Traditional Political Values and Political Development: The Case of
Native Indian Self-Government." *CPSA Papers/ACSP Contributions
1989*, Section F, paper 13, fiche 4. Paper presented at the 61st annual
meeting of the Canadian Political Science Association, June 1-3,
1989, Laval University, Quebec, P.Q.

1625   **Long, J. Anthony**
"Political Attitudes of Members of an Internal Colony: A Study of
Native Indian University Students in Canada." *Plural Societies*, vol.
14 nos. 3/4 (1983) p. 85-98.

1626   **Long, J. Anthony, Menno Boldt, and Leroy Little Bear, eds.**
Governments in Conflict: Provinces and Indian Nations in Canada.
Toronto: University of Toronto Press, 1988. 296 p.

1627   **Long, J. Anthony, Menno Boldt, and Leroy Little Bear**
"Barriers to Policy Development: Proposed Federal Policy Toward
Indian Governments and Perceptions of Self-government Among
Future Indian Leaders." *CPSA Papers/ACSP Contributions 1982*,
Section D, paper 4, fiches 11-12. Paper presented at the 54th annual
meeting of the Canadian Political Science Association, June 7-9,
1982, University of Ottawa, Ottawa, Ontario.

1628   **Loveday, P.**
"Indigens and Electoral Administration, Australia and Canada."
Electoral Studies, vol. 6 no. 1 (1987) p. 31-40.

1629   **Luciuk, Lubomyr Y.**
"Ukrainians and Internment Operations in Ontario During the First
World War." *Polyphony: The Bulletin of the Multicultural History
Society of Ontario*, vol. 10 no. 1/2 (1988) p. 27-31.

1630   **Lupul, Manoly R.**
"Political Implementation of Multiculturalism." *Journal of Canadian
Studies/Revue d'études canadiennes*, vol. 17 no. 1 (1982) p. 93-102.

1631   **Lyon, Peter**
"Is There an Anglo-Canadian Political Culture?" *Bulletin of Canadian
Studies*, vol. 6 no. 2 (1983) p. 95-108.

1632   **Manzer, Ronald**
"Policy, Administration and Political Culture: The Case of Education
in the Anglo-democracies." *CPSA Papers/ACSP Contributions*,
Section G, paper 9, fiche 20. Paper presented at the 56th annual
meeting of the Canadian Political Science Association, June 10-12,
1984, University of Guelph, Guelph, Ontario.

1633   **March, Roman R.**
"Ethnicity, Party Politics and Political Culture in Canada: A
Comparative Perspective." *CPSA Papers/ACSP Contributions*,
Section H, paper 9, fiche 3. Paper presented at the 61st annual
meeting of the Canadian Political Science Association, June 1-3,
1989, Laval University, Quebec, P.Q.

1634   **Marule, Marie Smallface**
"An Indian Perspective on Canadian Politics." In: *Politics: Canada*,
edited by Paul W. Fox and Graham White. 6th ed. Toronto:
McGraw-Hill Ryerson, 1987, p. 26-33.

1635   **McElroy, Ann**
"The Politics of Inuit Alliance Movements in the Canadian Arctic."
In: *Political Organization of Native North Americans*, edited by
Ernest Schusky. Lanham, Md.: University Press of America,
1980, p. 243-282.

1636   **McGee, Charles**
"Cultural Policies in the 1980s." *Canadian Issues*, vol. 9
(1988) p. 155-170.

1637   **Mellos, Koula**
"The Group in Pluralist Ideology and Politics." *Canadian Journal of
Political and Social Theory/Revue canadienne de la théorie politique
et sociale*, vol. 10 no. 3 (1986) p. 24-45.

1638   **Morse, Bradford W.**
"Government Obligations, Aboriginal Peoples and Section 91(24) of
the Constitution Act, 1867." In: *Aboriginal Peoples and Government
Responsibility: Exploring Federal and Provincial Roles*, edited by
David C. Hawkes. Ottawa: Carleton University Press, 1989, p. 59-91.

1639   **Moss, John E.**
"Native Proposals for Constitutional Reform." *Journal of Canadian
Studies/Revue d'études canadiennes*, vol. 15 no. 4 (1980-81) p. 85-
92.

1640   **Nevitte, Neil and Allan Kornberg, eds.**
Minorities and the Canadian State. Oakville, Ont.: Mosaic Press,
1985. 324 p.

1641   **Newman, Saul**
*The Ethnic Dilemma: The Rise and Decline of Ethnoregional
Political Parties in Scotland, Belgium, and Quebec*. Unpublished PhD
thesis, Princeton University, 1989.

1642   **Nordholt, Jan Willem Schulte**
"François Adriaan van der Kemp: How an Immigrant Changes from
a Liberal into a Conservative." In: *Dutch Immigration to North
America*, edited by Herman Ganzevoort and Mark Boekelman.
Toronto: Multicultural History Society of Ontario, 1983, p. 85-96.

1643   **O'Neil, Daniel J.**
"Leadership and the Ethnic Factor: The Case of John A. Macdonald."
Plural Societies, vol. 12 no. 3 (1981) p. 109-123.

1644   **Opekokew, Delia**
*The Political and Legal Inequities Among Aboriginal Peoples in
Canada*. Kingston, Ont.: Institute of Intergovernmental Relations,
Queen's University, 1987. 52 p.

1645   **Paquet, Gilles**
"Nouvelle-France, Québec, Canada: A World of Limited Identities."
In: *Colonial Identity in the Atlantic World: 1500-1800*, edited by
Nicholas Canny and Anthony Pagden. Princeton: Princeton University
Press, 1987.

1646   **Paton, Richard**
New Policies and Old Organizations: Can Indian Affairs Change?
Ottawa: Centre for Policy and Program Assessment, School of Public
Administration, Carleton University, 1982. 67 leaves.

1647   **Payne, Richard J.**
"Canada, South Africa and the Commonwealth." *International
Perspectives*, (1987) p. 9-11.

1648   **Penner, Keith**
"The Politics of Aboriginal Self-government." In: *Issues in
Entrenching Aboriginal Self-government*, edited by David C. Hawkes
and Evelyn Peters. Kingston, Ont.: Institute of Intergovernmental
Relations, Queen's University, 1987, p. 21-34.

1649   **Pennoyer, Gregory Brent**
*The 1987 Constitutional Accord: Solving Canada's Constitutional
Crisis.* Unpublished MA thesis, CBN University, 1988. 133 leaves.

1650   **Rasporich, A.W.**
"Ethnicity in Lakehead Politics, 1900-30." *Polyphony: The Bulletin of
the Multicultural History Society of Ontario*, vol. 9 no. 2
(1987) p. 61-66.

1651   **Rawson, Bruce**
"Federal Perspectives on Indian-Provincial Relations." In: *Governments in Conflict? Provinces and Indian Nations in Canada*, edited
by J. Anthony Long, Menno Boldt, and Leroy Little Bear. Toronto:
University of Toronto Press, 1988, p. 23-30.

1652   **Reitz, Jeffrey G.**
The Survival of Ethnic Groups. Montreal: McGraw-Hill Ryerson,
1980. 292 p.

1653   **Remillard, Gil**
"Quebec's Quest for Survival and Equality via the Meech Lake
Accord." In: *Meech Lake Primer: Conflicting Views of the 1987
Constitutional Accord*, edited by Michael D. Behiels. Ottawa:
University of Ottawa Press, 1989, p. 28-41.

1654 **Rioux, Marcel**
Two Nations: An Essay on the Culture and Politics of Canada and Quebec in a World of American Pre-eminence. Toronto: Lorimer, 1983, 167 p.

1655 **Robinson, Eric**
The Infested Blanket: Canada's Constitution: Genocide of Indian Nations. Winnipeg: Queenston House Publishing Co., 1985. 168 p.

1656 **Roy, Michel**
"Surveying the Francophone Summit/Conclusions du sommet de Québec." *Language and Society/Langue et société*, no. 24 (1987) p. 31-32.

1657 **Roy, Patricia E.**
"Citizens Without Votes: East Asians in British Columbia, 1872-1947." In: *Ethnicity, Power and Politics in Canada*, edited by Jorgen Dahlie and Tissa Fernando. Toronto: Methuen, 1981, p. 151-171.

1658 **Sancton, Andrew**
Governing the Island of Montreal, Language Differences and Metropolitan Politics. Berkeley: University of California Press, 1985. 213 p.

1659 **Sanders, Douglas E.**
"Some Current Issues Affecting Indian Government." In: *Pathways to Self-determination: Canadian Indians and the Canadian State*, edited by Leroy Little Bear, Menno Boldt and J. Anthony Long. Toronto: University of Toronto Press, 1984, p. 113-121.

1660 **Sawchuk, Joseph Samuel**
Metis Politics and Metis Politicians: A New Political Arena in Canada. Unpublished PhD thesis, University of Toronto, 1983. Canadian theses on microfiche, CT86-22500-3.

1661 **Sawchuk, Joseph Samuel**
"Some Early Influences on Metis Political Organization." *Culture*, vol. 2 no. 3 (1982) p. 85.

1662 **Schwartz, Bryan**
First Principles, Second Thoughts: Aboriginal Peoples, Constitutional Reform and Canadian Statecraft. Montreal: Institute for Research on Public Policy, 1986. 515 p.

1663 **Schwartz, Bryan**
First Principles: Constitutional Reform with Respect to the Aboriginal Peoples of Canada, 1982-1984. Kingston, Ont.: Institute of Intergovernmental Relations, Queen's University, 1985. 292 p.

1664 **Schwartz, Mildred A.**
"Political Support and Group Dominance." In: *Political Support in Canada: The Crisis Years,* edited by Allan Kornberg and Harold D. Clarke. Durham, N.C.: Duke University Center for International Studies Publication, Duke University Press, 1983, p. 49-72.

1665 **Shaffir, William**
"Hassidic Jews and Quebec Politics." *Jewish Journal of Sociology,* vol. 25 no. 2 (1983) p. 105-118.

1666 **Shanahan, David Frances**
The Irish Question in Canada: Ireland, the Irish and Canadian Politics, 1880-1922. Unpublished PhD thesis, Carleton University, 1989. DAI vol. 51-A, p. 265.

1667 **Silver, A.I.**
The French-Canadian Idea of Confederation, 1864-1900. Toronto: University of Toronto Press, 1982. 257 p.

1668 **Sillanpaa, Lennard**
"Voting Behavior of Finns in the Sudbury Area, 1930-1972." In: *Finnish Diaspora I: Canada, South America, Africa, Australia and Sweden,* edited by Michael G. Karni. Toronto: Multicultural History Society of Ontario, 1981, p. 101-116.

1669 **Simeon, Richard**
"Aboriginal Self-government and Canadian Political Values." In: *Issues in Entrenching Aboriginal Self-government,* edited by David C. Hawkes and Evelyn Peters. Kingston, Ont.: Institute of Intergovernmental Relations, Queen's University, 1987, p. 49-58.

1670 **Smiley, Donald Victor**
"The Canadian Federation and the Challenge of Quebec Independence." In: *Canadian Federalism: From Crisis to Constitution,* edited by Harold Waller, Filippo Sabetti, and Daniel J. Elazar. Lanham, Maryland: University Press of America, Centre for the Study of Federalism, 1988, p. 107-132.

1671   **Smiley, Donald Victor**
"Update: The Canadian Confederation in 1978." In: *Canadian Federalism: From Crisis to Constitution*, edited by Harold Waller, Filippo Sabetti, and Daniel J. Elazar. Lanham, Maryland: University Press of America, Centre for the Study of Federalism, 1988, p. 133-137.

1672   **Smith, Joel**
"The Quebec Referendum: National or Provincial Event?" In: *Political Support in Canada: The Crisis Years*, edited by Allan Kornberg and Harold D. Clarke. Durham, N.C.: Duke University Center for International Studies Publication, Duke University Press, 1983, p. 353-379.

1673   **Spiegel, Shelly**
"Ontario Provincial Native Policy and Directions." In: *Governments in Conflict? Provinces and Indian Nations in Canada*, edited by J. Anthony Long, Menno Boldt, and Leroy Little Bear. Toronto: University of Toronto Press, 1988, p. 102-108.

1674   **Stanislawski, Howard J.**
"Canadian Jewry and Foreign Policy in the Middle East." In: *Canadian Jewish Mosaic*, edited by Morton Weinfeld, W. Shaffir and I. Cotler. Toronto: John Wiley and Sons, 1981, p. 397-413.

1675   **Stasiulis, Daiva K.**
"Affirmative Action for Visible Minorities and the New Politics of Race in Canada." In: *Canada 2000: Race Relations and Public Policy*, edited by O.P. Dwivedi et al. Guelph, Ont.: Department of Political Studies, University of Guelph, 1989, p. 233-239.

1676   **Stasiulis, Daiva K.**
"Minority Resistance in the Local State: Toronto in the 1970s and 1980s." *Ethnic and Racial Studies*, vol. 12 no. 1 (1989) p. 63-83.

1677   **Stasiulis, Daiva K.**
"The Political Structuring of Ethnic Community Action: A Reformulation." *Canadian Ethnic Studies/Études ethniques au Canada*, vol. 12 no. 3 (1980) p. 19-44.

1678   **Stein, Lana**
"Representative Local Government: Minorities in the Municipal Work Force." *The Journal of Politics*, vol. 48 no. 3 (1986) p. 694-713.

1679   Stevenson, Garth, ed.
        Federalism in Canada: Selected Readings. Toronto: McClelland and
        Stewart, 1989. 520 p.

1680   Swanick, Eric L.
        The Lake Meech Accord (Canadian Constitution): A Bibliography.
        Monticello, Ill.: Vance Bibliographies, 1988. 22 p.

1681   Swankey, Ben
        "Reflections of a Communist: Canadian Internment Camps." *Alberta
        History,* vol. 30 no. 2 (1982) p. 11.

1682   Taras, David
        "From Passivity to Politics: Canada's Jewish Community and
        Political Support for Israel." In: *The Domestic Battleground: Canada
        and the Arab-Israeli Conflict,* edited by David Taras and David H.
        Goldberg. Montreal: McGill-Queen's University Press, 1989, p. 37-
        62.

1683   Tarnopolsky, Walter S.
        *Religious Freedom: Freedom of Religion in Canada: The Legal and
        Constitutional Basis.* Vancouver: Bible Holiness Movement, 1985.
        27 p.

1684   Taylor, Donald M.
        "Defining 'Quebecois': The Role of Ethnic Heritage, Language and
        Political Orientation." In: *Ethnicity and Ethnic Relations in Canada:
        A Book of Readings,* edited by Rita M. Bienvenue and Jay E. Gold-
        stein. Toronto: Butterworths, 1985, p. 125-137. Reprinted from
        Canadian Ethnic Studies/Études ethniques au Canada. vol. 14 no. 2
        (1982) p. 59-70.

1685   Taylor, John Leonard
        *Indian Band Self-government in the 1960's: A Case Study of Walpole
        Island.* Ottawa: Indian and Northern Affairs Canada, Treaties and
        Historical Research Centre, 1984. 147 p. French language title:
        "L'autonomie gouvernementale des bandes indiennes dans les années
        soixante."

1686   Thériault, J. Yvon
        "État, ethnie et démocratie: réflexions sur la question politique en
        Acadie." *Canadian Review of Studies in Nationalism/Revue
        canadienne des études sur le nationalisme,* vol. 11 no. 2
        (1984) p. 201-218.

1687   **Thiessen, H.W.**
"Indian Self-government: A Provincial Perspective." In: *Pathways to Self-determination: Canadian Indians and the Canadian State*, edited by Leroy Little Bear, Menno Boldt and J. Anthony Long. Toronto: University of Toronto Press, 1984, p. 85-89.

1688   **Thorburn, H.G.**
"The Political Foundations of Canada's Pluralistic Society." In: *Canada 2000: Race Relations and Public Policy*, edited by O.P. Dwivedi et al. Guelph, Ont.: Department of Political Studies, University of Guelph, 1989, p. 64-75.

1689   **Tung, Ko-Chih R.**
"Voting Rights for Alien Residents: Who Wants It?" *International Migration Review*, vol. 19 no. 3 (1985) p. 451-467.

1690   **Uhlaner, Carole Jean**
"Does Sex Matter? Participation by French and English Women in Mass Canadian Politics." *CPSA Papers/ACSP Contributions 1980*, Section: Political Behaviour, paper 2, fiche 4. Paper presented at the 52nd annual meeting of the Canadian Political Science Association, June 2-4, 1980, Université du Québec à Montréal.

1691   **Wearing, Joseph**
Strained Relations: Canadian Parties and Voters. Toronto: McClelland and Stewart, 1988. 318 p.

1692   **Weatherbe, Steve, Tim Gallagher, and Paul Bunner**
"B.C.'s Terrorist Mouthpiece [Francisco Nota Moises]: Three West Coast Cases [Moises, Pastora and Torres] Underscore Canada's Politically Inconsistent Immigration Process." *Alberta Report*, vol. 15 no. 29 (1988) p. 9-10.

1693   **Weaver, Sally M.**
"Indian Policy in the New Conservative Government, Part II, the Neilson Task Force in the Context of Recent Policy Initiatives." *Native Studies Review*, vol. 2 no. 2 (1986) p. 1-45.

1694   **Weaver, Sally M.**
"Federal Policy-making for Metis and Non-status Indians in the Context of Native Policy." *Canadian Ethnic Studies/Études ethniques au Canada*, vol. 17 no. 2 (1985) p. 80-102.

1695   **Weaver, Sally M.**
"Political Representivity and Indigenous Minorities in Canada and Australia." In: *Indigenous Peoples and the Nation-state: Fourth World Politics in Canada, Australia and Norway*, edited by Noel Dyck. St. John's, Nfld.: Institute of Social and Economic Research, Memorial University of Newfoundland, 1985, p. 113-150.

1696   **Weaver, Sally M.**
"Indian Government: A Concept in Need of a Definition." In: *Pathways to Self-determination: Canadian Indians and the Canadian State*, edited by Leroy Little Bear, Menno Boldt and J. Anthony Long. Toronto: University of Toronto Press, 1984, p. 65-68.

1697   **Weeks, Nancy**
"Northern Development and Political Change." In: *Strategy and the Arctic*, edited by Roddick B. Byers and Michael Slack. Toronto: Canadian Institute of Strategic Studies, 1986, p. 71-85.

1698   **Weinfeld, Morton**
"The Development of Affirmative Action in Canada." *Canadian Ethnic Studies/Études ethniques au Canada*, vol. 13 no. 2 (1981) p. 23-39.

1699   **Wickberg, Edgar**
"Chinese and Canadian Influences on China Politics in Vancouver." *B.C. Studies*, vol. 45 (1980) p. 37-55.

1700   **Wong, Yuwa**
Ethnicity and State Policy: The Canadian Case. Unpublished PhD thesis, Simon Fraser University, 1981. Canadian theses on microfiche, 51089.

1701   **Wood, John R.**
"A Visible Minority Votes: East Indian Electoral Behaviour in the Vancouver South Provincial and Federal Elections of 1979." In: *Ethnicity, Power and Politics in Canada*, edited by Jorgen Dahlie and Tissa Fernando. Toronto: Methuen, 1981, p. 177-201.

Human, Civil, and Cultural Rights

1702 **Abols, Imants J.**
The Charter of Rights and Freedoms: Equality Rights. Ottawa:
Library of Parliament, Research Branch, 1986. 22 p.

1703 **Acheampong, Kenneth Asamoa**
*Human Rights and Affirmative Action: A Conceptual Analysis of Bill
C-62, an Act Respecting Employment Equity.* Unpublished LLM
thesis, University of Saskatchewan, 1988.

1704 **Ahenakew, David**
"Aboriginal Title and Aboriginal Rights: The Impossible and
Unnecessary Task of Identification and Definition." In: *The Quest for
Justice: Aboriginal Peoples and Aboriginal Rights,* edited by Menno
Boldt, and J. Anthony Long, with Leroy Little Bear. Toronto:
University of Toronto Press, 1985, p. 24-30.

1705 **Anderson, Donald George**
The Development of Human Rights Protection in British Columbia.
Unpublished MA thesis, University of Victoria, 1986.
188 p. Canadian theses on microfiche, CT88-22552-1.

1706 **Arkelian, A.J.**
"The Right to a Passport in Canadian Law." *Canadian Yearbook of
International Law/Annuaire canadien de droit international,* vol. 21
(1983) p. 284-293.

1707 **Arnand, Raj**
"Ethnic Equality." In: *Equality Rights and the Canadian Charter of
Rights and Freedoms,* edited by Anne F. Bayefsky and Mary Eberts.
Toronto: Carswell, 1985, p. 81-129.

1708   **Auerbach, Arnold J.**
"Human Rights and Social Control." *The Journal of Intergroup Relations*, vol. 14 no. 2 (1986) p. 34-36.

1709   **Axworthy, Thomas S.**
"Colliding Visions: The Debate Over the Canadian Charter of Rights and Freedoms, 1980-81." *Journal of Commonwealth and Comparative Politics*, vol. 24 no. 3 (1986) p. 239-253.

1710   **Barsh, Russel Lawrence**
"Aboriginal Rights, Treaty Rights, and Human Rights: Indian Tribes and Constitutional Renewal." *Journal of Canadian Studies/Revue d'études canadiennes*, vol. 17 no. 2 (1982) p. 55-81.

1711   **Bartels, Dennis A.**
"Ktaqamkuk Ilnui Sagimawoutie: Aboriginal Rights and the Myth of the Micmac Mercenaries in Newfoundland." In: *Native People, Native Lands: Canadian Indians, Inuit and Metis*, edited by Bruce Alden Cox. Ottawa: Carleton Univeristy Press, 1988, p. 32-36.

1712   **Bartlett, Richard H.**
"Hydroelectric Power and Indian Water Rights on the Prairies." *Prairie Forum*, vol. 14 no. 2 (1989) p. 177-194.

1713   **Bartlett, Richard H.**
Subjugation, Self-management and Self-government of Aboriginal Lands and Resources in Canada. Kingston, Ont.: Institute of Intergovernmental Relations, Queen's University, 1986. 102 p.

1714   **Bartlett, Richard H.**
"Mineral Rights on Indian Reserves in Ontario." *Canadian Journal of Native Studies*, vol. 3 no. 2 (1983) p. 245-276.

1715   **Basso, Piero**
"Perspectives of the International League for the Rights and Liberation of Peoples." *Social Justice*, vol. 16 no. 1 (1989) p. 127-131.

1716   **Beal, Bob**
Prairie Fire: The 1885 North-west Rebellion. Edmonton: Hurtig, 1984. 384 p.

1717   **Beaudoin, Gerald A.**
"Constitutionalizing Quebec's Protection at the Supreme Court and in
the Senate." In: *Meech Lake Primer: Conflicting Views of the 1987
Constitutional Accord*, edited by Michael D. Behiels. Ottawa:
University of Ottawa Press, 1989, p. 385-390.

1718   **Beaudoin, Gérald A.**
"Le multiculturalisme et les droits confessionnels et linguistique: une
vue succincte."In: *Multiculturalism and the Charter: A Legal
Perspective*, edited by the Canadian Human Rights Foundation.
Toronto: Carswell, 1987, p. 15-28.

1719   **Beaudoin, Gerald A.**
"Les droits des minorités: mythe ou réalité? La protection constitutionnelle des minorités." *Cahiers de droit*, vol. 27 no. 1 (1986) p. 31-
52.

1720   **Beaupré, Rémi Michael**
"The Case of Manitoba Language Rights: Judicial Review of the
Legislative Process." *Canadian Parliamentary Review*, vol. 10 no. 4
(1987/88) p. 16-22.

1721   **Beckton, Clare F.**
"Freedom of Expression: Individual vs Collective Rights." *Cambridge
Lectures*, vol. 5 (1987) p. 31-51.

1722   **Beckton, Clare F.**
"Section 27 and Section 15 of the Charter." In: *Multiculturalism and
the Charter: A Legal Perspective*, edited by the Canadian Human
Rights Foundation. Toronto: Carswell, 1987, p. 1-14.

1723   **Belcher, Ruth C.**
"Choice of Language and Commercial Expression Under S. 2(b) of
the Canadian Charter: Case Comment." *Journal of Canadian Studies/
Revue d'études canadiennes*, vol. 4 no. 1 (1989) p. 1-11.

1724   **Berger, Thomas R.**
"Human Rights in Canada: The English, the French and the Native
Peoples." In: *The Forty-ninth and Other Parallels: Contemporary
Canadian Perspectives*, edited by David Staines. Amherst, Mass.:
University of Massachusetts Press, 1986, p. 19-33.

1725   **Berger, Thomas R.**
"The Establishment of Aboriginal Rights: The Case of the Nishgas in British Columbia." In: *Two Nations, Many Cultures: Ethnic Groups in Canada*, edited by Jean Leonard Elliott. 2nd ed. Scarborough, Ont.: Prentice-Hall of Canada, 1983, p. 19-31.

1726   **Berger, Thomas R.**
"Native Rights and Self-determination." *Canadian Journal of Native Studies*, vol. 3 no. 2 (1983) p. 363-375.

1727   **Berger, Thomas R.**
"Native Rights and Self-determination: An Address." *University of Western Ontario Law Review*, vol. 22 no. 1 (1983) p. 1-14. Paper first presented at the Conference on the Voices of Native People, September 25, 1983.

1728   **Berlin, Mark L.**
"Hate Unbridled." *Policy Options/Options politiques*, vol. 6 no. 6 (1985) p. 31-32.

1729   **Bernier, Chantal**
"Les droits territoriaux des inuit au large des côtes et le droit international." *Canadian Yearbook of International Law/Annuaire canadien de droit international*, vol. 24 (1986) p. 314-334.

1730   **Bienvenue, Rita M.**
"Colonial Status: The Case of Canadian Indians." In: *Ethnicity and Ethnic Relations in Canada: A Book of Readings*, edited by Rita M. Bienvenue and Jay E. Goldstein. 2nd ed. Toronto: Butterworths, 1985, p. 199-214.

1731   **Bissonnette, Alain**
"Les luttes autochtones et l'exigence de la lucidité." *Recherches amérindiennes au Québec*, vol. 13 no. 3 (1983) p. 163-168.

1732   **Bissonnette, Alain**
"Les droits des autochtones et les Territoires du Nord-Ouest." *Recherches amérindiennes au Québec*, vol. 11 nos. 2-3 (1981) p. 133-147; 181-192.

1733   **Block, Walter E.**
On Employment Equity: A Critique of the Abella Royal Commission Report. Vancouver: Fraser Institute, 1985. 111 p.

1734   **Bolaria, B. Singh**
"Theories and Policies of Racial Domination." In: *Racial Oppression in Canada*, edited by B. Singh Bolaria and Peter S. Li. Toronto: Garamond Press, 1985, p. 19-32.

1735   **Bolaria, B. Singh and Peter S. Li, eds.**
Racial Oppression in Canada. 2nd ed. Toronto: Garamond Press, 1988. 272 p.

1736   **Boldt, Menno**
"Tribal Philosophies and the Canadian Charter of Rights and Freedoms." *Ethnic and Racial Studies*, vol. 7 no. 4 (1984) p. 478-493.

1737   **Boldt, Menno and J. Anthony Long, eds., with Leroy Little Bear**
The Quest for Justice: Aboriginal Peoples and Aboriginal Rights. Toronto: University of Toronto Press, 1985. 406 p.

1738   **Borovoy, A. Alan**
"Language as Violence v. Freedom of Expression: Canadian and American Perspectives on Group Defamation." *Buffalo Law Review*, vol. 37 no. 2 (1989) p. 337-374.

1739   **Borovoy, A. Alan**
When Freedoms Collide: The Case for Civil Liberties. Toronto: Lester and Orpen Dennys, 1988. 419 p.

1740   **Bottos, Dino**
"Keegstra and Andrews: A Commentary on Hate Propaganda and the Freedom of Expression." *Alberta Law Review*, vol. 27 no. 3 (1989) p. 461-475.

1741   **Bottos, Dino**
"Multiculturalism: Section 27's Application in Charter Cases Thus Far." *Alberta Law Review*, vol. 26 no. 3 (1988) p. 621-633.

1742   **Bowerman, Jennifer K.**
"East Indians in Alberta: A Human Rights Viewpoint." In: *Visible Minorities and Multiculturalism: Asians in Canada*, edited by K. Victor Ujimoto and Gordon Hirabayashi. Toronto: Butterworths, 1980, p. 181-191.

1743   **Braen, Andre**
"Language Rights." In: *Language Rights in Canada*, edited by Michel
Bastarache. Montreal: Éditions Y. Blais, 1987, p. 3-66. Translation of
the author's "Les droits linguistiques" In: *Les droits linguistiques au
Canada*, sous la direction de Michel Bastarache. Montreal: Éditions
y. Blais, 1986, p. 4-70.

1744   **Braen, André**
"Les droits des minorités au Canada et la Constitution." *Revista de la
Facultad de Derecho de Mexico*, no. 151-153 (1987) p. 29-44.

1745   **Braen, André**
"The Enforcement of Language Rights." In: *Language Rights in
Canada*, edited by Michel Bastarache. Montreal: Éditions Y. Blais,
1987, p. 449-499. Translation of the author's "Les recours en matière
de droits linguistiques" In: *Les droits linguistiques au Canada*, sous
la direction de Michel Bastarache. Montreal: Éditions y. Blais,
1986, p. 465-519.

1746   **Braun, Stefan**
"Social and Racial Tolerance and Freedom of Expression in a
Democratic Society: Friends or Foes? Regina vs Zundel." *Dalhousie
Law Journal*, vol. 11 no. 2 (1988) p. 471-513.

1747   **Brecher, Irving, ed.**
*Human Rights, Development and Foreign Policy: Canadian
Perspectives*. Halifax: The Institute for Research on Public Policy/
L'institut de recherches politiques, 1989. 579 p.

1748   **Breton, Raymond**
"The Concepts of 'Distinct Society and Identity' in the Meech Lake
Accord." In: *Competing Constitutional Visions: The Meech Lake
Accord*, edited by Katherine E. Swinton and Carol J. Rogerson.
Toronto: Carswell, 1988, p. 3-10. Paper presented at a symposium
held at the University of Toronto on October 30, 1987.

1749   **British Columbia. Ministry of Attorney General**
Indian Land Claims in British Columbia. Victoria: Secretariat for
Indian Policy and Programs, Ministry of Attorney General, 1985. 6,
(2) leaves.

1750   **Brown, Douglas M.**
"Indian Hunting Rights and Provincial Law: Some Recent Developments." *University of Toronto Faculty of Law Review*, vol. 39 no. 2
(1981) p. 121-132.

1751   **Brun, Henri**
"Les statuts respectifs de citoyen, résident et étranger, à la lumière des chartes des droits." *Cahiers de droit*, vol. 29 no. 3 (1988) p. 689-731.

1752   **Bruyère, Louis**
"Aboriginal Peoples and the Meech Lake Accord." In: *Canadian Human Rights Year Book/Annuaire canadien des droits de la personne*, (1988) p. 49-80.

1753   **Buron, Denis**
"Liberté d'expression et diffamation de collectivites; quand le droit à l'égalité s'exprime." *Cahiers de droit*, vol. 29 no. 2 (1988) p. 491-534.

1754   **Cairns, Alan C.**
"Citizens and Their Charter: Democratizing the Process of Constitutional Reform." In: *Meech Lake Primer: Conflicting Views of the 1987 Constitutional Accord*, edited by Michael D. Behiels. Ottawa: University of Ottawa Press, 1989, p. 109-124.

1755   **Cairns, Alan C.**
"Political Science, Ethnicity and the Canadian Constitution." In: *Federalism and Political Community: Essays in Honour of Donald Smiley*, edited by David P. Shugarman and Reg Whitaker. Peterborough, Ont.: Broadview Press, 1989, 113-140.

1756   **Cairns, Alan C.**
"Constitutionalism, Citizenship and Society in Canada: An Overview." In: *Constitutionalism, Citizenship and Society in Canada*, research coordinators Alan Cairns and Cynthia Williams. Toronto: University of Toronto Press, 1985, p. 1-50.

1757   **Cairns, Alan and Cynthia Williams, research coords.**
Constitutionalism, Citizenship and Society in Canada. Toronto: University of Toronto Press, 1985. 231 p.

1758   **Caldwell, Gary and Eric Waddell, eds.**
The English of Quebec: From Majority to Minority Status, edited by Gary Caldwell and Eric Waddell. Québec, P.Q.: Institut québécois de recherche sur la culture, 1982. 464 p.

1759   **Canada. Commissioner of Official Languages**
The Minorities; Time for Solutions: Two Million Canadians in Search of Linguistic Equality. Ottawa: Commissioner of Official Languages, 1986. 64, 68 p. Proceedings of the colloquium sponsored by the Office of the Commissioner of Official Languages, Ottawa and Hull, October 18-19, 1985. French language title: *Les minorités, le temps des solutions: deux millions de canadiens en quête de l'égalite linguistique.*

1760   **Canada. Department of Indian Affairs and Northern Development.**
"In All Fairness: A Native Claims Policy, Comprehensive Claims." In: *People, Resources and the Environment North of '60: National and Regional Interests in the North ....* Ottawa: Canadian Arctic Resources Committee, 1984, p. 57-70.

1761   **Canada. Department of Indian Affairs and Northern Development. Office of Native Claims**
"Perspectives in Native Land-claims Policy." In: *People, Resources and the Environment North of '60: National and Regional Interests in the North ....* Ottawa: Canadian Arctic Resources Committee, 1984, p. 87-108.

1762   **Canada. Department of Indian Affairs and Northern Development**
In All Fairness: A Native Claims Policy: Comprehensive Claims. Ottawa: Supply and Services Canada, 1981. 30, 32 p. French language title: *En toute justice: une politique des revendictions.*

1763   **Canada. Indian and Northern Affairs Canada**
Report to Parliament: Implementation of the 1985 Changes to the Indian Act. Ottawa: Indian and Northern Affairs, 1987, 48 p.

1764   **Canadian Bar Association**
Current Issues in Aboriginal and Treaty Rights: Friday, May 25, 1984. Ottawa: Canadian Bar Association, 1984. 191 p. Chairmen: William B. Henderson and Brad Morse.

1765   **Canadian Ethnocultural Council**
"A Dream Deferred: Collective Equality for Canada's Ethnocultural Communities." In: *Meech Lake Primer: Conflicting Views of the 1987 Constitutional Accord,* edited by Michael D. Behiels. Ottawa: University of Ottawa Press, 1989, p. 335-348.

1766   **Canadian Human Rights Foundation**
Multiculturalism and the Charter: A Legal Perspective. Toronto:
Carswell, 1987. 192 p.

1767   **Cardinal, Harold**
"Indian Nations and Constitutional Change." In: *Governments in
Conflict? Provinces and Indian Nations in Canada,* edited by J.
Anthony Long and Menno Boldt, with Leroy Little Bear. Toronto:
University of Toronto Press, 1988, p. 83-89.

1768   **Carignan, Pierre**
"De la notion de droit collectif et de son application en matière
scolaire au Québec: la charte canadienne des droits et libertés:
concepts et impacts." *Revue juridique thémis,,* vol. 18 no. 1
(1984) p. 1-103.

1769   **Castel, James Garland**
"The Extradition of Canadian Citizens and Section 1 and 6(1) of the
Canadian Charter of Rights and Freedoms." *Canadian Yearbook of
International Law/Annuaire canadien de droit international,* vol. 25
(1987) p. 263-299.

1770   **Center for Migration Studies**
"Civil Rights and the Sociopolitical Participation of Migrants."
International Migration Review, vol. 19 no. 3 (1985) p. 398-661.

1771   **Chamberlin, J. Edward**
"Aboriginal Rights and the Meech Lake Accord." In: *Competing
Constitutional Visions: The Meech Lake Accord,* edited by Katherine
E. Swinton and Carol J. Rogerson. Toronto: Carswell, 1988, p. 11-19.

1772   **Chamberlin, J. Edward**
"Homeland and Frontier." *Queen's Quarterly,* vol. 89 no. 2
(1982) p. 325-337.

1773   **Charest, Paul**
"Contraintes écologiques et pêcheries sédentaires sur la Basse Côte
nord du Saint Laurent." *Anthropologie et sociétés,* vol. 5 no. 1
(1981) p. 29-56.

1774   **Chartier, Clem**
"Aboriginal Rights and Land Issues: The Metis Perspective." *The
Quest for Justice: Aboriginal Peoples and Aboriginal Rights,* edited
by Menno Boldt and J. Anthony Long, with Leroy Little Bear.
Toronto: University of Toronto Press, 1985, p. 54-61.

1775   **Chartier, Clem**
"The Nature of Indian Title." *Canadian Legal Aid Bulletin*, vol. 5 no. 2/3 (1982) p. 71-98.

1776   **Chouinard, Jean-Yves**
"Les droits collectifs inséparables des droits individuels." *Action nationale*, vol. 71 no. 3 (1981) p. 371-384.

1777   **Christopher, T.C.**
"The 1982 Canadian Charter of Rights and Freedoms and Multiculturalism." *Canadian Review of Studies in Nationalism/Revue canadienne des études sur le nationalisme*, vol. 14 no. 2 (1987) p. 331-343.

1778   **Christopher, T.C.**
"Section 27 of the Canadian Charter of Rights and Freedoms: Origin and Judicial Interpretation." *CPSA Papers/ACSP Contributions 1985*, Section C, paper 5, fiche 5. A paper presented at the 57th annual meeting of the Canadian Political Science Association, May 31-June 2, 1985, Université de Montréal.

1779   **Clark, Bruce A.**
Indian Title in Canada. Toronto: Carswell, 1987. 142 p.

1780   **Cloutier, Joe**
"Is History Repeating Itself at Lubicon Lake?" *Canadian Journal of Native Education*, vol. 15 no. 1 (1988) p. 1-17.

1781   **Coalition of NGOs [Non-Governmental Organizations]**
"About the Coalition of NGOs Concerned with Impunity for Violators of Human Rights." *Social Justice*, vol. 16 no. 1 (1989) p. 135-142.

1782   **Coates, Kenneth Stephen**
Treaty Research Report, Treaty Five (1875-1908). Ottawa: Treaties and Historical Research Centre, Indian and Northern Affairs Canada, 1987. 102 p.

1783   **Cohen, Fay G.**
Treaties on Trial: The Continuing Controversy Over Northwest Indian Fishing Rights. Seattle: University of Washington Press, 1986. 229 p.

1784   **Cohnstaedt, Joy**
"Human Rights and Canadian Cultural Policy." *Canadian Issues*, vol.
12 (1989) p. 51-64.

1785   **Coluin, Eric**
Legal Process and the Resolution of Indian Claims. Saskatoon:
University of Saskatchewan Native Law Centre, 1981. 29 p.

1786   **Conn, Stephen**
"Inuit Village Councils in Alaska: An Historical Model for
Effectuation of Aboriginal Right?" *Études Inuit Studies*, vol. 9 no. 2
(1985) p. 43-59.

1787   **Cook, George Ramsay**
"Alice in Meachland: Or the Concept of Quebec as 'A Distinct
Society'." In: *Meech Lake Primer: Conflicting Views of the 1987
Constitutional Accord*, edited by Michael D. Behiels. Ottawa:
University of Ottawa Press, 1989, p. 147-160.

1788   **Coon-Come, Matthew**
"Indian Rights in Canada: An International Issue." *Sakatchewan
Indian Federated College Journal*, vol. 4 no. 2 (1988) p. 91-98.

1789   **Council of Forest Industries of British Columbia**
*Native Indian Land Claims in British Columbia: A Background
Paper.* Prepared by the Council of Forest Industries of British
Columbia. Vancouver: The Council, 1986. 14 p.

1790   **Courchene, Thomas J.**
"Meech Lake and Socio-economic Policy." *Canadian Public Policy/
Analyse de politiques*, vol. 14 (1988 supplement) p. 63-80.

1791   **Courchene, Thomas J.**
Meech Lake and Federalism: Accord or Discord? North York, Ont.:
Robarts Centre for Canadian Studies, York University, 1987. 64 p.

1792   **Crossley, John Edward**
The Making of Canadian Indian Policy to 1946. Unpublished PhD
thesis, University of Toronto, 1987.

1793   **Cumming, Peter A.**
"Canada's North and Native Rights." In: *Aboriginal Peoples and the
Law: Indian, Metis and Inuit Rights in Canada*, edited by Bradford
Morse. Ottawa: Carleton University Press, 1989, p. 695-743.

1794   **Dacks, Gurston**
"Devolution and Political Development in the Canadian North."
CPSA Papers/ACSP Contributions 1989, Section A, paper 4, fiches
1-2. Paper presented at the 61st annual meeting of the Canadian
Political Science Association, June 1-3, 1989, Laval University,
Quebec, P.Q.

1795   **Dacks, Gurston**
"The Politics of Native Claims in Northern Canada." In: *The Quest
for Justice: Aboriginal Peoples and Aboriginal Rights*, edited by
Menno Boldt and J. Anthony Long, with Leroy Little Bear. Toronto:
University of Toronto Press, 1985, p. 251-264.

1796   **Davies, Alan T.**
"The Queen versus James Keegstra: Reflections on Christian
Antisemitism in Canada." *American Journal of Theology and
Philosophy*, vol. 9 nos. 1-2 (1988) p. 99-116.

1797   **Davies, Maureen**
"Aspects of Aboriginal Rights in International Law." In: *Aboriginal
Peoples and the Law: Indian, Metis and Inuit Rights in Canada*,
edited by Bradford Morse. Ottawa: Carleton University Press,
1989, p. 16-46.

1798   **Demers, Clovis**
"Administrative Change to Accomodate Self-government." In:
Current Issues in Aboriginal and Treaty Rights. Ottawa, Ont.:
Canadian Bar Association-Ontario Continuing Legal Education,
1984, p. 171-175.

1799   **Diamond, Billy**
"Aboriginal Rights: The James Bay Experience." In: *The Quest for
Justice: Aboriginal Peoples and Aboriginal Rights*, edited by Menno
Boldt and J. Anthony Long, with Leroy Little Bear. Toronto:
University of Toronto Press, 1985, p. 265-285.

1800   **Dion, Léon**
"Fondements de la distinction entre droits privés et droits publics."
*Royal Society of Canada. Proceedings and Transactions/Société
royale du Canada. Mémoirs et comptes rendus*, ser. 4, vol. 23
(1985) p. 69-90.

1801   **Document of the United Nations**
"Universal Declaration of Human Rights." *Social Justice*, vol. 16 no. 1 (1989) p. 150-154.

1802   **Donnelly, F.K.**
"The Battle Over Eckville: Prejudice in Canadian Provincial Politics." *Patterns of Prejudice*, vol. 18 no. 1 (1984) p. 16-22.

1803   **Donnelly, Jack**
"Human Rights: The Impact of International Action." *International Journal*, vol. 43 no. 2 (1988) p. 241-263.

1804   **Driben, Paul**
"As Equal as Others." *Policy Options/Options politiques*, vol. 6 no. 5 (1985) p. 7-8.

1805   **Driben, Paul**
"The Nature of Metis Claims." *Canadian Journal of Native Studies*, vol. 3 no. 1 (1983) p. 183-196.

1806   **Dupre, J. Stefan**
"Canadian Constitutionalism and the Sequel to the Meech Lake/ Langevin Accord." In: *Federalism and Political Community: Essays in Honour of Donald Smiley*, edited by David P. Shugarman and Reg Whitaker. Peterborough, Ont.: Broadview Press, 1989, p. 241-248.

1807   **Dyck, Noel**
"The Negotiation of Indian Treaties and Land Rights in Saskatchewan." In: *Aborigines, Land and Land Rights*, edited by N. Peterson and M. Langton. Canberra: Australian Institute of Aboriginal Studies, 1983, p. 405-415. Paper presented at the Aboriginal Land Right Symposium of the Australian Institute of Aboriginal Studies, May 21-22, 1989.

1808   **Dyck, Noel**
"The Politics of Special Status: Indian Associations and the Administration of Indian Affairs." In: *Ethnicity, Power, and Politics in Canada*, edited by Jorgen Dahlie and Tissa Fernando. Toronto: Methuen, 1981, p. 279-291.

1809   **Dyck, Noel**
"Indian, Metis, Native: Some Implications of Special Status." *Canadian Ethnic Studies/Études ethniques au Canada*, vol. 12 no. 1 (1980) p. 34-46.

1810   **Elias, Peter Douglas**
"Aboriginal Rights and Litigation: History and Future of Court
Decisions in Canada." *Polar Record*, vol. 25 [152] (1989) p. 1-8.

1811   **Elkins, David J.**
"Facing our Destiny: Rights and Canadian Distinctiveness." *Canadian
Journal of Political Science/Revue canadienne de science politique*,
vol. 22 no. 4 (1989) p. 699-716.

1812   **Elliot, David W.**
"Aboriginal Title." In: *Aboriginal Peoples and the Law: Indian,
Metis and Inuit Rights in Canada*, edited by Bradford Morse. Ottawa:
Carleton University Press, 1989, p. 48-121.

1813   **Elman, Bruce P.**
"The Promotion of Hatred and the Canadian Charter of Rights and
Freedoms: A Review of Keegstra vs the Queen." *Canadian Public
Policy/Analyse de politiques*, vol. 15 no. 1 (1989) p. 72-83.

1814   **Emond, D. Paul**
"Alternative Resolution Processes for Comprehensive Native Claims."
Current Issues in Aboriginal and Treaty Rights. Ottawa, Ont.:
Canadian Bar Association/Ontario Continuing Legal Education,
1984, p. 74-110.

1815   **Erasmus, Georges**
"The Solution We Favour for Change." In: *Drumbeat: Anger and
Renewal in Indian Country*, edited by Boyce Richardson. Toronto:
Summerhill Press, 1989, p. 295-303.

1816   **Erasmus, Georges**
"Native Rights." In: *Meech Lake and Canada: Perspectives from the
West*, edited by Roger Gibbins, Howard Palmer, Brian Rusted, and
David Taras. Edmonton: Academic Printing and Publishing,
1988, p. 179-184.

1817   **Ervin, Alexander M.**
"Contrasts Between the Resolution of Native Land Claims in the
United States and Canada: Based on Observations of the Alaska
Native Land Claims Movement." *Canadian Journal of Native Studies*,
vol. 3 no. 1 (1983) p. 123-139.

1818   **Federation of Saskatchewan Indian Nations. Indian Government Commission.**
"Indian Nations in Unity with the Sacred Treaties." *Sakatchewan Indian Federated College Journal*, vol. 4 no. 2 (1988) p. 63-78.

1819   **Feit, Harvey A.**
"Negotiating Recognition of Aboriginal Rights: History, Strategies and Reactions to the James Bay and Northern Quebec Agreement." In: *Aborigines, Land and Land Rights*, edited by N. Peterson and M. Langton. Canberra: Australian Institute of Aboriginal Studies, 1983, p. 416-438. Paper presented at the Aboriginal Land Rights Symposium of the Australian Institute of Aboriginal Studies, May 21-22, 1980.

1820   **Feit, Harvey, A.**
"Negotiating Recognition of Aboriginal Rights: History, Strategies and Reactions to the James Bay Northern Quebec Agreement." *Canadian Journal of Anthropology/Revue canadienne d'anthropologie*, vol. 1 no. 2 (1980) p. 159-172.

1821   **Felice, Bill**
"Rights in Theory and Practice: An Historical Perspective." *Social Justice*, vol. 16 no. 1 (1989) p. 34-55.

1822   **Filmon, Gary**
"The Opposition View: The Other side of the Question." *Language and Society/Langue et société*, no. 16 (1985) p. 13-15.

1823   **Findlay, Peter C.**
"The Implications of 'Sovereignty-Association' for Social Welfare in Canada: An Anglophone Perspective." *Canadian Journal of Social Work Education*, vol. 6 no. 1 (1980) p. 141-148.

1824   **Fisher, A.D.**
"The Concept of 'Affirmative Action' in Socialist and Capitalist Systems." *Canadian Journal of Native Education*, vol. 11 no. 2 (1984) p. 2-7.

1825   **Flanagan, Thomas**
"Metis Aboriginal Rights: Some Historical and Contemporary Problems." In: *The Quest for Justice: Aboriginal Peoples and Aboriginal Rights*, edited by Menno Boldt and J. Anthony Long, with Leroy Little Bear. Toronto: University of Toronto Press, 1985, p. 230-247.

1826   **Flanagan, Thomas**
"Metis Land Claims at St. Laurent: Old Arguments and New Evidence." *Prairie Forum*, vol. 12 no. 2 (1987) p. 245-256. Article designed as an answer to criticism of the author's book: *Riel and the Rebellion: 1885 Reconsidered*, 1983.

1827   **Flanagan, Thomas**
"The Case Against Metis Aboriginal Rights." *Canadian Public Policy /Analyse de politiques*, vol. 9 no. 3 (1983) p. 314-325.

1828   **Flavelle, Lucinda**
The Equality Rights Provisions of the Canadian Charter of Rights and Freedoms. Toronto: Ontario Legislative Library, Legislative Research Service, 1985. 20 leaves. (microform).

1829   **Fogarty, Kenneth H.**
Equality Rights and their Limitations in the Charter. Toronto: Carswell, 1987. 422 p.

1830   **Fontaine, André**
"L'insuffisance des garanties constitutionnelles relatives aux droits des acadiens."In: *Territoires et minorités: de l'Amérique française au lac Meech*, textes réunis par Gilles Sénécal. Montréal: Association canadienne-française pour l'avancement des sciences, 1989, p. 22-36. Actes du colloque organisé par l'Association professionnelle des Géographes du Québec.

1831   **Foster, Hamar**
"How Not to Draft Legislation: Indian Land Claims, Government Intransigence, and How Premier Walkem Nearly Sold the Farm in 1874." *Advocate*, vol. 46 (1988) p. 411-420.

1832   **Foster, William F.**
"Constitutional Protection and the Right to Education." *Dalhousie Law Journal*, vol. 11 no. 3 (1988) p. 759-832.

1833   **Foucher, Pierre**
"L'accord du lac Meech et les francophones hors Québec." *Canadian Human Rights Year Book/Annuaire canadien des droits de la personne*, (1988) p. 3-48.

1834   **Foucher, Pierre**
"The Right to Receive Public Services in Both Official Languages." In: *Language Rights in Canada*, edited by Michel Bastarache. Montreal: Éditions Y. Blais, 1987, p. 176-257. Translation of the author's "Le droit à la prestation des services publics dans les langues officielles" chapter in: *Les droits linguistiques au Canada*.

1835 **Foucher, Pierre**
"Les droits linguistiques en matière scolaire." In: *Les droits linguistiques au Canada*, sous la direction de Michel Bastarache. Montréal: Éditions Y. Blais, 1986, p. 269-325.

1836 **Foucher, Pierre**
Constitutional Language Rights of Official-language Minorities in Canada: A Study of the Legislation of the Provinces and Territories Respecting Education Rights of Official-language Minorities and Compliance with Section 23 of the Canadian Charter of Rights and Freedoms. Ottawa: Canadian Law Information Council, 1985. 460 p.

1837 **Foucher, Pierre**
"Les droits scolaires des acadiens et la Charte." *University of New Brunswick Law Journal/Revue de droit de l'Université de Nouveau-Brunswick*, vol. 33 (1984) p. 97-154.

1838 **Fournier, Francine**
"Collective Rights in the Area of Equality Rights: The Canadian Scene." *Cambridge Lectures*, vol. 5 (1987) p. 229-246.

1839 **Frideres, James S.**
"Native Claims and Settlement in Yukon." In: *Arduous Journey: Canadian Indians and Decolonization*, edited by J. Rick Ponting. Toronto: McClelland and Stewart, 1986, p. 284-301.

1840 **Frideres, James S.**
"Native Land Claims." In: *Ethnicity and Ethnic Relations in Canada: A Book of Readings*, edited by Rita M. Bienvenue and Jay E. Goldstein. 2nd ed. Toronto: Butterworths, 1985, p. 289-308.

1841 **Frideres, James S.**
"Native Settlements and Native Rights." *Canadian Journal of Native Studies*, vol. 1 no. 1 (1981) p. 59-85.

1842 **Gaffney, R.E.**
Broken Promises: The Aboriginal Constitutional Conferences. [s.l.]: New Brunswick Association of Metis and Non-status Indians, 1984. 115 p.

1843 **Gagnon, Alain-G.**
"Quebec and the Pursuit of Special Status." In: *Perspectives on Canadian Federalism*, edited by R.D. Olling and M.W. Westmacott. Scarborough, Ont.: Prentice-Hall Canada, 1988, p. 304-325.

1844   **Gewirth, Alan**
"Why There are Human Rights." *Social Theory and Practice*, vol. 11 no. 2 (1985) p. 235-248.

1845   **Gibbins, Roger, et al.**
Meech Lake and Canada: Perspectives from the West. Edmonton: Academic Printing and Publishing, 1988. 283 p.

1846   **Gibson, Dale**
"Protection of Minority Rights Under the Canadian Charter of Rights and Freedoms: Can Politicians and Judges Sing Harmony?" In: *Minorities and the Canadian State*, edited by Neil Nevitte and Allan Kornberg. Oakville, Ont.: Mosaic Press, 1985, p. 31-54.

1847   **Gibson, Dale**
"Stereotypes, Statistics and Slippery Slopes: A Reply to Professors Flanagan and Knopff and Other Critics of Human Rights Legislation." In: *Minorities and the Canadian State*, edited by Neil Nevitte and Allan Kornberg. Oakville, Ont.: Mosaic Press, 1985, p. 125-138. A critique of the essays on pages 87-124 of the book.

1848   **Gibson, Dale**
Impact of Canadian Charter of Rights and Freedoms on Manitoba Statutes. Winnipeg: Legal Research Institute, University of Manitoba, 1982. 151 leaves.

1849   **Gilbert, Anne**
"Les francophones hors Québec à la quête d'un territoire." In: *Territoires et minorités: de l'Amérique française au lac Meech: actes du colloque organisé par l'Association professionnelle des géographes du Québec*, textes réunis par Gilles Sénécal. Montréal: Association canadienne-française pour l'avancement des sciences, 1989, p. 37-49.

1850   **Glaser, Kurt**
"Canada's Native Minorities and Their Status." *Plural Societies*, vol. 17 no. 2 (1987) p. 52-74.

1851   **Gold, Gérald Louis**
"La revendication de nos droits: The Quebec Referendum and Francophone Minorities in Canada." *Ethnic and Racial Studies*, vol. 7 no. 1 (1984) p. 106-128.

1852   **Goodwin-Gill, Guy S.**
"International Law and the Detention of Refugees and Asylum
Seekers." *International Migration Review*, vol. 20 no. 2
(1986) p. 193-219.

1853   **Goodwin-Gill, Guy S.**
"Basic Humanitarian Principles Applicable to Non-nationals."
International Migration Review, vol. 19 no. 3 (1985) p. 556-569.

1854   **Goreham, Richard Alexander**
Group Language Rights in Plurilingual States. Unpublished LLM
thesis, McGill University, 1980. 204 leaves.

1855   **Gormley, Daniel J.**
"Aboriginal Rights as National Rights." *Canadian Journal of Native
Studies*, vol. 4 no. 1 (1986) p. 32-42.

1856   **Green, Leslie C.**
"Are Language Rights Fundamental?" *Osgoode Hall Law Journal*,
vol. 25 no. 4 (1987) p. 639-670.

1857   **Green, Leslie C.**
"Aboriginal Peoples, International Law and the Canadian Charter of
Rights and Freedoms." *Canadian Bar Review/Revue du Barreau
canadien*, vol. 61 no. 1 (1983) p. 339-353.

1858   **Grey, Julius H.**
"Canadian Citizenship Law and Human Rights Issues." In:
Challenging the Concept of Citizenship, edited by Rene R. Gadacz.
Edmonton: CSC Consulting Services, 1986, p. 29-45.

1859   **Guillaume, Pierre**
"Acadiens, droits linguistiques et rapatriement de la constitution."
Études canadiennes/Canadian Studies, no. 13 (1982) p. 153-156.

1860   **Hall, Tony**
"What are We? Chopped Liver? Aboriginal Affairs in the
Constitutional Politics of Canada in the 1980's." In: *Meech Lake
Primer: Conflicting Views of the 1987 Constitutional Accord*, edited
by Michael D. Behiels. Ottawa: University of Ottawa Press,
1989, p. 423-456.

1861   **Harakas, A.J.**
"Canadian Immigration Law and the Canadian Charter of Rights and Freedoms." *American Society of International Law. Proceedings of Annual Meeting*, vol. 79 (1987) p. 214-216. Paper presented at the 79th annual meeting of the American Society of International Law, New York, N.Y., April 25-27, 1985.

1862   **Harding, James**
Aboriginal Rights and Government Wrong: Uranium Mining and Neocolonialism in Northern Saskatchewan. Series in the Public Interest, Working Paper no. 1. Regina: Prairie Justice Research, University of Regina, 1988. 43 p.

1863   **Hardy, Richard I.**
"Metis Rights in the Mackenzie River District of the Northwest Territories." *Canadian Native Law Reporter*, vol. 2 no. 1 (1980) p. 1-33.

1864   **Harney, Jean-Paul**
"A la dérive sur le lac Meech." In: *L'adhésion du Québec à l'accord du lac Meech*, sous la direction de Réal A. Forest. Montréal: Éditions Thémis, 1988, p. 207- 217. Proceedings of the 1987 colloquium organised by the Quebecois section of the Association du Barreau canadien on Constitutional Rights and Civil Liberties.

1865   **Head, Wilson A.**
"Employment Agencies and Discrimination." *Currents*, vol. 1 no. 2 (1983) p. 34.

1866   **Headley, Bernard D.**
"Crime, Justice, and Powerless Racial Groups." *Social Justice*, vol. 16 no. 4 (1989) p. 1-9.

1867   **Henderson, James Youngblood**
"The Doctrine of Aboriginal Rights in Western Legal Tradition." In: *The Quest for Justice: Aboriginal Peoples and Aboriginal Rights*, edited by Menno Boldt and J. Anthony Long, with Leroy Little Bear. Toronto: University of Toronto Press, 1985, p. 185-220.

1868   **Henderson, William B.**
"Constitutional Affirmation of Aboriginal and Treaty Rights." In: *Current Issues in Aboriginal and Treaty Rights*. Ottawa, Ontario: Canadian Bar Association-Ontario Continuing Legal Education, 1984, p. 51-58.

1869   **Hodgins, Bruce W.**
The Temagami Experience: Recreation, Resources, and Aboriginal Rights in the Northern Ontario Wilderness. Toronto: University of Toronto Press, 1989. 370 p.

1870   **Hodgins, Bruce W.**
"'A Third Order of Government': The Claims of the Temagami Indians in the Context of the Current Debate Over Aboriginal Rights." In: *Cultural Dimensions of Canada's Geography*, edited by Frederick M. Helleiner. Peterborough, Ontario: Department of Geography, Trent University, 1983, p. 137-157. A paper presented to the German-Canadian Symposium, August 28-September 11, 1983.

1871   **Holleman, Warren Lee**
The Human Rights Movement: Western Values and Theological Perspectives. New York: Praeger Publishers, 1987. 247 p.

1872   **Hore, Edward**
"Caught in the Act: Mired in Controversy, Bureaucracy and Backlogs. How Can Human Rights Commissions Possibly Work?" *Saturday Night*, vol. 104 no. 9/3714 (1989) p. 25-28.

1873   **Howard, Rhoda E. and Jack Donnelly**
"Human Dignity, Human Rights and Political Regimes." *American Political Science Review*, vol. 80 no. 3 (1986) p. 801-817.

1874   **Hudson, Michael R.**
The Rights of Indigenous Populations in National and International Law: A Canadian Perspective. Montreal: McGill University, 1985. 295 leaves.

1875   **Hughes, Patricia**
"Indians and Lands Reserved for the Indians: Off-limits to the Provinces." *Osgoode Hall Law Journal*, vol. 21 no. 1 (1983) p. 82-112.

1876   **Hunter, Hope**
"Human Rights Legislation: Federal Charter of Rights and Alberta Individual Rights Protection Act." *First Reading: Edmonton Social Planning Council*, vol. 2 no. 6 (1985) p. 249-255.

1877   **Husak, Douglas N.**
"Why There are No Human Rights." *Social Theory and Practice*, vol. 10 no. 2 (1984) p. 125-141.

1878   **International League for the Rights and Liberation of Peoples**
"Universal Declaration of the Rights of People." *Social Justice*, vol.
16 no. 1 (1989) p. 155-158.

1879   **Ittinuar, Peter**
"The Inuit Perspective on Aboriginal Rights." In: *The Quest for
Justice: Aboriginal Peoples and Aboriginal Rights*, edited by Menno
Boldt and J. Anthony Long, with Leroy Little Bear. Toronto:
University of Toronto Press, 1986, p. 47-53.

1880   **Jackson, John D.**
"The Language Question in Quebec: On Collective and Individual
Rights." In: *The English of Quebec: From Majority to Minority
Status*, edited by Gary Caldwell and Eric Waddell. Québec, P.Q.:
Institut québécois de recherche sur la culture, 1982, p. 363-378.

1881   **Jackson, Michael**
"The Articulation of Native Rights in Canadian Law." *University of
British Columbia Law Review*, vol. 18 no. 2 (1984) p. 255-288.

1882   **Jaine, Linda**
"The Evolution of Comprehensive Land Claims Policies in Canada,
1973-1988: The Federal Government's Position in Relation to the
Aboriginal Claimant's Position." *Sakatchewan Indian Federated
College Journal*, vol. 4 no. 2 (1988) p. 99-114.

1883   **Jean, Joseph**
Statut juridique de l'immigrant au Canada. Unpublished LLM thesis,
Université Laval, 1985. 2 microfiches. Canadian theses on micro-
fiche, CT87-21710-0.

1884   **Johnston, Darlene M.**
"The Quest of the Six Nations Confederacy for Self-determination."
University of Toronto Faculty of Law Review, vol. 44 no. 1
(1986) p. 1-32.

1885   **Johnston, Darlene M.**
The Taking of Indian Lands: Consent or Coercion? Saskatoon:
University of Saskatchewan, Native Law Centre, 1989. 93 p.

1886   **Kallen, Evelyn**
Label Me Human: Minority Rights of Stigmatized Canadians.
Toronto: University of Toronto, 1989. 251 p.

1887   **Kallen, Evelyn**
"The Meech Lake Accord: Entrenching a Pecking Order of Minority
Rights." In: *Meech Lake Primer: Conflicting Views of the 1987
Constitutional Accord*, edited by Michael D. Behiels. Ottawa:
University of Ottawa Press, 1989, p. 349-370.

1888   **Kallen, Evelyn**
"The Charter's Omission: Group Rights of Canada's Minorities."
Plural Societies, vol. 18 no. 1 (1988) p. 41-55.

1889   **Kallen, Evelyn**
"The Meech Lake Accord: Entrenching a Pecking Order of Minority
Rights." *Canadian Public Policy/Analyse de politiques*, vol. 14 (1988
supplement) p. 107-120.

1890   **Kallen, Evelyn**
Ethnicity and Human Rights in Canada. Toronto: Gage, 1982. 268 p.

1891   **Kato, Hiroaki**
*Group Rights Democracy and the Plural Society: The Case of
Canada's Aboriginal Peoples*. Unpublished PhD thesis, Carleton
University, 1986. 4 microfiches. Canadian theses on microfiche, 87-
25826-5 MDRS.

1892   **Keenleyside, Terence A.**
"Foreign Aid and Human Rights." *International Perspectives*,
(1987) p. 15-18.

1893   **Keenleyside, T.A. and Patricia Taylor**
"The Impact of Human Rights Violations on the Conduct of
Canadian Bilateral Relations; A Contemporary Dilemma." *Behind the
Headlines*, vol. 42 no. 2 (1984) p. 1-27.

1894   **Keon-Cohen, B.A.**
"Native Justice in Australia, Canada and the U.S.A.: A Comparative
Analysis." *Monash University Law Review*, vol. 7 no. 3
(1981) p. 250-325.

1895   **Kerr, Robert William**
"The Remedial Power of the Courts After the Manitoba Language
Rights Case." *Windsor Yearbook of Access to Justice*, vol. 6
(1986) p. 252-267.

1896   **Kerr, Robert William**
"The Future of Language Right Under Canada's Constitutional
Options." In: *Canada and the New Constitution: An Unfinished
Agenda*, edited by Stanley H. Beck and Ivan Bernier. volume 1.
Montreal: Institute for Research on Public Policy, 1983, p. 307-331.

1897   **Khaki, Aziz, ed.**
Progress Towards Equality, compiled and edited by Aziz Khaki.
Vancouver: Committee for Racial Justice, 1989, 239 p. Proceedings
of the National Symposium on Progress Towards Equality, September
16-18, 1988, Vancouver.

1898   **Knopff, Rainer**
*Human Rights and Social Technology: The New War on
Discrimination*. Ottawa, Carleton University Press, 1989. 233 p.

1899   **Krasnick, Harry**
*English as a Second Language Problem in the Canadian Charter of
Rights and Freedoms*. Unpublished Ed.D. thesis, University of British
Columbia, 1987. 200 leaves. Canadian theses on microfiche, 400856.

1900   **Kuhlen, Daniel J.**
A Layperson's Guide to Treaty Rights in Canada, edited by Anne
Skarsgard. Saskatchewan: Native Law Centre, University of
Saskatchewan, 1985. 59 p.

1901   **Laforest, Guy**
"The Meaning and Centrality of Recognition." In: *Meech Lake and
Canada: Perspectives from the West*, edited by Roger Gibbins,
Howard Palmer, Brian Rusted and David Taras. Edmonton:
Academic Printing and Publishing, 1988, p. 73-90.

1902   **Lam, Lawrence**
"A Decade in Canada: Immigration, Human Rights and Racism."
New Community, vol. 14 no. 1/2 (1987) p. 234-240.

1903   **Language Rights in Canada**
"Language Rights in Canada." *Rights and Freedoms. Les droits et la
liberté*, no. 47 (1983) p. 2-20.

1904   **Laponce, J.A.**
"Protecting the French Language in Canada: From Neurophysiology
to Geography, to Politics: The Regional Imperative." In: *Regional
Development at the National Level: Canadian and African
Perspectives*, edited by Timothy M. Shaw and Yash Tandon.
Lanham, Md.: University Press of America, 1985, vol. 1, p. 47-66.

1905   **Laponce, J.A.**
"Protecting the French Language in Canada: From Neurophysiology to Geography to Politics: The Regional Imperative." *Journal of Commonwealth and Comparative Politics*, vol. 23 no. 2 (1985) p. 157-170.

1906   **Laponce, J.A.**
"Linguistic Minority Rights in the Light of Neurophysical and Geographical Evidence." *CPSA Papers/ACSP Contributions 1982*, Section G, paper 8, fiche 21. Paper presented at the 54th annual meeting of the Canadian Political Science Association, June 7-9, 1982, Ottawa University, Ottawa, Ontario.

1907   **Latouche, Daniel**
"Problems of Constitutional Design in Canada: Quebec and the Issue of Bicommunalism." *Publius*, vol. 18 no. 2 (1988) p. 131-146.

1908   **Laurin, Lucie**
Des luttes et des droits: antécédents et histoire de la ligue des droits de l'homme de 1936 à 1975. Montréal: Éditions du Méridien, 1985. 167 p.

1909   **Lebel, Michel**
"Quelques réflexions autour de l'article 27 de la Charte canadienne des droits." In: *Multiculturalism and the Charter: A Legal Perspective*, Canadian Human Rights Foundation. Toronto: Carswell, 1987, p. 139-144.

1910   **Légaré, Anne**
La société distincte de l'État: Québec-Canada 1930-1980. Montréal: Hurtubise, 1989. 240 p.

1911   **Legendre, Camille**
French Canada in Crisis: A New Society in the Making? London: Minority Rights Group, 1980. 20 p.

1912   **Lester, Geoffrey S.**
Inuit Territorial Rights in the Canadian Northwest Territories: A Survey of Legal Problems. Ottawa: Tungavik Federation of Nunavut, 1984. 54 p.

1913   **Lester, Geoffrey S.**
The Territorial Rights of the Inuit of the Canadian Northwest Territories: A Legal Argument. Unpublished PhD thesis, York University, 1981. 1530 leaves.

1914   **Little Bear, Leroy**
"Aboriginal Rights and the Canadian 'Grundnorm'." In: *Arduous Journey: Canadian Indians and Decolonization*, edited by J. Rick Ponting. Toronto: McClelland and Stewart, 1986, p. 243-259.

1915   **Little Bear, Leroy**
"The Concept of Native Title." *Canadian Legal Aid Bulletin/Bulletin canadien de l'aide juridique*, vol. 5 no. 2/3 (1982) p. 99-106.

1916   **Long, John S.**
"'No Basis for Argument': The Signing of Treaty Nine in Northern Ontario, 1905-1906." *Native Studies Review*, vol. 5 no. 2 (1989) p. 19-54.

1917   **Lui, May**
"Asians and Human Rights Legislation." In: *Asian Canadians: Regional Perspectives*, edited by K. Victor Ujimoto and Gordon Hirabayashi. [Guelph, Ont.: Univeristy of Guelph, 1989], p. 139-144. Paper presented at the 5th Asian Canadian Symposium held at Mount Saint Vincent University, Halifax, Nova Scotia, May 23 to May 26, 1981.

1918   **Lyon, Noel**
"Constitutional Issues in Native Law." In: *Aboriginal Peoples and the Law: Indian, Metis and Inuit Rights in Canada*, edited by Bradford Morse. Ottawa: Carleton University Press, 1989, p. 408-451.

1919   **Lyon, Noel**
Aboriginal Self-government: Rights of Citizenship and Access to Government Services. Kingston, Ont.: Institute of Intergovernmental Relations, Queen's University, 1984. 70 p.

1920   **Lyons, Oren**
"Traditional Native Philosophies Relating to Aboriginal Rights." In: *The Quest for Justice: Aboriginal Peoples and Aboriginal Rights*, edited by Menno Boldt and J. Anthony Long, with Leroy Little Bear. Toronto: University of Toronto Press, 1985, p. 19-23.

1921   **Lysyk, Kenneth M.**
"Rights and Freedoms of the Aboriginal Peoples of Canada." In: *The Canadian Charter of Rights and Freedoms*. Toronto: Carswell, 1982, Commentary edited by Walter S. Tarnopolsky and Gerald A. Beaudoin, p. 467-488.

1922   **M'Gonigle, R. Michael**
"Native Rights and Environmental Sustainability: Lessons from British Columbia Wilderness." *Canadian Journal of Native Studies*, vol. 8 no. 1 (1988) p. 107-130.

1923   **MacDonald, John A.**
Human Rights and Discrimination in B.C.: Past, Present and Future. Vancouver: The Author, 1983. 49, 6 leaves.

1924   **MacKay, A. Wayne**
"Linguistic Duality and the Distinct Society in Quebec: Declarations of Sociological Fact or Legal Limits on Constitutional Interpretation?" In: *Competing Constitutional Visions: The Meech Lake Accord*, edited by Katherine E. Swinton and Carol J. Rogerson. Toronto: Carswell, 1988, p. 65-79.

1925   **Mackey, William F.**
"La modification par la loi du comportement langagier." In: *Langue et Droit*, sous la direction de Paul Pupier et José Woehrling. Montréal: Wilson and Lafleur, 1989, p. 45-54. Paper presented at the First Conference of the International Institute of Comparative Linguistic Law, April 27-29, 1988 at the Université du Québec, Montréal, P.Q.

1926   **MacKinnon, Victor**
"Canadian Approaches: Assimilation or Separate Development? Canadian Approaches to the Promotion and Protection of the Rights of Minorities and Indigenous Peoples." In: *Self-determination in the Commonwealth*, edited by W.J. Allan Macartney. Aberdeen: Aberdeen University Press, 1988, p. 65-77.

1927   **MacMillan, C. Michael**
"The Rights of Citizen, Then and Now: The Canadian Case." *CPSA Papers/ACSP Contributions 1989*, Section B, paper 15, fiche 5. Paper presented at the 61st annual meeting of the Canadian Political Science Association, June 1-3, 1989, Laval University, Quebec, P.Q.

1928   **MacMillan, C. Michael**
"Language Issues and Nationalism in Quebec." *Canadian Review of Studies in Nationalism/Revue canadienne des études sur le nationalisme*, vol. 14 no. 2 (1987) p. 229-246.

1929   **MacMillan, C. Michael**
"The Practice of Language Rights: Notes Toward a Theory." *CPSA Papers/ACSP Contributions 1987*, Section B(b), paper 3, fiche 2, Paper presented at the 59th annual meeting of the Canadian Political Science Association, June 6-8, 1987, McMaster University, Hamilton, Ont.

1930   **MacMillan, C. Michael**
"Language Issues and Nationalism in Quebec." In: *Atlantic Provinces Political Studies Association. Proceedings*. Paper no. 4. [s.l.:] The Association, 1986. Paper presented at the 12th annual conference of the Atlantic Provinces Political Studies Association, held at Dalhousie University, Halifax, Nova Scotia, October 23-25, 1986.

1931   **MacMillan, C. Michael**
"Language Rights, Human Rights and Bill 101." *Bulletin of Canadian Studies*, vol. 7 no. 2 (1983/84) p. 73-80.

1932   **MacMillan, C. Michael**
"Language Rights, Human Rights and Bill 101." *Queen's Quarterly*, vol. 40 no. 2 (1983) p. 343-378.

1933   **Magnet, Joseph Eliot**
"Collective Rights, Cultural Autonomy and the Canadian State." *McGill Law Journal/Revue de droit de McGill*, vol. 3291 (1986) p. 170-186.

1934   **Magnet, Joseph Eliot**
"Minority Language Education Rights." *Supreme Court Law Review* vol. 4 (1982) p. 195-216.

1935   **Malbon, Justin Eugene**
Section 35, Canadian Constitution Act: The Aboriginal Right to Land. Unpublished LLM thesis, York University, 1987. 3 microfiches. Canadian theses on microfiche, CT89-21679-7.

1936   **Mandel, Michael**
The Charter of Rights and the Legalization of Politics in Canada. Toronto: Wall and Thompson, 1989. 368 p.

1937   **Manyfingers, Morris**
"Determination of Indian Band Membership: An Examination of Political Will." *Canadian Journal of Native Studies*, vol. 6 no. 1 (1986) p. 63-75.

1938   **Manyfingers, Wallace**
"Aboriginal Peoples and the Constitution: Commentary." *Alberta Law Review*, vol. 19 no. 3 (1981) p. 428-432.

1939   **Manzer, Ronald**
"Human Rights in Domestic Politics and Policy." In: *Human Rights in Canadian Foreign Policy*, edited by Robert O. Matthews and Cranford Pratt. Kingston: McGill-Queen's University Press, 1988, 23-45.

1940   **Maran, Rita**
"The Universal Declaration of Human Rights at 40." *Social Justice*, vol. 16 no. 1 (1989) p. 146-149.

1941   **Marchant, Cosmo Kenneth**
A Hierarchy of Rights: Linguistic, Religious, Racial and Ethnic Minorities in Canada. Unpublished D.Jur. thesis, York University, 1981. Canadian theses on microfiche, 47846.

1942   **Marquardt, Stephan**
The Right to Self-government of the Aboriginal Peoples of Canada Under Domestic and International Law. Unpublished LLM thesis, McGill University, 1988. 4 microfiches. Canadian theses on microfiche, CT90-22025-2.

1943   **Marule, Marie Smallface**
"Traditional Indian Government: of the People, for the People, by the People." In: *Pathways to Self-determination: Canadian Indians and the Canadian State*, edited by Leroy Little Bear, Menno Boldt, J. Anthony Long. Toronto: University of Toronto Press, 1984, p. 36-44.

1944   **Mason, Michael D.**
"Canadian and the United States Approaches to Indian Sovereignty." *Osgoode Hall Law Journal*, vol. 21 no. 3 (1983) p. 423-474.

1945   **Mathews, Robert O. and Cranford Pratt, eds.**
Human Rights in Canadian Foreign Policy. Montreal: McGill-Queen's University Press, 1988. 320 p.

1946   **McAllister, Anne B.**
James Bay Settlement. Kingston, Ont.: Centre for Resource Studies, Queen's University, 1985. 55 p.

1947   **McCaskill, Don**
"Native People and the Justice System." In: *As Long as the Sun Shines and Water Flows*, edited by Ian A.L. Getty and Antoine S. Lussier. Vancouver: University of British Columbia Press, 1983, p. 288-298.

1948   **McConnell, W.H.**
"Bilingualism on the Prairies: The Constitutional Status of French in Saskatchewan." *Saskatchewan Law Review*, vol. 53 no. 1 (1989) p. 143-152.

1949   **McConnell, W.H.**
"The Meech Lake Accord: Laws or Flaws?" *Saskatchewan Law Review*, vol. 52 no. 1 (1988) p. 115-141.

1950   **McConnell, W.H.**
"The Baker Lake Decision on Aboriginal Rights." *Musk-ox*, no. 26 (1980) p. 59-64. Article is followed by source documents p. 65-77.

1951   **McCurdy, Howard and Donald Lenihan**
"A Democratic Test for Foreign Aid: Countries Receiving Our Help Must Pass Minimal Tests for Progress in Human Rights." *Policy Options/Options politiques*, vol. 9 no. 7 (1988) p. 22-24.

1952   **McDonald, Michael**
"Indian Status: Colonialism or Sexism?" *Canadian Community Law Journal*, vol. 9 (1986) p. 23-48.

1953   **McEvoy, John P.**
"The Charter as a Bilingual Instrument." *Canadian Bar Review/Revue du Barreau du Canada*, vol. 64 no. 1 (1986) p. 155-171.

1954   **McLeod, M.**
"Legal Protection of Refugee Children Separated from Their Parents: Selected Issues." *International Migration/Migrations Internationales/ Migraciones Internacionales*, vol. 27 no. 2 (1989) p. 295-307.

1955   **McNeil, Kent**
"The Constitutional Rights of the Aboriginal Peoples of Canada." *Supreme Court Law Review*, vol. 4 (1982) p. 255-265.

1956   **McNeil, Kent**
Native Claims in Rupert's Land and the North-Western Territory: Canada's Constitutional Obligations. Saskatoon: Native Law Centre, University of Saskatchewan, 1982. 37 p.

1957   **McNeil, Kent**
Native Rights and the Boundaries of Rupert's Land and the North-Western Territory. Saskatoon: University of Saskatchewan Native Law Centre, 1981. 67 p.

1958   **McWhinney, Edward**
"The Language Problem in Quebec." *American Journal of Comparative Law*, vol. 29 (1981) p. 413-427.

1959   **Menczer, Micha J.**
"Existing and Potential Legislation Relating to Self-government." *Current Issues in Aboriginal and Treaty Rights.* Ottawa, Ont.: Canadian Bar Association/Ontario Continuing Legal Education, 1984, p. 127-170.

1960   **Minion, Robin, comp.**
Native Rights in Canada. Edmonton: Boreal Institute for Northern Studies, 1984. 102 p.

1961   **Mitchell, Leon**
"Indian Treaty Land Entitlement in Manitoba." In: *Governments in Conflict? Provinces and Indian Nations in Canada*, edited by J. Anthony Long and Menno Boldt, with Leroy Little Bear. Toronto: University of Toronto Press, 1988, p. 129-138.

1962   **Mitchell, Leon**
"Using Mediation to Resolve Disputes Over Aboriginal Rights; A Case Study." In: *The Quest for Justice: Aboriginal Peoples and Aboriginal Rights*, edited by Menno Boldt and J. Anthony Long, with Leroy Little Bear. Toronto: University of Toronto Press, 1985, p. 286-291.

1963   **Moisan, Gaston**
"Les droits des autochtones et les activités de chasse et de pêche." *Recherches Amérindiennes au Québec*, vol. 12 no. 4 (1982) p. 269-272.

1964   **Moodley, Kogila A.**
"The Predicament of Racial Affirmative Action: A Critical Review of 'Equality Now'." *Queen's Quarterly*, vol. 91 no. 4 (1984) p. 795-806.

1965   **Morel, Andre**
"La reconnaissance du Québec comme société distincte dans le respect de la charte." In: *L'adhésion du Québec à l'Accord du lac Meech*, sous la direction de Réal A. Forest. Montréal: Éditions Thémis, 1988, p. 55-63. Proceedings of the 1987 colloquium organised by the Quebecois section of the Association du Barreau canadien on Constitutional Rights and Civil Liberties.

1966   **Morse, Bradford W.**
"The Resolution of Land Claims." In: *Aboriginal Peoples and the Law: Indian, Metis and Inuit Rights in Canada*, edited by Bradford Morse. Ottawa: Carleton University Press, 1989, p. 617-682.

1967   **Morse, Bradford W.**
"Specific Claims: An Overview." In: *Current Issues in Aboriginal and Treaty Rights*. Ottawa, Ont.: Canadian Bar Association-Ontario Continuing Legal Education, 1984, p. 59-73.

1968   **Morse, Bradford W.**
"Native Land Rights and the Canadian Constitution." In: *Aspects of the Constitutional Debate, 1981*, edited by J. Clarke and S.F. Wise. Ottawa: Institute of Canadian Studies, Carleton University, 1982. p. 218-269.

1969   **Morton, F.L.**
"Group Rights Versus Individual Rights in the Charter: The Special Cases of Natives and Quebecois." In: *Minorities and the Canadian State*, edited by Neil Nevitte and Allan Kornberg. Oakville, Ont.: Mosaic Press, 1985, p. 71-86.

1970   **Moss, Wendy**
Aboriginal Rights. Current issue review, 89-11E. Ottawa: Library of Parliament, Research Branch, Law and Government Division, 1989. 16 p.

1971   **Moss, Wendy**
Dene/Metis Comprehensive Land Claim Agreement in Principle. Backgrounder, BP-195E. Ottawa: Library of Parliament, Research Branch, Law and Government Division, 1989. 14 p.

1972   **Moss, Wendy**
History of Discriminatory Laws Affecting Aboriginal People. Backgrounder, BP-175E. Ottawa: Library of Parliament, Research Branch, Law and Government Division, 1987. 29 p.

1973   **Mulroney, Brian**
"Notes for an Opening Statement to the Conference of First Ministers on the Rights of Aboriginal Peoples." In: *The Quest for Justice: Aboriginal Peoples and Aboriginal Rights*, edited by Menno Boldt and J. Anthony Long, with Leroy Little Bear. Toronto: University of Toronto Press, 1985, p. 157-164.

1974   **Nakatsuru, Shaun**
"A Constitutional Right of Indian Self-Government." *University of Toronto Faculty of Law Review*, vol. 43 no. 2 (1985) p. 72-99.

1975   **Nash, Alan E., ed.**
Human Rights and the Protection of Refugees Under International Law: Proceedings of a Conference Held in Montreal, November 29- December 2, 1987. Montreal: Canadian Human Rights Foundation, 1988. 338 p.

1976   **National Association of Japanese Canadians**
Democracy Betrayed: The Case for Redress. Ottawa: National Association of Japanese Canadians, 1984. 26 p. A submission to the Government of Canada on the violation of rights and freedoms of Japanese Canadian during and after World War II.

1977   **Native Affairs Secretariat**
The Concept and Nature of Aboriginal Rights: An Overview. Edmonton: Policy and Planning Branch, Native Affairs Secretariat, 1986. 29 p.

1978   **Nedeljkovic, Maryvonne**
"Liberté individuelle et collective: les immigrés et la citoyenneté canadienne." *Études Canadiennes/Canadian Studies*, vol. 21 no. 2 (1986) p. 229-236.

1979   **Niedermeier, Lynn**
"The Content of Aboriginal Rights." *Canadian Native Law Reporter*, vol. 3 no. 1 (1981) p. 1-26.

1980   **Niedermeier, Lynn**
"Aboriginal Rights: Definition or Denial?" *Queen's Law Journal*, vol. 6 no. 2 (1980/81) p. 568-686.

1981   **Nolan, Cathal J.**
"A Human Rights Advisory Service." *International Perspectives*, (1987) p. 19-20.

1982   O'Reilly, James
"Indian Land Claims in Quebec and Alberta." In: *Governments in Conflict? Provinces and Indian Nations in Canada*, edited by J. Anthony Long and Menno Boldt, with Leroy Little Bear. Toronto: University of Toronto Press, 1988, p. 139-147.

1983   Obieta-Chalbaud, Jose A. De
"Self-determination of Peoples as a Human Right." *Plural Sciences*, vol. 16 no. 1 (1986) p. 61-79.

1984   Odjig, Alfred
Aboriginal Rights in Canada. Ottawa: National Library of Canada, 1985. 17, 19 p. French language title: "Droits des autochtones du Canada.".

1985   Ortiz, Roxanne Dunbar
Indians of the Americas; Human Rights and Self-determination. London: Zed, 1984. 313 p.

1986   Paltiel, Khayyam Z.
"Group Rights in the Canadian Constitution and Aboriginal Claims to Self-determination." In: *Contemporary Canadian Politics: Readings and Notes*, edited by Robert J. Jackson, Doreen Jackson and Nicholas Baxter-Moore. Scarborough, Ont.: Prentice-Hall of Canada, 1987, p. 26-43.

1987   Parel, Anthony
"The Meech Lake Accord and Indo-Canadians." *Canadian Ethnic Studies/Études ethniques au Canada*, vol. 20 no. 1 (1988) p. 129-137.

1988   Parel, Anthony
"The Meech Lake Accord and Multiculturalism." In: *Meech Lake and Canada: Perspectives from the West*, edited by Roger Gibbins, Howard Palmer, Brian Rusted and David Taras. Edmonton: Academic Printing and Publishing, 1988, p. 171-178.

1989   Patenaude, Micheline
Le droit provincial et les terres indiennes. Montréal: Éditions Y. Blais, 1986. 198 p.

1990   Patenaude, Pierre
"L'objection éthique et de conscience: impact de la charte canadienne des droits et libertés." *Revue de droit*, vol. 13 no. 2, 1983 p. 315-352.

1991   **Patterson, E. Palmer**
"A Decade of Change: Origins of the Nishga and Tsimshian Land Protests in the 1880's." *Journal of Canadian Studies/Revue d'études canadiennes*, vol. 18 no. 3 (1983) p. 40-54.

1992   **Penner, Keith**
"Their Own Place: The Case for a Distinct Order of Indian First Nation Government in Canada." In: *Governments in Conflict? Provinces and Indian Nations in Canada*, edited by J. Anthony Long and Menno Boldt, with Leroy Little Bear. Toronto: University of Toronto Press, 1988, p. 31-37.

1993   **Penner, Keith**
"Report of the Special Committee on Indian Self-government in Canada." In: *Current Issues in Aboriginal and Treaty Rights*. Ottawa, Ont.: Canadian Bar Association-Ontario Continuing Legal Education, 1984, p. 116-126.

1994   **Pentney, William F.**
"Race Relations: The Legislative Base." In: *Canada 2000: Race Relations and Public Policy*, edited by O.P. Dwivedi et al. Guelph, Ont.: Department of Political Studies, University of Guelph, 1989, p. 53-63.

1995   **Pentney, William F.**
"The Rights of the Aboriginal Peoples of Canada and the Constitution Act, 1982, Pt. 1; The Interpretive Prism of Section 25." *University of British Columbia Law Review*, vol. 22 no. 1 (1988) p. 21-59.

1996   **Pentney, William F.**
"The Rights of the Aboriginal Peoples of Canada in the Constitutional Act, 1982, Pt. 2; Section 35, the Substantive Guarantee." *University of British Columbia Law Review*, vol. 22 no. 2 (1988) p. 207-278.

1997   **Penton, M. James**
"Collective Versus Individual Rights: The Canadian Tradition." In: *The U.S. Bill of Rights and the Canadian Charter of Rights and Freedoms*, edited by William R. Kercher. Toronto: Ontario Economic Council, 1983, p. 174-183.

1998   **Pitsula, James M.**
"The Blakeney Government and the Settlement of Treaty Indian Land Entitlements in Saskatchewan 1975-1982." *Historical Papers*, 1989, p. 190-209.

1999   **Plain, Fred**
"A Treatise on the Rights of the Aboriginal Peoples of the Continent of North America." In: *The Quest for Justice: Aboriginal Peoples and Aboriginal Rights*, edited by Menno Boldt and J. Anthony Long, with Leroy Little Bear. Toronto: University of Toronto Press, 1985, p. 31-40.

2000   **Pollard, Bruce G.**
"Minority Language Rights in Four Provinces." In: *Canada: The State of the Federation, 1985*, edited by Peter M. Leslie. Kingston, Ont.: Institute of Intergovernmental Relations, Queen's University, 1985, p. 193-222.

2001   **Pons-Ridler, Suzanne**
"The Territorial Concept of Official Bilingualism: A Cheaper Alternative for Canada?" *Language Sciences*, vol. 11 no. 2 (1989) p. 147-158.

2002   **Posluns, Michael**
Constitutional Development and the Protection of Aboriginal Rights. Kingston, Ont.: Institute of Local Government, Queen's University, 1983. 92, 13 p. Prepared for the Western Constitutional Forum.

2003   **Poulantzas, N.M.**
"Multiculturalism, Affirmative Action Programs Under the Canadian Charter of Rights and Freedoms, and the Protection of Minorities." *Revue de droit international, des sciences diplomatiques et politiques*, vol. 4 (1985) p. 309-322.

2004   **Proulx, Daniel**
"La précarité des droits linguistiques scolaires, ou les singulières difficultés de la mise en œuvre de l'article 23 de la Charte canadienne des droits et libertés." *Revue générale de droit*, vol. 14 no. 2 (1983) p. 335-370.

2005   **Pupier, Paul et José Woehrling, eds.**
Langue et droit. Montréal: Wilson and Lafleur, 1989. 641 p. English language title: *Language and Law: Proceedings of the First Conference of the International Institute of Comparative Linguistic Law.*

2006   **Quiroga, Cecilia Medina**
        The Battle of Human Rights: Gross Systematic Violations and the Inter-American System. Dordrecht, Netherlands: Martinus Nijhoff Publishers, 1988. 363 p.

2007   **Ratushny, Edward**
        "Security in the Multi-ethnic State: The Canadian Experience." *Ethnic Studies Report*, vol. 2 no. 2 (1984) p. 1-20.

2008   **Ray, Douglas**
        "Human Rights and Educational Policies." *MJE: The McGill Journal of Education*, vol. 23 no. 2 (1988) p. 161-169.

2009   **Reaume, Denise G.**
        "Language Rights, Remedies, and the Rule of Law." *Canadian Journal of Law and Jurisprudence*, vol. 1 no. 1 (1988) p. 35-62.

2010   **Reeves, William J.**
        "The Resolution of Complaints Based on Race and Origin: The Canadian Human Rights Commissions." In: *Minorities and the Canadian State*, edited by Neil Nevitte and Allan Kornberg. Oakville, Ont.: Mosaic Press, 1985, p. 139-154.

2011   **Reeves, W.J. and J.S. Frideres**
        "Individual Appeals for Government Intervention: The Ability to Implement Human Rights Legislation." *Ethnic Studies Report*, vol. 4 no. 1 (1986) p. 24-36.

2012   **Regel, Alan R.**
        "Hate Propaganda: A Reason to Limit Freedom of Speech." *Saskatchewan Law Review*, vol. 49 no. 2 (1984/85) p. 303-318.

2013   **Rentelin, Alison Dundes**
        "The Concept of Human Rights." *Anthropos*, vol. 83 no. 4-6 (1988) p. 343-364.

2014   **Rentelin, Alison Dundes**
        "Relativism and the Search for Human Rights." *American Anthropolgist*, vol. 90 no. 1 (1988) p. 56-72.

2015   **Richardson, Boyce**
        "Wrestling with the Canadian System: A Decade of Lubicon Frustration." In: *Drumbeat: Anger and Renewal in Indian Country*, edited by Boyce Richardson. Toronto: Summerhill Press, 1989, p. 229-264.

2016   **Riddell, Alan**
        "Á la recherche du temps perdu: la Cour suprême et l'interprétation
        des droits linguistiques constitutionnels dans les années 80." *Cahiers
        de droit*, vol. 29 no. 3 (1988) p. 829-855.

2017   **Riley, Del**
        "What Canada's Indians Want and the Difficulties of Getting It." In:
        *Pathways to Self-determination: Canadian Indians and the Canadian
        State*, edited by Leroy Little Bear, Menno Boldt and J. Anthony
        Long. Toronto: University of Toronto Press, 1984, p. 159-163.

2018   **Robe, Andrew Bear**
        *The Sovereign and Inherent Right to Indian Self-Government in
        Canada: From Theory and Principle to Implementation.* Unpublished
        MA thesis, University of Calgary, 1987 Canadian theses on
        microfiche, CT88-24147-0.

2019   **Romanow, Roy J.**
        "Aboriginal Rights in the Constitutional Process." In: *The Quest for
        Justice: Aboriginal Peoples and Aboriginal Rights*, edited by Menno
        Boldt and J. Anthony Long, with Leroy Little Bear. Toronto:
        University of Toronto Press, 1985, p. 73-82.

2020   **Ronaghan, Allen**
        "The Confrontation at Rivière aux Îlets de Bois." *Prairie Forum*, vol.
        14 no. 1 (1989) p. 1-7.

2021   **Rose, Loretta Lynn**
        "Foreign Aid and Human Rights: Aid for the Poor or the
        Oppressed?" *International Perspectives*, vol. 17 no. 4 (1988) p. 23-
        25.

2022   **Rozefort, Wallace**
        *Criminal Prosecutions: The Defense of Religious Freedom and the
        Canadian Charter.* Unpublished L.L.M. thesis, University of British
        Columbia, 1985. 188 leaves. Canadian theses on microfiche, CT87-
        20254-5.

2023   **Sanders, Douglas E.**
        "The Application of Provincial Laws." In: *Aboriginal Peoples and
        the Law: Indian, Metis and Inuit Rights in Canada*, edited by
        Bradford Morse. Ottawa: Carleton University Press, 1989, p. 452-
        465.

2024   **Sanders, Douglas E.**
"The Constitution, the Provinces, and Aboriginal Peoples." In: *Governments in Conflict? Provinces and Indian Nations in Canada*, edited by J. Anthony Long and Menno Boldt, with Leroy Little Bear. Toronto: University of Toronto Press, 1988, p. 151-174.

2025   **Sanders, Douglas E.**
"Article 27 and the Aboriginal Peoples of Canada." *Multiculturalism and the Charter: A Legal Perspective*. Toronto: Canadian Human Rights Foundation and Carswell, 1987, p. 155-166.

2026   **Sanders, Douglas E.**
"An Uncertain Path: The Aboriginal Constitutional Conferences." In: *Litigating the Values of a Nation: The Canadian Charter of Rights and Freedoms*, edited by Joseph M. Weiler and Robin M. Elliot. Toronto: Carswell, 1986, p. 63-77.

2027   **Sanders, Douglas E.**
"Aboriginal Rights: The Search for Recognition in International Law." In: *The Quest for Justice: Aboriginal Peoples and Aboriginal Rights*, edited by Menno Boldt and J. Anthony Long, with Leroy Little Bear. Toronto: University of Toronto Press, 1985, p. 292-303.

2028   **Sanders, Douglas E.**
"The Indian Lobby and the Canadian Constitution, 1978-1982." In: *Indigenous People and the Nation-state: 'Fourth World' Politics in Canada, Australia and Norway*, edited by Noel Dyck. St. John's, Nfld.: Institute of Social and Economic Research, Memorial University of Newfoundland, 1985, p. 151-189.

2029   **Sanders, Douglas E.**
"The Renewal of Indian Special Status." In: *Equality Rights and the Canadian Charter of Rights and Freedoms*, edited by Anne F. Bayefsky and Mary Eberts. Toronto: Carswell, 1985, p. 529-563.

2030   **Sanders, Douglas E.**
"The Indian Lobby." In: *And No One Cheered: Federalism, Democracy and the Constitution Act*, edited by Keith Banting and Richard Simeon. Toronto: Methuen, 1983, p. 301-332.

2031   **Sanders, Douglas E.**
"Prior Claims: Aboriginal People in the Constitution of Canada." In: *Canada and the New Constitution: An Unfinished Agenda*, edited by Stanley H. Beck and Ivan Bernier. volume 1. Montreal: Institute for Research on Public Policy, 1983, p. 225-279.

2032   **Sanders, Douglas E.**
"The Re-emergence of Indigenous Questions in International Law."
Canadian Human Rights Yearbook/Annuaire canadien des droits de la personne, 1983, p. 3-30.

2033   **Sanders, Douglas E.**
"The Rights of the Aboriginal Peoples of Canada." *Canadian Bar Review/Revue du Barreau canadien*, vol. 61 no. 1 (1983) p. 314-338.

2034   **Sautter, Udo**
"Aspects of the Canadian Constitutional Question." *Amerikastudien/American Studies*, vol. 25 no. 3 (1980) p. 294-317.

2035   **Scott, Ian G.**
"The Constitution as an Expression of Ideological Pluralism and Accommodation." In: *Meech Lake Primer: Conflicting Views of the 1987 Constitutional Accord*, edited by Michael D. Behiels. Ottawa: University of Ottawa Press, 1989, p. 53-59.

2036   **Scott, Ian G.**
"The Role of the Provinces in the Elucidation of Aboriginal Rights in Canada." In: *Governments in Conflict? Provinces and Indian Nations in Canada*, edited by J. Anthony Long and Menno Boldt, with Leroy Little Bear. Toronto: University of Toronto Press, 1988, p. 59-71.

2037   **Scott, Stephen Allan**
"'Meech Lake' and the Quebec Society: 'Distinct' or Distinctive?"
In: *Meech Lake Primer: Conflicting Views of the 1987 Constitutional Accord*, edited by Michael D. Behiels. Ottawa: University of Ottawa Press, 1989, p. 161-170.

2038   **Scott, Stephen Allan**
"Meech Lake and Quebec Society: 'Distinct' or Distinctive?" In: *L'adhésion du Québec à l'Accord du lac Meech*, sous la direction de Réal A. Forest. Montréal: Éditions Thémis, 1988, p. 41-53.

2039   **Selby, David**
Human Rights. Modern World Issues Series. Cambridge, U.K.: Cambridge University Press, 1987. 80 p.

2040   **Senecal, Andre**
"Article 23 of the New Canadian Constitution and the Quebec Language Issue." *Quebec Studies*, no. 2 (1984) p. 70-81.

2041   **Senese, Salvatore**
"External and Internal Self-determination." *Social Justice*, vol. 16 no. 1 (1989) p. 19-25.

2042   **Shank, Gregory, ed.**
"Human Rights and Peoples' Rights: View from North and South." *Social Justice*, vol. 16 no. 1 (1989) p. 1-163.

2043   **Slattery, Brian**
"Understanding Aboriginal Rights." *Canadian Bar Review/Revue du Barreau canadien*, vol. 66 no. 4 (1987) p. 727-783.

2044   **Slattery, Brian**
"The Hidden Constitution: Aboriginal Rights in Canada." In: *The Quest for Justice: Aboriginal Peoples and Aboriginal Rights*, edited by Menno Boldt and J. Anthony Long, with Leroy Little Bear. Toronto: University of Toronto Press, 1985, p. 114-138.

2045   **Slattery, Brian**
"The Hidden Constitution: Aboriginal Rights in Canada." *American Journal of Comparative Law*, vol. 32 no. 2 (1984) p. 361-392.

2046   **Slattery, Brian**
"The Constitutional Guarantee of Aboriginal and Treaty Rights." *Queen's Law Journal*, vol. 8 nos. 1-2 (1982/83) p. 232-273.

2047   **Smiley, Donald Victor**
"The Canadian Charter of Rights and Freedoms with Special Reference to Quebec-Canada Relations." In: *The U.S. Bill of Rights and the Canadian Charter of Rights and Freedoms*, edited by William R. Kercher. Toronto: Ontario Economic Council, 1983, p. 218-225.

2048   **Smith, Donald B.**
"Aboriginal Rights a Century Ago: The St. Catharines Milling Case of 1885." *The Beaver*, vol. 67 no. 1 (1987) p. 4-15.

2049   **Smith, Jennifer**
"Political Vision and the 1987 Constitutional Accord." In: *Competing Constitutional Visions: The Meech Lake Accord*, edited by Katherine E. Swinton and Carol J. Rogerson. Toronto: Carswell, 1988, p. 271-277.

2050   **Smith, Lynn**
"The Distinct Society Clause in the Meech Lake Accord: Could it
Affect Equality Rights for Women?" In: *Competing Constitutional
Visions: The Meech Lake Accord*, edited by Katherine E. Swinton
and Carol J. Rogerson. Toronto: Carswell, 1988, p. 35-54.

2051   **Snow, John**
"Identification and Definition of Our Treaty and Aboriginal Rights."
In: *The Quest for Justice: Aboriginal Peoples and Aboriginal Rights*,
edited by Menno Boldt and J. Anthony Long, with Leroy Little Bear.
Toronto: University of Toronto Press, 1985, p. 41-46.

2052   **Soucie, Rolande**
Section 23 of the Charter: Provincial Implementation. Current issue
review. Ottawa: Library of Parliament, Research Division, 1986.
22 p.

2053   **Stainsby, Jonathan**
"Education and Equality Rights in the Supreme Court." *University of
Toronto Faculty of Law Review*, vol. 46 no. 1 (1988) p. 259-270.

2054   **Sunstein, C.R.**
"Compelling Government Action: The Problem of Affirmative
Rights." *Cambridge Lectures*, vol. 5 (1987) p. 297-307.

2055   **Surtees, Robert J.**
"Indian Land Cessions in Upper Canada, 1815-1830." In: *As Long As
the Sun Shines and Water Flows*, edited by Ian A.L. Getty and
Antoine S. Lussier. Vancouver: University of British Columbia Press,
1983, p. 65-84.

2056   **Symonds, Glady L.**
"Ideology and Social Change: Meech Lake and National Identity." In:
*Meech Lake, from Centre to Periphery: The Impact of the 1987
Constitutional Accord on Canadian Settlements: A Speculation*, edited
by Hilda Symonds. Vancouver: Centre for Human Settlements,
University of British Columbia, 1988. p. 55-67.

2057   **Tarnopolsky, Walter S.**
"The Effect of Section 27 on the Interpretation of the Charter." In:
*Central and East European Ethnicity in Canada: Adaptation and
Preservation*, edited by T. Yedlin. Edmonton: Central and East
European Studies Society of Alberta, 1985, p. 1-8.

2058   **Tarnopolsky, Walter S.**
"The Critical Century: Human Rights and Race Relations." *Royal Society of Canada. Proceedings and Transactions/Sociéte royale du Canada. Mémoires et comptes rendus*, ser. 4, vol. 20 (1982) p. 309-322.

2059   **Taylor, Donald M.**
Les réactions des anglophones à la Charte de la langue française. Montréal: Office de la langue française, 1986. 176 p.

2060   **Tennant, Paul**
"Aboriginal Rights and the Penner Report on Indian Self-government." In: *The Quest for Justice: Aboriginal Peoples and Aboriginal Rights*, edited by Menno Boldt and J. Anthony Long, with Leroy Little Bear. Toronto: University of Toronto Press, 1985, p. 321-332.

2061   **Totten, Sam**
"Human Rights: A Unit." *The Social Studies*, vol. 76 no. 6 (1985) p. 240-243.

2062   **Tough, Frank J.**
"Economic Aspects of Aboriginal Title in Northern Manitoba: Treaty 5 Adhesions and Metis Scrip." *Manitoba History*, no. 15 (1988) p. 3-16.

2063   **Treaty and Aboriginal Rights Research Centre**
Debt to be Paid: Treaty Land Entitlement in Manitoba. Prepared by Staff of the Treaty and Aboriginal Rights Research Centre. Winnipeg: The Centre, 1984. 24 p.

2064   **Trudeau, Pierre Elliott**
"Statement by the Prime Minister of Canada to the Conference of First Ministers on Aboriginal Constitutional Matters." In: *The Quest for Justice: Aboriginal Peoples and Aboriginal Rights*, edited by Menno Boldt and J. Anthony Long, with Leroy Little Bear. Toronto: University of Toronto Press, 1985, p. 148-156.

2065   **Turi, Joseph G.**
"Introduction au droit linguistique." In: *Langue et droit*, sous la direction de Paul Pupier et José Woehrling. Montréal: Wilson and Lafleur, 1989, p. 55-84. Paper presented at the First Conference of the International Institute of Comparative Linguistic Law, April 27-29, 1988 at the Université du Québec, Montréal, P.Q.

2066   **Union of B.C. Indian Chiefs**
Support Conference on Aboriginal Title and Rights, 25-27 February 1983, Vancouver, Canada. Vancouver: Union of B.C. Indian Chiefs, 1983.

2067   **Vandycke, Robert**
"L'activisme judiciaire et les droits de la personne: émergence d'un nouveau savoir-pouvoir?" *CPSA Papers/ACSP Contributions 1989*, Section B, paper 23, fiche 7-8. Paper presented at the 61st annual meeting of the Canadian Political Science Association, June 1-3, 1989, Laval University, Quebec, P.Q.

2068   **Weaver, Sally M.**
"Federal Difficulties with Aboriginal Rights Demands." In: *The Quest for Justice: Aboriginal Peoples and Aboriginal Rights*, edited by Menno Boldt and J. Anthony Long, with Leroy Little Bear. Toronto: University of Toronto University Press, 1985, p. 139-147.

2069   **Westmoreland-Traore, Jaunita**
"Legal and Justice Issues: Constitutional Issues in Canada's Progress Towards Equality." In: *Progress Towards Equality*, compiled and edited by Aziz Khaki. Vancouver: Committee for Racial Justice, 1989, p. 35-42. Proceedings of the National Symposium on Progress Towards Equality, September 16-18, 1988 at Vancouver.

2070   **Whyte, John D.**
"The 1987 Constitutional Accord and Ethnic Accommodation." In: *Competing Constitutional Visions: The Meech Lake Accord*, edited by Katherine E. Swinton and Carol J. Rogerson. Toronto: Carswell, 1988, p. 263-270.

2071   **Whyte, Kenn**
"Aboriginal Rights: The Native American's Struggle for Survival." *Human Organization*, vol. 41 no. 2 (1982) p. 178-184.

2072   **Wildsmith, Bruce H.**
"Pre-Confederation Treaties." In: *Aboriginal Peoples and the Law: Indian, Metis and Inuit Rights in Canada*, edited by Bradford Morse. Ottawa: Carleton University Press, 1989, p. 122-271.

2073   **Wilson, Bill**
"Aboriginal Rights: The Non-status Indian Perspective." In: *The Quest for Justice: Aboriginal Peoples and Aboriginal Rights*, edited by Menno Boldt and J. Anthony Long, with Leroy Little Bear. Toronto: University of Toronto Press, 1985, p. 62-69.

2074   **Winn, Conrad**
"Affirmative Action and Visible Minorities: Eight Premises in Quest
of Evidence." *Canadian Public Policy/Analyse de politiques*, vol. 11
no. 4 (1985) p. 684-700.

2075   **Woehrling, José**
"A Critique of the Distinct Society Clause's Critics." In: *Meech Lake
Primer: Conflicting Views of the 1987 Constitutional Accord*, edited
by Michael D. Behiels. Ottawa: University of Ottawa Press,
1989, p. 171-207.

2076   **Woehrling, José**
"Les droits linguistiques des minorités et le projet de modification de
la constitution du Canada (l'Accord du lac Meech)" In: *Langue et
droit*, sous la direction de Paul Pupier et José Woehrling. Montréal:
Wilson and Lafleur, 1989, p. 291-322. Paper presented at the First
Conference of the International Institute of Comparative Linguistic
Law, April 27-29, 1988 at the Université du Québec, Montréal, P.Q.

2077   **Woehrling, José**
"La modification constitutionnelle de 1987, la reconnaissance du
Québec comme société distincte et la dualité linguistique du Canada."
Cahiers de droit, vol. 29 no. 1 (1988) p. 3-63.

2078   **Woehrling, José**
"La reconnaissance du Québec comme société distincte et la dualité
linguistique du Canada: conséquences juridiques et constitutionnelles." *Canadian Public Policy/Analyse de politiques*, vol. 14 (1988
supplement) p. 43-62.

2079   **Woehrling, José**
"La constitution canadienne et la protection des minorités ethniques."
Cahiers de droit, vol. 27 no. 1 (1986) p. 171-188.

2080   **Woehrling, José**
"L'État canadien et la protection constitutionnelle des minorités
ethniques." *Études Canadiennes/Canadian Studies*, vol. 21 no. 2
(1986) p. 269-278.

2081   **Woehrling, José**
"Minority and Equality Rights." *McGill Law Journal/Revue de droit
de McGill*, vol. 31 no. 1 (1985) p. 51-92.

2082   **Woehrling, José**
"Minority Cultural and Linguistic Rights and Equality Rights in the
Canadian Charter of Rights and Freedoms." *McGill Law Journal/
Revue de droit de McGill*, vol. 31 no. 1 (1985) p. 50-92.

2083   **Woloshyn, Donald F.**
*Canadian Compliance with International Law Respecting the Right of
Asylum of Refugees.* Unpublished thesis, McGill University, 1986.
210 leaves. Canadian theses on microfiche, 312920.

2084   **Wyman, Max**
"Human Rights, Human Freedom and Human Discrimination." In:
Civil Liberties in Canada: Entering the 1980's, edited by Gerald L.
Gall. Toronto: Butterworths, 1985, p. 53-80.

2085   **Yu, Miriam**
"Human Rights, Discrimination, and Coping Behaviour of the
Chinese in Canada." *Canadian Ethnic Studies/Études ethniques au
Canada*, vol. 19 no. 3 (1987) p. 114-124.

2086   **Zlotkin, Norman K.**
"Post-Confederation Treaties." In: *Aboriginal Peoples and the Law:
Indian, Metis and Inuit Rights in Canada*, edited by Bradford Morse.
Ottawa: Carleton University Press, 1989, p. 272-406.

2087   **Zlotkin, Norman K.**
*Unfinished Business: Aboriginal Peoples and the 1983 Constitutional
Conference.* Kingston, Ont.: Institute of Inter-governmental Relations,
Queen's University, 1983. 91 p.

Women

2088   **Almeida, Christine**
"No Help from Anyone: The Trials of Women Garment Workers."
The Asianadian, vol. 6 no. 2 (1985) p. 8-11.

2089   **Anderson, Joan M.**
"The Meaning of Work for Immigrant Women in the Lower
Echelons of the Canadian Labour Force." *Canadian Ethnic Studies
/Études ethniques au Canada,* vol. 19 no. 2 (1987) p. 67-90.

2090   **Anderson, Karen**
*Commodity Exchange and Subordination: A Comparison of
Montagnais-Naskapi Women circa 1600-1650.* Toronto: Department
of Sociology, University of Toronto, 1983.

2091   **Arat-Koc, Sedef**
"In the Privacy of Our Own Home: Foreign Domestic Workers as
Solution to the Crisis in the Domestic Sphere in Canada." *Studies In
Political Economy,* no. 28 (1989) p. 33-58.

2092   **Baines, Beverly**
"Gender and the Meech Lake Committee." In: *Navigating Meech
Lake: the 1987 Constitutional Accord,* edited by Clive Thomson.
Kingston, Ont.: Institute of Intergovernmental Relations, Queen's
University, 1988, p. 43-52. Reprinted from: *Queen's Quarterly,* vol.
94 no. 4 (1987) p. 807- 816.

2093   **Baines, Beverly**
"Gender and the Meech Lake Committee." *Queen's Quarterly,* vol.
94 no. 4 (1987) p. 807-816.

2094   **Barber, Marilyn**
"Immigrant Domestics 1900-30: The Use of the Tape Collection of
the Multicultural History Society." *Polyphony: The Bulletin of the
Multicultural History Society of Ontario*, vol. 9 no. 1 (1987) p. 83-
84.

2095   **Barber, Marilyn**
"In Search of a Better Life: A Scottish Domestic in Rural Ontario."
*Polyphony: The Bulletin of the Multicultural History Society of
Ontario*, vol. 8 no. 1/2 (1986) p. 13-16.

2096   **Bashevkin, Sylvia B.**
Toeing the Lines: Women and Party Politics in English Canada.
Toronto: University of Toronto Press, 1985. 222 p.

2097   **Bayor, Ronald H., ed.**
"Immigrant Women." *Journal of American Ethnic History*, vol. 8 no.
2 (1989) p. 1-199.

2098   **Beique, Marie**
*Gestes et paroles, ou, le savoir et sa transmission chez les femmes
inuits du Québec nordique (Kangirsuk).* Unpublished MA thesis,
Université Laval, 1986. 2 microfiches. Canadian theses on
microfiche, CT88-27223-6.

2099   **Béland, Francois and Michel De Sève**
"L'inégalité et la discrimination sexuelles et linguistiques au
Québec." *Canadian Review of Sociology and Anthropology/Revue
canadienne de sociologie et d'anthropologie*, vol. 23 no. 3
(1986) p. 309-330.

2100   **Belgrave, Linda Liska**
"The Effects of Race Differences in Work History, Work Attitudes,
Economic Resources and Health on Women's Retirement." *Research
on Aging*, vol. 10 no. 3 (1988) p. 383-398.

2101   **Bhagavatula, Lakshmi Sucharita**
A Study of Immigrant Women in Vancouver. Vancouver: Vancouver
Society of Immigrant Women, 1989. 79 p.

2102   **Blackman, Margaret B.**
Sadie Brower Neakok: An Inupiag Woman. Seattle and Vancouver:
University of Washington Press and Douglas and McIntyre, 1989.
275 p.

2103   Bohachcvsky-Chomiak, Martha
        Feminists Despite Themselves: Women in Ukrainian Community Life.
        1884-1939. Edmonton: Canadian Institute of Ukrainian Studies,
        University of Alberta, 1987. 470 p.

2104   Bourne, Paula, ed.
        Women's Paid and Unpaid Work: Historical and Contemporary
        Perspectives. Toronto: New Hogtown Press, 1985. 123 p.

2105   Boyd, Monica
        "Immigration and Income Security Policies in Canada: Implications
        for Elderly Immigrant Women." *Population Research and Policy*
        Review, vol. 8 no. 1 (1989) p. 5-24.

2106   Boyd, Monica
        "The Feminization of Temporary Workers: The Canadian Case."
        International Migration/Migrations Internationales/Migraciones Inter-
        nacionales, vol. 24 no. 4 (1986) p. 717-734.

2107   Boyd, Monica
        "Immigrant Women in Canada." In: *International Migration: The*
        Female Experience, edited by R.J. Simpson and C.B. Brettell.
        Totowa, N.J.: Rowman and Allanheld, 1986, p. 45-61.

2108   Boyd, Monica
        "At a Disadvantage: The Occupational Attainments of Foreign Born
        Women in Canada." *International Migration Review,* vol. 18 no. 4
        (1984) p. 1091-1119.

2109   Bradbury, Bettina
        "Women's History and Working-class History." *Labour/Le Travail,*
        no. 19 (1987) p. 23-43.

2110   Brady, Elizabeth and Shelagh Wilkinson, eds.
        "Mediterranean Women in Canada." *Canadian Woman Studies,* vol. 8
        no. 2 (1987) p. 1-73. Special monographic issue of the journal.

2111   Braithwaite, Diana
        "Reflections of a Black Historian." *Polyphony: The Bulletin of the*
        Multicultural History Society of Ontario, vol. 8 no. 1/2 (1986) p. 89-
        92.

2112   **Brand, Dionne**
"A Working Paper on Black Women in Toronto: Gender, Race and Class." *Fireweed*, no. 19 (1984) p. 26-43.

2113   **Brant, Beth, ed.**
A Gathering of Spirit: A Collection by North American Indian Women. 3rd ed. Toronto: The Women's Press, 1988. 238 p.

2114   **Brewer, Rose M.**
"Black Women in Poverty: Some Comments on Female Headed Families." *Signs: Journal of Women in Culture and Society*, vol. 13 no. 12 (1988) p. 331-339.

2115   **Brodribb, Somer**
"The Traditional Roles of Native Women in Canada and the Impact of Colonization." *The Canadian Journal of Native Studies*, vol. 4 no. 1 (1984) p. 85-104.

2116   **Brown, Jennifer H.**
"Women as Centre and Symbol in the Emergence of Metis Communities." *The Canadian Journal of Native Studies*, vol. 3 no. 1 (1983) p. 39-46.

2117   **Bundrock, Marianne**
German Immigrant Women in Saskatoon: Adaptation and Marginality. Unpublished MA thesis, University of Saskatchewan, 1989.

2118   **Burnet, Jean R.**
"Women and Ethnicity." *Polyphony: The Bulletin of the Multicultural History Society of Ontario*, vol. 8 no. 1/2 (1986) p. 1-2. Introduction to a monographic issue of *Polyphony* titled "Women and Ethnicity."

2119   **Burnet, Jean R.**
"Minorities I Have Belonged To." *Canadian Ethnic Studies/Études ethniques au Canada*, vol. 13 no. 1 (1981) p. 24-36.

2120   **Burnet, Jean R., ed.**
Looking Into My Sister's Eyes: An Exploration in Women's History. Toronto: Multicultural History Society of Ontario, 1986. 245 p.

2121   **Burnet, Jean R.Draper, ed.**
"Women and Ethnicity." *Polyphony: The Bulletin of the Multicultural History Society of Ontario*, vol. 8 nos. 1-2 (1986) 104 p. A monographic issue of the journal.

2122   **Bustamante, Rosalina E.**
"Filipino Women and Equality." *Polyphony: The Bulletin of the Multicultural History Society of Ontario*, vol. 8 no. 1/2 (1986) p. 77-79.

2123   **Bystydzicnski, Jill M.**
"Minority Women of North America: A Comparison of French-Canadian and Afro-American Women." *The American Review of Canadian Studies*, vol. 15 no. 4 (1986) p. 465-480.

2124   **Cairns, Alan and Cynthia Williams, eds.**
The Politics of Gender, Ethnicity and Language in Canada. Toronto: University of Toronto Press, 1986.

2125   **Canadian Pacific Railway**
"Women's Work in Alberta." *Alberta History*, vol. 34 no. 4 (1986) p. 24-32.

2126   **Canadian Radio-Television and Telecommunications Commission**
Images of Women: Report of the Task Force on Sex Stereotyping in the Broadcast Media. Ottawa: Ministry of Supply and Services, 1982. 189 p.

2127   **Carbert, Louise**
"Voices from the Hinterland: The Study of Women's Political Participation in English Canada." *CPSA Papers/ACSP Contributions 1989*, Section E, paper 7, fiche 2-3. Paper presented at the 61st annual meeting of the Canadian Political Science Association, June 1-3, 1989, Laval University, Quebec, P.Q.

2128   **Chan, Kwok B.**
"Coping with Aging and Managing Self-identity: The Social World of the Elderly Chinese Women." *Canadian Ethnic Studies/Études ethniques au Canada*, vol. 15 no. 3 (1983) p. 36-50.

2129   **Chong, Denise**
"The Concubine's Children: Secrets of Chinatown — Grandfather Kept His Secret Well." *Saturday Night*, vol. 103 no. 10/3703 (1988) p. 41-52.

2130   **Chow, Rita, Parameswara Krishman, and Nirannanilat Lalu**
"Female Working Life Expectancy, Canada 1921-1971: Results from an Application of Model Working Life Tables." *Canadian Studies in Population*, vol. 13. no. 2 (1986) p. 181-192.

2131   **Cohen, Yolande**
       Les thèses québécoises sur les femmes. Québec: Institut de recherche
       sur la culture, 1983.

2132   **Coomarasamy, Sudha,**
       "Sri Lankan Tamil Women: Resettlement in Montreal." *Canadian
       Woman Studies/Cahiers de la femme,* vol. 10 no. 1 (1989) p. 69-73.

2133   **Craig, Susan D.**
       *Qui prend mari, prend pays?: A Study of Women's Role in Ethnic
       Boundary in a Native Community in Quebec.* Unpublished MA thesis,
       Laval University, 1988. 2 microfiches. Canadian theses on micro-
       fiche, CT90-22914-4.

2134   **Creese, Gillian Laura**
       "The Politics of Dependence: Women, Work and Unemployment in
       Vancouver Labour Movement Before World War II." *Canadian
       Journal of Sociology/Cahiers canadiens de sociologie,* vol. 13 nos. 1-
       2 (1987/1988) p. 121-142.

2135   **Creese, Gillian Laura**
       *Working Class Politics, Racism and Sexism: The Making of a
       Politically Divided Working Class in Vancovuer, 1900-1939.*
       Unpublished PhD thesis, Carleton University, 1986. 323 p.

2136   **Curtin, Kaier**
       "Roaring Twenties Scandal: Yiddish Lesbian Play Rocks Broadway."
       Lilith: The Jewish Women's Magazine, no. 19 (1988) p. 13-14.

2137   **Danys, Milda**
       "Lithuanian DP's in Hospitals and Private Homes." *Polyphony: The
       Bulletin of the Multicultural History Society of Ontario,* vol. 8 no. 1/2
       (1986) p. 51-55.

2138   **Das Gupta, Tania**
       "Looking Under the Mosaic: South Asian Immigrant Women."
       *Polyphony: The Bulletin of the Multicultural History Society of
       Ontario,* vol. 8 no. 1/2 (1986) p. 67-69.

2139   **Davis, Nanciellen**
       "Acadian Women: Economic Development, Ethnicity and the Status
       of Women." In: *Two Nations, Many Cultures: Ethnic Groups in
       Canada,* edited by Jean Leonard Elliott. 2nd ed. Scarborough, Ont.:
       Prentice-Hall of Canada, 1983, p. 204-215.

2140   **Denis, A.B.**
"Femmes: ethnie et occupation au Québec et en Ontario (1931-
1971)" *Canadian Ethnic Studies/Études ethniques au Canada*, vol. 13
no. 1 (1981) p. 75-90.

2141   **Dexter, Jenny**
"Migrant Women: Their Experience and Language Needs."
Multicultural Australian Papers, no. 59 (1987) p. 1-26.

2142   **Dhar, Meena**
"Women Helping Immigrant Asian Women: Toronto's Riverdale
Immigrant Women's Centre." *The Asianadian*, vol. 5 no. 4
(1984) p. 18-22.

2143   **Dicosta, Diana Maria and Geoffrey Nelson**
"Family and Social Network Factors After Divorce in Catholic Italian
and Catholic Anglophone Women." *Journal of Divorce*, vol. 11 no. 2
(1987) p. 111-127.

2144   **Draper, Paula J. and Janice B. Karlinsky**
"Abraham's Daughters: Women, Charity and Power in the Canadian
Jewish Community." In: *Looking Into My Sister's Eyes: An
Exploration in Women's History*, edited by Jean Burnet. Toronto:
Multicultural History Society of Ontario, 1986, p. 75-90.

2145   **Draper, Paula J. and Janice B. Karlinsky**
"Jewish Women as Volunteers." *Polyphony: The Bulletin of the
Multicultural History Society of Ontario*, vol. 8 no. 1/2 (1986) p. 37-
39.

2146   **Dufour, Rose**
"L'otite chez les enfants inuit: une question de mode alimentaire?"
Études Inuit Studies, vol. 8 no. 2 (1985) p. 77-89.

2147   **Dumont, Micheline, et al.**
Quebec Women, a History. Toronto: The Women's Press, 1987.
396 p.

2148   **Eberts, Mary**
"The Constitution, the Charter, and the Distinct Society Clause: Why
are Women Being Ignored?" In: *Meech Lake Primer: Conflicting
Views of the 1987 Constitutional Accord*, edited by Michael D.
Behiels. Ottawa: University of Ottawa Press, 1989, p. 302-320.

2149   **Epp, Frank H. and Marlene G. Epp**
"The Diverse Roles of Ontario Mennonite Women." In: *Looking Into My Sister's Eyes: An Exploration in Women's History*, edited by Jean Burnet. Toronto: Multicultural History Society of Ontario, 1986, p. 223-242.

2150   **Epp, Marlene**
"Women in Canadian Mennonite History: Uncovering the 'Underside'." *Journal of Mennonite Studies*, vol. 5 (1987) p. 90-107.

2151   **Epp, Marlene**
"Mennonite Women Slowly Regain Equality." *Polyphony: The Bulletin of the Multicultural History Society of Ontario*, vol. 8 no. 1/2 (1986) p. 77-79.

2152   **Estable, Alma**
Immigrant Women in Canada: Current Issues. Ottawa: Canadian Advisory Council on the Status of Women, 1986. 35 p.

2153   **Evans, Barbara**
"'Yours for a Square Deal . . .': Women's Role in Saskatchewan Farm Movement and the Early CCF." *Canadian Dimension: A Socialist Newsmagazine*, vol. 21 no. 3 (1987) p. 7-12.

2154   **Evans, Vella Neil**
"The Mormon Women: Defined in Authoritative Church Discourse, 1830-1980." *Religious Studies and Theology*, vol. 7 no. 1 (1987) p. 31-42.

2155   **Fédération des femmes du Québec**
"Are Women's Rights Threatened by the Distinct Society Clause?" In: *Meech Lake Primer: Conflicting Views of the 1987 Constitutional Accord*, edited by Michael D. Behiels. Ottawa: University of Ottawa Press, 1989, p. 295-301.

2156   **Ferland, Jacques**
"In Search of the 'Unbound Prometheia': A Comparative View of Women's Activism in Two Quebec Industries, 1869-1908." *Labour/ Le Travail*, no. 24 (1989) p. 11-44.

2157   **Fiske, Jo-Anne**
"Fishing is Women's Business: Changing Economic Roles of Carrier Women and Men." In: *Native People, Native Lands: Canadian Indians, Inuit and Metis*, edited by Bruce Alden Cox. Ottawa: Carleton Univeristy Press, 1988, p. 186-198.

2158   **Forde, Jean**
"A Commitment to Serve - Three Jamaician Women in Toronto."
*Polyphony: The Bulletin of the Multicultural History Society of
Ontario*, vol. 8 no. 1/2 (1986) p. 80-82.

2159   **Forsyth, Louise H.**
"Les femmes de l'Ontario et du Québec: leur présence sur la place
publique des villes." *Études canadiennes/Canadian Studies*, vol. 19
(1985) p. 163-169.

2160   **Frager, Ruth A.**
"Class and Ethnic Barriers to Feminist Perspective in Toronto's
Jewish Labour Movement." *Studies in Political Economy*, no. 30
(1989) p. 143-166.

2161   **Freidenburg, Judith**
"Migrant Careers and Well-being of Women." *International
Migration Review*, vol. 22 no. 2 (1988) p. 208-225.

2162   **Fuchs, Linda**
*Social Support, Life Events, Self-concept and Happiness Among
Southeast Asian Refugee Women in Saskatoon.* Unpublished MA
thesis, University of Saskatchewan, 1987.

2163   **Ghosh, Ratna**
"Education, Gender, and the Immigrant Experience." In:
Multiculturalism in Canada: Social and Educational Perspectives,
edited by Ronald J. Samuda, John W. Berry and Michel Laferriere.
Toronto: Allyn and Bacon Inc., 1984, p. 327-333.

2164   **Ghosh, Ratna**
"South Asian Women in Canada: Adaptation." In: *South Asians in
the Canadian Mosaic*, edited by Rabindra N. Kanungo. Montreal:
Kala Bharati Foundation, 1984, p. 145-155.

2165   **Ghosh, Ratna**
"Minority Within a Minority: On Being South Asian and Female in
Canada." In: *Women in the Family and the Economy: An
International Comparative Survey*, edited by George Kurian and
Ratna Ghosh. Westport, Connecticut: Greenwood Press, 1981, p. 413-
426.

2166   **Ghosh, Ratna**
"Social and Economic Integration of South Asian Women in Montreal, Canada." In: *Women in the Family and the Economy: An International Comparative Survey*, edited by George Kurian and Ratna Ghosh. Westport, Connecticut: Greenwood Press, 1981, p. 59-71.

2167   **Godard, Barbara**
Talking About Ourselves: The Literary Productions of Native Women of Canada. Ottawa, Ont.: Canadian Research Institute for the Advancement of Women, 1985. 44 p.

2168   **Gondolf, Edward W., Ellen Fisher, and J. Richard McFerron**
"Racial Differences Among Shelter Residents: A Comparison of Anglo, Black and Hispanic Battered Women." *Journal of Family Violence*, vol. 3 no. 1 (1988) p. 39-52.

2169   **Green, Mary Jean**
"The 'Literary Feminists' and the Fight for Womens' Writing in Quebec." *Journal of Canadian Studies/Revue d'études canadiennes*, vol. 21 no. 1 (1986) p. 128-143.

2170   **Green, Mary Jean, Paula Gilbert Lewis, and Karen Gould**
"Inscriptions of the Feminine: A Century of Women Writing in Quebec." *American Review of Canadian Studies*, vol. 15 no. 4 (1986) p. 364.

2171   **Greschner, Donna**
"How Not to Drown in Meech Lake: Rules, Principles and Women's Equality Rights." In: *Competing Constitutional Visions: The Meech Lake Accord*, edited by Katherine E. Swinton and Carol J. Rogerson. Toronto: Carswell, 1988, p. 55-63.

2172   **Guenette, Cynthia**
The Effects of Ethnicity and Gender on Occupational Attainment: The Case of Quebec Teachers. Unpublished MA thesis, University of Ottawa, 1985. 3 microfiches. Canadian theses on microfiche, CT86-26634-6.

2173   **Hanson, Jody**
Luxemburg's Methodology: Implications for Northern Native Women. Unpublished MEd thesis, Francis Xavier University, 1989.

2174   **Harris, Ruth Lynnette**
The Transformation of Canadian Policies and Programs to Recruit Foreign Labour: The Case of Caribbean Female Domestic Workers, 1950's-1980's. Unpublished PhD thesis, East Lansing, Michigan State University, 1989. 334 p.

2175   **Hernandez, Carmencita R.**
"The Coalition of Visible Minority Women." In: *Social Movements/ Social Change,* edited by Frank Cunningham et al. Toronto: Between the Lines, 1988, p. 157-169.

2176   **Hobart, Charles W.**
"Changing Profession and Practice of Sexual Standards: A Study of Young Anglophone and Francophone Canadians." *Journal of Comparative Family Studies,* vol. 15 no. 2 (1984) p. 231-255.

2177   **Holt, Marjatta and Joyce Scane**
The Women Speak. Toronto: Ontario Institute for Studies in Education (OISE) Press, 1988. 17 p.

2178   **Hopkins, Elaine R.**
"Feminism and a Female Trinity in Denise Boucher's 'Les fées ont soif'." *The American Review of Canadian Studies,* vol. 14 no. 1 (1984) p. 63-71.

2179   **Hopkins, Elizabeth**
"A British Gentlewoman Immigrant: Susanna Moodie." *Polyphony: The Bulletin of the Multicultural History Society of Ontario,* vol. 8 no. 1/2 (1986) p. 5-8.

2180   **Hopkins, Elizabeth**
"Prison-house for Prosperity: The Immigrant Experience of the Nineteenth Century Upper-class British Woman." In: *Looking Into My Sister's Eyes: An Exploration in Women's History,* edited by Jean Burnet. Toronto: Multicultural History Society of Ontario, 1986, p. 7-20.

2181   **Horn, Michiel**
"Canadian Soldiers and Dutch Women after the Second World War." In: *Dutch Immigration to North America,* edited by Herman Ganzevoort and Mark Boekelman. Toronto: Multicultural History Society of Ontario, 1983, p. 187-196.

2182   **Horodyski, Mary**
"Women and the Winnipeg General Strike of 1919." *Manitoba History*, no. 11 (1986) p. 28-37.

2183   **Horrall, S.W.**
"The (Royal) North-West Mounted Police and Prostitution on the Canadian Prairies." *Prairie Forum*, vol. 10 no. 1 (1985) p. 105-127.

2184   **Howard, Irene**
"The Mothers' Council of Vancouver: Holding the Fort for the Unemployed, 1935-1938." *B.C. Studies*, nos. 69/70 (1986) p. 249-287.

2185   **Iacovetta, Franca**
"Trying to Make Ends Meet: An Historical Look at Italian Women, the State and Family Survival Strategies in Post-war Toronto." *Canadian Woman Studies/Cahiers de la femme*, vol. 8 no. 2 (1987) p. 6-11.

2186   **Iacovetta, Franca**
"From *Contadina* to Worker: Southern Italian Immigrant Working Women in Toronto, 1947-62." In: *Looking Into My Sister's Eyes: An Exploration in Women's History*, edited by Jean Burnet. Toronto: Multicultural History Society of Ontario, 1986, p. 195-222.

2187   **Iacovetta, Franca**
"'Primitive Villagers and Uneducated Girls': Canada Recruits Domestics from Italy, 1951-1952." *Canadian Woman Studies/Cahiers de la femme*, vol. 7 no. 4 (1986) p. 14-18.

2188   **Iacovetta, Franca**
"Southern Italian Working Women." *Polyphony: The Bulletin of the Multicultural History Society of Ontario*, vol. 8 no. 1/2 (1986) p. 56-60.

2189   **Iacovetta, Franca**
"From *Contadina* to Worker: Southern Italian Working Women in Toronto, 1947-62." *Polyphony: The Bulletin of the Multicultural History Society of Ontario*, vol. 7 no. 2 (1985) p. 91-97.

2190   **Imamura, Ann E.**
"The Loss that has No Name: Social Womanhood of Foreign Wives." *Gender and Society*, vol. 2 no. 3 (1988) p. 291-307.

2191   **Indra, Doreen M.**
"Invisible Mosaic: Women, Ethnicity and the Vancouver Press, 1905-1976." *Canadian Ethnic Studies/Études ethniques au Canada*, vol. 13 no. 1 (1981) p. 63-74.

2192   **Jain, Harish C.**
"Race and Sex Discrimination in Employment in Canada: Theories, Evidence and Policies." *Relations industrielles/Industrial Relations*, vol. 37 no. 2 (1982) p. 344-366.

2193   **Jain, Harish C.**
Race and Sex Discrimination in the Workplace: An Analysis of Theory, Research and Public Policy in Canada. Ottawa: Employment and Immigration Canada, 1981. 82 p.

2194   **Jameson, Elizabeth**
"Toward a Multicultural History of Women in the Western United States." *Signs: Journal of Women in Culture and Society*, vol. 13 no. 4 (1988) p. 761-791.

2195   **Jamieson, Kathleen**
Native Women in Canada: A Selected Bibliography. Ottawa: Social Science and Humanities Research Council of Canada, 1983.

2196   **Jamieson, Wanda**
Aboriginal Male Violence Against Aboriginal Women in Canada. Unpublished MA thesis, University of Ottawa, 1987. 3 microfiches. Canadian theses on microfiche, CT89-23724-7.

2197   **Jardine, Pauline O.**
"An Urban Middle Class Calling: Women and the Emergence of Modern Nursing Education at the Toronto General Hospital, 1881-1914." *Urban History Review/Revue d'histoire urbaine*, vol. 17 no. 3 (1989) p. 177-190.

2198   **Jellison, Katherine**
"Women and Technology on the Great Plains, 1910-40." *Great Plains Quarterly*, vol. 8. no. 3 (1988) p. 145-157.

2199   **Juhnke, Jim**
"The Role of Women in the Mennonite Transition from Traditionalism to Denominationalism." *Mennonite Life*, vol. 41 no. 3 (1986) p. 17-20.

2200   **Juteau, Danielle**
"Ethnicity and Femininity: [d']après nos expériences." *Canadian Ethnic Studies/Études ethniques au Canada*, vol. 13 no. 1 (1981) p. 1-23.

2201   **Kallen, Evelyn**
"Multiculturalism, Minorities and Motherhood: A Social Scientific Critique of Section 27." In: *Multiculturalism and the Charter: A Legal Perspective*, edited by Canadian Human Rights Foundation. Toronto: Carswell, 1987, p. 123-138.

2202   **Kalnins, Ilze**
"Women at the Centre: A Feminist Experiment in an Ethnic Milieu." *Polyphony: The Bulletin of the Multicultural History Society of Ontario*, vol. 8 no. 1/2 (1986) p. 83-88.

2203   **Kaprielian, Isabel**
"Armenian Refugee Women and the Maintenance of Identity and Heritage." *Polyphony: The Bulletin of the Multicultural History Society of Ontario*, vol. 8 no. 1/2 (1986) p. 33-36.

2204   **Kaprielian, Isabel**
"Creating and Sustaining an Ethnocultural Heritage in Ontario: The Case of Armenian Women Refugees." In: *Looking Into My Sister's Eyes: An Exploration in Women's History*, edited by Jean Burnet. Toronto: Multicultural History Society of Ontario, 1986, p. 139-153.

2205   **Kealey, Linda**
"Canadian Socialism and the Woman Question: 1900-1914." *Labour/ Le Travail*, no. 13 (1984) p. 77-100.

2206   **Kealey, Linda and Joan Sangster, eds.**
Beyond the Vote: Canadian Women and Politics. Toronto: University of Toronto Press, 1989. 349 p.

2207   **Khosla, Renu**
"The Changing Familial Role of South-Asian Women in Canada: A Study in Identity Transformation." In: *Asian Canadians: Regional Perspectives*, edited by K. Victor Ujimoto and Gordon Hirabayashi, [Guelph, Ont.: University of Guelph, 1989] p. 178-184. Paper presented at the 5th Asian Canadian Symposium held at Mount Saint Vincent University, Halifax, Nova Scotia, May 23 to May 26, 1981.

2208   **King, Deborah K.**
"Multiple Jeopardy, Multiple Consciousness: The Context of a Black Feminist Ideology." *Signs: Journal of Women in Culture and Society*, vol. 14 no. 1 (1988) p. 42-72.

2209   **Kinnear, Mary, ed.**
First Days, Fighting Days: Women in Manitoba History. Regina: Canadian Plains Research Center, University of Regina, 1987. 177 p.

2210   **Kojder, Apolonja**
"Women and the Polish Alliance of Canada." In: *Looking Into My Sister's Eyes: An Exploration in Women's History*, edited by Jean Burnet. Toronto: Multicultural History Society of Ontario, 1986, p. 91-106.

2211   **Kojder, Apolonja**
"Women and the Polish Alliance of Canada." *Polyphony: The Bulletin of the Multicultural History Society of Ontario*, vol. 8 no. 1/2 (1986) p. 40-41.

2212   **Koza, Kimberly Ann**
Women as Images of History: Contemporary Anglophone Fiction by Minority and Post-colonial Women Writers. Unpublished PhD thesis, Indiana University, 1988. 313 p.

2213   **Kraybill, Donald B.**
"Mennonite Woman's Veiling: The Rise and Fall of a Sacred Symbol." *The Mennonite Quarterly Review*, vol. 61 no. 3 (1987) p. 298-320.

2214   **Krosenbrink-Gelissen, Lilianne E.**
No Indian Women, No Indian Nation: Canadian Native Women in Search of Their Identity. Unpublished MA thesis, Nijmegen, Netherlands, Catholic University, 1984. 86 leaves.

2215   **Kurzon, Dennis**
"Sexist and Nonsexist Language in Legal Texts: The State of the Art." *International Journal of the Sociology of Language*, no. 80 (1988) p. 99-113.

2216   **La Prairie, Carol Pitcher**
"Selected Criminal Justice and Socio-demographic Data on Native Women." *Canadian Journal of Criminology*, vol. 26 no. 2 (1984) p. 161-170.

2217 **Lalonde, Richard N.**
"Social Integration Strategies of Haitian and Indian Immigrant Women in Montreal." In: *Ethnic Psychology: Research and Practice with Immigrants, Refugees, Native Peoples, Ethnic Groups and Sojourners*, edited by John W. Berry and R.C. Annis. Lisse: Swets and Zeitlinger, 1988, p. 114-124.

2218 **Lamarche, Lucie**
"Perspective féministe d'une certaine société distincte: les québécoises et l'accord du lac Meech." In: *Competing Constitutional Visions: The Meech Lake Accord*, edited by Katherine E. Swinton and Carol J. Rogerson. Toronto: Carswell, 1988, p. 21-33.

2219 **Lee, Christina Chau-Ping**
Acculturation and Value Change: Chinese Immigrant Women. Unpublished EdD thesis, University of British Columbia, 1984. 225 leaves. Canadian theses on microfiche, 66903.

2220 **Leveille, Danielle**
L'androcentrisme en anthropologie: un exemple, les femmes inuit. Unpublished MA thesis, Université Laval, 1985. 2 microfiches. Canadian theses on microfiche, CT88-23071-1.

2221 **Levine, Karen**
"A Jewish Working Woman's Career." *Polyphony: The Bulletin of the Multicultural History Society of Ontario*, vol. 8 no. 1/2 (1986) p. 93-95.

2222 **Lindgren, H. Elaine**
"Ethnic Women Homesteading on the Plains of North Dakota." *Great Plains Quarterly*, vol. 9 no. 3 (1989) p. 157-173.

2223 **Lindström-Best, Varpu**
"Finnish Socialist Women in Canada, 1890-1930." In: *Beyond the Vote: Canadian Women and Politics*, edited by Linda Kealey and Joan Sangster. Toronto: University of Toronto Press, 1989, p. 196-216.

2224 **Lindström-Best, Varpu**
Defiant Sisters: A Social History of Finnish Immigrant Women in Canada. Toronto: Multicultural History Society of Ontario, 1988. 205 p.

2225 **Lindström-Best, Varpu**
"Hide and Seek: Interviewing Immigrant Women." *Polyphony: The Bulletin of the Multicultural History Society of Ontario*, vol. 9 no. 1 (1987) p. 88-89.

2226 **Lindström-Best, Varpu**
Defiant Sisters: A Social History of the Finnish Immigrant Women in Canada, 1890-1930. Unpublished PhD thesis, York University, 1986. 6 microfiches. Canadian theses on microfiche, CT89-20732-1.

2227 **Lindström-Best, Varpu**
"Going to Work in America: Finnish Maids, 1911-30." *Polyphony: The Bulletin of the Multicultural History Society of Ontario*, vol. 8 no. 1/2 (1986) p. 17-20.

2228 **Lindström-Best, Varpu**
"'I Won't Be a Slave!'—Finnish Domestics in Canada, 1911-30." In: *Looking Into My Sister's Eyes: An Exploration in Women's History*, edited by Jean Burnet. Toronto: Multicultural History Society of Ontario, 1986, p. 33-54.

2229 **Lintelman, Joy K.**
"'America is the Woman's Promised Land': Swedish Immigrant Women and American Domestic Service." *Journal of American Ethnic History*, vol. 8 no. 2 (1989) p. 9-23.

2230 **Littlefield, Loraine**
"Women Traders in the Maritime Fur Trade." In: *Native People, Native Lands: Canadian Indians, Inuit and Metis*, edited by Bruce Alden Cox. Ottawa: Carleton University Press, 1988, p. 173-185.

2231 **Livesay, Dorothy**
"Two Women Writers: Anglophone and Francophone." In: *Language and Literature in Multicultural Contexts*, edited by Satendra Nandan. Suva: University of the South Pacific and the Association for Commonwealth Language and Literature Studies, 1983, p. 234-239. ACLALS Fifth Tri-ennial Conference Proceedings.

2232 **Loeb, Catherine**
North American Indian Women: Selected Sources. Madison, Wis.: University of Wisconsin System, Women's Studies Librarian, 1985. 19 p.

2233   **Lukian, Ludvika**
"Episodes from the Life of an Immigrant Women." *Ukrainian Canadian*, vol. 42 no. 735/229 (1989) p. 35-38; vol. 42 no. 736/230 (1989) p. 34-38.

2234   **MacGregor, Robert M.**
"The Distorted Mirror: Images of Visible Minority Women in Canadian Print Advertising." *Atlantis*, vol. 15 no. 1 (1989) p. 137-143.

2235   **Mahoney, Kathleen E.**
"Women's Rights." In: *Meech Lake and Canada: Perspectives from the West*, edited by Roger Gibbins et al. Edmonton: Academic Printing and Publishing, 1988, p. 159-170.

2236   **Mann, Coramae Richey**
"Minority and Female: A Criminal Justice Double Bind." *Social Justice*, vol. 16 no. 4 (1989) p. 95-114.

2237   **Maroney, Heather Jon and Meg Luxton, eds.**
Feminism and Political Economy: Women's Work, Women's Struggles. Toronto: Methuen Publications, 1987. 333 p.

2238   **Martin, Michele**
"Feminization of the Labour Process in the Communications Industry: The Case of the Telephone Operators, 1876-1904." *Labour/ Le Travail*, no. 22 (1988) p. 139-162.

2239   **Maryn, Sonia**
"Ukrainian-Canadian Women in Transition: From Church Basement to Board Room." *Journal of Ukrainian Studies/Zhurnal Ukrajinoznavchnyk Studij*, vol. 10 no. 1 (1985) p. 89-96.

2240   **McGregor-Brand, Dionne**
A Conceptual Analysis of How Gender Roles are Racially Constructed: Black Women. Unpublished MA thesis, University of Toronto: 1989.

2241   **McMullen, Lorraine**
"Ethnicity and Femininity: Double Jeopardy." *Canadian Ethnic Studies/Études ethniques au Canada*, vol. 13 no. 1 (1981) p. 52-62.

2242 **Medicine, Beatrice**
"Native American (Indian) Women: A Call for Research."
Anthropology and Education Quarterly, vol. 19 no. 2 (1988) p. 86-92.

2243 **Merlet, Myriam**
Situation économique des femmes immigrantes haïtiennes.
Unpublished MSc thesis, Université du Québec à Montréal, 1985. 4 microfiches. Canadian theses on microfiche, CT88-25781-4.

2244 **Miedema, Baukje**
"Second Class Status: An Analysis of the Lived Experiences of Immigrant Women in Fredericton." *Canadian Ethnic Studies/Études ethniques au Canada*, vol. 21 no. 2 (1989) p. 63-73.

2245 **Mitchell, Marjorie**
"When You Don't Know the Language, Listen to the Silence: An Historical Overview of Native Indian Women in B.C." In: *History of British Columbia: Selected Readings*, edited by Patricia Roy.
Toronto: Copp Clark Pitman Ltd., a Longman Co., 1989, p. 49-68.

2246 **Moghaddam, Fathali M.**
"Integration Strategies and Attitudes Toward the Built Environment: A Study of Haitian and Indian Immigrant Women in Montreal."
Canadian Journal of Behavioural Science/Revue canadienne des sciences de comportement, vol. 21 no. 2 (1989) p. 160-173.

2247 **Moghaddam, Fathali M.**
"The Meaning of Multiculturalism for Visible Minority Immigrant Women." *Canadian Journal of Behavioural Science/Revue canadienne des sciences de comportement*, vol. 19 no. 2 (1987) p. 121-136.

2248 **Montgomery, Maureen F.**
'Gilded Prostitution': Status, Money, and Transatlantic Marriage, 1870-1914. London, U.K.: Routledge, 1989. 342 p.

2249 **Moore, Timothy E.**
"The Representation of Women, the Elderly and Minorities in Canadian Television Commercials." *Canadian Journal of Behavioural Science/Revue canadienne des sciences de comportement*, vol. 17 no. 3 (1985) p. 215-225.

2250   **Muszynski, Alicja**
"Race and Gender: Structural Determinants in the Formation of British Columbia's Salmon Labour Forces." *Canadian Journal of Sociology/Cahiers canadien de sociologie*, vol. 13 nos. 1-2 (1987/ 1988) p. 103-120.

2251   **Muszynski, Alicja**
"The Organization of Women and Ethnic Minorities in a Resource Industry: A Case Study of the Unionization of Shore Workers in the B.C. Fishing Industry 1937-1949." *Journal of Canadian Studies/ Revue d'études canadiennes*, vol. 19 no. 1 (1984) p. 89-107.

2252   **Naidoo, Josephine C.**
"Canadian South Asian Women in Transition: A Dualistic View of Life." *Journal of Comparative Family Studies*, vol. 19 no. 2 (1988) p. 311-328.

2253   **Naidoo, Josephine C.**
"Women of South Asian Origins: Status of Research, Problems, Future Issues." In: *The South Asian Diaspora in Canada*, edited by Milton Israel. Toronto: Multicultural History Society of Ontario, 1987, p. 27-58.

2254   **Naidoo, Josephine C.**
"Value Conflicts for South Asian Women in Multicultural Canada." In: *Ethnic Minorities and Immigrants in a Cross-cultural Perspective: Selected Papers*, edited by Lars H. Ekstrand. Berwyn: Swets North America, 1986, p. 132-148. Paper presented at the first Circum-Mediterranean Regional IACCP Conference, Malmo, Sweden, 1985.

2255   **Naidoo, Josephine C.**
"A Cultural Perspective on the Adjustment of South Asian Women in Canada." In: *From a Different Perspective. Studies of Behaviour Across Cultures*, edited by Isabel Reyes Lagunes and Ype H. Poortinga. Lisse: Swets and Zeitlainger, 1985, p. 76-92.

2256   **Naidoo, Josephine C.**
"South Asian Women in Canada: Self Perceptions, Socialization, Achievement, Aspirations." In: *South Asians in the Canadian Mosaic*, edited by Rabindra N. Kanungo. Montreal: Kala Bharati Foundation, 1984, p. 123-142.

2257   **Naidoo, Josephine C.**
"Stressful and Facilitating Life Experiences for South Asian Women in Canada." In: *Asian Canadians: Aspects of Social Change*, edited by K. Victor Ujimoto and Josephine Naidoo. Guelph, Ont.: University of Guelph, 1984, p. 90-111. Paper presented at the 6th Asian Canadian Symposium, University of Guelph, June 6-8, 1984.

2258   **Naidoo, Josephine C.**
"East Indian Women in the Canadian Context: A Study in Social Psychology." In: *Visible Minorities and Multiculturalism: Asians in Canada*, edited by K. Victor Ujimoto and Gordon Hirabayashi. Toronto: Butterworths, 1980, p. 193-218.

2259   **Naidoo, Josephine C.**
"Women of South Asian and Anglo-Saxon Origins in the Canadian Context: Self-perceptions, Socialization, Achievement Aspirations." In: *Sex Roles: Origins, Influences, and Implications for Women*, edited by Cannie Stark-Ademec. 1st ed. Montreal: Eden Press, Women's Publications, 1980, p. 50-88.

2260   **Naidoo, Jospehine C. and J. Campbell Davis**
"Canadian South Asian Women in Transition: A Dualistic View of Life." *Journal of Comparative Family Studies*, vol 19 no. 2 (1988) p. 311-327.

2261   **Ng, Roxana**
"Immigrant Women and Institutionalized Racism." In: *Changing Patterns: Women in Canada*, edited by Sandra Burt, Lorraine Code, and Lindsay Dorney. Toronto: McClelland and Stewart, 1988, p. 184-203.

2262   **Ng, Roxana**
The Politics of Community Services: Immigrant Women, Class and State. Toronto: Garamond, 1988. 113 p.

2263   **Ng, Roxana**
Immigrant Women and the State: A Study in the Social Organization of Knowledge. Unpublished PhD thesis, University of Toronto: 1984. 3 microfiches. Canadian theses on microfiche, 65081.

2264   **Nicolson, Murray W.**
"Women in the Irish-Canadian Catholic Family." *Polyphony: The Bulletin of the Multicultural History Society of Ontario*, vol. 8 no. 1/2 (1986) p. 9-12.

2265   **Niesiobedzka, Stefania**
"A Polish Displaced Person's Memories." *Polyphony: The Bulletin of the Multicultural History Society of Ontario*, vol. 8 no. 1/2 (1986) p. 96-98.

2266   **Nipp, Dora**
"But Women Did Come: Working Chinese Women in the Interwar Years." In: *Looking Into My Sister's Eyes: An Exploration in Women's History*, edited by Jean Burnet. Toronto: Multicultural History Society of Ontario, 1986, p. 179-194.

2267   **Nipp, Dora**
"Working Chinese Women in the Interwar Period." *Polyphony: The Bulletin of the Multicultural History Society of Ontario*, vol. 8 no. 1/2 (1986) p. 45-46.

2268   **Norell, Donna**
"The Most Humane Institution in All the Village: The Women's Rest Room in Rural Manitoba." *Manitoba History*, no. 11 (1986) p. 38-50.

2269   **Nunes, Fernando**
"Portuguese-Canadian Women: Problems and Prospects." *Polyphony: The Bulletin of the Multicultural History Society of Ontario*, vol. 8 no. 1/2 (1986) p. 61-66.

2270   **Ong, Amoy Yuk Mui**
An Exploratory Study of the Life of the Single Asian Immigrant Woman in Winnipeg: Implications for Social Work Practice. Unpublished MSW thesis, University of Manitoba, 1987. 3 microfiches. Canadian theses on microfiche, CT88-26970-7.

2271   **Ontario Native Women's Association**
What Does the Future Hold for Native Women — Aboriginal Entitlement? Thunder Bay, Ont.: Ontario Native Women's Association, 1982. 90 p.

2272   **Patrias, Carmela**
"Passages from the Life...: An Italian Woman in Welland, Ontario." *Canadian Woman Studies/Cahiers de la femme*, vol. 8 no. 2 (1987) p. 69-73.

2273   **Perillo, Carmen**
"Multicultural Policy: Women Beware." *Canadian Woman Studies/Cahiers de la femme*, vol. 8 no. 2 (1987) p. 27-29.

2274 **Papp, Susan M.**
"Hungarian Immigrant Women." *Polyphony: The Bulletin of the Multicultural History Society of Ontario*, vol. 8 no. 1/2 (1986) p. 42-44.

2275 **Petroff, Lillian**
"Contributors to Ethnic Cohesion: Macedonian Women in Toronto to 1940." In: *Looking Into My Sister's Eyes: An Exploration in Women's History*, edited by Jean Burnet. Toronto: Multicultural History Society of Ontario, 1986, p. 125-138.

2276 **Petroff, Lillian**
"Macedonian Women in Toronto to 1940." *Polyphony: The Bulletin of the Multicultural History Society of Ontario*, vol. 8 no. 1/2 (1986) p. 24-28.

2277 **Petryshyn, Marusia K.**
"The Changing Status of Ukrainian Women in Canada, 1921-1971." In: *Changing Realities: Social Trends Among Ukrainian Canadians*, edited by W. Roman Petryshyn. Edmonton: Canadian Institute of Ukrainian Studies, 1980, p. 189-209.

2278 **Pichini, Lia**
"Two Generations in Conflict: Sex Role Expectations Among Italian-Canadian Women." *Canadian Woman Studies/Cahiers de la femme*, vol. 8 no. 2 (1987) p. 22-23.

2279 **Pivato, Joseph**
"An Immigrant Daughter and a Female Writer: Mary de Michele." *Vice Versa*, vol. 1 no. 5/6 (1984) p. 21-22.

2280 **Poirier, Marie**
Les femmes immigrées au Québec: bibliographie annotée. Montréal: Direction des communications et direction de la recherche, Ministère des Communautés culturelles et de l'immigration, 1985. 51 p.

2281 **Poirier, Suzanne**
"Emma Goldman, Ben Reitman and Reitman's Wives: A Study in Relationships." *Women's Studies*, vol. 14 no. 3 (1988) p. 277-297.

2282 **Polyzoi, Eleoussa**
"Greek Immigrant Women from Asia Minor: Philoptoho and Languages Schools." *Polyphony: The Bulletin of the Multicultural History Society of Ontario*, vol. 11 no. 1/2 (1989) p. 28-35.

2283   **Polyzoi, Eleoussa**
"Greek Immigrant Women from Asia Minor in Prewar Toronto: The
Formative Years." In: *Looking Into My Sister's Eyes: An Exploration
in Women's History*, edited by Jean Burnet. Toronto: Multicultural
History Society of Ontario, 1986, p. 107-124.

2284   **Polyzoi, Eleoussa**
"Greek Immigrant Women from Asia Minor: Philoptoho and
Language Schools." *Polyphony: The Bulletin of the Multicultural
History Society of Ontario*, vol. 8 no. 1/2 (1986) p. 29-32.

2285   **Polyzoi, Eleoussa**
"The Greek Ladies' Philoptoho Society: Its Early Years in Toronto."
*Polyphony: The Bulletin of the Multicultural History Society of
Ontario*, vol. 6 no. 1 (1984) p. 79-82.

2286   **Porter, Marilyn**
"'She Was Skipper of the Shore Crew': Notes on the History of the
Sexual Division of Labour in Newfoundland." *Labour/Le Travail*, no.
15 (1985) p. 105-124.

2287   **Preyra, Cecilia Maria**
*Experiences of South Asian Women in a Canadian Shelter for
Battered Women*. Unpublished MA thesis, University of Toronto:
1989.

2288   **Ralston, Helen**
"Ethnicity, Class and Gender Among South Asian Women in Metro
Halifax: An Exploratory Study." *Canadian Ethnic Studies/Études
ethniques au Canada*, vol. 20 no. 3 (1988) p. 63-83.

2289   **Riley, Glenda**
"Women's Responses to the Challenges of Plains Living." *Great
Plains Quarterly*, vol. 9 no. 3 (1989) p. 174-184.

2290   **Riutort, Monica**
"Latin-American Women in Toronto." *Polyphony: The Bulletin of the
Multicultural History Society of Ontario*, vol. 8 no. 1/2 (1986) p. 73-
74.

2291   **Robinson, Gwen**
"Pioneer Women in Southwestern Ontario." *Polyphony: The Bulletin
of the Multicultural History Society of Ontario*, vol. 8 no. 1/2
(1986) p. 3-4.

2292   **Rodriguez-Elizalde, Jorge**
"La discrimination et les femmes francophones du corridor bilingue de l'Ontario." *Bulletin du Centre de recherche en civilisation canadienne-française* no. 27 (1983) p. 17-29.

2293   **Romanyshyn, Oleh**
"The Canadian League for the Liberation of Ukraine and its Women's Association." *Polyphony: The Bulletin of the Multicultural History Society of Ontario*, vol. 10 no. 1/2 (1988) p. 153-166.

2294   **Sabia, Laura**
"'You Are Not One of Us': The Roots of My Militant Feminism." *Canadian Woman Studies/Cahiers de la femme*, vol. 8 no. 2 (1987) p. 32-36.

2295   **Sangster, Joan**
"The Communist Party and the Woman Question, 1922-1929." *Labour/Le Travail*, no. 15 (1985) p. 25-56.

2296   **Sangster, Joan**
"Social History of Finns in Ontario: Finnish Women in Ontario, 1890-1930." *Polyphony: The Bulletin of the Multicultural History Society of Ontario*, vol. 3 no. 2 (1981) p. 46-54.

2297   **Scane, Joyce and Marjatta Holt**
Immigrant Women: Their Untold History /Immigrant Women: Their Untold History - Teacher's Guide. Toronto: Ontario Institute for Studies in Education (OISE) Press, 1988. 44 p., 32 p.

2298   **Schneider, Aili Gronlund**
The Finnish Baker's Daughters. Toronto: The Multicultural History Society of Ontario and the Ontario Heritage Foundation, 1986. 105 p.

2299   **Seager, Joni**
"The Other Two Solitudes: Gender and Canadian Studies." *The American Review of Canadian Studies*, vol. 15 no. 4 (1986) p. 497-508.

2300   **Séguin, Claire**
"Essai sur la condition de la femme indienne au Canada." *Recherches amerindiennes au Québec*, vol. 10 no. 4 (1981) p. 251-260.

2301   **Seller, Maxine S.**
"World of Our Mothers: The Women's Page of *The Jewish Daily Forward.*" *The Journal of Ethnic Studies*, vol. 16 no. 2 (1988) p. 95, 118.

2302   **Seller, Maxine S.**
"Defining Socialist Womanhood: The Women's Page of *The Jewish Daily Forward* in 1919." *American Jewish History*, vol. 76 no. 4 (1987) p. 416-438.

2303   **Seward, Shirley B.**
Immigrant Women in Canada: A Policy Perspective. Ottawa: Canadian Advisory Council on the Status of Women, 1988. 75 p.

2304   **Seward, Shirley B. and Kathryn McDade**
"A New Deal for Immigrant Women." *Policy Options/Options politiques*, vol. 9 no. 5 (1988) p. 15-18.

2305   **Shapiro, Daniel M.**
"The Persistence of the Male—Female Earnings Gap in Canada, 1970-1980: The Impact of Equal Pay Laws and Language Policies." *Canadian Public Policy/Analyse de politiques*, vol. 13 no. 4 (1987) p. 462-476.

2306   **Shapiro, Daniel M.**
"Language Legislation and Male—Female Earning Differentials in Quebec." *Canadian Public Policy/Analyse de politiques*, vol. 8 no. 1 (1982) p. 106-113.

2307   **Shapiro, Daniel M.**
"Male—Female Earnings Differentials and the Role of Language in Canada, Ontario, and Quebec." *Canadian Journal of Economics/ Revue canadienne d'économique*, vol. 14 no. 2 (1981) p. 341-348.

2308   **Sheehan, Nancy M.**
"Women and Imperialism: The I.O.D.E. (Imperial Order Daughters of the Empire) Propaganda and Patriotism in Canadian Schools, 1900-1940." *Aspects of Education: Journal of the Institute of Education, University of Hull*, no. 40 (1989) p. 11-34.

2309   **Shibata, Yuko**
"Coping with Values in Conflict: Japanese Women in Canada." In: *Visible Minorities and Multiculturalism: Asians in Canada*, edited by K. Victor Ujimoto and Gordon Hirabayashi. Toronto: Butterworths, 1980, p. 257-276.

2310   **Silman, Janet, ed.**
Enough is Enough: Aboriginal Women Speak Out. Toronto: Women's
Press, 1987. 253 p.

2311   **Sims-Wood, Janet**
"Researching Black Women's History Resources and Archives at the
Moorland-Spingarn Research Center." *Ethnic Forum*, vol. 7. no. 1
(1987) p. 38-47.

2312   **Smith, Lynn**
"The Distinct Society Clause in the Meech Lake Accord: Could It
Affect Equality Rights for Women?" In: *Competing Constitutional
Visions: The Meech Lake Accord*, edited by Katherine E. Swinton
and Carol J. Rogerson. Toronto: Carswell, 1988, p. 35-54.

2313   **Struser, Halina Gail**
Childbearing Experience of Indo-Canadian Immigrant Women.
Unpublished MSA thesis, University of British Columbia, 1985. 147
leaves.

2314   **Sturino, Franc**
"The Role of Women in Italian Immigration to the New World." In:
Looking Into My Sister's Eyes: An Exploration in Women's History,
edited by Jean Burnet. Toronto: Multicultural History Society of
Ontario, 1986, p. 21-32.

2315   **Sturino, Franc**
"Women and the Italian Immigrant Family." *Polyphony: The Bulletin
of the Multicultural History Society of Ontario*, vol. 8 no. 1/2
(1986) p. 21-23.

2316   **Swampy, Grace Marie**
"The Role of the Native Woman in the Native Society." *Canadian
Journal of Native Education*, vol. 9 no. 2 (1982) p. 2-20.

2317   **Swyripa, Frances**
"The Ideas of the Ukrainian Women's Organization of Canada, 1930-
1945." In: *Beyond the Vote: Canadian Women and Politics*, edited by
Linda Kealey and Joan Sangster. Toronto: University of Toronto
Press, 1989, p. 239-257.

2318   **Swyripa, Frances**
*From Princess Olha to Baba: Images, Roles and Myths in the History of
Ukrainian Women in Canada.* Unpublished PhD thesis, University of
Alberta, 1988. Canadian theses on microfiche, CT90-22251-4.

2319   **Swyripa, Frances**
"Outside the Block Settlement: Ukrainian Women in Ontario During the Formative Years of Community Consciousness." In: *Looking Into My Sister's Eyes: An Exploration in Women's History*, edited by Jean Burnet. Toronto: Multicultural History Society of Ontario, 1986, p. 179-194.

2320   **Swyripa, Frances**
"Ukrainian Women in Ontario." *Polyphony: The Bulletin of the Multicultural History Society of Ontario*, vol. 8 no. 1/2 (1986) p. 47-50.

2321   **Szado, Daniela**
"The Social Roots of Wife Battering: An Examination of the Phenomenon in Mediterranean Immigrant Communities." *Canadian Woman Studies/Cahiers de la femme*, vol. 8 no. 2 (1987) p. 41-42.

2322   **Tazmani, Parvin**
Immigration, adaptation et problèmes de santé mentale chez les femmes professionnelles d'origine iranienne au Québec. Unpublished MSc thesis, Université de Montréal, 1986. 1 microfiche.

2323   **Teal, Gregory L.**
The Organization of Production and the Heterogeneity of the Working Class: Occupation, Gender and Ethnicity Among Clothing Workers in Quebec. Unpublished PhD thesis, McGill University, 1986. 6 microfiches. Canadian theses on microfiche, CT89-20784-4.

2324   **Theresa-Larain, Maria**
"Immigrant Women: An Exploited Class." *The Asianadian*, vol. 5 no. 2 (1983) p. 10-13.

2325   **Thomas, Geraldine**
"Women in the Greek Community of Nova Scotia." *Canadian Ethnic Studies/Études ethniques au Canada*, vol. 20 no. 3 (1988) p. 84-93.

2326   **Ticoll, Ellen**
"Double Discrimination: Problems of Immigrant Women." *First Reading: Edmonton Social Planning Council*, vol. 3 no. 6 (1984) p. 6-7.

2327   **Trovato, Frank**
"Economic Status: A Census Analysis of Thirty-year-old Immigrant Women in Canada." *Canadian Review of Sociology and Anthropology/Revue canadienne de sociologie et d'anthropologie*, vol. 23 no. 4 (1986) p. 569-587.

2328   Uhlaner, Carole Jean
"Does Sex Matter? Participation by French and English Women in Mass Canadian Politics." *CPSA Papers/ACSP Contributions 1980*, Section: Political Behaviour, paper 2, fiche 4. Paper presented at the 52nd annual meeting of the Canadian Political Science Association, June 2-4, 1980, Université du Québec à Montréal.

2329   Van Kirk, Sylvia
"'Women in Between': Indian Women in Fur Trade Society in Western Canada." In: *Out of the Background: Readings on Canadian Native History*, edited by Robin Fisher and Kenneth Coates. Toronto: Copp Clark Pitman, 1988, p. 150-166.

2330   Van Kirk, Sylvia
Many Tender Ties: Women in Fur-trade Society in Western Canada, 1670-1870. Winnipeg: Watson and Dwyer Pub. Ltd., 1980. 303 p.

2331   Verma, Ravi B.P.
"Variations in Family Size Among Canadian Women by Generation and Ethnic Groups." *International Journal of Comparative Sociology*, vol. 20 nos. 3-4 (1980) p. 293-303.

2332   Wargelin, Kaarina and Raymond
"Pioneer Pastors' Wives Chose the Role of Service: 'A Noble But Often Difficult Calling'." *Siirtolaisuus - Migration*, no. 1 (1989) p. 16-24.

2333   Weaver, Sally M.
"The Status of Indian Women." In: *Two Nations, Many Cultures: Ethnic Groups in Canada*, edited by Jean Leonard Elliott. 2nd ed. Scarborough, Ont.: Prentice-Hall of Canada, 1983, p. 56-81.

2334   White, Pamela M.
Native Women: A Statistical Overview. Ottawa: Department of the Secretary of State of Canada, 1985. 31, 31 p. French language title: *Les femmes autochtones: un aperçu statistique*.

2335   Williams, Delores S.
"The Color of Feminism: Or Speaking the Black Women's Tongue." *The Journal of Religious Thought*, vol. 43 no. 1 (1986) p. 42-58.

2336   Winters, Jacqueline
Women in Indian Development: The Dawn of a New Consciousness. Unpublished MA thesis, McGill University, 1987. 2 microfiches. Canadian theses on microfiche, CT89-28538-1.

2337   **Wolowelsky, Joel B.**
"Modern Orthodoxy and Women's Changing Self-perception." *Tradition: Journal of Orthodox Jewish Thought*, vol. 22 no. 1 (1986) p. 65-81.

2338   **Wynnyckyj, Iroida L.**
"Oral History: Ukrainian Women's Voices." *Polyphony: The Bulletin of the Multicultural History Society of Ontario*, vol. 10 no. 1/2 (1988) p. 251-255.

2339   **Yee, May**
"Out of a Silent History: Voices of Chinese-Canadian Women." *Polyphony: The Bulletin of the Multicultural History Society of Ontario*, vol. 9 no. 1 (1987) p. 85-87.

2340   **Yoon, Bok-Nam**
The Adjustment Problems and Educational Needs of Korean Immigrant Women in the Winnipeg Garment Industry. Unpublished MEd thesis, University of Manitoba, 1983. 2 microfiches. Canadian theses on microfiche, 54374.

Language and Linguistics

2341   **Adiv, Ellen**
An Analysis of Second Language Performance in Two Types of Immersion Programs. Unpublished PhD thesis, McGill University, 1980. 4 microfiches. Canadian theses on microfiche, 50374.

2342   **Adiv, Ellen**
"An Analysis of Second Language Performance in Two Types of Immersion Programs." *Canadian Association of Applied Linguistics Bulletin*, vol. 2 no. 2 (1980) p. 139-152.

2343   **Albert, Luc**
"Language in Canada." *Canadian Social Trends*, no. 12 (1989) p. 9.

2344   **Aleong, Stanley, et al.**
"The Role of the Technical School in the Implementation of Proposed Automotive Terminology in Quebec French, A First Report." *Language Problems and Language Planning*, vol. 5 no. 3 (1981) p. 221-239.

2345   **Allen, Virginia, G.**
"Story Retelling: Developmental Stages in Second-language Acquisition." *Canadian Modern Language Review/Revue canadienne des langues vivantes*, vol. 41 no. 4 (1985) p. 686-691.

2346   **Amyot, Gérard et Michel Amyot, eds.**
L'état de la langue française au Québec: Bilan et prospective. Textes corrigés et presentés par Gérard Lapointe et Michel Amyot. 2 vols. Québec, P.Q.: Service des communications, Conseil de la langue française, 1986.

2347   **Anctil, Pierre**
"Linguistic Legislation and Ethnic Enrollment in Montreal's French Language Schools." *Journal of Cultural Geography*, vol. 8 no. 2 (1988) p. 17-27.

2348   **Andres, Myrna Louise**
Integrating Language and Culture in the Classroom: A Module for Junior High Core French Programs. Unpublished MA thesis, University of Calgary, 1984. 5 microfiches. illus. Canadian theses on microfiche, CT86-27931-6.

2349   **Andrew, Edward**
"Pierre Trudeau on the Language of Values and the Value of Languages." *Canadian Journal of Political and Social Theory/Revue canadienne de la théorie politique et sociale*, vol. 6 nos. 1-2 (1982) p. 143-159.

2350   **d'Anglejan, Alison**
"Déterminants socio-culturels de l'apprentissage du discours décontextualisé en milieu scolaire: vers un cadre théorique intégré." *Revue québécoise de linguistique*, vol. 16 no. 2 (1987) p. 145-162.

2351   **d'Anglejan, Alison**
"Beyond the Language Classroom: A Study of Communicative Abilities in Adult Immigrants Following Intensive Instruction." *TESOL Quarterly*, vol. 20 no. 2 (1986) p. 185-205.

2352   **d'Anglejan, Alison**
"Learner Characteristics and Second Language Acquisition: A Multivariate Study of Adult Immigrants and Some Thoughts on Methodology." *Language Learning*, vol. 35 no. 1 (1985) p. 1-19.

2353   **d'Anglejan, Alison**
"Language Planning in Quebec: An Historical Overview and Future Trends." In: *Conflict and Language Planning in Quebec*, edited by Richard Y. Bourhis. Clevedon, Avon: Multilingual Matters, 1984, p. 29-52.

2354   **d'Anglejan, Alison**
"The Education of Minorities in Canada: An Examination of Policies." *World Yearbook of Education*, 1981, p. 85-94.

2355   **Anthony, Robert J.**
"An Educational Perspective on Native Language Literacy."
*Canadian Journal of Anthropology/Revue canadienne
d'anthropologie*, vol. 1 no. 2 (1980) p. 219-227.

2356   **Aoki, Ted T.**
"The Dialectic of Mother Language and Second Language." In:
Language, Culture and Literary Identity in Canada, edited by J.M.
Bumsted. Vancouver: University of British Columbia, 1987, p. 38-47.
Paper presented at the 1984 Ottawa Conference on Language, Culture
and Literary Identity in Canada. Published as Supplement 1 of
Canadian Literature/Littérature canadienne, May 1987, issue no.
112.

2357   **Aunger, Edmund A.**
"Language and Law in the Province of Alberta." In: *Langue et droit*,
sous la direction de Paul Pupier et José Woehrling. Montréal: Wilson
and Lafleur, 1989, p. 203-229. Paper presented at the First Conference of the International Institute of Comparative Linguistic Law,
April 27-29, 1988 at the Université du Québec, Montréal, P.Q.

2358   **Baggio, Daniela G.**
Ethnic Differentiation and Minority Language Maintenance.
Unpublished MA thesis, Carleton University, 1984. 2 microfiches.
Canadian theses on microfiche, CT86-29846-9.

2359   **Bagin, Ladislav**
"Slovak Language Schools in Windsor, Ontario." *Polyphony: The
Bulletin of the Multicultural History Society of Ontario*, vol. 11 no.
1/2 (1989) p. 72-74.

2360   **Baillargeon, Mireille**
*Langue maternelle: importance des populations linguistiques du
Québec et de la région de Montréal en 1986*. Québec, P.Q.:
Gouvernement du Québec, Ministère des communautés culturelles et
de l'immigration, Direction de la planification et de l'évaluation,
1988. 41 p.

2361   **Baillargeon, Mireille**
Les futurs linguistiques possibles de la région en 2001. Nouv.
version. Québec, P.Q.: Gouvernement du Québec, Ministère de
l'immigration, Direction de la recherche, 1981. 285 p.

2362   **Bain, Bruce**
"Cognitive Consequences of Raising Children Bilingually: One
Parent, One Language." *Canadian Journal of Psychology*, vol. 34 no.
4 (1980) p. 304-314.

2363   **Balan, Vasyl**
"Ukrainian Language Education in Canada: Summary of Statistical
Data." In: *New Soil, Old Roots: The Ukrainian Experience in
Canada*, edited by Jaroslav Rozumnyi, Oleh W. Gerus and Mykhailo
H. Marunchak. Winnipeg: Ukrainian Academy of Arts and Sciences,
Canada, 1983, p. 276-287.

2364   **Baranczak, StanisLaw**
"Tongue-tied Eloquence: Notes on Language, Exile and Writing."
*University of Toronto Quarterly: A Canadian Journal of the
Humanities*, vol. 58 no. 4 (1989) p. 429-438.

2365   **Barat, Pradip K.**
"Bengali Language Learning: Opportunities in and Around Toronto."
*Polyphony: The Bulletin of the Multicultural History Society of
Ontario*, vol. 11 no. 1/2 (1989) p. 117-120.

2366   **Barbaud, Philippe**
"Retour sur l'énigme de la francisation des premiers canadiens: le
choc des patois en Nouvelle-France." In: *Language, Culture and
Literary Identity in Canada*, edited by J.M. Bumsted. Vancouver:
University of British Columbia, 1987, p. 51-57. Paper presented at
the 1984 Ottawa Conference on Language, Culture and Literary
Identity in Canada. Published as Supplement 1 of *Canadian
Literature/Littérature canadienne*, May 1987, issue no. 112.

2367   **Bastarache, Michel**
"L'impact de l'entente du lac Meech sur les minorités linguistiques
provinciales." *University of New Brunswick Law Journal/Revue de
droit de l'Université de Nouveau-Brunswick*, vol. 38 (1989) p. 217-
226.

2368   **Bastarache, Michel**
"Le statut du français dans l'ouest canadien." In: *Langue et droit*,
sous la direction de Paul Pupier et José Woehrling. Montréal: Wilson
and Lafleur, 1989, p. 231-242. Paper presented at the First Conference of the International Institute of Comparative Linguistic Law,
April 27-29, 1988 at the Université du Québec, Montréal, P.Q.

2369 **Bastarache, Michel**
"La clause relative à la dualité linguistique et la reconnaissance du Québec comme société distincte." In: *L'adhésion du Québec à l'Accord du lac Meech*, sous la direction de Real A. Forest. Montréal: Éditions Thémis, 1988, p. 33-39.

2370 **Bastarache, Michel**
"Bilingualism and the Judicial System." In: *Language Rights in Canada*, edited by Michel Bastarache. Montreal: Editions Y. Blais, 1987, p. 123-174. Translation of the author's "Le bilinguisme dans le domaine judiciaire," In: *Les droits linguistiques au Canada*, p. 125-179.

2371 **Bastarache, Michel**
"The Principle of Equality of the Official Languages." In: *Language Rights in Canada*, edited by Michel Bastarache. Montreal: Editions Y. Blais, 1987, p. 501-521. Translation of the author's "Le principe d'égalité des langues officielles." In: *Les droits linguistiques au Canada*, p. 521-547.

2372 **Bastarache, Michel, ed.**
Les droits linguistiques au Canada. Montréal: Éditions Y. Blais, 1986. 576 p. English translation published under title: *Language Rights in Canada*, edited by Michel Bastarache. Montreal: Editions Y. Blais, 1987.

2373 **Batts, Michael S.**
"Literary History and National Identity." In: *Language, Culture and Literary Identity in Canada*, edited by J.M. Bumsted. Vancouver: University of British Columbia, 1987, p. 104-111. Paper presented at the 1984 Ottawa Conference on Language, Culture and Literary Identity in Canada. Published as Supplement 1 of *Canadian Literature/Littérature canadienne*, May 1987, issue no. 112.

2374 **Beaty, Stuart**
"A New Official Languages Act for Canada: Its Scope and Implications." In: *Langue et droit*, sous la direction de Paul Pupier et José Woehrling. Montréal: Wilson and Lafleur, 1989, p. 185-193. Paper presented at the First Conference of the International Institute of Comparative Linguistic Law, April 27-29, 1988 at the Université du Québec, Montréal, P.Q.

2375   **Beaudoin, Gérald A.**
"La protection de la langue française au Canada." *Revue générale de droit*, vol. 19 no. 2 (1988) p. 479-492.

2376   **Beaujot, Roderic P.**
"The Decline of Official Language Minorities in Quebec and English Canada." *Canadian Journal of Sociology/Cahiers canadiens de sociologie*, vol. 7 no. 4 (1982) p. 367-389.

2377   **Beaupre, Remi Michael**
Interpreting Bilingual Legislation. 2nd ed. Toronto: Carsell, 1986. 236 p. First edition published under title: *Construing Bilingual Legislation in Canada.*

2378   **Bhatnager, Joti K.**
"Linguistic Behaviour and Adjustment of Immigrant Children in French and English Schools in Montreal." *International Review of Applied Psychology*, vol. 29 nos. 1-2 (1980) p. 141-159.

2379   **Bienvenue, Rita M.**
"Language Politics and Social Divisions in Manitoba." *American Review of Canadian Studies*, vol. 19 no. 2 (1989) p. 187-202.

2380   **Bienvenue, Rita M.**
"Ethnolinguistic Attitudes and French Immersion Enrollments." *Canadian Ethnic Studies/Études ethniques au Canada*, vol. 16 no. 2 (1984) p. 15-29.

2381   **Bilodeau, Roger**
"La judiciarisation des conflits linguistiques au Canada." *Cahiers de droit*, vol. 1 (1986) p. 215-225.

2382   **Bilodeau, Roger**
"La langue, l'éducation et les minorités: avant et depuis la Charte canadienne des droits et libertés." *Manitoba Law Journal*, vol. 13 no. 3 (1983) p. 371-388.

2383   **Binot-Tessier, Emilie**
Analyse des attitudes parentales sous-jacentes à l'apprentissage d'une langue seconde chez l'adolescent anglophone, âge de 12 à 18 ans. Unpublished MEd thesis, Université du Québec à Montréal, 1983. 3 microfiches. Canadian theses on microfiche, CT85-23448-4.

2384 **Borins, Sandford F.**
"Language Use in the Federal Public Service: Some Recent Survey Results." *Canadian Public Administration*, vol. 27 no. 2 (1984) p. 262-268.

2385 **Borins, Sandford F.**
Language of the Skies: The Bilingual Air Traffic Control Conflict in Canada. Montreal and Kingston: McGill-Queen's University Press, 1983.

2386 **Bostock, William Walter**
"The Commissioner of Official Languages: A Canadian Response to a Situation of Ethnolinguistic Cleavage." *Ethnic and Racial Studies*, vol. 3 no. 4 (1980) p. 415-426.

2387 **Bouchard, Chantal**
"De la 'langue du grand siècle' à la 'langue humiliée': les canadiens français et la langue populaire, 1879-1970." *Recherches sociographiques*, vol. 29 no. 1 (1988) p. 7-23.

2388 **Boulanger, Jean-Claude**
"La néologie et l'aménagement linguistique du Québec." *Language Problems and Language Planning*, vol. 10 no. 1 (1986) p. 14-29.

2389 **Bourbeau, Robert**
Canada, A Linguistic Profile. Ottawa: Statistics Canada, 1989. 37 p. French language title: *Le Canada, un profil linguistique.*

2390 **Bourbeau, Robert**
"Trends in Language Mobility Between French and English." In: *Social Inequality in Canada: Patterns, Problems, Policies*, edited by James E. Curtis et al. Scarborough, Ont.: Prentice-Hall Canada, 1988, p. 221-229. A revision of the author's: "Canada's Language Transfer Phenomenon." *Language and Society/Langue et société*, vol. 11 (1982) p. 14-22.

2391 **Bourbeau, Robert**
Linguistic Characteristics of Young People and Their Attitudes to Language Issues. Hull, P.Q.: Secretary of State, Policy Coordination Analysis and Management Systems Branch, 1984. 46, 48 p. French Language title: *Caractéristiques et attitudes des jeunes face aux questions linguistiques.*

2392   **Bourbeau, Robert**
"Les transferts linguistiques au Canada." *Language and Society/
Langue et société*, no. 11 (1983) p. 14-22.

2393   **Bourhis, Richard Y.**
"Aménagement linguistique, statut et usage du français au Québec."
Présence francophone, no. 33 (1988) p. 9-32.

2394   **Bourhis, Richard Y.**
"The Charter of the French Language and Cross-cultural Communications in Montreal." In: *Conflict and Language Planning in Quebec*,
edited by Richard Y. Bourhis. Clevedon, Avon: Multilingual Matters,
1984, p. 174-204.

2395   **Bourhis, Richard Y., ed.**
Conflict and Language Planning in Quebec. Clevedon, Avon: Multilingual Matters, 1984. 304 p.

2396   **Bourhis, Richard Y.**
"Language Policies in Multilingual Settings." In: *Conflict and
Language Planning in Quebec*, edited by Richard Y. Bourhis.
Clevedon, Avon, Multilingual Matters, 1984, p. 1-28.

2397   **Bourhis, Richard Y.**
"Social Psychology and Heritage Language Research: A
Retrospective View and Future Trends for Canada." In: *Heritage
Languages in Canada: Research Perspectives*, edited by Jim
Cummins. Ottawa: Department of the Secretary of State of Canada,
1984, p. 13-44. Paper presented at the Heritage Language Research
Conference, convened by the Multiculturalism Program, Ottawa, May
1984.

2398   **Bourhis, Richard Y.**
"Vitality Perceptions and Language Attitudes: Some Canadian Data."
Journal of Language and Social Psychology, vol. 3 no. 2
(1984) p. 97-126.

2399   **Bourhis, Richard Y.**
"Language Attitudes and Self Reports of French Language Usage in
Quebec." *Journal of Multilingual and Multicultural Development*, vol.
4 nos. 2-3 (1983) p. 163-180.

2400 **Bourhis, Richard Y.**
"Language Policies and Language Attitudes: le monde de la francophonie." In: *Attitudes Towards Language Variation: Social and Applied Contexts*, edited by Ellen Bouchard Ryan and Howard Giles. London: E. Arnold, 1982, p. 34-62.

2401 **Bouthillier, Guy**
"La question linguistique." *Année politique au Québec*, vol. 1 (1987/88) p. 125-128.

2402 **Bouthillier, Guy**
"Aux origines de la planification linguistique québécoise." In: *L'État et la planification linguistique*, sous la direction d'André Martin. Québec, P.Q.: Office de la langue française, 1981, vol. 2, p. 7-22.

2403 **Bouthillier, Guy**
"Éléments d'une chronologie politique de l'action linguistique du Québec pour la décennie 1960-1969, précédée d'un aperçu sur la période 1935-1965." In: *L'État et la planification linguistique*, sous la direction d'André Martin. Québec, P.Q.: Office de la langue française, 1981, vol. 2, p. 23-42.

2404 **Braen, Andre**
"Bilingualism and Legislation." In: *Language Rights in Canada*, edited by Michel Bastarache. Montreal: Éditions Y. Blais, 1987, p. 68-121. Translation of the author's "Le bilinguisme dans le domaine législatif" In: *Les droits linguistiques au Canada*, edited by Michel Bastarache. Montréal: Éditions Y. Blais, 1986, p. 69-123.

2405 **Buch, Alfred-Charles**
L'attitude des élèves anglophones d'Ottawa du niveau secondaire à l'égard de leur langue seconde. Unpublished MA thesis, Université de Montréal: 1983. 1 microfilm.

2406 **Burnaby, Barbara J.**
The Use of Aboriginal Languages in Canada: An Analysis of 1981 Census Data. Ottawa: Secretary of State, 1987. 79, 85 p. French language title: *L'utilisation des langues autochtones au Canada.*

2407 **Burnaby, Barbara J.**
Aboriginal Languages in Ontario. Toronto: Ontario Ministry of Education, 1984. 41, 24 p.

2408   **Burnaby, Barbara J.**
Language in Education Among Canadian Native People. Toronto:
The Ontario Institute for Studies in Education, 1982. 45 p.

2409   **Burns, George E.**
"French Immersion Implementations in Ontario: Some Theoretical,
Policy and Applied Issues." *Canadian Modern Language
Review/Revue canadienne des langues vivantes*, vol. 42 no. 3
(1986) p. 572-591.

2410   **Bustamante, Rosalina E.**
"Filipino Canadians: Where is our Heritage Language Going?."
*Polyphony: The Bulletin of the Multicultural History Society of
Ontario*, vol. 11 no. 1/2 (1989) p. 112-115.

2411   **Canada. Statistics Canada**
Language. The Nation. Census Canada 1986. 1 vol. Ottawa: Statistics
Canada, 1987. French language title: *Langue.*

2412   **Canada. Statistics Canada**
Language Retention and Transfer. Dimensions. Census Canada, 1986.
1 vol. Ottawa: Statistics Canada, 1989. French language title:
Rétension et transfert linguistique.

2413   **Canada. Statistics Canada**
Language in Canada. Ottawa: Statistics Canada, Supply and Services
Canada, 1985. 18 p.

2414   **Carey, Stephen T.**
"Reflections on a Decade of French Immersion." *Canadian Modern
Language Review/Revue canadienne des langues vivantes*, vol. 41 no.
2 (1984) p. 246-259.

2415   **Carson, Bruce**
The Meech Lake Accord: Linguistic Duality and the Distinct Society.
Ottawa: Library of Parliament, Research Branch, Law and Govern-
ment Division, 1989. 13 p.

2416   **Cartwright, Donald G.**
"Language Policy and Internal Geo-politics: The Canadian Situation."
In: *Languages in Geographic Context*, edited by Colin H. Williams.
Clevedon, Eng.: Multilingual Matters, 1988, p. 238-266.

2417 **Cartwright, Donald G.**
"Linguistic Territorialization: Is Canada Approaching the Belgian Model?" *Journal of Cultural Geography*, vol. 8 no. 2 (1988) p. 115-134.

2418 **Cartwright, Donald G.**
"Accommodation Among the Anglophone Minority in Quebec to Official Language Policy: A Shift in Traditional Patterns of Language Contact." *Journal of Multilingual and Multicultural Development*, vol. 8 no. 1/2 (1987) p. 187-212.

2419 **Cartwright, Donald G.**
"An Official-languages Policy for Ontario." *Canadian Public Policy/ Analyse de politiques*, vol. 11 no. 3 (1985) p. 561-577.

2420 **Cartwright, Donald G.**
"Bilingual Districts as an Instrument of Canadian Language Policy." *Institute of British Geographers. Transactions*, vol. 7 no. 4 (1982) p. 474-493.

2421 **Cartwright, Donald G.**
"Language Policy and the Political Organization of Territory: A Canadian Dilemma." *Canadian Geographer/Le géographe Canadien*, vol. 25 no. 3 (1981) p. 205-224.

2422 **Cartwright, Donald G.**
Bilingual Districts: The Elusive Territorial Component in Canada's Official Languages Act. Stafford, U.K.: North Staffordshire Polytechnic, Department of Geography and Sociology, 1980. 40 p.

2423 **Cartwright, Donald G.**
"Language Legislation and the Potential for Redistribution of the Anglophone Population in Quebec." *Ontario Geography*, no. 15 (1980) p. 65-81.

2424 **Cartwright, Donald G.**
Official-language Populations in Canada: Patterns and Contacts. Montreal: Institute for Research on Public Policy, 1980. 160 p.

2425 **Castonguay, Charles**
"The Anglicization of Canada, 1971-1981." *Language Problems and Language Planning*, vol. 11 no. 1 (1987) p. 22-34.

2426   **Castonguay, Charles**
"Transferts et semi-transferts linguistiques au Québec d'après le recensement de 1981." *Cahiers québécois de démographie*, vol. 14 no. 1 (1985) p. 241-257.

2427   **Castonguay, Charles**
"L'orientation linguistique des marriages mixtes dans la région de Montréal." *Recherches sociographiques*, vol. 21 no. 3 (1980) p. 225-252.

2428   **Cheung, Yuet-Wah**
"Effects of Parents' Ethnic Language Retention by Children: The Case of Chinese Urban Canada." *Sociological Focus*, vol. 1 (1981) p. 33-48.

2429   **Christmas, Peter J.**
"How Can We Preserve Our Native Language?" *Canadian Issues*, vol. 9 (1988) p. 171-177.

2430   **Chumak-Horbatsch, Roma**
"Language Use in the Ukrainian Home: A Toronto Sample." *International Journal of the Sociology of Language*, no. 63 (1987) p. 99-118.

2431   **Chumak-Horbatsch, Roma**
Language in the Ukrainian Home: Its Use in Ten Toronto Families Attempting to Preserve Their Mother Tongue. Unpublished PhD thesis, University of Toronto, 1984. 3 microfiches. Canadian theses on microfiche: no. 65155.

2432   **Clarini, Janice Paola**
Determinants of Language Assimilation in Three Ethnic Groups in Canada. Unpublished MA thesis, Concordia University, 1987. 2 microfiches. Canadian theses on microfiche, CT88-23866-6.

2433   **Cleghorn, Ailie**
"Languages in Contact: An Ethnographic Study of Interaction in an Immersion School." *TESOL Quarterly*, vol. 18 no. 4 (1984) p. 595-626.

2434   **Clement, Richard**
"Second Language Proficiency and Acculturation: An Investigation of the Effects of Language Status and Individual Characteristics." *Journal of Language and Social Psychology*, vol. 5 no. 4 (1986) p. 271-290.

2435   **Clement, Richard**
"Aptitude, Attitude and Motivation in Second Language Proficiency: a Test of Clement's Model." *Journal of Language and Social Psychology*, vol. 4 no. 1 (1985) p. 21-37.

2436   **Clement, Richard**
"Orientations in Second Language Acquisition: The Effects of Ethnicity, Milieu, and Target Language on Their Emergence." *Language Learning*, vol. 33 no. 3 (1983) p. 273-291.

2437   **Clement, Richard**
"Social and Individual Factors in Second Language Acquisition." *Canadian Journal of Behavioural Science/Revue canadienne des sciences de comportement*, vol. 12 no. 4 (1980) p. 293-302.

2438   **Coleman, William D.**
"From Bill 22 to Bill 101: The Politics of Language Under the Parti Québécois." In: *Quebec Since 1945: Selected Readings*, edited by Michael D. Behiels. Toronto: Copp Clark Pitman, 1987, p. 241-262.

2439   **Coleman, William D.**
"Class Bases of Language Policy in Quebec, 1949-1983." In: *Quebec: State and Society*, edited by Alain G. Gagnon. Toronto: Methuen, 1984, p. 388-409.

2440   **Coleman, William D.**
"Social Class and Language Policies in Quebec." In: *Conflict and Language Planning in Quebec*, edited by Richard Y. Bourhis. Clevedon, Avon: Multilingual Matters, 1984, p. 130-147.

2441   **Coleman, William D.**
"A Comparative Study of Language Policy in Quebec: A Political Economy Approach." In: *The Politics of Canadian Public Policy*, edited by Michael M. Atkinson and Marsha A. Chandler. Toronto: University of Toronto Press, 1983, p. 21-42.

2442   **Coleman, William D.**
"From Bill 22 to Bill 101: The Politics of Language Under the Parti Quebecois." *Canadian Journal of Political Science/Revue canadienne de science politique*, vol. 14 no. 3 (1981) p. 459-485.

2443   **Coleman, William D.**
"The Class Bases of Language Policy in Quebec 1949-1975." *Studies in Political Economy*, vol. 3 (1980) p. 93-117.

2444   **Colletta, Salvadore Pietro**
Community and Parental Influence: Effects on Student Motivation and French Second Language Proficiency. Unpublished PhD thesis, University of Ottawa, 1983. 3 microfiches. Canadian theses on microfiche, 64047.

2445   **Conseil de la langue française**
Aspects de l'évolution de la situation linguistique au Québec: quatre textes de chercheurs de la direction des études et recherches, Conseil de la langue française. Québec, P.Q.: Le Conseil de la langue française, 1986. 65 p.

2446   **Corbeil, Jean-Claude**
L'aménagement linguistique du Québec. Montréal: Guérin, 1980. 154 p.

2447   **Corbeil, Jean-Claude**
"Aspects sociolinguistiques de la langue française au Québec." *French Review*, vol. 53 no. 6 (1980) p. 834-838.

2448   **Corbeil, Pierre**
"Back to Basics: Language and Politics in Quebec." *Ethnic Studies Report*, vol. 7 no. 1 (1989) p. 1-19.

2449   **Cumbo, Richard S.**
"A History of the Maltese Heritage Programme in Toronto." *Polyphony: The Bulletin of the Multicultural History Society of Ontario*, vol. 11 no. 1/2 (1989) p. 85-88.

2450   **Cummins, Jim**
"Psychological Assessment of Minority Language Students." In: *Multiculturalism in Canada: Social and Educational Perspectives*, edited by Ronald J. Samuda, John W. Berry and Michel Laferriere. Toronto: Allyn and Bacon Inc., 1984, p. 238-249.

2451   **Cummins, Jim**
"Language Proficiency, Bi-literacy and French Immersion." *Canadian Journal of Education/Revue canadienne de l'education*, vol. 8 no. 2 (1983) p. 117-138.

2452 **Cummins, Jim**
"Age on Arrival and Immigrant Second Language Learning in Canada: a Reassessment." *Applied Linguistics*, vol. 2 no. 2 (1981) p. 132-149.

2453 **Curat, Hervé**
Gustave, Guillaume et la psycho-systématique du language: bibliographie annotée. Québec: Presses de l'Université Laval, 1983.

2454 **Danesi, Marcel**
"Canadian Italian: A Case in Point of How Language Adapts to Environment." *Polyphony: The Bulletin of the Multicultural History Society of Ontario*, vol. 7 no. 2 (1985) p. 111-113.

2455 **Danesi, Marcel**
"Ethnic Language and Acculturation: The Case of Italian Canadians." *Canadian Ethnic Studies/Études ethniques au Canada*, vol. 17 no. 1 (1985) p. 48-103.

2456 **Daoust-Blais, Denise**
"Corpus and Status Language Planning in Quebec: A Look at Linguistic Education." In: *Progress in Language Planning: International Perspectives*, edited by Juan Cobarrubias and Joshua A. Fishman. New York: Mouton Publishers, 1983, p. 207-234.

2457 **Daoust-Blais, Denise**
"La planification linguistique au Québec: Aménagement du corpus linguistique et promotion du statut du français." In: *L'état et la planification linguistique*. Sous la direction d'André Martin. Québec, P.Q.: Office de la langue française, 1981, vol. 2, p. 43-70.

2458 **Darnell, Regna**
"A Linguistic Classification of Canadian Native Peoples: Issues, Problems and Theoretical Implications." In: *Native Peoples: The Canadian Experience*, edited by R. Bruce Morrison and C. Roderick Wilson. Toronto: McClelland and Stewart, 1986, p. 22-44.

2459 **DaRosa, Victor M.P.**
"Espaces ethniques et question linguistique au Québec: à propos des communautés italienne et portugaise." *Canadian Ethnic Studies/ Études ethniques au Canada*, vol. 18 no. 2 (1986) p. 143-150.

2460   **Davids, Leo**
"Yiddish in Canada: Picture and Prospects." *Canadian Ethnic Studies /Études ethniques au Canada*, vol. 16 no. 2 (1984) p. 89-101.

2461   **Davies, Susan**
English Language Skills of Minority Language Children in a French Immersion Program. Unpublished MSc thesis, University of British Columbia, 1985, 125 leaves. Canadian theses on microfiche, 258721.

2462   **Day, Elaine M.**
"Provincial Assessment of French Immersion Programs in British Columbia, Canada." *Evaluation and Research in Education/Revue canadienne de l'education*, vol. 2 no. 3 (1989) p. 1-17.

2463   **Day, Elaine M.**
"A Comparison of Early and Late French Immersion Programmes in British Columbia." *Canadian Journal of Education/Revue canadienne de l'education*, vol. 13 no. 2 (1988) p. 290-305.

2464   **Day, Elaine M.**
"Assessment of Oral Communicative Skills in Early French Immersion Programs." *Journal of Multilingual and MultiCultural Development*, vol. 8 no. 3 (1987) p. 237-260.

2465   **Déchênes, Jules, comp.**
Ainsi parlèrent les tribunaux: Conflits linguistiques au Canada, 1968-1980. Montréal: Wilson and Lafleur, 1980-1985. 2 vols.

2466   **Defoe, Tracy A.**
English as a Second Language Teachers and Culture: An Interview Study of Role Perceptions. Unpublished MA thesis, University of British Columbia, 1986. 144 leaves. Canadian theses on microfiche, CT88-24626-X.

2467   **Deschamps, Gilles et Marie-Rita Boucher**
Représentation cartographiée de la population allophone de la zone métropolitaine de Montréal selon la langue maternelle en 1981. Montréal: Ministère des communautés culturelles et de l'immigration, Direction de la recherche, 1983. 44 p.

2468   **Deshaies, Denise**
"Disglossie et alternance de code: Un examen des concepts en fonction des comportements bilingues." *Revue québécoise de linguistique théorique et appliquée*, vol. 8 no. 2 (1989) p. 57-73.

2469   **Deshaies, Denise**
Étude des comportements langagiers dans deux entreprises en début de processus de francisation. Québec, P.Q.: Centre international de recherche sur le bilinguisme, 1982. 260 p.

2470   **Deshaies, Denise**
Le français parlé dans la ville de Québec: Une étude sociolinguistique. Québec, P.Q.: Centre international de recherche sur le bilinguisme, 1981. 137 p.

2471   **Desrochers, Alain M.**
Second Language Acquisition: An Investigation of a Bi-cultural Excursion Experience. Québec, P.Q.: International Centre for Research on Bilingualism, Laval University, 1981. 35 p.

2472   **Didier, Emmanuel**
"The Private Law of Language." In: *Language Rights in Canada,* edited by Michel Bastarache. Montreal: Éditions Y. Blais, 1987, p. 317-447. Translation of the author's "Le droit linguistique privé" chapter in the book: *Les droits linguistiques au Canada,* 1986, p. 331-463.

2473   **Dion, Léon**
"The Impact of Demolinguistic Trends on Canadian Institutions." *Canadian Issues,* (1989) p. 57-72. Special monographic volume in the *Canadian Issues* series titled *Demolinguistic Trends and the Evolution of Canadian Institutions.* Montreal: Association for Canadian Studies, 1989. French language title: "Les incidences démolinguistiques sur les institutions canadiennes." p. 59-74. Paper presented at a Colloquium on Demolinguistic Trends and the Evolution of Canadian Institutions, held in Hull, February 10, 1989.

2474   **Doern, Russell**
The Battle Over Bilingualism: The Manitoba Language Question, 1983-1985. Winnipeg: Cambridge Publishers, 1985. 227 p.

2475   **Dorais, Louis-Jacques**
"Religion and Refugee Adaptations: The Vietnamese in Montreal." *Canadian Ethnic Studies/Études ethniques au Canada,* vol. 21 no. 1 (1989) p. 19-29.

2476   **Dorais, Louis-Jacques**
"Language Use and Adaptation." In: *Uprooting, Loss and Adaptation: The Resettlement of Indochinese Refugees in Canada*, edited by Kwok B. Chan and Doreen Marie Indra. Ottawa: Canadian Public Health Association, 1987, p. 52-64.

2477   **Douaud, Patrick C.**
Ethnolinguistic Profile of the Canadian Metis. Ottawa: National Museums of Canada, 1985. 109 p.

2478   **Driedger, Leo**
"Non-official Multilingualism: Factors Affecting German Language Competence, Use and Maintenance in Canada." *Canadian Ethnic Studies/Études ethniques au Canada*, vol. 18 no. 3 (1986) p. 90-108.

2479   **Driedger, Leo**
"Sociology of Language and Canadian Heritage Language Research." In: *Heritage Languages in Canada: Research Perspectives*, edited by Jim Cummins. Ottawa: Department of the Secretary of State of Canada, 1984, p. 63-71.

2480   **Druke, Mary E.**
"Iroquois and Iroquoian in Canada." In: *Native Peoples: The Canadian Experience*, edited by R. Bruce Morrison and C. Roderick Wilson. Toronto: McClelland and Stewart, 1986, p. 302-324.

2481   **Ducharme, Jean-Charles**
Official Languages Act. Ottawa: Library of Parliament, Research Branch, 1988. 12 p.

2482   **Ducharme, Jean-Charles**
Minority Language Education Rights. Ottawa: Library of Parliament, Research Branch, 1984. 20 p. (Current issue review) Produced by the Library of Parliament, Research Branch, Law and Government Division. Reviewed 25 February, 1988.

2483   **Edwards, Henry P.**
"Second Language Acquisition Through Subject-matter Learning: A Study of Sheltered Psychology Classes at the University of Ottawa." *Canadian Modern Language Review/Revue canadienne des langues vivantes*, vol. 41 no. 2 (1984) p. 268-282.

2484   **Edwards, Henry P.**
"Psychological and Social Factors Influencing Second Language Acquisition." *Canadian Modern Language Review/Revue canadienne des langues vivantes*, vol. 36 no. 3 (1980) p. 481-484.

2485   **Edwards, John**
"Language, Multiculturalism and Identity: A Canadian Study." *Journal of Multilingual and Multicultural Development*, vol. 8 no. 5 (1987) p. 391-408.

2486   **Edwards, John**
"The Social and Political Context of Bilingual Education" In: *Multiculturalism in Canada: Social and Educational Perspectives*, edited by Ronald J. Samuda, John W. Berry and Michel Laferriere. Toronto: Allyn and Bacon Inc., 1984, p. 184-200.

2487   **Feuerverger, Grace**
"Ethnolinguistic Vitality of Italo-Canadian Students in Integrated Heritage Language Programs in Toronto." *Canadian Modern Language Review/Revue canadienne des langues vivantes*, vol. 46 no. 1 (1989) p. 50-72.

2488   **Feuerverger, Grace**
"Jewish-Canadian Ethnic Identity and Non-native Language Learning: a Social-psychological Study." *Journal of Multilingual and Multicultural Development*, vol. 10 no. 4 (1989) p. 327-357.

2489   **Feuerverger, Grace**
Jewish-Canadian Ethnic Identity and Non-native Language Learning. Unpublished PhD thesis, University of Toronto, 1986.

2490   **Fiddler, Margaret Ann**
Implementing Indian Control of Education in Sandy Lake, Ontario. Unpublished MEd thesis, University of Saskatchewan, 1989.

2491   **Fong, Henry**
English as a Second Language Programs and Students' Social Integration. Unpublished MSW thesis, University of Windsor, 1981. 2 microfiches. Canadian theses on microfiche, 53382.

2492   **Fortin, Conrad**
"Bilingualism in Canada." *Journal of American and Canadian Studies*, no. 2 (1988) p. 21-68.

2493   **Fortner, Robert S.**
"Significance and Legitimacy in Public Policy Debate: The Canadian Public and the Politics of Language in Canadian Broadcasting Development." *Journal of Canadian Studies/Revue d'études canadiennes*, vol. 23 no. 4 (1988/89) p. 82-108.

2494   **Foster, Gilbert**
Language and Poverty: The Persistence of Scottish Gaelic in Eastern Canada. St. John's, Nfld.: Institute of Social and Economic Research, Memorial University of Newfoundland, 1989. 138 p.

2495   **Foster, Lois**
"The Politicization of Language Issues in 'Multicultural' Societies: Some Australian and Canadian Comparisons." *Canadian Ethnic Studies/Études ethniques au Canada*, vol. 21 no. 3 (1989) p. 55-73.

2496   **Foster, Michael**
"Canada's Indigeneous Languages: Present and Future." *Language and Society/Langue et société*, vol. 7, 1982 p. 7-16.

2497   **Foucher, Pierre**
"L'interprétation des droits linguistiques constitutionnels par la Cour suprême du Canada." *Ottawa Law Review*, vol. 19 no. 2 (1987) p. 381-411.

2498   **Frideres, James S.**
"Visible Minority Groups and Second Language Programs: Language Adaptation." *International Journal of the Sociology of Language*, no. 80, 1989, p. 83-98.

2499   **Gardner, Ethel B.**
"Recognition and Legitimization of First Nations Languages." *Canadian Journal of Native Education*, vol. 16 no. 2 (1989) p. 3-24.

2500   **Gardner, Robert C.**
"Second Language Learning in an Immersion Programme: Factors Influencing Acquisition and Retention." *Journal of Language and Social Psychology*, vol. 8 no. 5 (1989) p. 287-305.

2501   **Gardner, Robert C.**
"The Socio-educational Model of Second Language Learning: Assumptions, Findings and Issues." *Language Learning*, vol. 38 no. 1 (1988) p. 101-126.

2502   **Gardner, Robert C.**
"Second Language Attrition: The Role of Motivation and Use."
Journal of Language and Social Psychology, vol. 6 no. 1
(1987) p. 29-47.

2503   **Gardner, Robert C.**
"The Role of Attitudes and Motivation in Second-language Learning:
Correlational and Experimental Considerations." *Language Learning*,
vol. 35 no. 2 (1985) p. 207-227.

2504   **Gardner, Robert C.**
"Social Factors in Second-language Attrition." *Language Learning*,
vol. 33 no. 4 (1985) p. 519-540.

2505   **Gardner, Robert C.**
*Social Psychology and Second Language Learning: The Role of
Attitudes and Motivation*. London: E. Arnold, 1985. 208 p.

2506   **Gardner, Robert C.**
"Learning Another Language: A True Social Psychological
Experiment." *Journal of Language and Social Psychology*, vol. 2 nos.
2-4 (1983) p. 219-239.

2507   **Gardner, Robert C.**
"The Socio-educational Model of Second Language Acquisition: An
Investigation Using LISREL Causal Modeling." *Journal of Language
and Social Psychology*, vol. 2 no. 1 (1983) p. 1-15.

2508   **Gardner, Robert C.**
"Second Language Acquisition and Bilingualism: Research in Canada
1970-1980." *Canadian Psychology*, vol. 22 no. 2 (1981) p. 146-162.

2509   **Gardner, Robert C.**
"Second Language Learning." In: *Canadian Social Psychology of
Ethnic Relations*, edited by Robert C. Gardner and Rudolf Kalin.
Toronto: Methuen, 1981, p. 92-114.

2510   **Gardner, Robert C.**
"On the Validity of Affective Variables in Second Language
Acquisition: Conceptual, Contextual and Statistical Considerations."
Language Learning, vol. 30 no. 2 (1980) p. 255-270.

2511   **Garigue, Philippe**
"Francophonie et bilinguisme à Toronto." *Royal Society of Canada. Proceedings and Transactions/Société royale du Canada. Mémoirs et comptes rendus*, ser. 5, vol. 1 (1986) p. 179-189.

2512   **Gatt-Rutter, John**
"Languishing Languages." *Australian-Canadian Studies*, vol. 7 nos. 1-2 (1989) p. 145-153.

2513   **Gémar, Jean-Claude**
Les trois états de la politique linguistique du Québec: D'une société traduite à une société d'expression. Québec, P.Q.: Éditeur officiel du Québec, 1983. 201 p. Étude présentée au Conseil de la langue française.

2514   **Gendron, Jean-Denis**
"Langue et société au Canada." *Zeitschrift der Gesellschaft für Kanada-Studien*, vol. 4 no. 2 (1984) p. 33-56.

2515   **Genesee, Fred**
"Early Bilingual Development: One Language or Two?" *Journal of Child Language*, vol. 16 no. 1 (1989) p. 161-179.

2516   **Genesee, Fred**
"Evaluative Reactions to Language Choice Strategies: The Role of Sociostructural Factors." *Language and Communication*, vol. 8 nos. 3-4 (1988) p. 229-250.

2517   **Genesee, Fred**
"La adquisición de una segunda lengua mediante la imersión: el enfoque canadiense." *Infancia y aprendizaje*, vol. 33 no. 1 (1986) p. 27-36.

2518   **Genesee, Fred**
"Beyond Bilingualism: Social Psychological Studies of French Immersion Programme in Canada." *Canadian Journal of Behavioural Science/Revue canadienne des sciences de comportement*, vol. 16 no. 4 (1984) p. 338-352.

2519   **Genesee, Fred**
"The Social Psychological Significance of Bilingual Code Switching for Children." *Applied Psycholinguistics*, vol. 5 no. 1 (1984) p. 3-20.

2520 **Genesee, Fred**
"Social Psychology Applied to Social Issues in Canada." *Canadian Journal of Behavioural Science/Revue canadienne des sciences de comportement*, vol. 16 no. 1 (1984) p. 338-352.

2521 **Genesee, Fred**
"The Social Psychology of Second Language Learning: Another Point of View." *Language Learning*, vol. 33 no. 2 (1983) p. 209-224.

2522 **Genesee, Fred**
"The Social Psychological Significance of Code-switching in Cross-cultural Communication." *Journal of Language and Social Psychology*, vol. 1 no. 1 (1982) p. 1-27.

2523 **Genesee, Fred**
"Cognition and Social Consequences of Bilingualism." In: *Canadian Social Psychology of Ethnic Relations*, edited by Robert C. Garner and Rudolf Kalin. Toronto: Methuen, 1981, p. 114-130.

2524 **Genesee, Fred**
"A Comparison of Early and Late Second Language Learning." *Canadian Journal of Behavioural Science/Revue canadienne des sciences de comportement*, vol. 13 no. 2 (1981) p. 115-128.

2525 **Genesee, Fred**
"Bilingualism and Biliteracy: A Cross-cultural Contact in a Bilingual Community." In: *The Social Psychology of Reading*, edited by J. Edwards. Silver Springs, Md.: Institute of Modern Languages, 1980, p. 147-171.

2526 **Genesee, Fred**
"Individual Differences in Second Language Learning." *Applied Psycholinguistics*, vol. 1 no. 1 (1980) p. 95-110.

2527 **Genty, Michel**
"Le trillium et le lys: Ou quelques observations sur les classes d'immersion en français, à Toronto et en Ontario." *Études canadiennes*, no. 22 (1987) p. 81-102.

2528 **Gibson, Dale**
"The Rule of Non-law: Some Implications of the Manitoba Language Reference." *Royal Society of Canada. Proceedings and Transactions/Société royale du Canada. Mémoirs et comptes rendus*, ser. 5, vol. 1 (1986) p. 31-39.

2529   **Gill, Robert M.**
"Language Policy in Saskatchewan, Alberta and British Columbia and the Future of French in the West." *The American Review of Canadian Studies*, vol. 15 no. 1 (1985) p. 16-37.

2530   **Gill, Robert M.**
"Federal and Provincial Language Policy in Ontario and the Future of the Franco-Ontarians." *The American Review of Canadian Studies*, vol. 13 no. 1 (1983) p. 13-43.

2531   **Gill, Robert M.**
"Federal, Provincial and Local Language Legislation in Manitoba and the Franco-Manitobans." *American Review of Canadian Studies*, vol. 12 no. 1 (1982) p. 30-52.

2532   **Gill, Robert M.**
"Bilingualism in New Brunswick and the Future of L'Acadie." *American Review of Canadian Studies*, vol. 10 no. 2 (1980) p. 56-74.

2533   **Godin, Gerard**
"Quebec: Language Question." In: *The Forty-ninth and Other Parallels: Contemporary Canadian Perspectives*, edited by David Staines. Amherst: University of Massachusetts Press, 1986, p. 34-40.

2534   **Goudreau, Michel**
Le rôle des caractéristiques personnelles et situationnelles sur l'attitude et les atteintes des professeurs d'anglais langue seconde au Québec. Unpublished MA thesis, University of Montreal, 1982. 1 microfilm.

2535   **Grant, Agnes**
Native Literature in Junior and Senior High School Programs. Unpublished PhD thesis, University of Manitoba, 1985. 3 microfiches. Canadian theses on microfiche, CT86-23204-2.

2536   **Grenier, Gilles**
"Bilingualism Among Anglophones and Francophones in Canada." *Canadian Issues*, (1989) p. 35-46. Special monographic volume in the *Canadian Issues* series titled *Demolinguistic Trends and the Evolution of Canadian Institutions*. Montreal: Association for Canadian Studies, 1989. French language title: "Le bilinguisme chez les anglophones et les francophones au Canada." p. 35-46. Paper presented at a Colloquium on Demolinguistic Trends and the Evolution of Canadian Institutions, held in Hull, February 10, 1989.

2537 **Grover, C.**
"Intonation in English, French and German: Perception and Production." *Language and Speech*, vol. 30 no. 3 (1987) p. 277-295.

2538 **Gryz, Zbigniew Jan**
Socio-demographic Determinants of Language Shifts in Canada.
Unpublished PhD thesis, Carleton University, 1980.

2539 **Haigh-Brown, Alan**
"British Columbia Indian Language: A Crisis of Silence." *B.C. Studies*, no. 57 (1983) p. 57-67.

2540 **Hall, D. Geoffrey**
"French Immersion and Hemispheric Language Processing: A Dual-task Study." *Canadian Journal of Behavioural Science/Revue canadienne des sciences de comportement*, vol. 20 no. 1 (1988) p. 1-14.

2541 **Hamers, Josiane F.**
"L'évolution des attitudes envers la langue seconde et l'identité culturelle chez les jeunes québécoises francophones et anglophones." *Canadian Modern Language Review/Revue canadienne des langues vivantes*, vol. 41 no. 2 (1984) p. 283-307.

2542 **Hamers, Josiane F.**
"Towards a Social Psychological Model of Bilingual Development." *Journal of Language and Social Psychology*, vol. 1 no. 1 (1982) p. 29-49.

2543 **Hammerly, Hector**
French Immersion: Myths and Reality. Calgary: Detseling Enterprises Ltd., 1989. 164 p.

2544 **Hammerly, Hector**
"French Immersion (Does it Work?) and the Development of Bilingual Proficiency Report." *Canadian Modern Language Review/Revue canadienne des langues vivantes*, vol. 45 no. 3 (1989) p. 567-578.

2545 **Harley, Birgit**
"The Effects of Early Bilingual Schooling on First Language Skills." *Applied Psycholinguistics*, vol. 7 no. 4 (1986) p. 295-321.

2546 **Harmon, Lesley D.**
The Modern Stranger: On Language and Membership. Unpublished
PhD thesis, York University, 1983. 3 microfiches. Canadian theses on
microfiche, 61481.

2547 **Harney, Robert F.**
"Communist Schools: Heritage Language and the RCMP."
*Polyphony: The Bulletin of the Multicultural History Society of
Ontario*, vol. 11 no. 1/2 (1989) p. 45-48.

2548 **Harney, Robert F.**
"Introduction." *Polyphony: The Bulletin of the Multicultural History
Society of Ontario*, vol. 11 no. 1/2 (1989) p. 1-12. Introduction to a
monographic issue of *Polyphony* "Heritage Languages in Ontario."

2549 **Harrison, B.R.**
"Language Maintenance and Language Shift in Canada." *Migration
Today*, vol. 13 (1985) p. 13-17.

2550 **Harvey, Fernand**
"Les groupes ethniques: Enjeu de la lutte linguistique au Québec."
Journal of Canadian Studies/Revue d'études canadiennes, vol. 23 no.
4 (1988/89) p. 37-43.

2551 **Hauptman, Philip C.**
"Second Language Acquisition Through Subject-matter Learning: A
Follow-up Study at the University of Ottawa." *Language Learning*,
vol. 38 no. 3 (1988) p. 439-482.

2552 **Hauptman, Philip C., Raymond LeBlanc, and Marjorie Bingham
Wesche, eds.**
*Second Language Performance Testing/L'évaluation de la
performance en langue seconde.* Ottawa: University of Ottawa Press,
1985. 308 p.

2553 **Hébert, Léo-Paul**
"Le père Jean-Baptiste de la Brosse, profeseur, linguiste et
ethnographe chez les montagnais du Saguenay (1766-1782)." *La
société canadienne d'histoire de l'Église catholique: Sessions d'étude*
no. 55 (1988) p. 7-40.

2554   **Hebert, Yvonne**
"The Socio-political Context of Native Indian Language Education in British Columbia." *Canadian Journal of Native Studies*, vol. 4 no. 1 (1984) p. 121-137.

2555   **Hegedus, Istvan**
"Flight and Settlement: The '56ers: Maintaining Hungarian in Canada." *Polyphony: The Bulletin of the Multicultural History Society of Ontario*, vol. 2 no. 2/3 (1980) p. 76-80.

2556   **Heller, Monica**
"The Role of Language in the Formation of Ethnic Identity." In: *Children's Ethnic Socialization: Pluralism and Development*, edited by Jean S. Phinney and Mary Jane Rotheram. Beverly Hills, California: Sage Publications, 1986, p. 180-199.

2557   **Heller, Monica**
"Anthropological Perspectives on Heritage Language Research." In: *Heritage Languages in Canada: Research Perspectives*, edited by Jim Cummins. Ottawa: Department of the Secretary of State of Canada, 1984, p. 72-82. Paper presented at the Heritage Language Research Conference, convened by the Multiculturalism Program, Ottawa, May 1984.

2558   **Heller, Monica**
Language, Ethnicity and Politics in Quebec, Unpublished PhD thesis, University of California, Berkeley, 1982. 340 p.

2559   **Heller, Monica**
"Negotiations of Language Choice in Montreal." In: *Language and Social Identity*, edited by John J. Gumperz. Cambridge: Cambridge University Press, 1982, p. 101-118.

2560   **Henripin, Jacques**
"Le québécois dont la langue est flottante et la mobilité linguistique." *Cahiers québécois de démographie*, vol. 14 no. 1 (1985) p. 87-98.

2561   **Holobow, Naomi E.**
"Effectiveness of Partial French Immersion for Children from Different Social Class and Ethnic Backgrounds." *Applied Psycholinguistics*, vol. 8 no. 2 (1987) p. 137-152.

2562   **Howard, Philip G.**
"History of the Use of Dene Languages in Education in the
Northwest Territories." *Canadian Journal of Native Education*, vol.
10 no. 2 (1983) p. 1-18.

2563   **Huel, Raymond**
"The Dilemmas of French Language Education in Saskatchewan:
L'Association Interprovinciale and the Recruitment of Bilingual
Teachers, 1917-25." *Canadian Ethnic Studies/Études ethniques au
Canada*, vol. 20 no. 2 (1988) p. 20-35.

2564   **Hutchings, David**
"Language Policy: Ontario, New Brunswick and Manitoba." In:
Provincial Policy-making: Comparative Essays, edited by Donald C.
Rowat. Ottawa: Department of Political Science, Carlton University,
1981, p. 283-304.

2565   **Irvine, William P.**
"Segmented Language Communites and Bilingualism: Towards
Segmented Language Use?" *Canadian Issues*, (1989) p. 47-56.
Special monographic volume in the *Canadian Issues* series titled
Demolinguistic Trends and the Evolution of Canadian Institutions.
Montreal: Association for Canadian Studies, 1989. French language
title: "La segmentation des communautés linguistiques et le
bilinguisme: l'utilisation de la langue sera-t-elle segmentée?" p. 47-
58. Paper presented at a Colloquium on Demolinguistic Trends and
the Evolution of Canadian Institutions, held in Hull, February 10,
1989.

2566   **Jalava, Mauri**
"Finnish Language and Culture in Canada." *Polyphony: The Bulletin
of the Multicultural History Society of Ontario*, vol. 11 no. 1/2
(1989) p. 110-111.

2567   **Jarvis, George K.**
"Language Shift Among Those of Aboriginal Tongue in Canada."
Canadian Studies in Population, vol. 16 no. 1 (1989) p. 25-42.

2568   **Jones, Richard**
"Politics and the Reinforcement of the French Language in the
Province of Quebec, 1960-1986." In: *Quebec Since 1945: Selected
Readings*, edited by Michael D. Behiels. Toronto: Copp Clark
Pitman, 1987, p. 223-240.

2569   **Julien, Richard Alben**
        *Cheticamp: An Acadian Community Divided by a French Language
        Conflict.* Unpublished MEd thesis, University of Alberta, 1987. 3
        microfiches. Canadian theses on microfiche, CT89-22921-x.

2570   **Kalbach, Warren and Madeline A. Richard**
        "Differential Effects of Ethno-religious Structure on Linguistic
        Trends and Economic Achievements of Ukrainian Canadians." In:
        Changing Realities: Social Trends Among Ukrainian Canadians,
        edited by W.R. Petryshyn. Edmonton: Canadian Institute of Ukrainian
        Studies, 1980 p. 78-96.

2571   **Kernaghan, Kenneth**
        "Bilingualism in the Public Service of Canada." In: *Public
        Administration in Canada: Selected Readings*, edited by Kenneth
        Kernaghan. 5th ed. Toronto: Methuen, 1985, p. 244-248.

2572   **Kernaghan, Kenneth**
        "Bilingualism in the Public Service of Canada." In: *Public
        Administration in Canada: Selected Readings*, edited by Kenneth
        Kernaghan. 4th ed. Toronto: Methuen, 1982, p. 94-98.

2573   **Khleif, B.B.**
        "Ethnicity and Language in Understanding the New Nationalism: The
        North Atlantic Region." *International Journal of Comparative
        Sociology*, vol. 23 no. 1/2 (1982) p. 114-121.

2574   **Kojder, Apolonja**
        "Ontario Polish Language Preservation." *Polyphony: The Bulletin of
        the Multicultural History Society of Ontario*, vol. 11 no. 1/2
        (1989) p. 13-17.

2575   **Kuplowska, Olga M.**
        "Language Retention Patterns Among Ukrainian Canadians." In:
        Changing Realities: Social Trends Among Ukrainian Canadians,
        edited by W.R. Petryshyn. Edmonton: Canadian Institute of Ukrainian
        Studies, 1980 p. 134-60.

2576   **Laberge, Daniel Gene**
        *Language Retention Among the Members of the French Club in
        Thunder Bay.* Unpublished MA thesis, University of Lakehead, 1980.
        1 microfiche. Canadian theses on microfiche, 47490

2577   **Labrie, Normand**
"Ethnolinguistic Vitality, Self-confidence and Second Language
Proficiency: An Investigation." *Journal of Multilingual and
Multicultural Development*, vol. 7 no. 4 (1984) p. 269-282.

2578   **Lachapelle, Réjean**
"Evolution of Language Groups and the Official Languages Situation
in Canada." *Canadian Issues*, (1989) p. 7-35. Special monographic
volume in the *Canadian Issues* series titled *Demolinguistic Trends
and the Evolution of Canadian Institutions*. Montreal: Association for
Canadian Studies, 1989. French language title: "Évolution des
groupes linguistiques et situations des langues officielles au
Canada." p. 7-35. Paper presented at a Colloquium on Demolinguistic
Trends and the Evolution of Canadian Institutions, held in Hull,
February 10, 1989.

2579   **Lachapelle, Réjean**
Aspects linguistiques de l'évolution démographique au Canada.
Ottawa: Health and Welfare Canada, 1988. 205 p. Report prepared
for the Review of Demography and its Implications for Economic
and Social Policy.

2580   **Lachapelle, Réjean**
"Change in Fertility Among Canada's Linguistic Groups." *Canadian
Social Trends*, (Autumn 1988) p. 2-8.

2581   **Lachapelle, Réjean**
"The Strengthening of Majority Positions: Recent Developments in
the Language Situation." *Report on the Demographic Situation in
Canada*. Ottawa: Statistics Canada, Demography Division, vol. 3
(1986) p. 109-125.

2582   **Lachapelle, Rejean**
"Analyse de la mobilité linguistique: Indices, observations et
modèles." *Cahiers québécois de démographie*, vol. 13 no. 2
(1984) p. 247-280.

2583   **Lachapelle, Réjean**
*The Demolinguistic Situation in Canada: Past Trends and Future
Prospects*, translated by Deirdre A. Mark. Montreal: Institute for
Research on Public Policy, 1982. 387 p.

2584 **Lachapelle, Réjean**
"Evolution of Ethnic and Linguistic Composition." In: *Cultural Boundaries and Cohesion of Canada*, edited by Raymond Breton et al. Montreal: Institute for Research on Public Policy, 1980, p. 15-44.

2585 **Lachapelle, Réjean**
La situation démolinguistique au Québec: évolution passée et prospective. Montréal: Institut de recherches politiques, 1980. 391 p.

2586 **Laguerre, Pierre Michel**
Situation socio-linguistique des enfants d'immigrants haïtiens au Québec. Unpublished MA thesis, McGill University, 1983. 3 microfiches. Canadian theses on microfiche, CT87-24300-4.

2587 **Lalonde, Richard N.**
"Investigating a Causal Model of Second Language Acquisition: Where Does Personality Fit?" *Canadian Journal of Behavioural Science/Revue canadienne des sciences de comportement*, vol. 16 no. 3 (1984) p. 224-237.

2588 **Lambert, Ronald D.**
"The French-and English-Canadian Language Communities and Multicultural Attitudes." *Canadian Ethnic Studies/Études ethniques au Canada*, vol. 14 no. 2 (1982) p. 43-58.

2589 **Lambert, Wallace E.**
"Language in the Education of Ethnic Minority Children in Canada." In: *Multiculturalism in Canada: Social and Educational Perspectives*, edited by Ronald J. Samuda, John W. Berry and Michel Laferrière. Toronto: Allyn and Bacon Inc., 1984, p. 201-215.

2590 **Lambert, Wallace E.**
"The Social Psychology of Language: A Perspective for the 1980's." In: *Language: Social Psychological Perspectives, Selected Proceedings*, edited by Howard Giles, W. Peter Robinson, and Philip M. Smith. Oxford: Pergamon Press, 1980, p. 415-424. Paper presented at the International Conference on Social Psychology and Language, University of Bristol, 1979.

2591 **Landry, Réjean**
"Bilinguisme additif, bilinguisme soustractif et vitalité ethnolinguistique." *Recherches sociographiques*, vol. 25 no. 2/3 (1984) p. 337-358.

2592   **Landry, Rodrigue**
"Choix de la langue d'enseignement: une analyse chez des parents
francophones en milieu bilingue soustractif." *Canadian Modern
Language Review/Revue canadienne des langues vivantes*, vol. 41 no.
3 (1985) p. 480-500.

2593   **Lapkin, Sharon**
"How Well Do Immersion Students Speak or Write French?"
*Canadian Modern Language Review/Revue canadienne des langues
vivantes*, vol. 40 no. 4 (1984) p. 575-585.

2594   **Lapkin, Sharon**
"Late Immersion in Perspective: The Peel Study." *Canadian Modern
Language Review/Revue canadienne des langues vivantes*, vol. 39 no.
2 (1983) p. 182-206.

2595   **Laponce, J.A.**
"L'aménagement linguistique et les effets pervers." In: *Langue et
droit*, sous la direction de Paul Pupier et José Woehrling. Montréal:
Wilson and Lafleur, 1989, p. 35-43. Paper presented at the First
Conference of the International Institute of Comparative Linguistic
Law, April 27-29, 1988 at the Université du Québec, Montréal: P.Q.

2596   **Laponce, J.A.**
"The French Language in Canada: Tensions Between Geography and
Politics." *Political Geography Quarterly*, vol. 3 no. 2 (1984) p. 91-
104.

2597   **Laporte, Pierre-Etienne**
"Status Language Planning in Quebec: An Evaluation." In: *Conflict
and Language Planning in Quebec*, edited by Richard Y. Bourhis.
Clevedon, Avon: Multilingual Matters, 1984, p. 53-80.

2598   **Laporte, Pierre-Etienne**
"Language Planning and the Status of French in Quebec." In: *Two
Nations, Many Cultures: Ethnic Groups in Canada*, edited by Jean
Leonard Elliott. 2nd ed. Scarborough, Ontario: Prentice-Hall of
Canada, 1983, p. 91-109.

2599   **Lauren, Christer**
*Canadian French and Finland Swedish: Minority Languages with
Outside Standards, Regionalisms, and Adstrata*. Québec, P.Q.:
International Center for Research on Bilingualism, 1983. 28 p.

2600   **Leclerc, Jacques**
"La dynamique des langues dans la fédération canadienne." *Études canadienne/Canadian Studies*, no. 25 (1988) p. 7-22.

2601   **Leclerc, Jacques**
Langue et société. Laval, P.Q.: Mondia, 1986. 530 p.

2602   **Legerstee, Maria**
"Implantation et évaluation d'un programme d'intervention motiva-tionnelle en classe d'immersion." *Canadian Modern Language Review/Revue canadienne des langues vivantes*, vol. 39 no. 1 (1982) p. 18-23.

2603   **Lerthirunwong-Diong, Malai**
Problems of Adjustment and Attitudes of Indochinese Refugees Towards Their Language Maintenance: A Case Study of the Lao Community in Toronto. Unpublished PhD thesis, University of Toronto, 1989. 3 microfiches. Canadian theses on microfiche, CT90-21762-6.

2604   **Letellier, Armand**
DND Language Reform: Staffing the Bilingualism Programs, 1967-1977. Ottawa: Directorate of History, Department of National Defence, 1987. 260 p. French language title: *Réforme linguistique de la défense nationale: la mise en marche des programmes de bilinguisme, 1967-1977*.

2605   **Levine, Marc V.**
"Language Policy and Quebec's 'visage français': New Directions in 'la question linguistique'." *Quebec Studies*, no. 8 (1989) p. 1-16.

2606   **Levine, Marc V.**
"The Language Question in Quebec: A Selected, Annotated Bibliography." *Quebec Studies*, no. 8 (1989) p. 37-41.

2607   **Levine, Marc V.**
"Language Policy, Education, and Cultural Survival: Bill 101 and the Transformation of Anglophone Quebec 1977-1985." *Quebec Studies*, no. 4 (1986) p. 3-27.

2608   **Leyssac, Andre de**
Decline of Civilization in Canada. Regina: les Éditions Louis Riel, 1985. 104 p. French language title: *Recul de la civilisation au Canada*.

2609   **Lortie, Pierre**
"The Achilles Heel of Bilingualism in Canada." *Language and Society/Langue et société*, no. 10 (1983) p. 19-23.

2610   **Low, D. Martin**
"Les droits linguistiques en matière judiciaire devant les tribuneaux fédéraux du Canada." In: *Langue et droit*, sous la direction de Paul Pupier et José Woehrling. Montréal: Wilson and Lafleur, 1989, p. 195-201. Paper presented at the First Conference of the International Institute of Comparative Linguistic Law, April 27-29, 1988 at the Université du Québec, Montréal: P.Q.

2611   **Luciani, Gérard**
"Les immigrants d'origine italienne au Canada anglophone (Toronto): situation linguistique, problèmes et essai de solution." In: *Le facteur ethnique aux États-Unis et au Canada*, études réunies par Monique Lecomte et Claudine Thomas. Lille, France: Université de Lille, 1983, p. 213-224.

2612   **MacIntyre, Peter D.**
"Anxiety and Second Language Learning: Toward a Theoretical Clarification." *Language Learning*, vol. 39 no. 2 (1989) p. 251-275.

2613   **MacIntyre, Peter D.**
The Measurement of Anxiety and Applications to Second Language Learning: An Annotated Bibliography. London, Ont.: University of Western Ontario, 1988. 39 p.

2614   **Mackay, Murdo**
The Language Problem and Schoolboard Reform on the Island of Montreal. Unpublished MA thesis, McGill University, 1987. 3 microfiches. Canadian theses on microfiche, CT89-21185-X.

2615   **MacMillan, C. Michael**
"Henri Bourassa on the 'Defence of Language Rights'." *Dalhousie Review*, vol. 62 no. 3 (1982) p. 413-430.

2616   **Maheu, R.**
"La partie cachée de la mobilité linguistique." In: *Démographie et destin des sous-populations*. Paris: L'Association, 1983, p. 249-259. Association internationale des démographes de langue française, Colloque de Liège.

2617   **Mallen, Pierre-Louis**
"Problèmes actuels des nations bilingues." *Revue des sciences morales et politiques*, vol. 138 no. 3 (1983) p. 475-489.

2618   **Marcos, Gamila, ed.**
Bilinguisme et enseignement du français. Montréal: Méridien, 1989. 217 p.

2619   **Martin, André, ed.**
L'État et la planification linguistique: langues et sociétés. 2 vols. Québec: Office de la langue française, 1981.

2620   **Masliah, Daphne-Laure**
"Majorités et minorités officielles: politiques linguistiques au Canada." *Études canadienne/Canadian Studies*, vol. 21 no. 2 (1986) p. 253-267.

2621   **Masny, Diana**
"Language, Cognition, and Second Language Grammaticality Judgements." *Journal of Psycholinguistic Research*, vol. 14 no. 2 (1985) p. 175-197.

2622   **Matiss, Ilze A. and Solveiga Miezitis**
"Meeting the Challenge of Heritage Language Retention at the Toronto Latvian School Valodina." *Polyphony: The Bulletin of the Multicultural History Society of Ontario*, vol. 11 no. 1/2 (1989) p. 121-124.

2623   **Maurais, Jacques**
"L'expérience québécoise d'aménagement linguistique." In: *Politique et aménagement linguistique*, textes publiés sous la direction de J. Maurais. Québec, P.Q.: Conseil de la langue française, 1987, p. 359-416.

2624   **Maurais, Jacques**
Aspects de l'aménagement linguistique du Québec. Québec: Conseil de la langue française, Direction des études et recherches, 1985. 135 p.

2625   **Mazurkiewicz, Irene**
"A New Look at Language Attitudes in Montreal." *Psychology Monographs*, vol. 1/2 no. 2 (1986) p. 203-217.

2626   **McEachern, Ron**
"Materials Development for Native Language Programs." *Canadian Journal of Native Education*, vol. 15 no. 1 (1988) p. 39-42.

2627   **McEachern, William**
"Indian/Metis Language Programs and French Immersion: First Cousins or Distant Relations?" *Journal of Indigenous Studies*, vol. 1 no. 1 (1989) p. 21-26.

2628   **McKee, B. Brian**
A Socio-demographic Analysis of Language Groups in Quebec. Ottawa: Center for Research on Ethnic Minorities, 1984. 41 leaves.

2629   **McRoberts, Kenneth**
"Making Canada Bilingual: Illusions and Delusions of Federal Language Policy." In: *Federalism and Political Community: Essays in Honour of Donald Smiley*, edited by David P. Shugarman and Reg Whitaker. Peterborough, Ont.: Broadview Press, 1989, p. 141-171.

2630   **Meisel, John**
"L'identification du problème linguistique: données sociolinguistiques d'enquête." In: *L'État et la planification linguistique*, sous la direction d'André Martin. Volume 1. Québec, P.Q.: Office de la langue française, 1981, p. 57-82.

2631   **Michaud, Daniel**
L'enseignement de la langue seconde à des adultes immigrants: une approche centrée sur l'auto développement de la personne et l'insertion sociale. Unpublished MA thesis, Université de Montréal, 1982.

2632   **Monnier, Daniel**
La langue d'affichage: analyse d'un sondage CROP réalisé en juin 1986. Québec, P.Q.: Conseil de la langue française, 1986. 45 p.

2633   **Monnier, Daniel**
"Portrait en rose et gris: Quelques conclusion de recherche sur la situation linguistique au Québec." In: *Aspects de l'évolution de la situation Linguistique au Québec: Quatre textes de chercheurs de la direction des études et recherches*, Conseil de la langue française. Québec, P.Q.: Le Conseil, 1986, p. 7-21. Communication presentée au congrès de l'Association canadienne de recherche sociale appliquée (1985).

2634 **Monnier, Daniel**
"La volonté de franciser: Qu'en est-il?" In: *Aspects de l'évolution de la situation linguistique au Québec: Quatre textes de chercheurs de la direction des études et recherches*, Conseil de la langue française. Québec, P.Q.: Le Conseil, 1986, p. 23-37. Une analyse de données recuillies dans le cadre du sondage omnibus du Centre de sondage de l'Université de Montréal (1984).

2635 **Monnier, Daniel**
La question linguistique: l'état de l'opinion publique: analyse du sondage de Sondagex Inc., mars-avril 1983. Québec, P.Q.: Conseil de la langue française, 1983. 68 p.

2636 **Munro, Kenneth**
"Official Bilingualism in Alberta." *Prairie Forum*, vol. 12 no. 1 (1987) p. 37-47.

2637 **Nelson, John E.**
"A Sociolinguistic Study of Montreal." *Canadian Modern Language Review/Revue canadienne des langues vivantes*, vol. 40 no. 3 (1984) p. 360-373.

2638 **Noro, Hiroko**
Family and Language Maintenance: An Exploratory Study of Japanese Language Maintenance Among Children of Postwar Japanese Immigrants in Toronto. Unpublished PhD thesis, University of Toronto, 1987. 124 leaves. Canadian theses on microfiche, CT89-22288-6.

2639 **Obadia, Andre A.**
"La crise est arrivée: la croissance des programmes de français langue seconde et ses repercussions sur la qualité et le nombre des enseignants." *Canadian Modern Language Review/Revue canadienne des langues vivantes*, vol. 45 no. 3 (1989) p. 435-444.

2640 **Olson, Paul**
"Politics, Class, and Happenstance: French Immersion in a Canadian Context." *Interchange*, vol. 14 no. 1 (1983) p. 1-16.

2641 **Olynyk, Marian**
"A Quantitative and Qualitative Analysis of Speech Markers in the Native and Second Language Speech of Bilinguals." *Journal of Applied Psycholinguistics*, vol. 8 no. 2 (1987) p. 121-136.

2642   **Owens, Thompson W.**
"Linguistic Insecurity in Winnipeg: Validation of a Canadian Index of Insecurity." *Language in Society*, vol. 13 no. 3 (1984) p. 337-350.

2643   **Paille, Michel**
"Aménagement linguistique et population au Québec." *Journal of Canadian Studies/Revue d'études canadiennes*, vol. 23 no. 4 (1988/ 89) p. 54-69.

2644   **Paille, Michel**
"Conséquences des politiques linguistiques québécoises sur les effectifs scolaires selon la langue d'enseignement."In: *Aspects de l'évolution de la situation linguistique au Québec: Quatre textes de chercheurs de la direction des études et recherches*, Conseil de la langue française. Québec, P.Q.: Le Conseil, 1986, p. 39-51.

2645   **Paille, Michel**
"Effets démographiques de l'application de la 'clause Canada' sur la langue d'enseignement au Québec." In: *Aspects de l'évolution de la Situation Linguistique au Québec: Quatre textes de chercheurs de la direction des études et recherches*, Conseil de la langue française. Québec, P.Q.: Le Conseil, 1986, p. 53-65.

2646   **Paille, Michel**
Contribution à la démolinguistique du Québec. Québec, P.Q.: Direction des études et recherches, Conseil de la langue française, 1985. 246 p.

2647   **Pak, Anita Wan-Ping**
"Correlates of Self-confidence with English Among Chinese Students in Toronto." *Canadian Journal of Behavioural Science/Revue canadienne des sciences de comportement*, vol. 17 no. 4 (1985) p. 369-378.

2648   **Pampalon, Janet O'Donnell**
Evolution of Anglo-Canadian Attitudes Towards Canadian Language Policy, 1967-1977. Unpublished MA thesis, Laval University, 1981. 4 microfiches. Canadian theses on microfiche, 56318.

2649   **Parsons, Arthur S.**
"The Conventions of the Senses: The Linguistic and Phenomeno- logical Contributions to a Theory of Culture." *Human Studies*, vol. 11 no. 1 (1988) p. 3-42.

2650   **Peeters, Yvo J.D.**
        "Le droit à la langue en tant que droit collectif." *Plural Sciences*, vol.
        16 no. 1 (1986) p. 41-51

2651   **Pellerin, Micheline**
        "L'expression orale après treize ans d'immersion Française."
        *Canadian Modern Language Review/Revue canadienne des langues
        vivantes*, vol. 42 no. 3 (1986) p. 592-606.

2652   **Penigault-Duhet, Paule-Marie**
        "Les problèmes linguistiques au Nouveau-Brunswick d'après les
        rapports du commissaire aux langues officielles." *Études
        canadienne/Canadian Studies*, no. 13 (1982) p. 165-172.

2653   **Piotrowski, Andrzej**
        "Sociology and Socio-linguistics: A Comment on Some Splits and
        Selective Affinities." *International Journal of Sociology of Language*
        no. 78 (1989) p. 72-82.

2654   **Prattis, J. Ian**
        "Inuktitut-English Bilingualism in the Northwest Territories of
        Canada." *Anthropologica*, vol. 25 no. 1 (1983) p. 85-105.

2655   **Price, John A.**
        "The Viability of Indian Languages in Canada." *Canadian Journal of
        Native Studies*, vol. 1 no. 2 (1981) p. 339-346.

2656   **Priest, Gordon E.**
        Aborigine Languages in Canada. Ottawa: Statistics Canada, 1984.
        20 p.

2657   **Proulx, Daniel**
        "La loi 101, la clause-Québec et la Charte canadienne devant la Cour
        suprême: Un cas d'espèce?" *Revue générale de droit*, vol. 16 no. 1
        (1985) p. 167-193.

2658   **Prujiner, Alain**
        "Les enjeux politiques de l'intervention juridique en matière
        linguistique." In: *Langue et droit*, sous la direction de Paul Pupier et
        José Woehrling. Montréal: Wilson and Lafleur, 1989, p. 103-115.
        Paper presented at the First Conference of the International Institute
        of Comparative Linguistic Law, April 27-29, 1988 at the Université
        du Québec, Montréal, P.Q.

2659   **Quan, Ping Shao**
"Chinese Heritage Language Education in Metro Toronto."
Polyphony: The Bulletin of the Multicultural History Society of Ontario, vol. 11 no. 1/2 (1989) p. 125-129.

2660   **Québec. Conseil de la langue française**
La crise des langues. Textes corrigés et présentés par Jacques Maurais. Québec, P.Q.: Gouvernement du Québec, Conseil de la langue française, 1985. 490 p.

2661   **Ravault, René-Jean**
Perceptions de deux solitudes: Étude sur les relations entre les deux communautés de langues officielles du Nouveau-Brunswick. Québec, P.Q.: Centre international de recherche sur le bilinguisme, 1983. 101 p.

2662   **Raynauld, André**
"The Advancement of the French Language in Canada." *Canadian Issues*, (1989) p. 93-104. Special monographic volume in the *Canadian Issues* series titled *Demolinguistic Trends and the Evolution of Canadian Institutions.* Montreal: Association for Canadian Studies, 1989. French language title: "L'avancement du français au Canada." p. 95-106. Paper presented at a Colloquium on Demolinguistic Trends and the Evolution of Canadian Institutions, held in Hull, February 10, 1989.

2663   **Read, Catherine**
Some Aspects of the Need for Official Language/Literacy Training Among Adult Immigrants in Canada. Unpublished MA thesis, Concordia Univesity, 1985. Canadian theses on microfiche, CT87-20527-7.

2664   **Reid, Sharon Lyn**
The 1988 Survey of Pupils for Whom English is a Second Language in Vancouver Schools. Vancouver: Student Assessment and Research, Vancouver School Board, 1988.

2665   **Reitz, Jeffrey G.**
"Language and Ethnic Community Survival." In: *Ethnicity and Ethnic Relations in Canada: A Book of Readings*, edited by Rita M. Bienvenue and Jay E. Goldstein. 2nd ed. Toronto: Butterworths, 1985, p. 105-123. Reprinted from *Canadian Review of Sociology and Anthropology/Revue canadienne de sociologie et d'anthropologie* vol. 11 no. 1 (1974) p. 104-122.

2666   **Reitz, Jeffrey G.**
"Ukrainian Language and Identity Retention in Urban Canada."
Canadian Ethnic Studies/Études ethniques au Canada, vol. 12 no. 2
(1980) p. 33-54.

2667   **Richstone, Jeffrey**
"La protection juridique des langues autochtones au Canada." In:
Langue et droit, sous la direction de Paul Pupier et José Woehrling.
Montréal: Wilson and Lafleur, 1989, p. 259-278. Paper presented at
the First Conference of the International Institute of Comparative
Linguistic Law, April 27-29, 1988 at the Université du Québec,
Montréal: P.Q.

2668   **Robertson, Barbara Mae**
*The Socio-cultural Determiners of French Language Maintenance:
The Case of Niagara Falls, Ontario.* Unpublished PhD thesis, State
University of New York (Buffalo), 1980. 168 leaves. Canadian theses
on microfiche, 1089.

2669   **Robertson, Gordon**
"Principle and the Art of the Possible." *Language and Society/Langue
et société*, no. 10 (1983) p. 12-18.

2670   **Robichaud, Armand G.**
"Langue et minorité en milieu urbain." *Études canadienne/Canadian
Studies*, no. 19 (1985) p. 55-65.

2671   **Robinson, Patricia A.**
"French Mother Tongue Transmission in Mixed Mother Tongue
Families." *Canadian Journal of Sociology/Cahiers canadiens de
sociologie*, vol. 14 no. 3 (1989) p. 317-334.

2672   **Robinson, Patricia A.**
"Mother Tongue and Marriage: The French and English in Canada."
Canadian Studies in Population, vol. 16 no. 2 (1989) p. 187-200.

2673   **Robinson, Patricia A.**
"Language Retention Among Canadian Indians: A Simultaneous
Equations Model with Dichotomous Endogenous Variables."
American Sociological Review, vol. 50 no. 4 (1985) p. 515-529.

2674   **Rudnyckyj, Jaroslav B.**
Languages of Canada. Ottawa: [s.n.], 1987. 86 p. French language
title: *Langues du Canada*: Ukrainian language title: *Movy Kanady.*

2675   **Rudzik, Orest H.T.**
"Literary Norms and Translation." In: *Language, Culture and
Literary Identity in Canada,* edited by J.M. Bumsted. Vancouver:
University of British Columbia, 1987. p. 27-32. Paper presented at
the 1984 Ottawa Conference on Language, Culture and Literary
Identity in Canada. Published as Supplement 1 of *Canadian
Literature/Littérature canadienne,* May 1987, issue no. 112.

2676   **Sabetti, Filippo**
*Covenant Language in Canada: Continuity and Change in Political
Discourse.* Philadelphia: Workshop on Covenant and Politics of the
Center for the Study of Federalism, Temple University, 1980. 26 p.

2677   **Sabourin, Conrad F.**
La francité canadienne. 2 volumes. Montréal: Université de Montréal,
Faculté des sciences de l'éducation, 1985-1987. Vol. 1: *Aspects
linguistiques,* Vol. 2: *Sociologie et politologie de la langue.*

2678   **Safty, Adel**
"French Immersion and the Making of a Bilingual Society: A Critical
Review and Discussion." *Canadian Journal of Education,* vol. 13 no.
2 (1988) p. 243-262.

2679   **Saint-Germain, Maurice**
"Les disparités linguistiques de revenue dans la région d'Ottawa-
Hull." *Cahiers de géographie du Québec,* vol. 33 no. 89
(1989) p. 217-240.

2680   **Salle, Émile-Lesage**
*Origine ethnique et attitude à l'égard de l'enseignement de la langue
duale.* Unpublished MA thesis, Université Laval, 1982. Canadian
theses on microfiche, CT87-22572-3.

2681   **Senecal, Andre J.**
"The Growing Role of the Quebec State in Language Corpus
Planning." *The American Review of Canadian Studies,* vol. 13 no. 2
(1983) p. 52-63.

2682   **Sengupta, Smita**
       *Integration and Maintenance of Ethnic Identity: A Case Study of an
       East Indian Heritage Language Program in Greater Toronto.*
       Unpublished PhD thesis, University of Toronto, 1987. Canadian
       theses on microfiche, CT89-22226-6.

2683   **Shapson, Stanley M.**
       "A Comparison Study of Three Late Immersion Programs." *Alberta
       Journal of Educational Research*, vol. 28 no. 2 (1982) p. 135-148.

2684   **Short, David E.**
       "Restrictions on Access to English Language Schools in Quebec: An
       International Human Rights Analysis." *Canada-United States Law
       Journal*, vol. 4 (1981) p. 1-38.

2685   **Simulik, Anthony P.**
       *Language Usage Amongst Selected Groups of Slavic-Speaking
       Immigrants in Edmonton.* Unpublished MA thesis, University of
       Alberta, 1984. Canadian theses on microfiche, CT87-20129-8.

2686   **Singh, Hardev**
       "Punjabi Language Education for Children in Toronto." *Polyphony:
       The Bulletin of the Multicultural History Society of Ontario*, vol. 11
       no. 1/2 (1989) p. 130-131.

2687   **Sotiriadis, Caterina Maria**
       *The Development of French Second Language Programs in Manitoba
       1880-1980.* Unpublished MEd thesis, University of Manitoba, 1981.
       Canadian theses on microfiche, CT89-22972-4.

2688   **Soucie, Rolande**
       Official Bilingualism in Canada: The Second Decade. Ottawa:
       Library of Parliament, Research Branch, Political and Social Affairs
       Division, 1986. 21 p.

2689   **St.-Laurent, Gilles**
       Origine et évolution du bilinguisme judiciaire au Québec. Québec,
       P.Q.: Centre international de recherche sur le bilinguisme, 1985. 61,
       20 p.

2690   **Stadler, Beatrice**
       *Language Maintenance and Assimilation: The Case of the German-
       speaking Immigrants.* Unpublished MA thesis, Simon Fraser
       University, 1983, 195 p. Canadian theses on microfiche, 62339.

2691   **Stadler, Beatrice**
"A Sociolinguistic Study of the Integration of German Immigrants in Vancouver: Approach and Methodology." In: *German-Canadian Studies: Critical Approaches*, edited by Peter Liddell. Vancouver: CAUTG, 1983, p. 78-86.

2692   **Stone, Arthur N.**
"Bilingual Drafting in a Common Law Jurisdiction in Canada." *Canadian Parliamentary Review*, vol. 9 no. 2 (1986) p. 20-21.

2693   **Swain, Merrill**
"Canadian Immersion and Adult Second Language Teaching: What's the Connection?" *Modern Language Journal*, vol. 73 no. 2 (1989) p. 150-159.

2694   **Swain, Merrill**
"Early French Immersion Later On." *Journal of Multilingual and Multicultural Development*, vol. 2 no. 1 (1981) p. 1-23.

2695   **Swain, Merrill**
"Lingusitic Expectations: Core, Extended and Immersion." *Canadian Modern Language Review/Revue canadienne des langues vivantes*, vol. 37 no. 3 (1981) p. 486-497.

2696   **Taddeo, Donat J.**
Le débat linguistique au Québec: la communauté italienne et la langue d'enseignement. Traduit de l'anglais par Brigitte Morel-Nish. Montréal: Les Presses de l'université de Montréal, 1987. 246 p.

2697   **Tardif, Claudette**
"French Immersion Research: A Call for New Perspectives." *Canadian Modern Language Review/Revue canadienne des langues vivantes*, vol. 44 no. 1 (1987) p. 67-77.

2698   **Tardif, Claudette**
"Les erreurs en français langue seconde et leur effets sur la communication orale." *Canadian Modern Language Review/Revue canadienne des langues vivantes*, vol. 37 no. 4 (1981) p. 706-723.

2699   **Taylor, Donald M.**
"Language Attitudes in a Multilingual Northern Community." *Canadian Journal of Native Studies*, vol. 9 no. 1 (1989) p. 85-120.

2700   **Taylor, Donald M.**
"Language Planning and Inter Group Relations: Anglophone and Francophone Attitudes Toward the Charter of the French Language." In: *Conflict and Language Planning in Quebec*, edited by Richard Y. Bourhis. Clevedon, Avon: Multilingual Matters, 1984, p. 148-173.

2701   **Tetley, William**
"Language and Education Rights in Quebec and Canada: A Legislative History and Personal Political Diary." In: *Reshaping Confederation: The 1982 Reform of the Canadian Constitution*, edited by Paul Davenport and Richard H. Leach. Durham, N.C.: Duke University Press, 1984, p. 177-220.

2702   **Tetley, William**
"The English and Language Legislation: A Personal History." In: *The English of Quebec: From Majority to Minority Status*, edited by Gary Caldwell and Eric Waddell. Quebec, P.Q.: Institut québécois de recherche sur la culture, 1982, p. 379-398.

2703   **Tetley, William**
"Language and Education Rights in Quebec and Canada." *Law and Contemporary Problems*, vol. 45 no. 4 (1982) p. 177-219.

2704   **Thériault, J. Yvon**
"The Future of French-speaking Community Outside Quebec: A Tug-of-war." *Canadian Issues*, (1989) p. 131-140. Special monographic volume in the *Canadian Issues* series titled *Demolinguistic Trends and the Evolution of Canadian Institutions*. Montreal: Association for Canadian Studies, 1989. French language title: "Lourdeur ou légèreté du devenir de la francophonie hors Québec." p. 135-144. Paper presented at a Colloquium on Demolinguistic Trends and the Evolution of Canadian Institutions, held in Hull, February 10, 1989.

2705   **Toohey, Kelleen**
"Northern Native Canadian Language Education." *Canadian Review of Sociology and Anthropology/Revue canadienne de sociologie et d'anthropologie*, vol. 22 no. 1 (1985) p. 93-101.

2706   **Toohey, Kelleen**
Northern Native Canadian Second Language Education: A Case Study of Fort Albany, Ontario. Unpublished PhD thesis, Ontario Institute for Studies in Education, 1982. 248 p. Canadian theses on microfiche, 55716.

2707   **Tucker, G. Richard**
"Social Policy and Second Language Teaching." In: *Canadian Social Psychology of Ethnic Relations*, edited by Robert C. Gardner and Rudolf Kalin. Toronto: Methuen, 1981, p. 77-91.

2708   **Vaillancourt, Francois**
"The Economics of Language and Language Planning." *Language Problems and Language Planning*, vol. 7 no. 2 (1983) p. 162-178.

2709   **Vardy, Brian William.**
An Examination of English Language Teaching Practices in an Innu Setting from 1951-1982. Unpublished MEd thesis, Memorial University of Newfoundland, 1983. Canadian theses on microfiche, 63604.

2710   **Veltman, Calvin J.**
"Assessing the Effects of Quebec's Language Legislation." *Canadian Public Policy/Analyse de politiques*, vol. 12 no. 2 (1986) p. 314-319.

2711   **Veltman, Calvin J.**
"The Interpretation of the Language Question of the Canadian Census." *Canadian Review of Sociology and Anthropology/Revue canadienne de sociologie et d'anthropologie*, vol. 23 no. 3 (1986) p. 412-422.

2712   **Veltman, Calvin J.**
"L'évolution de la ségrégation linguistique à Montréal: 1961-1971." *Recherches sociologiques*, vol. 24 no. 3 (1983) p. 379-390.

2713   **Vries, John de**
"Towards Sociology of Language in Canada." In: *Social Issues: Sociological Views of Canada*, edited by Dennis Forcese and Stephen Richer. Scarborough, Ont.: Prentice-Hall, Canada, 1982, p. 167-210.

2714   **Waddell, Eric**
"State, Language and Society: The Vicissitudes of French in Quebec and Canada." In: *Language and Society/Langue et société*, Alan Cairns and Cynthia Williams, research coordinators. Toronto: University of Toronto Press, 1986, p. 67-110.

2715   **Wagner, Mary Catherine**
Student Perceptions of Culture in Second Language Learning. Unpublished MEd thesis, University of Alberta, 1986. 2 microfiches. Canadian theses on microfiche, CT89-20953-7.

2716   **Wardhaugh, Ronald**
Language and Nationhood: The Canadian Experience. Vancouver: New Star Books, 1983. 269 p.

2717   **Williams, Colin H.**
"Official Language Districts: A Gesture of Faith in the Future of Canada." *Ethnic and Racial Studies*, vol. 4 no. 3 (1981) p. 334-347.

2718   **Wilman, David**
The Natural Language of Inuit Children: A Key to Inuktitut Literacy. Unpublished PhD thesis, University of New Mexico, 1988.

2719   **Woehrling, José**
"La reconnaissance du Québec comme société distincte et la dualité linguistique du Canada: Conséquences juridiques et contitutionnelles." *Canadian Public Policy/Analyse de politiques*, vol. 14 (1988 supplement) p. 43-62.

2720   **Wolowyna, Oleh**
"Significance of the Rural-Urban Shift in Linguistic Assimilation and Socioeconomic Status of Ukrainians in Canada." *Canadian Ethnic Studies/Études ethniques au Canada*, vol. 12 no. 2 (1980) p. 17-32.

2721   **Woolfson, Peter**
"Language Policy in Quebec: La survivance, 1967-1982." *Quebec Studies*, no. 2 (1984) p. 55-69.

2722   **Woolfson, Peter**
"Language in Quebec: Legal and Societal Issues." *The American Review of Canadian Studies*, vol. 13 no. 2 (1983) p. 42-51.

2723   **Wright, Ronald**
"Beyond Words: Why Should Anyone Care if the Languages of the Yukon Indians are Dying?" *Saturday Night*, vol. 103 no. 4/3697 (1988) p. 38-46.

2724   **Wu, Zhou**
Linguistic Shaping of Thought Revisited: Do English and Chinese Speakers Really Think Differently. Unpublished MEd thesis, University of Alberta, 1988. 2 microfiches. Canadian theses on microfiche, CT90-22550-5.

2725   **Yalden, Maxwell F.**
"An Overview of Language Reform." *Language and Society/Langue et société*, no. 10 (1983) p. 4-11.

2726   **Yalden, Maxwell F.**
"Language and the State: A Canadian Perspective." *Zeitschrift der Gesellschaft für Kanada-Studien*, vol. 2 no. 1 (1982) p. 95-101.

2727   **Yalden, Maxwell F.**
"Language and Power in Canada." *Society*, vol. 19 no. 1 (1981) p. 45-50.

2728   **Yalden, Maxwell F.**
"The Bilingual Experience in Canada." In: *The New Bilingualism: An American Dilemma*, edited by Martin Ridge. Los Angeles: University of Southern California Press, 1980, p. 71-87.

2729   **Youngs, Fred**
"Linguistic Wrongs and Rights: A Political Football." *Language and Society/Langue et société*, no. 16 (1985) p. 3-8.

Mass Media

2730 **Abu-Laban, Baha**
"Multiculturalism and Canadian Television: A Critical Review."
Multiculturalism, vol. 5 no. 1 (1981) p. 3-7.

2731 **Alexander, Don**
"Mohawk Radio: A Nation Rebuilds Through Broadcasting." *Fuse*,
vol. 9 no. 4 (1985) p. 24-28.

2732 **Allen, Richard L. and Shirley Hatchett**
"The Media and Social Reality Effects: Self and System Orientations
of Blacks." *Communication Research*, vol. 13 no. 1 (1986) p. 97-123.

2733 **Anctil, Pierre**
"Aspects de la thématique juive de la *Canadian Jewish News* édition
de Montréal, 1977-1982." *Canadian Ethnic Studies/Études ethniques
au Canada*, vol. 16 no. 1 (1984) p. 29-58.

2734 **Apramian, John**
"Ararat Monthly: The Only Armenian Publication in British North
America." *Polyphony: The Bulletin of the Multicultural History
Society of Ontario*, vol. 4 no. 1 (1982) p. 58-63.

2735 **Audley, Paul**
"The Agenda for Broadcasting Policy: Reflections on the Caplan-
Sauvageau Task Force." In: *Communication Canada: Issues in
Broadcasting and New Technology*, edited by Rowland M. Lorimer
and Donald C. Wilson. Toronto: Kagan and Woo, 1988, p. 199-213.

2736 **Audley, Paul**
*Canada's Cultural Industries: Broadcasting, Publishing, Records and
Film*. Toronto: James Lorimer and Co., in association with the
Canadian Institute for Economic Policy, 1983. 346 p.

2737   **Bathalon, Réal and Nicole Jetté, comps.**
Répertoire des organismes des communautés ethnoculturelles au Québec. Montréal: Centre interculturel Monchanin, 1983.

2738   **Bathalon, Réal and Nicole Jetté, comps.**
The Bulletin of the Canadian Celtic Arts Association. vol. 1 no. 1 (1982).

2739   **Bisztray, George**
"Hungarian Immigration After 1945: The Hungarian Canadian Press." *Polyphony: The Bulletin of the Multicultural History Society of Ontario,* vol. 2 no. 2/3 (1980) p. 54-58.

2740   **Black, Hawley L.**
The Role of the Canadian Press News Agency in Gatekeeping Canada's News. Unpublished PhD thesis, McGill University, 1980. Canadian theses on microfiche, 50394.

2741   **Black, Jerome H.**
"Patterns of Ethnic Media Consumption: A Comparative Examination of Ethnic Groupings in Toronto." *Canadian Ethnic Studies/Études ethniques au Canada,* vol. 19 no. 1 (1987) p. 21-41.

2742   **Boardman, Anthony E.**
"Canadian and British TV Markets: Why the CBC Should Not be Like the BBC." *Canadian Public Policy/Analyse de politiques,* vol. 10 no. 3 (1984) p. 347-358.

2743   **Bolubash, Anna**
"The Ukrainian Press in Ontario." *Polyphony: The Bulletin of the Multicultural History Society of Ontario,* vol. 10 no. 1/2 (1988) p. 213-220.

2744   **Boon, John**
"Telecommunications and the Constitution in an Information Age." *Saskatchewan Law Review,* vol. 49 no. 1 (1984/85) p. 69- 87.

2745   **Brisebois, Debbie**
"The Inuit Broadcasting Corporation." *Anthropologica,* vol. 25 no. 1 (1983) p. 107-115.

2746   **Bustamante, Rosalina E.**
"Filipino Ethnic Newspapers in Metropolitan Toronto." *Polyphony: The Bulletin of the Multicultural History Society of Ontario*, vol. 4 no. 1 (1982) p. 75-76.

2747   **Carr, Graham**
"Design as Content: Foreign Influences and the Identity of English-Canadian Intellectual Magazines, 1919-39." *American Review of Canadian Studies*, vol. 18 no. 2 (1988) p. 181-193.

2748   **Chopra, Anju**
Design and Evaluation of Experimental Multicultural Television Segments for Preschool Children. Unpublished MA thesis, Concordia University, 1981. 2 microfiches, illustrations. Canadian theses on microfiche, 49589.

2749   **Coldevin, Gary O.**
"Effects of a Decade of Satellite Television in the Canadian Arctic: Euro-Canadian and Inuit Adolescents Compared." *Journal of Cross-cultural Psychology*, vol. 16 no. 3 (1985) p. 329-354.

2750   **Coldevin, Gary O.**
"Longitudinal Influences of Satellite Television on Canadian Inuit Adolescents." In: *Communications and the Canadian North.* Montreal: Department of Communication Studies, Concordia University, 1983, p. 68-98.

2751   **Collins, Richard**
"Broadcasting and National Culture in Canada." *Journal of Canadian Studies/Revue d'études canadiennes*, vol. 4 no. 1 (1989) p. 35-57.

2752   **Comeau, Paul Andre**
"French Language Broadcasting in Canada." In: *Bilingualism and the Media in Canada and Wales.* [s.l.]: Canadian Studies in Wales Group, 1983. p. 21-27.

2753   **Conte, Franco**
"Editorial Views: Nuovo Mondo." *Polyphony: The Bulletin of the Multicultural History Society of Ontario*, vol. 4 no. 1 (1982) p. 126.

2754   **Cox, Kirwan**
The National Film Board and Television: A Report Prepared for the Task Force on Broadcasting Policy. Rigaud: [s.n.], 1986. 60 p.

2755   **Cranston, Paul**
Inuit Television Broadcasting: Cultural Identity and Expression in a New Medium. Unpublished MA thesis, McGill University, 1985. 2 microfiches. Canadian theses on microfiche, CT86-26964-7.

2756   **Czarnecki, Mark**
The Creation of Program Material. Task Force on Broadcasting Policy, vol. 13. [s.l.:s.n.], 1986.

2757   **Dahlie, Jorgen**
"The Ethnic Press as a Cultural Resource: Canada Scandinavian and the Norwegian-Swedish Community in B.C., 1910-1930." In: *Proceedings: Association for the Advancement of Scandinavian Studies in Canada, First Annual Meeting,* edited by Edward W. Laine. Ottawa: The Association, 1983, p. 15-26.

2758   **Demay, Joël**
"Le journalisme indien à la croisée des 'courants d'action journalistique'." *Anthropologica,* vol. 25 no. 1 (1983) p. 31-35.

2759   **Desaulniers, Jean-Pierre**
"What Does Canada Want: l'histoire sans leçon." *Media, Culture and Society,* vol. 9 no. 2 (1987) p. 149-158.

2760   **Dick, Ronald S.**
"Minorities and the Canadian Visual Media." In: *Minorities and the Canadian State,* edited by Neil Nevitte and Allan Kornberg. Oakville, Ont.: Mosaic Press, 1985, p. 157-192.

2761   **Dragasevic, Draga**
"The Serbian Patriotic Media in Ontario Since 1916." In: *Serbs in Ontario: A Socio-cultural Description,* edited by Sofija Skoric and George Vid Tomashevich. Toronto: Serbian Heritage Academy, 1987, p. 128-146.

2762   **DuCharme, Michele**
"The Coverage of Canadian Immigration Policy in the *Globe and Mail,* 1980-1985." *Currents: Readings in Race Relations,* vol. 3 no. 3 (1986) p. 6-11.

2763   **Eaman, Ross Allan**
The Media Society: Basic Issues and Controversies. Toronto: Butterworths, 1987. 188 p.

2764   **Evans, Karen**
"Edmund James Peck: His Contribution to Eskimo Literacy and Publishing." *Journal of the Canadian Church Historical Society*, vol. 26 no. 2 (1984) p. 58-68.

2765   **Fortner, Robert S.**
"Significance and Legitimacy in Public Policy Debate: The Canadian Public and the Politics of Language in Canadian Broadcasting Development." *Journal of Canadian Studies/Revue d'études canadiennes*, vol. 23 no. 4 (1988/89) p. 82-108.

2766   **Fortner, Robert S.**
"The System of Relevances and the Politics of Language in Canadian Public Policy Formulation: The Case of Broadcasting." *Canadian Public Policy/Analyse de politiques*, vol. 12 nos. 3-4 (1986) p. 19-36.

2767   **Freiman, Mark**
"Canadian Content in Private Television: An Innisian Analysis." *University of Toronto Faculty of Law Review*, vol. 41 no. 1 (1983) p. 19-33.

2768   **Gathercole, Sandra**
"Changing Channels: Canadian Television Needs to Switch to a New Format." In: *Contemporary Canadian Politics: Readings and Notes*, edited by Robert J. Jackson, Doreen Jackson and Nicholas Baxter-Moore. Scarborough, Ont.: Prentice-Hall of Canada, 1987, p. 79-86.

2769   **Gay, Daniel**
"L'information sur l'Amérique latine et les silences de la presse québécoise." *Études internationales*, vol. 13 no. 4 (1982) p. 679-690.

2770   **Giuliani, Maura**
"The Inuit Broadcasting Corporation." *North/Nord*, vol. 30 no. 1 (1983) p. 16-19.

2771   **Gomez, Henry**
"The Invisible Visibles." *Currents*, vol. 1 no. 2 (1983) p. 12.

2772   **Granzberg, Gary**
"Television as a Storyteller: The Algonkion Indians of Central Canada." *Journal of Communication*, vol. 32 no. 1 (1982) p. 43-52.

2773   **Gregg, Andrew**
"Broadcasting in the North: Natives Shift from Fear of Losing Their
Souls to Proficiency Behind the Camera." *Broadcaster: Canada's
Communications Magazine*, vol. 47 no. 9 (1988) p. 30-32.

2774   **Gregorovich, Andrew**
"Canadian Multilingual Press Federation: David Crombie Introduces
Multiculturalism Bill." *Forum: A Ukrainian Review*, no. 72
(1987) p. 26-28.

2775   **Grohovaz, Gianni**
"Editorial Views: Toronto's Italian Press After the Second World
War." *Polyphony: The Bulletin of the Multicultural History Society of
Ontario*, vol. 4 no. 1 (1982) p. 105-113.

2776   **Hackett, Robert A.**
"For a Socialist Perspective in the News Media." *Studies in Political
Economy*, no. 19 (1986) p. 141-156.

2777   **Hall, Joy**
"Native Communications: Top Priority/La priorité des autochtones: la
communication." *Parallélogramme*, vol. 14 no. 3 (1988/89) p. 25-31.

2778   **Hannigan, John A.**
"Ideology, Elites and the Canadian Mass Media." In:
Communications in Canadian Society, edited by Benjamin D. Singer.
Don Mills, Ontario: Addison-Wesley Publishers, 1983, p. 55-61.

2779   **Harney, Robert F.**
"Editorial Views: Interview with Jonas Yla." *Polyphony: The Bulletin
of the Multicultural History Society of Ontario*, vol. 4 no. 1
(1982) p. 128-132.

2780   **Harney, Robert F.**
"Preface" and "The Ethnic Press in Ontario." *Polyphony: The
Bulletin of the Multicultural History Society of Ontario*, vol. 4 no. 1
(1982) p. 1-14.

2781   **Hathaway, Thomas**
"CBC-FM Radio: Clearing the Air." *Queen's Quarterly*, vol. 92 no. 1
(1985) p. 21-35.

2782   **Heydenkorn, Benedykt**
"Editorial Views: The Nature of the Ethnic Press." *Polyphony: The Bulletin of the Multicultural History Society of Ontario*, vol. 4 no. 1 (1982) p. 99-103.

2783   **Heydenkorn, Benedykt**
"Polish Press — *Gazeta Katolicka.*" *Polyphony: The Bulletin of the Multicultural History Society of Ontario*, vol. 4 no. 1 (1982) p. 52-57.

2784   **Heydenkorn, Benedykt**
"The Polish Press in Canada." *Polyphony: The Bulletin of the Multicultural History Society of Ontario*, vol. 4 no. 1 (1982) p. 35-36.

2785   **Hill, Daniel G.**
"The Black Press." *Polyphony: The Bulletin of the Multicultural History Society of Ontario*, vol. 4 no. 1 (1982) p. 43-48.

2786   **Hoerder, Dirk**
"Reports: Labour Newspaper Preservation Project." *Polyphony: The Bulletin of the Multicultural History Society of Ontario*, vol. 4 no. 1 (1982) p. 142-143.

2787   **Hutner, Susan Cohen**
"*The Canadian Jewish Review.*" *Polyphony: The Bulletin of the Multicultural History Society of Ontario*, vol. 4 no. 1 (1982) p. 37-42.

2788   **Ipellie, Alootook**
"*Inuit Today Magazine.*" *North/Nord*, vol. 30 no. 1 (1983) p. 20-23.

2789   **Itroc [Corti, Enrico]**
"Can an Italo-Canadian be a Fascist?" *Polyphony: The Bulletin of the Multicultural History Society of Ontario*, vol. 7 no. 2 (1985) p. 52-53.

2790   **Kaprielian, Isabel**
"The Armenian Political Press and its Reading Rooms." *Polyphony: The Bulletin of the Multicultural History Society of Ontario*, vol. 4 no. 1 (1982) p. 30-34.

2791 **Kariel, Herbert G.**
"Cultural Affinity Displayed in Canadian Daily Newspapers."
Journalism Quarterly, vol. 60 no. 3 (1983) p. 431-436.

2792 **Kayfetz, Ben**
"Recollections and Experiences with the Jewish Press in Toronto."
*Polyphony: The Bulletin of the Multicultural History Society of
Ontario*, vol. 6 no. 1 (1984) p. 228-231.

2793 **Kayfetz, Ben**
"The Toronto Yiddish Press." *Canadian Jewish Historical Society
Journal société de l'histoire juive canadienne*, vol. 7 no. 1
(1983) p. 39-54.

2794 **Kayfetz, Ben**
"Editorial Views: Recollections and Experiences with the Jewish
Press." *Polyphony: The Bulletin of the Multicultural History Society
of Ontario*, vol. 4 no. 1 (1982) p. 120-122.

2795 **Ke, Vera, et al. eds.**
Mosaic in Media: Selected Works of Ethnic Journalists and Writers.
Toronto: Canadian Ethnic Journalists and Writers' Club, 1986. 239 p.

2796 **Kelly, Michael J.**
*The Media and Terrorism: An Examination of News Coverage of
Armenian Terrorism in Canada.* Unpublished PhD thesis, Carleton
University, 1987.

2797 **Khaki, Aziz**
"The Role and Function of the Media in Depiction and Portrayal of
Visible Minorities in the Media and Society at Large." In: *Progress
Towards Equality*, edited and compiled by Aziz Khaki. Vancouver:
Committee for Racial Justice, p. 17-21.

2798 **Kim, Jung G.**
"Korean-language Press in Ontario." *Polyphony: The Bulletin of the
Multicultural History Society of Ontario*, vol. 4 no. 1 (1982) p. 82-
86.

2799 **Kim, Jung G.**
"Reports: Ontario Ethnocultural Newspapers: Bibliography and
Microfilming Project — Its Inception and Progress." *Polyphony: The
Bulletin of the Multicultural History Society of Ontario*, vol. 4 no. 1
(1982) p. 139-141.

2800   **King, Christopher**
"Images of South Asians in the Media and in Educational Materials."
In: *Canada and South Asia: Issues and Opportunities*, edited by
Arthur G. Rubinoff. Toronto: Centre for South Asian Studies,
1988, p. 69-73.

2801   **Koebberling, Ursel**
*Industrialization, Telecommunication and Broadcasting Development
in the Western Arctic: Political-economic and Socio-cultural
Implications for the Inuit.* Unpublished MA thesis, Simon Fraser
University, 1984. 3 microfiches. Canadian theses on microfiche,
68215.

2802   **Kruger, Martin**
"Öeknomische Aspekte der Rundfunkordnung." *Zeitschrift der
Gesellschaft für Kanada-Studien*, vol. 8 no. 1 (1988) p. 89-105.

2803   **L'Allier, Jean-Paul**
La spécificité québécoise et les medias électroniques. Québec, P.Q.:
Jean-Paul L'Allier et associés inc., 1986. 97 p.

2804   **Laba, Martin**
"Popular Culture as Local Culture: Regions Limits and Canadian-
ism." In: *Communication Canada: Issues in Broadcasting and New
Technology*, edited by Rowland M. Lorimer and Donald C. Wilson.
Toronto: Kagan and Woo, 1988, p. 82-101.

2805   **Laferrière, Michel**
"Media et groupes minoritaire: quelques réflexions à partir du cas du
Québec." *Études canadiennes/Canadian Studies*, (1982) p. 65.

2806   **Lam, Lawrence**
"The Role of Ethnic Media for Immigrants: A Case Study of Chinese
Immigrans and Their Media in Toronto." *Canadian Ethnic Studies/
Études ethniques au Canada*, vol. 12 no. 1 (1980) p. 74-92.

2807   **Lehr, John C.**
"Texas (When I Die): National Identity and Images of Place in
Canadian Country Music Broadcasts." *Canadian Geographer/Le
géographe canadien*, vol. 27 no. 4 (1983) p. 361-369.

2808   **Lindström-Best, Varpu**
"*Vapaa Sana* 1931-81: The Largest Finnish-language Newspaper in North America." *Polyphony: The Bulletin of the Multicultural History Society of Ontario*, vol. 4 no. 1 (1982) p. 49-51.

2809   **Lindström-Best, Varpu**
"Culture and Politics in Finnish Canada: Fist Press: A Study of the Finnish Canadian Handwritten Newspapers." *Polyphony: The Bulletin of the Multicultural History Society of Ontario*, vol. 3 no. 2 (1981) p. 65-73.

2810   **Liska, Peter**
"An Oriental Window: Chinavision Expands to New Markets Nationwide." *Broadcaster: Canada's Communications Magazine*, vol. 47 no. 8 (1988) p. 28-29.

2811   **Lonsdale, Cliff**
"The Canadian Media and National Unity." In: *Bilingualism and the Media in Canada and Wales*, [s.l.]: Canadian Studies in Wales Group, 1983. p. 9-14.

2812   **Luciuk, Lubomyr**
"Two English-language Ukrainian Newspapers." *Polyphony: The Bulletin of the Multicultural History Society of Ontario*, vol. 4 no. 1 (1982) p. 77-81.

2813   **Magder, Ted**
The Political Economy of Canadian Cultural Policy: The Canadian State and Feature Films, 1917-84. Unpublished PhD thesis, York University, 1988.

2814   **Maistre, Gilbert**
"L'influence de la radio et de la télévision américaines au Canada." *Recherches sociographiques*, vol. 12 no. 1 (1971) p. 51-76.

2815   **Marquand, John**
"Inuit Use of Radio and Television in Arctic Quebec." In: *Communications and the Canadian North.* Montreal: Department of Communication Studies, Concordia University, 1983, p. 99-119.

2816   **Mauko, Vladimir**
"Editorial Views: The Ethnic Press Association of Ontario." *Polyphony: The Bulletin of the Multicultural History Society of Ontario*, vol. 4 no. 1 (1982) p. 115-119.

2817 **Mauko, Vladimir**
"Editorial Views: *Slovenska Drzava.*" *Polyphony: The Bulletin of the Multicultural History Society of Ontario*, vol. 4 no. 1 (1982) p. 114-114.

2818 **Meyer, Marion E.**
"The Jews of Kingston: A Comparative Study of Organized and Non-Affiliated Jews (A Preliminary Report)." *Canadian Jewish Historical Society Journal société de l'histoire juive canadienne*, vol. 6 no. 2 (1982) p. 87-98.

2819 **Miller, Earl**
"Portrayal of Non-Whites in Advertising." *Currents*, vol. 1 no. 2 (1983) p. 26.

2820 **Mitchell, David J.**
"Culture as Political Discourse." In: *Communication Canada: Issues in Broadcasting and New Technology*, edited by Rowland M. Lorimer and Donald C. Wilson. Toronto: Kagan and Woo, 1988, p. 157-174.

2821 **Monnier, Daniel**
La situation de la langue française au Québec: statistiques récentes pour les domaines du travail, du commerce et des médias. Québec, P.Q.: Conseil de la langue française, 1984. 25 p.

2822 **National Forum on Multiculturalism in Broadcasting**
Reflections from the Electronic Mirror: Report of the National Forum on Multiculturalism in Broadcasting. Toronto: Canadian Multiculturalism Council, 1988. 155, 165 p. Forum held in Toronto, Ontario, May 13 and 14, 1988.

2823 **Nipp, Dora**
"The Ethnic Press Project." *Polyphony: The Bulletin of the Multicultural History Society of Ontario*, vol. 9 no. 1 (1987) p. 59-62.

2824 **Papp, Susan M.**
"The Hungarian Press in Ontario." *Polyphony: The Bulletin of the Multicultural History Society of Ontario*, vol. 4 no. 1 (1982) p. 64-68.

2825   **Payne, David E.**
"Anglophone Canadian and American Mass Media: Use and Effect on Quebecois Adults." *Communication Research*, vol. 9 no. 1 (1982) p. 113-144.

2826   **PEAC Media Research**
The Presence and Portrayal of Non-whites in English-language Television Advertising in Canada: Final Report. Toronto: PEAC Media Research, 1982. 22 p.

2827   **Peers, Frank W.**
CBC: The Big Picture. A Paper Prepared for the Task Force on Broadcasting Policy. Toronto: [s.n.], 1985. 137 p.

2828   **Pelletier, Clotilde**
Les radios communautaires au Nouveau-Québec inuit: outils de dépendence ou de développement? Unpublished MSc thesis, Université de Montréal, 1985.

2829   **Pendakur, M.**
"Cultural Dependency in Canada's Feature Film Industry." *Journal of Communications*, vol. 31 no. 1 (1981) p. 48-57.

2830   **Petryszak, Nicholas G.**
"The Nature of the Canadian Television Audience: A Case Study." *Canadian Journal of Communication*, vol. 7 no. 2 (1980) p. 50-71.

2831   **Pidzamecky, Taras**
"Ukrainian National Youth Federation of Canada: Fifty Decades of Youth Leadership." *Forum: A Ukrainian Review*, no. 58 (1984) p. 12-17.

2832   **Pilli, Arja**
"The Finnish Experience: The Origins of *Canadan Uutiset*." *Polyphony: The Bulletin of the Multicultural History Society of Ontario*, vol. 9 no. 2 (1987) p. 39-42.

2833   **Principe, Angelo**
"The Italo-Canadian Anti-fascist Press in Toronto, 1922-40." *Polyphony: The Bulletin of the Multicultural History Society of Ontario*, vol. 7 no. 2 (1985) p. 43-51.

2834   **Principe, Angelo**
"The Multicultural Press." *Polyphony: The Bulletin of the Multicultural History Society of Ontario*, vol. 4 no. 1 (1982) p. 94-94.

2835   **Pronko, Jerry**
"Ethno Press 88." *Forum: A Ukrainian Review*, no. 75 (1988) p. 13-14.

2836   **Raudsepp, Enn**
"Emergent Media: The Native Press in Canada." *Canadian Journal of Communication*, vol. 11 no. 2 (1985) p. 193-209.

2837   **Raudsepp, Enn**
"Media Use and Satisfaction Patterns Among English-speaking Audiences in Montreal." *Canadian Journal of Communication*, vol. 8 no. 3 (1982) p. 12-41.

2838   **Ridington, Robin**
"Texts that Harm: Journalism in British Columbia." *Currents*, vol. 3 no. 4 (1986) p. 6-12.

2839   **Riggins, Stephen Harold**
"The Organizational Structure of the *Toronto Native Times* (1968-1981)." *Anthropologica*, vol. 25 no. 1 (1983) p. 37-52.

2840   **Rogoff, Edmond Marc du**
"Les médias franco-ontariens: ou comment survivre dans les îlots." *Zeitschrift der Gesellschaft für Kanada-Studien*, vol. 7 no. 1 (1987) p. 83-102.

2841   **Rome, David**
Early Anti-semitism: The Voice of the Media. 2 volumes. Montreal: National Archives, Canadian Jewish Congress, 1983.

2842   **Rosenthal, Heather Angela**
Ethnic Discourse in CBC Radio Drama and Government Immigration Policies. Unpublished MA thesis, Concordia University, 1987. Canadian theses on microfiche, CT89-21844-7.

2843   **Rosenthal, Henry M. and S. Cathy Berson, eds.**
The 'Canadian Jewish Outlook' Anthology. Vancouver: New Star Books, 1988. 381 p.

2844   **Roth, Lorna**
"Inuit Media Project and Northern Communication Policy." In:
Communications and the Canadian North. Montreal: Department of
Communication Studies, Concordia University, 1983, p. 42-67.

2845   **Roth, Lorna**
*The Role of Communication Projects and Inuit Participation in the
Formation of a Communication Policy for the North*. Unpublished
MA thesis, McGill University, 1982. Canadian theses on microfiche,
64416.

2846   **Rupert, Robert**
"Native Broadcasting in Canada." *Anthropologica*, vol. 25 no. 1
(1983) p. 53-61.

2847   **Russell, Catherine**
"The Politics of Putting Art on Film: Derek May and the National
Film Board of Canada." *Journal of Canadian Studies/Revue d'études
canadiennes*, vol. 21 no. 1 (1986) p. 104-115.

2848   **Santo, Odoardo Di**
"Editorial Views: *Forze Nuove*." *Polyphony: The Bulletin of the
Multicultural History Society of Ontario*, vol. 4 no. 1 (1982) p. 123-
125.

2849   **Shanahan, David Frances**
*Irish Catholic Journalists and the New Nationality in Canada, 1858-
1870*. Unpublished MA thesis, Lakehead University, 1984. Canadian
theses on microfiche, 67698.

2850   **Shepherd, John**
"Music Consumption and Cultural Self-identities: Some Theoretical
and Methodological Reflections." *Media, Culture and Society*, vol. 8
no. 3 (1986) p. 305-330.

2851   **Silver, A.I.**
"The French-Canadian Press and 1885." *Native Studies Review*, vol. 1
no. 1 (1984) p. 2-15.

2852   **Simons, Gary C.**
*Agent, Editor, and Native: The Attitudes of the Western Canadian
Press to the Department of Indian Affairs, 1880-1891*. Unpublished
MA thesis, Queen's University, 1984. Canadian theses on microfiche,
CT87-21000-9.

2853   **Singer, Benjamin D.**
"Minorities and the Media: A Content Analysis of Native Canadians in the Daily Press." In: *Communications in Canadian Society*, edited by Benjamin D. Singer. Don Mills, Ont.: Addison-Wesley Publishers, 1983, p. 226-236.

2854   **Singer, Benjamin D.**
"Minorities and the Media: A Content Analysis of Native Canadian in the Daily Press." *Canadian Review of Sociology and Anthropology/Revue canadienne de sociologie et d'anthropologie*, vol. 19 no. 3 (1982) p. 348-359.

2855   **Sloan, Tom**
"Press Review: Bill C-72/Échos de la presse: le projet de Loi C-72." *Language and Society/Langue et société*, no. 25 (1988) p. 35-36.

2856   **Stenbaek, Marianne**
"The Politics of Cultural Survival: Towards a Model of Indigenous Television." *American Review of Canadian Studies*, vol. 18 no. 3 (1988) p. 331-340.

2857   **Stiles, J. Mark**
The Educational and Developmental Aspects of Native Broadcasting in Canada. Unpublished MA Ed thesis, St. Francis Xavier University, 1987.

2858   **Stone, Daniel**
"Winnipeg's Polish Language Newspapers and Their Attitude Towards Jews and Ukrainians Between the Two World Wars." *Canadian Ethnic Studies/Études ethniques au Canada*, vol. 21 no. 2 (1989) p. 27-37.

2859   **Subervi-Velez, Federico A.**
"The Mass Media and Ethnic Assimilation and Pluralism: A Review and Research Proposal with Special Focus on Hispanics." *Communication Research*, vol. 13 no. 1 (1986) p. 71-96.

2860   **Sugiman, Momoye**
"A Minority Within a Minority—Midi Ondera: A Film Maker Talks About Her Art." *The Asianadian*, vol.6 no. 2 (1985) p. 26-29.

2861   **Sutherland, Anthony X.**
        The Canadian Slovak League: A History, 1932-1982. Toronto: The
        Canadian Slovak League, 1984.

2862   **Toffler, Alvin**
        "Mass Media: A Force in Identity Change." In: *Communications in
        Canadian Society,* edited by Benjamin D. Singer. Don Mills, Ont.:
        Addison-Wesley Publishers, 1983, p. 133-137.

2863   **Tomovic, Vladislav**
        "The Serbian Press in Canada, 1916-82." *Polyphony: The Bulletin of
        the Multicultural History Society of Ontario,* vol. 4 no. 1
        (1982) p. 87-93.

2864   **Turek, Victor**
        "The Polish-language Press in Canada." *Polyphony: The Bulletin of
        the Multicultural History Society of Ontario,* vol. 6 no. 2
        (1984) p. 88-92.

2865   **Urion, Carl**
        "An Interview with Freelance Broadcaster Kin Kopola."
        Anthropologica, vol. 25 no. 1 (1983) p. 63-69.

2866   **Valaskakis, Gail**
        "Television and Cultural Integration: Implications for Native
        Communities in the Canadian North." In: *Communication Canada:
        Issues in Broadcasting and New Technology,* edited by Rowland M.
        Lorimer and Donald C. Wilson. Toronto: Kagan and Woo,
        1988, p. 124-138.

2867   **Waters, David**
        "The English Media and the New Quebec." In: *English of Quebec:
        From Majority to Minority Status,* edited by Gary Caldwell and Eric
        Waddell. Québec, P.Q.: Institut québécois de recherche sur la culture,
        1982, p.307-324.

2868   **Weatherford, Elizabeth and Emelia Seubert**
        Native Americans on Film and Video. Volume 2. New York:
        Museum of the American Indian, 1988. 113 p.

2869   **Whitehouse, Anab**
        "Prejudice: The Canadian Media and Islam." *Currents: Readings in
        Race Relations,* vol. 3 no. 3 (1986) p. 18-19.

2870 **Wong, Mina and I. Preyra**
"CBS's Visible Minority Training Program." *The Asianadian*, vol. 5 no. 3 (1984) p. 18-22.

2871 **Ziniak, Madeline**
"The Development of a Byelorussian Press in Canada." *Polyphony: The Bulletin of the Multicultural History Society of Ontario*, vol. 4 no. 1 (1982) p. 69-73.

2872 **Zolf, Dorothy**
"Comparisons of Multicultural Broadcasting in Canada and Four Other Countries." *Canadian Ethnic Studies/Études ethniques au Canada*, vol. 21 no. 2 (1989) p. 13-26.

2873 **Zybala, Stanley**
"The Ethnic Press in Ontario." *Polyphony: The Bulletin of the Multicultural History Society of Ontario*, vol. 4 no. 1 (1982) p. 3-29.

Culture

2874 **Abramowitz, David**
"Soviet-Yiddish Writer [Hershel Polianker] in Canada." *Outlook: Canada's Progressive Jewish Magazine*, vol. 27 no. 12 (1989) p. 5-6.

2875 **Ackerman, Marianne**
"A Crisis of Visions: Anglophone Theatre in Montreal." *Canadian Theatre Review*, no. 46 (1986) p. 21-27.

2876 **Adams, Dawn**
Haida Art. Vancouver: Wedge, 1983.

2877 **Adams, Robert**
The Life and Work of Alexander Bercovitch, Artist. Montreal: Editions Marlowe, 1988. 134 p.

2878 **Adilman, Mona Elaine**
"Sholem Aleichem's Uncle and Cousins in Canada." *Outlook: Canada's Progressive Jewish Magazine*, vol. 27 no. 4 (1989) p. 10-11.

2879 **Adrizzi, Maria J.**
The Emigrant Cycle. Toronto: Toma Publishing, 1982.

2880 **Ahermaa, Martin**
"The Call of Ancestral Voices." *Polyphony: The Bulletin of the Multicultural History Society of Ontario*, vol. 5 no. 2 (1983) p. 104-106.

2881 **Allaby, Ian**
"Citizen Zeidler: An Architect for Better City Living." *Canadian Geographic/De géographe canadien*, vol. 105 no. 2 (1985) p. 8-17.

2882   **Alleyne, Mervyn C.**
Roots of Jamaican Culture. London, U.K.: Pluto Press, 1988. 186 p.

2883   **American Jewish Historical Society**
"Revisiting a Classic: Nathan Glazer's 'American Judaism'."
American Jewish History, vol. 77 no. 2 (1987) p. 208-284.

2884   **Ames, Michael A.**
"Bill Holm, Willie Seaweed and the Problem of Northwest Coast Indian
'Art': A Review Article." *B.C. Studies*, no. 64 (1984/85) p. 74-81.

2885   **Anderson, Adrienne E. and Louise Penner**
"Namaka Mennonite Cemetery." *Alberta Family Histories Society*,
vol. 6 no. 1 (1985) p. 6-8.

2886   **Anselmi, William**
"A Survey on Italo-Canadian Literature: A Paradoxical Panorama
Unresolved." *Vice Versa*, no. 16 (1986) p. 41-43.

2887   **Anthony, Brian**
"Negotiating Canadian Culture: What's at Stake?" *Canadian Business
Review*, vol. 13 no. 2 (1986) p. 14-17.

2888   **Arnold, Abraham J.**
"Writing Canadian Jewish History." *Outlook: Canada's Progressive
Jewish Magazine*, vol. 26 no. 1/2 (1988) p. 10-11.

2889   **Artinian, Hagop**
"Armenian General Sports Union." *Polyphony: The Bulletin of the
Multicultural History Society of Ontario*, vol. 7 no. 1 (1985) p. 38.

2890   **Asch, Michael**
Kinship and the Drum Dance in a Northern Dene Community. The
Circumpolar Research Series. Edmonton: The Boreal Institute for
Northern Studies and Academic Printing and Publishing, 1989. 113 p.

2891   **Association française d'études canadiennes**
"L'homme et la fôret." *Études canadiennes/Canadian Studies*, no. 23
(1987) p. 1-201.

2892   **Atkinson, Thomas**
*Values, Domains and the Perceived Quality of Life: Canada and the
United States.* Toronto: Institute for Behavioral Research, 1980. 36
leaves.

2893   **Baglo, Fredy**
"Art that Speaks in the Language of Today: A Conversation About
Artistic Expression in the Church with Lutz Haufschild." *Canada
Lutheran*, vol. 4 no. 11 (1989) p. 8-13.

2894   **Bailey, Cameron**
"Hip Hop Infects Toronto: Overview, Interview and Record Primer."
Fuse Magazine, vol. 12 no. 3/52 (1988) p. 16-28.

2895   **Bailey, Cameron**
"Writing B(l)ack: The Call and Response of Black Literary
Criticism." *Border/Lines*, no. 11 (1988) p. 36-40.

2896   **Baillargeon, Jean-Paul, ed.**
*Les pratiques culturelles des québécois: Une autre image de nous-
mêmes.* Québec, P.Q.: Institut québécois de recherche sur la culture,
1986. 394 p.

2897   **Balan, Jars**
Salt and Braided Bread: Ukrainian Life in Canada. Toronto: Oxford
University Press, 1984.

2898   **Balan, Jars and Yuri Klynovy, eds.**
*Yarmarok: Ukrainian Writing in Canada Since the Second World
War.* Edmonton: Canadian Institute of Ukrainian Studies, University
of Alberta, 1987. 352 p.

2899   **Barbeau, Marius**
Art of the Totem. Revised ed. Surrey, B.C.: Hancock House, 1983.

2900   **Barber, Crystal**
A Metis Wedding. Regina: Gabriel Dumont Institute of Native Studies
and Applied Research, 1985. 28 p.

2901   **Barclay, Harold B.**
Culture: The Human Way. Edmonton: Department of Anthropology,
University of Alberta, 1983.

2902   **Barer-Stein, Thelma**
"Experiencing the Unfamiliar: Culture Adaptation and Culture Shock
as Aspects of a Process of Learning." *Canadian Ethnic Studies/
Études ethniques au Canada*, vol. 20 no. 2 (1988) p. 71-91.

2903 **Barnes, Thomas G.**
"'Canada, True North': A 'Here There' or a Boreal Myth?" *American Review of Canadian Studies*, vol. 19 no. 4 (1989) p. 369-379.

2904 **Beal, A. Lynne**
"Canadian Content in the WISC-R: Bias or Jingoism?" *Canadian Journal of Behavioural Science/Revue canadienne des sciences de comportement*, vol. 20 no. 2 (1988) p. 154-166.

2905 **Beaton-Planetta, Elizabeth**
"A Tale of Three Churches: Ethnic Architecture in Sydney, Nova Scotia." *Canadian Ethnic Studies/Études ethniques au Canada*, vol. 14 no. 3 (1984) p. 89-107.

2906 **Beck, Brenda E.F.**
"Bread Crumbs or Yeast: Indo-Canadian Popular Culture and its Growth Potential." In: *The South Asian Diaspora in Canada*, edited by Milton Israel. Toronto: Multicultural History Society of Ontario, 1987, p. 59-72.

2907 **Beck, Brenda E.F.**
"Indo-Canadian Popular Culture: Should Writers Take the Lead in its Development?" In: *A Meeting of Streams: South Asian Canadian Literature*, edited by M.G. Vassanji. Toronto: TSAR Publications, 1985, p. 121-132.

2908 **Beck, Ervin**
"Mennonite and Amish Painting on Glass." *The Mennonite Quarterly Review*, vol. 63 no. 2 (1989) p. 115-149.

2909 **Beck, Marion**
Notebook of an Immigrant. Regina: Clover Press, 1983.

2910 **Begin, Carmelle and Pierre Crepeau**
Dance! Roots, Ritual and Romance. Hull: Canadian Museum of Civilization/Musée canadien des civilisations, 1989. 49 p.

2911 **Bell, Gay**
"An Interview with Andri Zhina [A Jamaican-Canadian Poet and Playwright]." *Fuse*, vol. 10 no. 1/2 (1986) p. 58-63.

2912   **Bennett, Margaret**
The Last Stronghold: Scottish Gaelic Traditions in Newfoundland.
Canada's Atlantic Folklore - Folklife Series. St. John's: Breakwater
Books, 1989. 200 p.

2913   **Bently, Allen**
"From Spain to New Brunswick: The Art of Angel Gomez-
Miguelanez." *Arts Atlantic*, vol. 8 no. 4/32 (1988) p. 36-39.

2914   **Bérard, Chantal**
"L'importance de l'utilisation du folklore dans 'Tchipayuk ou le
chemin du loup'." *Cahiers franco-canadiens de l'Ouest*, vol. 1 no. 2
(1989) p. 213-222.

2915   **Berg, Wesley**
"From Piety to Sophistication: Developments in Canadian-Mennonite
Music After World War II." *Mennonite Studies*, vol. 6 (1988) p. 89-
99.

2916   **Berg, Wesley**
"Gesangbuch, Ziffern and Deutschtum: A Study of the Life and
Work of J.P. Claszn, Mennonite Hymnologist." *Journal of Mennonite
Studies*, vol. 4 (1986) p. 8-30.

2917   **Berg, Wesley**
*From Russia with Music: A Study of the Mennonite Choral Singing
Tradition in Canada.* Winnipeg: Hyperion Press, 1985. 151 p.

2918   **Berger, Jeniva**
"A Coat of Many Colours: The Multicultural Theatre Movement in
Canada." In: *Contemporary Canadian Theatre: New World Visions, A
Collection of Essays Prepared by the Canadian Theatre Critics
Association*, edited by Anton Wagner. Toronto: Simon and Pierre,
1985, p. 216-226.

2919   **Berry, John Widdup**
"Cultural Psychology and Ethnic Psychology: A Comparative
Analysis." In: *From a Different Perspective: Studies of Behavior
Across Cultures*, edited by Isabel Reyes Lagunes and Ype H.
Poortinga. Lisse: Swets and Zeitlinger; Berwyn, Pa.: Swets North
America, 1985, p. 3-15. Paper presented at the 7th International
Conference of the International Association for Cross-cultural
Psychology held at Acapulco, Mexico, August 29-Sepember 1, 1984.

2920 **Berton, Pierre**
Why We Act Like Canadians: A Personal Exploration of our National Character. Toronto: McClelland and Stewart Ltd., 1982. 113 p.

2921 **Bertrand, Pierre**
"Le voyage immobile: le Québec de l'an 2000 face au défi de la transculture-une perspective." *Vice Versa*, no. 22-23 (1988) p. 8-9.

2922 **Birch, Jack Stephan**
Ascriptive and Performance Predictors of Attainment of Success in Professional Hockey. Unpublished PhD thesis, University of Waterloo, 1989.

2923 **Bird, Michael S.**
Canadian Folk Art: Old Ways in a New Land. Toronto: Oxford University Press, 1983.

2924 **Bird, Michael S. and Terry Kobayashi**
A Splendid Harvest: Germanic Folk and Decorative Arts in Canada. Toronto: Van Nostrand Reinhold, 1981.

2925 **Biron, Normand**
"Clement Greenburg, la qualité exemplaire d'un regard." *Vice Versa*, no. 25 (1988) p. 32-33.

2926 **Bisztray, George**
Canadian-Hungarian Literature: A Preliminary Survey. Ottawa: Department of the Secretary of State of Canada, Multiculturalism, 1988. 48 p.

2927 **Bisztray, George**
Hungarian Canadian Literature. Toronto: University of Toronto Press, 1987. 116 p.

2928 **Bisztray, George**
"Flight and Settlement: The '56ers: Cultural Institutions." *Polyphony: The Bulletin of the Multicultural History Society of Ontario*, vol. 2 no. 2/3 (1980) p. 70-76.

2929 **Blackman, Margaret B.**
"Contemporay Northwest Coast Art for Ceremonial Use." *American Indian Art*, vol. 10 no. 3 (1985) p. 24-37.

2930   **Blank, Hedy**
        The Prohibition Against Making Images: Teaching Art in the
        Orthodox Jewish Schools in Montreal, The Context for this Problem
        and an Examination of Art Teaching Practice in Two Orthodox
        Schools. Unpublished MA thesis, Concordia University, 1986. 1
        microfiche. Canadian theses on microfiche, CT88-20749-3.

2931   **Blicq, Andrew and Ken Gigliotti**
        People of the Interlake. Winnipeg: Turnstone Press, 1986. 129 p.

2932   **Blodgett, Jean**
        "Jessie Oonark: A Retrospective." *The Wag Magazine*, (1986) p. 4-7.

2933   **Blundell, Valda**
        "Speaking the Art of Canada's Native Peoples: Anthropological
        Discourse and the Media." *Australian-Canadian Studies*, vol. 7 no.
        1/2 (1989) p. 23-43.

2934   **Blundell, Valda**
        "Une Approche Semiologique du Pow Wow Canadien Contempor-
        ain." *Recherches Amerindiennes au Québec*, vol. 15 no. 4
        (1985/86) p. 53-66.

2935   **Blundell, Valda and Ruth Phillips**
        "If it's Not Shamanic, is it Sham? An Examination of Media
        Responses to 'Woodland School' Art." *Anthropologica*, vol. 25 no. 1
        (1983) p. 117-132.

2936   **Boekestijn, Cees**
        "Intercultural Migration and the Development of Personal Identity:
        The Dilemma Between Identity Maintenance and Cultural Adapta-
        tion." *International Journal of Intercultural Relations*, vol. 12 no. 2
        (1988) p. 83-106.

2937   **Borso, Diana**
        Holman Island 1980/81: Prints. Holman Island, N.W.T.: Holman
        Eskimo Co-operative, 1981.

2938   **Bosley, Vivien**
        "Edmonton: Alive, Well, and in French." *Canadian Theatre Review*,
        no. 47 (1986) p. 140-143.

2939   **Bouchard, Claude**
"Genetic Basis of Racial Differences [In Performance]." *Canadian Journal of Sport Sciences/Journal canadien des sciences du sport,* vol. 13 no. 2 (1988) p. 103-108.

2940   **Boucher, Bernard**
"Le controle du développement culturel et ses enjeux: Le cas des conseils de la culture au Québec." *Canadian Issues,* vol. 9 (1988) p. 123-132.

2941   **Boucher, Michel**
"Côuts de transaction et faible nombre relatif des canadiens-français dans la LNH." *Actualité économique,* vol. 61 no. 3 (1985) p. 388-393.

2942   **Boucher, Michel**
"Les canadiens-français dans la ligue nationale de hockey: une analyse statistique." *Actualité économique,* vol. 60 no. 3 (1984) p. 308-325.

2943   **Bradford, Dorothy**
"Chinese Connections: Art and Craft Work Resulting from a Link-up with a School in China." *Art and Craft: A Scholastic Magazine,* no. 337 (1986) p. 16-19.

2944   **Brake, Michael**
Comparative Youth Culture: The Sociology of Youth Culture and Youth Subcultures in America, Britain and Canada. London: Routledge and Kegan Paul, 1985. 228 p.

2945   **Brasser, Ted J.**
"Backrest Banners Among the Plains Cree and Plains Ojibwa." *American Indian Art,* vol. 10 no. 1 (1984) p. 56-63.

2946   **Brenner, Rachel Feldhay**
A.M. Klein: The Father of Canadian Jewish Literature. Lewiston, N.Y.: Millen Press, 1989. 144 p.

2947   **Brenner, Rachel Feldhay**
"A.M. Klein and Mordecai Richler: Canadian Responses to the Holocaust." *Journal of Canadian Studies/Revue d'études canadiennes,* vol. 24 no. 2 (1989) p. 65-77.

2948   **Brenner, Rachel Feldhay**
Assimilation and Assertion: The Response to the Holocaust in Mordecai Richler's Writing. New York: P. Lang, 1989. 219 p.

2949   **Bringhurst, Robert, et al. eds.**
Visions: Contemporary Art in Canada. Vancouver: Douglas and McIntyre, 1983.

2950   **Brown, Ian W.**
"Soft Gold: A Northwest Coast Exhibition at the Peabody Museum, Harvard University." *American Indian Art*, vol. 10 no. 4 (1985) p. 24-29.

2951   **Brown, Lennox**
Cultural Crises: A Look at Cultural Impacts in Canada, the Caribbean and England. Toronto: Calypso House, 1981.

2952   **Bruchac, Joseph, ed.**
New Voices from the Longhouse: An Anthology of Contemporary Iroquois Writing. Greenfield Centre: The Greenfield Review Press, 1989. 294 p.

2953   **Brydon, Diana**
"Discovering 'Ethnicity': Joy Kogawa's *Obasan* and Mena Abdullah's *Time of the Peacock*." In: *Australian/Canadian Literatures in English: Comparative Perspectives*, edited by Russell McDougall and Gillian Whitlock. Melbourne: Methuen Australia, 1987, p. 94-110.

2954   **Bumsted, J.M.**
"Toward An Understanding of Popular Culture." *Alberta*, vol. 2 no. 1 (1989) p. 1-15.

2955   **Bumsted, J.M., ed.**
Language, Culture and Literary Identity in Canada/La langue, la culture et l'identité littéraire au Canada. Vancouver: University of British Columbia, 1987. 150 p. Papers presented at the 1984 Ottawa Conference on Language, Culture and Literary Identity in Canada. Published as Supplement 1 of *Canadian Literature/Littérature canadienne*, May 1987, follows issue no. 112 of that journal.

2956   **Burnett, Ron**
"Developments in Cultural Identity Through Film: The Documentary Film, the National Film Board and Quebec Nationalism." *Australian - Canadian Studies*, vol. 3 (1985) p. 44-52.

2957   **Bustamante, Rosalina E.**
"Filipinos and Sports." *Polyphony: The Bulletin of the Multicultural History Society of Ontario*, vol. 7 no. 1 (1985) p. 13-16.

2958   **Bustamante, Rosalina E.**
"Filipino Traditions in Music, Dance and Drama." *Polyphony: The Bulletin of the Multicultural History Society of Ontario*, vol. 5 no. 2 (1983) p. 99-103.

2959   **Busza, Andrew**
"Cultural Dislocation and Poetry." In: *Language, Culture and Literary Identity in Canada*, edited by J.M. Bumsted. Vancouver: University of British Columbia, 1987, p. 62-74. Papers presented at the 1984 Ottawa Conference on Language, Culture and Literary Identity in Canada. Published as Supplement 1 of *Canadian Literature/Littérature canadienne*, May 1987, follows issue no. 112 of that journal.

2960   **Butler, Barbara Louise**
The Persistence of Traditional Ways in an Inuit Community. Unpublished MA thesis, University of British Columbia, 1985. 158 leaves. Canadian theses on microfiche, 23637.

2961   **Byfield, Ted**
"Alberta's 'Genuine' Culture." *Alberta*, vol. 2 no. 1 (1989) p. 125-130.

2962   **Caccia, Fulvio**
"Le monde selon Nick: Rencontre avec le jeune peintre montrélais Nicola Palazzo." *Vice Versa*, vol. 2 no. 5 (1985) p. 12-15.

2963   **Caccia, Fulvio**
"L'ethnicité comme post-modernité." *Vice Versa*, vol. 2 no. 1 (1984) p. 12-13, 22.

2964   **Canada. Secretary of State. Multiculturalism Directorate**
Publications Supported by the Multiculturalism Directorate, Government of Canada. 2nd ed., revised. Ottawa: Secretary of State, 1982. 71, 31 p.

2965   **Canada. Task Force on Broadcasting Policy**
Report on Broadcasting Policy. Ottawa: Minister of Supply and Services, 1986. 731 p. Chairmen: Gerald Lewis Caplan and Florian Sauvageau. French language title: *Rapport du groupe de travail sur la politique de la radiodiffusion.*

2966   **Canadian Centre for Folk Culture: National Museum of Man**
Massey Foundation Collection: Works of Craft from the Massey Foundation Collection. Ottawa: Balmuir Book Publishers in cooperation with the National Museum of Man, National Museums of Canada, 1984.

2967   **Canadian Conference of the Arts**
"Searching for a Federal Cultural Policy/Á la recherche d'une politique culturelle fédérale." *Arts Bulletin/Bulletin arts*, vol. 12 no. 2 (1988) p. 1-24.

2968   **Canadian Conference of the Arts**
"Free Trade and Culture: Who Cares?/Le libre-échange et la culture: qui s'en fiche?" *Arts Bulletin/Bulletin arts*, vol. 11 no. 1 (1986) p. 1-25.

2969   **Canadian-U.S. Conference on Communications Policy**
Cultures in Collision: The Interaction of Canadian and U.S. Television Broadcasting Policies. New York: Praeger, 1983. 207 p. Conference held in 1983 in New York and sponsored by Syracuse University, the University of Toronto and the Americas Society.

2970   **Cardinal-Shubert, Joane**
"In the Red: Money, Appropriation, and Native Imagery." *Fuse Magazine*, vol. 13 no. 1/2 (1989) p. 20-28.

2971   **Carlson, Roy L., ed.**
Indian Art Traditions of the Northwest Coast. Burnaby, B.C.: Archaeology Press, Simon Fraser University, 1983.

2972   **Carpenter, Carole H.**
"Ethnic Joke-telling among Canadian Children." *Culture and Tradition*, vol. 9 (1985) p. 31-40.

2973   **Carpenter, Carole H. and Edith Fowke, comps.**
Explorations in Canadian Folklore. Toronto: McClelland and Stewart, 1985. 400 p.

2974   **Carpenter, Inta Gale**
Being Latvian in Exile: Folklore as Ideology. Unpublished PhD thesis, Indiana University, 1989. 292 pages.

2975   **Carr, Graham**
English-Canadian Literary Culture in the Modernist Milieu, 1920-40.
Unpublished PhD thesis, University of Maine, 1983. 316 p. Canadian
theses on microfiche, CT86-22788-X.

2976   **Carter, Susan**
"Theatre Employment for Asians: It's Not Easy, But There's Hope."
The Asianadian, vol. 6 no. 3 (1985) p. 16-18.

2977   **Centre d'études franco-canadiennes de l'Ouest**
La langue, la culture et la société des francophones de l'Ouest,
textes établis par Annette Saint-Pierre et Liliane Rodrigues. Saint-
Boniface, Man.: Le centre, 1985. 251 p. Les actes du quatrième
colloque du Centre d'études franco-canadiennes de l'Ouest tenu au
Collège universitaire de Saint-Boniface les 23 et 24 novembre 1984.

2978   **Chacko, James, ed.**
Cultural Sovereignty, Myth or Reality. Windsor, Ont.: Centre for
Canadian-American Studies, University of Windsor, 1987.
373 p. Conference held at the University of Windsor, Windsor,
Ontario, November 5-7, 1986

2979   **Chamberlain, Nigel C.**
Soccer Multiculturalism and the Canadian State. Unpublished MA
thesis, University of Alberta, 1983. 2 microfiches. Canadian theses on
microfiche, CT87-22627-4.

2980   **Chan, Anthony B.**
"Born Again Asian: The Making of a New Literature." *The Journal
of Ethnic Studies,* vol. 11 no. 4 (1984) p. 57-74.

2981   **Chan, Teri**
"Growing Up with Gung Fu or How to Learn Commitment." *The
Asianadian,* vol. 6 no. 3 (1985) p. 11-15.

2982   **Cheska, Alyce Taylor**
"Ethnicity, Identity, and Sport: The Persistence of Power."
International Review for the Sociology of Sport, vol. 22 no. 2
(1987) p. 99-110.

2983   **Cheska, Alyce Taylor**
"The Antigonish Highland Games: A Community's Involvement in
the Scottish Festival of Eastern Canada." *Nova Scotia Historical
Quarterly,* vol. 3 no. 1 (1983) p. 51-63.

2984   **Chiasson, Zenon**
"The Acadian Theatre." *Canadian Theatre Review*, no. 46
(1986) p. 50-57.

2985   **Chicules, Helen**
"Macedonian Sports." *Polyphony: The Bulletin of the Multicultural
History Society of Ontario*, vol. 7 no. 1 (1985) p. 44-46.

2986   **Chong, Jean**
"Can an Asian Play Lady Macbeth? - Jean Yoon Discusses Her
Theatre Experiences." *The Asianadian*, vol. 6 no. 2 (1985) p. 21-23.

2987   **Christensen, Rolf Buschardt**
"A Danish Contribution to Gymnastics: John A. Madsen."
*Polyphony: The Bulletin of the Multicultural History Society of
Ontario*, vol. 7 no. 1 (1985) p. 39-42.

2988   **Christopher, Robert**
"Narrators of the Arctic: Images and Movements in Northern
Narratives." *American Review of Canadian Studies*, vol. 18 no. 3
(1988) p. 259-270.

2989   **Cipywnyk, Raissa Sonia**
*The Effect of a Cultural Program in the Visual Arts on Students'
Ethnic Attitudes.* Unpublished MA thesis, University of British
Columbia, 1988. 134 p. Canadian theses on microfiche, 447370.

2990   **Cleland, Charles E.**
"Naub-Cow-Zo-Win Discs and Some Observations on the Origin and
Development of Ojibwa Iconography." *Arctic Anthropology*, vol. 22
no. 1 (1985) p. 131-140.

2991   **Clermont, Norman**
Le site iroquoien de Lanoraie: témoignage d'une maison-longue.
Montréal: Recherches amerindiennes au Québec, 1983.

2992   **Clift, Dominique**
The Secret Kingdom: Interpretations of the Canadian Character.
Toronto: McClelland and Stewart, 1989. 240 p.

2993   **Cody, Glenn**
"Difference with a Difference: World Of Music, Art and Dance
(WOMAD) Harbourfront, Toronto, August 9-14, 1988." *Fuse
Magazine*, vol. 12 no. 3/52 (1988) p. 42-43.

2994   Coe, Ralph T.
        Lost and Found Traditions: Native American Art, 1965-1985.
        Vancouver: Douglas and McIntyre, 1986. 288 p.

2995   Cohnstaedt, Joy
        "Human Rights and Canadian Cultural Policy." *Canadian Issues,* vol.
        12 (1989) p. 51-64.

2996   Cole, Douglas
        Captured Heritage: The Scramble for Northwest Coast Artifacts.
        Vancouver: Douglas and McIntyre, 1985.

2997   Collinson, Helen
        "Lars Haukaness: Artist and Instructor." *Alberta History,* vol. 32 no.
        4, (1984) p. 11-20.

2998   Colloque du Centre d'études franco-canadiennes de l'Ouest.
        La langue, la culture et la société des francophones de l'Ouest.
        Textes établis par Pierre-Yves Macquais, André Lalonde et Bernard
        Wilhelm. Régina, Sask.: Institute de recherche au Centre d'études
        bilingues, 1984. 258 p.

2999   Colombo, John Robert
        "Our Cosmopolitans: The Ethnic Canadian Writer in a Provincial
        Society." In: *Language, Culture and Literary Identity in Canada,*
        edited by J.M. Bumsted. Vancouver, B.C.: University of British
        Columbia, 1987, p. 90-100. Papers presented at the 1984 Ottawa
        Conference on Language, Culture and Literary Identity in Canada.
        Published as Supplement 1 of *Canadian Literature/Littérature
        canadienne,* May 1987, follows issue no. 112 of that journal.

3000   Colombo, John Robert, ed.
        Songs of the Indians. Ottawa: Oberon Press, 1983.

3001   Comeau, André
        *Artistes plasticiens: Canada, régime français et conquête, Bas-
        Canada et le Québec.* Montréal: Éditions Bellarmin, 1983.

3002   Comeault, Gilbert Louis
        "L'Affaire Forest: Franco-Manitobans in Search of Cultural and
        Linguistic Duality." In: *Quebec and Acadian Diaspora in North
        America,* edited by Raymond Breton and Pierre Savard. Toronto:
        Multicultural History Society of Ontario, 1982, p. 101-122.

3003 **Condon, Richard G.**
"The History and Development of Arctic Photography." *Arctic Anthropology*, vol. 26 no. 1 (1989) p. 46-87.

3004 **Conn, Richard**
"Blackfeet Slumak Necklaces." *Northwest Anthropological Research Notes*, vol. 21 no. 1/2 (1987) p. 111-120.

3005 **Conway, John F.**
"An 'Adapted Organic Tradition'." In: *In Search of Canada*, edited by Stephen R. Graubard. New Brunswick: Transaction Publishers, 1989, p. 381-396.

3006 **Conway, John F.**
"An 'Adapted Organic Tradition'." *Daedalus*, vol. 117 no. 4 (1988) p. 381-396.

3007 **Cook, Ramsay**
"Raising Kane: Noble Savagery and the Perils of Nineteenth-century Patronage — How Paul Kane Composes Canvases on Demand, Catering to Victorian Preconceptions." *Canadian Art*, vol. 2 no. 3 (1985) p. 60-63.

3008 **Cooke, Lanny**
"Don Cardinal — Bush Painter of the North." *The Beaver*, vol. 313 no. 4 (1983) p. 54-57.

3009 **Cooper, Andrew Fenton, ed.**
Canadian Culture: International Dimensions (Contemporary Affairs 50). Waterloo, Ont.: Centre on Foreign Policy and Federalism, University of Waterloo/Wilfrid Laurier University and Canadian Institute of International Affairs, 1985. 160 p.

3010 **Coulombe, Serge**
"Discrimination à l'embauche et performance supérieure des franco-québécois dans la LNH: une mise au point." *Actualité économique*, vol. 61 no. 4 (1985) p. 527-530.

3011 **Coulombe, Serge**
"Les francophones dans la Ligue nationale de hockey: une analyse économique de la discrimination." *Action économique*, vol. 61 no. 1 (1985) p. 73-91.

3012   **Cowan, Edward J.**
"Ethnic Sports in Canada: The Scottish Contribution." *Polyphony: The Bulletin of the Multicultural History Society of Ontario*, vol. 7 no. 1 (1985) p. 17-20.

3013   **Craig, Terrence**
Racial Attitudes in English-Canadian Fiction, 1905-1980. Waterloo, Ont.: Wilfrid Laurier University Press, 1987. 163 p.

3014   **Creighton, Helen**
La Fleur du Rosier: Acadian Folksongs. Sydney, N.S.: University College of Cape Breton Press, 1988.

3015   **Crumrine, N. Ross and Marjorie Helm, eds.**
The Power of Symbols: Masks and Masquerade in the Americas. Vancouver: University of British Columbia Press, 1983.

3016   **Cumbo, Enrico**
"Material Culture and Ethnic Studies." *Polyphony: The Bulletin of the Multicultural History Society of Ontario*, vol. 9 no. 1 (1987) p. 79-82.

3017   **Cumbo, Enrico**
"Recreational Activity at the Hamilton Venetian Club." *Polyphony: The Bulletin of the Multicultural History Society of Ontario*, vol. 7 no. 1 (1985) p. 59-63.

3018   **Cumbo, Enrico**
"Sports and Inter-ethnic Relations at Camp Petawawa." *Polyphony: The Bulletin of the Multicultural History Society of Ontario*, vol. 7 no. 1 (1985) p. 31-34.

3019   **Cumbo, Enrico**
"The Feast of the Madonna del Monte." *Polyphony: The Bulletin of the Multicultural History Society of Ontario*, vol. 5 no. 2 (1983) p. 84-85.

3020   **Cyr, J.J.**
"Test Item Bias in the WISC-R." *Canadian Journal of Behavioural Science/Revue canadienne des sciences de comportement*, vol. 19 no. 1 (1987) p. 101-107.

3021   **Czuboka, Michael**
"Canada's National Ukrainian Festival at Dauphin." *Forum: A Ukrainian Review*, no. 62 (1985) p. 12-15.

3022   **Da Breo, Hazel**
"Black Art in Ontario: Accepting Responsibility/L'art de noirs en Ontario: La prise de responsabilité." *Parallélogramme*, vol. 1 no. 3 (1988/89) p. 17-24.

3023   **Dabyeen, Cyril**
"Compromise and Self-expression: Problems of the Third World Writer in Canada." In: *Visible Minorities and Multiculturalism: Asians in Canada*, edited by K. Victor Ujimoto and Gordon Hirabayashi. Toronto: Butterworths, 1980, p. 329-334.

3024   **Dagg, Melvin Harold**
Beyond the Garrison: A Study of the Image of the Indian in Canadian Literature. Unpublished PhD thesis, University of New Brunswick, 1983. 3 microfiches. Canadian theses on microfiche, 64200.

3025   **Dalpé, Jean-Marie, et al.**
"Formes théâtrales et communauté franco-ontarienne," *Études canadiennes/Canadian Studies*, no. 15 (1983) p. 89-100.

3026   **Danys, Milda**
"Lithuanian Theatre in Canada after the Second World War." *Polyphony: The Bulletin of the Multicultural History Society of Ontario*, vol. 5 no. 2 (1983) p. 15-21.

3027   **Darch, Heather Anne**
The Breakdown of the Cultural Imperatives for the Establishment of Alliances Among the Native Tribes of the Great Lakes. Unpublished MA thesis, University of Guelph, 1988. 3 microfiches. Canadian theses on microfiche, CT89-28384-2.

3028   **Darewych, Daria**
"Ukrainian Art and Artists in Ontario." *Polyphony: The Bulletin of the Multicultural History Society of Ontario*, vol. 10 no. 1/2 (1988) p. 202-212.

3029   **Davis, Ann**
"Reflections: A Lacanian Approach to Christiane Pflug's Art." The *American Review of Canadian Studies*, vol. 15 no. 4 (1986) p. 433-448.

3030   **Davis, Ann and Robert Thacker**
"Pictures and Prose: Romantic Sensibility and the Great Plains in
Catlin, Kane and Miller." *Great Plains Quarterly*, vol. 6 no. 1
(1986) p. 3-20.

3031   **Day, Lois**
"Canadian North-west Coast Cultural Revival." *Anthropology Today*,
vol. 1 no. 4 (1985) p. 16-18.

3032   **Dayan-Davis, Claire**
"La femme, la tradition littéraire et la roman de l'Ouest." *Cahiers
franco-canadiens de l'Ouest*, vol. 1 no. 2 (1989) p. 185-196.

3033   **De Sousa, Alan**
"The First Portuguese Canadian Club." *Polyphony: The Bulletin of
the Multicultural History Society of Ontario*, vol. 7 no. 1
(1985) p. 65-66.

3034   **De Kerckhove, Derrick**
"Control of the Collective Mind: Free Trade and Canada's Cultural
Industries." *The Canadian Forum*, vol. 68 no. 782 (1989) p. 20-23.

3035   **De Lagrave, Jean-Paul**
"Les débuts de la maçonnerie au Québec." *Man and Nature/L'homme
et la Nature*, vol. 7 (1988) p. 195-207.

3036   **Deel, T. Van**
"Some Aspects of Dutch Literature." *Vice Versa*, vol. 2 (1985) p. 28-
30.

3037   **Delay, Florence and Jacques Roubaud**
Partition Rouge: poèmes et chants des indiens d'Amérique du Nord.
Paris: Seuil, 1988. 240 p.

3038   **Delgoy, Reva**
"Jewish Painters and Modernity—Montreal 1930-1945." *Outlook:
Canada's Progressive Jewish Magazine*, vol. 26 no. 3 (1988) p. 12-
13, 22.

3039   **Desaulniers, Jean-Pierre**
"La sociologie de la culture: problèmes d'adéquation." *Recherches
sociographiques*, vol. 26 no. 3 (1985) p. 458-484.

3040   **Deschamps, Carole**
*L'intégration et l'adaptation socioscolaire des jeunes immigrants:
une étude de cas.* Unpublished MSc thesis, Université de Montréal,
1987. 1 microfilm.

3041   **Deschênes, Gaston**
*Amable Charron et Chrysostôme Perrault, sculpteurs de Saint-Jean-Port-
Joli.* La Pocatière, Qué.: Société historique de la Côte-du-Sud, 1983.

3042   **DeShane, Nina**
"Ethnomusicology and the Study of North American Indian Music."
Queen's Quarterly, vol. 90 no. 1 (1983) p. 45.

3043   **DeSousa, Alan**
"The First Portuguese Canadian Club." *Polyphony: The Bulletin of the
Multicultural History Society of Ontario,* vol. 7 no. 1 (1985) p. 65-66.

3044   **Desrosiers, Roland**
La musique traditionelle au Québec: focale et instruments. Montréal:
Conseil canadien des arts populaires, Centre de documentation, 1980.

3045   **DeVarennes, Fernard**
Lieux et monuments historiques de l'Acadie. Moncton: Les éditions
d'Acadie, 1987. 245 p.

3046   **Deverell, Rita Shelton**
"When the Performer is Black." *Canadian Theatre Review,* no. 47
(1986) p. 56-62.

3047   **Dewar, John D.**
"The Introduction of Western Sports to the Indian People of Canada's
Prairie West." In: *Sport, Culture, Society: International and Sociological
Perspectives,* edited by J. A. Mangan and R. B. Small. London: E. and
F.N. Spon, 1986, p. 27-32. Proceedings of the 8th Commonwealth and
International Conference on Sport, Physical Education, Dance, Recreation
and Health, 1986, Glasgow.

3048   **Dhar, Meena**
"I Live By My Dance: A Conversation with Rina Singha." *The
Asianadian,* vol. 6 no. 2 (1985) p. 24-26.

3049   **Di Giovanni, Caroline**
"The Ontario Multicultural Theatre Association: the First Decade,
1971-81." *Polyphony: The Bulletin of the Multicultural History
Society of Ontario,* vol. 5 no. 2 (1983) p. 112-118.

3050 **Di Giovanni, Caroline, ed.**
Italian-Canadian Voices: An Anthology of Poetry and Prose, 1946-1983. Oakville, Ontario: Mosaic Press, 1984. 205 p.

3051 **Dimic, Milan**
"Canadian Literatures of Lesser Diffusion: Observations from a Systematic Standpoint." *Canadian Review of Comparative Literature/Revue canadienne de littérature comparée,* vol. 16 no. 3/4 (1989) p. 565-574.

3052 **Dion, Léon**
"The Mystery of Quebec." In: *In Search of Canada,* edited by Stephen R. Graubard. New Brunswick: Transaction Publishers, 1989, p. 283-217.

3053 **Dion, Léon**
"The Mystery of Quebec." *Daedalus,* vol. 117 no. 4 (1988) p. 283-318.

3054 **Doerksen, Victor G.**
"Arnold Dyck's Only Poem 'Keine Heimat — No Homeland'." *Mennonite Studies,* vol. 6 (1988) p. 134-143.

3055 **Doerksen, Victor G.**
"New Voices, New Issues in Mennonite Poetry." *Journal of Mennonite Studies,* vol. 5 (1987) p. 138-143.

3056 **Doerksen, Victor G.**
"In Search of a Mennonite Imagination." *Journal of Mennonite Studies,* vol. 2 (1984) p. 104-112.

3057 **Dorsinville, Max**
Le pays natal: Essais sur les littératures du Tiers-monde et du Québec. Montréal: Nouvelles éditions africaines, 1984.

3058 **Doucette, Leonard E.**
Theatre in French Canada 1606-1867. Toronto: University of Toronto Press, 1984.

3059 **Doucette, Leonard E.**
J'ai tant dansé: répertoire de danses québécoises. 2nd ed. Montréal: Éditions les sortilèges, 1981.

3060   **Dowsett, Gwendolyne Edna**
        The Vernacular Architecture of Three Ethnic Groups in Manitoba: A
        Comparative Analysis. Unpublished MA thesis, University of
        Manitoba, 1984. 3 microfiches. Canadian theses on microfiche,
        62383.

3061   **Dreisziger, N.F.**
        "*Sporthiradó*: Hungarian Sports News." *Polyphony: The Bulletin of*
        the Multicultural History Society of Ontario, vol. 7 no. 1
        (1985) p. 47-50.

3062   **Drew, Leslie,**
        Haida: Their Art and Culture. Surrey, B.C.: Hancock House, 1982.

3063   **Duerden, Charles**
        "Feast of Lebanon [Levee Hosted by Prince Edward Island's
        Lebanese Association]." *Atlantic Advocate*, vol. 80 no. 4
        (1989) p. 39-41.

3064   **Duffek, Karen**
        "'Authenticity' and the Contemporary Northwest Coast Indian Art
        Market." *B.C. Studies*, no. 57 (1983) p. 99.

3065   **Duffek, Karen**
        The Contemporary Northwest Coast Indian Art Market. Unpublished
        MA thesis, University of British Columbia, 1983. 310 leaves.
        Canadian theses on microfiche, 64918.

3066   **Duffek, Karen, and Bill Reid**
        Beyond the Essential Forum. U.B.C. Museum of Anthropology Note
        no. 19. Vancouver: University of British Columbia Press, 1986.

3067   **Duffus, Allan**
        Early Architecture of Portage la Prairie. Winnipeg, Manitoba:
        Historic Resources Branch, 1983.

3068   **Duffus, Allan, et al.**
        The Dwellings Fair: Churches of Nova Scotia, 1750-1830. Hantsport,
        N.S.: Lancelot Press, 1982.

3069   **Dumont, Fernand and Fernand Harvey**
        "La recherche sur la culture." *Recherches sociographiques*, vol. 26
        no. 1/2 (1985) p. 119-135.

3070 **Duthie, Beth**
"Reiss, Kihn and Tailfeathers: They Painted the Indians." *Glenbow*, vol. 5 no. 4 (1985) p. 4-7.

3071 **Dutton, Sue**
"Libraries are for Everyone: Public Libraries in Alberta Keep People Informed and Reading in More than Thirty Languages Other than English." *Heritage*, vol. 13 no. 1 (1985) p. 12-13.

3072 **Edson, Carol**
"Mormon Gravestones: A Folk Expression of Identity and Belief." *Dialogue: A Journal of Mormon Thought*, vol. 22 no. 4 (1989) p. 88-94.

3073 **Edwards, G.J. and G.T.**
"Langdon Kihn: Indian Portrait Artist." *The Beaver*, vol. 315 no. 3 (1985) p. 4-11.

3074 **Eklund, William**
"The Formative Years of the Finnish Organization of Canada." In: *Finnish Diaspora I: Canada, South America, Africa, Australia and Sweden*, edited by Michael G. Karni. Toronto: Multicultural History Society of Ontario, 1981, p. 49-61.

3075 **Elder, Bruce R.**
Image and Identity: Reflections on Canadian Film and Culture. Waterloo, Ont.: Wilfred Laurier University Press, 1989. 483 p.

3076 **Enninger, Werner**
"The Semiotic Structure of Amish Folk Costume and Its Function in the Organization of Face to Face Interaction." *Multimedial Communications*, no. 8 (1982) p. 86-124.

3077 **Epp, George K.**
"Der mennonitische Beitrag zur deutsch kanadischen Literatur." *German-Canadian Year Book/Deutschkanadisches jahrbuch*, vol. 6 (1981) p. 140.

3078 **Etungat, Kania**
Kania Etungat: Sculpture. Ottawa: Canadian Arctic Producers Co-operative, 1982.

3079   **Evan-Jones, Sandra**
"Shumka: Edmonton's Ukrainian Shumka Dancers, A Whirlwind of Dance, Color and Music!" *Dance in Canada/Danse au Canada*, no. 40 (1984) p. 2-4.

3080   **Everest, Beth**
"The Dance of the Stoneys: A Moral Issue." *Canadian Journal of Native Education*, vol. 16 no. 1 (1989) p. 1-5.

3081   **Feder, Norman**
"Museum Exhibition: The Jasper Grant Collection." *American Indian Art*, vol. 10 no. 3 (1985) p. 46-51.

3082   **Feder, Norman**
"The Side Fold Dress." *American Indian Art*, vol. 10 no. 1 (1984) p. 48-55.

3083   **Feldman, Anna**
"Yiddish Song." *Canadian Jewish Outlook*, vol. 23 no. 1-2, (1985) p. 7-8.

3084   **Fenton, William N.**
The False Faces of the Iroquois. The Civilisation of the American Indian Series. Norman, Oklahoma: University of Oklahoma Press, 1987. 522 p.

3085   **Fenton, William N.**
Masked Medicine Societies of the Iroquois. Ohsweken, Ont.: Iroqrafts, 1984.

3086   **Field, D.**
"Reminiscences of Samuel Rothschild." *Polyphony: The Bulletin of the Multicultural History Society of Ontario*, vol. 7 no. 1 (1985) p. 117-119.

3087   **Fitzhugh, William W.**
"The Nulliak Pendants and Their Relation to Spiritual Traditions in Northeast Prehistory." *Arctic Anthropology*, vol. 22 no. 1 (1985) p. 87-109.

3088   **Flannery, Regina and Mary Elizabeth Chambers**
"Each Man Has His Own Friends: The Role of Dream Visitors in Traditional East Cree Belief and Practice." *Arctic Anthropology*, vol. 22 no. 1 (1985) p. 1-22.

3089   **Flores, Toni**
"Art, Folklore, Bureaucracy and Ideology." *Dialectical Anthropology*, vol. 10 no. 3/4 (1986) p. 249-264.

3090   **Forbes, Ernest R.**
Challenging the Regional Stereotype: Essays on the 20th Century Maritimes. Fredericton, N.B.: Acadiensis Press, 1989. 220 p.

3091   **Forde, Jean**
"West Indian Sports and Recreation in Ontario." *Polyphony: The Bulletin of the Multicultural History Society of Ontario*, vol. 7 no. 1 (1985) p. 53-55.

3092   **Fowke, Edith**
Canadian Folklore. Don Mills, Ont.: Oxford University Press, 1988. 144 p.

3093   **Fowke, Edith, comp. and trans.**
Folktales of French Canada. Toronto: NC Press, 1982. 151 p.

3094   **Friesen, Gerhard K.**
"Life as a Sum of Shattered Hopes: Arnold Dyck's Letters to Gerhard J. Friesen (Fritz Senn)." *Mennonite Studies*, vol. 6 (1988) p. 124-135.

3095   **Froeschle, Hartmut**
"Foreward." In: *Nachrichten aus Ontario: Deutschsprachige Literatur in Kanada*. Hildesheim: Olms Presse, 1981. 290 p.

3096   **Frye, Northrop**
"Sharing the Continent." In: *A Passion for Identity: Introduction to Canadian Studies*, edited by Eli Mandel and David Taras. Toronto: Methuen, 1987, p. 206-215.

3097   **Fuerstenberg, Adam**
"From Yiddish to 'Yiddishkeit': A.M. Klein, J.I. Segal and Montreal's Yiddish Culture." *Journal of Canadian Studies/Revue d'études canadiennes*, vol. 19 no. 2 (1984) p. 66-81.

3098   **Fung, Richard**
"Eyes on Black Britain: An Interview with Filmmaker Issac Julien." *Fuse*, vol. 11 no. 4 (1987/88) p. 25-28.

3099   **Gabor, Bob**
        Costume of the Iroquois. Ohsweken, Ont.: Iroqrafts, 1983.

3100   **Gagnon, Gabriel**
        "Plaidoyer pour la convergence culturelle." *Possibles*, vol. 12 no. 3
        (1988) p. 37-44.

3101   **Gamble, Donald J.**
        "Crushing of Cultures: Western Applied Science in Northern
        Societies." *Arctic*, vol. 39 no. 1 (1986) p. 20-23.

3102   **Garfield, Viola E.**
        "Making a Bird or Chief's Rattle? Making a Box Design." *Northwest
        Anthropological Research Notes*, vol. 21 no. 1/2 (1987) 159-174.

3103   **Gates, Henry Louis, Jr.**
        "Authority, (White) Power and the (Black) Critic: It's All Greek to
        Me." *Cultural Critique*, no. 7 (1987) p. 19-46.

3104   **Georges, Robert A.**
        "Research Perspectives in Ethnic Folklore Studies." *Folklore and
        Mythology Studies*, vol. 7 (1983) p. 1-23.

3105   **Gibbins, Roger and Nel Nevitt**
        "A Comparison of English Canadian, Quebecois and American
        Respondents." *CPSA Papers/ACSP Contributions 1984*, Section D,
        paper 5, fiche 11. Paper presented at the 56th annual meeting of the
        Canadian Political Science Association, June 10-12, 1984, University
        of Guelph, Guelph, Ontario.

3106   **Gidmark, David**
        Birchbark Canoe: The Story of an Apprenticeship with the Indians.
        Brunstown, Ont.: General Store Publishing House, 1989. 160 p.

3107   **Gil-del-Real, Maria T.**
        "Potlatching and Face-maintenance Among the Kwakiutl of British
        Columbia." *Journal of Psychoanalytic Anthropology*, vol. 3 no. 3
        (1980) p. 295-308.

3108   **Glenbow — Alberta Institute**
        "The Spirit Sings: Artistic Traditions of Canada's First People."
        Glenbow, vol. 8 no. 1 (1988) p. 1-30.

3109   **Globerman, Steven**
Cultural Regulation in Canada. Toronto: Institute for Research on
Public Policy, 1983.

3110   **Goretz, Joel**
"A Disappearing Tradition: Mennonite Hog Butchering." *Mennonite
Life*, vol. 39 no. 4 (1984) p. 4-8.

3111   **Gorlach, Manfred**
"Die Stellung des Kanadischen Englisch." *Zeitschrift der Gesellschaft
für Kanada-Studien*, vol. 7 no. 1 (1987) p. 205-220.

3112   **Gowans, Alan**
"The Way We Look and What Makes Our Built Environment
Distinctively Canadian?" *Canadian Heritage*, no. 41 (1983) p. 9-24.

3113   **Grant, Barry K.**
"'Across the Great Divide': Initiation and Inflection in Canadian
Rock Music." *Journal of Canadian Studies/Revue d'études
canadiennes*, vol. 21 no. 1 (1986) p. 116-127.

3114   **Graubard, Stephen R., ed.**
In Search of Canada. New Brunswick, N.J.: Transaction Publishers,
1989. 396 p.

3115   **Greenstein, Michael**
"Secular Chassidism in Canadian Literature." *Outlook: Canada's
Progressive Jewish Magazine*, vol. 27 no. 4 (1989) p. 17-18; vol. 27
no. 5 (1989) p. 17-18.

3116   **Greenstein, Michael**
*Third Solitudes: Tradition and Discontinuity in Jewish-Canadian
Literature*. Montreal and Kingston: McGill-Queen's University Press,
1989.

3117   **Gregorovich, Andrew**
"Canada's Ukrainian Icon Stamp." *Forum: A Ukrainian Review*, no.
76 (1988) p. 2-3.

3118   **Gregorovich, Andrew**
"Mike Bossy: Ukrainian-Canadian All-time Hockey Great Retires."
Forum: A Ukrainian Review, no. 76 (1988) p. 24-25.

3119   **Gregorovich, Andrew**
"Ukrainian Film Festival 1988: Held at Ontario Film Theatre, Ontario Science Centre, Toronto, March 1-9, 1988." *Forum: A Ukrainian Review*, no. 73 (1988) p. 12-13.

3120   **Gregorovich, Andrew**
"Ukrainian Wooden Church in Niagara Falls." *Forum: A Ukrainian Review*, no. 72 (1987) p. 15-17.

3121   **Gregorovich, Andrew**
Gum San: Gold Mountain: Images of Gold Mountain, 1886-1947; March 30 to June 16, 1985, Vancouver Art Gallery. [catalogue] Vancouver: Vancouver Art Gallery, 1985, 80 p. Text in English and Chinese.

3122   **Gregorovich, Andrew**
"Ukrainian Slo-pitch Softball League." *Forum: A Ukrainian Review*, no. 62 (1985) p. 28-31.

3123   **Gregorovich, Andrew**
"Ukrainian Museum of Canada." *Forum: A Ukrainian Review*, no. 53 (1983/84) p. 11-13.

3124   **Gregorovich, Andrew**
"Alberta Ukrainian Pioneer Monument." *Forum: A Ukrainian Review*, no. 54 (1983) p. 6-9.

3125   **Gregorovich, Andrew**
"Ukrainian Christmas." *Forum: A Ukrainian Review*, no. 56 (1983) p. 6-9.

3126   **Gregorovich, Andrew**
"Tenth Vesna Festival, 1983: The World's Largest Ukrainian Cabaret." *Forum: A Ukrainian Review*, no. 53 (1982/83) p. 2-7.

3127   **Gregorovich, Andrew**
"International Exhibit of Ukrainian Artists." *Forum: A Ukrainian Review*, no. 52 (1982) p. 10-13.

3128   **Gregorovich, Andrew**
"Sports Achievements of Ukrainian Canadians." *Forum: A Ukrainian Review*, no. 52 (1982) p. 23-28.

3129 **Gregorovich, Andrew**
"Steve Podborske: World Ski Champion." *Forum: A Ukrainian Review*, no. 50 (1982) p. 3-10.

3130 **Gregorovich, Andrew and Joy Brittan**
"Joy Brittan: Our Very Own [Ukrainian] Cinderella." *Forum: A Ukrainian Review*, no. 57 (1983/84) p. 24-28.

3131 **Griffiths, Naomi**
"The Golden Age: Acadian Life, 1713-1748." *Histoire Sociale/Social History*, vol. XVII no. 33 (1984) p. 21-34.

3132 **Grohovaz, Gianni A.**
"If You Don't Know How to Play Bocce, Don't Come a Courting My Sister." *Polyphony: The Bulletin of the Multicultural History Society of Ontario*, vol. 7 no. 1 (1985) p. 129-130.

3133 **Grohovaz, Gianni A.**
"See You at Brandon Hall. Oh! ...I Mean the Italo-Canadian Recreation Club." *Polyphony: The Bulletin of the Multicultural History Society of Ontario*, vol. 7 no. 2 (1985) p. 98-104.

3134 **Grohovaz, Gianni**
"A Quest for Heritage: Piccolo Teatro Italiano." *Polyphony: The Bulletin of the Multicultural History Society of Ontario*, vol. 5 no. 2 (1983) p. 47-55.

3135 **Grubisic, Vinko**
"Croatian Athletes in Toronto." *Polyphony: The Bulletin of the Multicultural History Society of Ontario*, vol. 7 no. 1 (1985) p. 56-58.

3136 **Gruending, Dennis**
Gringo: Poems and Journals from Latin America. Moose Jaw: Coteau Books, 1983.

3137 **Gudjonsdottir, Elsa E.**
"Description of the Icelandic National Costume, Twentieth Century Version." *The Icelandic Canadian*, vol. 44 no. 1 (1985) p. 25-29.

3138 **Gundy, Jeff**
"Humility in Mennonite Literature." *The Mennonite Quarterly Review*, vol. 63 no. 1 (1989) p. 5-21.

3139   **Gundy, Jeff**
"Separation and Transformation: Tradition and Audience for Three Mennonite Poets." *Journal of Mennonite Studies*, vol. 4 (1986) p. 53-69.

3140   **Gunther, Erna**
"The Social Organization of the Haida as Reflected in Their State Carving." *Northwest Anthropological Research Notes*, vol. 21 no. 1/2 (1987) p. 345-352.

3141   **Hallett, Susan**
"Stan Hill: [Iroquois] Bone Carver." *The Beaver*, vol. 316 no. 1 (1985) p. 56-57.

3142   **Halpin, Marjorie M.**
Jack Shadbolt and the Coastal Indian Image. U.B.C. Museum of Anthropology Note no. 18. Vancouver: University of British Columbia Press, 1986. 58 p.

3143   **Handler, Richard**
"On Sociocultural Discontinuity: Nationalism and Cultural Objectification in Quebec." *Current Anthropology*, vol. 25 no. 1 (1985) p. 55-71.

3144   **Harding-Milburn, Wanda**
"The Chatham All-stars." *Polyphony: The Bulletin of the Multicultural History Society of Ontario*, vol. 7 no. 1 (1985) p. 111-116.

3145   **Harney, Robert F.**
"The Immigrant City." *Vice Versa*, no. 24, (1988) p. 4-6.

3146   **Harney, Robert F.**
"Immigrant Theatre." *Polyphony: The Bulletin of the Multicultural History Society of Ontario*, vol. 5 no. 2 (1983) p. 1-14.

3147   **Haseltine, Patrica, ed.**
East and Southeast Asian Material Culture in North America: Collections, Historical Sites and Festivals. New York: Greenwood Press, 1989. 163 p.

3148 **Haughton, Harry S.**
Social and Cultural Reproduction in the (Music) Curriculum Guideline Process in Ontario Education: Ethnic Minorities and Cultural Exclusion. Unpublished PhD thesis, University of Toronto, 1984. 4 microfiches. Canadian theses on microfiche, 65121.

3149 **Heath, Terrence**
Unrooted: The Life and Art of Ernest Lindner. Saskatoon, Sask.: Fifth House, 1983.

3150 **Helleiner, Frederick M., ed.**
Cultural Dimensions of Canada's Geography. Peterborough, Ont.: Dept of Geography, Trent University, 1984. 357 p. Proceedings of the German-Canadian Symposium, August 28-September 11, 1983.

3151 **Henry, Victoria**
"Breaking the Bonds of Art History: Robert Howle Puts His 'Native' Art Beyond the Reach of Anthropologists." *Canadian Forum,* vol. 68 no. 783 (1989) p. 22-23.

3152 **Hersch, Hank**
"Cat's Meow in Montréal: That's Andreas Galarraga—Le Grand Chat to Expo Fans." *Sports Illustrated,* vol. 69 no. 6 (1988) p. 50-52.

3153 **Hesje, Angeline**
"Pysanky: The Spiritual Meaning of Ukrainian Easter Egg Art Is Revealed." *Canadian Lutheran,* vol. 3 no. 4 (1988) p. 10-11, 26.

3154 **B.H. [Benedykt Heydenkorn]**
"Paderewski in Toronto." *Polyphony: The Bulletin of the Multicultural History Society of Ontario,* vol. 6 no. 2 (1984) p. 68.

3155 **B.H. [Benedykt Heydenkorn]**
"Polish Theatre." *Polyphony: The Bulletin of the Multicultural History Society of Ontario,* vol. 6 no. 2 (1984) p. 110-112.

3156 **Heydenkorn, Benedykt**
"Polish Theatre." *Polyphony: The Bulletin of the Multicultural History Society of Ontario,* vol. 5 no. 2 (1983) p. 78-80.

3157 **Hickey, Clifford G.**
"An Examination of Processes of Cultural Change Among Nineteenth Century Copper Inuit." *Études Inuit Studies,* vol. 8 no. 1 (1984) p. 13-35.

3158   **Highwater, Jamake**
"North American Indian Art: A Special Way of Seeing," *Arts West*, vol. 8 no. 5 (1983) p. 12-17.

3159   **Hill, Gordon**
Journey Through Time: An Introduction to the Archaeology and Cultural History of the MSTW Planning District. Winnipeg: Department of Culture, Heritage and Recreation, 1984.

3160   **Hilliker, Rebecca**
"Alaska's Lost Heritage: The Unprecedented Flowering of Drama, Dance and Song in the 19th Century Potlatch of the Northwest Coast Indians." *Journal of Popular Culture*, vol. 21 no. 4 (1988) p. 63-76.

3161   **Himes, John H.**
"Racial Variation in Physical and Body Composition." *Canadian Journal of Sport Sciences/Journal Canadien des sciences du sport*, vol. 13 no. 2 (1988) p. 117-126.

3162   **Hirabayashi, Joanne**
"The Chilkat Weaving Complex." *Northwest Anthropological Research Notes*, vol. 21 no. 1/2 (1987) p. 49-61.

3163   **Hirabayashi, Richard**
"Ethnic Consciousness and an Analytical Framework for Culturally Sensitive Material." *Canadian Children*, vol. 10 nos. 1/2 (1985-86) p. 81-89.

3164   **Hoag, Peter Lochrie**
Acculturating Eskimo Arts: The Diffusion of Government Sponsored Production Facilities in Alaska and Canada. Unpublished PhD thesis, University of Michigan, 1981. Canadian theses on microfiche, 1139.

3165   **Hoe, Ban Seng**
"Chinese Cultural Traditions in Canada: Main Themes of an Ethnic Hall Exhibition at a Federal Museum." *Canadian Ethnic Studies/ Études ethniques au Canada*, vol. 19 no. 3 (1987) p. 148-162.

3166   **Holeton, Lise**
"The Tourbillions: The Dancers of the Good Old Times!/Les Tourbillions: Les danseurs du bon vieux temps!" *Heritage Link*, vol. 4 no. 2 (1989) p. 21-33.

3167   **Holmes, Douglas**
Northerners: Profiles of People in the Northwest Territories. Toronto:
James Lorimer and Co., 1989. 190 p.

3168   **Houle, Alain**
"Fleurimond Constantineau: mémorialiste d'un mode de vie." *North/
Nord,* vol. 28 no. 2 (1981) p. 46-49.

3169   **Houston, Alma and Helen Burgess, eds.**
Inuit Art: An Anthology. Winnipeg: Watson and Dwyer, 1988. 128 p.

3170   **Hubbard, Lorraine D.**
"Black Theatre Canada: A Decade of Struggle." *Polyphony: The
Bulletin of the Multicultural History Society of Ontario,* vol. 5 no. 2
(1983) p. 57-65.

3171   **Hungarian Studies Review**
"Hungarian Cultural Presence in North America." Special issue,
Hungarian Studies Review, vol. 8 no. 2 (1981).

3172   **Ingber, Judith Brin, ed.**
"Dancing into Marriage: Collected Papers on Jewish Wedding
Dances." *Dance Research Journal,* vol. 17/18 no. 1/2 (1985/
1986) p. 49-86.

3173   **Injejikian, Hasmig**
"The Musical Repertory of Early Armenian Settlers." *Polyphony: The
Bulletin of the Multicultural History Society of Ontario,* vol. 4 no. 2
(1982) p. 107-116.

3174   **Institut für Auslandersbeziehungen, Stuttgart**
"Auf dem Wege zu einer Kulturengesellschaft? Die Jahrestagung
1989 des Arbeitskreises Kultur und Entwicklung." *Zeitschrift für
Kuluraustausch,* vol 39 no. 2 (1989) p. 123-234.

3175   **Ipellie, Alootook**
"My Story." *North/Nord,* vol. 30 no. 1 (1983) p. 54-58.

3176   **Islam, Sadequl**
"The Political Economy of Free Trade and Cultural Sovereignty."
CPSA Papers/ACSP Contributions 1987, Section L, paper 7, fiche 2.
Paper presented at the 59th annual meeting of the Canadian Political
Science Association, June 6-8, 1987, McMaster University, Hamilton,
Ontario.

3177   **Israel, Milton and Kalyan Banerjee**
"Bengali Theatre in Toronto." *Polyphony: The Bulletin of the Multicultural History Society of Ontario*, vol. 5 no. 2 (1983) p. 22-24.

3178   **Isseman, Betty**
"Inuit Skin Clothing: Construction and Motifs." *Études Inuit Studies*, vol. 9 no. 2 (1985) p. 101-119.

3179   **Jackson, David**
"Union Activism: Punjabi Theatre in B.C." *Fuse*, vol. 9 no. 3 (1985) p. 10-14.

3180   **Jackson, Marion E.**
Baker Lake Inuit Drawings: A Study in the Evolution of Artistic Self-consciousness. Unpublished PhD thesis, University of Michigan, 1985. 347 p. Canadian theses on microfiche, CT87-23944-9.

3181   **Jalava, Mauri A.**
"National Finnish Organizations in Canada: Finnish Cultural Associations in Ontario, 1945-80." *Polyphony: The Bulletin of the Multicultural History Society of Ontario*, vol. 3 no. 2 (1981) p. 104-110.

3182   **Jenkins, Rita-Marie**
"Anatomy of a Community Festival: Brantford's International Village Festival." *Recreation Canada*, vol. 44 no. 3 (1986) p. 23-30.

3183   **Johannsen, Christina B. and John P. Ferguson**
Iroquois Arts: A Directory of a People and Their Work. Southworld: Association for the Advancement of Native North American Arts and Crafts, 1983. 406 p.

3184   **Johnston, Thomas F.**
"Community History and Environment as Wellspring of Inupiaq Eskimo Songtexts." *Anthropos*, vol. 83, nos. 1-3 (1988) p. 162-171.

3185   **Johnston, Thomas F.**
"Blacks in Art and Music in Western Canada: Jazz and Classical." *Anthropological Journal of Canada/Journal anthropologique du Canada*, vol. 19 no. 2 (1981) p. 23-30.

3186 **Jonaitis, Aldona**
From the Land of the Totem Poles: The Northwest Coast Indian Art Collection at the American Museum of National History. New York: American Museum of Natural History, 1988. 271 p.

3187 **Jonasson, Eric**
"The Husavick 'Rune Stone'." *The Icelandic Canadian*, vol. 44 no. 4 (1986) p. 11-15.

3188 **Jorgensen, Joseph G.**
"Land is Cultural, So is a Commodity: The Locus of Differences Among Indians, Cowboys, Sod-busters, and Environmentalists." *The Journal of Ethnic Studies*, vol. 12 no. 3 (1984) p. 1-22.

3189 **Jurak, Mirko, ed.**
Cross-cultural Studies: American, Canadian, and European Literatures, 1945-1985. Ljubljana, Yugoslavia: English Department, Filozofska fakulteta, Edvard Kardelj University, 1988. 521 p.

3190 **Kahn, Lisa**
"Culture: International Bridge or Barrier? Literary Reflections on Their Acculturation Process by Contemporary Emigrant and Immigrant Writers." *Zeitschrift für Kulturaustausch*, vol. 39 no. 1 (1989) p. 9-13.

3191 **Kalsey, Surjeet**
"Canadian Punjabi Literature." In: *A Meeting of Streams: South Asian Canadian Literature*, edited by M.G. Vassanji. Toronto: TSAR Publications, 1985, p. 109-119.

3192 **Kaprielian, Isabel**
"From Baronian to Adamov: A Brief Sketch of Armenian Drama in Ontario." *Polyphony: The Bulletin of the Multicultural History Society of Ontario*, vol. 5 no. 2 (1983) p. 107-111.

3193 **Kaprielian, Isabel**
"Armenian Folk-belief with Special Emphasis on *Veeag*." *Polyphony: The Bulletin of the Multicultural History Society of Ontario*, vol. 4 no. 2 (1982) p. 101-106.

3194 **Karp, Ellen, comp.**
Many are Strong Among Strangers: Canadian Songs of Immigration. Ottawa: National Museums of Canada, 1984. 138 p.

3195   **Karsh, Yousuf**
Karsh, A Fifty-year Retrospective. Toronto: University of Toronto Press, 1983.

3196   **Keilor, Elaine**
"Les tambours des athapascans du nord." *Recherches amérindiennes au Québec,* vol. 15 no. 4 (1985/86) p. 43-52.

3197   **Khan, Nuzrat Yar**
Urdu Literature in Canada: A Preliminary Survey. Edited by Michael S. Batts. [Ottawa]: Department of the Secretary of State of Canada, Multiculturism, 1988. 45 p.

3198   **Khan, Nuzrat Yar**
"Urdu Language and Literature in Canada." In: *A Meeting of Streams: South Asian Canadian Literature,* edited by M.G. Vassanji. Toronto: TSAR Publications, 1985, p. 95-108.

3199   **Kidd, Bruce**
"The Worker's Sports Movement in Canada, 1924-40: The Radical Immigrant's Alternative." *Polyphony: The Bulletin of the Multicultural History Society of Ontario,* vol. 7 no. 1 (1985) p. 80-88.

3200   **Kidd, Ross**
"Reclaiming Culture: Indigenous Performers Take Back Their Show." *The Canadian Journal of Native Studies,* vol. 4 no. 1 (1984) p. 105-20.

3201   **King, Carolyn**
"Cultural Collision and a Collection: Tracing a Collection of West Coast Indian Art." *Alberta Report,* vol. 15 no. 45 (1988) p. 42-43.

3202   **King, Thomas, Chery Calver, and Helen Hoy, eds.**
Native in Literature. Toronto: ECW Press, 1987. 232 p.

3203   **Kjeldsen, Erik K.M.**
"Integration of Minorities into Olympic Sport in Canada and the U.S.A." *Journal of Sport and Social Issues,* vol. 8 no. 2 (1984) p. 30-44.

3204   **Klassen, Doreen Helen**
Singing Mennonite: Low German Songs Among the Mennonites. Winnipeg: University of Manitoba Press, 1989. 330 p.

3205   **Klymasz, Robert B. and Kenneth Peacock**
The Ukrainian Folk Ballad in Canada. Immigrant Communities and
Ethnic Minorities in the United States and Canada, no. 65. New
York: AMS Press, 1989. 333 p.

3206   **Knowles, Valerie**
"Sculptor of the North: [Harold Pfeiffer]." *North/Nord*, vol. 30 no. 2
(1983) p. 46-49.

3207   **Kocjancic, Cvetka**
"Slovenians Love Sports." *Polyphony: The Bulletin of the Multicultural
History Society of Ontario*, vol. 7 no. 1 (1985) p. 27-28.

3208   **Kolessa, Filiaret**
Ukrains' ka usna slovensnist. Edmonton: Canadian Institute of
Ukrainian Studies, Kacmac Alliance of Gaspesia, 1981.

3209   **Konrad, Victor A.**
"Against the Tide: French Canadian Barn Building Traditions in the
St. John Valley of Maine." *The American Review of Canadian
Studies*, vol. 12 no. 2 (1982) p. 22-36.

3210   **Kostyniuk, Brent**
"The Art of Chinese Brush Painting [Wang Ziho]." *Heritage*, vol. 13
no. 2 (1985) p. 11-12.

3211   **Krashinsky, Michael**
"Do Hockey Teams Discriminate Against French Canadians?: A
Comment on 'Discrimination and Performance Differentials in the
National Hockey League'." *Canadian Public Policy/Analyse de
politiques*, vol. 15 no. 1 (1989) p. 94-97. A critique of an article by
M. Lavoie, G. Grenier and S. Coulombe: "Discrimination and
Performance Differentials in the National Hockey League." *Canadian
Public Policy/Analyse de politiques*, vol. 13 no. 4 (1987) p. 407-422.

3212   **Krawchuk, Peter**
"Our Ukrainian Symbols." *Ukrainian Canadian*, vol. 42 no. 736/230
(1989) p. 7-9.

3213   **Kreisel, Henry**
"The 'Ethnic' Writer in Canada." In: *Identifications: Ethnicity and
the Writer in Canada*, edited by Jars Balan. Edmonton: Canadian
Institute of Ukrainian Studies, 1982, p. 1-13.

3214   **Kremblewski, Ed Zbys**
"Polish Canadian Community Sports." *Polyphony: The Bulletin of the Multicultural History Society of Ontario*, vol. 7 no. 1 (1985) p. 64.

3215   **Krishnan, V.**
"The Relationship Between Income and Fertility: The Role of Immigrant Culture."In: *Contributions to Demography, Methodological and Substantive: Essays in Honour of Dr. Karol J. Krotki.* Edmonton: University of Alberta, Department of Sociology, 1987, p. 483-504.

3216   **Kristjanson, Gustaf**
"Sveinbjörn Sveinbjörnsson, Musician." *The Icelandic Canadian*, (1983) p. 42-44.

3217   **Kroetsch, Robert**
"The Grammar of Silence: Narrative Patterns in Ethnic Writing." *Canadian Literature*, no. 106 (1985) p. 65-74.

3218   **Kroker, Arthur**
"The Cultural Imagination and the National Questions." *Canadian Journal of Political and Social Theory*, vol. 6 no. 1/2 (1982) p. 5-11.

3219   **Kroller, Eva-Marie**
"The Cultural Contribution of the 'Other' Ethnic Groups: A New Challenge to Comparative Canadian Literature." In: *Critical Approaches to the New Literatures in English: A Selection of Papers*, edited by Dieter Riemenschneider. Essen, Germany: Berlag die Blaue Eule, 1989, p. 83-90. Paper presented at the 10th annual Conference on 'Commonwealth' Literature and Language Studies, Koenigstein, June 11-14, 1987.

3220   **Kumove, Shirley**
Words Like Arrows: A Collection of Yiddish Folk Sayings. Toronto: University of Toronto Press, 1984.

3221   **Kurelek, William and Joan Murray**
Kurelek's Vision of Canada. Edmonton: Hurtig, 1983; Oshawa, Ont: Robert Mclaughlin Gallery, 1982.

3222   **Labelle, Ronald, ed.**
Inventaire des sources en folklore acadien. Moncton, N.B.: Centre d'études acadiennes, Université de Moncton, 1984.

3223 **Laine, Edward W.**
"National Finnish Organizations in Canada: The Finnish Organization of Canada, 1923-40, and the Development of a Finnish Canadian Culture." *Polyphony: The Bulletin of the Multicultural History Society of Ontario*, vol. 3 no. 2 (1981) p. 81-90.

3224 **Lambert, Wallace E.**
"The Fate of Old-Country Values in a New Land: A Cross-national Study of Child-rearing." *Canadian Psychology/Psychologie canadienne*, vol. 28 no. 1 (1987) p. 9-20.

3225 **Lamonde, Yvan**
"American Cultural Influence in Quebec: A One-way Mirror." In: *Problems and Opportunities in U.S.-Quebec Relations*, edited by Alfred O. Hero, Jr., and Marcel Daneau. Boulder, Colorado: Westview Press, 1984, p. 106-126.

3226 **Lamy, Laurent and Jean-Claude Hurni**
Architecture contemporaine au Québec, 1960-70. Montréal: L'héxagone, 1983.

3227 **Langelle, Jean and Ian Badgley**
"The Ancient Dwellings of Arctic Québec." *The Beaver*, vol. 312 no. 4 (1982) p. 26-31.

3228 **Laroque, Erma**
"The Metis in English Canadian Literature." *The Canadian Journal of Native Studies*, vol. 3 no.1 (1983) p. 85-94.

3229 **Lau, Paulus**
"Faces of Enigma: The Art of Shuk Cheung." *The Asianadian*, vol. 6 no. 3 (1985) p. 19-20.

3230 **Lavoie, Laurent**
"La vie intellectuelle et les activitiés culturelles à la forteresse de Louisbourg, 1713-1758." *Man and Nature/L'Homme et nature*, vol. 4 (1985) p. 129-138.

3231 **Lavoie, Marc**
"Discrimination and Performance Differentials in the National Hockey League." *Canadian Public Policy/Analyse de politiques*, vol. 13 no. 4 (1987) p. 407-422.

3232 **Le Blanc, Alonzo**
Arthur Le Blanc, acadien: violoniste-virtuose. Moncton, N.B.: Musée acadien, 1982.

3233 **Lea, Joanne**
House and Heritage: A Study of Ethnic Vernacular Architecture of 1880-1920 in Rural Alberta. Unpublished MA thesis, University of Calgary, 1985. 2 microfiches. Canadian theses on microfiche, CT86-27127-7.

3234 **Lea-McKeown, Mark Young**
The Importance of Native Music Culture in Education at a Manitoba Ojibwa Reserve from an Ethnological Perspective. Unpublished PhD thesis, University of Alberta, 1987. 3 microfiches. Canadian theses on microfiche, CT89-24428-6.

3235 **Ledohowski, Edward M.**
Architectural Heritage, the Eastern Interlake Planning District. Winnipeg, Manitoba: Historic Resources Branch, 1983.

3236 **Ledohowski, Edward M.**
Les arts populairs acadiens de l'Île-du-Prince-Édouard. Charlottetown, P.E.I.: The Prince Edward Island Heritage Foundation and La Société Saint-Thomas d'Aquin, 1982.

3237 **Lee, Molly**
"Objects of Knowledge: The Communicative Aspect of Baleen Baskets." *Études Inuit Studies*, vol. 9 no. 1 (1985) p. 163-182.

3238 **Lee, Molly and Nelson H.H. Graburn**
"The Living Arctic: Hunters of the Canadian North—An Exhibit at the Museum of Mankind." *American Indian Art Magazine*, vol. 14 no. 1 (1988) p. 54-59.

3239 **Lehto, Lilian K.**
"Some Cross-cultural Observations of a Third Generation Finnish-American." *Siirtolaisuus-Migration*, no. 3, 1988 p. 16-18.

3240 **Leonard, Wilbert M. II**
"Salaries and Race in Professional Baseball: The Hispanic Component." *Sociology of Sport*, vol. 5 no. 3 (1988) p. 278-284.

3241   **Lesoway, Marie**
*Out of the Peasant Mold: A Structural History of the M. Hawreliak
Home in Shandro, Alberta.* Historical Resources Division, Historic
Sites Service, Occasional Paper no. 16. Edmonton: Alberta Culture
and Multiculturalism, Historical Resources Division, Historic Sites
Service, 1989. 166 p.

3242   **Levental, Igar and Jessica**
"Russian Dancers in Alberta: The Start of a New Era of Cultural
Exchange." *Dance in Canada/Danse au Canada,* no. 47 (1986) p. 18-
21.

3243   **Levesque, George A.**
"Black Culture, the Black Esthetic, Black Chauvinism: A Mild
Dissent." *The Canadian Review of American Studies,* vol. 12 no. 3
(1981) p. 275-285.

3244   **Levin, Martin**
"The Founding and Restoration of Canada's Oldest Surviving
Synagogue: A Different Jewish History." *Canadian Jewish Historical
Society Journal/Société de l'histoire juive canadienne,* vol. 8 no. 1
(1984) p. 1-11.

3245   **Levitan, Seymour**
"Canadian Yiddish Writers." In: *Identifications, Ethnicity and the
Writer in Canada: Conference Papers,* edited by Jars Balan.
Edmonton: Canadian Institute of Ukrainian Studies, 1982, p. 116-134.

3246   **Levitt, Cyril and William Shaffir**
"Baseball and Ethnic Violence in Toronto: The Case of the Christie
Pits Riot, August 16, 1933." *Polyphony: The Bulletin of the
Multicultural History Society of Ontario,* vol. 7 no. 1 (1985) p. 67-
72.

3247   **Lewis, Tom and Robert Jungman, eds.**
*On Being Foreign: Cultural Shock in Short Fiction — An
International Anthology.* Burlington: Intercultural Books, 1986. 308 p.

3248   **Li, Jian**
Cultural Conventions in Greetings Between Chinese and Canadians.
Unpublished MA thesis, University of Toronto, 1987.

3249   **Ligocki, Gordon**
"Lithuanian Art '89." *Lituanus*, vol. 35 no. 4 (1989) p. 44-55.

3250   **Lipset, Seymour Martin**
"Canada and the United States: The Cultural Dimension." *Canada and the United States: Enduring Friendship, Persistent Threat*, edited by Charles F. Doran and John H. Sigler. Englewood Cliffs, N.J.: Prentice-Hall, 1985, p. 109-160.

3251   **Livingstone, Donna**
"She Walks in Two Worlds: Canadian Indian Author Eleanor Bass." *Glenbow*, vol. 8 no. 2 (1988) p. 8-9.

3252   **Livingstone, Donna**
"The Spirit Sings: Artistic Tradititions of Canada's First Peoples." *Journal of the West*, vol. 27 no. 1 (1988) p. 84-88.

3253   **Loewen, Harry**
"Leaving Home: Canadian-Mennonite Literature in the 1980s." *Ethnic Forum*, vol. 8 no. 1 (1988) p. 94-105.

3254   **Loewen, Harry**
"The Mennonite Writer as Witness and Critic." *Journal of Mennonite Studies*, vol. 2 (1984) p. 113-123.

3255   **Loewen, Harry**
"Mennonite Literature in Canada: Beginnings, Reception and Study." *Journal of Mennonite Studies*, vol. 1 (1983) p. 119-132.

3256   **Loriggio, Francesco**
"The Question of the Corpus: Ethnicity and Canadian Literature." In: *Future Indicative: Literary Theory and Canadian Literature*, edited by John Moss. Ottawa: University of Ottawa Press, 1986, p. 53-68.

3257   **Low, Jean**
"Dr. Charles Frederick Newcombe: The Alienist Who Became Collector of the Native Treasures of the Pacific Northwest." *The Beaver*, vol. 312 no. 4 (1982) p. 32-39.

3258   **Lowe, Jeff**
"Canada's Cities and the American Psyche." *City Magazine*, vol. 10 no. 1 (1988) p. 11-12.

3259 **Lukic, Milka**
"The Serbian Folklore Ensemble 'Kolo'." In: *Serbs in Ontario: A Socio-cultural Description*, edited by Sofija Skoric and George Vid Tomashevich. Toronto: Serbian Heritage Academy, 1987, p. 176-182.

3260 **Lupul, Manoly R., ed.**
Continuity and Change: The Cultural Life of Alberta's First Ukrainians. Edmonton: Canadian Institute of Ukrainian Studies, University of Alberta, 1988. 268 p.

3261 **Lupul, Manoly R., ed.**
Visible Symbols: Cultural Expression Among Canada's Ukrainians. Edmonton: Canadian Institute of Ukrainian Studies, 1984. 204 p.

3262 **Lyford, Carrie**
Iroquois: Their Art and Crafts. Surrey, B.C.: Hancock House Publishers, 1989. 128 p.

3263 **Lyford, Carrie**
Iroquois: Their Art, Craft and Culture. Surrey, B.C.: Hancock House, 1985.

3264 **Lynge, Finn**
"Cultural Genocide of Tomorrow or: A Future for Us All?" *Études Inuit Studies*, vol. 9 no. 2 (1985) p. 21-26.

3265 **Lyons, Douglas C.**
"Blacks and 50 Years of T.V.: Ten Memorable Moments." *Ebony*, vol. 44 no. 11 (1989) p. 70, 72, 74, 76.

3266 **Lyons, Douglas C.**
"Ben Johnson: The World's Fastest Human." *Ebony*, vol. 43 no. 7 (1988) p. 76-78, 82-85.

3267 **MacKinnon, Neil**
"A Caustic Look at Shelburne Society in 1781." *Acadiensis*, vol. 17 no. 2 (1988) p. 139-142.

3268 **MacLean, John**
"A Tribute to the Red River Cart." *Alberta History*, vol. 31 no. 1 (1983) p. 33-37.

3269   **Maddin, Guy**
"An Interview with Lorna Tergesen, President, Icelandic Festival of Manitoba." *The Icelandic Canadian*, vol. 67 no. 1 (1988) p. 10-16.

3270   **Mah, Daniel**
"Early Chinese Sports in Toronto." *Polyphony: The Bulletin of the Multicultural History Society of Ontario*, vol. 7 no. 1 (1985) p. 120-122.

3271   **Maillet, Marguerite**
Histoire de la littérature acadienne: de rêve en rêve. Moncton, N.B.: Éditions d'Acadie, 1983.

3272   **Makaryk, Irena R., ed.**
"Contemporary Ukrainian Poetry." *Studia Ucrainica*, no. 4 (1988) p. 1-128.

3273   **Maley, Alan and Alan Duff**
The Inward Ear: Poetry in the Language Classroom. Cambridge: Cambridge University Press, 1989. 186 p.

3274   **Malin, Edward**
Totem Poles of the Pacific Northwest Coast. Portland, Oregon: Timber Press, 1986. 187 p.

3275   **Malina, Robert M.**
"Racial/Ethnic Variation in the Motor Development and Performance of American Children." *Canadian Journal of Sport Sciences/Journal canadien des sciences du sport*, vol. 13 no. 2 (1988) p. 136-143.

3276   **Man, Alfred Young**
"Token and Taboo: Academia vs. Native Art." *Fuse*, vol. 11 no. 6 (1988) p. 46-48.

3277   **Markoff, Irene**
"Persistence of Old-world Cultural Expression in the Traditional Music of Bulgarian Canadians." *Polyphony: The Bulletin of the Multicultural History Society of Ontario*, vol. 6 no. 1 (1984) p. 73-74.

3278   **Marimer, Jean**
"L'Acadie dans son théâtre." *Études canadiennes/Canadian Studies*, no. 13 (1982) p. 201-207.

3279   **Marmier, Jean**
"Les ouvrages d'histoire littéraire française du Canada." *Études canadiennes/Canadian Studies*, no. 13 (1982) p. 125.

3280   **Marquis, Greg**
"Country Music: The Folk Music in Canada." *Queen's Quarterly*, vol. 95 no. 2 (1988) p. 291-309.

3281   **Marr, Carolyn J.**
"Taken Pictures: On Interpreting Native American Photographs of the Southern Northwest Coast." *Pacific Northwest Quarterly*, vol. 80 no. 2 (1989) p. 52-61.

3282   **Marsh, Winifred Petchey**
People of the Willow: The Padlimiut Tribe of the Caribou Eskimo Portrayed in Watercolors. Toronto: Anglican Book Centre, 1983.

3283   **Martin, Ged and Jeffrey Simpson**
Canada's Heritage in Scotland. Toronto: Dundurn Press, 1989. 245 p.

3284   **Martin, Nicole V.**
"Les modèles de financement de la culture au Canada." *Canadian Issues*, vol. 9 (1988) p. 143-154.

3285   **Massey, Norman**
"Montréal Yiddish Conference." *Outlook: Canada's Progressive Jewish Magazine*, vol. 26 no. 5 (1988) p. 7, 9.

3286   **Matsumoto, David and Tsutomu Kudoh**
"Cultural Similarities and Differences in Semantic Dimensions of Body Postures." *Journal of Nonverbal Behavior*, vol. 11 no. 3 (1987) p. 166-179.

3287   **Matthews, K.**
Our Newfoundland and Labrador Cultural Heritage. Scarborough, Ont.: Prentic-Hall, 1984.

3288   **Maud, Ralph**
A Guide to B.C. Indian Myth and Legend: A Short History of Myth Collecting and a Survey of Published Texts. Vancouver: Talonbooks, 1982. 218 p.

3289   **May, Cedric**
       Minorities and Mother Country Imagery. St. John's: Institute of
       Social and Economic Research, Memorial University, 1984.

3290   **May, Cedric**
       "Les chances pour la parole acadienne de se faire entendre: étude
       d'un recueil d'Herménégilde Chiasson." *Études canadiennes/
       Canadian Studies*, no. 13 (1982) p. 209-17.

3291   **Mazza, Antonino**
       "The Ethnic Imagination or Writing the Trans-individual Subject."
       *Polyphony: The Bulletin of the Multicultural History Society of
       Ontario*, vol. 7 no. 2 (1985) p. 137-140.

3292   **McCann, Phillip**
       "Culture, State Formation and the Invention of Traditions:
       Newfoundland, 1832-1855." *Journal of Canadian Studies/Revue
       d'études canadiennes*, vol. 23 no. 1/2 (1988) p. 86-103.

3293   **McCormack, Thelma**
       "Culture and the State." *Canadian Public Policy/Analyse de
       politiques*, vol. 10 no. 3 (1984) p. 267-277.

3294   **McCracken, Jane W.**
       "Stephan G. Stephansson: Icelandic-Canadian Poet and Free
       Thinker." *Canadian Ethnic Studies/Études ethniques au Canada*, vol.
       15 no. 1 (1983) p. 33-53.

3295   **McCue, Wilson**
       "Involving Ethnic Older Adults in Community Recreation Programs."
       Recreation Canada, vol. 44 no. 3 (1986) p. 15-17.

3296   **McDonnell, Roger F.**
       "Symbolic Orientations and Systematic Turmoil: Centering on the
       Kaska Symbol of Dene." *Canadian Journal of Anthropology/Revue
       canadienne d'anthropologie*, vol. 4 no. 1 (1984) p. 39-56.

3297   **McDougall, R.L.**
       "The Literary Influence of Sir Walter Scott in Canada." *British
       Journal of Ethnic Studies*, vol. 2 no. 2 (1987) p. 304-314.

3298   **McGrath, Robin**
"Monster Figures and Unhappy Endings in Inuit Literature."
Canadian Journal of Native Education, vol. 15 no. 1 (1988) p. 51-58.

3299   **McGrath, Robin**
"Images of the Land in Inuit Literature." *Études Inuit Studies*, vol. 9
no. 2 (1985) p. 133-139.

3300   **McGrath, Robin**
Canadian Inuit Literature: The Development of a Tradition. Ottawa:
National Museums of Canada, 1984. 230 p.

3301   **McKendry, Blake**
Folk Art Primitive and Native Art in Canada. Toronto: Methuen
Publications, 1983.

3302   **McKinney, Rhoda F.**
"What's Behind the Rise of Rap? Rappers Transform Music Charts
with Streetwise Rhythmic Rhymes." *Ebony*, vol. 44 no. 3
(1989) p. 66-68, 70.

3303   **McLarty, Lianne**
"'Seeing Things': Canadian Popular Culture and the Experience of
Marginality." In: *Communication Canada: Issues in Broadcasting
and New Technology*, edited by Rowland M. Lorimer and Donald C.
Wilson. Toronto: Kagan and Woo, 1988, p. 102-109.

3304   **McLuhan, Elizabeth and Tom Hill**
Norval Morisseau and the Emergence of the Image Makers. Toronto:
Methuen, 1984. 183 p.

3305   **McMillan, Alan D. and Denis E. St. Claire**
*Alberni Prehistory: Archaeological and Ethnographic Investigations
on Western Vancouver Island.* Penticton, B.C.: Theytus Books, 1982.

3306   **McNab, Elizabeth**
"West Indian Children's Literature." *Canadian Children*, vol. 10, nos.
1/2 (1985/86) p. 73-79.

3307   **McNair, Peter L.**
*The Legacy: Continuing Traditions of Canadian Northwest Coast
Indian Art.* Vancouver: Douglas and McIntyre, 1984.

3308   **Meisel, John**
"Escaping Extinction: Cultural Defence of an Undefended Border."
In: *Southern Exposure: Canadian Perspectives on the United States*,
edited by David H. Flaherty and William R. McKercher. Toronto:
McGraw-Hill Ryerson, 1986, p. 152-168.

3309   **Mellis, John Charles**
*God of the Potlatch: Christian Theology and the Kwakiutl
Worldview.* Unpublished ThM thesis, Fuller Theological Seminary,
School of World Mission, 1981. 168 leaves.

3310   **Messenger, Phyllis Mauch, ed.**
*The Ethics of Collecting Cultural Property: Whose Culture? Whose
Property?* Alberquerque: University of New Mexico Press, 1989.
266 p.

3311   **Michaelson, David Rubin**
*From Ethnography to Ethnology: A Study of the Conflict of
Interpretations of the Southern Kwakiutl Potlatch.* Unpublished PhD
thesis, New School for Social Research, 1980. 159 p.

3312   **Mifflen, Jessie**
Journal to Yesterday in the Out-harbours of Newfoundland. St.
John's, Nfld: H. Cuff Publications, 1983.

3313   **Millman, Lawrence**
"The Saga of Redhead." *The Icelandic Canadian*, (1984) p. 23-29.

3314   **Mitcham, Allison**
The Northern Imagination: A Study of Northern Canadian Literature.
Moonbeam, Ont.: Penumbra Press, 1983.

3315   **Mizynec, Victor**
Folk Instruments of Ukraine. Doncaster, Australia: Bayda Books,
1987. 48 p.

3316   **Mol, Leo**
Leo Mol Sculpture 1952-1979. Kleinburg, Ontario: McMichael
Canadian Collection, *c.* 1980. 24 p. illus.

3317   **Momatiuk, Yua and John Eastcott**
This Marvellous Terrible Place: Images of Newfoundland and Labrador. Camden East, Ont.: Camden House Publishing, 1988. 159 p.

3318   **Moore, Charles G.**
"Mathematics-like Principles Inferred from The [American Indian] Petroglyphs." *Journal of American Indian Education*, vol. 27 no. 2 (1988) p. 30-36.

3319   **Moore, William**
The Northwest — A Collector's Vision: An Exhibition of Native Art of the Pacific Northwest from the Peacock Collection, November 7-27, 1988. Barrie: The Barrie Art Gallery, 1988. 21 p.

3320   **Moreno, Maria V.**
"Theatre in Spanish-speaking Toronto." *Polyphony: The Bulletin of the Multicultural History Society of Ontario*, vol. 6 no. 1 (1984) p. 214-216.

3321   **Morgan, Lael**
Art and Eskimo Power: The Life and Times of Alaskan Howard Rock. Fairbanks: Epicenter Press, 1988. 259 p.

3322   **Morley, Patricia**
Kurelek: A Biography. Toronto: MacMillan of Canada, 1986. 338 p.

3323   **Morton, David**
"Signs of the Rising Sun: When is a Japanese Garden More than a Japanese Garden? Mystic Messages of Kannosuke Mori in the Nitobe Memorial Garden [Vancouver, B.C.]." *Saturday Night*, vol. 103 no. 8 /3701 (1988) p. 42-28.

3324   **Moskal, George**
"Ivan Honchar, Sculptor and Curator." *Ukrainian Canadian*, vol. 41 no. 726/220 (1988) p. 15-16.

3325   **Moyer, David S.**
"Sinterklass in Victoria: St. Nicholaas as a Symbol of Dutch Ethnicity." *Canadian Journal of Netherlandic Studies*, vol. 5 no. 2 (1984) p. 24-30.

3326   **Mukherjee, Arun Prabha**
"South Asian Poetry in Canada: In Search of a Place." In: *A Meeting of Streams: South Asian Canadian Literature*, edited by M.G. Vassanji. Toronto: TSAR Publications, 1985, p. 7-25.

3327   **Multicultural History Society of Ontario**
Polyphony: The Bulletin of the Multicultural History Society of Ontario, vol. 7 no. 1 (1985). Monographic issue of the journal devoted to sports and ethnicity in Ontario: "Czech Sports." p. 104-105; "Dutch Sports." p. 100-101; "Estonian Sports." p. 106-107; "Goan Sports." p. 89-93; "Lithuanian Sports." p. 96-99; "Native Sports." p. 108-110; "Slovak Sports." p. 29-30; "Swiss Sports." p. 94-95.

3328   **Muro, Margaret**
"Indian Art Comes to Light: Infra-red Photography is Revealing the Faded Masterpieces of Our Northwest Coast." *Canadian Geographic/ De géographe canadien*, vol. 108 no. 4 (1988) p. 66-70.

3329   **Myers, Marybelle**
"Northern Artists: Different Rules for Different Artists." *Inuit Art Quarterly*, vol. 3 no. 1 (1988) p. 9-11.

3330   **Myers, Marybelle**
"Who Will Control? Who Will Pay?: Is There a Future for Inuit Printmaking?" *Inuit Art Quarterly*, vol 3 no. 1 (1988) p. 3-8.

3331   **Nagel, Frank Norbert**
"Die Magdalenen-Inseln/Îles-de-la-Madeleine, Québec. Kultur-landschaft, Ressourcen und Entwicklungsperspektiven eines kanadis-chen Peripherraumes." In: *Mitteilungen der Geographischen Gesellschaft in Hamburg*. Hamburg: Weisbaden, 1985. p. 115-156.

3332   **Nakayama, Reverend**
"Japanese Canadian Poet and Farmer, Mr. Denbeikobayashi." *Okanagan Historical Society: 47th Annual Report*, (1983) p. 99-103.

3333   **Nardocchio, Elaine F.**
"Church and State, Religion and Politics in Quebec Theatre." *Bulletin of Canadian Studies*, vol. 7 no. 2 (1983/84) p. 73-80.

3334   **Narine, Dalton**
"Are Whites Taking Over Rhythm and Blues?" *Ebony*, vol. 44 no. 9
(1989) p. 90, 92, 94.

3335   **National Museum of Man and Canadian Centre for Folk Culture
Studies**
From the Heart: Folk Art in Canada. National Museum of Man and
Canadian Centre for Folk Culture Studies. Toronto: McClelland and
Stewart, 1983.

3336   **Native Indian/Inuit Photographers Association**
'Visions': An Exhibition of Contemporary Native Photography.
Ottawa: Department of Indian and Northern Affairs, 1985. 41 p.

3337   **Nattiez, Jean-Jacques**
"Le disque de musique amérindienne: IV nouveaux disques et
cassettes de musique inuit." *Recherches amérindiennes au Québec*,
vol. 15 no. 4 (1985/86) p. 67-77.

3338   **Neal, Arthur G.**
"Symbolism of the Canadian-U.S. Border." *Journal of American
Culture*, vol. 9 no. 1 (1986) p. 2-6.

3339   **Neal, Arthur G.**
"Animism and Totemism in Popular Culture." *Journal of Popular
Culture*, vol. 19 no. 2 (1985) p. 15-23.

3340   **Neaman, Evelyn Celia**
*Effects of a Cultural Curriculum in Changing Children's Inter-ethnic
Attitudes.* Unpublished MA thesis, University of British Columbia,
1987. 68 p. Canadian theses on microfiche, CT89-28471-7.

3341   **Neary, Kevin**
"Arts of the Sacred Cedar: A Totem Pole for the Southwest
Museum." *Master Key*, vol. 59 no. 4 (1986) p. 3-10.

3342   **Nipp, Dora**
"Toronto Chinese Drama Associations." *Polyphony: The Bulletin of
the Multicultural History Society of Ontario*, vol. 5 no. 2
(1983) p. 71-74.

3343   **Nkolo, Jean-Victor**
"Les immigrants sont des poèmes: un entretien avec Gérald Godin."
Vice Versa, vol. 2 no. 4 (1985) p. 5-7.

3344   **Nunley, John W. and Judith Bettelheim**
Caribbean Festival Arts: Each and Every Bit of Difference. Seattle:
The Saint Louis Art Museum and University of Washington Press,
1988. 218 p.

3345   **O'Connell, Sheldon**
"The Drum Dance/La danse au tambour." *North/Nord*, vol. 31 no. 1
(1985) p. 32-38.

3346   **O'Connell, Sheldon**
"Music of the People/La musique autochtone d'aujourd'hui." *North/
Nord*, vol. 31 no. 1 (1985) p. 57-63.

3347   **O'Dea, Shane**
"Simplicity and Survival: Vernacular Response in Newfoundland
Architecture." *Newfoundland Quarterly*, vol. 78 no. 3 (1983) p. 19-
31, Reprinted in *SSAC Bulletin*, vol. 8 no. 2 (1983) p. 3-11.

3348   **O'Neill, John**
"Techno-culture and the Specular Functions of Ethnicity: With a
Methodological Note." In: *Ethnicity in a Technological Age*, edited
by Ian H. Angus. Edmonton: Canadian Institute of Ukrainian Studies,
University of Alberta, 1988, p. 17-29.

3349   **Oberman, Sheldon and Elaine Newton, eds.**
*Mirror of a People: Canadian Jewish Experience in Poetry and
Prose.* Winnipeg: Jewish Educational Publishers of Canada, 1985.
250 p.

3350   **Olson, Stephanie**
"Canadian Indian Legends." *The Medium*, vol. 28 no. 3 (1987) p. 30-
36.

3351   **Omner, Rosemary E.**
"Primitive Accumulation and the Scottish 'Clann' in the Old World
and the New." *Journal of Historical Geography*, vol. 12 no. 2
(1986) p. 121-141.

3352   **Overton, James**
"A Newfoundland Culture?" *Journal of Canadian Studies/Revue d'études canadiennes*, vol. 23 no. 1/2 (1988) p. 5-22.

3353   **Ozog, Edward L.**
Polish-Canadian Immigrant Literature, 1918-1940. Unpublished MA thesis, University of Ottawa, 1984. 4 microfiches. Canadian theses on microfiche, 67588.

3354   **Pacey, Elizabeth**
More Stately Mansions: Churches of Nova Scotia, 1830-1910. Hantsport, N.S.: Lancelot Press, 1983.

3355   **Pache, Walter**
"Literary History in Canada and the Ethnic Factor." *Cross-cultural Studies: American, Canadian, and European Literatures, 1945-1985,* edited by Mirko Jurak. Ljubljana, Yugoslavia: English Department, Filozofska fakulteta, Edvard Kardelj University, 1988, p. 323-328. Paper presented at the Symposium on Contemporary Literatures and Cultures of the United States of America and Canada, held in Bled, Yugoslavia, May 9-14, 1988.

3356   **Paci, F.G.**
"Tasks of the Canadian Novelist Writing on Immigrant Themes." In: *Contrasts: Comparative Essays on Italian Canadian Writing,* edited by Joseph Pivato. Montreal: Guernica Editions, 1985, p. 35-60.

3357   **Padolsky, Enoch**
"Canadian Minority Writing and Acculturation Options." *Canadian Review of Comparative Literature*, vol. 16 nos. 3-4 (1989) p. 600-618.

3358   **Padolsky, Enoch**
"The Place of Italian-Canadian Writing." *Journal of Canadian Studies/Revue d'études canadiennes*, vol. 21 no. 4 (1986/87) p. 138-152.

3359   **Pain, Howard**
Heritage of Upper Canadian Furniture: A Study in the Survival of Formal and Vernacular Styles from Britain, America and Europe, 1780-1900. Toronto: Key Porter, 1984.

3360   **Palmer, Tamara**
"The Fictionalization of the Vertical Mosaic: The Immigrant Success and National Mythology." *Canadian Review of Comparative Literature*, vol. 16 nos. 3/4 (1989) p. 619-655.

3361   **Papp, Susan M.**
"Hungarian Canadian Dramatic Productions." *Polyphony: The Bulletin of the Multicultural History Society of Ontario*, vol. 5 no. 2 (1983) p. 33-36.

3362   **Papp, Susan M.**
"Oral History Sources' Collection: Hungarian-Canadian Cultural Centre-Hungarian House." *Polyphony: The Bulletin of the Multicultural History Society of Ontario*, vol. 2 no. 2/3 (1980) p. 89-92.

3363   **Parson, Alison**
"Keiko Shintani: Two Worlds on One Warp." *Ontario Craft*, vol. 9 no. 2 (1984) p. 16-18.

3364   **Patterson, Nancy-Lou**
"'See the Vernacular Landscape Glowing': The Symbolic Landscape of the Swiss-German Mennonite Settlers in Waterloo County." *Mennonite Life*, vol. 38 no. 4 (1983) p. 8-16.

3365   **Patterson, Nancy-Lou**
"Death and Ethnicity: Swiss-German Mennonite Gravestones of the 'Pennsylvania Style' (1804-1854) in the Waterloo Region, Ontario." *Mennonite Life*, vol. 37 no. 3 (1982) p. 4-7.

3366   **Pauls, Leonora Mary**
The English Language Folk and Traditional Songs of Alberta: Collection and Analysis for Teaching Purposes. Unpublished MMus thesis University of Calgary, 1981. 4 microfiches. Canadian theses on microfiche, 55393.

3367   **Pawlowski, Andrew**
"A Polish Way to Canadian Art: Contemporary Painters and Sculptors in Toronto." *Polyphony: The Bulletin of the Multicultural History Society of Ontario*, vol. 6 no. 2 (1984) p. 113-117.

3368   **Peers, Frank W., Robert Babe and Ian Parker**
"The Strategy of Canadian Culture in the 21st Century: Public Policy and Market Forces, Copyright and Culture, the Free Trade Challenge." *Canadian Forum*, vol. 67 no. 776/777 (1988) p. 19-35.

3369   **Perreault-Dorval, Gaby**
"Culture de survie, survie d'une culture." *North/Nord*, vol. 30 no. 1 (1983) p. 44-50.

3370   **Pestre De Almeida, Lilian**
Quêtes: textes d'auteurs italo-québecois. Montréal: Éditions Guernica, 1983.

3371   **Pestre De Almeida, Lilian**
"Regard péripherique sur la francophonie ou pourquoi et comment enseigner les littératures francophones dans les Amériques." *Études littéraires*, vol. 16 no. 2 (1983) p. 253-74.

3372   **Peters, Gordon**
"Portrait of A New Inuit Artist: Mary Okleena." *The Northern Review*, no. 2 (1988) p. 141-143.

3373   **Petroff, Lillian**
"Balkanski Unak: Exercise and Fellow Feeling in Toronto's Cabbagetown." *Polyphony: The Bulletin of the Multicultural History Society of Ontario*, vol. 7 no. 1 (1985) p. 43.

3374   **Petroff, Lillian**
"Prosperity and Patriotism: Macedonian Theatre in Toronto, 1910-1940." *Polyphony: The Bulletin of the Multicultural History Society of Ontario*, vol. 5 no. 2 (1983) p. 81-83.

3375   **Petrone, Penny**
First People, First Voices. Toronto: University of Toronto Press, 1983. 221 p.

3376   **Petrone, Penny, ed.**
Northern Voices: Inuit Writing in English. Toronto: University of Toronto Press, 1988. 314 p.

3377   **Philip, Marlene Nourbese**
"Black and White: No Laughing Matter." *Fuse*, vol. 11 no. 6 (1988) p. 30-31.

3378   **Philip, Marlene Nourbese**
"Who's Listening? Artists, Audiences and Language." *Fuse*, vol. 12
no. 1/2 (1988) p. 14-24.

3379   **Pietropaolo, Vincenzo**
"Did You Come by Photograph or Train?" *Polyphony: The Bulletin
of the Multicultural History Society of Ontario*, vol. 7 no. 2
(1985) p. 141.

3380   **Pivato, Joseph**
Italian-Canadian Writers: A Preliminary Survey, edited by Michael
S. Batts. [Ottawa]: Department of the Secretary of State of Canada,
Multiculturalism, 1988. 53 p.

3381   **Pivato, Joseph**
"Ethnic Writing and Comparative Canadian Literature." In:
Contrasts: Comparative Essays on Italian Canadian Writing, edited
by Joseph Pivato. Montreal: Guernica Publications, 1985, p. 15-34.

3382   **Pivato, Joseph**
"Italian Writers in Ontario: A Brief Review." *Polyphony: The
Bulletin of the Multicultural History Society of Ontario*, vol. 7 no. 2
(1985) p. 133-136.

3383   **Pivato, Joseph**
"A Literature of Exile: Italian Language Writing in Canada." In:
Contrasts: Comparative Essays on Italian Canadian Writing, edited
by Joseph Pivato. Montreal: Guernica Editions, 1985, p. 169-188.

3384   **Pivato, Joseph**
"Shock of Recognition: Italian-Canadian Writers." *Vice Versa*, vol. 2
no. 3 (1985) p. 29-30.

3385   **Plocher, Hanspeter**
"Soziale Aspekte in modernen franko-kanadischen Theater." *Zeitshrift
der Gesellschaft fur Kanada-Studien*, no. 4/2 (1984) p. 21-32.

3386   **Plumet, Patrick**
"Cairns-Balisis et mégalithes de l'Ungava." *Études Inuit Studies*, vol.
9 no. 2 (1985) p. 61-99.

3387   **Preston, Richard J.**
"Transformations musicales et culturelles chez les cris de l'Est."
Recherches amérindiennes au Québec, vol. 15 no. 4 (1985/86) p. 19-
28.

3388   **Principe, Angelo**
*The Concept of Italy in Canada and in Italian-Canadian Writings
from the Eve of Confederation to the Second World War.*
Unpublished PhD thesis, University of Toronto, 1989.

3389   **Prokopowich, Mary**
"Ukrainian Festival: Dauphin Manitoba, All Decked Out for 20th-
year Celebration." *Canadian Geographic/De géographe canadien*,
vol. 105 no. 3 (1985) p. 44-49.

3390   **Pronovost, Gilles**
*Temps, culture et société: essai sur le processus de formation du
loisir et des sciences de loisir dans les sociétés occidentales.* Sillery,
P.Q.: Presses de l'université du Québec, 1983.

3391   **Proulx, Richard**
*Exercices de lecture: introduction à la musique folklorique de langue
française.* Hull, Qué.: R. Proulx, 1983.

3392   **Pucci, Antonio**
"Ethnic Theatre in Thunder Bay." *Polyphony: The Bulletin of the
Multicultural History Society of Ontario*, vol. 5 no. 2 (1983) p. 37-
39.

3393   **Rahatyn, Levko**
"Ukrainian Sports Activity in the Sudbury Region." *Polyphony: The
Bulletin of the Multicultural History Society of Ontario*, vol. 7 no. 1
(1985) p. 73-75.

3394   **Ramirez, Bruno**
"Cosmopolitanism and Ethnicity: A View from the Kitchen." *Vice
Versa*, no. 15 (1986) p. 40-41.

3395   **Rapp, Eugene**
"Sports in the German Club of Hamilton." *Polyphony: The Bulletin
of the Multicultural History Society of Ontario*, vol. 7 no. 1
(1985) p. 51-52.

3396   **Rasporich, Beverly**
"Alberta Cartoonists Stewart Cameron, and Everett Soop: Cowboys, Indians and Political Protest." *Alberta*, vol. 2 no. 1 (1989) p. 16-34.

3397   **Rasporich, Beverly**
"Canadian Humour and Culture: Regional and National Expressions." *Canadian Issues*, vol. 9 (1988) p. 99-119.

3398   **Ray, Dorothy Jean**
"Happy Jack: King of the Eskimo Ivory Carvers." *American Indian Art*, vol. 10 no. 1 (1984) p. 32-47.

3399   **Rear, John**
"A Root Awakening: Some Sense and Value in Transcultural Music." *Vice Versa*, no. 25 (1988) p. 8-10.

3400   **Redekop, Calvin**
"Mennonites, Aesthetics and Buildings." *Mennonite Life*, vol. 41 no. 3 (1986) p. 27-29.

3401   **Redekop, Magdalene**
"The Literary Politics of the Victim: Interview with Joy Kogawa about the Experience of *Obasan* and the Sequel Now Being Written." *Canadian Forum*, vol. 68 no. 783 (1989) p. 14-17.

3402   **Redmond, Gerald**
The Sporting Scot of Nineteenth-Century Canada. London, Toronto: Associated University Press; Rutherford, N.J.: Farleigh Dickinson University Press, 1982.

3403   **Reich, David**
Design Criteria for Native Housing in Canada. Montreal: Concordia University, 1985. Unpublished MEng thesis Concordia University, 1985. Canadian theses on microfiche, CT87-20546-3.

3404   **Reid, Dennis**
From the Four Quarters: Native and European Art in Ontario, 5000 BC to 1867 AD. Toronto: Art Gallery of Ontario, 1984.

3405   **Reid, Martine J.**
"Le mythe de Baxbakwalanuxsiwae: une affaire de famille." *Recherches amerindiennes au Québec*, vol. 14 no. 2 (1984) p. 25-33.

3406   **Reimar, Al, Anne Reimar, and Jack Thiessen, eds.**
Répertoire littéraire de l'ouest canadien. Saint-Boniface, Man.:
Centre d'études franco-canadiennes de l'Ouest, 1984.

3407   **Reimar, Al, Anne Reimar, and Jack Thiessen, eds.**
*A Sackful of Plautdietsch: A Collection of Mennonite Low German
Stories and Poems.* Winnipeg: Hyperion Press, 1983.

3408   **Reimer, Mavis**
"A Question of Audience? Two Views of Home in the Russian-
Mennonite Novels of Barbara Smucker." *Mennonite Studies,* vol. 6
(1988) p. 165-173.

3409   **Revutsky, Valerian**
A History of Ukrainian Theatre, 1619-1975. Edmonton: Canadian
Institute of Ukrainian Studies, 1984.

3410   **Richardson, Sara L. and John L. Crompton**
"Latent Demand for Vacation Travels: A Cross-cultural Analysis of
French-and-English-speaking Residents of Ontario and Québec."
Leisure Sciences, vol. 10 no. 1 (1988) p. 17-26.

3411   **Ridington, Robin**
*Trail to Heaven: Knowledge and Narrative in a Northern Native
Community.* Vancouver: Douglas and McIntyre, 1988. 30 p.

3412   **Riedal, Walter E., ed.**
*The Old and the New World: Literary Perspectives of German-
speaking Canadians.* Toronto: University of Toronto Press, 1984.
191 p.

3413   **Rioux, Marcel**
"Requiem pour un rêve." *Canadian Journal of Sociology/Cahiers
canadiens de sociologie,* vol. 12 nos. 1-2 (1987) p. 8-15.

3414   **Rioux, Marcel**
"Une fête populaire et développement de la culture populaire au
Québec: une approche critique." *Loisir et société,* vol. 4 no. 1
(1981) p. 55-82.

3415   **Rioux, Monique**
"Discovering the Inuit People." *Canadian Theatre Review,* no. 46
(1986) p. 72-78.

3416   **Robertson, Clive**
"Art and Issues of Native Identity." *Fuse*, vol. 12 no. 6 (1989) p. 3-4.

3417   **Robertson, Heather**
"Against All Odds and Expectations: The Recent Success of Native Artists is Threatening the Imported European Traditions that Still Dominate Canadian Art." *Canadian Forum*, vol. 68 no. 782 (1989) p. 4-6.

3418   **Robichaud, Armand G.**
"Culture majoritaire, culture minoritaire: aspects psycho-sociaux." *Études canadiennes/Canadian Studies*, no. 21 vol. 2 (1986) p. 237-251.

3419   **Robinson, Harry, ed.**
Write it on Your Heart: The Epic World of an Okanagan Storyteller. Vancouver: Talonbooks, 1989. 319 p.

3420   **Rohatyn, Levko**
"Ukrainian Sports Activity in the Sudbury Region." *Polyphony: The Bulletin of the Multicultural History Society of Ontario*, vol. 7 no. 1 (1985) p. 73-75.

3421   **Romero, Jorge E.**
"History of LEFA [Educadorian League of Amateur Soccer]" *Polyphony: The Bulletin of the Multicultural History Society of Ontario*, vol. 7 no. 1 (1985) p. 29-30.

3422   **Rose, Mildred A.**
Old Belly Dancing Moon: A Collection of Haiku and Senryn. Moose Jaw, Sask.: Music Press, 1983.

3423   **Rosenberg, Neil V.**
"Ethnicity and Class: Black Country Musicians in the Maritimes." *Journal of Canadian Studies/Revue d'études canadiennes*, vol. 23 nos.1/2 (1988) p. 138-147.

3424   **Rosenthal, Henry, ed.**
"Aaron Kramer: Poet Laureate of the Jewish Left." *Outlook: Canada's Progressive Jewish Magazine*, vol. 27 no. 12 (1989) p. 12-13.

3425 **Ross, W. Gilles**
"The Sound of Eskimo Music." *The Beaver*, vol. 315 no. 3 (1985) p. 28-36.

3426 **Rothschild, Samuel**
"Reminiscences." *Polyphony: The Bulletin of the Multicultural History Society of Ontario*, vol. 7 no. 1 (1985) p. 117-119.

3427 **Routledge, Marie**
"Community Profiles: The Central Arctic." p. 4-5; "Spence Bay." p. 6-11; "Gjoa Haven." p. 12-16; "Pelly Bay." p. 17-21; "Focus on Artists: Samuel Nahaulaitug." p. 22-23; "Maudie Okittug." p. 24-26; "Judas Oolooah," p. 30-33; "Collections: The Macdonald Stewart Art Centre." p. 34-41; "Drawings by Etidlooie Etidlooie." p. 42-47, *Inuit Arts and Crafts/L'art et l'artisanat Inuit*, no. 2 (1984).

3428 **Ruger, Hendrika, ed.**
Dutch Voices: A Collection of Stories and Poems by Dutch-Canadians. [Kevin Van Tighem, Cornelia Hoogland, John Schoutsen, Mary Steenlan, John Weier]. Windsor, Ont.: Netherlandic Press, 1989. 87 p.

3429 **Rusconi, Marisa**
"Nouveaux itinéraires entre experience et écriture: voyage à travers la 'Jeune' génération de romancières italiennes." *Vice Versa* no. 25 (1988) p. 22-23.

3430 **Russell, Kelly**
Rufus Guinchard: The Man and His Music. St. John's, Nfld.: H. Cuff, 1982.

3431 **Sadowska-Guillon, Irène**
"Nouvelles voies de la dramaturgie française." *Vice Versa*, no. 25 (1988) p. 29-30.

3432 **Salerno, Henry and Ronald Ambrosetti, eds.**
"Ethnic Theatre." *Journal of Popular Culture*, vol. 19 no. 3 (1985) p. 91-162.

3433 **Saloman, Kathryn**
Jewish Ceremonial Embroidery. London, U.K.: B.T. Batsford, 1988. 168 p.

3434 **Salvatore, Filippo**
"The Italian Writers of Quebec: Language, Culture and Politics." In: *Contrasts: Comparative Essays on Italian Canadian Writing*, edited by Joseph Pivato. Montreal: Guernica Editions, 1985, p. 189-206.

3435 **Samson, Jacques and Magdeleine Yeries**
"Racial Differences in Sports Performance." *Canadian Journal of Sport Sciences/Journal canadien des sciences du sport*, vol. 13 no. 2 (1988) p. 109-116.

3436 **Sandberg, L. Anders**
"Literature as Social History: A Swedish Novelist [Sven Delblanc] in Manitoba." *Prairie Forum*, vol. 13 no. 1 (1988) p. 83-98.

3437 **Saucier, Céline and Eugen Kedl**
Image inuit de Nouveau-Québec. [Montréal]: Éditions Fides and Musée de la civilisation, 1988. 256 p.

3438 **Savard, Pierre, comp.**
Aspects de la civilisation canadienne-française: textes. Ottawa: Éditions de l'Université d'Ottawa, 1983. 341 p.

3439 **Schaefer, Ewald and Gerhard Hauck**
"A Fresh Start in a Series of Beginnings: Deutsches Theater Toronto 1983." *Polyphony: The Bulletin of the Multicultural History Society of Ontario*, vol. 5 no. 2 (1983) p. 25-28.

3440 **Scott, Colin**
"Knowledge Construction Among Cree Hunters: Metaphors and Literal Understanding." *Journal de la Société des américanistes*, vol. 75 (1989) p. 193-208.

3441 **Scott, Colin**
"Hunting Territories, Hunting Bosses and Communal Production Among Coastal James Bay Cree." *Anthropologica*, n.s. vol. 28 nos. 1-2 (1986) p. 163-173.

3442 **Scott, Jay**
"I Lost It at the Trading Post: Indian Art is Dead, Long Live Art by Indians." *Canadian Art*, vol. 2 no. 4 (1985) p. 33-39.

3443   **Seguin, Margaret**
"Understanding Tsimshian 'Potlatch'." In: *Native Peoples: The Canadian Experience*, edited by R. Bruce Morrison and C. Roderick Wilson. Toronto: McClelland and Stewart, 1986, p. 473-500.

3444   **Shackleton, Philip and Kenneth Roberts**
"The Skin Boats: Kayaks and Umiaks." *The Beaver*, vol. 314 no. 1 (1983) p. 52-57.

3445   **Shadbolt, Doris**
Bill Reid [Haida Artist]. Vancouver: Douglas and McIntyre, 1986. 192 p.

3446   **Shemie, Bonnie**
Houses of Snow, Skin and Bones - Native Dwellings: The Far North. Montréal, P.Q.: Tundra Books, 1989. 24 p.

3447   **Shepherd, John**
"The Politics of Silence: Problematics for the Analysis of English Canadian Musical Culture." *Australian-Canadian Studies*, vol. 7 nos. 1/2 (1989) p. 113-125.

3448   **Shepherd, John**
"Music Consumption and Cultural Self-Identities: Some Theoretical and Methodological Reflections." *Media, Culture and Society*, vol. 8 no. 3 (1986) p. 305-330.

3449   **Sheppard, Janice R.**
"The Dog Husband: Structural Identity and Emotional Specificity in Northern Athapaskan Oral Narrative." *Arctic Anthropology*, vol. 20 no. 1 (1983) p. 89-101.

3450   **Sherbaniuk, Richard**
"Architecture and Ethnicity." *Heritage*, vol. 13 no. 4 (1985) p. 1-3.

3451   **Shifrin, Ellen**
"Traditional French-Canadian Social Dance: Working with the Iconography." In: *Proceedings 5th Canadian Symposium on the History of Sport and Physical Education*, Toronto: University of Toronto Press. 1982. p. 298.

3452   **Showalter, Shirley Hershey**
"Bringing the Muse Into Our Country: A Response to Jeff Gundy's 'Humility in Mennonite Literature'." *The Mennonite Quarterly Review*, vol. 63 no. 1 (1989) p. 22-29.

3453   **Shuba, Rev. Msgr. Michael**
"I'm Just Reminiscing." *Polyphony: The Bulletin of the Multicultural History Society of Ontario*, vol. 7 no. 1 (1985) p. 124-126.

3454   **Sillanpaa, Nelma**
"Revonatulet Athletic Club of Timmins." *Polyphony: The Bulletin of the Multicultural History Society of Ontario*, vol. 7 no. 1 (1985) p. 76-79.

3455   **Silver, Judith A.**
Therapeutic Aspects of Folk Dance: Self-concept, Body Concept, Ethnic Distancing and Social Distancing. Unpublished PhD thesis University of Toronto, 1981. Canadian theses on microfiche, 53155.

3456   **Simard, Jean and Françoise Brault**
Les arts sacrés au Québec. Ottawa: Éditions de Mortagne, 1989. 319 p.

3457   **Simms, Glenda and Wes Stevenson**
"Cross-cultural Education Through Recreational Services." *Recreation Canada*, vol. 44 no. 3 (1986) p. 18-20.

3458   **Simon, Sherry**
"The Language of Difference: Minority Writers in Quebec." In: *Language, Culture and Literary Identity in Canada*, edited by J.M. Bumsted. Vancouver, B.C.: University of British Columbia, 1987, p. 119-128. Paper presented at the 1984 Ottawa Conference on Language, Culture and Literary Identity in Canada. Published as a Supplement 1 of *Canadian Literature/Littérature canadienne*, May 1987, follows issue no. 112 of that journal.

3459   **Sirois, Antoine et Agnès Bastin, eds.**
L'essor culturel de Sherbrooke et de la région depuis 1950. Sherbrooke, P.Q.: Dép. d'études françaises, Université de Sherbrooke, 1985. 292 p.

3460   **Sitwell, O.F.G. and Olenka S.E. Bilash**
"Analysing the Cultural Landscape as a Means of Probing the Non-Material Dimension of Reality." *Canadian Geographer/Le géographe Canadien*, vol. 30 no. 2 (1986) p. 132-145.

3461   **Skulason, Hrund**
"The Icelandic Male Voice Choir of Winnipeg." *The Icelandic Canadian*, vol. 44 no. 3 (1986) p. 18-23.

3462   **Skvorecky, Josef**
"Some Problems of the Ethnic Writer in Canada." In: *Language, Culture and Literary Identity in Canada*, edited by J.M. Bumsted. Vancouver, B.C.: University of Britiwsh Columbia, 1987, p. 82-89. Paper presented at the 1984 Ottawa Conference on Language, Culture and Literary Identity in Canada. Published as Supplement 1 of *Canadian Literature*, May 1987, follows issue no. 112 of that journal.

3463   **Slater, Dennis**
"A Culture in Miniature: The World of Japanese Netsuke." *Glenbow*, vol. 8 no. 4 (1988) p. 12-14.

3464   **Slavutych, Yar**
"Expectations and Reality in Early Ukrainian Literature in Canada, 1897-1905." In: *Identifications, Ethnicity and the Writer in Canada*, edited by Jars Balan. Edmonton: Canadian Institute of Ukrainian Studies, 1982, p. 14-21.

3465   **Smieja, Florian**
"Notes on Polish Canadian Creative Literature." *Polyphony: The Bulletin of the Multicultural History Society of Ontario*, vol. 6 no. 2 (1984) p. 105-109.

3466   **Smith, Molly**
"Chinese Artistry and Malaysian Color [Willie Wong]." *Heritage*, vol. 14 no. 2 (1986) p. 6-7.

3467   **Snider, Norman**
"O Canada Revisited: A Cultural Update/Le Canada anglais et la culture au fil du temps." *Language and Society/Langue et société* no. 24 (1987) p. 44-45.

3468   **Sokolsky, Zoriana**
"An Interview with Dr. Elias Wachna." *Polyphony: The Bulletin of the Multicultural History Society of Ontario*, vol. 7 no. 1 (1985) p. 127-128.

3469   **Sokolyk, K.W.**
"Vedmedyky-Volleyball Champions." *Polyphony: The Bulletin of the Multicultural History Society of Ontario*, vol. 10 no. 1/2 (1988) p. 241-244.

3470   **Solomon, Rovell Patrick**
The Creation of Separatism: The Lived Culture of West Indian Boys in a Toronto High School. Unpublished PhD thesis, State University of New York at Buffalo, 1987. Canadian theses on microfiche, CT88-22273-5.

3471   **Sparling, Mary**
Great Expectations: The European Vision in Nova Scotia, 1749-1848. Halifax, N.S.: Art Gallery, Mount Saint Vincent University, 1980.

3472   **Speisman, Stephen**
"Yiddish Theatre in Toronto." *Polyphony: The Bulletin of the Multicultural History Society of Ontario*, vol. 5 no. 2 (1983) p. 95-98.

3473   **Spiro, Solomon J.**
Tapestry for Design: Judaic Allusions in the Second Scroll and the Collected Poems of A.M. Klein. Vancouver: University of British Columbia Press, 1984.

3474   **Stefon, Frederick J. and Martha Hadsel**
"Immigrant Images: A Photographic Essay." *Journal of Ethnic Studies*, vol. 17 no. 1 (1989) p. 53-96.

3475   **Stefura, Mary**
"Aspects of Culture in the Ukrainian Community of the Sudbury Area." *Polyphony: The Bulletin of the Multicultural History Society of Ontario*, vol. 5 no. 2 (1983) p. 29-32.

3476   **Steltzer, Ulli**
A Haida Potlatch. Vancouver: Douglas and McIntyre, 1984. 81 p.

3477   **Steven, James R.**
"Susan Ross - A Northern Journey: Etchings and Drawings." *Northward Journal: A Quarterly of Northern Arts*, no. 38 (1986) p. 20-47.

3478   **Stevenson, Mark**
"Cricket Makes a Come-back: Expatriate Colonists Breathe New Life into an Unbearably Gentlemanly Sport." *Alberta Report*, vol. 15 no. 29 (1988) p. 46-47.

3479   **Stevenson, Mark**
"Larry Lemieux, Seoul's Saviour: A Heroic Prairie Yachtsman Exudes Olympic Spirit and Lives Out of a Ford Van." *Alberta Report*, vol. 15 no. 43 (1988) p. 41-43.

3480   **Stilz, Gerhard**
"Resisting the 'Second Emigration': German-Canadian Writers in a Multicultural Context." In: *Cross-cultural Studies: American, Canadian, and European Literatures, 1945-1985*, edited by Mirko Jurak. Ljubljana, Yugoslavia: English Department, Filozofska fakulteta, Edvard Kardelj University, 1988, p. 353-361. Paper presented at the Symposium on Contemporary Literatures and Cultures of the United States of America and Canada, held in Bled, Yugoslavia, May 9-14, 1988.

3481   **Stockdale, John**
"Racial Stereotypes in the Canadian Novel, 1920-1950." *Études canadiennes/Canadian Studies*, no. 12 (1982) p. 145-152.

3482   **Struk, Danylo**
"Ukrainian Emigre Literature in Canada." In: *Identifications, Ethnicity and the Writer in Canada*, edited by Jars Balan. Edmonton: Canadian Institute of Ukrainian Studies, 1982, p. 88-103.

3483   **Sugunasiri, Suwanda H.J.**
"Emerging Themes in South Asian Canadian Literature." *The Asianadian*, vol. 5 no. 3 (1984) p. 26-28.

3484   **Sugunasiri, Suwanda H.J., and Michael S. Batts, eds.**
The Search for Meaning: The Literature of Canadians of South Asian Origin. Ottawa: Department of the Secretary of State of Canada: Multiculturalism, 1988. 215 p.

3485   **Sundstén, Taru**
"The Theatre of the Finnish-Canadian Labour Movement and its Dramatic Literature, 1900-1939." In: *Finnish Diaspora I: Canada, South America, Africa, Australia and Sweden*, edited by Michael G. Karni. Toronto: Multicultural History Society of Ontario, 1981, p. 77-92.

3486   **Surette, Paul**
        Benoit Poirier: la vie d'un musicien acadien, 1882 à 1965. Tignish,
        Î.P.É.: Société culturelle Ti-Pa, 1982.

3487   **Szczesny, Wilfred**
        "Canadian-Soviet Cultural Exchanges Expanding." *Ukrainian
        Canadian*, vol. 41 no. 727/221 (1988) p. 15-17.

3488   **Tacou, P.S.C.**
        "An Analysis of Dorset Art in Relation to Prehistoric Cultural
        Stress." *Études Inuit Studies*, vol. 7 no. 1 (1983) p. 41-66.

3489   **Takehara, Gordon**
        "Terry Watada: Singing the Asian Canadian Blues." *The Asianadian*,
        vol. 5 no. 3 (1984) p. 14-17.

3490   **Tanner, Adrian**
        "The Significance of Hunting Territories Today." In: *Native People,
        Native Lands: Canadian Indians, Inuit and Metis*, edited by Bruce
        Alden Cox. Ottawa: Carleton University Press, 1988, p. 60-74.

3491   **Tarvainen, Eino and Varpu Lindström-Best**
        "Culture and Politics in Finnish Canada: The Finnish Immigrant
        Theatre." *Polyphony: The Bulletin of the Multicultural History
        Society of Ontario*, vol. 3 no. 2 (1981) p. 74-76.

3492   **Taxel, Joel**
        "The Black Experience in Children's Fiction: Controversies
        Surrounding Award Winning Books." *Curriculum Inquiry*, vol. 16 no.
        3 (1986) p. 245-281.

3493   **Temelini, Walter**
        "The Growth of Sports Involvement in the Windsor Area."
        *Polyphony: The Bulletin of the Multicultural History Society of
        Ontario*, vol. 7 no. 1 (1985) p. 21-26.

3494   **Terrell, Kingsley**
        "The Chatham All-Stars." *Polyphony: The Bulletin of the
        Multicultural History Society of Ontario*, vol. 7 no. 1 (1985) p. 111-
        116.

3495   **Thibault, André, ed.**
"Le Québec des différences: culture d'ici." *Possibles*, vol. 12 no. 3
(1988) p. 7-167.

3496   **Thompson, Maurice O.**
"Cricket, Lovely Cricket." *Polyphony: The Bulletin of the
Multicultural History Society of Ontario*, vol. 7 no. 1 (1985) p. 35-
37.

3497   **Thorpe, Edward**
Black Dance. London: Chatto and Windus, 1989. 192 p.

3498   **Thunder Bay Art Gallery**
Woodlands: Comtemporary Art of the Anishnabe. Thunder Bay, Ont.:
Thunder Bay Art Gallery, 1989. 47 p.

3499   **Thurston, Harry**
"Nova Scotia Traditions: It's Just Plain Simple Art." *Equinox*, no. 39
(1988) p. 48-57.

3500   **Tippett, Maria**
*The Making of English-Canadian Culture, 1900-1939: External
Influences*. North York, Ont.: Robarts Centre for Canadian Studies,
York University, 1987. 16 p.

3501   **Tomovic, Vladislav**
"Theatre among Serbs, Croats and Slovenes." *Polyphony: The
Bulletin of the Multicultural History Society of Ontario*, vol. 5 no. 2
(1983) p. 75-77.

3502   **Tracz, Orysia Paszczak**
"Oseredok [Ukrainian Culture and Educational Center] A Very
Special Space." *Forum: A Ukrainian Review*, no. 76 (1988) p. 16-23.

3503   **Trigger, Bruce G.**
"A Present of Their Past? Anthropologists, Native People and Their
Heritage." *Culture*, vol. 8 no. 1 (1988) p. 71-80.

3504   **Trudel, F.**
"Les relations entre les français et les inuit au Labrador méridional,
1660-1760." *Études Inuit Studies*, vol. 4 no. 1/2 (1980) p. 135-145.

3505   **Tsangaris, John**
"Cretan Theatre." *Polyphony: The Bulletin of the Multicultural History Society of Ontario*, vol. 5 no. 2 (1983) p. 42-46.

3506   **Tulurialik, Ruth Annaqtuusi and David F. Pelly**
Qikaaluktut: Images of Inuit Life. Toronto: Oxford University Press, 1986. 100 p.

3507   **Tuomi-lee, Sirkka**
"Stage Recollections among the Finns." *Polyphony: The Bulletin of the Multicultural History Society of Ontario*, vol. 5 no. 2 (1983) p. 67-70.

3508   **Ukrainian Museum of Canada, Saskatoon, Saskatchewan**
"Division III - Exploring Ukrainian Culture; Division II - Exploring Ukrainian Settlement; Division I - Exploring the Ukrainian Home." *The Medium*, vol. 28 no. 3 (1987) p. 26-29, 37-39, 40-42.

3509   **Urry, James**
"'All That Glisters...': Delbert Plett and the Place of the 'Kleine Gemeinde' in Russian-Mennonite History." *Journal of Mennonite Studies*, vol. 4 (1986) p. 228-250.

3510   **Vandall, Peter, Joe Douguette and Freda Ahenakew**
Wâskahikaniwiyiniw-Acimowina/Stories of the House People. Collections of the Algonquian Text Society/Collections de la Société d'edition de textes Algonquiens. Winnipeg: University of Manitoba Press, 1987. 240 p.

3511   **Vanderburgh, Rosamund M.**
"The Impact of Government Support for Indian Culture on Canada's Aged Indians." In: *North American Elders: United States and Canadian Perspectives*, edited by Eloise Rathbone-McCuan and Betty Havens. New York: Greenwood Press, 1988, p. 221-234.

3512   **Vickers, Roy Henry**
Solstice ['A Turning Point']: The Art of Roy Henry Vickers. Tofino, B.C.: Eagle Dancer Enterprises, 1988. 145 p.

3513   **Vikis-Freibergs, Vaira, ed.**
Linguistics and Poetics of Latvian Folksong. Montreal: McGill-Queen's University Press, 1988. 328 p.

3514   **Virgo, Sean**
"Decoding Tony Hunt: Making and Wearing the Masks of His People, He's a Complex Figure in a Tribal Tradition," *Canadian Art*, vol. 5 no. 1 (1988) p. 72-79.

3515   **Vovchok, Marko**
Ukrainian Folk Stories. Saskatoon: Western Producer Prairie Books, 1983.

3516   **Walkingstick, Kay**
"'Like A Longfish Out of Water': Interview with George Longfish." *Northeast Indian Quarterly*, vol. 6 no. 3 (1989) p. 16-23.

3517   **Wallace, Robert**
"A Tale of Two Cities: Maurice Podbrey of Montreal's Centaur Theatre and John Van Burek of Toronto's Theatre Du P'tit Bonheur Discuss Minority-language Theatre." *Canadian Theatre Review*, no. 46 (1986) p. 6-20.

3518   **Warner, John Anson**
"New Visions in Canadian Plains Painting." *American Indian Art*, vol. 10 no. 2 (1985) p. 46-53.

3519   **Warner, John Anson**
"Contemporary Canadian Indian Art." *Masterkey: Anthropology of the Americas*, vol. 58 no. 4 (1984) p. 3-14.

3520   **Warner, John Anson**
Heritage of Raven: Classical and Contemporary Art of The Northwest Coast Indians. Surrey, B.C.: Hancock House, 1984.

3521   **Webber, Alika Poddinsky**
North American Indian and Eskimo Footwear: A Typology and Glossary. Toronto: Bata Shoe Museum, 1989. 88 p.

3522   **Weber, Ronald L.**
"Photographs as Ethnographic Documents." *Arctic Anthropology*, vol. 22 no. 1 (1985) p. 67-78.

3523   **Weiss, Jonathan M.**
"Québec Theatre in the 80s: The End of an Era." *American Review of Canadian Studies*, vol. 13 no. 2 (1983) p. 64-73.

3524   **Westfall, William**
"The Regional Patterns in Canada and Canadian Culture." *Canadian Issues*, vol. 5 (1983) p. 2-15.

3525   **Whidden, Lynn**
"Les hymnes, une anomalie parmi les chants traditionnels des cris du Nord." *Recherches Amérindiennes au Québec*, vol. 15 no. 4 (1985/86) p. 29-36.

3526   **Whithers, Josephine**
"Inuit Women Artists: An Art Essay." *Feminist Studies*. vol. 10 no 1 (1984) p. 85-96.

3527   **Wight, Darlene**
"Oonark's Family." *The Wag Magazine*, (1986) p. 14-15.

3528   **Wilkenson, Doris Y.**
"The Doll Exhibit: The Psycho-cultural Analysis of Black Female Role Stereotypes." *Journal of Popular Culture*, vol. 21 no. 2 (1987) p. 19-29.

3529   **Williams, Robert**
"Culture in the Service of the State: Canadian and Australian International Cultural Policy." *Australian-Canadian Studies*, vol. 5 no. 1 (1987) p. 49-60.

3530   **Wilms, Oonagh Haldane**
An Analysis of the Implementation of an Art Program in an Indigenous Culture: With Particular Reference to the Six Nations Reserve, Ohsweken. Unpublished EdD thesis University of Toronto, 1986. 3 microfiches. Canadian theses on microfiche, CT88-25284-7.

3531   **Wilson, William A.**
"The Study of Mormon Folklore: An Uncertain Mirror For Truth." *Dialogue: A Journal of Mormon Thought*, vol. 22 no. 4 (1989) p. 95-111.

3532   **Winks, Robin W.**
"The Sinister Oriental: Thriller Fiction and the Asia Scene." *Journal of Popular Culture*, vol. 19 no. 2 (1985) p. 49-61.

3533   **Winnipeg Real Estate News**
"'New Iceland' Fishing Village [Hecla] Being Restored to Life." *The Icelandic Canadian*, vol. 43 no. 3 (1985) p. 40-42.

3534   **Wirsig, Kirk H.**
"The Ukrainian Easter Egg." *Prism International*, vol. 27 no. 3
(1989) p. 49-62.

3535   **Wong, Mina and Satish Dhar**
"Face to Face with Rick Shiomi." *The Asianadian*, vol. 5 no. 3
(1984) p. 10-13.

3536   **Wong-Chu, Jim**
"Ten Years of Asian Canadian Literary Arts in Vancouver." *The
Asianadian*, vol. 5 no. 3 (1984) p. 23-25.

3537   **Wynnyckyj, Andriy and Sophie Gagat**
"Uciecha: a Repertory of Polish Plays." *Polyphony: The Bulletin of
the Multicultural History Society of Ontario*, vol. 5 no. 2
(1983) p. 40-41.

3538   **Wynnyckyj, Andriy and Zofia Shahrodi**
"Uciecha: a Repertory of Polish Plays." *Polyphony: The Bulletin of
the Multicultural History Society of Ontario*, vol. 6 no. 2
(1984) p. 69-70.

3539   **Wynnyckyj, Iroida L.**
"Amateur Theatre in Canadian Ukrainian Community Halls."
*Polyphony: The Bulletin of the Multicultural History Society of
Ontario*, vol. 5 no. 2 (1983) p. 87-94.

3540   **Young, Judy**
"Canadian Literature in the Non-official Languages." *Canadian Ethnic
Studies/Études ethniques au Canada*, vol. 14 no. 1 (1982) p. 138-149.

3541   **Young, Judy**
"The Unheard Voices: Ideological or Literary Identification of
Canada's Ethnic Writers." *Identifications: Ethnicity and the Writer in
Canada*, edited by Jars Balan. Edmonton: Canadian Institute of
Ukrainian Studies, 1982, p. 104-115.

3542   **Zepp, Norman**
*Pure Vision: The Keewatin Spirit/Un vision pure: l'esprit du
Keewatin*. Regina: Norman Mackenzie Art Gallery, University of
Regina, 1986. 140 p.

3543   **Zhaotao, Liang and Zhang Shouqi**
"On 'Ethnoarchaeology'." *Chinese Sociology and Anthropology*, vol. 20 no. 4 (1988) p. 93-111.

3544   **Ziniak, Madeline**
"Byelorussian Literature in Toronto." *Polyphony: The Bulletin of the Multicultural History Society of Ontario*, vol. 6 no. 1 (1984) p. 120-122.

Education and Research

3545 **Adams, David W.**
"Before Canada: Toward an Ethnohistory of Indian Education."
History of Education Quarterly, vol. 28 no. 1 (1988) p. 95-105.

3546 **Allen, P.**
"A Three-level Curriculum Model for Second Language Education."
*Canadian Modern Language Review/Revue canadienne des langues
vivantes*, vol. 40 no. 1 (1983) p. 23-43.

3547 **Allison, D.J.**
"4th-World Education in Canada and the Faltering Promise of Native
Teacher Education Programs." *Journal of Canadian Studies/Revue
d'études canadiennes*, vol. 18 no. 3 (1983) p. 102-118.

3548 **Amenu-Tekaa, Christian**
*Perceptions of Community Participation in Education on Canadian
Indian Reserves: A North-central Alberta Case Study.* Unpublished
PhD thesis, University of Pittsburgh, 1988. 176 p.

3549 **American Association for Higher Education**
"Hispanics and the Academy." *Change: Magazine of Higher
Learning*, vol. 20 no. 3 (1988) p. 1-70.

3550 **American Association of Colleges for Teacher Education**
"Theme: Minorities." *Journal of Teacher Education*, vol. 39 no.1
(1988) p. 2-27.

3551 **American Council on Education**
"Minorities in the Education Pipeline." *Educational Record: The
Magazine of Higher Education*, vol. 68 no. 4; vol. 69 no. 1
(1988) p. 1-126.

3552   **Anisef, Paul**
        *Accessibility to Postsecondary Education in Canada: A Review of
        Literature.* Ottawa, Education Support Branch, Department of the
        Secretary of State, 1985. 243 p.

3553   **Anisef, Paul**
        *Losers and Winners: The Pursuit of Equality and Social Justice in
        Higher Education.* Toronto: Butterworth, 1982. 225 p.

3554   **Ashworth, Mary**
        *Blessed with Bilingual Brains: Education of Immigrant Children with
        English as a Second Language.* Vancouver: Pacific Educational
        Press, University of British Columbia, 1988. 290 p.

3555   **Avis, James**
        "White Ethnicity White Racism: Teacher and Student Perceptions of
        FE (Further Education)." *The Journal of Moral Education*, vol. 17
        no. 1 (1988) p. 52-60.

3556   **Aziz-al Ahsan, Syed**
        "School Texts and the Political Culture of British Columbia, 1880-
        1980." *B.C. Studies*, no. 63 (1984) p. 55-72.

3557   **Baer, Douglas E.**
        "Education and Support for Dominant Ideology." *Canadian Review of
        Sociology and Anthropology/Revue canadienne de sociologie et
        d'anthropologie*, vol. 19 no. 2 (1982) p. 173-195.

3558   **Bagley, Chris**
        "Multiculturalism and the Classroom." *Canadian Children*, vol. 9 no.
        1 (1984) p. 75-77.

3559   **Bain, Bruce**
        "Issues in Second Language Education in Canada." In: *Contemporary
        Educational Issues: The Canadian Mosaic*, edited by Leonard Stewin
        and Stewart J.H. McCann. Toronto: Copp Clark, 1987, p. 215-227.

3560   **Bale, Gordon**
        "Law, Politics and the Manitoba School Question: Supreme Court
        and Privy Council." *Canadian Bar Review/Revue du Barreau
        canadien*, vol. 63 no. 3 (1985) p. 461-518.

3561   **Balthazar, Louis**
L'école détournée. Montréal: Boréal, 1989. 214 p.

3562   **Barman, Jean**
"The Legacy of the Past: An Overview." In: *Indian Education in Canada*, edited by Jean Barman, Yvonne Hebert and Don McCaskill. vol. 1. Vancouver: University of British Columbia Press, 1986, p. 1-22.

3563   **Battiste, Marie**
"Micmac Literacy and Cognitive Assimilation." In: *Indian Education in Canada*, edited by Jean Barman, Yvonne Hebert and Don McCaskill. vol. 1. Vancouver: University of British Columbia Press, 1986, p. 23-44.

3564   **Bauer, Julien**
"Jewish Communities, Jewish Education and Quebec Nationalism." *Social Compass*, vol. 31 no. 4 (1984) p. 391-407.

3565   **Behiels, Michael D.**
"The Commission des écoles catholiques de Montréal and the Neo-Canadian Question, 1947-63." *Canadian Ethnic Studies/Études ethniques au Canada*, vol. 18 no. 2 (1986) p. 38-64.

3566   **Berryman, Jack**
Implementation of Ontario's Heritage Languages Program: A Case Study of the Extended School Day Model. Unpublished EdD thesis, University of Toronto, 1986. 603 leaves. Canadian theses on microfiche, CT88-23798-8.

3567   **Bezeau, Lawrence M.**
"The Constitutional and Legal Basis for Education of Canadian Indians." *Canadian Journal of Native Education*, vol. 12 no. 1 (1984) p. 38-46.

3568   **Bhatnagar, Joti**
"Adjustment and Education of South Asian Children in Canada." In: *South Asians in the Canadian Mosaic*, edited by Rabindra N. Kanungo. Montreal: Kala Bharati Foundation, 1984, p. 49-66.

3569   **Bhatnagar, Joti, ed.**
Educating Immigrants. New York: St. Martins Press; London: Croom Helm, 1981. 241 p.

3570 **Bindseil, Gerhart Andre**
"Higher Education Policy Implications for Franco-Ontarians: Towards a Basis and Direction for Further Development of University Programs." In: *Readings in Canadian Higher Education*, [compiled by] Higher Education Group, The Ontario Institution for Studies in Education. Toronto: The Group, 1988, p. 77-93.

3571 **Blondin, Georgina**
"The Development of the Zhahti Koe Slavey Language Program." *Canadian Journal of Native Education*, vol. 16 no. 2 (1989) p. 89-106.

3572 **Bourdages, Johanne S.**
Étude comparative de la performance en langue seconde de jeunes anglophones à l'école française et à l'immersion. Unpublished MA thesis, Université d'Ottawa, 1982. 2 microfiches. Canadian theses on microfiche, 56471.

3573 **Bouthillier, Guy**
"L'école anglaise: la pénétration des valeurs québécoises." *Action nationale*, vol. 78 no. 7 (1988) p. 561-565.

3574 **Braen, Andre**
"Les droits scolaires des minorités de langue officielle au Canada et l'interpretation judiciaire." *Revue generale de droit*, vol. 19 no. 2 (1988) p. 311-337.

3575 **Brazeau, Jacques**
"Pertinence de l'enseignement des relations ethniques et caracterisation de ce champ d'etudes au Canada et au Québec." *Sociologie et sociétés*, vol. 15 no. 2 (1983) p. 133-146.

3576 **Brown, Winston Lloyd**
West Indian Youth in Metro Toronto: The Relative Effects of Home and School Related Variables on their Attitudes Towards Participation in Post-secondary Education. Unpublished EdD thesis, University of Toronto, 1984. 274 leaves. Canadian theses on microfiche, CT86-28514-6.

3577 **Bubrin, Vladmir**
"Three Decades of Croatian Heritage Language in Toronto." *Polyphony: The Bulletin of the Multicultural History Society of Ontario*, vol. 11 no. 1/2 (1989) p. 80-84.

3578   **Buchanan, Alan G.**
"Education and Ethnic Attitudes: Some Observations on Anglophones in New Brunswick." *Canadian Ethnic Studies/Études ethniques au Canada*, vol. 19 no. 2 (1987) p. 110-116.

3579   **Buchignani, Norman**
"Research on South Asians in Canada: Retrospect and Prospect." In: *The South Asian Diaspora in Canada: Six Essays*, edited by Milton Israel. Toronto: Multicultural History Society of Ontario, 1987, p. 87-112.

3580   **Burgess, D.A.**
"The Ile-Perrot School Question: A Quebec Case Study." *Canadian and International Education*, vol. 10 no. 1 (1981) p. 32-41.

3581   **Burke, Mavis E.**
"Educational Implications of Cultural Diversity: Dilemma and Direction." In: *Multiculturalism in Canada: Social and Educational Perspectives*, edited by Ronald J. Samuda, John W. Berry and Michel Laferrière. Toronto: Allyn and Bacon Inc., 1984, p. 3-17.

3582   **Burnaby, Barbara J.**
"Language Policy and the Education of Native Peoples: Identifying the Issues." In: *Langue et droit*, sous la direction de Paul Pupier et José Woehrling. Montréal: Wilson and Lafleur, 1989, p. 279-289. Paper presented at the First Conference of the International Institute of Comparative Linguistic Law, April 27-29, 1988 at the Université du Québec, Montréal, P.Q.

3583   **Burnaby, Barbara J.**
Languages and Their Role in Educating Native Children. Toronto: OISE Press, 1980. 417 p.

3584   **Burt, Eric C.**
"Citizenship and Social Participation: Rudiments of Grounded Theory in Civic Education." In: *Challenging the Concept of Citizenship*, edited by René R. Gadacz. Edmonton: CSC Consulting Services, 1986, p. 46-75.

3585   **Canadian Council of Ministers of Education, Toronto (Ontario)**
Opportunities: Postsecondary Education and Training for Students with Special Needs. Toronto: [s.n.], 1987. 59 p. French language title: *Possibilités de formation et d'enseignement postsecondaire pour les étudiants ayant des besoins spéciaux.*

3586   **Carey, Stephen T.**
"Communication Skills in Immersion Programs." *Alberta Journal of Educational Research*, vol. 30 no. 4 (1984) p. 270-283.

3587   **Carey, Stephen T.**
"Achievement, Behavioural Correlates and Teachers' Perceptions of Francophone and Anglophone Immersion Students." *Alberta Journal of Educational Research*, vol. 29 no. 3 (1983) p. 159-167.

3588   **Carney, Robert**
"Teacher Education in the Northwest Territories: Cultural Inclusion, Cultural Imperialism and Teacher Autonomy." *History of Education Review*, vol. 17 no. 1 (1988) p. 18-26.

3589   **Chalmers, John W.**
"Northland: The Founding of a Wilderness School System." *Canadian Journal of Native Education*, vol. 12 no. 3 (1985) p. 2-45.

3590   **Chan, Elaine Y.**
Chinese Students from Hong Kong at the University of Calgary: Their Problems and Sociocultural Orientation. Unpublished MA thesis, University of Calgary, 1987. 2 microfiches. Canadian theses on microfiche, CT89-20766-6.

3591   **Clarke, Sandra**
"Education in the Mother Tongue: Tokenism Versus Cultural Autonomy in Canadian Indian Schools." *Canadian Journal of Anthropology/Revue canadienne d'anthropologie*, vol. 1 no. 2 (1980) p. 205-217.

3592   **Clifton, Rodney A.**
"The Effects of Ethnicity and Sex on Teachers' Expectations of Junior High School Students." *Sociology of Education*, vol. 59 no. 1 (1986) p. 58-67.

3593   **Clifton, Rodney A.**
"Ethnic Differences in the Academic Achievement Process in Canada." *Social Science Research*, vol. 11 no. 1 (1982) p. 67-87.

3594   **Clow, Michael and Terry Conlin**
"The Introductory Canadian Politics Course and Textbook Debate Revisited." *CPSA Papers/ACPS Contributions 1984*, Section A, paper 2, fiche 1-2. Paper presented at the 56th Annual Canadian Political Science Association Meeting, June 10-12, 1984, University of Guelph, Guelph, Ontario.

3595   **Coelho, Elizabeth**
Caribbean Students in Canadian Schools: Book 1. Toronto: Carib-Can Publishers, 1988. 219 p.

3596   **Cohen, Patti K.**
The Formation of a Board of Jewish Education: A Policy Analysis. Unpublished MEd thesis, University of Manitoba, 1984. 2 microfiches. Canadian theses on microfiche, 57854

3597   **Coldevin, G. and T. Wilson**
"Éducation, télévision par satellite et impuissance apprise chez des adolescents Inuit du Canada." *Études Inuit Studies,* vol. 6 no. 1 (1982) p. 29-37.

3598   **Conrad, Brenda Dorm**
"Cooperative Learning and Prejudice Reduction." *Social Education,* vol. 52 no. 4 (1988) p. 283-286.

3599   **Cordeau, Richard**
Attitudes des étudiants en formation des maîtres à l'université du Québec à Montréal vis-à-vis des groupes ethniques: évaluation des changements intervenus au niveau de ces attitudes au cours des dix dernières années. Unpublished MA thesis, Université de Québec à Montréal, 1987. 3 microfiches. Canadian theses on microfiche, CT90-22204-2.

3600   **Courtney, Richard**
"Islands of Remorse: Amerindian Education in the Contemporary World." *Curriculum Inquiry,* vol. 16 no.1 (1986) p. 43-64.

3601   **Cram, Jack**
"Northern Teachers for Northern Schools: An Inuit Teacher-training Program." *McGill Journal of Education,* vol. 20 no. 2 (1985) p. 113-132.

3602   **Craven, Stewart**
"The Education of Native Children." *Comment on Education,* vol. 16 no. 2 (1985) p. 14-17.

3603   **Crawford, James**
Bilingual Education: History, Politics, Theory and Practice. Trenton, Ont.: Crane Publishing, 1989. 204 p.

3604   **Crump, Elizabeth Rose De Filippo**
The Multicultural Orientations of Elementary and Junior High School Children: Edmonton, Alberta. Unpublished PhD thesis, University of Toronto, 1986. 4 microfiches. Canadian theses on microfiche, CT88-24670-7.

3605   **Cullinane, Debra**
"Native Indian Education: A Practical Approach that Works." *The B.C. Teacher,* vol. 66 no. 3 (1987) p. 28-29.

3606   **Cummins, Bryan**
"Indian Control of Indian Education: A Burkian Interpretation." *Canadian Journal of Native Education,* vol. 12 no. 3 (1985) p. 15-20.

3607   **Cummins, Jim**
"Immersion Programs: Current Issues and Future Directions." In: *Contemporary Educational Issues: The Canadian Mosaic,* edited by Leonard L. Stewin and Stewart J.H. McCann. Toronto: Copp Clark, 1987, p. 192-206.

3608   **Cummins, Jim**
"Educational Linguistics and its Sociological Context in Heritage Language Research." In: *Heritage Languages in Canada: Research Perspectives,* edited by Jim Cummins. Ottawa: Department of the Secretary of State of Canada, 1984, p. 45-62. Paper presented at the Heritage Language Research Conference, convened by the Multiculturalism Program, Ottawa, May 1984.

3609   **Cummins, Jim, ed.**
Heritage Language Education: Issues and Directions: Proceedings of a Conference Organized by the Multiculturalism Directorate of the Department if the Secretary of State, Saskatoon, June 1981. Ottawa: Multiculturalism Canada, 1983. 91 p.

3610   **Cziko, Gary A.**
"The Impact of Immersion in a Foreign Language on Pupils' Social Attitudes." *Working Papers on Bilingualism,* vol. 19 (1980) p. 13-28.

3611   **D'Oyley, Vincent**
"Race and Education in Canada." In: *Canada 2000: Race Relations and Public Policy,* edited by O.P. Dwivedi et al. Guelph, Ont.: Department of Political Studies, University of Guelph, 1989, p. 200-203.

3612   **Dandurand, Pierre**
"Les rapports ethniques et le champ universitaire." *Recherches sociographiques*, vol. 27 no. 1 (1986) p. 41-77.

3613   **Danesi, Marcel**
"Heritage Languages in Canadian Elementary Schools: An Educational Experiment Comes of Age." *Polyphony: The Bulletin of the Multicultural History Society of Ontario*, vol. 11 no. 1/2 (1989) p. 49-55.

3614   **Danesi, Marcel and Alberto Di Giovanni**
"Italian as a Heritage Language in Ontario: A Historical Sketch." *Polyphony: The Bulletin of the Multicultural History Society of Ontario*, vol. 11 no. 1/2 (1989) p. 89-94.

3615   **Danys, Milda**
"Lithuanian Collections at the Multicultural History Society." *Polyphony: The Bulletin of the Multicultural History Society of Ontario*, vol. 9 no. 1 (1987) p. 35-38.

3616   **Davis, Sydney**
"The Participation of Indian and Metis Parents in the School System." *Canadian Journal of Native Education*, vol. 13 no. 2 (1986) p. 32-39.

3617   **Dawson, Don**
"Ethnic Language Programs and Policies in Canadian Education: A Typology and Critique." *Education and Society*, vol. 7 no. 1 (1989) p. 3-8.

3618   **Dawson, Don**
"The Politics of Ukrainian Education in Alberta." In: *Osvita: Ukrainian Bilingual Education*, edited by Manoly R. Lupul. Edmonton: Canadian Institute of Ukrainian Studies, University of Alberta, 1985, p. 231-245.

3619   **Dawson, Don**
Community Power Structure and the Rise of Ethnic Language Programs in Public Schooling. Unpublished PhD thesis, University of Alberta, 1982. 4 microfiches. Canadian theses on microfiche, 60269.

3620   **Dawson, Don**
"Ethnic Language and Cultural Maintenance in Canadian Education:
The Trend Towards 'Public Bilingual' Schooling." *Prairie Forum*,
vol. 7 no. 2 (1982) p. 197-212.

3621   **Dawson, Janis**
"'If My Children are Proud': Native Education and the Problem of
Self-esteem." *Canadian Journal of Native Education*, vol. 13 no. 1
(1988) p. 43-50.

3622   **DeFaveri, Ivan**
"Education and the Limits of Tolerance." In: *Essays on Canadian
Education*, by Nick Kach, Kas Mazurek, Robert S. Patterson, Ivan
DeFaveri. Calgary: Detselig Enterprises, 1986, p. 197-205.

3623   **Deines, John Allen**
*A Study of the Cree Culture Course: An Educational Innovation by
the James Bay Cree of Quebec*. Unpublished PhD thesis, University
of Calgary, 1984. 3 microfiches. Canadian theses on microfiche,
66231.

3624   **Denis, Ann B.**
"Education and Ethnic Relations." In: *Two Nations, Many Cultures:
Ethnic Groups in Canada*, edited by Jean Leonard Elliott. 2nd ed.
Scarborough, Ont.: Prentice-Hall of Canada, 1983, p. 110-122.

3625   **Devasahayam, Vaidyanathan S.**
*The Effects of Reading Passages with Indian and Non-Indian Content
on the Silent Reading Comprehension of Native Indian Students*.
Unpublished MEd thesis, University of Regina, 1984. 71 leaves.
Canadian theses on microfiche, CT86-28492-1.

3626   **Dickinson, Greg**
"Toward 'Equal' Status for Catholic Schools in Ontario: The
Supreme Court of Canada Examines Constitutional Issues." *Canadian
and International Education/Éducation canadienne et internationale*,
vol. 16 no. 2 (1987) p. 5-23.

3627   **Divoky, Diane**
"The Model Minority Goes to School." *Phi Delta Kappan*, vol. 70
no. 3 (1988) p. 219-222.

3628   **Donneur, Andre**
"L'évaluation des politiques en relations internationales: le cas de la cooperation franco-québécoise en éducation." *Études internationales*, vol. 14 no. 2 (1983) p. 237-254.

3629   **Downey, Lawrence William**
The Story of Ts'kel: A Program in Educational Administration for Native Educational Leaders. [s.l.: s.n.] 1987. 111p.

3630   **Ducharme, Jean-Charles**
Minority Language Education Rights: Section 23 of the Charter. Current issue review, 89-6E. Ottawa: Library of Parliament, Research Branch, 1989. 18 p. Prepared by the the Library of Parliament, Research Branch, Law and Government Division.

3631   **Ducharme, Jean-Charles**
Minority Language Education Rights. Current issue review. Ottawa: Library of Parliament, Research Branch, 1984. 20 p. Produced by the Library of Parliament, Research Branch, Law and Government Division. Reviewed 25 February, 1988.

3632   **Duhamel, Ronald J.**
"French-language Programme in Manitoba and Saskatchewan: Post-secondary Education Challenges." *Canadian Modern Language Review/Revue canadienne des langues vivantes*, vol. 41 no. 5 (1985) p. 819-826.

3633   **Duquette, Georges J.**
An Ethnographic Study on Language Acquisition in a Culturally Enriched Kindergarten Environment. Unpublished PhD thesis, State University of New York-Buffalo, 1986.

3634   **Dyck, John Edgar**
Religious and Moral Education in Ontario Public Schools: A Pluralist Response. Unpublished MCS thesis, Regent College (University of British Columbia), 1983. 3 microfiches. Canadian theses on microfiche, CT88-22495-9.

3635   **Edwards, Henry P.**
"Partial Immersion for English-speaking Pupils in Elementary School: The Ottawa Roman Catholic Separate School Board in Grade One to Four." *Canadian Modern Language Review/Revue canadienne des langues vivantes*, vol. 37 no. 2 (1981) p. 283-296.

3636   **Eiseman, Thomas Owen**
"Research Report: Caribbean Students in Montreal Schools." *McGill Journal of Education*, vol. 21 no. 2 (1986) p. 163-168.

3637   **Elish, Barbara**
"Should Jewish Supplementary Religious Schools be Like the Public Schools?" *Jewish Education*, vol. 57 nos. 2/3/4 (1989) p. 45-52.

3638   **Elofson, Warren and Betty-Lou**
"Improving Native Education in the Province of Alberta." *Canadian Journal of Native Education*, vol. 15 no. 1 (1988) p. 31-38.

3639   **Fahlman, Ruth**
"What to Say and When to Say It: Interaction in the Multicultural Classroom." *Prime Areas: Journal of British Columbia Teachers Assocation*, vol. 28 no. 3 (1986) p. 16-17.

3640   **Fiordo, Richard**
"The Great Learning Enterprise of the Four World Development Project." *Journal of American Indian Education*, vol. 27 no. 3 (1988) p.24-34.

3641   **Flanagan, Patrick**
Schooling, Souls and Social Class: The Labrador Inuit. Unpublished MA thesis, University of New Brunswick, 1984. Canadian theses on microfiche, CT87-20787-3.

3642   **Forgues, Louis**
L'action du gouvernement fédéral chez les inuits du Nouveau-Québec: le cas de l'éducation, 1949-1975. Unpublished MA thesis, Université Laval, 1987. 2 microfiches. Canadian theses on microfiche, CT89-24762-5.

3643   **Foucher, Pierre**
"Language Rights and Education." In: *Language Rights in Canada*, edited by Michel Bastarache. Montreal: Editions Y. Blais, 1987, p. 259-315. Translation of the author's "Les droits linguistiques en matière scolaire" chapter in the book: *Les droits linguistiques au Canada*, p. 273-329.

3644   **Francis, Mary Annexstad**
The Role of Values Education in Multicultural Education. Unpublished PhD thesis, University of Toronto, 1980. 3 microfiches. Canadian theses on microfiche, 47049.

3645   **Freedman, Philip I.**
"Multiethnic/Multicultural Education: Establishing the Foundations."
The Social Studies, vol. 75 no. 5 (1984) p. 200-202.

3646   **Frideres, James S.**
"Native People and Canadian Education." In: *The Political Economy
of Canadian Schooling*, edited by Terry Wotherspoon. Toronto:
Methuen, 1987. p. 275-289.

3647   **Friesen, John W.**
"Education and Effective Interpersonal Relationships: A Multicultural
Prospective." *The Alberta Counsellor*, vol. 14 no.1 (1985) p. 31-37.

3648   **Friesen, John W.**
"Establishing Objectives for a Multicultural Program." *The History
and Social Science Teacher*, vol. 21 no. 1 (1985) p. 34-38.

3649   **Friesen, John W.**
"Lest We Forget ..." *Multicultural Education Journal*, vol. 3 no. 1
(1985) p. 2-4.

3650   **Friesen, John W. and Esha R. Chaudhuri**
"Developing a School Multicultural Program." *Multicultural
Education Journal*, vol. 4 no. 1 (1986) p. 35-79.

3651   **Gayle, C.**
"Effective Second Language Teaching Styles." *Canadian Modern
Language Review/Revue canadienne des langues vivantes*, vol. 40 no.
4 (1984) p. 525-541.

3652   **Genesee, Fred**
"Three Elementary School Alternatives for Learning Through a
Second Language." *Modern Language Journal*, vol. 73 no. 3
(1989) p. 250-263.

3653   **Genesee, Fred**
"The Linguistic and Academic Development of English-speaking
Children in French Schools: Grade 4 Outcomes." *Canadian Modern
Language Review/Revue canadienne des langues vivantes*, vol. 41 no.
4 (1985) p. 669-685.

3654 **Genesee, Fred**
"French Immersion Programs." In: *Bilingual and Multicultural Education: Canadian Perspectives*, edited by S.M. Shapson and V. D'Oyley. Avon, Eng.: Multicultural Matters, 1984, p. 33-54.

3655 **Genesee, Fred**
"Bilingual Education of Majority-language Children: The Immersion Experiments in Review." *Applied Psycholinguistics*, vol. 4 no. 1 (1983) p. 1-46.

3656 **Genesee, Fred**
"Trilingual Education for Majority-language Children." *Child Development*, vol. 54 no. 1 (1983) p. 105-114.

3657 **Gerlai, Esther**
Differences in Reading Attainment Among Ethnic Minority Children in the Primaries from a Social Perspective. Unpublished MA thesis, University of Toronto, 1980.

3658 **Ghosh, Ratna and Douglas Ray, eds.**
Social Change and Education in Canada. Don Mills, Ont.: Harcourt Brace Jovanovich, 1987. 288 p.

3659 **Gillett, James Stephen**
"Ethnic Bilingual Education for Canada's Minority Groups." *Canadian Modern Language Review/Revue canadienne des langues vivantes*, vol. 43 no. 2 (1987) p. 337-356.

3660 **Gillett, James Stephen**
Student Achievement in Canadian Heritage Language Partial Immersion Programs: A Meta-evaluation. Unpublished MEd thesis, University of Saskatchewan, 1984.

3661 **Givan, David**
"Private Lives and Teacher Discipline [New Brunswick's Malcolm Ross Case]." *The Canadian School Executive*, vol. 8 no. 3 (1988) p. 3-7.

3662 **Gliksman, L.**
"The Role of Intergrative Motive on Students' Participation in the French Classroom." *Canadian Modern Language Review/Revue canadienne des langues vivantes*, vol. 38 no. 4 (1982) p. 625-647.

3663   **Grant, Linda**
"Regenerating and Refocusing Research on Minorities and Education." *The Elementary School Journal*, vol. 88 no. 5 (1988) p. 441-448.

3664   **Grant, Linda, ed.**
"Minorities." *The Elementary School Journal*, vol. 88 no. 5 (1988) p. 441-571.

3665   **Gray, Vicky A.**
"A Summary of the Elementary School Evaluation of the Early French Immersion Program in Fredericton, New Brunswick." *Canadian Modern Language Review/Revue canadienne des langues vivantes*, vol. 42 no. 5 (1986) p. 940-951.

3666   **Grossman, Judith F.**
"Curriculum and Ideology: Indoctrination as an Inappropriate Approach to Conservative Jewish Education." *Jewish Education*, vol. 57 nos. 2-4 (1989) p. 39-41.

3667   **Grove, D. John**
"Cultural Participation and Educational Achievement: A Cross-cultural Analysis." *International Journal of Comparative Sociology*, vol. 26 no. 3/4 (1985) p. 232-240.

3668   **Guimond, Serge**
"Education, Academic Program and Intergroup Attitudes." *Canadian Review of Sociology and Anthropology/Revue canadienne de sociologie et d'anthropologie*, vol. 26 no. 2 (1989) p. 193-216.

3669   **Hammerly, Hector**
"The Immersion Approach: Litmus Test of Second Language Acquisition Through Classroom Communication." *Modern Language Journal*, vol. 71 no. 4 (1987) p. 395-401.

3670   **Harney, Robert F.**
"Ethnic Archival and Library Materials in Canada: Problems of Bibliographic Control and Preservation." *Ethnic Forum*, vol. 2 no. 2 (1982) p. 3-31.

3671   **Henchey, Norman**
Between Past and Future: Quebec Education in Transition. Calgary: Detselig Enterprises, 1987. 294 p.

3672   **Henley, Richard**
"The Campaign for Compulsory Education in Manitoba." *Canadian Journal of Education/Revue canadienne de l'education*, vol. 7 no. 1 (1982) p. 59-83.

3673   **Herberg, Edward Norman**
Education Through the Ethnic Looking-glass: Ethnicity and Education in Five Canadian Cities. Unpublished PhD thesis, University of Toronto, 1980. 728 p. Canadian theses on microfiche, 47074.

3674   **Heydenkorn, Benedykt**
"The Canadian Polish Research Institute and the MHSO." *Polyphony: The Bulletin of the Multicultural History Society of Ontario*, vol. 9 no. 1 (1987) p. 28-30.

3675   **B.H. [Benedykt Heydenkorn]**
"Polish Voices." *Polyphony: The Bulletin of the Multicultural History Society of Ontario*, vol. 6 no. 2 (1984) p. 122.

3676   **Hirschberg, Jack Jacob**
Secular and Parochial Education of Ashkenazi and Sephardi Jewish Children in Montreal: A Study in Ethnicity. Unpublished PhD thesis, McGill University, 1989.

3677   **Hull, Jeremy**
Overview of the Educational Characteristics of Registered Indians in Canada. Winnipeg: Working Margins Consulting Group for Indian and Northern Affairs Canada, 1987. 223 p.

3678   **Hurlbert, Earl Leroy**
School Law Under the Charter of Rights and Freedoms. Calgary: University of Calgary Press, 1989. 254 p.

3679   **Ijaz, M. Ahmed**
Ethnic Attitudes of Elementary School Children Toward Blacks and East Indians and the Effect of a Cultural Program on These Attitudes. Unpublished EdD thesis, University of Toronto, 1980. 4 microfiches. Canadian theses on microfiche, 50277.

3680   **Impara, Marta Maria**
A Comparative Study of Educational Programs for Linguistic Minorities in Three Pluralistic Nations: Canada, Peru, and Sweden. Unpublished PhD thesis, Florida State University, 1986. 343 p. Canadian theses on microfiche, CT87-25462-6.

3681   **Irving, Hyacinth Michele**
        An Analysis of Ontario's Junior Division Social Studies Textbooks in Relation to Multiculturalism. Unpublished MA thesis, University of Ottawa, 1986. 2 microfiches. Canadian theses on microfiche, CT88-21920-3.

3682   **Irwin, Leslie**
        Attitudes of Southern Alberta Elementary School Teachers Toward Multicultural Education. Unpublished EdD thesis, Brigham Young University (Provost, Utah), 1988. 2 microfiches. Canadian theses on microfiche, CT89-26828-2.

3683   **Isser, Natalie and Lita Linzer Schwartz**
        The American School and the Melting Pot: Minority Self-esteem and Public Education. Bristol: Wyndham Hall Press, 1985. 271 p.

3684   **Jackman, Martha**
        "Minority Language Education Rights Under the Charter." *University of Toronto Faculty of Law Review*, vol. 43 no. 2 (1985) p. 16-71.

3685   **Jamieson, Margaret**
        The Immigrant Child and Adjustment to Learning in a Second Culture. Unpublished PhD thesis, Univesity of Alberta, 1982. 3 microfiche. Canadian theses on microfiche, no. 56827.

3686   **Jansen, Clifford J.**
        Education and Social Mobility of Immigrants: A Pilot Study Focussing on Italians in Vancouver. Downsview, Ontario: Institute for Behavioural Research, York University, 1981. 100 p.

3687   **Javed, Tahir**
        Concepts and Issues in Multicultural Education: A Conceptual Analysis. Unpublished MA thesis, Concordia University, 1987. 2 microfiches, illustrations. Canadian theses on microfiche, CT89-20363-6.

3688   **Johnston, Eric and Diane Longboat**
        "Sovereignty, Jurisdiction and Guiding Principles in Aboriginal Education in Canada." *The Canadian Journal of Native Studies*, vol. 6 no. 1 (1986) p. 173-180.

3689   **Jones, Frank E.**
"Age at Immigration and Education: Further Explorations."
International Migration/Migrations Internationales/Migraciones Inter-nacionales, vol. 21 no. 1 (1987) p. 70-85.

3690   **Jones, Frank E.**
"Age at Immigration and Educational Attainment." *Canadian Review of Sociology and Anthropology/Revue canadienne de sociologie et d'anthropologie*, vol. 18 no. 3 (1981) p. 393-404.

3691   **Jones, Robert**
"Teachers' Freedom of Expression [New Brunswick's Malcolm Ross Case]." *The Canadian School Executive*, vol. 8 no. 3 (1988) p. 8-9.

3692   **Josephson, M.I. (Joe)**
"TEFL and the Case for Indian Universities." *Canadian Journal of Native Education*, vol. 13 no. 2 (1986) p. 3-10.

3693   **Kach, Nick**
"Education and Ethnic Acculturation: A Case Study." In: *Essays on Canadian Education*, edited by Nick Kach, Kas Mazurek, Robert S. Patterson and Ivan DeFaveri. Calgary: Detselig Enterprises, 1986, p. 41-60.

3694   **Kach, Nick, Kas Mazurek, Robert S. Patterson, and Ivan DeFaveri**
Essays on Canadian Education. Calgary: Detselig Enterprises, 1986. 244 p.

3695   **Kaprielian, Isabel**
"Armenian Supplementary Schools in Southern Ontario." *Polyphony: The Bulletin of the Multicultural History Society of Ontario*, vol. 11 no. 1/2 (1989) p. 18-23.

3696   **Kaprielian, Isabel**
"Multiple Uses of an Ethnic Archives." *Polyphony: The Bulletin of the Multicultural History Society of Ontario*, vol. 9 no. 1 (1987) p. 73-74.

3697   **Kayfetz, Ben**
"My Life at Cheder." *Polyphony: The Bulletin of the Multicultural History Society of Ontario*, vol. 11 no. 1/2 (1989) p. 144-147.

3698   **Kehoe, Jack**
"Achieving the Goals of Multicultural Education in the Classroom."
In: *Multiculturalism in Canada: Social and Educational Perspectives,*
edited by Ronald J. Samuda, John W. Berry and Michel Laferrière.
Toronto: Allyn and Bacon Inc., 1984, p. 139-153.

3699   **Kendall, Janet Ross**
"English Reading Skills of French Immersion Students in Kindergarten and Grades 1 and 2." *Reading Research Quarterly,* vol. 22 no.
2 (1987) p. 135-159.

3700   **Kim, Jung G.**
"Ontario Ethnocultural Newspapers: Bibliography and Microfilming
Project—Its Inception and Progress." *Polyphony: The Bulletin of the
Multicultural History Society of Ontario,* vol. 4 no. 1 (1982) p. 139-
140.

3701   **Kleinfeld, Judith, Joe Cooper, and Nathan Kyle**
"Post Secondary Counselors: A Model for Increasing Native
American College Success." *Journal of American Indian Education,*
vol. 27 no. 1 (1987) p. 9-16.

3702   **Koens, Peter R.**
"Local Control Within a Model of the Sociology of Knowledge: A
Study in Curriculum." *Canadian Journal of Native Education,* vol. 16
no. 1 (1989) p. 37-44.

3703   **Kojder, Apolonja**
"Polish Schools in Toronto." *Polyphony: The Bulletin of the
Multicultural History Society of Ontario,* vol. 6 no. 2 (1984) p. 41-
46.

3704   **Kroeh-Sommer, Helma**
Ethnicity, Individual Modernity, and Academic Attributions. Unpub-
lished MA thesis, University of Concordia, 1986. 2 microfiches.
Canadian theses on microfiche, CT88-20756-6.

3705   **Laferrière, Michel**
"L'éducation des enfants des groupes minoritaires au Québec: de la
définition des problèmes par les groupes eux-mêmes à l'intervention
de l'État." *Sociologie et sociétés,* vol. 15 no. 2 (1984) p. 117-132.

3706   **Laferrière, Michel**
"Languages, Ideologies, and Multicultural Education in Canada:
Some Historical and Sociological Perspectives." In: *Multiculturalism
in Canada: Social and Educational Perspectives*, edited by Ronald J.
Samuda, John W. Berry and Michel Laferrière. Toronto: Allyn and
Bacon Inc., 1984, p. 171-183.

3707   **Laferrière, Michel**
"The Education of West Indian and Haitian Students in the Schools
of Montreal: Issues and Prospects." In: *Two Nations, Many Cultures:
Ethnic Groups in Canada*, edited by Jean Leonard Elliott. 2nd ed.
Scarborough, Ontario: Prentice-Hall of Canada, 1983, p. 158-172.

3708   **Laferrière, Michel**
"Éducation interculturelle et multiculturalism: ambiguités et occulta-
tions." *Canadian Society for the Study of Education, Yearbook*, vol. 8
(1981) p. 27-37.

3709   **Laine, Edward W.**
*Archival Sources for the Study of Finnish Canadians/Sources
d'archives sur les finno-canadiens*. Ottawa: National Archives of
Canada/Archives nationales du Canada, 1989. 104 p.

3710   **Laine, Edward W.**
*On the Archival Heritage of the Finnish Canadian Working-class
Movement: A Researcher's Guide and Inventory to the Finnish
Organization of Canada Collection at the National Archives of
Canada*. Research Report no. 5. Turku, Finland: Institute of
Migration, 1987. 455 p. (Siirtolaisuusinstituutti: Tutkimuksia/
Migrationsinstitutet: Forskningsrapporter/Institute of Migration)

3711   **Lalonde Emile**
*A Case Study of the Development of Indian Autonomy of Reserve
Schools in a Saskatchewan District*. Unpublished MEd thesis,
University of Regina, 1986. 2 microfiches. Canadian theses on
microfiche, CT88-21992-0.

3712   **Laperrière, Anne**
"L'intégration scolaire d'enfants immigrants en milieu populaire
montréalais: vers une autre école." *Cahiers de recherche
sociologique*, vol. 2 no. 2 (1984) p. 91-113.

3713   **Larose, François**
"Perspectives de développement des services universitaires sur le terrain en milieux algonquins et développement pédagogique communautaire." *The Canadian Journal of Native Studies*, vol. 6 no. 1 (1986) p. 181-195.

3714   **Lavoie-Roux, Therese**
"Education, Cultural Survival and National Identity." In: *Federal-provincial Relations: Education Canada*, edited by J.W. George Ivany and Michael E. Manley-Casimir. Toronto: OISE, 1981, p. 73-79.

3715   **Lawrence, Glace W.**
"Preserving Ontario's Black Heritage: The Ontario Black History Society." *Polyphony: The Bulletin of the Multicultural History Society of Ontario*, vol. 9 no. 1 (1987) p. 56-58.

3716   **Leduc, Yvan**
"The French-Canadian Bourgeoisie, the Clergy, and Physical Education in Canada East and Quebec, 1840-1875." In: *Proceedings 5th Canadian Symposium on the History of Sports and Physical Education*. Toronto: University of Toronto Press, 1982, p. 386.

3717   **Lee, Jena Chi-Yung**
Chinese-English Bilingual Education: Parental Attitudes and Bilingual Schooling. Unpublished MEd thesis, University of Alberta, 1984. 125 leaves. Canadian theses on microfiche, CT87-22660-6.

3718   **Lee, John D.**
"Psychosocial Differences Among Chinese Canadian and Non-Chinese Students." *Canadian Ethnic Studies/Études ethniques au Canada*, vol. 14 no. 3 (1982) p. 43-56.

3719   **Lee, Keng Mun**
Chinese Foreign Students' Adjustment at the University of Windsor: A Social Constructionist Perspective. Unpublished MA thesis, University of Windsor, 1986. 2 microfiches. Canadian theses on microfiche, CT88-25384-3.

3720   **Less, John D.**
"Education of Native Adolescents in Inner-city Schools." *Canadian Journal of Native Education*, vol. 13 no. 2 (1986) p. 22-26.

3721   **Lin, Ruey-Lin, Deborah La Counte and Jeanne Eder**
"A Study of Native American Students in a Predoniinantly White College." *Journal of American Indian Education*, vol. 27 no. 3 (1988) p. 8-15.

3722   **Lindsay, Anne Crawford**
A Study of the Oral Narrative Discourse Style of Young Indian Children in a School-related Activity. Unpublished MA thesis, University of Victoria, 1988. 4 microfiches. Canadian theses on microfiche, CT90-21341-8.

3723   **Lindsey, Edward H.**
"Linguistic Minority Educational Rights in Canada: An International and Comparative Perspective." *Georgia Journal of International and Comparative Law*, vol. 13 no. 3 (1983) p. 515-547.

3724   **Lingard, John**
Multicultural Education: Perception and Implementation at the School Division Level in Saskatchewan. Unpublished MEd thesis, University of Saskatchewan, 1988.

3725   **Lorimer, Rowland M.**
The Nation in the Schools: Wanted: A Canadian Education. Toronto: OISE Press, 1984. 113 p.

3726   **Luciuk, Lubomyr**
"Canadian Ucrainica at the MHSO." *Polyphony: The Bulletin of the Multicultural History Society of Ontario*, vol. 9 no. 1 (1987) p. 23-25.

3727   **Magnet, Joseph Eliot**
"A New Deal in Minority Language Education." In: *Courts in the Classroom: Education and the Charter of Rights and Freedoms*, edited by Michael E. Manley-Casimir, and Terri A. Sussel. Calgary: Detselig Enterprises, 1986, p. 105-114. Paper presented at The 4th National Educational Policy Conference: The Charter of Rights and Freedoms: Catalyst for Educational Reform, held at Simon Fraser University, June 1983.

3728   **Magocsi, Paul Robert**
"The Chair of Ukrainian Studies at the University of Toronto." *Polyphony: The Bulletin of the Multicultural History Society of Ontario*, vol. 10 no. 1/2 (1988) p. 221-228.

3729   **Magor, Murray C.**
The Language of Education in Quebec: A Study of Bill 101 in Terms of Constitutional and Natural Law. Unpublished MA thesis, McGill University, 1982. 2 microfiches. Canadian theses on microfiche, 61106.

3730   **Mah, Hilda**
A History of the Education of Chinese Canadians in Alberta, 1885-1947. Unpublished MEd thesis University of Alberta, 1987. 3 microfiches.

3731   **Mahe, Y.T.M.**
"Two Teachers' Perspectives on Social Studies Teaching in French Immersion." *Alberta Journal of Educational Research*, vol. 32 no. 3 (1986) p. 201-211.

3732   **Mallea, John R.**
Schooling in a Plural Canada. Clevedon, Eng.: Multilingual Matters Ltd., 1989. 143 p.

3733   **Mallea, John R.**
"Cultural Diversity in Canadian Education: A Review of Contemporary Developments." In: *Multiculturalism in Canada: Social and Educational Perspectives*, edited by Ronald J. Samuda, John W. Berry and Michel Laferrière. Toronto: Allyn and Bacon Inc., 1984, p. 78-97.

3734   **Mallea, John R.**
"Heritage Languages, Culture and Schooling." In: *Heritage Languages in Canada: Research Perspectives*, edited by Jim Cummins. Ottawa: Department of the Secretary of State of Canada, 1984, p. 83-95. Paper presented at the Heritage Language Research Conference, convened by the Multiculturalism Program, Ottawa, May 1984.

3735   **Mallea, John R.**
"Minority Language Education in Quebec and Anglophone Canada." In: *Conflict and Language Planning in Quebec*, edited by Richard Y. Bourhis. Clevedon, Avon, [Eng.]: Multilingual Matters, 1984, p. 222-260.

3736   **Mallea, John R.**
"Cultural Diversity and Canadian Education." In: *Federal-provincial Relations: Education Canada*, edited by J.W. George Ivany and Michael E. Manley-Casimir. Toronto: OISE, 1981, p. 91-104.

3737   **Manicom, Ann**
"Ideology and Multicultural Curriculum: Deconstructing Elementary Texts." In: *Breaking the Mosaic*, edited by Jon Joung. Toronto: Garamond Press, 1987, p. 75-103.

3738   **Manley-Casimir, Michael E. and Terri A. Sussel**
Courts in the Classroom: Education and the Charter of Rights and Freedoms. Calgary: Detselig Enterprises, 1986. 244 p.

3739   **Marcuzzi, Rose Marie**
"Urban Education of Indian/Native Children." *Canadian Journal of Native Education*, vol. 13 no. 2 (1986) p. 27-31.

3740   **Martel, Angeline**
"The Canadian Constitution and Issues of Power Structures in Minority Education." In: *Breaking the Mosaic*, edited by Jon Joung. Toronto: Garamond Press, 1987, p. 247-275.

3741   **Masemann, V.L.**
"Comparative Perspectives on Multicultural Education." *Canadian Society for the Study of Education, Yearbook*, vol. 8 (1981) p. 38-48.

3742   **Matiss, Ilze A. and Solveiga Miezitis**
"Meeting the Challenge of Heritage Language Retention at the Toronto Latvian School Valodina." *Polyphony: The Bulletin of the Multicultural History Society of Ontario*, vol. 11 no. 1/2 (1989) p. 121-124.

3743   **Mazurek, Kas**
"Initiatives and Opportunities in Native American Education at the University of Lethbridge." *Canadian Journal of Native Education*, vol. 15 no. 1 (1988) p. 84-89.

3744   **Mazurek, Kas**
"Multiculturalism, Education and the Ideology of the Meritocracy." In: *The Political Economy of Canadian Schooling*, edited by Terry Wotherspoon. Toronto: Methuen, 1987. p. 141-179.

3745   **Mazurek, Kas**
"Culture and Power: Educational Ideologies in Multicultural Canada."
In: *Essays on Canadian Education*, edited by Nick Kach, Kas
Mazurek, Robert S. Patterson, and Ivan DeFaveri. Calgary: Detselig
Enterprises, 1986, p. 161-181.

3746   **Mazurek, Kas**
"Culture and Power: Educational Ideologies in Multicultural Canada."
New Education, vol. 5 no. 2 (1983) p. 47-59.

3747   **McCall, D.**
"Evolution and Revolution, Secondary School Changes for Ontario
and Quebec." *McGill Journal of Education*, vol. 17 no. 2
(1982) p. 111-119.

3748   **McCarthy, Cameron**
"Rethinking Liberal and Radical Perspectives on Racial Inequality in
Schooling: Making the Case for Nonsynchrony." *Harvard
Educational Review*, vol. 58 no. 3 (1988) p. 265-279.

3749   **McCarthy-Senebald, Maryanne**
*Native Peoples' Access to Adult Basic Education: Factors for
Consideration in Program Planning*. Unpublished M.Ad.Ed. thesis,
St. Francis Xavier University, 1989.

3750   **McInnes, Alan Douglas Ian**
Blue Quills: A Case Study in Locally Controlled Indian Education.
Unpublished MEd thesis, University of Alberta, 1987. 3 microfiches.
Canadian theses on microfiche, CT88-27083-7.

3751   **McLeod, Keith A.**
"Multiculturalism and Multicultural Education: Policy and Practice."
In: *Multiculturalism in Canada: Social and Educational Perspectives*,
edited by Ronald J. Samuda, John W. Berry and Michel Laferrière.
Toronto: Allyn and Bacon Inc., 1984, p. 30-49.

3752   **McLeod, Keith A.**
"Multicultural Education: A Decade of Development." In: *Two
Nations, Many Cultures: Ethnic Groups in Canada*, edited by Jean
Leonard Elliott. 2nd ed. Scarborough, Ont.: Prentice-Hall of Canada,
1983, p. 243-259.

3753   **McLeod, Keith A.**
"Multiculturalism and Multicultural Education; Policy and Practice."
In: *Canadian Society for the Study of Education. Yearbook*, vol. 8
(1981) p. 12-26.

3754   **McLeod, Keith A., ed.**
Canada and Citizenship Education. Toronto: Canadian Educational
Association, 1989. 199 p.

3755   **McLeod, Keith A., ed.**
Multicultural Early Childhood Education. Toronto: Guidance Centre,
Faculty of Education, University of Toronto, 1984. 155 p.

3756   **McMahon, Francis**
*Significations de la culture dans l'école française hors Québec: le
cas de la Citadelle.* Unpublished PhD thesis, Université de Montréal,
1986. 1 microfilm.

3757   **McNeely, David Douglas**
*An Analysis of the Learning Styles of Native Indian Students in
Grades One Through Seven.* Unpublished MSc thesis, University of
Calgary, 1985. 2 microfiches. Canadian theses on microfiche, CT86-
26384-3.

3758   **McPhie, Judith Lynn**
"Attitude Change Through Cultural Immersion: A Grade Four
Enrichment Curriculum." *Canadian Ethnic Studies/Études ethniques
au Canada*, vol. 21 no. 1 (1989) p. 65-76.

3759   **McPhie, Judith Lynn**
*Attitude Change Through Cultural Immersion: A Grade Four Enrich-
ment Curriculum in Pre-contact Squamish Longhouse Life.*
Unpublished MA thesis, Simon Fraser University, 1987. 2
microfiches. Canadian theses on microfiche, CT89-26529-1.

3760   **Mellouki, M'hammed**
*Savoir enseignant et idéologie réformiste: la formation des maitres,
1930-1964.* Quebec, P.Q.: Institut québécois de recherche sur la
culture, 1989. 392 p.

3761   **Melnyk, Iryna**
Ukrainian Bilingual Education in the Montreal Public School System.
Unpublished MA thesis, McGill University.

3762   **Mercier, Jean**
"L'apprentissage politique des jeunes québécois dans les écoles." In: *Political Education in Canada*, edited by Jon H. Pammett and Jean-Luc Pepin. Halifax: Institute for Research on Public Policy, 1988, p. 53-64.

3763   **Migué, Jean-Luc**
Le monopole public de l'éducation: l'économie politique de la mediocrité. Sillery, P.Q.: Les Presses de l'Université du Québec, 1989. 195 p.

3764   **Milner, Henry**
"Quebec Educational Reform and the Protestant School Establishment." In: *Quebec: State and Society.* edited by Alain G. Gagnon. Toronto: Methuen, 1984, p. 410-425.

3765   **Milner, Henry**
"The Deconfessionalization of Montreal's School System: The Rights of Entrenched Minorities Versus the Capacity of Institutions to Evolve with Their Community." In: *CPSA Papers 1981/ACSP Contributions 1981*, Section: Public Policy, paper 3, fiches 1-2. Paper presented at the 53rd annual meeting of the Canadian Political Science Association, May 27-29, 1981, Dalhousie University, Halifax, N.S.

3766   **Miodunka, Wladyslaw**
"The Polonia Research Institute of the Jagiellonian University." *Polyphony: The Bulletin of the Multicultural History Society of Ontario*, vol. 9 no. 1 (1987) p. 92-93.

3767   **Mollica, Tony**
"Teaching Heritage Languages: What the Teachers Need to Know." *Polyphony: The Bulletin of the Multicultural History Society of Ontario*, vol. 11 no. 1/2 (1989) p. 62-66.

3768   **Moodley, Kogila, ed.**
Race Relations and Multicultural Education. Vancouver: Centre for the Study of Curriculum and Instruction, University of British Columbia, 1985. 123 p.

3769   **Mori, G.A.**
Educational Attainment of Canadians. 1986 Census of Canada, Focus on Canada. Ottawa: Statistics Canada, 1989. 50, 52 p. French language title: *Niveau de scolarité des canadiens.*

3770   **Morris, Sonia V., ed.**
Multicultural and Intercultural Education: Building Canada. Calgary: Detselig Enterprises Ltd., 1989. 255 p. Papers presented at a conference sponsored by the Canadian Council for Multicultural and Intercultural Education, held in Edmonton in 1987.

3771   **Morrison, Frances C.**
Aspects of French Immersion at the Primary and Secondary Levels: Evaluation of the Second Language Learning (French) Programs in the Schools of the Ottawa and Carleton Boards of Education. Toronto: Ontario Ministry of Education, 1986. 91 p.

3772   **Morrison, Frances C.**
Evaluation of the Second Language Learning (French) Programs in the Schools of Ottawa and Carleton Boards of Education. 3 vols. Toronto: Ontario Ministry of Education, 1986.

3773   **Morrison, Frances C.**
After Immersion: Ottawa and Carleton Students at the Secondary and Post-secondary Level: Evaluation at the Second Language Learning (French) Programs in the Schools of Ottawa and Carleton Boards of Education. Ottawa: Ottawa Board of Education, Research Centre, 1982. 157 p.

3774   **Moreau, Bernice M.**
"Adult Education Among Black Nova Scotians: 1750-1945." *Journal of Education,* (1987) p. 29-35.

3775   **Morrow, Robert D.**
"Cultural Differences — Be Aware!: The Vast Differences in Various Cultures Require that Teachers, When Conferencing with Southeast Asian Parents, Approach the Subject of Exceptionality with Insight and Caution." *Academic Therapy,* vol. 23 no. 2 (1987) p. 143-149.

3776   **Mougeon, Raymond**
"The Social and Historical Context of Minority French Language Education in Ontario." *Journal of Multilingual and Multicultural Development,* vol. 7 no. 2/3 (1986) p. 199-227.

3777   **Mougeon, Raymond**
"Le problème des élèves anglo-dominants dans les écoles ontariennes de langue française: acquisition, emploi et enseignement du français." *Canadian Modern Language Review/Revue canadienne des langues vivantes,* vol. 41 no. 2 (1984) p. 336-352.

3778   **Mu, Hai**
A Study of Characteristics of Chinese ESL Learners in MBA
Programs at Canadian Universities. Unpublished PhD thesis,
University of Alberta, 1987. 250 p. Canadian theses on microfiche,
CT89-21976-1.

3779   **Murdoch, John**
"Ethnic-relativism in Cree Curriculum Development."
Multiculturalism in Canada: Social and Educational Perspectives,
edited by Ronald J. Samuda, John W. Berry and Michel Laferrière.
Toronto: Allyn and Bacon Inc., 1984, p. 292-300.

3780   **Myles, David W.**
Teacher Bias Towards Visible Ethnic Minority Groups in Special
Education Referrals. Unpublished MA thesis, University of British
Columbia, 1987. 162 p. Canadian theses on microfiche, 417773.

3781   **Myles, David W. and Harold C. Ratzlaff**
"Teachers' Bias Towards Visible Ethnic Minority Groups in Special
Education Referrals." B.C. Journal of Special Education, vol. 12 no.
1 (1988) p. 19-28.

3782   **NS [Anonymous]**
"Toronto Greek Communal School, 1930-33." Polyphony: The
Bulletin of the Multicultural History Society of Ontario, vol. 6 no. 1
(1984) p. 233-236.

3783   **Nagy, Philip**
"Attitudes to, and Impact of French Immersion." Canadian Journal
of Education/Revue canadienne de l'éducation, vol. 13 no. 2
(1988) p. 263-276.

3784   **Nakonechny, Carole**
Classroom Communication: A Case Study of Native Indian
Adolescents. Unpublished MA thesis, University of British Columbia,
1986. 150 leaves. Canadian theses on microfiche, CT88-23753-8.

3785   **National Indian Brotherhood**
"Indian Control of Indian Education." In: Cultural Diversity and
Canadian Education: Issues and Innovations, edited by John R.
Mallea and Jonathan C. Young. Ottawa: Carleton University Press,
1984, p. 131-149.

3786   **Native Indian Pre-school Curriculum Research Project**
Native Indian Pre-school Curriculum Resources Bibliography.
Vancouver: Urban Native Indian Education Society, 1983.

3787   **Netten, Joan E.**
"Student-teacher Interaction Patterns in the French Immersion
Classroom: Implications for Levels of Achievement in French
Language Proficiency." *Canadian Modern Language Review/Revue
canadienne des langues vivantes*, vol. 45 no. 3 (1989) p. 483-501.

3788   **Nigro, Saverio**
"Heritage Language Teaching in Thunder Bay." *Polyphony: The
Bulletin of the Multicultural History Society of Ontario*, vol. 11 no.
1/2 (1989) p. 116.

3789   **Oishi, Mitsuko**
Native Education and Labour Market Segmentation. Unpublished
MEd thesis University of Alberta, 1985. 3 microfiches. Canadian
theses on microfiche, CT86-25523-9.

3790   **Olthuis, J.A.**
"Collective Rights in Education." In: *Courts in the Classroom:
Education and the Charter of Rights and Freedoms*, edited by
Michael E. Manley-Casimir and Terri A. Sussel. Calgary: Detselig
Enterprises, 1986, p. 125-132. Paper presented at the 4th National
Educational Policy Conference: The Charter of Rights and Freedoms;
Catalyst for Educational Reform, held at Simon Fraser University,
June 1983.

3791   **Pacquette, Jerald**
"Policy, Power and Purpose: Lessons from Two Indian Education
Scenarios." *Journal of Canadian Studies/Revue d'études canadiennes*,
vol. 24 no. 2 (1989) p. 78-94.

3792   **Painchaud, Giséle, Allison d'Anglejan, et Claude Renaud**
Acquisition du français par des immigrants adultes du Québec.
Montréal: Université de Montréal, Faculté des sciences de
l'éducation, 1984. 75 p.

3793   **Papp, Susan M.**
"Hungarian Language Education in Ontario." *Polyphony: The Bulletin
of the Multicultural History Society of Ontario*, vol. 11 no. 1/2
(1989) p. 75-79.

3794   **Parsonson, Karen**
Ethnic Heritage and Perceived Control: Implications for the College Classroom. Unpublished MA thesis, University of Manitoba, 1984. 2 microfiches. Canadian theses on microfiche, 57770.

3795   **Paul, Philip**
"The First Nations, Canada and Education." In: *Federal-provincial Relations: Education Canada,* edited by J.W. George Ivany and Michael E. Manley-Casimir. Toronto: OISE, 1981, p. 87-90.

3796   **Paulet, Robert**
"Special Education Programs for Northern Clients." *Multicultural Education,* vol. 5 no. 2 (1987) p. 14-23.

3797   **Pawley, Catherine**
"How Bilingual are French Immersion Students?" *Canadian Modern Language Review/Revue canadienne des langues vivantes,* vol. 41 no. 5 (1985) p. 865-876.

3798   **Pejovic, Zoran**
Boulevard of Dreams: Croatians and Education in Ontario. Unpublished PhD thesis, York University, 1989.

3799   **Pennacchio, Luigi G.**
"Italian Heritage Language Classes in Pre-second World War Toronto." *Polyphony: The Bulletin of the Multicultural History Society of Ontario,* vol. 11   no. 1/2 (1989) p. 36-44.

3800   **Pépin, Gilles**
"L'article 93 de la Constitution et des droits relatifs à la confessionalité des écoles du Québec." *Revue du Barreau,* vol. 48 no. 3 (1988) p. 427-465.

3801   **Persi, Joseph**
"Cognitive Measures and Cultural Bias: A Comparison of the Performances of Native and Non-native Low Achievers." *Canadian Journal of Native Education,* vol. 14 no. 1 (1987) p. 15-18.

3802   **Pertusati, Linda**
"Beyond Segregation or Integration: A Case Study from Effective Native American Education." *Journal of American Indian Education,* vol. 27 no. 2 (1988) p. 10-20.

3803   **Peterson, Kenneth D., Donna Deyhle, and William Watkins**
"Evaluation that Accommodates Minority Teacher Contributions."
Urban Education, vol. 23 no. 2 (1988) p. 133-149.

3804   **Petroff, Lillian**
"An All-important Business: Educating Macedonian Youth in Toronto
Before World War II." *Polyphony: The Bulletin of the Multicultural
History Society of Ontario*, vol. 11 no. 1/2 (1989) p. 24-27.

3805   **Poisson, Rene Emile**
*Teacher Perception of Socio-cultural Factors Affecting Education in
Multicultural Classrooms.* Unpublished MEd thesis, University of
Saskatchewan, 1982. 113 leaves.

3806   **Polyzoi, Eleoussa**
"The Experience of One Teacher in Greek Communal Schools."
*Polyphony: The Bulletin of the Multicultural History Society of
Ontario*, vol. 11 no. 1/2 (1989) p. 148-152.

3807   **Potestio, John**
"The Thunder Bay Multicultural Association." *Polyphony: The
Bulletin of the Multicultural History Society of Ontario*, vol. 9 no. 2
(1987) p. 104-108.

3808   **Pratt, David**
"Bias in Textbooks: Progress and Problems." In: *Multiculturalism in
Canada: Social and Educational Perspectives*, edited by Ronald J.
Samuda, John W. Berry and Michel Laferrière. Toronto: Allyn and
Bacon Inc., 1984, p. 152-166.

3809   **Pratt, David**
"The Social Role of School Textbooks in Canada." In: *Cultural
Diversity and Canadian Education: Issues and Innovations*, edited by
John R. Mallea and Jonathan C. Young. Ottawa: Carleton University
Press, 1984, p. 290-312.

3810   **Prymak, Thomas M.**
"The Persian Language School in Toronto." *Polyphony: The Bulletin
of the Multicultural History Society of Ontario*, vol. 11 no. 1/2
(1989) p. 132-136.

3811   **Pucci, Antonio**
"Thunder Bay's Relationship with the Multicultural History Society."
*Polyphony: The Bulletin of the Multicultural History Society of
Ontario*, vol. 9 no. 1 (1987) p. 26-27.

3812   **Quan, Ping Shao**
"Chinese Heritage Language Education in Metro Toronto."
*Polyphony: The Bulletin of the Multicultural History Society of
Ontario*, vol. 11 no. 1/2 (1989) p. 125-129.

3813   **Raben, Harvey A.**
"Bringing Order to Chaos: The Centralization of Jewish Education in
Toronto." *Canadian Jewish Historical Society Journal/Société de
l'histoire juive canadienne*, vol. 10 no. 1 (1988) p. 34-45.

3814   **Rajwani, Farida A.**
The Development of Isma'ili Religious Education in Canada.
Unpublished MA thesis, McGill University, 1983. 2 microfiches.
Canadian theses on microfiche, CT87-23041-7.

3815   **Ram, Bali**
"Anglophone-Francophone Differences in Returns to Schooling in
Canada." *International Journal of Comparative Sociology*, vol. 21
nos. 1-2 (1980) p. 49-64.

3816   **Ramcharan, Subhas**
"The Role of Education in Multi-racial Canada." In: *Canada 2000:
Race Relations and Public Policy*, edited by O.P. Dwivedi et al.
Guelph, Ont.: Department of Political Studies, University of Guelph,
1989, p. 191-199.

3817   **Ray, Douglas W.**
"Cultural Identity and Education." In: *Multiculturalism in Canada:
Social and Educational Perspectives*, edited by Ronald J. Samuda,
John W. Berry and Michel Laferrière. Toronto: Allyn and Bacon Inc.,
1984, p. 50-61.

3818   **Regehr, T.D.**
"The Writing of Canadian Mennonite History." *Journal of Mennonite
Studies*, vol. 1 (1983) p. 11-32.

3819   **Rhamey, Margaret Anne**
The Relationship of Locus of Control and Self-concept to Ethnicity in School Children. Unpublished MA thesis, University of Toronto, 1982. Canadian theses on microfiche.

3820   **Richards, Gerald R.**
"Ready, Aim... (misfire): Aims of Second Education in Canada." *Education Canada,* vol. 21 no. 2 (1981) p. 29-31, 46.

3821   **Richer, Stephen**
"French Immersion and Classroom Behaviour." *Canadian Journal of Sociology/Cahiers canadiens de sociologie,* vol. 8 no. 4 (1982) p. 377-393.

3822   **Richmond, Anthony H.**
"Ethnogenerational Variations in Educational Achievement." *Canadian Ethnic Studies/Études ethniques au Canada,* vol. 18 no. 3 (1986) p. 75-89.

3823   **Ricker, John**
"The Contribution of Ontario's Schools to Political Education." In: *Political Education in Canada,* edited by Jon H. Pammett and Jean-Luc Pepin. Halifax: Institute for Research on Public Policy, 1988. p. 65-74.

3824   **Riddle, David K.**
Discovering the Past: An Introduction to the Archaeology and Culture History of the Neepawa and Area Planning District. Winnipeg: Department of Culture, Heritage and Recreation, 1983.

3825   **Rose, Sheila Dianne**
The Effects of Participation in the Global Education Project on Children's Attitudes Toward Foreign People. Unpublished thesis, University of Connecticut, 1988. 119 leaves.

3826   **Roy, Basabi**
Formal Education As Status Reconfirmation: The Indian Context. Unpublished M.Ed. thesis, University of Alberta, 1985. Canadian theses on microfiche, CT86-27609-0.

3827   **Roy-Nicklen, Louise**
Multicultural Education: An Attempt to Meet the Needs of Native Students in the Northwest Territories. Unpublished MA thesis, Dalhousie University, 1986. 118 leaves. Canadian theses on microfiche, 29760.

3828   **Ryan, James J.**
"Disciplining the Inuit: Normalization, Characterization and Schooling." *Curriculum Inquiry*, vol. 19 no. 4 (1989) p. 381-403.

3829   **Ryan, James J.**
Disciplining the Inuit: Social Form and Control in Bush, Community and School. Unpublished PhD thesis, University of Toronto, 1988. 305 leaves.

3830   **Saindon, Jacques**
Conception et élaboration d'un programme éducatif dans le but d'intégrer la culture canadienne-française dans les classes d'immersion française au deuxième cycle du secondaire des écoles du Nouveau-Brunswick. Unpublished MEd thesis, Université de Moncton, 1986. 2 microfiches. Canadian theses on microfiche, CT89-20700-3.

3831   **Samuda, Ronald J.**
Assessment and Placement of Minority Students. Toronto: C.J. Hogrefe and Intercultural Social Sciences Publications, 1989. 231 p.

3832   **Samuda, Ronald J.**
"Assessing the Abilities of Minority Students Within a Multiethnic Milieu." In: *Multiculturalism in Canada: Social and Educational Perspectives,* edited by Ronald J. Samuda, John W. Berry and Michel Laferrière. Toronto: Allyn and Bacon Inc., 1984, p. 353-367.

3833   **Sandahl, Peder**
"Teaching Human Rights: Why, What and How?" *The History and Social Science Teacher*, vol. 22 no. 2 (1986/87) p. 85-87.

3834   **Saskatchewan. Saskatchewan Human Rights Commission**
Education Equity: A Report on Indian/Native Education. Ronald J. Kruzenski, Chief Commissioner. Saskatoon: Saskatchewan Human Rights Commission, 1985. 83 p.

3835   **Savard, Pierre**
"Le Centre de recherche en civilisation canadienne-française." *Polyphony: The Bulletin of the Multicultural History Society of Ontario*, vol. 9 no. 1 (1987) p. 90-91.

3836   **Schafler, Samuel**
"God and the Jewish School." *Jewish Education*, vol. 57 no. 1
(1989) p. 4-44.

3837   **Shilling, Rachel and Bill Novak**
"Wandering Spirit Survival School-Toronto Native Way School."
*Polyphony: The Bulletin of the Multicultural History Society of
Ontario*, vol. 11 no. 1/2 (1989) p. 95-98.

3838   **Schmeiser, Douglas A.**
"Multiculturalism in Canadian Education." In: *Multiculturalism and
the Charter: A Legal Perspective*. Canadian Human Rights
Foundation. Toronto: Carswell, 1987, p. 167-186.

3839   **Seasay, Alieu**
*The Role of Multi-cultural Community Officers in the Ontario School
System: A Case Study*. Unpublished PhD thesis, University of
Toronto, 1982. Canadian theses on microfiche, 58360.

3840   **Serrano, Ricardo**
Un cas d'éducation ethnique au Québec; celui des espagnols.
Unpublished PhD thesis, Université de Montréal, 1987.

3841   **Shamai, Shmuel**
"The Jews and the Public Education System: The Students' Strike
over the 'Flag Fight' in Toronto after the First World War."
*Canadian Jewish Historical Society Journal/Societe de l'historie juive
canadienne*, vol. 10 no. 1 (1988) p. 46-53.

3842   **Shamai, Shmuel**
"Critical Theory of Education and Ethnicity: The Case Study of the
Toronto Jewish Community." *Journal of Education*, vol. 169 no. 2
(1987) p. 89-114.

3843   **Shamai, Shmuel**
Ethnic and National Identity Among Jewish Students in Toronto.
Unpublished PhD thesis, University of Toronto, 1986. Canadian
theses on microfiche, CT88-26152-8.

3844   **Shamai, Shmuel**
*Ethnicity, Gender and Educational Achievement in Canada: An
Historical-statistical Analysis, Based on Censal Data 1921-1981*.
Toronto: Department of Sociology of Education, Ontario Institute of
Schooling in Education, 1986. 24 leaves.

3845   **Shapson, Stanley M.**
"Post-secondary Bilingual Education: Identifying and Adapting to the Shift in Second-language Demands." *Canadian Modern Language Review/Revue canadienne des langues vivantes*, vol. 41 no. 5 (1985) p. 827-834.

3846   **Shapson, Stanley M. and Vincent D'Oyley, eds.**
Bilingual and Multicultural Education: Canadian Perspectives. Avon, England: Multicultural Matters, 1984. 170 p.

3847   **Shapson, Stanley M., Vincent D'Oyley, and Anne Lloyd, eds.**
Bilingualism and Multiculturalism in Canadian Education. Vancouver: Centre for the Study of Curriculum and Instruction, University of British Columbia, 1982. 129 p.

3848   **Shearwood, P.**
"Literacy Among the Aboriginal Peoples of the Northwest Territories." *Canadian Modern Language Review/Revue canadienne des langues vivantes*, vol. 43 no. 4 (1987) p. 630-642.

3849   **Shkedi, Asher**
"Curriculum Change in a Jewish Day School from a Principal's Point of View." *Jewish Education*, vol. 57 no. 1 (1989) p. 15-21.

3850   **Singh, Hardev**
"Punjabi Language Education for Children in Toronto." *Polyphony: The Bulletin of the Multicultural History Society of Ontario*, vol. 11 no. 1/2 (1989) p. 130-131.

3851   **Slobod, Shirley**
Program Planning in English As a Second Language at the Protestant School Board of Greater Montreal: A Historical Study. Unpublished MA thesis, Concordia University, 1982. Canadian theses on microfiche, 55695.

3852   **The Society for the Advancement of Native Studies**
"Universities and Self Determination." *The Canadian Journal of Native Studies*, vol. 6 no. 1 (1986) p. 1-195.

3853   **Souaid, Carolyn**
"Inuit-controlled School System Clashes with Traditional Lifestyle." *Information North*, vol. 14 no. 1 (1988) p. 1-4.

3854   **Sower, Ruth**
"Towards Achieving an Interactive Education Model for Special
Needs Students: The Computer Writing Project for Native American
Students." *Journal of American Indian Education*, vol. 27 no. 1
(1987) p. 30-38.

3855   **Spaights, Ernest, Derek Kenner, and Harold E. Dixon**
"The Relationship of Assertiveness and the Academic Success of
Black Students in Predominantly White Institutions of Higher
Education." *Psychology*, vol. 24 no. 3 (1987) p. 9-16.

3856   **Stainsby, Jonathan**
"Plus ça change ...: Education and Equality Rights in the Supreme
Court [Funding of Separate Schools in Ontario]." *University of
Toronto Faculty of Law Review*, vol. 46 no. 1 (1988) p. 259-270.

3857   **Steele, Catherine Laramy**
*Mohawk Cultural Perspectives: A Curriculum Data Base for Mohawk
Cross-cultural Curriculum.* Unpublished EdD thesis, University of
New York, 1986. Canadian theses on microfiche, CT88-21933-5.

3858   **Sterling, Robert**
"Non-authority in Nicola Valley Indian Culture and Implications for
Education." *Canadian Journal of Native Studies*, vol. 4 no. 2
(1984) p. 293-302.

3859   **Stern, H.H.**
"Second Language Education in Canada: Innovation, Research, and
Policies." *Interchange*, vol. 17 no. 2 (1986) p. 41-56.

3860   **Stuart, Richard**
"Duff Pattullo and the Yukon Schools Question of 1937." *Canadian
Historical Review*, vol. 64 no. 1 (1983) p. 25-44.

3861   **Subotic, Christie Milana**
*The Hidden Curriculum as a Method of Cultural Production:
Primary/Junior Levels in Ontario Elementary Schooling.* Unpublished
MA thesis, University of Toronto, 1989.

3862   **Swain, Merrill**
Evaluating Bilingual Education: A Canadian Case Study. Clevedon,
England: Multilingual Matters, 1986. 117 p.

3863   **Swain, Merrill**
"Immersion Education: Applicability for Nonvernacular Teaching to Vernacular Speakers." *Studies in Second Language Acquisition*, vol. 4 no. 1 (1981) p. 1-17.

3864   **Swainson, Donald**
"Separate Schools and the Question of Canadian Identity." *Queen's Quarterly*, vol. 96 no. 1 (1989) p. 14-21.

3865   **Swerhun, Stan Rodger**
Guidelines for Bicultural Education of Minority Group Children in Alberta. Unpublished MA thesis, University of Calgary, 1981. 2 microfiches. Canadian theses on microfiche, 55415.

3866   **Tamaoka, Katsuo**
An Assessment of Congruence Between Learning Styles of Cree, Chipweyan, Metis, and Non-Native Students and Instructional Styles of Native and Non-Native Teachers in Selected Northern Saskatchewan Schools. Unpublished MEd thesis, University of Saskatchewan, 1986.

3867   **Taplin, John Mark**
A Study of Educational Policy Towards Immigrants in Alberta, with Emphasis Upon English as a Second Language Instruction and the Indo-Chinese Refugee Movement. Unpublished MA thesis, University of Calgary, 1987. 2 microfiches. Canadian theses on microfiche, CT89-21686-X.

3868   **Taylor, Simon**
"Teaching About Racism: An Adult Approach." *Adult Education*, vol. 61 no. 2 (1988) p. 129-133.

3869   **Tetley, William**
"Language and Education Rights in Quebec and Canada: A Legislative History and Personal Political Diary." In: *Reshaping Confederation: The 1982 Reform of the Canadian Constitution*, edited by Paul Davenport and Richard H. Leach. Durham, N.C.: Duke University Press, 1984, p. 177-220.

3870   **Tetley, William**
"Language and Education Rights in Quebec and Canada." *Law and Contemporary Problems*, vol. 45 no. 4 (1982) p. 177-219.

3871   **Tippeconnic, John W., III**
"A Survey: Attitudes Toward the Education of American Indians."
Journal of American Indian Education, vol. 28 no. 1 (1988) p. 34-36.

3872   **Toronto Board of Education**
*Consultative Committee on the Education of Black Students in
Toronto Schools.* Toronto: Board of Education, 1987.

3873   **Trueba, Henry T.**
"Culturally Based Explanations of Minority Students' Academic
Archievement." *Anthropology and Education*, vol. 19 no. 3
(1988) p. 270-287.

3874   **Turcotte, Paul-André**
"Éducation catholique et nationalisme dans enseignement secondaire
québécois." *Social Compass*, vol. 31 no. 4 (1984) p. 356-377.

3875   **Ullman, Rebecca**
"Recent Developments in Heritage Language Teacher Education."
*Polyphony: The Bulletin of the Multicultural History Society of
Ontario*, vol. 11 no. 1/2 (1989) p. 49-55.

3876   **Walker, Franklin A.**
"The History of Ontario Separate Schools: Sources and Problems."
The Canadian Catholic Historical Association: Historical Studies, no.
55 (1988) p. 7-20.

3877   **Walton, Patrick**
"The Native Indian Education Advisory Committee." *Canadian
Journal of Native Education*, vol. 16 no. 1 (1989) p. 6-11.

3878   **Wangler, David G.**
"Science, Nature and Man: A Brief Investigation of the Art of
Knowing as Practiced by Scientific and Non-scientific Cultures."
Canadian Journal of Native Education, vol. 11 no. 1 (1983) p. 46-51.

3879   **Ward, Margaret**
*Indian Education in Canada: Implementation of Educational Policy,
1973-1978.* Unpublished MEd thesis, University of Saskatchewan,
1988.

3880   **Welch, David**
The Social Construction of Franco-Ontarian Interests Toward French Language Schooling: 19th Century to 1980s. Unpublished PhD thesis, University of Toronto, 1988. 5 microfiches. Canadian theses on microfiche, CT90-21390-6.

3881   **White, Clovis L.**
"Ethnic Identity and Academic Performance Among Black and White College Students: An Interactionist Approach." *Urban Education,* vol. 23 no. 3 (1988) p. 219-240.

3882   **Wilson, J. Donald**
"Multicultural Programmes in Canadian Education." In: *Multiculturalism in Canada: Social and Educational Perspectives,* edited by Ronald J. Samuda, John W. Berry and Michel Laferrière. Toronto: Allyn and Bacon Inc., 1984, p. 62-77.

3883   **Wiss, Corrinne A.**
"Early French Immersion Programs May Not be Suitable for Every Child." *Canadian Modern Language Review/Revue canadienne des langues vivantes,* vol. 45 no. 3 (1989) p. 517-529.

3884   **Wiss, Corrinne A.**
"Issues in the Assessment of Learning Problems in Children from French Immersion Programs: A Case Study Illustration in Support of Cummins." *Canadian Modern Language Review/Revue canadienne des langues vivantes,* vol. 43 no. 2 (1987) p. 302-313.

3885   **Wood, Dean**
"Social Studies Textbooks in a Multicultural Society." *The History and Social Science Teacher,* vol. 17 no. 1 (1981) p. 21-29.

3886   **Woods, Devon**
"Studying ESL (English as a Second Language) Teachers' Decision Making: Rationale, Methodological Issues and Initial Results." *Carleton Papers in Applied Language Studies,* vol. 6 (1989) p. 107-124.

3887   **Woolstencroft, Peter**
"Politics and Education: Issues of Public Policy and Political Philosophy." *CPSA Papers/ACSP Contributions 1983,* Section F, paper 7, fiches 15-16. Paper presented at the 55th annual meeting of the Canadian Political Science Association, June 6-8, 1983, University of British Columbia, Vancouver, B.C.

3888   **Wynnyckyj, Iroida L.**
"The Ukrainian Collection of the Multicultural History Society of Ontario." *Polyphony: The Bulletin of the Multicultural History Society of Ontario*, vol. 10 no. 1/2 (1988) p. 256-263.

3889   **Wynnyckyj, Oksana A.**
"St. Sofia School: A Ukrainian Community and Heritage Language School." *Polyphony: The Bulletin of the Multicultural History Society of Ontario*, vol. 11 no. 1/2 (1989) p. 137-143.

3890   **Wynnyckyj, Oksana A.**
"Hryhorij Skovoroda Kursy in Toronto: A Model for a Ukrainian Educational Network." *Polyphony: The Bulletin of the Multicultural History Society of Ontario*, vol. 10 no. 1/2 (1988) p. 229-240.

3891   **Younes, Fatima-Zohra**
L'algérienne immigrée au Québec et l'education de ses Enfants. Unpublished MA thesis, Université du Québec à Montréal, 1987.

3892   **Young, Jonathan C.**
Multicultural Education: Dilemmas and Contradictions in an Elementary School Setting. Unpublished PhD thesis, University of Toronto, 1984. 5 microfiches. Canadian theses on microfiche, 62244.

3893   **Young, Jonathon C., ed.**
Breaking the Mosaic: Ethnic Identities in Canadian Schooling. Toronto: Garamond Press, 1984. 302 p. Papers presented at a working symposium titled Race, Ethnicity, and Education: Critical Perspectives, held at the Ontario Institute for Studies in Education, in October 1984.

3894   **Young, Judy and Carole Walker**
"The Federal Government's Cultural Enrichment Programme." *Polyphony: The Bulletin of the Multicultural History Society of Ontario*, vol. 11 no. 1/2 (1989) p. 67-71.

3895   **Young, Lee D.**
"Attracting Minority Students with Effective Campus Progams." *College and University*, vol. 63 no. 1 (1987) p. 23-32.

3896   **Young, Lynne**
"Can Linguistic Descriptions Help Language Learners to Develop Realistic Expectations About Academic Discourse?" *Carleton Papers in Applied Language Studies*, vol. 6 (1989) p. 40-63.

3897 **Yung, Wing K.**
"A Prelude to the Heritage Language Programme: The Chinese
Canadian Bicultural-bilingual Programme." *Polyphony: The Bulletin
of the Multicultural History Society of Ontario*, vol. 11 no. 1/2
(1989) p. 99-109.

3898 **Zakydalsky, Taras**
"Encyclopedia of Ukraine." *Polyphony: The Bulletin of the
Multicultural History Society of Ontario*, vol. 10 no. 1/2
(1988) p. 228.

3899 **Zucchi, Flavia**
"A First Experiment in Friulan Heritage Language Teaching."
*Polyphony: The Bulletin of the Multicultural History Society of
Ontario*, vol. 11 no. 1/2 (1989) p. 154-156.

Religion

3900 **Adams, William Seth**
"Christian Liturgy, Scripture and the Jews: A Problem in Jewish-Christian Relations." *Journal of Ecumenical Studies*, vol. 25 no. 1 (1988) p. 39-55.

3901 **Adrian, Marlian**
"'In Like Manner': Religious Paradigms and the Motivation for General Conference Mennonite Missions Among Native Americans." *Mennonite Life*, vol. 43 no. 3 (1988) p. 4-9.

3902 **Akenson, Donald Harman**
Small Differences: Irish Catholics and Irish Protestants, 1815-1922, an International Perspective. Montreal: McGill-Queen's University Press, 1988. 237 p.

3903 **Anderson, Charles P., Tirthankar Bose, and Joseph L. Richardson, eds.**
Circle of Voices: A History of the Religious Communities in British Columbia. Lantzville, B.C.: Oolichan Books, 1983. 288 p.

3904 **Archer, John H.**
"The Anglican Church and the Indian in the Northwest." *Journal of the Canadian Church Historical Society*, vol. 28 no. 1 (1986) p. 19-30.

3905 **Baglo, Fredy**
"Chinese Ministry in Canada." *Canada Lutheran*, vol. 2 no. 2 (1987) p. 12-15.

3906   **Bainbridge, William Sims**
"Church and Cult in Canada." *Canadian Journal of Sociology/
Cahiers canadiens de sociologie*, vol. 7 no. 4 (1982) p. 351-366.

3907   **Beaton, Elizabeth**
"Religious Affiliation and Ethnic Identity of West Indians in Whitney
Pier." *Canadian Ethnic Studies/Études ethniques au Canada*, vol. 20
no. 3 (1988) p. 112-131.

3908   **Beaudoin, Réjean**
"Considérations sur le messianisme canadien-français." *Écrits du
Canada français*, no. 53 (1984) p. 105-125.

3909   **Beaulieu, Alain**
"Réduire et instruire: deux aspects de la politique missionaire des
Jésuites face aux amérindiens nomades (1632-1642)." *Recherches
amerindiennes au Québec*, vol. 17 no. 1/2 (1987) p. 129-154.

3910   **Beyer, Peter**
"The Mission of Quebec Ultramontanism: A Luhmannian Perspective." *Sociological Analysis: A Journal of the Sociology of Religion*,
vol. 46 no. 2 (1985) p. 37-48.

3911   **Bibby, Reginald W. and Peter D. McCormick**
"Religion and Party Preference in Canada: Toward Clarification of
the Relationship. " *CPSA Papers/ACSP Contributions 1984*, Section
D, paper 2, fiche 10. Paper presented at the 56th annual meeting of
the Canadian Political Science Association, June 10-12, 1984,
University of Guelph, Guelph, Ontario.

3912   **Black, William W.**
"Religion and the Right of Equality." In: *Equality Rights and the
Canadian Charter of Rights and Freedoms*, edited by Anne F.
Bayefsky and Mary Eberts. Toronto: Carswell, 1985, p. 131-182.

3913   **Blodgett, Jean**
"Christianity and Inuit Art." *The Beaver*, vol. 315 no. 2 (1984) p. 16-
25.

3914   **Bodrug, John**
*Independent Orthodox Church: Memoirs Pertaining to the History of
a Ukrainian Canadian Church in the Years 1903 to 1913*, edited by
J.B. Gregorovich. Toronto: Ukrainian Canadian Research Foundation,
1980.

3915　**Boldt, Ed**
"The Baptism Issue: An Episode in the History of the Ontario Mennonite Brethren Churches." *Mennonite Historian*, vol. 13 no. 2 (1987) p. 1-2.

3916　**Bolt, Clarence R.**
"The Conversion of the Port Simpson Tsimshian: Indian Control or Missionary Manipulation?" In: *Out of the Background: Readings on Canadian Native History*, edited by Robin Fisher and Kenneth Coates. Toronto: Copp Clark Pitman, 1988, p. 219-235.

3917　**Bolt, Clarence R.**
"The Conversion of the Port Simpson Tsimshian: Indian Control or Missionary Manipulation?" *B.C. Studies*, no. 57 (1983) p. 38.

3918　**Bourgeault, Guy**
"Le nationalisme québecois et l'Église." *Canadian Review of Studies in Nationalism/Revue canadienne des études sur le nationalisme*, vol. 5 no. 2 (1986) p. 189-207.

3919　**Brace, Faith**
"Winging North with the Gospel: LAMP (Lutheran Association of Missionaries and Pilots)." *Canadian Lutheran*, vol. 3 no. 5 (1988) p. 10-11, 26-28.

3920　**Bratt, James D.**
"Dutch Calvinism in the United States in the 1920s: Americanization and Self-Definition." In: *Dutch Immigration to North America*, edited by Herman Ganzevoort and Mark Boekelman. Toronto: Multicultural History Society of Ontario, 1983, p. 167-186.

3921　**Brinks, H.J.**
"Immigrant Letters: The Religious Context of Dutch American Ethnicity." In: *Dutch Immigration to North America*, edited by Herman Ganzevoort and Mark Boekelman. Toronto: Multicultural History Society of Ontario, 1983, p. 131-146.

3922　**Brodeur, Leo A.**
"Quebec Separatism and Christianity: Or a Highly Successful Cultural Pluralism: 2,000 Years of Roman Christianity." In: *The Canadian Alternative: Cultural Pluralism and Canadian Unity*, edited by Hedi Bouraoui. Downsview, Ont.: ECW Press, 1980, p. 43-49. Paper presented at the Conference on Cultural Pluralism and the Canadian Unity held at Stong College, York University, 1979.

3923 **Bros, Alex**
Polish Immigrant Relations with the Roman Catholic Church in Urban Ontario, 1896-1923. Unpublished MA thesis, Wilfred Laurier University, 1986. 2 microfiches. Canadian theses on microfiche, CT88-22920-9.

3924 **Brown, Teddi**
"A Heritage of Hope: Mennonite Volunteer Crews Go 'Wherever God's Children are Hurting'." *Canadian Heritage*, vol. 12 no. 1 (1986) p. 21-24.

3925 **Buchanan, Frederick S.**
"Mormons Meet the Mennonites: A View from 1884." *The Mennonite Quarterly Review*, vol. 62 no. 2 (1988) p. 159-166.

3926 **Burns, Robert I.**
"The Missionary Syndrome: Crusader and Pacific Northwest Religious Expansionism." *Comparative Studies in Society and History*, vol. 30 no. 2 (1988) p. 271-285.

3927 **Burrows, Rufus, Jr.**
"Who Teaches Black Theology?" *The Journal of Religious Thought*, vol. 43 no. 2 (1986-87) p. 7-18.

3928 **Carter, Sarah**
"The Missionaries' Indian: The Publications of John McDougall, John Maclean and Egerton Ryerson Young." *Prairie Forum*, vol. 9 no. 1 (1984) p. 27-44.

3929 **Chalmers, John W.**
"The Church at Spring Lake." *Alberta History*, vol. 31 no. 4 (1983) p. 33-36.

3930 **Chalmers, John W.**
"Missions and Schools in the Athabasca." *Alberta History*, vol. 31 no. 1 (1983) p. 24-29.

3931 **Cheal, David J.**
"Ontario Loyalism: A Socio-religious Ideology in Decline." *Canadian Ethnic Studies/Études ethniques au Canada*, vol. 13 no. 1 (1981) p. 40-51.

3932   **Chell, Jim**
"Native Ministry in Canada: Historically, the Ministry to Canada's Native People Has Not Been a Lutheran Affair." *Canada Lutheran*, vol. 4 no. 2 (1989) p. 8-12.

3933   **Choquette, Diane, comp.**
New Religious Movements in the United States and Canada: A Critical Assessment and Annotated Bibliography. Westport, Conn.: Greenwood Press, 1985. 235 p.

3934   **Choquette, Robert**
La foi gardienne de la langue en Ontario, 1900-1950. Montréal: Éditions Bellarmin, 1987. 282 p.

3935   **Choquette, Robert**
L'Église catholique dans l'Ontario française du dix-neuvième siècle. Ottawa: Editions de l'Universite d'Ottawa, 1984. 365 p.

3936   **Christie, J. Lee**
"Seekers of the Sacred Circle." *Calgary*, vol. 10 no. 11 (1988) p. 27-29, 36.

3937   **Clermont, Norman**
"Le pouvoir spirituel chez les iroquoiens de la période du contact." *Recherches amérindiennes au Québec*, vol. 18 no. 2/3 (1988) p. 61-68.

3938   **Cliche, Marie Aimée**
Les pratiques de dévotion en Nouvelle-France: comportment populaires et encadrement ecclésial dans le gouvernement de Québec. Quebec: Les Presses de l'Université Laval, 1988. 355 p.

3939   **Coates, Kenneth Stephen**
"'Betwixt and Between': The Anglican Church and the Children of the Carcross (Chooutla) Residential School, 1911-1954." In: *Interpreting Canada's North: Selected Readings*, edited by Kenneth S. Coates and William R. Morrison. Toronto: Copp Clark Pitman Ltd., 1989, p. 150-168.

3940   **Cohen, Arthur A.**
"On Judaism and Modernism." *Partisan Review*, vol. 54 no. 3 (1987) p. 437-442.

3941   **Cohn-Sherbok, Dan**
"Judaism and the Theology of Liberation." *Modern Theology*, vol. 3
no. 1 (1986) p. 1-20.

3942   **Cooper, Carol Ann**
Anglican Missions and the Subarctic Fur Trade: A Study of Rt.
Reverend John Horden and the Native Peoples of Moosonee, 1851-
1893. Unpublished MA thesis, University of Waterloo, 1986. 3
microfiches. Canadian theses on microfiche, CT88-21500-3.

3943   **Coriaty, Msgr.**
"Rapport sur la communauté grècque melchite catholique."
Polyphony: The Bulletin of the Multicultural History Society of
Ontario, vol. 9 no. 1 (1987) p. 70-72.

3944   **Cowan, Trudy**
"Glossary of Jewish Terms." *Glenbow*, vol. 6 no. 1 (1986) p. 12-14.

3945   **Coward, Harold G.**
"Religious Experience of the South Asian Diaspora in Canada." In:
The South Asian Diaspora in Canada, edited by Milton Israel.
Toronto: Multicultural History Society of Ontario, 1987, p. 73-86.

3946   **Crabbs, Fred**
"The Church in the North." In: *Rupert's Land: A Cultural Tapestry*,
edited by Richard C. Davis. Waterloo, Ont.: Wilfrid Laurier
University Press, 1988, p. 213-266.

3947   **D'Allaire, Micheline**
"Les religieuses enseignantes au Canada français, au XIXème siècle."
Cultures du Canada français no. 6 (1989) p. 86-97.

3948   **D'Anglure, Bernard Saladin**
"Penser le féminin chamanique, ou le 'tiers-sexe' des chamanes
inuit." *Recherches amérindiennes au Québec*, vol. 18 no. 2/3
(1988) p. 19-50.

3949   **Danys, Milda**
"Lithuanian Parishes in Toronto." *Polyphony: The Bulletin of the*
Multicultural History Society of Ontario, vol. 6 no. 1 (1984) p. 104-
109.

3950   **Daschko, Walter**
"Tserkvy: a Survey of Ukrainian-Canadian Church Architecture in
Ontario, Its Major Roots and Trends." *Polyphony: The Bulletin of the
Multicultural History Society of Ontario*, vol. 10 no. 1/2
(1988) p. 191-201.

3951   **Davies, Allan and Marilyn F. Nefsky**
"The Church of England in Canada and the Jewish Plight during the
Nazi Era." *Canadian Jewish Historical Society Journal/Société de
l'histoire juive canadienne*, vol. 10 no. 1 (1988) p. 1-19.

3952   **Davis, Davena Gwendolen Monk**
*The Day Spring from on High Hath Visited Us: An Examination of
the Missionary Endeavours of the Moravians and the Anglican
Church Missionary Society Among the Inuit in the Arctic Regions of
Canada and Labrador, 1880s-1920s.* Unpublished PhD thesis, McGill
University, 1987. 3 microfiches. Canadian theses on microfiche,
CT89-28012-6.

3953   **Davis, Richard C., ed.**
Rupert's Land: A Cultural Tapestry. Waterloo, Ont.: Wilfrid Laurier
University Press, 1988. 314 p.

3954   **Desrosiers, Yvon, ed.**
Religion et culture au Québec: figures contemporaines du sacre.
Montréal: Fides, 1986. 422 p.

3955   **Dhruvarajan, Vanaja**
"Religious Ideology and Interpersonal Relationships Within the
Family." *Journal of Comparative Family Studies*, vol. 19 no. 2
(1988) p. 273-285.

3956   **Dossa, Parin Aziz**
*Ritual and Daily Life: Transmission and Interpretation of the Ismaili
Tradition in Vancouver.* Unpublished PhD thesis, University of
British Columbia, 1983. 301 leaves. Canadian theses on microfiche,
241527.

3957   **Dossa, Parin Aziz**
"The Shi'a-Isma'ili Muslim Community in British Columbia." In:
*Circle of Voices: A History of the Religious Communities in Britsh
Columbia*, edited by Charles P. Anderson et al. Lantzville, B.C.:
Oolichan Books, 1983. p. 232-239.

3958   **Doyle, Denise Joan**
        Religious Freedom in Canada. Unpublished DCL thesis, St. Paul's
        University, 1982. 3 microfiches. Canadian theses on microfiche,
        60142.

3959   **Driedger, Leo**
        "Jewish Identity: The Maintenance of Urban Religious and Ethnic
        Boundaries." *Ethnic and Racial Studies*, vol. 3 no. 1 (1980) p. 67-88.

3960   **Dueck, Ronald Peter**
        *Some Relationships of Religious and Personality Factors to Science
        Attitudes of Adolescents in a Mennonite Community.* Unpublished
        MEd thesis, University of Manitoba, 1981. 1 microfiche, illustrations.
        Canadian theses on microfiche, CT89-25829-5.

3961   **Enns-Rempel, Kevin**
        "The Fellowship of Evangelical Bible Churches and the Quest for
        Religious Identity." *The Mennonite Quarterly Review*, vol. 63 no. 3
        (1989) p. 247-264.

3962   **Erb, Peter**
        "A Reflection on Mennonite Theology in Canada." *Journal of
        Mennonite Studies*, vol. 1 (1983) p. 179-190.

3963   **Fisher, Eugene J.**
        "Covenant Theology and Jewish-Christian Dialogue." *American
        Journal of Theology and Philosophy*, vol. 9 no. 1/2 (1988) p. 5-40.

3964   **Fortin, Denis**
        "Être québécois et protestant aujourd'hui." In: *Religion et culture au
        Québec: figures contemporaines du sacré*, en collaboration, sous la
        direction de Yvon Desrosiers. Montréal: Fides, 1986, p. 137-152.

3965   **Fraser, Jean**
        "Hanukkah." *Heritage*, vol. 14 no. 4 (1986) p. 8-9.

3966   **Fretz, J. Winfield**
        The Waterloo Mennonites: A Community in Paradox. Waterloo, Ont.:
        Wilfrid Laurier University Press & Conrad Grebel College, 1989.
        391 p.

3967   **Friesen, John**
"The GC/MC [General Conference/Mennonite Church] Merger
Proposal: Some Historical Considerations." *Mennonite History*, vol.
15 no. 2 (1989) p. 1-2.

3968   **Gadon, Sean**
"The Syrian Religious Experience in Toronto, 1896-1920s."
*Polyphony: The Bulletin of the Multicultural History Society of
Ontario*, vol. 6 no. 1 (1984) p. 65-67.

3969   **Gagat, Zofia**
"St. Stanislaus Parish: The Heart of Toronto Polonia." *Polyphony:
The Bulletin of the Multicultural History Society of Ontario*, vol. 6
no. 1 (1984) p. 50-54.

3970   **Gagnon, Anne C.**
*The Pensionnat Assumption: Religious Nationalism in a Franco-
Albertan Boarding School for Girls, 1926-1960.* Unpublished MEd
thesis, University of Alberta, 1988. 2 microfiches. Canadian theses on
microfiche, CT89-25977-1.

3971   **Gagnon, Serge and Louise Lebel-Gagnon**
"Le milieu d'origine du clergé québécois, 1775-1840: mythes et
réalites." *Revue d'histoire de l'Amérique française*, vol. 37 no. 3
(1983) p. 373-397.

3972   **Gay, Paul**
"La religion dans la littérature franco-ontarienne contemporaine."
Bulletin du Centre de recherche en civilisation canadienne-française,
no. 26 (1983) p. 2-6.

3973   **Goa, David J., ed.**
*The Ukrainian Religious Experience: Tradition and the Canadian
Cultural Context.* Edmonton: Canadian Institute of Ukrainian Studies,
University of Alberta, 1989. 244 p.

3974   **Goldring, Philip**
"Religion, Missions and Native Culture." *Journal of the Canadian
Church Historical Society*, vol. 27 no. 2 (1984) p. 43-49.

3975   **Granite, Morris J.**
"History of (Jewish) Secularism." *Canadian Jewish Outlook*, vol. 24 no. 4
(1986) p. 17-18; vol. 24 no. 5 (1986) p. 7-8, 16; vol. 24 no. 6 (1986) p. 7-
8; vol. 24 no. 7-8 (1986) p. 7-8; and vol. 24 no. 9 (1986) p. 7-8, 21, 23.

3976 **Grant, John Webster**
Moon of Wintertime: Missionaries and the Indians of Canada in Encounter Since 1534. Toronto: University of Toronto Press, 1984.

3977 **Gregorovich, Andrew**
"Ukrainian Orthodox Church in Canada." *Forum: A Ukrainian Review*, no. 74 (1988) p. 28-30.

3978 **Gregorovich, Andrew**
"Ukrainian Orthodox Church in North America." *Forum: A Ukrainian Review*, no. 74 (1988) p. 25-27.

3979 **Gregorovich, Andrew**
"Forty Years of Service: Metropolitan Mstyslav of the Ukrainian Orthodox Church." *Forum: A Ukrainian Review*, no. 66 (1986) p. 81-86.

3980 **Gresko, Jacqueline**
"Creating Little Dominions Within the Dominion: Early Catholic Indian Schools in Saskatchewan and British Columbia." In: *Indian Education in Canada*, edited by Jean Barman, Yvonne Hebert and Don McCaskill. Vancouver: University of British Columbia Press, 1986, vol. 1, p. 88-109.

3981 **Gross, Rita M.**
"Religious Pluralism: Some Implications for Judaism." *Journal of Ecumenical Studies*, vol. 26 no. 1 (1989) p. 29-44.

3982 **Guédon, Marie-Françoise**
"Du rêve à l'ethnographie: explorations sur le monde personnel du chammanisme nabesna." *Recherches amérindiennes au Québec*, vol. 18 no. 2/3 (1988) p. 5-18.

3983 **Gutmann, Joseph**
"The Precious Legacy: Images of Judaism." *Glenbow*, vol. 6 no. 1 (1986) p. 1-7, 16-17.

3984 **Handera, Vladimir I.**
"The Russian Orthodox Church in Toronto." *Polyphony: The Bulletin of the Multicultural History Society of Ontario*, vol. 6 no. 1 (1984) p. 83-85.

3985   **Harvey, Louis-Charles**
"Black Gospel Music and Black Theology." *The Journal of Religious Thought*, vol. 43 no. 2 (1987) p. 19-37.

3986   **Hayward, M. Ann**
"R[egina] v[ersus] Jack and Charlie and the Constitution Act 1982: Religious Freedom and Aboriginal Rights in Canada." *Queen's Law Journal*, vol. 10 no. 1 (1984) p. 165-182.

3987   **Heilman, Samuel C. and Steven M. Cohen**
Cosmopolitans and Parochials: Modern Orthodox Jews in America. Chicago: University of Chicago Press, 1989. 248 p.

3988   **B.H. [Benedykt Heydenkorn]**
"The Polish Canadian Parish as a Social Entity: A Hamilton Example." *Polyphony: The Bulletin of the Multicultural History Society of Ontario*, vol. 6 no. 2 (1984) p. 37-40.

3989   **Hill, Margaret**
"The Detention of Freedomite Children, 1953-59." *Canadian Ethnic Studies/Études ethniques au Canada*, vol. 18 no. 3 (1986) p. 47-60.

3990   **Hogan, Brian F.**
"Catechising Culture: Assumption College, The Pius XI Labour School, and the United Automobile Workers, Windsor, 1940-1950." *The Canadian Catholic Historical Association: Historical Studies*, no. 55 (1988) p. 79-95.

3991   **Homer, Stephen**
"Upholders of the Faith: Not that Hasidim Hate Anybody, But When it Comes to Religion We Have to Be Very Strict." *Equinox*, no. 26 (1986) p. 44-45.

3992   **Hryniuk, Stella**
"Pioneer Bishop, Pioneer Times: Nykyta Budka in Canada." *The Canadian Catholic Historical Association: Historical Studies*, no. 55 (1988) p. 21-42.

3993   **Hubbard, R.H.**
"From Rocks and Ice to Leafy Isles: Bermuda's Links with the Dioceses of Nova Scotia and Newfoundland." *Journal of the Canadian Church Historical Society*, vol. 29 no. 1 (1987) p. 3-11.

3994 **Huel, Raymond**
"When a Minority Feels Threatened: The Impetus for French Catholic Organization in Saskatchewan." *Canadian Ethnic Studies/ Études ethniques au Canada*, vol. 18 no. 3 (1986) p. 1-16.

3995 **Hutterian Bretheren, ed.**
The Chronicle of the Hutterian Brethren, Volume I. Ste. Agathe: Plough Publishing House and Hutterian Bretheren, 1987. 887 p.

3996 **Institute of Formative Spirituality**
"Spiritual Formation: Contemporary Jewish Perspectives Studies in Formative Spirituality." *The Journal of Ongoing Formation*, vol. 8 no. 1 (1987) p. 1-158.

3997 **Johnson, Richard**
"The Reproduction of the Religious Cleavage in Canadian Elections." *Canadian Journal of Political Science/Revue canadienne de science politique*, vol. 18 no. 1 (1985) p. 99-117.

3998 **Johnston, Andrew John B.**
"Popery and Progress: Anti-Catholicism in Mid-19th Century Nova Scotia." *Dalhousie Review*, vol. 64 no. 1 (1984) p. 146-183.

3999 **Jones, Rev. Humphreys J.**
"A Short History of the Dewi Sant Welsh United Church." *Polyphony: The Bulletin of the Multicultural History Society of Ontario*, vol. 6 no. 1 (1984) p. 75-78.

4000 **Joseph, Howard, Jack N. Livingstone, and Michael D. Oppenheim, eds.**
Truth and Compassion: Essays on Judaism and Religion in Memory of Rabbi Dr. Solomon Frank. Waterloo, Ont.: Published for the Canadian Corporation for Studies in Religion by Wilfrid Laurier University Press, 1983. 217 p.

4001 **Juhnke, James C.**
"The Daniel Explosion: Bethel College's First Bible Crisis." *Mennonite Life*, vol. 44 no. 3 (1989) p. 20-25.

4002 **Kan, Sergei, ed.**
"Native Cultures and Christianity in Northern North America." *Arctic Anthropology*, vol. 24 no. 1 (1987) p. 1-66.

4003   **Kaplan, William**
State and Salvation: The Jehovah's Witnesses and Their Fight for Civil Rights. Toronto: University of Toronto Press, 1989. 340 p.

4004   **Klassen, William**
"Mennonite Studies as a Part of Religious Studies." *Journal of Mennonite Studies*, vol. 1 (1983) p. 161-174.

4005   **Koontz, Ted**
"Mennonites and 'Postmodernity'." *The Mennonite Quarterly Review*, vol. 63 no. 4 (1989) p. 401-427.

4006   **Korol, Yaroslav**
"Bishop Isidore of Toronto Visits Ukraine." *Ukrainian Canadian*, vol. 41 no. 727/221 (1988) p. 7-9.

4007   **Krentzman, Meir**
Lexique de concepts judaïques choisis. Québec: Office de la langue française, 1983.

4008   **Kyle, Richard**
"The Mennonite Brethren and the Denominational Model of the Church: An Answer to the Pressures of North American Society." *Mennonite Life*, vol. 42 no. 3 (1987) p. 30-36.

4009   **La Barne, Weston**
The Peyote Cult. 5th ed. Norman: University of Oklahoma Press, 1989. 334 p.

4010   **Lacroix, Benoît and Jean Simard, eds.**
Religion populaire, religion de clercs? Collection: Culture populaire no. 2. Québec: Institut québécois de recherche sur la culture, 1984. 444 p.

4011   **Larson, Lyle E. and Brenda Munro**
"Religious Intermarriage in Canada, 1974-1982." *International Journal of Sociology of the Family*, vol. 15 no. 1/2 (1985) p. 31-49.

4012   **Lazerwitz, Bernard, Alan Winter, and Arnold Dashefsky**
"Localism, Religiosity, Orthodoxy and Liberalism: The Case of Jews in the United States." *Social Forces*, vol. 67 no. 1 (1988) p. 229-242.

4013 **Lebel, Marc**
"Livres et bibliothèques chez les ursulines de Québec." *Bulletin du Centre de recherche en civilisation canadienne-française*, no. 26 (1983) p. 15-20.

4014 **Legge, Russel D.**
"Religious Pluralism and the Study of Religion." In: *Pluralism, Tolerance and Dialogue: Six Studies*, edited by Darrol M. Bryant. Waterloo, Ontario: University of Waterloo Press, 1989, p. 41-67.

4015 **Leighton, Douglas**
"The Ethnohistory of Missions in Southwestern Ontario." *Journal of the Canadian Church Historical Society*, vol. 26 no. 2 (1984) p. 50-57.

4016 **Lewis, I.M.**
Ecstatic Religion: A Study of Shamanism and Spirit Possession. 2nd ed. New York: Routledge, 1989. 200 p.

4017 **Lewis, James R.**
"Shamans and Prophets: Continuities and Discontinuities in Native American New Religions." *The American Indian Quarterly*, vol. 12 no. 3 (1988) p. 221-228.

4018 **Lightstone, Jack**
"Mythe, Rituels et Institutions de la religion civile de la communauté juive canadienne." *Religion et culture au Québec: figures contemporaines du sacré*, en collaboration, sous la direction de Yvon Desrosiers. Montréal: Fides, 1986, p. 119-138.

4019 **Locust, Carol**
"Wounding the Spirit: Discrimination and Traditional American Indian Belief Systems." *Harvard Educational Review*, vol. 58 no. 3 (1988) p. 315-330.

4020 **Loewen, Harry**
"Echoes of Drumbeats: The Movement of Exuberance Among the Mennonite Brethren." *Journal of Mennonite Studies*, vol. 3 (1985) p. 118-127.

4021 **Long, John H.**
Mosaic of a Maverick: Memoirs of a Missionary in the North. Toronto: Initiative Publishing House, 1983.

4022   **Long, John S.**
"The Cree Prophets: Oral and Documentary Accounts." *Journal of the Canadian Church Historical Society*, vol. 31 no. 1 (1989) p. 3-14.

4023   **Long, John S.**
"Archdeacon Thomas Vincent of Moosonee and the Handicap of 'Metis Racial Status'." *The Canadian Journal of Native Studies*, vol. 3 no. 1 (1983) p. 95-116.

4024   **Lowig, Fr. Evan**
"Conference on the Ukrainian Religious Experience: Tradition and the Canadian Cultural Context." *St. Vladimir's Theological Quarterly*, vol. 30 no. 2 (1986) p. 158-161.

4025   **Mair, Nathan H.**
"The Quebec Protestant Churches and the Question of Nationalism." *Social Compass*, vol. 31 no. 4 (1984) p. 379-390.

4026   **Marchetto, Father Ezio**
"The Catholic Church and Italian Immigration to Toronto: An Overview." *Polyphony: The Bulletin of the Multicultural History Society of Ontario*, vol. 7 no. 2 (1985) p. 107-110.

4027   **Martens, Hildegard**
"German Roman Catholics in Toronto." *Polyphony: The Bulletin of the Multicultural History Society of Ontario*, vol. 9 no. 1 (1987) p. 31-32.

4028   **Martens, Hildegard**
"The German Community of St. Patrick's Parish, 1929 to the Present." *Polyphony: The Bulletin of the Multicultural History Society of Ontario*, vol. 6 no. 1 (1984) p. 98-100.

4029   **Martin, Dennis D.**
"Nothing New Under the Sun? Mennonites and History." *The Conrad Grebel Review*, vol. 5 no. 1/2 (1987) p. 1-27 and p. 147-153.

4030   **Mauthe, Rene**
"So Where are the Results? Mennonites Question Their 50-year-old Indian Connection." *Alberta Report*, vol. 15 no. 34 (1988) p. 30-31.

4031   McCaskill, Don, ed.
"Amerindian Cosmology." Special joint issue of *Canadian Journal of Native Studies*, vol. 7 no. 2 (1987) and *Cosmos*, vol. 4 (1988) p. 1-420.

4032   McCurley, Donna Anne
The Effect of Ethnic Diversity Within Catholicism on Differential Catholic Fertility in Canada, 1971. Unpublished PhD thesis, Tulane University, 1983. 208 p. Canadian theses on microfiche, CT86-24161-0.

4033   McGowan, Mark George
"We Are All Canadians": A Social, Religious and Cultural Portrait of Toronto's English Speaking Roman Catholics, 1890-1920. Unpublished PhD thesis, University of Toronto, 1988.

4034   McKerrow, Peter E.
A Brief History of the Coloured Baptists of Nova Scotia and Their First Organization as Churches, A.D. 1832. Halifax: Nova Scotia Print Co., 1983. Reprint, Halifax, 1895.

4035   McLelland, Janet
"Religion and Ethnicity: The Role of Buddhism in Maintaining Ethnic Identity Among Tibetans in Lindsay, Ontario." *Canadian Ethnic Studies/Études ethniques au Canada*, vol. 19 no. 1 (1987) p. 63-76.

4036   Migliore, Sam
"Religious Symbols and Cultural Identity: A Sicilian-Canadian Example." *Canadian Ethnic Studies/Études ethniques au Canada*, vol. 20 no. 1 (1988) p. 78-94.

4037   Millett, David
"Ethnic Survival in Canada: The Role of the Minority Church." In: *Two Nations, Many Cultures: Ethnic Groups in Canada*, edited by Jean Leonard Elliott. 2nd ed. Scarborough, Ont.: Prentice-Hall of Canada, 1983, p. 260-288.

4038   Milner, Henry
"Quebec Educational Reform and the Protestant School Establishment." In: *Quebec: State and Society*, edited by Alain G. Gagnon. Toronto: Methuen, 1984, p. 410-425.

4039   **Mohs, Gordon**
Spiritual Sites, Ethnic Significance, and Native Spirituality: The Heritage and Heritage Sites of the Sto: Lo Indians of British Columbia. Unpublished MA thesis, Simon Fraser University, 1987. 3 microfiches. Canadian theses on microfiche, CT89-26587-9.

4040   **Moody, Barry, ed.**
Repent and Believe: The Baptists Experience in Maritime Canada. Wolfville, Nova Scotia: Lancelot Press, 1980.

4041   **Mori, George**
"Religious Affiliation in Canada." *Canadian Social Trends,* no. 6, (1987) p. 12-16.

4042   **Mullins, Mark R.**
"The Organizational Dilemmas of Ethnic Churches: A Case Study of Japanese Buddhism in Canada." *Sociological Analysis,* vol. 49 no. 3 (1988) p. 217-233.

4043   **Mullins, Mark R.**
"The Life-cycle of Ethnic Churches in Sociological Perspective." *Japanese Journal of Religious Studies,* vol. 14 no. 4 (1987) p. 321-334.

4044   **Murphy, Terrence**
"The Emergence of Maritime Catholicism, 1781-1830." *Acadiensis,* vol. 13 no. 2 (1984) p. 29-49.

4045   **Nagata, Judith A.**
"Is Multiculturalism Sacred? The Power Behind the Pulpit in the Religious Congregations of Southeast Asian Christians in Canada." *Canadian Ethnic Studies/Études ethniques au Canada,* vol. 19 no. 2 (1987) p. 26-43.

4046   **Nardocchio, Elaine F.**
"Church and State, Religion and Politics in Quebec Theatre." *Bulletin of Canadian Studies,* vol. 7 no. 2 (1983/84) p. 73-80.

4047   **Neufeld, Arnie**
"Canada's First Mennonite Brethren Church at Winkler, Manitoba." *Mennonite Historian,* vol. 14 no. 2 (1988) p. 1-3; vol. 14 no. 3 (1988) p. 3.

4048   **Neufeld, Tom Yoder**
"Christian Counterculture: Ecclesia and Establishment." *The Mennonite Quarterly Review*, vol. 63 no. 2 (1989) p. 193-209.

4049   **Nicolson, Murray W.**
"The Role of Religion in Irish-North American Studies." *Ethnic Forum*, vol. 4 no. 1/2 (1984) p. 64-77.

4050   **Nicolson, Murray W.**
The Catholic Church and the Irish in Victorian Toronto. Unpublished PhD thesis, University of Guelph, 1981.

4051   **Nikiforuk, Andrew**
"The Community Life: For Hutterites, 'Good Times Don't Make Good Christians'." *Equinox*, no. 33 (1987) p. 22-43.

4052   **Nock, David N.**
A Victorian Missionary and Canadian Indian Policy: Cultural Synthesis vs. Cultural Replacement. Waterloo: Canadian Corporation for Studies in Religion/Corporation canadienne des sciences religieuses, Wilfrid Laurier University Press, 1988. 194 p.

4053   **Novak, David**
Jewish-Christian Dialogue: A Jewish Justification. Oxford, U.K.: Oxford University Press, 1989. 194 p.

4054   **Olender, Vivian**
"The Canadian Methodist Church and the Gospel of Assimilation: 1900-1925." *Journal of Ukrainian Studies/Zhurnal Ukrajinoznavchnyk Studij*, vol. 7 no. 2 (1982) p. 61-74.

4055   **Olender, Vivian**
The Reaction of the Canadian Presbyterian Church Towards Ukrainian Immigrants (1900-1925): Rural Home Missions as Agencies of Assimilation. Unpublished DTh thesis, University of St. Michael's College, 1984. 3 microfiches. Canadian theses on microfiche, 65064.

4056   **Paleczny, Tadeusz**
"Ruch Apostolatu Emigracyjnego: Geneza, Zalozenia I Cele/The Emigration Apostolate Movement—The Origins, The Principles, The Objectives." *Przeglad Polonijny*, vol. 15 no. 4 (1989) p. 109-112, 167.

4057   **Palmer, Howard**
"The Religious Ethic and the Spirit of Immigration: The Dutch in Alberta." In: *Peoples of Alberta: Portraits of Cultural Diversity*, edited by Howard and Tamara Palmer. Saskatoon: Western Producer Prairie Books, 1985, p. 143-173.

4058   **Palmer, Howard**
"The Religious Ethic and the Spirit of Immigration: The Dutch in Alberta." *Prairie Forum*, vol. 7 no. 2 (1982) p. 237-266.

4059   **Papp, Susan**
"Interview with Father Laszlo Forgach." *Polyphony: The Bulletin of the Multicultural History Society of Ontario*, vol. 2 no. 2/3 (1979-80) p. 33-35.

4060   **Patrias, Carmela**
"Community Building: Churches." *Polyphony: The Bulletin of the Multicultural History Society of Ontario*, vol. 2 no. 2/3 (1979-80) p. 27-31.

4061   **Pawlikowski, John T.**
"Toward a Theology for Religious Diversity: Perspectives from the Christian-Jewish Dialogue." *Journal of Ecumenical Studies*, vol. 26 no. 1 (1989) p. 138-153.

4062   **Perin, Roberto**
"Clerics and the Constitution: The Quebec Church and Minority Rights in Canada." *Canadian Catholic Historical Studies*, no. 56 (1989) p. 31-48.

4063   **Perin, Roberto**
"Religion, Ethnicity and Identity: Placing the Immigrant Within the Church." *Canadian Issues*, vol. 7 no. 1 (1985) p. 212-231.

4064   **Peters, Jacob**
Organizational Change Within a Religious Denomination: A Case Study of the Conference of Mennonites in Canada, 1903-1978. Unpublished PhD thesis, University of Waterloo, 1987. 5 microfiches. Canadian theses on microfiche, CT88-25688-5.

4065   **Piatocha, Alex**
"Evangelical Mission to Ukraine Report." *Challenger: Western Canada Ukrainian Evangelical Baptist English Fellowship*, vol. 20 no. 10-12 (1989) p. 4-5.

4066   **Pillidbeit, Jakob**
"German Interest Conference." *Canada Lutheran*, vol. 4 no. 4
(1989) p. 18-19, 34.

4067   **Pion, Denis**
"Croyance et incroyance chez les nord-ontariens: bilan de la dernière
décennie." *Bulletin du Centre de recherche en civilisation
canadienne-française*, no. 26 (1983) p. 7-14.

4068   **Powell, Trevor**
"The Church of England and the 'Foreigner' in the Dioceses of
Qu'Appelle and Saskatchewan." *Journal of the Canadian Church
Historical Society*, vol. 28 no. 1 (1986) p. 31-43.

4069   **Praszalowicz, Dorota**
"Amerykanskie Koscioly O Genzie Etnicznej-Suomi Synod I Finska
Grupa Etniczna W. Stanach Zjednoczonych/American Churches of
Ethnic Origin-The Evangelical Lutheran Church-Suomi Synod in the
Finnish Ethnic Group in the U.S.A.." *Przeglad Polonijny*, vol. 15 no.
4 (1989) p. 73-98, 165.

4070   **Protich, George**
"Serbian Religious Tradition in Ontario." In: *Serbs in Ontario: A
Socio-cultural Description*, edited by Sofija Skoric and George Vid
Tomashevich. Toronto: Serbian Heritage Academy, 1987, p. 86-98.

4071   **Provincial Museum of Alberta**
"Seasons of Celebration: Ritual in Eastern Church Culture/Temps de
célébration: les rites dans la culture chrétienne d'Orient." *Heritage
Link*, vol. 4 no. 2 (1989) p. 12-14.

4072   **Randolph, Laura B.**
"What's Behind the Black Rebellion in the Catholic Church." *Ebony*,
vol. 45 no. 1 (1989) p. 160-162, 164.

4073   **Rasporich, Anthony W.**
"Utopia, Sect and Millennium in Western Canada, 1870-1940."
Prairie Forum, vol. 12 no. 2 (1987) p. 217-244.

4074   **Remie, Cornelius H.W.**
"Culture Change and Religious Continuity Among the
Arviligdjuarmiut of Pelly Bay, N.W.T., 1935-1963." *Études Inuit
Studies*, vol. 7 no. 2 (1983) p. 53-78.

4075   **Rempel, Peter H.**
"On the Origins of the Conference of Mennonites in Manitoba."
Mennonite Historian, vol. 13 no. 4 (1987) p. 1-2.

4076   **Richling, Barnett**
"'Very Serious Reflections': Inuit Dreams about Salvation and Loss
in Eighteenth-century Labrador." *Ethnohistory*, vol. 36 no. 2
(1989) p. 148-169.

4077   **Rollmann, Hans**
"Inuit Shamanism and the Moravian Missionaries of Labrador: A
Textual Agenda for the Study of Native Inuit Religion." *Études Inuit
Studies*, vol. 8 no. 2 (1985) p. 131-138.

4078   **Rosenweig, Bernard**
"The Rabbinical Council of America: Retrospect and Prospect."
Tradition: Journal of Orthodox Jewish Thought, vol. 22 no. 1
(1986) p. 2-15.

4079   **Rouillard, Jacques**
"Major Changes in the Confederation des Travailleurs Catholiques du
Canada, 1940-1960." In: *Quebec Since 1945: Selected Readings*,
edited by Michael D. Behiels. Toronto: Copp Clark Pitman,
1987, p. 111-132. Translation of the author's: "Mutations de la
Confédération des travailleurs catholiques du Canada." *Revue
d'histoire de l'Amérique française* vol. 34 no. 3 (1980) p. 377-405.

4080   **Rozefort, Wallace**
*Criminal Prosecutions: The Defense of Religious Freedom and the
Canadian Charter*. Unpublished L.L.M. thesis, University of British
Columbia, 1985. 188 leaves. Canadian theses on microfiche, CT87-
20254-5.

4081   **Ruddel, David-Thiery**
*Le protestantisme français au Québec, 1840-1919: images et
témoignages*. Ottawa: Musées Nationaux de Canada/National
Museums of Canada, 1983.

4082   **Safran, William**
"Ethnic Mobilization, Modernization, and Ideology: Jacobinism,
Marxism, Organicism, and Functionalism." *The Journal of Ethnic
Studies*, vol. 15 no. 1 (1987) p. 1-32.

4083   **Scheffel, David Z.**
"Russian Old Believers and Canada: A Historical Sketch." *Canadian Ethnic Studies/Études ethniques au Canada*, vol. 21 no. 1 (1989) p. 1-18.

4084   **Schijn, Herman**
"Concerning the Non-swearing of Oaths [By Mennonites]." *The Mennonite Quarterly Review*, vol. 61 no. 2 (1987) p. 228-235.

4085   **Schindler, Albert E.**
"Our Easter Tradition." *Heritage Link*, vol. 4 no. 2 (1989) p. 9-11.

4086   **Schmidt, Jeremy**
"Spirit Wrestlers: The Uneasy Life of British Columbia's Doukhobors." *Equinox*, no. 25 (1986) p. 60-69.

4087   **Schoenfeld, Stuart**
"Rereading a Canadian Classic: Crestwood Heights as a Study of the Invisible Religion." *Canadian Review of Sociology and Anthropology/ Revue canadienne de sociologie et d'anthropologie*, vol. 25 no. 3 (1988) p. 456-463.

4088   **Segal, Benjamin J.**
"Teaching Prayer: Considerations." *Jewish Education*, vol. 57 no. 2/3 /4 (1989) p. 72-76.

4089   **Sell, Alan P.F.**
"Anabaptist-congregational Relations and Current Mennonite-Reformed Dialogue." *The Mennonite Quarterly Review*, vol. 61 no. 3 (1987) p. 321-334.

4090   **Shaffir, William**
"Separation from the Mainstream in Canada: The Hassidic Community of Tash." *The Jewish Journal of Sociology*, vol. 29 no. 1 (1987) p. 19-35.

4091   **Shahrodi, Zofia**
"St. Stanislaus' Parish: The Heart of Toronto Polonia." *Polyphony: The Bulletin of the Multicultural History Society of Ontario*, vol. 6 no. 2 (1984) p. 27-32.

4092   **Shek, Ben Z.**
"Bulwark to Battlefield: Religion in Québec Literature." *Journal of Canadian Studies/Revue d'études canadiennes*, vol. 18 no. 2 (1983) p. 42-57.

4093   **Shelly, Harold P.**
"Born of the Current of Revivalism: Origin of the Bible Fellowship Church." *The Mennonite Quarterly Review*, vol. 63 no. 3 (1989) p. 265-284.

4094   **Shreve, Dorthy Shadd**
The AfriCanadian Church: A Stablizer. Jordan Station, Ont.: Paideia Press, 1983. 138 p.

4095   **Simpson, John H.**
"Religion and Churches." In: *Understanding Canadian Society*, edited by James Curtis and Lorne Tepperman. Toronto: McGraw-Hill Ryerson, 1988, p. 345-369.

4096   **Singh, Mohinder**
Basics of Sikhism. Vancouver: Sikh Education Society, 1988. 50 p.

4097   **Slonim, Reuben**
To Kill a Rabbi. Toronto: ECW Press, 1987. 354 p.

4098   **Smith, Donald B.**
Sacred Feathers: The Story of the Rev. Peter Jones (Kahkewaquonaby) and the Mississauga Indians of Upper Canada. Toronto: University of Toronto Press, 1987. 344 p.

4099   **Smits, Cornelis**
"Secession, Quarrels, Emigration and Personalities." In: *Dutch Immigration to North America*, edited by Herman Ganzevoort and Mark Boekelman. Toronto: Multicultural History Society of Ontario, 1983, p. 97-110.

4100   **Stekelenburg, Henry van**
"Tracing the Dutch Roman Catholic Emigrants to North America in the Nineteenth and Twentieth Centuries." In: *Dutch Immigration to North America*, edited by Herman Ganzevoort and Mark Boekelman. Toronto: Multicultural History Society of Ontario, 1983, p. 57-84.

4101 **Stobbe, Abe John**
South Abbotsford Mennonite Brethren Church: A History from 1932-1982. Abbotsford, B.C.: South Abbotsford Mennonite Brethren Church, 1982.

4102 **Suderman, Elmer**
"Early Mennonite Observers' Perceptions of the Great Plains." *Journal of Canadian Culture*, vol. 2 no. 1 (1985) p. 1-11.

4103 **Sugunasiri, Suwanda H.J.**
"Buddhism in Metropolitan Toronto: Preliminary Overview." *Canadian Ethnic Studies/Études ethniques au Canada*, vol. 21 no. 2 (1989) p. 83-103.

4104 **Sugunasiri, Suwanda H.J.**
"Buddhists in Ontario." *Polyphony: The Bulletin of the Multicultural History Society of Ontario*, vol. 9 no. 1 (1987) p. 78.

4105 **Suokonautio, Markku**
"National Finnish Organizations in Canada: Reorganization of the Finnish Lutherans in Canada." *Polyphony: The Bulletin of the Multicultural History Society of Ontario*, vol. 3 no. 2 (1981) p. 91-96.

4106 **Swomley, John M.**
Religious Liberty and the Secular State: The Constitutional Context. Buffalo, N.Y.: Prometheus Books, 1987. 148 p.

4107 **Symposium Planning and Findings Committee [Mennonite Brethren Conference]**
"A Symposium on Faith and Ethnicity Among the Mennonite Brethren: Summary and Findings Statement." *Journal of Mennonite Studies*, vol. 6 (1988) p. 51-59. Symposium held November 19-21, 1987.

4108 **Talamantez, Inez M.**
"Use of Dialogue in the Reinterpretation of American Indian Religious Traditions: A Case Study." *American Indian Culture and Research Journal*, vol. 9 no. 2 (1985) p. 33-48.

4109 **Talbot, Steve**
"Desecration and American Indian Religious Freedom." *The Journal of Ethnic Studies*, vol. 12 no. 4 (1985) p. 1-18.

4110   **Taskey, Lu**
"The Religious Life Cycle: A Photographic Essay." *Polyphony: The Bulletin of the Multicultural History Society of Ontario*, vol. 10 no. 1/2 (1988) p. 17-20.

4111   **Thériault, Serge**
"Le mouvement canadien-français dans l'Eglise épiscopale—rite vieux-catholique." *Journal of the Canadian Church Historical Society*, vol. 30 no. 1 (1988) p. 20-31.

4112   **Toews, John B.**
"Brethren and Old Church Relations in Pre-World War I Russia: Setting the Stage for Canada." *Journal of Mennonite Studies*, vol. 2 (1984) p. 42-59.

4113   **Toews, Paul**
"Mennonites in American Society: Modernity and the Persistence of Religious Community." *The Mennonite Quarterly Review*, vol. 63 no. 3 (1989) p. 227-246.

4114   **Toews, Paul**
"Faith in Culture and Culture in Faith: The Mennonite Brethren in North America." *Mennonite Studies*, vol. 6 (1988) p. 36-50.

4115   **Torosian, Hygus**
"The First Armenian Church in Canada: St. Gregory the Illuminator." *Polyphony: The Bulletin of the Multicultural History Society of Ontario*, vol. 4 no. 2 (1982) p. 87-94.

4116   **Treplin, Ulrike**
"Die Deutsche Kanada-Auswanderung in der Weimarer Zeit und die Evangelisch-lutherische Auswanderermission in Hamburg." *Zeitschrift der Gesellschaft für Kanada-Studien*, vol. 7 no. 1 (1987) p. 167-192.

4117   **Turner, Edith**
"From Shamans to Healers: The Survival of an Inupiaq Eskimo Skill." *Anthropologica*, vol. 31 no. 1 (1989) p. 3-24.

4118   **Ukrainian Catholic National Shrine - Ukrajins'kyj Katolyts'kyj Krajovyj Sobor**
Millennium in Ottawa/Tysjacholittja V Ottavi. Ottawa: Ukrainian Catholic National Shrine/Ukrains'kyj Katolyts'kyj Krajovyj Sobor, 1988. 20 p.

4119   **Ukrainian Fraternal Association**
"Millennium of Christianity in Ukraine, 988-1988." *Forum: A Ukrainian Review*, no. 66 (1986) p. 1-100.

4120   **Ward, Kenn**
"The Baltic Deportation: The Baltic Special Interest Conference of the Evangelical Lutheran Church in Canada." *Canada Lutheran*, vol. 2 no. 5 (1987) p. 12-113.

4121   **Washington, Joseph R., Jr.**
Race and Religion in Early Nineteenth Century America, 1800-1850: Constitution, Conscience and Calvinist Compromise, vols. 1 and 2, Studies in American Religion, vol. 39. Queenston: Edwin Mellen Press, 1988. 998 p.

4122   **Weaver, Laura H.**
"Forbidden Fancies: A Child's Vision of Mennonite Plainness." *Mennonite Life*, vol. 43 no. 2 (1988) p. 20-23.

4123   **Weingartner, Erich**
"Hope in the Midst of Despair: A Memorable Encounter with a Korean Pastor is Recounted." *Canada Lutheran*, vol. 4 no. 6 (1989) p. 16-18.

4124   **Whitfield, Stephen J.**
"Jewish History and the Torment of Totalitarianism." *Judaism*, vol. 36 no. 3 (1987) p. 304-319.

4125   **Wiens, Delbert**
"Ethos, Ethoi and Ethics: The Moralities of the Mennonite Brethren." *The Conrad Grebel Review*, vol. 6 no. 1 (1988) p. 45-64.

4126   **Woocher, Jonathan S.**
Sacred Survival: The Civil Religion of American Jews. Bloomington, Ind.: Indiana University Press, 1986. 245 p.

4127   **Wood, Marjorie Rodgers**
"Hinduism in Vancouver: Adjustments in the Home, the Temple, and the Community." In: *Visible Minorities and Multiculturalism: Asians in Canada*, edited by K. Victor Ujimoto and Gordon Hirabayashi. Toronto: Butterworths, 1980, p. 277-288.

4128   **Wurzburger, Walter S.**
"Cooperation with Non-Orthodox Jews." *Tradition: Journal of Orthodox Jewish Thought*, vol. 22 no. 1 (1986) p. 33-40.

4129   **Yoder, Paton**
"The Structure of the Amish Ministry in the Nineteenth Century." *The Mennonite Quarterly Review*, vol. 61 no. 3 (1987) p. 280-197.

4130   **Zmiyiwsky, Daria and Suaan Soldan**
"Ukrainian Millennnium Celebrations [Thunder Bay, Ontario]." *Northern Mosaic*, vol. 12 no. 3 (1988) p. 1, 8-9.

4131   **Zylberberg, Jacques**
"La régulation etatique des minorités religieuses." In: *Minorités et l'État*, sous la direction de Pierre Guillaume, Jean-Michel Lacroix, Rejean Pelletier, et Jacques Zylberberg. Bordeaux, France: Presses Universitaires de Bordeaux, 1986, p. 117-132.

Index

Entries in this index are referenced according to their running numbers and not according to page numbers. They are indexed by authors, joint authors, and editors. Organizations or government departments are treated as corporate authors. Where none of these authors are available an entry is indexed by its title.   GPS

A

Allison, D.J., 3547
Almeida, Christine, 2088
Ama, Pierre F.M., 0694
Ambrosetti, Ronald, 3432
Amenu-Tekaa, Christian, 3548
*American and Canadian Immi-
grant and Ethnic Folklore*,
0001
American Association for Higher
Education, 3549
American Association of
Colleges for Teacher
Education, 3550
American Council on Education,
3551
American Jewish Historical
Society, 2883
Ames, Michael A., 2884
Ames, Michael M., 0625
Amyot, Gérard, 2346
Amyot, Michel, 2346
Anctil, Pierre, 0149, 0626, 2347,
2733
Anderson, Adrienne E., 2885
Anderson, Alan B., 0627-0628
Anderson, Charles P., 3903
Anderson, Donald George, 1705
Anderson, Joan M., 2089
Anderson, Karen, 2090
Anderson, W.W., 0002
Andiappan, Palaniappan, 0629
Andres, Myrna Louise, 2348
Andrew, Edward, 2349
Angel, Sam Sumayya, 1516
Angus, Ian H., 0630
Angus, William H., 0192
Anisef, Paul, 3552-3553
Annis, R.C., 0673
Annis, Robert C., 0631-0633
Anselmi, William, 2886
Anthony, Brian, 2887
Anthony, Robert J., 2355
Aoki, Ted T., 2356
Appleby, David F., 0094

Apramian, John, 2734
Arat-Koc, Sedef, 2091
Archer, John H., 3904
Ares, Georges, 1517
Arkelian, A.J., 1706
Armitage, Peter, 0634
Armour, Leslie, 0635-0636
Armstrong, Robin, 1191
Arnand, Raj, 1707
Arnold, Abraham J., 2888
Arsenault, Pierre, 1518
Artinian, Hagop, 2889
Asch, Michael, 1192, 2890
Ashworth, Mary, 3554
Association Canadienne-
Française de l'Ontario, 1519
Association française d'études
canadiennes, 2891
Association haïtienne des
travailleurs du taxi
(A.H.T.T.), 1265-1266
Atchison, John, 0193-0194
Atkinson, Thomas, 2892
Audet, B., 0293
Audet, Benoit, 0195-0197
Audley, Paul, 2735-2736
Auerbach, Arnold J., 1708
Aunger, Edmund A., 2357
Avery, Donald, 0198-0199, 1267
Avery, R., 0200
Avis, James, 3555
Axelrod, Harvey S., 0062
Axworthy, Thomas S., 1709
Ayabe, Tsuneo, 1417
Aziz-al Ahsan, Syed, 3556

B

B.H. [Benedykt Heydenkorn],
1325, 3154-3155, 3988, 3368
Bacchi, Carol Lee, 0637
Badets, Jane, 0201

Dofny, Jacques, 0801
Donegan, Rosemary, 1305
Donnelly, F.K., 1802
Donnelly, Jack, 1803, 1873
Donneur, Andre, 3628
Dorais, Louis-Jacques, 0035,
    0802, 2475-2476
Dorotich, Dan, 1433
Dorsinville, Max, 3057
Dossa, Parin Aziz, 3956-3957
Douaud, Patrick C., 2477
Doucette, Leonard E., 3058-3059
Douguette, Joe, 3510
Dow, Bradley, 1402
Downey, Lawrence William, 3629
Dowsett, Gwendolyne Edna, 3060
Doyle, Denise Joan, 3958
Dragasevic, Draga, 2761
Draper, Paula J., 0274, 2121,
    2144-2145
Dreisziger, Nandor A.F., 0275,
    1434, 3061
Drew, Leslie,, 3062
Driben, Paul, 1804-1805
Driedger, Leo, 0535-0536, 0803-
    0810, 0811-0812, 1435,
    2478-2479, 3959
Drolet, Gaëtan, 0036
Druke, Mary E., 2480
Drummond, L., 0813
Drystek, Henry F., 0276
Dubeau, Sharon, 0277
Ducharme, Jean-Charles, 2481-
    2482, 3630-3631
DuCharme, Michele, 0814, 2762
Dueck, Ronald Peter, 3960
Duerden, Charles, 3063
Duff, Alan, 3273
Duffek, Karen, 3064-3066
Duffus, Allan, 3067-3068
Dufour, Rose, 2146
Duhaine, Gérard, 0537, 1209
Duhamel, Ronald J., 3632
Dumon, W.A., 0278

Dumont, Fernand, 3069
Dumont, Micheline, 2147
Dunae, Patrick A., 0279-0280
Duncan, James S., 0538
Dunsiger, Jane Catherine, 0281
Dupre, J. Stefan, 1806
Duquette, Georges J., 3633
Durst, Russel K., 0037
Dusenberry, Lynne Marie, 0815
Dutcher, Stephen Wayne, 0816
Duthie, Beth, 3070
Dutil, P.A., 1565
Dutton, Alan, 0817
Dutton, Alan, 1306
Dutton, Sue, 3071
Dwivedi, O.P., 0818-0819
Dworaczek, Marian, 0038
Dwyer, Aldrich J., 0039
Dwyer, Melva J., 0040
Dyck, John Edgar, 3634
Dyck, Noel, 1807-1809

E

Eaman, Ross Allan, 2763
Earle, Michael J., 1307-1309
Eastcott, John, 3317
Eastman, Julia Antonia, 0820
Eberts, Mary, 2148
Ebona, Andrew, 1566
Eder, Jeanne, 3721
Edson, Carol, 3072
Edwards, G.J., 3073
Edwards, G.T., 3073
Edwards, Henry P., 2483-2484, 3635
Edwards, John, 0821, 2485-2486
Eiseman, Thomas Owen, 3636
Eisenbruch, Maurice, 0282
Eklund, William, 3074
Elder, Bruce R., 3075
Elias, Peter Douglas, 1810
Eliefja, Chaya, 0822

Pollock, Norman, 0365
Polyzoi, Eleoussa, 0421, 2282-
    2285, 3806
Pons-Ridler, Suzanne, 2001
Ponterotto, Joseph G., 1051
Ponting, J. Rick, 1052-1053,
    1240
Porter, James N., 1491
Porter, Marilyn, 2286
Posluns, Michael, 2002
Potestio, John, 0180, 1492, 3807
Potvin, Claude, 0116
Poulantzas, N.M., 2003
Powell, Thomas J., 0831
Powell, Trevor, 4068
Prange, Mark, 1070
Prasad, Kamal Kant, 1241
Praszalowicz, Dorota, 4069
Pratt, Cranford, 1945
Pratt, David, 3808-3809
Prattis, J. Ian, 0588, 2654
Preston, Richard J., 3387
Preyra, Cecilia Maria, 2287
Preyra, I., 2870
Price, John A., 2655
Priest, Gordon E., 2656
Principe, Angelo, 2833-2834,
    3388
Prokopowich, Mary, 3389
Pronko, Jerry, 2835
Pronovost, Gilles, 3390
Protich, George, 4070
Proudfoot, Bruce, 0422
Proulx, Daniel, 2004, 2657
Proulx, Richard, 3391
Provincial Museum of Alberta,
    4071
Prujiner, Alain, 2658
Prymak, Thomas M., 3810
Pryor, Edward T., 0423
Pucci, Antonio, 0180, 1492,
    3392, 3811
Pupier, Paul, 2005
Putnam, S.L., 0444

Q

Quan, Ping Shao, 2659, 3812
Quebec Movement to Combat
    Racism (QMCR), 1054
Québec. Conseil de la langue
    française, 2660
Quenneville, Ginette, 1055
Quiroga, Cecilia Medina, 2006
Qureshi, Regula B., 1511

R

Raben, Harvey A., 3813
*Race and Sex Equality in the
    Workplace: A Challenge and
    Opportunity*, 1056
Radforth, Ian, 1372
Rahatyn, Levko, 3393
Rajwani, Farida A., 3814
Ralston, Helen, 2288
Ram, Bali, 0589, 3815
Ramcharan, Subhas, 0424, 1057-
    1058, 1493, 3816
Ramirez, Bruno, 0425-0426,
    1059, 1373-1375, 3394
Ramrattan, Annette, 0117
Randolph, Laura B., 4072
Rao, G. Lakshmana, 0181
Rapp, Eugene, 3395
Rasporich, Anthony W., 0427,
    1650, 4073
Rasporich, Beverly, 3396-3397
Ratushny, Edward, 2007
Ratzlaff, Harold C., 3781
Raudsepp, Enn, 2836-2837
Ravault, René-Jean, 2661
Rawson, Bruce, 1651
Ray, Dorothy Jean, 3398
Ray, Douglas, 0118, 2008, 3658,
    3817
Raynauld, André, 2662

DATE DUE

			Printed in USA